Public
Administration

DISCARD

Public Administration

Second Edition

Readings in institutions,
processes, behavior

Edited by
Robert T. Golembiewski, University of Georgia
Frank Gibson, University of Georgia
Geoffrey Y. Cornog, Sangamon State University

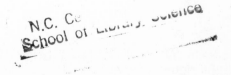

Rand McNally & Company   Chicago

Rand McNally Political Science Series
Advisory editor
Morton Grodzins, *late of the University of Chicago*

Preface

There is a narrow band indeed that separates being informative from being defensive. Our defense against being defensive in this volume of readings is to be brief in our editorial comments as well as to eschew interpretation of the several selections reprinted below, all the more fully to allow the several selections to stand on their own merits in exploring what we believe are significant problem areas in ways we consider particularly fruitful.

Our defense, like defenses all, is not foolproof. This Preface is congruent with our defense, for what we have to say about the motivation of this volume will be brief indeed. But the following Introduction comes less clearly from the same mold. Although that Introduction will not interpret individual items, it will sketch three broad approaches to the study of Public Administration and it will present designs of three course outlines consistent with these approaches (after the example of Harold Stein). Our editorial responsibility, then, is defined in terms of the selection of titles that help encompass the totality of Public Administration as we believe it to be variously understood by the vast majority of observers and participants. The individual titles adequately and articulately make their own case; of that we are convinced, and that we are willing to let them do. But more of this issue in due time.

Immediately, this book of readings has a straightforward rationale. We shall outline only two major components of that supporting rationale. First, a selection of readings can serve many useful purposes in a program of instruction in Public Administration. The coeditors felt the impact of this point acutely when they began to develop such a program of substantial scope for the University of Georgia in its dual capacities as a state university and as a regional center of instruction in the administrative arts and sciences. For example, multiple-section courses in Public Administration raise the complicated issue of the balance between uniformity and flexibility. The goal is a relative uniformity between sections, which however does not go so far as to immobilize the differential interests of the teaching staff. A comprehensive set of readings can permit relative uniformity between sections in supplementing texts and case studies; such a set of readings can also permit individual staff members some flexibility in pursuing their own particular interests; and such readings can conveniently present materials of a scope and depth beyond any textbook.

Second, no easy exploitation of the usefulness of a book of readings was possible. For no selection of readings in Public Administration exists which meets these two criteria: a recent publication date, and a coverage that includes traditional materials as well as contributions from the newly developing mathematical and behavioral approaches to administrative phenomena. Perhaps Waldo[1] and Lepawsky[2] did their work so well and so comprehensively in compiling their books of readings in the period following World War II that they thereby discouraged competitive efforts. Perhaps, as some judge, Public Administration as a discipline went into temporary decline after the salad days of the thirties and forties. In any case, the two volumes edited by Waldo and Lepawsky have seen few challengers of comparable comprehensiveness. Success should never be denigrated. Much analytical water has flowed under many research bridges in recent years, however. The consequence is a major gap between the materials conveniently available and the existing states of the science and the art of Public Administration.

These are the two major and uncomplicated motivations of this volume. We trust that the product will serve both introductory and advanced students, for that is our intention. And we trust that the product also highlights much of the contemporary spectrum of administratively relevant work, for nothing less than an appreciation of the full spectrum will satisfy us as teachers in an area crucial to man's coming to grips with his ever more complex environment.

To act on our motivation was to accumulate many indebtednesses, which unfortunately can be acknowledged only by a brief note. First and foremost, authors and publishers of the reprinted materials were unusually kind in helping us compile this volume, and this kindness came in the face of sometimes awkward and bothersome requests. We applaud

---

[1]Dwight Waldo, editor, *Ideas and Issues in Public Administration* (New York: McGraw-Hill, 1953).

[2]Albert Lepawsky, editor, *Administration: The Art and Science of Organization and Management* (New York: Knopf, 1949).

these many efforts of scholarship as well as the publishing talents which brought them to light. Moreover, various services provided by the University of Georgia also were indispensable in developing this compilation. The Social Science Research Institute and Sandra Daniels deserve especial mention. Finally, Gloria Hawkins ably provided many of the multitudinous clerical and typing services required.

Robert T. Golembiewski

Frank Gibson

Geoffrey Y. Cornog

Athens, Georgia

September 1, 1965

Preface to the Second Edition

The seven years following the publication of the first edition of this volume have seen unparalleled developments in the field of Public Administration. Examples are everywhere:

- We have seen the wind-down of this country's involvement in Viet Nam, an involvement that has surely had a substantial impact on policy decisions and their implementation at all levels of government in the United States.
- We have seen the climax of our "man on the moon" drive and the subsequent reallocation of funds from N.A.S.A. to other agencies, a reallocation that has caused reverberations throughout that assemblage of organizations dependent upon continued explorations in space.
- We have seen numerous attempts to meet the social needs of this country, attempts having diverse degrees of success. OEO, Model Cities, Headstart, Minimum Income Plans, LEAA and other programs have contended for support in the allocation of scarce resources.

Perhaps most suggestive of the real-time span between the editions is that the first was published during a major economic boom when serious discussions were underway to discover ways of sharing the anticipated and massive federal budget surpluses. The situation is considerably different today.

In a basic sense, these momentous zigs and zags all contribute to the rationale underlying this volume. Through it all, we see a rising clamor for more efficiency and effectiveness in the management of governmental programs. And through it all, we see an even greater need for this reader.

Like the world, this reader has changed in major ways. For example, it places more emphasis on newer techniques in management science than did the first edition. Thus, PPBS, Systems Analysis, EDP, and the like receive substantially more space. And since the constraints of size place us in a zero-sum game we have had to delete some traditional pieces. We hope that the new balance is somewhere close to the current mainstream of Public Administration, while adding some forward thrust as well.

Again we wish to express grateful appreciation to the numerous authors and publishers who have permitted us reprint rights. The acts of creation of the authors and of kindness by the publishers has made this volume possible. And acknowledgment must also go to Mrs. Jackie Hall for her most able assistance in the preparation of copy and in the numerous other details that accompany this type of endeavor.

Robert T. Golembiewski
Frank K. Gibson
Geoffrey Y. Cornog

Contents

26 Cti

Introduction

A book of readings in Public Administration should be like a smorgasbord for both teacher and student. To whet the appetites of instructors who are designing a course—where a book of readings is used as a supplement for a text—the selections should provide flexibility enough so that faculty with their varying backgrounds, different training, and diverse preferences for empirical and philosophical approaches can pick and choose among the selections to develop a stimulating program of readings. Moreover, the interested student deserves a nourishing selection of readings that will provide depth and breadth for central subjects treated by the text he has used. And whatever the student's motivational state, he requires nothing less than the opportunity to sample distinguished items from the full range of administratively relevant research and thought. To lay our culinary analogy forever to rest, finally, a successful course always depends upon the meat-and-potatoes of established knowledge and insight; and the impact of a course often will be heightened if students are exposed to the more exotic flavors of research at the frontiers of new thought and knowledge.

The guidelines underlying the selection of the following readings, then, may be given in shorthand fashion. These guidelines include:

—illuminating the most diverse possible classes of administrative phenomena;

—raising the widest possible range of philosophical and empirical issues;

—illustrating a wide sample of new aids to administration, including the computer, electronic data-processing equipment, and various approaches to decision-making;

—relying on the full panoply of disciplines and resources relevant to administrative analysis, including the literatures of Political Science and Public Administration, the behavioral science literatures in the several disciplines, and aspects of the mathematical sciences and the new computer technology;

—emphasizing the most contemporary materials;

—contributing to the flexibility of programs of instruction in Public Administration fielded by the most diverse kinds of users.

In most cases, the available literatures permitted us to meet these guidelines. However, in several cases where the published literature did not meet our needs, selections were prepared specifically for this volume.

The rationale underlying these guidelines is obvious, in general. At the expense of belaboring that which is already patent, however, the reasons will be sketched which support the decision to illuminate the most diverse classes of administrative phenomena.

The wide scope of the present selections has this prime motivation: Perforce, the public administrator operates in many "worlds," or problem environments, and a sense of the variegated cues to which he must respond is an important element in learning how administrators react and why they do so. There is no end to the problem environments, or administrative worlds, that might have been selected for emphasis here. Three such worlds have been selected, however, and their basic rationale is that for the coeditors of this volume they have proved useful ways of approaching the diverse subject matter of Public Administration. Since we recognize considerable differences among ourselves in emphases and preferred paths of approach, we have some hope that in accommodating to our own diverse needs we also represent in microcosm a broad part of the spectrum of approaches characteristic of students of the administrative processes.

The three administrative worlds chosen for emphasis may be enumerated and identified briefly. By way of preview, the emphasis is upon these worlds in which the administrator operates: the behavioral, the institutional and functional, and the processual.

First, the administrator is enmeshed in a *behavioral* world of self and others in dynamic interplay. From this first standpoint, administrative activity is an incredibly complex amalgam of the urgencies of personal needs, of the exigencies of interpersonal relations, and of the subtleties of small and large social groupings. The behavioral worlds of all administrators have much in common, in public agencies and in business enterprises alike. Hence particularly wide use will be made of research in the behavioral sciences to give specific substance to the dimensions of the behavioral aspects relevant for the public administrator. Such research covers the fields of business administration, psychology, sociology, and industrial administration, primarily.

One need not labor hard to establish the importance of this first administrative world. Its importance, for example, is implied by the excesses committed in its name. Thus some students have become so enamored of personal and social dynamics in administration that they see but little else, and recognize hardly any of that. Hence one acute student complained that some of his colleagues were abortively preoccupied with the isolated relations of individual men, or at best with small aggregates of men in face-to-face situations. They were, he noted caustically, fascinated by *men without organizations.*[1] The mischief is patent. As a matter of sharply contrasting fact, administrative man is *man within organizations,* and often very large organizations. Preoccupation with man and those human relations close to him, then, misses much of the administrative forest by focusing upon the separate trees.

Second, the administrator also operates within an *institutional* world. It differs significantly on many dimensions from his behavioral world, and also influences it greatly. This institutional environment is a world in whose building the administrator commonly does not share; moreover, it is a world imposed upon him by frequently compelling sanctions; and it is of a scale that far surpasses the relatively narrow confines of interpersonal and group relations. This massive institutional environment consists of the formally defined contexts within which the administrator works, of the policies and procedures which formally structure these contexts. On one level, for example, the administrator's environment comprises his formal work unit within some larger formal organization. At another level, this massive environment also consists of the specialized *functions* that individuals perform within their formal organizations. Thus an individual may be a training officer within the Office of Career Development; he will also be an employee of the parent U.S. Civil Service Commission; the latter has institutionalized relations with (for example) certain committees of Congress; and these relations, in turn, are determined by such broad institutional arrangements as the "sharing of powers" prescribed by the Constitution. The individual—to a greater or lesser degree—simultaneously feels the resultant impact of all

[1]Warren G. Bennis, "Leadership Theory and Administrative Behavior: The Problem of Authority," *Administrative Science Quarterly,* 4 (December, 1959), pp. 259–301.

of these various levels of institutional and functional restraints on his behavior.

Institutions and functions, as broadly defined here, share common major elements that affect the administrator. To a far more substantial degree than is true of his behavioral world, for instance, the institutional and functional world of an administrator represents a pattern from which he cannot escape. The imposed pattern may be so dominant, in fact, that it completely determines administrative behavior. In the more usual case, an administrator's institutions and functions are important constraints that help channel (but do not determine) his various behaviors. Thus, commonly, the individual will experience multiple pushes and pulls from various institutional and functional forces—as we have roughly defined these terms—which forces commonly are at cross-purposes. Here some individuals can be torn apart emotionally trying to react consistently to inconsistent cues. Here, also, some individuals find an opportunity to shape their own environment by acute management of the conflicting institutional forces exerted upon them. Selections below will dwell on the causes and consequences of these two typical adaptations.

The public administrator's institutional world also has important unique features, however. That is, the specifics of the institutions and functions—to which administrators may be subject, or from which they may manage to gain personal or sub-organizational aims—will differ in important respects in different contexts. These differences may be marked even between two units within the same larger government agency or business firm. Significant institutional differences also exist between public and business enterprises, in general, although the distinctions between organizations within each category commonly are as great as—if not greater than—the differences between public agencies on one hand and businesses on the other. The "public-private" institutional differences particularly concern us here. In a rough but useful sense, the business of governments takes place in a significantly different environment than does the governance of businesses. The specific characteristics of the public institutional environment thus will receive special attention in the readings reprinted below. The literature of Political Science proper is the main source of selections bearing on this second of the public administrator's worlds.

Again, the proof of the significance of the institutional and functional world is provided by the extreme devotion often accorded this second approach to administrative phenomena. So obsessed have some observers been with the legalisms and formalisms of institutions and functions, we have been warned, that much relevant literature reflects a focus on *organizations without men.*[2] Whatever the automated world of tomorrow brings—and it is not likely to be a general pattern of organizations without men—the myopia of much of the literature therefore neglects elements of great significance in the administrator's worlds of today. The challenge, then, is to keep the focus on institutions within reasonable bounds, thereby asserting its importance without denigrating the significance of other foci.

Third, administrators also operate in a world of major *processes.* These we conceive as the major tasks of management, as ways of building bridges between the behavioral and institutional worlds. These major processes of management include: communicating, coordinating, motivating, and controlling. In a simple sense, these major processes have a "horizontal" thrust. They provide general categories for guiding and analyzing behavior in small social groupings as well as within massive organizations, although the methods for analysis and action often will differ and the details usually do.

All organizations—whether public or private—can be viewed usefully in terms of general managerial processes. Relevant selections below, therefore, will come from a wide variety of disciplines. And particular attention will be given to various tools and techniques—such as the computer and electronic data-processing—that can be of tremendous aid to the manager in the several major processes through which he integrates his enterprise or agency. The proper techniques, then, require careful husbanding.

An emphasis upon managerial processes can serve the student, but there are problems. Thus the emphasis can encourage neglect of both the institutional and behavioral worlds of the administrator. For example, much of the literature is hortatory. It is preoccupied with convincing managers that they ought (for example) to coordinate, more or less as an abstract principle. In cases, an extreme emphasis upon processes neglects both specific behavior and specific institutional contexts. This

[2] *Ibid.*

neglects too much. The opposed ambition here is to respect the importance of the emphasis on managerial processes without becoming its slave.

The distinctions between behaviors, institutions, and processes will not be drawn more sharply here. This is a necessity, and also will prove convenient in several senses. Thus—to dwell on the necessity for general differentiation only—the three managerial worlds are not discrete, logically neat categories. Rather, they are three loosely defined points of approach to phenomena that occur together in nature. Reality defines our position for us in this respect, then. Nature does not permit precise differentiation of our three categories. The implied procedural guideline deserves explicit statement. Whichever vertex of the triangle in the figure one chooses to begin from, eventually—providing that one sticks to his last and that he labors well—one will "get all around" the complex problems of administration. Little attention, therefore, needs be given to the point at which the student should be introduced to the subject matter. The stress should be upon getting on with it and pushing forward through the full range of related phenomena we call "administration." This set of readings accepts this dictum as a basic criterion for the selection and presentation of readings.

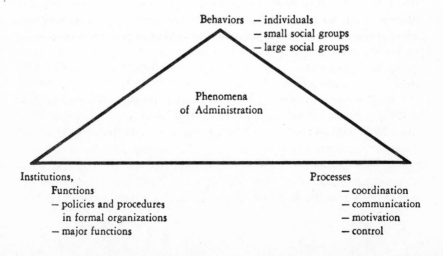

Behaviors — individuals
— small social groups
— large social groups

Phenomena
of Administration

Institutions,
Functions
— policies and procedures
in formal organizations
— major functions

Processes
— coordination
— communication
— motivation
— control

Necessity has independent virtues in this case, moreover. Consider only a single feature. Our main objective in this book of readings is to present a set of stimulating readings that will assist the possible range of students and staff in making exploration of the field more interesting and fruitful. The three imprecisely defined emphases reflected in the readings do service to this objective, and not only in a general sense. Specifically, considerable thought was given to alternative possible uses of the reprinted materials in programs of instruction. For our own edification, and we trust that of our readers as well, three alternative course outlines were designed. One course outline was built around each of the three emphases. The designations of these three alternative outlines are self-explanatory: Institutions and Functions as a Focus; The Process of Coordination as a Focus; and Behavior as a Focus. Each outline lists in the second column the readings in this volume considered appropriate for exploiting specific topics within a number of broad subject-matter areas. For the convenience of the user, various available case studies also are classified under specific headings within each of the three course outlines in the third column. This classification of case studies is the product of our own needs, but we trust it will also serve others.

There are many possible combinations of the selections reprinted here, of course, and any number make perfectly good sense. Therefore, the three course outlines merely illustrate some possible accommodations to the diverse needs and interests of student and teacher. Despite this fact, and despite the fact that most of the selections each treat a wide range of issues and thus cannot be pigeonholed neatly, the classification of the materials was considered worthwhile. At the very least, it demonstrates three diverse ways of using the reprinted materials—of getting on with it and pushing forward through the full range of phenomena we call administration, whatever the specific vantage point from which one desires to introduce the student to the subject matter of Public Administration. And this dynamic feature, of course, primarily motivates this volume.

Table 1   xxi

Table 1   The process of coordination as a focus

Coordination as a resultant process: Some perspectives

Public administration as coordination of systems: Social, cultural, governmental, political	Millett, "The Constitution and Public Administration," *page 355*	"A City Manager Tries to Fire His Police Chief," Inter-University Case Program Pamphlet No. 76
	Price, "The Diffusion of Sovereignty," *page 435*	"Health Centers and Community Needs," Inter-University Case Program Pamphlet No. 105
Public administration as coordination of sub-systems: Authority and the concept of "overlays"	Pfiffner and Sherwood, "Organization as Overlays," *page 423*	"The Blast at Centralia No. 5," pp. 2–22, in Dwight Waldo. ed., *Ideas and Issues in Public Administration* (New York: McGraw-Hill, 1953)

Administrative coordination: Goals and values

Administration as value-laden	Leys, "Good Judgment," *page 302*	"The Glavis-Ballinger Dispute," pp. 77–87, in Harold Stein, ed., *Public Administration and Policy Development* (New York: Harcourt, Brace, 1952)
	Schubert, "Is There a Public Interest Theory?," *page 487*	"Indonesian Assignment," pp. 53–62, in Stein. *op. cit.*
Levels of goals and ethics		
Individual systems: The needs and values of people	Argyris, "Basic Self-Actualization Trends of the Human Personality," *page 23*	"General Patton and the Sicilian Slapping Incidents," pp. 93–96, in Golembiewski. *op. cit.*
Group and institutional systems	Advisory Commission on Intergovernmental Relations, "The Evolution of Collective Negotiations in State and Local Government," *page 1*	"The Lamson Company," pp. 83–88, in Paul R. Lawrence et al., eds., *Organizational Behavior and Administration* (Homewood, Ill.: Dorsey Press and Irwin, 1961)

Table 1 xxiii

	Fesler, "Selecting Field Service Areas," page 122	Frederick C. Mosher and John Haar, Programming Systems and Foreign Affairs Leadership (New York: Oxford University Press. 1970)

Coordination of administration by the legislative branch

Some issues of legislative control: Narrow and broad	Burnham, "Some Administrators Unkindly View Congress," page 56	"Coalition-Building for Depressed Areas Bills," Inter-University Case Program Pamphlet No. 103
	Harris, "Various Vehicles for Legislative Control of Administration," page 224	"Super Carriers and B-36 Bombers," pp. 465–568, in Harold Stein, ed., American Civil-American Decisions (University. Ala.: University of Alabama Press. 1963)
	Moore, "To ... Provide for the Common Defense," page 371	
Specific vehicles of legislative control: The purse strings and parliamentary questions	Fisher, "The Politics of Impounded Funds," page 134	"The Defense Appropriations Rider," Inter-University Case Program Pamphlet No. 59
	Moore, "To ... Provide for the Common Defense," page 371	

Coordination by the executive branch

On being an executive: Some perspectives	Neustadt, "The President as Leader and Clerk: Command, Persuasion, and Public Prestige," page 401	"The Kings River Project," pp. 533–71, in Stein. op. cit.
	Selznick, "Leadership in Administration," page 510	
	Tannenbaum and Massarik, "Leadership: A Frame of Reference," page 573	

Table 1 xxv

Institutions for employee influence

Advisory Commission on Intergovernmental Relations, "The Evolution of Collective Negotiations in State and Local Government," *page 1*

Coordination of various administrative and governmental levels: Delegation, field administration, and federalism

Two varieties of delegation: Centralized and decentralized

Golembiewski, "Organization Development in Public Agencies: Perspectives on Theory and Practice," *page 190*

Kristol, "Decentralization for What?," *page 263*

Price, "The Diffusion of Sovereignty," *page 435*

"Reorganization and Reassignment in the California Highway Patrol," Inter-University Case Program Pamphlet No. 75

"The New York City Health Centers," pp. 609–28, in Edwin A. Bock. ed., *State and Local Government* (New York: 1963)

Field administration: Various patterns of delegation to various areas

Fesler, "Selecting Field Service Areas," *page 122*

"The Regionalization of Business Services in the Agricultural Research Service," Inter-University Case Program Pamphlet No. 106

"Three Cases in Field Administration," Inter-University Case Program Pamphlet No. 16

Federalism: Constitutional decentralization and some consequences

Grodzins, "The Many American Governments and Outdoor Recreation," *page 210*

"The Battle of Blue Earth Country," pp. 89–105, in Stein, *op. cit.*

"The Upstream-Downstream Controversy," Inter-University Case Program Pamphlet No. 55

Intra-agency coordination: Four aspects of the managerial job

Organizing work

Golembiewski, "Civil Service and Managing Work," *page 164*

Shaul, "What's Really Ahead for Middle Management," *page 524*

"Reorganization of the U.S. Public Health Service," Inter-University Case Program Pamphlet No. 89

"The Transfer of the Children's Bureau," pp. 15–30, in Stein, *op. cit.*

"Utility Power Co.," pp. 218–24, in Golembiewski, *op. cit.*

Motivating work

Individual systems

Argyris, "Basic Self-Actualization Trends of the Human Personality," *page 23*

Tannenbaum and Massarik, "Leadership: A Frame of Reference," *page 573*

"The Corelli Case," pp. 681–85, in John D. Glover and Ralph M. Hower, eds., *The Administrator* 3d ed. (Homewood, Ill.: Irwin, 1957)

Group and institutional systems

Cornog, "The Personnel Administrator: His Role and His Role Conflicts," *page 78*

Golembiewski, "Civil Service and Managing Work," *page 164*

March and Simon, "Delegation: Anticipated and Unanticipated Consequences," *page 331*

"Administrative Procedure in A Regulatory Agency," Inter-University Case Program Pamphlet No. 85

"Reorganization of the California State Personnel Board," Inter-University Case Program Pamphlet No. 32

Table 2 **xxix**

Table 2 Institutions and functions as a focus

The place of administration	Millett, "The Constitution and Public Administration," *page 355*	"The Blast At Centralia No. 5," pp. 2–22, in Dwight Waldo, ed., *Ideas and Issues in Public Administration* (New York: McGraw-Hill, 1953) "Health Centers and Community Needs," Inter-University Case Program Pamphlet No. 105
The matter of structure		
The theoretical nature of organization	Kuriloff, "An Experiment in Management: Putting Theory Y to the Test," *page 274*	"Production Planning in the Patent Office," pp. 1–14, in Harold Stein, ed. *Public Administration and Policy Development* (New York: Harcourt, Brace, 1952) "Utility Power Company," pp. 218–24, in Robert T. Golembiewski, *Perspectives on Public Management* (Itasca, Ill.: Peacock, 1968)
The politics of organization	Lee, "Behavioral Theory vs. Reality," *page 286*	"The Office of Education Library," pp. 31–52, in *ibid.*
The matter of reorganization	Golembiewski, "Organization Development in Public Agencies: Perspectives on Theory and Practice," *page 190*	Stephen K. Bailey and Edith K. Mosher, *E.S.E.A.: The Office of Education Administers A Law* (Syracuse, N.Y.: Syracuse University Press, 1968) "Reorganization and Reassignment in the California Highway Patrol," pp. 185–216, in Frederick C. Mosher, ed., *Governmental Reorganization* (New York: Bobbs-Merrill, 1967)

Table 2   xxxi

The structure and the employee organization

Advisory Commission on Intergovernmental Relations, "The Evolution of Collective Negotiations in State and Local Government," *page 1*

"The Glavis-Ballinger Dispute," pp. 77–88, in Stein. *op. cit.*

The finance system

Who gets what?

Hatry and Cotton, "What is a PPBS System?," *page 230*

Quade, "Systems Analysis Techniques for Planning—Programming—Budgeting," *page 457*

Turnbull, "PPBS in Perspective," *page 598*

"The FBI Retirement Bill," pp. 649–60, in Stein. *op. cit.*

Who controls?

Fisher, "The Politics of Impounded Funds," *page 134*

"The King's River Project," pp. 533–57, in Stein. *op. cit.*

Control of administration

Congressional relations

Burnham, "Some Administrators Unkindly View Congress," *page 56*

Harris, "Various Vehicles for Legislative Control of Administration," *page 224*

Moore, "To . . . Provide for the Common Defense," *page 371*

Gibson, "Organizations and Their Environments: The School System as a Focus," *page 156*

"The Defense Appropriations Rider," Inter-University Case Program Pamphlet No. 59

"Coalition-Building for Depressed Areas Bills," Inter-University Case Program No. 103

Interest group representation: Organized and unorganized

"Noerr Motor Freight vs. E.R.P.C.," pp. 140–58, in Golembiewski. *op. cit.*

Table 2   xxxiii

Table 3 Behavior as a focus

The objectives of the world of organization: Values as a framework of behavior

Schubert, "Is There a Public Interest Theory," *page 487*

"Gotham in the Air Age," in Harold Stein, ed., *Public Administration and Policy Development* (New York: Harcourt, Brace, 1952), pp. 143–97

"The Blast at Centralia No. 5: Mine Disaster No One Stopped," pp. 2–22, in Dwight Waldo, ed., *Ideas and Issues in Public Administration* (New York: McGraw-Hill, 1953)

"R.E.A. Personnel Report," pp. 621–32, in Stein, *op. cit.*

The psychological world: Individual behavior in organization

Argyris, "Basic Self-Actualization Trends of the Human Personality," *page 23*

"Joseph Longman," pp. 159–63, in John D. Glover and Ralph M. Hower, eds., *The Administrator* (Homewood, Illinois: Irwin, 1957)

Cornog, "The Personnel Administrator: His Role and His Role Conflicts," *page 78*

"The NLRB Field Examiner," pp. 63–75, in Stein, *op. cit.*

Kuriloff, "An Experiment in Management: Putting Theory Y to the Test," *page 274*

"Veteran's Hospital Social Service Department," pp. 495–98, in Robert Dubin, *Human Relations in Administration: The Sociology of Organization* (Englewood Cliffs, N.J.: Prentice-Hall, 1956)

Table 3   xxxv

Lee, "Behavioral Theory vs. Reality,"
page 286

The sociological world: Group behavior and organization

The group

Blau, "The Taboo on Reporting Offers
of Bribes," *page 27*

"Cal Young," pp. 548–49, in Dubin. *op.
cit.*

Inter-group relations

Advisory Commission on
Intergovernmental Relations, "The
Evolution of Collective Negotiations in
State and Local Government," *page 1*

"Lamson Company," pp. 45–48, in
Glover and Hower, *op. cit.*

Stephen Bailey and Edith K. Mosher,
*E.S.E.A.: The Office of Education
Administers A Law* (Syracuse, N.Y.:
Syracuse University Press, 1968)

Worlds into universe: Individuals, groups, and formal organization

Theory of formal organization

Golembiewski, "Civil Service and
Managing Work," *page 164*

"Production Planning in the Patent
Office," pp. 1–13, in Stein. *op. cit.*

Pfiffner and Sherwood, "Organization
as Overlays," *page 423*

"Utility Power Company," pp. 218–24,
in Robert T. Golembiewski, *Perspectives
on Public Management* (Itasca, Ill.:
Peacock, 1968)

Methods of formalizing behavior

Fesler, "Selecting Field Service Areas,"
page 122

"Indonesian Assignment," *ibid.* pp.
53–61.

Kristol, "Decentralization for What?,"
page 263

"Regionalization of Business Services in
the Agricultural Research Service,"
Inter-University Case Program No. 106

Impact of structure	Miller and Rein, "Participation, Poverty, and Administration," *page 335*	"A Case Study of Innovation," pp. 38–44, in Golembiewski, *op. cit.*
	Argyris, "Basic Self-Actualization Trends of the Human Personality," *page 23*	
	Cornog, "The Personnel Administrator: His Role and His Role Conflicts," *page 78*	"Grand City School System," pp. 464–70, in Dubin, *op. cit.*
		"Reorganization of the California State Personnel Board," Inter-University Case Program Pamphlet No. 32
	Dumont, "Down the Bureaucracy!," *page 112*	
	March and Simon, "Delegation: Anticipated and Unanticipated Consequences," *page 331*	
	Shaul, "What's Really Ahead for Middle Management," *page 524*	

Defining the universe of organization: Leadership and headship

Goals and leadership	Committee for Economic Development "The Federal Service: Those Who Serve at the Top," *page 63*	"The Martin Company," pp. 81–86, in Golembiewski, *op. cit.*
	Neustadt, "The President as Leader and Clerk: Command, Persuasion, and Public Prestige," *page 401*	"The American Decision to Rearm Germany," pp. 643–46, in Harold Stein, ed., *American Civil Military Decisions* (University, Ala.: University of Alabama Press, 1963)
	Selznick, "Leadership in Administration," *page 510*	
	Tannenbaum and Massarik, "Leadership: A Frame of Reference," *page 573*	

Table 3 **xxxvii**

Unifying the universe: Communication and information

The communications process

Johnson, "The Fateful Process of Mr. A Talking to Mr. B," *page 248*

Boss, "Decision-Making in the Budgetary Process," *page 36*

"Dashman Company," pp. 741-42, in Glover and Hower, *op. cit.*

"The Air Search and Rescue Program," pp. 363-90, in Stein, *op. cit.*

The decision-making process

Dill, "Administrative Decision-Making," *page 90*

Lindblom, "The Science of Muddling Through," *page 311*

Leys, "Good Judgment," *page 302*

Technology of information processing

Schumacher, "An Electronic Data Processing System," *page 501*

"Personnel Problems in Converting to Automation," Inter-University Case Program Pamphlet No. 44

Dividing the universe: The strategies of politics and power

Cornog, "Influence, Power, and Authority in Organization," *page 72*

Dumont, "Down the Bureaucracy!," *page 112*

Gibson, "Organizations and Their Environments: The School System as a Focus," *page 156*

Golembiewski, "Civil Service and Managing Work," *page 164*

Grodzins, "The Many American Governments and Outdoor Recreation," *page 210*

"Architects, Politics and Bureaucracy: Reorganization of the California Division of Architecture," pp. 441-74, in Mosher, *op. cit.*

"The Battle of Blue Earth County," pp. 89-105, in Stein, *op. cit.*

Price, "The Diffusion of Sovereignty," *page 435*

Subramaniam, "Representative Bureaucracy: A Reassessment," *page 535*

Controlling the universe: Responsibility, ethics, and control

Performance and its evaluation

Ridgway, "Dysfunctional Consequences of Performance Measurements," *page 478*

"The Kings River Project," pp. 533–72. in *op. cit.*

"The REA Personnel Report," *ibid.,* pp. 621–32.

Suchman, "Evaluation and Program Administration," *page 552*

Frederick Mosher and John Haar, *Programming Systems and Foreign Affairs Leadership* (New York: Oxford University Press, 1970)

Plans, budgets, legislatures, and courts: The formal controls

Fisher, "The Politics of Impounded Funds," *page 134*

"The Departmental Expense Ledger," pp. 558–60. in Dubin, *op. cit.*

Harris, "Various Vehicles for Legislative Control of Administration," *page 224*

"The General Accounting Office: Two Glimpses," Inter-University Case Program Pamphlet No. 35

Hatry and Cotton, "What is a PPBS System?," *page 230*

Moore, "To . . . Provide for the Common Defense," *page 371*

Nixon, "Reorganization Plan No. 2 of 1970," *page 408*

Quade, "Systems Analysis Techniques for Planning—Programming—Budgeting," *page 457*

"Noerr Motor Freight vs. E.R.P.C.," pp. 140–58. in Golembiewski, *op. cit.*

Table 3   **xxxix**

Attitudes and opinions: Informal controls	Turnbull, "PPBS in Perspective," *page 598*	
	Advisory Commission on Intergovernmental Relations, "The Evolution of Collective Negotiations in State and Local Government," *page 1*	"State Highway Department." pp. 33–40, in R. Joseph Novogorod. Gladys O. Dimock. and Marshall E. Dimock. eds.. *Casebook in Public Administration* (New York: Holt, Rinehart, and Winston. 1969)
	Burnham, "Some Administrators Unkindly View Congress," *page 56*	
	Price, "The Diffusion of Sovereignty," *page 435*	"The Emergency Rubber Project." pp. 633–48, in Stein, *op. cit.*

The Evolution of Collective Negotiations in State and Local Government

Advisory Commission
on Intergovernmental Relations

Before examining current employer-employee practices at the state and local levels of government, a brief historical look should be taken at the growth of public employee organizations and the factors contributing to their drive for recognition and a voice in matters affecting the terms and conditions of work. The wisdom of according public employees a participatory role is accepted today by a large segment of public officials and administrators. The real question is not whether but how much participation. How and why has this come about?

Public employee organizations

While the growth of public employee organizations at local, state, and national levels has not been commensurate with the growth of government itself, the organizations affiliated with national unions nevertheless comprise the most rapidly expanding sector of unionized labor. In 1956, the 915,000 organized government employees constituted approximately 5 percent of the total AFL-CIO membership; by 1964, 1.45 million such employees represented 8 percent of the total. The unionized public sector reached the 1.7 million mark in 1966 (the latest year for

Reprinted from Advisory Commission on Intergovernmental Relations, *Labor-Management Policies For State And Local Government* (Washington, D.C.: U.S. Government Printing Office, 1969), pp. 5–27. Footnotes have been renumbered.

reliable figures) or 9 percent of all union members.[1] In addition, while the proportion of unionized workers in relation to the entire labor force had dropped in recent years, the proportion of government employees—unionized and nonunionized—in the country's labor force rose from 12 percent in 1956 to 16 percent in 1964, but dipped to 15.4 percent in 1966 and 15.0 percent in 1968.

Unionization efforts, however, have scored differing records at the various levels of government, with the greatest success occurring at the federal level. Fifty-two percent, or 1.4 million members, of all federal executive branch employees in 1968 belonged to unions recognized for discussion purposes. Only 8 percent, or 644,000 members, of all state and local government workers belonged to affiliates of national unions in 1966. Two years later the figure edged up to 9.6 percent or approximately 890,000 members. These figures, of course, do not include professional associations such as those affiliated with the National Educational Association (NEA) or independent unions. Of the 1,026 organized cities over 10,000 population responding to a 1969 Advisory Commission survey made in cooperation with the International City Management Association (ICMA) and the National Association of Counties (NACO), 38 percent of the reporting jurisdictions with organized employees indicated that some of their employees were members of national unions, while 48 percent reported that organized employees belonged only to nationally affiliated local unions. Of the 117 organized metropolitan counties participating in the survey, 48 percent stated that some of their employees were members of national unions and 38 percent replied that their organized personnel were wholly in the unionized sector.

Yet unions constitute only one portion of the organized sector. Independent state and local employee associations loom large in the overall organized personnel picture with more than one-fifth of the total. For the municipalities participating in the ACIR-ICMA survey, 38 percent reported that some of their personnel were members of such associations

---

[1]Everett M. Kassalow, "Trade Unionism Goes Public," *The Public Interest,* No. 14, Winter 1969 p. 122. Three public unions have been at the forefront of this general advance: the American Federation of Government Employees, the American Federation of State, County and Municipal Employees, and the American Federation of Teachers.

and 14 percent indicated that their organized employees were exclusively associational members. Of the organized counties participating in the ACIR-NACO poll, 48 percent had some of their organized employees belonging to local associations and 14 percent had all such personnel in these organizations. Finally, professional associations with or without national organizations account for over 45 percent of the total organized state and local public sector.

Most public employee organizations at the state, county, and municipal levels may be divided into three major categories.[2] The professional associations include—among others—employee groups for teachers and school administrators, nurses, and social and welfare workers. The craft unions primarily consist of single occupational groups of employees—while the industrial type of union or association cuts across broad occupational categories in various departments and sometimes in whole governmental jurisdictions.

Professional associations. Professional associations represent a great variety of professional and semi-professional public employees at the state and local levels. All of them, however, are concerned with certification, training, codes of ethics, the right to exclude nonprofessionals from their organization, and the economic and social welfare of their members. Some of them are hardly distinguishable from unions with respect to employer relations and other related activities.

Among the largest is the National Education Association (NEA) with approximately one million members. Public school teachers constitute approximately 85 percent of the total membership of NEA with supervisors, principals, administrators and other school specialists accounting for the remaining 15 percent. This policy underscores a major difference between the NEA and the American Federation of Teachers, which limits its membership only to classroom teachers. Members of each of the 50 NEA state affiliates and most of the 8,000 local associations include

[2]Benjamin Werne, *Unit Report: Structure of Unions in the Public Employment Sector* (Washington, D.C.: National City-County Services on Management-Labor Relations, a joint service of the National League of Cities and the National Association of Counties, August 1967), p. 2.

teachers, supervisors, and administrators.[3] At the same time, the state affiliates enjoy a relatively high degree of autonomy in membership policies as well as in other matters.

* * *

Another professional association, the National Association of Social Workers (NASW), was established in 1955 with the merger of several professional groups. As of December 1968, it had an overall membership of slightly over 50,000 including student and private sector worker members. "Bread-and-butter" economic activities are carried on only in a limited way by NASW, but they are a focal point of concern of separate, local social worker unions. The Association, however, has never viewed the latter as a threat to its existence, probably because less than 15 percent of all social welfare workers are unionized. The American Nurses Association is another such professional group with 204,000 members (1967) or 31 percent of all nurses working in public and private institutions. The ANA is concerned with more than just professional standards. It actively engages in employer discussions and collective bargaining, seeks exclusive recognition, negotiates contracts and agreements, and has, on a few occasions, engaged in walkouts. In the summer of 1968, the ANA removed the clause from its constitution prohibiting strikes.

Another national organization, the Fraternal Order of Police, is independent of labor movement organizations and is the principal professional organization for policemen. FOP does not consider itself a union, although local lodges in some communities engage in collective bargaining, handle grievances and represent the interests of their members to their employer. In general, however, the FOP concentrates on police pension matters and improvement in police working conditions. The Grand Lodge of FOP was organized in 1915 and today claims to have over 620 lodges in 18 states, with a total of 62,600 members.

Craft-type unions. One of the largest among the craft-type unions is the International Association of Firefighters (IAFF), an affiliate of the

---

[3]However, an increasing number of bargaining agreements involving NEA locals divide representation into two categories—teachers and supervisors—thereby avoiding the issue of "divided loyalty."

AFL-CIO. The organization had its origins in the fraternal and social clubs of the 1880's and today claims that better than 90 percent of the nation's uniformed firemen are enrolled within its membership. In 1935, Association members numbered approximately 26,000. Nearly three decades later, the union claimed 115,000 members. Last year (1968), the total came to 131,356. The Association has operated traditionally without written contracts or agreements and adhered loyally to its constitutional ban on strikes. At its 1968 convention, however, the membership removed the fifty-year-old no-strike pledge from its constitution.

* * *

Another major public employee "craft" union is the American Federation of Teachers, which affiliated with the old American Federation of Labor in 1919. Their greatest success has been in the large cities with about 80 percent of the Federation's members employed in school systems with an enrollment of 100,000 or more. In terms of size, the AFT has a membership of 175,000 or about 20 percent of the country's organized teachers. For collective negotiation and discussion purposes, the AFT claims that their locals, in effect, serve as the representatives of approximately a quarter of a million school teachers.

Blue collar craft unions also are found frequently at national, state, county and municipal levels. Organization of some of these governmental employees has kept pace with the unionization of the counterpart trades in private industry.

* * *

No accurate count, however, is available concerning the number of state and local employees belonging to these craft unions.

Finally, establishment of a national police union has been announced with the goal of enrolling 325,000 law enforcement officers.

Industrial-type unions. The dominant "industrial-type" union at these levels is the American Federation of State, County, and Municipal Employees (AFSCME), an affiliate of the AFL-CIO. AFSCME traces its ancestry back to 1932 when a small group of Wisconsin State employees formed the Wisconsin State Employees Association and received an AFL charter. A month later, the local had 53 members. Within a year, the organization was exploring the possibility of establishing a national union, but this effort soon generated jurisdictional problems with the American Federation of Government Employees, another AFL affiliate. AFGE's charter from the AFL gave it ill-defined jurisdiction over all government employees, but its organizational activity had been confined almost exclusively to the federal service. With the emerging threat of a rival national organization, the union's leadership decided to clarify AFGE's position and in 1935 amended its constitution to claim jurisdiction over state and local employees as well as those in the federal sector.

At that time, the AFL leadership generally was indifferent to the unionization of public employees. Some heads of the older craft unions wanted no part of the public employee field. Yet, the AFL faced another far more difficult problem in 1935: the withdrawal of industrial unions to form the Congress of Industrial Organizations under the leadership of the Mineworker's President, John L. Lewis. The AFL leadership realized that unless the jurisdictional disputes between AFGE and the new organization of state and local employees were resolved, the newly organized CIO might issue a national charter to the ambitious newcomers.

Consequently, the AFL Executive Council promoted an agreement whereby the state and local group would become a semi-autonomous affiliate of AFGE, with its own convention and leadership. In effect, the AFGE would be merely the channel of communication with the parent AFL. The new group then held its first national convention in December 1935 and ratified the agreement. The organization thus formally became the American Federation of State, County, and Municipal Employees, adopted a constitution and elected its own officers.

But the AFGE-AFSCME relationship continued to be competitive. AFGE sought to limit AFSCME organizing to white-collar workers in state and local agencies—a restriction AFSCME would not accept. When AFGE voted in new leadership in 1936, the matter again was placed before the AFL Executive Council, and it finally decided to grant AFSCME independent status.

While the early growth of AFSCME was not impressive, its membership, as of July 1969, had soared to 425,000. It claims—with good reason—to be the fastest growing union in the country. Although two-thirds of its members hold blue collar jobs, its occupational categories range from garbage collectors to zoo keepers, from architects to psychologists, from laborers to lawyers. The Federation's chief aim is to achieve establishment of a system of collective bargaining which produces written agreements. Its basic procedural concerns then center on recognition, bargaining, union security, checkoff, and the use of signed contracts. In recent years, the union's members have not hesitated to strike even in jurisdictions where walk-outs are not permitted. In December 1968, the Federation reported that of its 700 local agreements 16 percent provided for a union shop, 12 percent for a modified union shop, and 10 percent contained a maintenance of membership provision. Five percent of the total stipulated an "agency shop" arrangement and half of the 700 agreements, concluded with jurisdictions in at least 24 states, call for binding arbitration of grievance disputes.

AFSCME reports that to date more than 1,850 local affiliates have been organized. Locals may represent an entire city or county, or alternatively a particular department, part of a department, or a group of employers in a particular occupational classification which cuts across many departments.

In addition to AFSCME, independent unaffiliated associations of public employees exist in at least 37 state governments and an indeterminate number of local governments. Their membership is drawn from all departments and agencies of these jurisdictions. Nearly all have nonselective enrollment policies and may count as members elected and appointive officials, department heads, supervisors, as well as rank and file workers. At least 14 states have two or more statewide public employee organizations and several associations have local unit affiliates organized on a substate regional basis.

These associations in the past generally have been satisfied with informal recognition by employers, and membership has never been required as a condition of employment. They usually have relied on lobbying to achieve better working conditions and have depended upon civil service procedures rather than on collective negotiations to settle disputes. Their affiliated competitors have frequently referred to them as "company unions."

With the recent passage of public labor-management legislation, however, a good deal of competition has been generated between these independent associations and the affiliated unions, both for membership and exclusive recognition rights.

* * *

A number of associations at both the state and local levels now are beginning to scrap their traditional passive practices and are adopting a fairly militant stance.

* * *

Published material on these unaffiliated organizations is limited and detailed analysis of the scope and nature of their membership and activities is virtually nonexistent.[4] What evidence there is, however, suggests that some of them are more than holding their own against unions in representation elections, partly because of their own increased militance and concern with establishing viable discussion and negotiation procedures.[5]

* * *

Factors contributing to the growth and militancy of public employee organization

Historically, professional and white-collar public employees have been reluctant to join labor unions. Nor have they displayed a high degree of interest in independent employee organizations. Today, however, dramatic changes are taking place. Not only have more government workers been joining public employee organizations and unions, but they have become more and more militant in their relationships with their employers. A number of factors have contributed to this trend, including the greater need for certain occupational groups to make themselves heard by employers, the new interest of the labor movement in organizing public personnel, the rivalry for recognition between public em-

[4]For a brief overview of the general characteristics of independent public employee organizations, see Kenneth O. Warner and Mary L. Hennessy, *Public Management at the Bargaining Table,* (Chicago: Public Personnel Association, 1967), pp. 28–31, 220–24.

[5]Everett M. Kassalow, "Canadian and U.S. White-Collar Union Increases," *Monthly Labor Review,* Vol. 91, No. 7, (July 1968), p. 43.

ployee professional organizations and unions, the experience of several pioneering cities, the promulgation of Federal Executive Order 10988, and the reluctance of many public employers to face up to new personnel administration problems.

The pressures of the non-PAT sector. The percentage of governmental employees that possesses considerable formal education, and has close ties with professional associations concerned with standards of work performance, is steadily increasing.[6] At the same time, the proportion of skilled and specialized technical employees also is rising in the public sector work force. The demand for these professional, administrative, and technical (PAT) personnel has created a shortage of persons possessing these skills. Hence, these persons are able to bargain individually and effectively with potential and actual employers and usually are able to secure quite favorable salaries and working conditions. If not satisfied with their present work assignment, they can move from one employer to another, from one part of the country to another, and still remain committed to one type of career employment in today's job market.

The semi-skilled, clerical, and even unskilled workers (the non-PAT sector), on the other hand, still make up a considerable part of the public personnel work force. Unlike their better-paid counterparts, they do not have the individual advantage of possessing skills in short supply or of having job mobility. In short, they do not possess, as individuals, a good bargaining position concerning their wages, hours of work, or working conditions. In the past, many governments have induced such persons to accept employment with the assurance that tenure and certain fringe benefits would be provided, possibly for the entire span of the individual's productive work career. But as the cost and standards of living have risen, especially during the past decade, this group of employees has become much more dependent on employee associations or unions to increase their earning power by dealing collectively with their employers.

[6]Winston W. Crouch, *Employer-Employee Relations in Council-Manager Cities,* (Washington, D.C.: International City Managers' Association, 1968), pp. 1-2.

Union effectiveness in private industry. The effectiveness of labor unions in the private sector, notably in salary and fringe benefit matters, has also influenced public employee organizations at the state and local levels. As a result, the value of the collective bargaining technique in private industry was and is appreciated and public employees have begun to be more receptive to organizing efforts. Hence, public employee organizations, in relatively short order, have been able to organize, present their demands to management, and, in some instances, when it was deemed necessary, to use the outlawed weapon of work stoppage.

Changes in labor movement membership strategies. In addition to the above factors, the recent drives of the labor movement to organize public employees also can be attributed partly to the failure of unions to increase their membership in proportion to the number of workers in the rapidly growing total labor force. The total civilian labor force has now reached a new high of approximately 80 million, but labor union membership (18,325,000) has not risen proportionately—with only somewhat more than 2 million added to the membership rolls between 1955 and 1967. Put another way, two out of every five workers eligible for union membership in 1955 carried union cards; now only two out of every six do.

Labor traditionally has been strong in organizing blue collar workers, especially those working in production and maintenance jobs in the industrial plants, and in the skilled and semiskilled trades. But opportunities for expansion in the blue collar work force have been shrinking. Automation and other technological changes have eliminated many production jobs. At the same time, the "service" industry (retail and wholesale trade, finance, insurance, and government) has been expanding. Moreover, white collar workers are now more numerous than is the blue collar sector. Yet, the former generally has been much more difficult to organize. No wonder labor has turned its attention to government, particularly when total employment in the public sector now is only about one million less than the total membership of the AFL-CIO.

Professional employee association and union rivalry. The emerging aggressiveness of the union movement in the public sector has come about in part as a result of confrontations between long-established public employee professional organizations and labor unions. As these groups fight for recognition and control, each often finds itself attempting to outdo the other in obtaining benefits for its members. Some observers feel that this is a primary cause of the militance now found in the education field.

Pioneering labor relations experience. Certain authorities also claim that the earlier experience in the cities of New York, Philadelphia, and Cincinnati also has played a part in setting the stage of today's activity. New York's former Mayor Robert F. Wagner issued an executive order in 1958 permitting city employees limited use of collective negotiations; Philadelphia since 1939 has had labor agreements containing provisions for union security and exclusive recognition; and employee organizations in Cincinnati have enjoyed *de facto* recognition since 1951. These early agreements served as examples for other cities. As the 1967 Task Force Report of the National Governors' Conference points out:[7]

> Neither the pillars of city halls nor the foundations of the civil service crumbled when conditions of employment were negotiated instead of being fixed unilaterally. But it took a bit of adjustment. The spontaneous reaction of many personnel directors was: "It's against civil service regulations. We can't agree to this." But they somehow managed to work things out.

In a like fashion, some contend that recent state labor relations legislation has served to generate organizational militance, even in small and rural local jurisdictions.

Federal labor-management policy. Executive Order 10988, issued by President Kennedy in 1962 to establish a uniform policy on employee-management relations in the federal service, also helped to stimulate organizational growth at the state and local levels. The Order, considered by many a landmark in the public labor relations field, was

[7]National Governors' Conference, *Report of Task Force on State and Local Government Labor Relations,* (Chicago, Ill.: Public Personnel Association for the 1967 Executive Committee of the National Governors' Conference, 1967), p. 32.

unequivocal in its support for union recognition and for establishing a meet and confer system in the public sector. In terms of its state and local impact, Jerry Wurf, president of the AFSCME, stated:[8]

> His (President Kennedy's) action, which gave federal employees the right to organize and set an example that has been followed by many states, counties, and cities, probably was a major contributing factor in the rapid growth of the American Federation of State, County, and Municipal Employees.

Other observers in and out of government, however, deplored the Kennedy Order since they felt that it opened a Pandora's box.

Nevertheless, on October 29, 1969, President Nixon moved to revamp the 1962 Order. His Executive Order 11491, "Labor-Management Relations in the Federal Service," made significant changes in the membership rights of certain types of personnel; in the status accorded to employee organizations in the negotiations process; and in the machinery available to administer and supervise the federal employer-employee relations program, to settle policy issues, and to handle disputes and grievances. Despite these modifications, wages and salaries and related "bread and butter" issues remained outside of the scope of negotiable items. Agencies and employee organizations were required to meet and negotiate "in good faith" only with respect to grievances, personnel practices and policies, and other matters affecting conditions of work.

A matter of mood? Still others explain public employee aggressiveness as an extension of the contemporary revolt against authority and as a spill-over from the civil rights movement and protest groups involved in direct confrontation with governmental power. From this vantage point, organizational militance becomes a matter of mood, of questioning traditional procedures for seeking redress, of emulating direct action tactics that appear to produce results. Moreover, in this instance, the aggressiveness is displayed by persons charged with the difficult task on a day-to-day basis of carrying on the many public services demanded by the electorate. At the same time, so the reasoning runs, this sector of

[8]Jerry Wurf, "Unions Enter City Hall," *Public Management, Journal of the International City Managers' Association*, (September 1966), p. 245.

the work force is most victimized by the distance, impersonality, and inflexible procedures of government and most subject to abusive and annoying treatment from the press and the public-at-large. Group militance thus becomes a matter of building vocational esteem, of asserting the members' individual worth, of forcing the impersonal "them" to recognize their existence and role in society and in the "system."

Management lethargy. Finally, the "head-in-the-sand" attitude of many public administrators has forced increasing militancy on the part of public employees.[9] For example, many government employers fail, either through carelessness or by design, to consult with their employees about procedures and policies that affect them. Many are wedded to an absolutist management ethic, which has long since been modified by governing bodies in other jurisdictions. Some governmental employers still refuse to have anything to do with unions or employee organizations, despite court decisions upholding the employee's right to join such organizations. These practices are frustrating to employees and do nothing to generate positive labor-management relations. In such cases, it is not surprising that unions attempt to reach beyond the administrator's authority to legislative bodies, the courts, and even the public to achieve their objectives. It is an unfortunate fact that this route is the only one for public employees in some jurisdictions to follow, if they are to be heard.

State legal and administrative authorization

Until 1959, when Wisconsin enacted a labor relations law for the public sector, there was no state statutory obligation on public management to deal collectively with its employees.[10] But action on this front has accelerated with each legislative session during the past decade. Witness the fact that in 1967 alone new legislation covering some as-

[9]Felix A. Nigro, "Collective Negotiations in the Public Service," *Public Administration Review,* (March-April 1968), pp. 115–117.

[10]The following discussion is based partly on *Report of Task Force on State and Local Government Labor Relations, op. cit.*

pect of labor relations in the public sector was adopted by 17 states.[11] In the 1968 and 1969 legislative sessions, ten states enacted new or significantly amended statutes affecting local and state public employees. At the present time, wide variations exist in state legal and administrative authorizations regarding labor relations in the public service.

* * *

Meet and confer and collective negotiations. Two general approaches characterize state legislation dealing with public employer-employee relations: meet and confer or collective negotiations. The basic and most significant difference between the two types of laws is the status accorded to the public employer in discussions over wages, hours, and conditions of work with employee organizations. The employer, under a meet and confer system, is given authority to make the final decision on most of the issues. This system is rooted in the assumption that there are basic differences between public and private employment, and that the distinctive features of the former require a significantly different approach in public labor management relations, one that is somewhat more protective of management's prerogatives. Under a collective negotiation system the public employer and representatives of an employee organization meet more nearly as equals. To put it another way, management's rights are less broad than under meet and confer and employee participation is somewhat better protected. As a result this system tends to resemble the labor relations pattern found in business and industry, although the right to strike is prohibited.

* * *

Statutory provisions affecting local public employees. Generally, four broad approaches characterize the various state policies relating to the obligations of *local* officials with their employees in the field of labor relations.

[11]Richard S. Rubin, *A Summary of State Collective Bargaining Law in Public Employment,* Public Employee Relations Report, No. 3, (Ithaca, N.Y.: New York State School of Industrial and Labor Relations, 1968), p. i.

- Avoidance of any recognition of employee organizations and silence concerning methods for resolving labor-management disputes at the local government level. (In some states where no such legislation exists, however, local jurisdictions have established their own negotiating procedures either by ordinance, executive order, or on a more informal basis.)
- Strengthening the hand of city officials who may wish to seek injunctions against striking public employees. The statutes here deal almost exclusively with controlling strikes, and ignore other facets of labor relations.
- Legislation giving certain local government occupational groups special consideration regarding organizing, presenting grievances, and negotiations. The groups frequently singled out include teachers, firemen, law enforcement officers, and utility and transit workers.
- A broad comprehensive statute setting forth policies and procedures, based on the meet and confer or collective negotiation concepts and covering all local employees and sometimes state personnel as well. These statutes usually offer the services of a state administrative agency as a third party to settle disputes.

Statutory provisions affecting state employees. State employee organizations in 26 states have been accorded meet and confer or collective negotiation rights by law, attorneys general opinions, executive orders, or court decisions. These legal and administrative actions cover state employees separately from local employees in 12 of the states. Of the 26 states, ten have laws or rules permitting or requiring administrators to meet and confer with state employee groups; 16 permit or require employers to establish collective negotiations with such groups. Employers in five states (California, Hawaii, Minnesota, Missouri, and South Dakota) are required to meet and confer with employees while in ten states (Delaware, Massachusetts, New Hampshire, New Jersey, New York, Oregon, Rhode Island, Vermont, Washington, and Wisconsin) they are required to bargain collectively with employee organizations.

On the other hand, Texas and Virginia forbid their officials to negotiate with unions and Alabama and North Carolina prohibit their employees from joining unions. In general, state practice tends to be more restrictive in collective bargaining matters for their own employees than for local government personnel.[12]

Permitting or mandating discussions or negotiations for local and state employees. In terms of *mandating* collective negotiations, 14 states—Connecticut, Delaware, Maine, Massachusetts, Michigan, Nevada, New Hampshire, New Jersey, New York, Oregon, Rhode Island, Vermont, Washington, and Wisconsin—have enacted a labor relations law requiring this for either local or state employees, or both. . . .[13] Alaska, Nebraska, and North Dakota statutes *permit* collective bargaining. Moreover, seven others, Arkansas, Idaho, Iowa, Montana, North Dakota, Utah and Virginia permit the state, localities, or both, but at their discretion, to undertake collective negotiations as a result of attorneys general opinions.

Five states—California, Hawaii, Minnesota, Missouri and South Dakota—have statutes that require management to meet and confer with public employees concerning wages and conditions of work. In three states, Indiana, Kentucky, and New Mexico, local public employees may, as a result of attorneys general opinions, be accorded meet and confer rights. The Pennsylvania attorney general has ruled that state employers *may* establish meet and confer procedures with their employees.

Finally, a number of states have enacted statutes requiring management to bargain collectively only with certain occupational categories, such as teachers, policemen, and firemen.

Legal bases of the right to organize. While nearly two-fifths of the states have enacted legislation requiring negotiations or discussions, the right to organize is protected for substantially all public employees in 33 states either by law, attorneys general opinions, court decisions, or executive orders. In two other states (Illinois and Oklahoma), this right is given only to state employees, while in three others (Connecticut, Nebraska, and Nevada) only local employees are permitted to organize.

---

[12] *Report of Task Force on State and Local Government, op.cit.,* p. 30.

[13] Opinions vary as to whether Minnesota and Missouri should be included within this group of states. See Rubin, *op.cit.,* p.i.

In 12 states no legal or administrative authorization is provided for public employees—either at the state or local levels—to organize. Some of these jurisdictions, however, have made exceptions in that certain occupational groups, such as teachers, policemen, and firemen, are allowed to establish public employee organizations.

Coverage, administrative machinery, dispute settlement, and unfair practices. The other basic provisions of these state laws sometimes highlight and sometimes reveal no differences between the states adopting the meet and confer or collective negotiation system.[14] A single law may cover all state and local public employees as is the case in 11 states, or legislation may be enacted separately for state and local employees—Massachusetts, Michigan, Rhode Island, Vermont, and Wisconsin. Four states—Minnesota, Nebraska, Oregon, and Washington—have single legislation for state and local employees, but have enacted separate laws covering negotiations between teachers and their employers. Coverage clearly does not serve as a differentiating factor between the meet and confer and collective negotiations systems.

A new independent state-level agency may be established to settle representation disputes, investigate unfair labor practices, determine bargaining units, and conduct elections as in Connecticut, Massachusetts, Michigan, New Hampshire, Rhode Island, New Jersey, New York, Vermont, and Wisconsin. On the other hand, a civil service board or commission, as in California, may be assigned responsibility for administering the act. Statutes covering school personnel in Connecticut, Minnesota, and Oregon designate an *ad hoc* committee or local school boards as the administering unit to settle disputes. Here again no clear differences emerge as between the two contrasting systems.

[14]In addition to material in the *Report of Task Force on State and Local Government Labor Relations, Ibid.,* pp. 50–61, see also Kurt L. Hanslowe, *The Emerging Law of Labor Relations in Public Employment,* New York State School of Industrial and Labor Relations, Cornell University, Ithaca, New York, 1967, pp. 59–70; AFL-CIO Maritime Trades Department, Executive Board, *Collective Bargaining in the Public Sector,* An Interim Report (Washington, D.C.: February 13, 1969), pp. 33–43, 52–61.

Analysis of the various provisions covering settlement of disputes indicates that all of the 16 collective negotiation statutes, save for Alaska's, have one feature in common. Although there are differences of terminology and detail, these laws call for fact-finding and binding or non-binding arbitration to resolve bargaining or negotiating impasses. By way of contrast, dispute settlement provisions of the five meet and confer states are limited to mediation of recognition and representation disputes. Fact-finding and arbitration procedures can be used but only with the concurrence of the employer.

Finally, the fourth area of comparison—unfair labor practices—the laws are uneven in dealing with actions of employers and employees harmful to the discussion or negotiating process. All five meet and confer states include a non-interference clause in their laws. Two of these state laws (California's and Minnesota's) deal with the refusal of either party to meet and confer "in good faith," thus affording employee organizations legal recourse if management is obstructionist. The collective negotiation states, as in Connecticut, Maine, Massachusetts, New York, Rhode Island, Vermont, Washington, and Wisconsin, set forth in detail actions that are prohibited on the part of either the employer or employee. The procedures for handling charges of unfair labor practices are in the general public employee relations acts of all these states, save for Wisconsin, where they are in the laws covering private industry. The provisions concerning prohibited practices in the remaining collective bargaining states are much more general. Most of them merely provide for the right of a public employee to join or not to join a labor or employee organization. Procedural provisions for investigating and hearing complaints concerning unfair practices and assessing penalties, for the most part, are lacking.

* * *

Strikes and other "work stoppages" in government

In 1958, . . . there were only 15 work stoppages. This involved 1,720 public employees and a loss of 7,520 man-days. . . . In 1966, there were

142 strikes, a nine-fold increase, involving 105,000 workers and the loss of 455,000 man-days. In 1968, the number of stoppages was almost double the 1966 figure; 254 strikes took place involving nearly 202,000 workers and causing a loss of over two and one-half million man-days.

The U.S. Bureau of Labor Statistics reported that public schools were the most frequently struck government service in 1968.[15] Teachers were involved in 112 school strikes. The sanitation services category was the governmental function next most frequently affected by work stoppages. Until 1966, sanitation was the prime arena for strike action.

Approximately 70 percent of the 1967 stoppages, involving 90 percent of the striking workers, centered around disputes over salaries and fringe benefits or over professional standards. In that year, union recognition or security was the second most frequent cause of work stoppages. In 1968 only 45 percent of the stoppages, involving 54 percent of the striking workers, were over salaries and fringe benefit disputes. Approximately 25 percent of the 1968 work stoppages were over recognition and union security issues.

Finding solutions to the strike issue in the public sector is just about the most difficult issue to resolve in the field of public employee relations. In spite of the increasing incidence of work stoppages, the laws, court decisions, and attorneys general opinions in at least 32 states specifically prohibit strikes by all government workers. ... In four others, the ban applies to state employees only. Employees of government-run public utilities and mass transportation systems constitute one of the most notable exceptions to these bans, especially where the facilities were privately owned prior to being run by the government.

* * *

Summary observations

The growth of public employee organizations and the development over the past decade of state legislative and administrative authoriza-

---

[15]U.S. Department of Labor, Bureau of Labor Statistics, "Work Stoppages in Government," *Monthly Labor Review,* Vol. 91 no. 7, July 1968, p. 53. Unpublished data for 1968 provided by the Bureau of Labor Statistics.

tions for direct discussions on collective bargaining are highlighted in the following summary findings:

- Government has become a major source of employment within the total labor force. While government employee unions and associations at the federal, state and local levels have not kept pace with this rapid rise, their membership still constitutes the fastest-growing sector of organized labor, jumping from slightly over five percent of total trade union membership in 1955 to nine percent or 1.7 million members by the end of 1966.

- In terms of the public sector, 52 percent of all federal employees (1.4 million workers) belonged to unions in 1968 and 8.6 percent of all state and local public employees (770,000 workers) were union members in that year. When the estimated membership of the independent state and local employee associations and the figures for NEA and other professional associations are added to the unionized sector, the "organized" portion of state and local employees rises to over one-fourth of the total.

- While public employee organizations affiliated with national unions, such as the American Federation of State, County, and Municipal Employees (AFL-CIO), the American Federation of Teachers (AFL-CIO), and the International Association of Firefighters (AFL-CIO), have always sought exclusive recognition and collective bargaining, only fairly recently have the large national professional associations, such as the National Education Association, become activist and endorsed exclusive representation for dealings with employers. Increased militancy among the local or state independent associations is also becoming more evident, although many still depend on lobbying and the establishment of favorable civil service rules rather than on collective negotiations or discussions to achieve better wages, working conditions, and satisfactory procedures to settle disputes.

- While the causes for the increased militancy among public employees are many, some of the basic factors include: the inability of individual employees in a large bureaucracy to be "heard" by his employers unless he speaks in a collective voice; a growing appreciation by public employee organizations of the effectiveness of collective bargaining techniques in the private sector; the financial resources and expertise of national unions in assisting public employee organizations to organize and present their demands to management; and the aggressiveness of public employee unions which caused many long-established professional and independent unaffiliated associations to adopt a more belligerent stance.

- The right of both state and local public employees to organize is either sanctioned by law, attorneys general opinions, court decisions, or executive orders in 33 states. Two other states recognize this right for state employees only and another three for local employees only. Fourteen of these 38 states have gone further and enacted a labor relations law which mandates collective negotiations for either state or local public employees, or both, while two states permit their local governments to adopt such procedures. Five states have mandated the meet and confer approach and require local public employers to discuss the terms and conditions of employment with employee organizations. In 12 states there is no statutory, judicial or administrative authorization permitting public employees at the state or local levels to organize, although special occupational groups (teachers, firemen, law enforcement) in many instances are given special consideration.

- Most of the state legislative and administrative activity in the field of collective bargaining for public employees has taken place since 1964. With the exception of the 1959 Wisconsin act, the passage by 15 states of broad comprehensive statutes or major amendments based on the collective negotiation concept occurred between 1965 and August 1969. All five meet and confer statutes were either enacted or significantly changed during the past four years. These recent enactments suggest a trend toward state establishment of positive procedures for handling public employee-management relations at both the state and local levels.

- Despite the fact that no state gives public employees at the state or local levels an unqualified right to strike, there were 254 strikes or other work stoppages in 1968—a seventeen-fold increase since 1958 with public school systems carrying the major burden. Forty-five percent of the work stoppages in 1968 involved disputes over wages or over professional standards. Surprisingly, even though almost four-fifths of the states give public employees the right to organize, the second most frequent cause of stoppages (25 percent) centered on the refusal of employers to recognize an employee union or provide security.

2

Basic Self-Actualization
Trends of the Human Personality

Chris Argyris

All organizations may be said to strive to achieve their objectives, maintain themselves internally, and adapt to their external environment. This multidimensional process may be called self-actualization. In order to make more precise predictions about the problems involved when human beings are considered for employment by the formal organization, it is necessary to be more explicit, if possible, about the demands the former will tend to make upon the latter. Since the human personality is a developing organism, one way to become more precise is to define the basic growth or development trends "inherent" in it (so long as it remains in the same culture). One can then logically assume that, at any given moment in time, the human personality will be predisposed to find expression for these developmental trends. Such an assumption implies another, namely, that there are basic development trends characteristic of a relatively large majority of the population being considered. This assumption might seem strained, especially to the psychologists inclined to stress individual differences. However, individual differences need not necessarily be ignored. As Kluckhohn and Murray point out, people tend to have some similar basic psychological characteristics because of their biological inheritance and the socio-cultural matrix within which they develop. This does not preclude the possibility that each individual can express these basic characteristics in his own idiosyncratic manner. Thus the concept of individual differences is still held.

So much for the logic behind the developmental trends listed below. It is assumed that human beings in our culture:

Reprinted with permission of author and publisher. From *Personality and Organization* by Chris Argyris. Copyright © 1957 by Harper & Row, Publishers, Inc., pp. 49–52.

1. Tend to develop from a state of passivity as infants to a state of increasing activity as adults. (This is what Erikson has called self-initiative and Bronfenbrenner has called self-determination.)

2. Tend to develop from a state of dependence upon others as infants to a state of relative independence as adults. Relative independence is the ability to "stand on one's own two feet" and simultaneously to acknowledge healthy dependencies. It is characterized by the liberation of the individual from his childhood determiners of behavior (e.g., family) and developing his own set of behavioral determiners. This individual does not tend to react to others (e.g., the boss) in terms of patterns learned during childhood.

3. Tend to develop from being capable of behaving only in a few ways as an infant to being capable of behaving in many different ways as an adult.

4. Tend to develop from having erratic, casual, shallow, quickly-dropped interests as an infant to having deeper interests as an adult. The mature state is characterized by an endless series of challenges, where the reward comes from doing something for its own sake. The tendency is to analyze and study phenomena in their full-blown wholeness, complexity, and depth.

5. Tend to develop from having a short time perspective (i.e., the present largely determines behavior) as an infant to a much longer time perspective as an adult (i.e, where the behavior is more affected by the past and the future). Bakke cogently describes the importance of time perspective in the lives of workers and their families and the variety of foresight practices by means of which they seek to secure the future.

6. Tend to develop from being in a subordinate position in the family and society as an infant to aspiring to occupy an equal and/or superordinate position relative to their peers.

7. Tend to develop from a lack of awareness of self as an infant to an awareness of and control over self as an adult. The adult who tends to experience adequate and successful control over his own behavior tends to develop a sense of integrity (Erikson) and feelings of self-worth. Bakke shows that one of the most important needs of workers is to enlarge those areas of their lives in which their own decisions determine the outcome of their efforts.

These dimensions are postulated as being descriptive of a basic multidimensional developmental process along which the growth of individuals in our culture may be measured. Presumably, every individual, at any given moment in time, can have his degree of development plotted along these dimensions. The exact location on each dimension will probably vary with each individual, and even within the same individual at different times. Self-actualization may now be defined more precisely as the individual's plotted scores (or profile) along the above dimensions.

It may be helpful to add a few words of explanation concerning these dimensions of personality development.

1. They comprise only one aspect of the total personality. All the properties of personality described previously must be used in trying to understand the behavior of a particular individual. Much depends upon the individual's self-concept, his degree of adaptation and adjustment, and the way in which he perceives his private world.

2. The dimensions are continua where the growth to be measured is assumed to be continuously changing in degree. An individual is presumed to develop continuously in degree, from the infant end to the adult end of each continuum.

3. The only characteristic assumed to hold for all individuals is that, barring unhealthy personality development, they will be predisposed toward moving from the infant end to the adult end of each continuum. This is a model (a construct) describing the basic growth trends. As such, it does not make any predictions about any specific individual. It *does,* however, presume to supply the researcher with basic developmental continua along which the growth of any individual in our culture may be described and measured.

4. So long as one develops in a particular culture one will never obtain maximum expression of these developmental trends. Clearly, all individuals cannot be maximally independent, active, and so forth all the time and still maintain an organized society. It is the function of culture (e.g., norms and mores) and society (e.g., family, friends, schools, churches, and laws) to inhibit maximum expression and to help an individual adjust and adapt by finding his optimum expression.

A second factor that prevents maximum expression and fosters optimum expression is the individual's own finite limits set by his personality. Some people fear the same amount of independence and activity that others desire. Also, it is commonplace to find some people who do not have the necessary abilities to perform specific tasks. No given individual is known to have developed all known abilities to their full maturity.

Finally, defense mechanisms also are important factors operating to help an individual to deviate from the basic developmental trends.

5. The dimensions described above are constructed in terms of latent or genotypical characteristics. If one states that an individual needs to be dependent, this need will probably be ascertained by clinical inference because it is one that individuals are not usually aware of. Thus, if one observes an employee acting as though he were independent, it is possible that if one goes below the behavioral surface, the individual may be quite dependent. The obvious example is the employee who always seems to behave in a contrary manner to that desired by management. Although his behavior may give the appearance that he is independent, his contrariness may be due to his great need to be dependent upon management, which he dislikes to admit to himself and to others.

3

The Taboo on Reporting
Offers of Bribes

Peter M. Blau

Agent Croner had uncovered serious violations in a firm. The manager of this firm brought employee Smith to the agency, whose testimony was intended to show that the alleged violations had not taken place. In a cleverly conducted cross-examination, Mr. Croner forced Mr. Smith to admit that his statements were untrue and that the violations had in fact occurred.[1] Upon leaving, Mr. Smith whispered to Mr. Croner, in a foreign

Reprinted with permission of author and publisher from *The Dynamics of Bureaucracy* (Chicago: University of Chicago Press, 1955), pp. 148–55. Footnotes have been renumbered.

[1]The technique of cross-examination can be described as an alternation between "whip" and "candy." First, Mr. Croner reminded the client in a serious voice of the long prison sentences given to those who commit perjury. Then he asked him factual questions concerning his statements in several different ways, involving the unsophisticated Mr. Smith in many contradictions. Mr. Croner pointed these contradictions out to the manager, who began to worry whether Mr. Smith might not involve him in additional conflicts with the law and with his employer, and therefore admonished Mr. Smith to be careful of what he said. By discrediting Mr. Smith as a witness, Mr. Croner had won the manager partly to his side. Next, he turned to the frightened and confused Mr. Smith with some words in the latter's native tongue, making him feel comfortable with a compatriot. Continuing the examination, he asked Mr. Smith whether he could write English; he, not wanting to acknowledge his illiteracy, said, "Of course." Mr. Croner, knowing that this was not so, told Mr. Smith to fill out a form, thus undermining his security by forcing him to admit that he could not write and that he had lied. Mr. Croner then adopted a very friendly tone, telling Mr. Smith that he knew that he was not a perjurer but only afraid of his employer and that he probably suffered more from the very violations he attempted to deny than any other employee; Mr. Smith laughingly agreed. This final piece of "candy" led to the admission that the testimony had been false.

language that he knew the latter understood, asking whether they could talk about this informally. Mr. Croner answered loudly in English, "No, nothing can be done; this is what the law says." Such a "feeler," more or less persistently pursued, is the typical starting point of a bribe. And such a blunt rejection usually ends the incident, despite an unequivocal rule that all offers of bribes must be reported to higher authorities for possible prosecution.

Right after this incident, the observer asked Mr. Croner what agents generally do about clients who offer bribes.

> *Croner:* We do what I just did. We never get bribes offered, because we usually stop it before we get an offer. [Turning to his neighbor:] Bert, come over here. [To the observer:] You don't mind if I call him over; I like him. [To the other agent:] What do you do about bribe offers, Bert?
> *Bert Lehmann:* Squelch it right away; you stop his talking, and that's all.
> *Observer:* That's very interesting. You never turn a man in?
> *Lehmann:* There's no possibility of turning a man in. It doesn't get to that point. Nobody offers you a bribe. The only thing they sometimes do is to make some vague suggestions. Then you stop it, and no bribe is offered to you. If you don't, you would have to enter into the proposition, and tell him that you're interested. For instance, once a man asked me whether we could talk it over outside. I knew what that was. So I said, "No; why should we go outside?" If somebody makes an offer like that, you would have to enter into collusion with him before you could report it. You would have to accept his suggestion, and meet him some place, and say that you will take the money. If you do that, you're just as guilty as he is.

Clients recurrently made offers of bribes, and some were quite direct, but all agents were strongly opposed to reporting such offers for prosecution, regardless of their attitudes toward clients. They not only failed to make such reports but considered it *wrong* to do so. The taboo on reporting attempted bribes was the strongest unofficial norm of the group. When the observer questioned it by asking whether prosecuting employers who tried to bribe officials would not show the public how honest civil servants are, agents became aggressive and defended the righteousness of the norm in emotional language, such as, "We don't like squealers!"

Strong mores are rarely violated. Just two cases of bribes had been reported and prosecuted in the entire agency in recent years. Only one of the officials who had made such a report continued to defend this action, which violated the unofficial norm of the work group. A possible reason for his persisting nonconformist attitude is that he was no longer a member of any group of agents; he had been promoted and given a different assignment. The other violator of this unofficial taboo, a member of Department Y, questioned his own wisdom in having reported the attempt at bribery. He explained that he had received such offers before but had merely discouraged them. Only the special circumstances in this case, the repeated and insistent way in which the offer had been made in the presence of third persons, had induced him to report it. He added that he would not report an offer of a bribe again under any condition—"It's too unpleasant." Even the deviant agreed with the fundamental validity of the norm.

The major reason for this agent's change of attitude was that the group had responded to his violation of an important norm by ostracizing him. One of his colleagues explained, referring to this person without naming him: "One fellow did turn in a guy once. After that, nobody in the office talked to him for a year." This was not literally true, of course, but the others confirmed that he had been ostracized. He himself said: "Nobody talked to me directly, criticizing me for it, but you can feel it if your fellow-agents disapprove of you." Several years later, this agent continued to occupy an isolated position in the group.

Why did these officials object so strongly to having employers prosecuted for attempted bribery?[2] They explained that they disapproved of their colleague's conduct because they considered it the act of an informer:

[2]One possible explanation of this norm is that it protected dishonest practices. Although the observer found no indication that any official ever accepted a bribe, one or the other may have successfully concealed such behavior from him. There can be little doubt, however, that accepting graft was *not* considered *a legitimate practice* in this group. *This*—namely that agents socially approved of taking bribes—could hardly have been concealed from an observer in daily contact with them for over three months. It must be remembered that *all* agents condemned the divulging of attempts at bribery, including those of whose honesty the observer was especially convinced, and those who strongly disapproved of employers who tried to evade their financial obligations to their own employees through bribes. It therefore seems justifiable to conclude that this *norm* was not intended to conceal dishonest practices. (This conclusion does not depend on the assumption that all agents were, in fact, perfectly honest.)

He didn't have to do that. Besides, he eggs them on. He acts as if he would be willing to accept some money, and then he denounces them. ... You don't go and denounce a guy.

We felt you shouldn't conspire to get an employer into such a situation. And he did try to get him into it. He met him midtown and had the F.B.I. agents there. It would be different, if all government employees were honest [referring to previously mentioned reputed dishonesties of Internal Revenue agents].

The condemnation of this agent was justified by the accusation that he had assumed the contemptible role of an *agent provocateur*. Indeed, he had agreed to meet the employer under the pretense of being willing to accept the money. But he had done so only by order of his superiors, who had decided, after he had reported the original offer to them, that this was the only way to obtain sufficient evidence for prosecution. His colleagues not only disrespected him for having let himself be used in this manner but also implied that he had deliberately provoked the initial offer of the bribe. This suspicion was not based on factual knowledge, since he, the only person who could have provided this information, insisted that quite the contrary had been the case: he had repeatedly refused the bribe, which the employer persisted in offering, before he had finally reported it.

The unsubstantiated charge that "he eggs them on" may well have been a projection of the agents' feeling that their own behavior in negotiations unwittingly invited offers of bribes. A comment of one agent indicates that he realized this: "I think it's a reflection on my own inspection technique if I'm offered something. If my bearing is firm, it's unlikely that they'll try to offer me anything." There is reason to assume, as will be seen presently, that the attitudes of these investigators were partly responsible for the attempts of clients to bribe them.

Agents objected to the general principle of reporting bona fide bribes as well as to the allegedly unfair methods used in the specific case cited. The following statement is typical:

I don't believe it's right to punish a businessman because he does something that every businessman has to do in order to stay in business. I feel that it's the fault of our system, not of the individual. So I don't think he should be punished. ... You might think that I don't feel strongly about bribes, because I don't turn them in. I feel very strongly about them, but I don't think it's fair to punish an employer; he has to do this.[3]

Tout comprendre c'est tout pardonner. Agents did not blame an employer for trying to bribe them and did not interpret such an attempt as an insult to their integrity, because they understood that he merely acted under the pressure of the business economy. Many pointed out that offering money to government inspectors is an old-established business practice. This empathy with the subjects of their investigations on the part of law-enforcement officials would be, indeed, remarkable, were it not for the special orientation that prevailed in this agency.

Violators of the laws the agency administered were looked upon as honest businessmen who had inadvertently engaged in practices that conflicted with some of the complex legal regulations. The agent was expected to understand their predicament and to help them to correct their mistakes. To be sure, violators were ordered to cease their illegal practices, but only a very small proportion of them, typically willful repeated offenders, were brought into court to be penalized for having broken the law. This tolerant orientation was reflected in the attitudes of agents toward bribes.

A major function of this conciliatory approach, as has been pointed out, was to enable the agent to convince violators to make retroactive adjustments *voluntarily.* If he had antagonized employers by treating them as culprits, he would have invited their refusal to co-operate. Of course, an agent's friendly smile did not suffice to motivate them to make these costly adjustments. His major weapon in negotiations was the disadvantaged position of the employer who had violated the law and was confronted by an official representative of the government. The skillful agent—sympathetic with the client's plight, yet sternly expecting him to make restitution as evidence of his basic honesty—could exploit this discomfort to obtain voluntary agreements in many cases.

Being offered a bribe constituted a special tactical advantage for an

[3]This agent, as a ardent union member and a progressive in politics, is not suspect of being personally identified with employers as a group. Evidently, his private convictions cannot explain his tolerance of illegal practices of businessmen; but his role as an agent helps to explain it.

agent. An employer who had violated one law was caught in the act of compounding his guilt by violating another one. He could no longer claim ignorance or inadvertence as an excuse for his violation. Agents exploited this situation to strengthen their position in negotiations. This is implied by the following remark concerning offers of small sums of money: "There's no sense in turning in a man for a small thing like that. You assume the role of the judge, and tell him what's right." Such a superordinate position, created by putting the briber in his place and maintained by his fear that this incorruptible public official may report him for prosecution, made it much easier to induce him to make retroactive adjustments. Refusing but not reporting bribes enabled agents to carry out their duties, which they considered important and on the basis of which they were evaluated, more effectively.

Since bribe offers helped agents in their work, there existed a perennial temptation, consciously or unconsciously, to provoke employers to make such overtures. Of course, we do not know, and neither do these agents, to what extent their attitudes invited the many offers of bribes they, according to their own statements, received. In any case, to preserve the advantageous position into which such an offer had put an agent, he had to reject it outright rather than appear hesitant in anticipation of reporting it for prosecution.

The fact that failing to report bribes facilitated the agent's task can only explain why this was rarely done, but not why there was a social norm prohibiting it. The existence of this norm suggests that this act might actually have some advantages for the actor and must therefore be proscribed if it also has disadvantages for the rest of the group. Indeed, some agents suspected their colleague of having sought personal gain when he had reported the bribe:

> I'll tell you why he did it. He was a war service appointee. He got a job when they were standing on street corners trying to get men into the [agency]. He figured he's one of many. "Later, these people will be laid off. If I make a name for myself, they'll keep me." But he was ostracized for two years!
>
> He thought he'd get glory; he was looking for a promotion. He heard that [the commissioner] had gotten a case like that and wanted another one, and he thought that this was the way to get a promotion. He's sorry now, and wouldn't do it again. Nobody in the office talked to him for a while.

This agent himself said: "They thought I wanted to make a hero of myself, I wanted to get some special credit."

The insistent demand of high administrative officials that bribes be reported to them provided inducements for doing so in order to impress superiors. This pattern of "excessive" compliance with requests of superiors has often been noted in hierarchical organizations, where it generally evokes strong negative reactions among the peer group.[4] The taboo on reporting bribes curbed resort to this short cut for gaining recognition from superordinate officials. Its first social function, therefore, was the protection of the reputations and promotion chances that agents had established in the course of performing their regular duties. A second function of this unofficial norm was that it inhibited behavior in investigations that was detrimental to future operations.

An agent thoroughly antagonized an employer whom he reported for attempting to bribe him. Since he had evidently decided to use this case, not to improve his record of successful negotiations, but to impress his superiors in a different way, the employer's hostility did not interfere with his objectives.[5] However, agents who will be assigned this case at some future date and even those who will investigate firms of friends of this employer are likely to encounter such antagonism that they can hardly succeed in convincing the client to make *voluntary* adjustments. If bribes were frequently prosecuted, agents would often find it difficult, if not impossible, to obtain these important voluntary concessions. This is precisely the situation which requires a strong social taboo: the actor benefits from an action that disadvantages the rest of the group. The prosecution of employers who tried to bribe civil servants, which was not

---

[4] For a discussion of the reactions of soldiers to such "excessive" compliance of comrades, see Stouffer *et al.* (1949), pp. 264–67, and the comments by Merton and Kitt (1950), p. 94.

[5] The violation of the taboo on "squealing" did, however, disturb the emotional equilibrium of an individual. Both agents who had reported a bribe said they had felt guilty afterward. One explained that he felt "horrible," because his client "was seventy years old and had a heart condition." But even the other agent, whose client had not been a pitiable old man and who continued to defend his action, stated: "It's not pleasant to turn somebody in. I felt sick afterward. (Why?) Oh, you think about being responsible for having somebody get into trouble. (Pause.) I guess I'm not the prosecuting type."

a basic objective of this agency, would have interfered with the accomplishment of its own objectives.[6] The taboo on reporting bribes, although contrary to an official rule, not only facilitated the task of agents but also contributed to the achievement of the goals of this agency.

The enforcement of group norms

The unofficial norms of work groups in a bureaucratic organization are, of course, not labeled as such. Their existence is only revealed by their characteristics, which may be briefly summarized:

1. *Acceptance by all members of the group,* regardless of differences in attitudes on related subjects. Some agents were very friendly, and others were stern or domineering, toward clients; some refused even the offer of a cigar, and others considered the acceptance of small favors, such as invitations to lunch, legitimate; but they all condemned the reporting of bribes. Even the violator of the taboo agreed with it in principle, and explained his violation as due to exceptional circumstances. (For less basic norms, this agreement existed only on the verbal level, and agents tried to hide their violations from colleagues.)

2. *Endeavors to conceal violations,* since they are considered to be shameful, not only from other members of the group, but also from outsiders; indeed, in this case, the reticence extends to violations of colleagues. Several agents refused to talk to the observer about the cases where a bribe had been reported, and most of the others did not mention the names of the two officials who had made the reports. Typically, it was the badly integrated official who named violators of norms. The counterpart of this concealment, stemming from the same assumption of the intrinsic shamefulness of these acts, is the use of the statement that a person has committed such an act as a deliberate insult. Thus an agent

---

[6]Of course, the prosecution of the violators of the laws this agency administered also aroused hostility, which spelled future difficulties. This was probably a main reason for prosecuting only the most serious offenders. However, these prosecutions, in contrast to those of bribers, were a major responsibility of the agency, and so viewed by agents.

climaxed his derogatory remarks about a colleague by saying that he even had "denounced an employer" who had offered him a bribe.

3. *Questioning provokes hostility* and emotional reactions. Many agents became resentful or aggressive when the observer asked why bribes are not reported, and defended the taboo with irrational phrases, such as, "We don't like squealers."

4. *Myths develop* with the theme that it is advantageous to conform. For example: "I'll tell you of one case. . . . He did exactly what you say. He went into a bar with a guy who had promised him money. He was supposed to give it to him in the bar. Then the F.B.I. came in, and they actually came in just like in the movies; the sirens were blasting. They happened to be late, and could only get there on time by using their sirens. And they came in with their guns, asking, 'Who is offering a bribe here?' By that time, the client had said, 'Excuse me, I have to go to the washroom,' and had left the place. You know what happened? The F.B.I. didn't say it had made a mistake. It wrote to the [commissioner] telling him that the agent had handled the case badly. So, you get into all kinds of trouble if you turn a man in."

5. *Ostracism is the penalty* only for violations of the most basic norms. Since the agent who had reported a bribe was cold-shouldered, none of the other members of Department Y made such reports, despite demands from superiors to do so.

4

Decision-Making
in the Budgetary Process

Russell Wayne Boss

Introduction

The budget is the key instrument in national policy-making.[1] Through
the budget elected officials are able to choose what services are to be
provided by government and which areas are to be left to the private
sector of the economy. The budget also expresses the decisions of the
elected officials about services which should be provided by the federal
government, rather than at the state and local levels. The degree of
activity and cost, as well as the specific programs and instruments to be
used in implementing these programs, are also specified in the budget.
Furthermore, the budget serves as a principal instrument of fiscal policy
for encouraging prosperity, stable growth, and high employment in the
economy.

Numerous reasons can be given for the necessity of rational decisions in government, particularly in the budgetary process. Arthur Smithies maintains that "almost every government decision has budgetary
implications, since the process of decision-making almost invariably involves the allocation of scarce resources among alternative uses. The
entire process of decision-making is improved to the extent that these
choices are made explicitly and deliberately."[2] Jack Carlson suggests
several other reasons.[3] First, the amount of resources available to govern-

---

[1]"Purposes of the Budget of the United States," *Report of the President's
Commission on Budget Concepts* (Washington, D.C.: U.S. Government Printing
Office, 1967), pp. 11–23.

[2]Arthur Smithies, *The Budgetary Process in the United States* (New York:
McGraw-Hill Book Company, 1955), p. 20.

[3]Jack Carlson, "The Status and Next Steps for Planning, Programming, and
Budgeting," *The Analysis and Evaluation of Public Expenditures: The PPB System*
(Washington, D.C.: U.S. Government Printing Office, 1969), pp. 613–47.

ment is limited, and the demand for government programs is usually much greater than the supply. Second, only a relatively small portion of the budget is controllable, due to the legal and moral obligations and commitments made by past decision-makers. Third, the budget process should insure that public funds be distributed most effectively and efficiently in achieving national priorities and objectives. Thus, it is not only highly desirable, but also necessary that the decision-making process functions in such a way as to insure the optimum distribution of government services with maximum efficiency.

In view of the importance of the budget, the following questions immediately come to mind: How do those involved in the budgetary process reach their decisions? Are they completely objective in their approach to problems? Or do they arbitrarily respond to the numerous pressures placed upon them by the various internal and external interest groups and power centers?

Numerous theories exist concerning how government decision-makers operate. These range from the antiseptically rational to the virulently political. Some offer empirical evidence to support their views. Most do not.

The purpose of this paper is to present a brief explanation of a number of major approaches to decision-making in the public sector, particularly as it relates to the budgetary process. These approaches take the following forms: (1) General theoretical explanations of the decision-making process; (2) Conditioning factors that affect the process, such as organizational structure and the political environment; (3) Research relevant to decision-making theories which suggest a type of movement of informal opinion between sharply-contrasting theories; and (4) The major development of PPBS and its effects upon decision-making.

General theories of decision-making

The rational approach to decision-making

Perhaps the best known and most widely accepted theory is the

Rational Approach to decision-making.[4] This approach includes some or all of the following notions:

1. The decision-maker is faced with a specific problem which can be isolated from other problems or which can be considered meaningfully in comparison with all other problems.
2. The goals or values are selected and ranked according to their importance.
3. All possible approaches in achieving the goals or values are known.
4. The consequences and costs of each alternative approach can be predicted.
5. The consequences for any approach can be compared with those of all other alternatives.
6. The decision-maker then chooses the alternative which has consequences most clearly matching the predetermined goals.

The goal of this method is a rational decision built upon the clarification of values or objectives prior to an empirical analysis of alternative policies. The ultimate test of a good policy is that it can be shown to be the most effective means to the desired end.

According to the Rational theory, the process sketched above should be followed explicitly by the administrator or legislator in each decision sequence. The result will be a maximum return from public funds in meeting public objectives.

Numerous scholars have challenged the Rational Approach to deci-

---

[4]See Charles E. Lindblom, "The Science of Muddling Through," *Public Administration Review* 19 (Spring 1959): 79–88; Lindblom, *The Policy Making Process* (Englewood Cliffs, N.J.: Prentice-Hall, Inc., 1968); Lindblom, "Decision-Making in Taxation and Expenditures," *Public Finances: Needs, Sources, and Utilization* (Princeton, N.J.: Princeton University Press, 1961); Frank K. Gibson, "Scientific Decision-Making: Some Fact and Some Fiction," *Association of Management in Public Health: Proceedings of the Annual Meeting* (Miami Beach, Florida, 15–19 October 1962), pp. 56–63; Amitai Etzioni, "Mixed-Scanning: A Third Approach to Decision-Making," *Public Administration Review* 27 (December 1967): 385–92; James D. Barber, *Power in Committees* (Chicago: Rand McNally and Company, 1966).

sion-making.[5] They point out the limits of its underlying requirements and challenge the degree to which these requirements must be followed. For example, Charles Lindblom points out that the model involves a number of underlying principles, particularly as it pertains to the budgetary process. These requirements include:

1. A comprehensive overview of the factors relevant to the decision;
2. Clarity of definition of social objectives;
3. A means-end approach to policy-making;
4. A deliberate and explicit choice among policies;
5. A calculation and minimization of cost;
6. Reason and cooperation rather than arbitrariness, coercion, and conflict; and
7. A unified decision-making process for decisions that are highly interdependent.[6]

Lindblom's major criticism of the Rational Approach is the difficulty in identifying and isolating a given problem. All too often, the specific problem cannot be isolated. More often, the cause or source of the problem is even more difficult to pinpoint. Further, the Rational Approach suggests no useful techniques that can facilitate "problem-identification."

Three other criticisms of the Rational Approach deserve note. Frequently the decision-maker has neither the time, the capacity, nor the information necessary to make the in-depth study that this method requires. Moreover, identifying the universal values required by the Rational Approach can be difficult or impossible. All values cannot be considered. Some must be sacrificed in order to achieve others. Furthermore, there is much disagreement among the values themselves, not only among people but between the inconsistent values of the analyst himself. Then too, no empirical proof of values is possible. It is, therefore, very difficult to rank what cannot be defined. Finally, the Rational Approach rests on an unambiguous relationship between "means" and

---

[5]Among this group are such authors as Charles E. Lindblom, Frank Gibson, Amitai Etzioni, James D. Barber, Wallace H. Best, Ira Sharkansky, Augustus B. Turnbull III, Aaron Wildavsky, Arthur Smithies, and Richard Fonno, Jr.

[6]Lindblom, "Decision-Making in Taxation," and "The Science of Muddling Through," *op. cit.*

"ends"; but Lindblom maintains that the relationship is clear only to the extent that ultimate values can be agreed upon. The usual situation is that one person's goal may be another person's means to achieving an entirely different goal.

The incremental approach to decision-making

Lindblom then suggests a method that he believes can overcome these inherent problems of the Rational Approach. This he calls the Incremental Approach. Here, the administrator specifically considers only a limited set of policy alternatives which are incremental additions or modifications of a broader set of policies that are considered "givens." For example, the incrementalist administrator uses this year's budget as the base from which next year's budget is considered; and only the increment is analyzed in any detail.

Lindblom's approach is not as "tidy" as the Rational Approach. The decision-making process, for example, is a series of partial and often discontinuous choices, rather than one major decision. Only the marginal values of various social objectives and constraints are considered. The Incremental Approach implies a combination of empirical analysis and value judgments, all the while emphasizing only a small number of relevant values. The Rational Approach, on the other hand, emphasizes the separate empirical analysis of each alternative. Finally, Incrementalism concentrates on only a small number of relevant values, while the Rational Approach attempts to cope with all values that could be related to all decisions.

Lindblom's Model simplifies the decision-making process of the individual administrator, reduces the "value" problems, and diminishes the general complexity of the entire process. Problems are handled by marginal comparisons; and the official makes choices only at the margins, rather than having to consider each program or alternative in its entirety. Both empirical analysis and value judgments are considered at the same time. Furthermore, the measure of a "good" decision is the degree to which the decision-makers are in agreement, while a poor decision excludes or ignores participants capable of influencing the projected course of action.

Of course, the simplifications of the Incremental Approach may become oversimplifications, and it is little consolation that an administrator is making only marginal adjustments in a policy network that is chronically out of touch with the needs of society. According to Lindblom, such weaknesses in the Incremental Approach are compensated for by the process of "Partisan Mutual Adjustment." Since the participants do not share common criteria, they differ in the values they think are important. Thus, they are highly partisan. Moreover, they do not necessarily cooperate with each other or recognize any common problem. They simply minimize their problems by concentrating on some values, excluding others, and adjusting to the circumstances over which they have no control.

Partisan Mutual Adjustment provides opportunities for the necessary coordination among the numerous decision-makers. Unlike the Rational Approach, which links consequences with goals, "Partisan Mutual Adjustment" links the decisions to the decision-makers. Furthermore, instead of a "means-end" sequence, it becomes an "interest-mean" sequence, with one person's goal perhaps serving as the means toward the goal of another. Crudely, the test is whether a tolerable agreement between the numerous decision-makers is possible, given the different values and interests and given the incredible complexity of the problem-situations.

Lindblom holds that Incrementalism and Partisan Mutual Adjustment make agreement possible in three different ways. First, ideological and other differences in values are less likely to stand in the way of agreed upon marginal values. Second, evaluating only actual "choice" situations leads decision-makers to reconsider values in the light of practical constraints, and such reconsideration often moves decision-makers toward agreement on programs. Finally, individuals can often agree on policies or programs even if they hold conflicting values.

The mixed-scanning approach

Amitai Etzioni agrees with Lindblom's attack on the superiority of the Rational Approach.[7] But he also believes that the Incremental Approach

[7]Etzioni, *op. cit.*, 385–92.

has serious flaws which cannot be overcome by Partisan Mutual Adjustment. For example, the interests of the most powerful and organized partisans probably will get most or all the attention from Incremental decision-makers. In addition, basic social innovation is not encouraged by this approach. Indeed, innovation may even be severely inhibited by it. Furthermore, the Incremental Approach does not apply to fundamental decisions, such as a declaration of war. These fundamental decisions cannot be ignored simply because they are few in number. As Etzioni explains:

> . . . it is often the fundamental decisions which set the context for numerous incremental ones. Although fundamental decisions are frequently "prepared" by incremental ones in order that the final decisions will initiate a less abrupt change, these decisions may still be considered relatively fundamental. The incremental steps which follow cannot be understood without them, and the preceding steps are useless unless they lead to fundamental decisions.
>
> Thus, while the incrementalists hold that decision-making involves a choice between two kinds of decision-making models, it should be noted that (a) the cumulative value of the incremental decisions specify or anticipate fundamental decisions, and (b) the cumulative value of the incremental decisions is greatly affected by the related fundamental decisions.[8]

Hence, Etzioni suggests a "Mixed-Scanning" Approach. This method provides for a ". . . high-order, fundamental policy-making process which prepares for fundamental decisions and works them out after they have been reached."[9] It does so by combining the Rational analysis of some problem-elements with the Incremental and less detailed approach to others. Etzioni explains his Mixed-Scanning Approach by a simple illustration:

> Assume we are about to set up a worldwide weather observation system using weather satellites. The rationalistic approach would seek an exhaustive survey of weather conditions by using cameras capable of detailed observations and by scheduling reviews of the entire sky as often as possible. This would yield an avalanche of details, costly to analyze and likely to overwhelm our action capacities. . . . Incrementalism would focus on those

[8] *Ibid.*, 387–88.
[9] *Ibid.*, 388.

areas in which similar patterns developed in the recent past and, perhaps, on a few nearby regions; it would thus ignore all formations which might deserve attention if they arose in unexpected areas.

A mixed-scanning strategy would include elements of both approaches by employing two cameras: a broad-angle camera that would cover all parts of the sky but not in great detail, and a second one which would zero in on those areas revealed by the first camera to require a more in-depth examination. While mixed-scanning might miss areas in which only a detailed camera could reveal trouble, it is less likely than incrementalism to miss obvious trouble spots in unfamiliar areas.[10]

Mixed-Scanning has a number of advantages. First, it permits taking advantage of both Incrementalism and the Rational Approach in different situations. Note, for example, that ranking organizational officials often focus on the overall picture and are impatient with details. The lower ranks, especially experts, are more likely to focus on details.[11] Mixed-Scanning can be applied to both levels of analysis.

Second, Mixed-Scanning permits adjustments to a rapidly changing environment by providing the flexibility necessary to adapt decision-making to the specific circumstance. In some situations, Incrementalism will suffice. In others, the more thorough Rational Approach is needed.

Third, Mixed-Scanning considers the capacity of the decision-maker. All do not enjoy the same ability. Generally speaking, the greater the capacities of the decision-maker, the more encompassing the level of Scanning he can undertake. And the more Scanning, generally speaking, the more effective the decision-making process becomes.

The crucial questions regarding the usefulness of Mixed-Scanning are twofold: (1) determining the conditions under which it, rather than the Incremental or Rational Approach, should be used; and (2) determining the extent to which each should be applied. Etzioni is not clear in explaining either of these questions. The reader is left to assume that the decision will apparently vary according to the circumstances involved.

[10] *Ibid.*, 389.
[11] *Ibid.*, 391.

Conditioning factors of decision-making

Decision-making: a function of organizational structure and specific procedures

Arthur Smithies discusses decision-making in the budgetary process from the viewpoint of the structure and procedures of a complicated organization.[12] His approach is both Incremental and Rational, and his optimistic viewpoint about the administrator's ability to make choices concerning the allocation of scarce resources is based on the assumption that "... the entire process of decision-making is improved to the extent that these choices are made explicitly and deliberately."[13]

The decision-making process, as he describes it, is made up of a number of specific stages. The nature of each stage is determined by the complexity of the organization. In less complex organizations the stages may be combined into a single step, while in larger and more complex structures they will probably be distinctly separate.

The first stage in the decision-making process is the determination of policy objectives. Since this is often done under conditions of great uncertainty, policy determination often approaches the Incremental philosophy of "extensions and reversals" of previous decisions. Therefore, an effective review of past performance is an essential part of this stage.[14]

Smithies' second stage includes the preparation of alternative plans that will further particular policy objectives in varying measure. In this planning stage, the bounds of feasibility are a focal point of concern.

Programming is the next stage in the process and includes a greater degree of finality and feasibility. It may involve either the selection of a single plan from a number of alternatives or a combination of elements from numerous plans. All programming decisions, Smithies suggests, should be based on the relative costs of the various alternatives.

[12]Smithies, *op. cit.*, pp. 20–34.
[13]*Ibid.*, p. 20.
[14]*Ibid.*, p. 21.

Budget formulation is merely an extension of the programming stage. It is also the first point at which rational economic calculations come fully into play. Consideration of the optimum use of scarce resources among various alternatives usually takes place at this stage. Since each alternative is expressed in the denominator of money, all can be compared in terms of taxation and borrowing. Smithies argues that expenditure commitments for any particular program should not be made until this stage, since the process of rational calculation and comparison can further the total objectives of the organization.

The two final stages in the decision-making process are program execution and program review. The first is important to insure that scrupulous adherence to the budgetary intent is maintained. The second insures that legality and propriety of expenditures are maintained, that a link between past and future policy objectives can be established, and that management can be aided by the review of its activities. The effectiveness of the decision-making process in an organization depends upon the way in which it performs each of these operations, as well as the way in which each of the separate stages relates to the others in Smithies' model.

Decision-making as political

In the final analysis, no matter how effective and proficient the subordinate decision-maker has been in creating a budget, it cannot escape the political scrutiny of the legislative arena. Aaron Wildavsky points this out in *The Politics of the Budgetary Process.*[15]

Wildavsky believes that the Rational Approach to budget making is highly useful for internal purposes, particularly at the lower levels of the organization. It can aid greatly in deciding among competing programs, maintaining control of the agency's operations, and giving the participants the feeling that they know what they are doing, finding the cost of the complex items, and providing support for the agency's demands and decisions.

[15]Aaron Wildavsky, *The Politics of the Budgetary Process* (Boston: Little, Brown & Company, 1964).

Legislative treatments of budgets, however, have a major political thrust. The budget document may be completely logical and appropriate when it is presented to the House Appropriations Committee; but from there on, budgetary precision and exactness are of little value. In order to get the budget approved by Congress, Wildavsky maintains that "it's not what's in your estimates, but how good a politician you are that matters."[16] Thus, it is of utmost importance that the administrator employ those skills that can best prepare him to anticipate or to cope with the political influences that will inevitably confront him as his budget request passes through the various stages of congressional review.

Wildavsky suggests three essential characteristics of a good administrator/politician. The first relates to the importance of cultivating an active clientele. Wildavsky reports that the "need for obtaining support of an active clientele is so firmly fixed a star in the budgetary firmament that it is perceived by everyone and uniformly taken into account."[17] Great emphasis is placed on effectively using the present clientele, as well as expanding that clientele. In any case, clientele activities should be directed toward influencing the constituencies of powerful congressmen and providing the legislators with feedback about the benefits of the agency's programs. Without effective feedback, Wildavsky maintains that congressmen tend to assume that either no one cares or that the program is of little value.

Wildavsky's second general suggestion deals with the development of confidence between governmental officials. The tremendous complexity and size of budgetary matters necessitates that some people trust others. This is particularly true in the budgetary process, since the decision-makers can only periodically check on subordinates. Wildavsky concludes that "committee members will treat an agency much better if they feel that its officials will not deceive them."[18]

Gearing one's behavior to fit the expectations of the committee members is one way in which the desired level of confidence can be obtained. Others include:

[16] *Ibid.,* p. 64.
[17] *Ibid.,* p. 65.
[18] *Ibid.,* p. 74.

1. being above-board and playing it straight at all times, since a lie can lead to irreparable loss of confidence;
2. developing the opinion that the agency official is a man of high integrity who can be trusted; and
3. developing a close personal relationship with members of the agency's appropriations subcommittee, particularly the chairman.

The third essential quality of a good administrator/politician is skill in following strategies that exploit one's opportunities to the maximum. These are largely situational and depend upon the conditions of time, place, circumstance, and the agency's attitude toward perceived opportunities. The ability of the individual agency in highlighting the merit of its programs is indispensible and provides substantial leverage at the bargaining table. The administrator must always keep in mind that his goal should be to get his budget at least approved by the president and Congress, and preferably increased in the process.

In all this political activity the Incremental Approach is dominant. Wildavsky concludes:

> Budgeting turns out to be an incremental process, proceeding from a historical base, guided by accepted notions of fair shares, in which decisions are fragmented, made in sequence by specialized bodies, and coordinated through repeated attacks on problems and through multiple feedback mechanisms. The role of the participants, and their perceptions of each other's powers and desires, fit together to provide a reasonably stable set of criteria on which to base calculations.[19]

Selected research: decision-making as it seems to be

Research has substantiated some of the above theories. Three studies are discussed here to illustrate that research. The first deals with the first-hand observation of small groups working on budget-making tasks in a laboratory environment. The second is an empirical study of agencies in the federal government. The third involves a comparative study of decision-making in the states of Wisconsin and Georgia.

[19] *Ibid.,* p. 20.

"More or less" incrementalism with "more or less" rationality

James D. Barber studied the techniques for simplifying budgetary decision-making by observing a number of boards of finance under laboratory conditions.[20] All deliberations were tape recorded and later analyzed in terms of the processes employed in reaching their conclusions. After careful study, Barber concluded that budgetary decision-making is *neither* completely Rational *nor* completely Incremental. Rather, it is more accurately described as "more or less" Incrementalism with "more or less" Rationality.

Barber observed that the budget-maker pursues specific Incremental strategies which simplify the budgetary process. These include the distinction between controllable and uncontrollable costs, concentration on both the size of the increased and the actual size of the request, the search for some element or set of elements with which the decision-maker has had much concrete experience, and the restriction of attention to the present and near future, rather than long-range projects.

The danger of neglecting Rational strategies was also highlighted by Barber. For example, some decision-makers simplified their decisions by concentrating on the "dollars and cents" calculations of the problem. They became so absorbed with the figures that they lost track of their meaning. This approach, Barber warns, is dangerous and can easily undermine the entire decision-making process.[21]

Decision-making in federal nondefense agencies

One of the few empirical studies of the actual budgetary decision-making process at the federal level was reported by Davis, Dempster, and Wildavsky in 1966.[22] They studied time series data which were collected from fifty-six nondefense agencies for the period 1947–1963. Eight

[20]Barber, *op. cit.,* pp. 36–46.

[21]*Ibid.,* p. 42.

[22]Otto A. Davis, M. A. H. Dempster, and Aaron Wildavsky, "A Theory of the Budgetary Process," *The American Political Science Review* 60 (September 1966): 529–47.

different models were constructed, and each was tested by appropriate statistical techniques.

The authors found two types of behavior to be most responsible for the final budgetary decision. First, "the agency request (through the Budget Bureau) for a certain year is a fixed mean percentage of *the Congressional appropriation for that agency in the previous year* plus a random variable (normally distributed with mean zero and unknown but finite variance) for that year"[23] (Italics added). The second finding was the "Congressional appropriation for an agency in a certain year is a fixed mean percentage of *the request in that year* plus a stochastic disturbance"[24] (Italics added).

Thus, last year's appropriation is used as a base against which agencies seek incremental increases; and actual increases depend upon the size of the requested increment. The data suggests that to be successful in getting the desired appropriation, an agency should "come in a little too high (padding), but not too high (loss of confidence)."[25]

However, it may be dangerous to generalize the results of this study to all areas of the budgetary process. The authors restrict their findings to the nondefense agencies of the federal government. They provide no information about how decisions are made for the Department of Defense; and it may be that these findings do not apply to this formidable portion of the budget. Nonetheless, the empirical evidence adds support to the idea of the Incremental budgetary process.

Decision-making at the state level

Ira Sharkansky and Augustus B. Turnbull III found support for both the Incremental and Political viewpoints when they studied budgetary decision-making in Wisconsin and Georgia.[26] In examining agency suc-

---

[23] *Ibid.,* 532.

[24] *Ibid.,* 534.

[25] *Ibid.,* 530.

[26] Ira Sharkansky and Augustus B. Turnbull III, "Budget Making in Georgia and Wisconsin: A Test of a Model." *Midwest Journal of Political Science* 13 (November 1969): 631–45.

cess in both budget approval and budget expansion, a number of general tendencies were found in the two states. First, only weak relationships existed between the actual size of the agency request, the governor's recommendation, and the legislative appropriation. Second, the legislature not only responded favorably to the governor's recommendations, but it relied heavily upon them. Third, the budget reviewers concentrated most heavily upon the increment. The sheer size of the request was less important than the requested increase. Finally, the legislators generally cut the requests of agencies that sought the largest increments; but they gave budget increases to only those agencies which requested them. Thus, empirical support is again provided for both Incrementalism and the proposition that politics and partisan influences, particularly on the part of the governor, determine the contents of the final decision reached in the legislative arena.

An emphasis on rationality: planning–programming–budgeting system

Current decision-making practices suggest a swing of the pendulum of theory and practice away from the Incrementalism emphasized in the research viewed above. The vehicle employed to encourage more rational decision-making is Planning-Programming-Budgeting System, or PPBS. A thorough explanation of the purpose and characteristics of PPBS has been given by Jack W. Carlson, former Assistant Director for Program Evaluation of the U.S. Bureau of the Budget.[27] Carlson points out that twenty-six federal agencies have adopted PPBS since August 25, 1965, when President Lyndon Johnson announced:

> . . . a very new and very revolutionary system of planning and programming and budgeting throughout the vast federal government—so that through the tools of modern management the full promise of finer life can be brought to every American at the lowest possible cost.[28]

[27]Carlson, *op. cit.*, pp. 613–47.

[28]President Lyndon Johnson, Transcript of the President's News Conference on Foreign and Domestic Matters," *New York Times,* 26 August 1965.

According to Carlson, the basic purposes of PPBS are to aid decision-makers in:

1. Allocating limited public resources more effectively;
2. Decreasing the portion of the budget that is "uncontrollable";
3. Understanding the impact and results of public programs;
4. Insuring the well-regulated presentation of relevant analysis for decision-making;
5. Identifying programs that have outlived their usefulness;
6. Integrating long-range objectives with the current year budget; and
7. Coordinating budgeting and planning with actual performance.[29]

Carlson points out that "PPBS was designed as a process that would encourage the analysis of major policy issues and provide a method of making explicit tradeoffs among programs aimed at similar objectives. It was tied to the budget cycle to assure relevance and organized flexibility to allow adaptation to the unique characteristics of each agency."[30]

Allen Schick suggests three major developments which he sees as responsible for the evolution and wide-scale acceptance of PPBS. First, increased sophistication of economic analytical methods has played a major role in shaping modern fiscal and budgetary policy. Second, the "development of new informational and decisional technologies has enlarged the applicability of objective analysis to policy making."[31] And finally, the planning and budgeting processes have converged, bringing with them the increased awareness of the need for a more rational basis upon which to make decisions.

The PPB System is divided into five major parts: Program Structures, Issue Letters, Program and Financial Plans, Program Memoranda, and Special Analytic Studies. *Program Structure* is defined as a grouping of "agency activities into objective-oriented classifications so that programs with common objectives or common outputs are considered together, along with the cost of each."[32]

---

[29]Carlson, *op. cit.,* p. 613.

[30]*Ibid.*

[31]Allen Schick, "The Road to PPB: The Stages of Budget Reform," *Public Administration Review* 26 (December 1966): 243–58.

[32]Carlson, *op. cit.,* p. 615.

The main purpose of the Program Structure is to facilitate more accurate analysis of "agency programs by organizing cost and output information" in a way that includes all "areas relevant to the problem." This stage not only forces attention to the differences, similarities, and objectives of agency programs, but it should also suggest possible alternatives and "reveal gaps in agency programs or new alternatives which have not yet been considered before."[33]

The second formal part of PPBS is the *Issue Letters*. These are letters which "define the major program issues that should receive attention during the current planning and budgeting cycle." They originate with the budget bureau and are sent to each agency.[34]

The purposes of the Issue Letters are threefold: (1) To assist the agency in focusing its limited analytic resources on its more crucial problems; (2) To help the decision-makers understand and agree upon the nature of the problems involved; and (3) To increase the quality of analysis, which will, in turn, broaden the range of alternatives that can be considered by both the agency and the administration.[35]

The *Program and Financial Plan* is a document which contains program financial information for the next five years; it also includes information for the previous two years as a basis for comparison. Using the program category as a unit of analysis, it explains the financial commitments of previous decisions and, when possible, projects outputs for the same period.

> The Program and Financial Plan is intended as a bridge to relate annual budget allocations more closely to longer-term plans and priorities, and thus provide a tool for department heads to gain more discretion over future budgets.[36]

The fundamental purpose of the Program and Financial Plan is "to identify the extent to which future budget choices are already foreclosed, so that remaining options are identified, and so that future consequences

---

[33] *Ibid.*
[34] *Ibid.,* p. 618.
[35] *Ibid.*
[36] *Ibid.,* p. 619.

of present decisions are routinely identified and considered during the decision process."[37]

A *Program Memorandum* is a brief document which summarizes the agency's decisions on major issues in the program category. It also contains an explanation of the reasons behind these decisions. "It should incorporate the results of any analysis bearing on the issue, identify the alternatives considered, and state explicitly the assumptions made in the evaluation.[38] The Program Memorandum currently includes only the major issues in each program category.

Special Analytic Studies, the fifth major stage of PPBS, are studies which analyze particular problems, in hopes that the conclusions can be used in the policy-making process. Almost anything that is appropriate to the issue may be included in these studies. Appropriate areas include data collection efforts, sociological evaluations, economic analysis, mathematical models, and development of useful techniques. Generally speaking, there are two basic types of Studies: "those which analyze questions which must be decided in the course of the current planning and budgeting cycle, and those that develop concepts or information for decisions which must be made in the future."[39]

Most observers agree that, when compared to the ideal set forth in 1965, current PPBS programs haven fallen short. Schick evaluates PPBS performance in the following manner:

> PPB has had a rough time these past few years. Confusion is widespread; results are meager. The publicity has outdistanced the performance by a wide margin. In the name of analysis, bureaus have produced reams of unsupported, irrelevant justification and description. As Shumpeter said of Marxism: it is preaching in the garb of analysis. Plans have been formulated without serious attention to objectives, resource constraints, and alternative opportunities. PPB's first years have been an exercise in technique. There have been the bulletins and the staffings, the program memoranda, and the program and financial plans. Those who have been apprehensive over possible threats to cherished political values can find no support for their fears in what has happened during these years.[40]

[37] *Ibid.*

[38] *Ibid.,* p. 618.

[39] *Ibid.,* p. 619.

[40] Allen Schick, "Systems Politics and Systems Budgeting," *Public Administration Review* 29 (March/April 1969): 149.

Aaron Wildavsky is even less sympathetic of the results of the PPB System. In reviewing the general success of the program, he concludes that:

> It would have been sufficient to say that the wholesale introduction of PPBS presented insuperable difficulties of calculation. All the obstacles previously mentioned, such as lack of talent, theory, and data, may be summed up in a single statement: *no one knows how to do program budgeting.* Another way of putting it would be to say that many know what program budgeting should be like in general, but no one knows what it should be in any particular case. Program budgeting cannot be stated in operational terms. There is no agreement on what the words mean, let alone an ability to show another person what should be done. The reason for the difficulty is that telling an agency to adopt program budgeting means telling it to find better policies and there is no formula for doing that. One can (and should) talk about measuring effectiveness, estimating costs, and comparing alternatives, but that is a far cry from being able to take the creating leap of formulating a better policy.[41]

Carlson also agrees that PPBS has not lived up to the expectations of those who introduced the program. When compared to the ideal, the success of the PPB System has been limited. However, this does not mean that progress has not been made. As a result of PPBS, the amount of useful analysis "has increased by about 200 percent during the last 4 [sic] years. This may mean only that it has gone from 5 to 15 [sic] on a scale that has 100 as a maximum, but it still represents considerable progress."[42]

As to the future of PPBS, Schick believes that there will be a continual upgrading in the sophistication of the budgeting process, and PPBS will play a vital part. But, since PPB is "an idea whose time has not quite come,"[43] organizational capabilities, political conditions, analysis techniques, and informational resources will have to be improved before PPBS can make the contributions to resource allocation and decision-making that were expected at the time of its conception.

---

[41] Aaron Wildavsky, "Rescuing Policy Analysis from PPBS," *Public Administration Review* 29 (March/April 1969): 193.

[42] Carlson, *op. cit.,* p. 623.

[43] Schick, "Systems Politics and Systems Budgeting," p. 150.

Conclusion

It may be most accurate to conclude that different approaches exist to the study of decision-making in the budgetary process. The Rational Approach, Incrementalism, and Mixed-Scanning each represent a theoretical explanation of what "is" or what "ought to be" the best method of decision-making. Wildavsky's "politics" and Smithies' "Organizational Structure and Strategies" represent certain conditioning factors that affect the process. And PPBS is certainly a tool that is being employed to swing the pendulum back toward the Rational Approach.

Broadly speaking, however, evidence suggests that the nature of the system largely determines the extent to which each process will be used for decision-making. In a highly dynamic environment, a predominately Incremental or Mixed-Scanning Approach can greatly simplify the decision process. In a more stable system, where decisions can be isolated and the programs can be agreed upon, the advantages of PPBS and the Rational Approach come into play.

5

Some Administrators Unkindly View Congress

James Burnham

No one any longer questions the fact, but only the degree and the merits of this century's aggrandizement of the executive branch within the aggrandized central government. But here we must return to the distinction that we found it necessary to make in Chapter IV, in discussing the diffusion of power within the American system. Just as the commission bureaucracies have ceased to be—if they ever were—mere delegated agents of Congress, the permanent "executive" bureaucracy is no longer a mere agent of the president. The combined bureaucracy has become, rather, a fourth primary branch of the central government.

In theory the permanent civil servants are only technicians, carrying out the president's will in accord with the laws enacted by Congress. They are theoretically distinguished by the protected, permanent and formalized status of their jobs from those who have a voice in policy. The policy posts remain under a spoils system, filled not by civil service examination but by specific presidential appointment (with Senate confirmation), and exposed to instant dismissal with or without stated cause. Because of their merely temporary service and their immediate, continuous dependence on the presidential will, the "policy echelon," headed by the cabinet members, usually functions in fact as the mere agent or "arm" of the executive that it is supposed to be in theory. But, generally speaking, the huge mass of the permanent bureaucracy is not temporary, and not dependent in any direct, continuous way on the executive will;

Reprinted with permission of author and publisher from *Congress and the American Tradition* (Chicago: Henry Regnery, 1959), pp. 159–64, 165, 166. Footnotes have been renumbered.

nor, in practice, is it really possible to preserve the distinction between "policy-making" and "non-policy-making" posts.

The Civil Service Act of 1883 was in part the result of decades of ideological agitation. The government, it was held, would be best served by a permanent career staff selected on the basis of training and ability, and protected by law and regulation against the vagaries of political struggle or popular passion. Apart from the ideological agitation—and without prejudice to its merits—civil service reform, with its guarantee of job security, was a natural social target for the government employees *in situ* as well as for those who might be considered to belong to the potential-bureaucratic type: citizens aspiring to careers in the government service, but more suited by nature to passing examinations and manipulating files than to the rougher, man-to-man battles of elections or the spoils system.

Before the event, both Congress and the president managed to persuade themselves that they might be able to gain something, in power terms, from a solid civil service system. The president could hope to get a more efficient and even more docile instrument to carry out the executive purpose. Congress could imagine that, with the governmental apparatus made secure from the arbitrary purges of a Jacksonian president, it would be more difficult for the executive to thwart the legislative will; and that, even if the permanent bureaucrats should lose their franchise by becoming residents of the District of Columbia, their job contentment would spread to their voting cousins in the hinterland.

Both Congress and the president failed to take into account the fact that the bureaucracy itself, once it had reached a certain size and was performing a variety of functions, would be a power element with interests and aims of its own, and that the protective ramparts of civil service "reform" must enhance its independent power. In our day only the very naive can suppose the civil bureaucracy, with its base peacetime number nearly 3,000,000, supported most of the time by the socially similar military bureaucracy, to be a mere agent of the president, meticulously obeying the orders of his appointive officials under the laws passed by Congress. The bureaucracy, like the Carolingian Mayors of the Palace in 8th-century France, not merely wields its own share of the sovereign power but begins to challenge the older branches for supremacy.

This emergence of the bureaucracy is a creeping growth, expressed most tellingly in the day to day, unpublicized activities of the governmental colossus, though on occasion it is more openly marked. What most plainly reveals the independent power of the bureaucracy are those cases where the bureaucrats of some department, agency or office persist in a policy that is contrary to the policy held by both Congress and the president. Under such circumstances—which are not at all unusual —it is obviously an illusion to believe that the civil servants are in reality subject to the "policy-making" appointive official who is their nominal superior, or to the laws that have been enacted by Congress. In a process well known to modern Washington, the official, who may be the secretary or assistant secretary of one of the major departments, becomes the dupe or tool or front of the permanent civil servants whom he is assigned to direct.

For example, many of the permanent officers of the Public Health Service have long favored an expansion of the government's role in the field of medicine, and both inside and outside the governmental apparatus have advocated measures that, in practical effect, move toward the progressive socialization of medicine. This is natural enough from the standpoint of their own jobs and interests. Moving on the inside track, their power and influence necessarily increase with every advance in a statist direction.[1] Probably few of the permanent officers are doctrinaire socialists; but most of them tend much closer to a medical socialism, or statism, than either the President, their appointive policy-making superiors, or Congress.

A similar pattern of relations is observable in government offices dealing with education, social insurance, agriculture, electric power and housing, and from the same organic cause. It is often forgotten that governmental "social insurance," for example, whatever its objective merits, is ineluctably bound up with the incomes and careers of tens of thousands of lesser and greater bureaucrats who administer it; and, more generally, the livelihood, power and prestige of the members of the permanent bureaucracy are bound up with the state. Once the bureaucracy has grown beyond the limits within which personal acquaintance and inspection can fairly well comprehend it, once it has taken on an institu-

---

[1] The well-known bureaucratic phenomenon of "empire building" arises not from accidents of individual psychology but out of the inner imperatives of the bureaucratic situation.

tional life of its own, an average bureaucrat (whatever he may say in public for discretion's sake) cannot be expected to support measures that would lead to the decrease of government's funds, functions and personnel. An exceptional individual strongly indoctrinated in anti-statist ideology or carefully watched by an anti-statist superior, might do so, but for the bureaucrat to advocate anti-statism is equivalent to asking for his economic throat to be cut. Thus the huge modern bureaucracy is both a product of statist tendencies and simultaneously a cause of the persistence of those tendencies.

The independent policy of the bureaucracy is manifest in connection not only with the general issue of statism but with a multitude of other problems as well, some of them minor and accidental, perhaps springing from no more complex cause than the ingrained ideas of a long-lasting individual bureaucrat or a particular bureau's fossilized work habits. It has been evident for some years that the permanent staff of the State Department, especially the career officers of the Foreign Service, have—besides their technical abilities—policy ideas of their own that do not readily yield to the directives of the president and the appointive heads of the department, and that are at a still further remove from the notions that congressmen try to incorporate in laws. The independent power of the foreign affairs bureaucracy is so widely recognized that it has given birth to a special term ("Indians") to designate the bureaucratic assistants to the appointive "policy-makers." "Some high officials have in part attributed to these juniors the 'force of inertia' that unduly delays, or leaves unconsummated, the execution of presidential policy."[2] There is substantial evidence that a number of important foreign policy decisions of the past generation—on the Nazis, China, Tito, Nasser, for example—were the will of the permanent bureaucracy rather than of the president and his supposedly policy-making appointees.[3] The conduct of the inde-

[2] Arthur Krock in the *New York Times,* December 14, 1956.

[3] The curious procedure usually employed in recent years to arrive at policy decisions automatically increases the weight of the bureaucracy. An outsider would assume that a policy-making official (or the president, if the matter were important enough) would issue a general directive, and instruct his staff to elaborate it, show how it would be implemented, etc. This is not what happens. The official instructs his staff to prepare *a policy* (on China, Yugoslavia, Germany or whatever) for him to adopt.

pendent regulatory agencies—such as the National Labor Relations Board or the Federal Communications Commission, to cite two conspicuous examples—departs still more widely at times from the intent of Congress and the president.

These observations apply to the military as well as the civil bureaucracy. In theory the president as chief administrator directs the civil bureaucracy, and as commander-in-chief directs the military bureaucracy. In practice each escapes from his control when it becomes large, technically complex, and permanent. The two bureaucracies have both common and special interests. In recent decades the power of the military has particularly expanded because of the increase in the size of the permanent military establishment, the immense sums of money put at its disposition, and the influence of military procurement on finance and industry. In spite of the doctrine of civilian supremacy, the influence of the military bureaucracy has come to be felt, and is sometimes decisive, not only in military and foreign affairs but in the domestic economy.[4]

The expanded power and autonomy of the bureaucracy is expressed in the symbols of personal conduct and social intercourse. Most citizens, lost in the mazes of tax or subsidy or license rules, have had immediate experience of that "bureaucratic arrogance" or insolence that the chroniclers of other bureaucratized societies have often described. All who have had business to do at the nation's capital will have discovered how long and perilous is the path to the desk of a high-ranking official of a departmental or agency office, and how small a chance there is that one's troubles will be promptly adjusted when one finally scales the last precipice. It is far easier, as anyone may readily confirm for himself, to get to talk with a member of Congress than with a bureaucrat of the middle or higher grades.

The bureaucratic arrogance has in recent years come to be directed against Congress and congressmen as well as the lay public. For appointments between congressmen and bureaucrats, the bureaucrats are more likely to be late than the congressmen. In their endogamous conversations, at their parties, the upper strata of the bureaucracy do not hide

---

[4] In *The Power Elite,* Prof. C. Wright Mills contends that the upper level of the military bureaucracy is integrally linked with the managerial group in industry to constitute the nation's now dominant stratum.

their feeling that Congress is a road block that they must somehow bypass if the country is to progress, a kind of idiot boy who must be pushed, teased and cozened. Reporting to Congress, testifying before its committees, "briefing" its leaders, is, as much of the bureaucracy judges it, a painful waste of time that can do nothing but interfere with the proper—i.e., bureaucratic—guidance of the nation's affairs.

This arrogance of the bureaucrat toward Congress—so significant a symptom of the altered power relations—has not been much studied in public. In order to give it a more precise specification, I shall quote from some unpublished material that has been made available to me by Anne Brunsdale. The following excerpts are transcribed "raw" (to use the bureaucratic dialect) from confidential interviews—wire or stenographically recorded—with higher level (GS16-18) governmental officials whose names, by the nature of the case, must be omitted.

An official recently transferred to the Department of Agriculture from the State Department:

> You hear them talking around the department about what they can get away with. It's always a question of, given this piece of legislation and this bunch of people in Congress, what can we get by with. . . . Often a bureaucrat has got to pretend that he is representing the people—and he does it honestly, and what action he takes [against congressional sanction] *is* in the public interest. He never takes any action like this without clearing it with his counterparts in other agencies and everybody else who would have any interest in it. And generally I think he comes out with something that represents a consensus all around the place. . . .
>
> The bureaucrat has a program to carry out that he believes in. The question of whether or not Congress has authorized it is not so important to him. He figures that if Congress really had the facts and knew what was right, it would agree with him. So he goes right ahead, getting away with as much as he can.
>
> I've attended lots of these meetings within the department where budget questions and the like were decided, and I never heard a respectful word spoken about Congress at one of them.

An official of another department:

> The real hard fact about life on the hill [i.e., in Congress] is that very few times does Congress, acting together and well-informed, pass the laws. . . . You [an administrative official] go up there and explain to the subject-matter committee how these things work and why. . . . We [administrators] draw up

good legislation in the national interest with all the parts fitting into the whole properly, and what happens to it when it hits the hill is like a Christian among the heathen. . . . So we spend lots of time figuring out how we can do something we want to do and think we should do, without taking a new piece of legislation over to Congress. . . .

Another, in reply to the question, "What's your estimate of the individual Congressmen?":

They're a pretty dumb bunch. They have to voice an opinion about something they know nothing about. . . . I can't think of a more unhappy fate for me than to be put in the position of a congressman. . . . On the other hand, most people in administrative jobs are there because they are trained for the job; they are employed in the field they are qualified for.

An official of the Post Office Department (some of whose remarks indirectly show the key role of the civil service job-guarantee in determining the power relations):

Everything that Congress does is wrapped up with the matter of votes. Theoretically the congressman is supposed to vote as to what is going to help the country. . . . But of course we might as well be practical and realize he doesn't do this. . . . Congress represents the selfish wishes of the people. It is concerned with getting votes, whereas the bureaucracy isn't. . . . I don't think Congress has any business supervising the activities of the administrative branch. The minute that Congress had the power to fire me, they would have a political weapon in their hands that would entirely destroy the civil service. . . . Our biggest problem with Congress is getting money and the fact that Congress is always passing laws without considering their effect upon the matter of operating the service. . . . [In an indignant tone:] We have to have a man here doing nothing but keeping up contacts with Congress, answering letters, giving congressmen information, etc.

6

The Federal Service:
Those Who Serve at the Top
Committee for Economic Development

Most Americans think that all federal civilian employees are members of a uniform civil service system. This impression is, however, incorrect. The competitive civil service is composed of more than two million civilians who come under the entrance examination, promotion, and related employment programs administered by the Civil Service Commission. But with respect to pay systems, only one-half of these competitive service employees come under the Classification Act administered by the Civil Service Commission, while 600,000 are paid on scales set by wage boards in accordance with prevailing local rates in private enterprise, and another 500,000 or more serve under a separate Postal Field Service salary system.

Completely separate personnel systems—outside the standard civil service systems—include most employees in the foreign affairs agencies who serve under the Foreign Service Act, employees of the Department of Medicine and Surgery in the Veterans Administration, employees of the Tennessee Valley Authority, the Atomic Energy Commission, and a number of other agencies. Then there are, of course, some 2.6 million active duty military personnel.

All these groups are responsible to the president, in whom "the Executive Power shall be vested." He is expected to see to it that the military and Foreign Service officers, political officials, and career civilians in the more than 80 departments and agencies of the executive establishment are properly utilized. At the same time, however, he must

Reprinted with permission of author and publisher from *Improving Executive Management in the Federal Government* (New York: 1964), pp. 10–12, 14, 15–20. Footnotes have been renumbered.

lead and speak for the nation, conduct foreign affairs, formulate legislative programs and present them to Congress, and give political leadership to his party.

This places a tremendous burden on the president. American businessmen know from their own experience in organizing and managing large-scale operations on a continental and world-wide stage that a system of unified management and leadership is workable and effective only if there is a sound organizational structure staffed by an adequate number of capable and properly trained personnel.

To meet these requirements and to make his burdens bearable the president relies on his cabinet and agency heads and, through them, on some 8,600 key political, career, and military executives. In addition to chiefs of bureaus and divisions, these include the high-level professional, advisory and managerial staff members who mold platforms into programs and programs into accomplishments. In view of the enormous responsibilities burdening the president, it is imperative that these top management team members be qualified, dedicated, and competent.

The changing environment

No generation in history has seen greater changes in the lives and governments of men than have occurred in the past thirty-five years: ten years of depression, a long war, and nineteen years of cold war and a succession of crises. The population of the United States has grown rapidly and the national economy has expanded vigorously. Science and technology have produced a revolution in the daily life of every citizen that would have been hard to imagine thirty-five years ago.

Constant ideological, economic, and technological changes have added new dimensions to the size and complexity of the federal government, and to the variety and difficulty of the managerial tasks within it.

—The goals of government are increasingly numerous and involved.

—The degree of specialization has increased. The basic disciplines of physics, chemistry, and biology are split and joined, as in bionics, astro-physics, and microelectronics.

—There are many more kinds of specialists whose work the executive must manage and coordinate. Foreign aid teams may include scientists and technicians in education, agriculture, engineering, credit and banking, municipal government, and industrial development.

—The constituencies with which the executive is concerned are more vociferous and more powerful. The federal executive faces special interest groups and competing agencies that are better fortified and better armed than ever. These interests must be weighed and balanced within a constitutional and statutory framework.

—The management tools at the federal executive's disposal are ever more sophisticated, efficient, and expensive. There are new machines, and there are new skills—in operations research, in systems management, and in mathematical programming.

Today's executive in government—as in business, science, or engineering—needs a broader range of competence than was required in earlier times. The bureau chief or division director must understand a wide assortment of specialties and have at least a working familiarity with new fields of knowledge. His successes in program management rest heavily on his understanding of the capabilities of specialists, and on the inter-relationships between their specializations. And he can succeed only under severe pressures from forceful constituencies and on harried time schedules.

* * *

The main burden of assuring that the resources of the federal government are well managed falls on relatively few of the five million men and women whom it employs. Under the department and agency heads there are 8,600 political, career, military, and foreign service executives—the top managers and professionals—who exert major influence on the manner in which the rest are directed and utilized. Below their level there are other thousands with assignments of some managerial significance, but we believe that the line of demarcation selected is the best available for our purposes in this statement.

In addition to presidential appointees in responsible posts, the 8,600 include the three highest grades under the Classification Act; the three highest grades in the postal field service; comparable grades in the foreign service; general officers in the military service; and similar classes in other special services and in agencies or positions excepted from the Classification Act.

There is no complete inventory of positions or people in federal service at this level. The lack may be explained by separate agency statutes and personnel systems, diffusion among so many special services, and absence of any central point (short of the president himself) with jurisdiction over all upper-level personnel of the government.

* * *

The 8,600 key people are found in four categories—presidential appointees, civilian career executives and professionals, military officers, and foreign service officers.

1. Top presidential appointees, about 500 of them, bear the brunt of translating the philosophy and aims of the current administration into practical programs.[1] This group includes the secretaries and assistant secretaries of cabinet departments, agency heads and their deputies, heads and members of boards and commissions with fixed terms, and chiefs and directors of major bureaus, divisions, and services. Appointments to many of these politically sensitive positions are made on recommendation by department or agency heads, but all are presumably responsive to presidential leadership.

One qualification for office at this level is that there be no basic

---

[1]There are other presidential appointments to lower-echelon posts, such as U.S. marshalls and attorneys, with a traditional patronage aspect. These are excluded from our total of 500 because they have little or no management responsibility.

GS is an abbreviation for "General Schedule." Grades GS-1 through GS-4 are low-level clerical and comparable workers; university graduates usually enter at grades GS-5 or GS-7; holders of master's degrees usually enter at GS-9; doctoral degree holders may enter at GS-11; and holders of GS-13, GS-14, and GS-15 grades usually have significant supervisory or managerial duties, or responsible professional or staff support roles.

The "supergrades", GS-16, GS-17, and GS-18, superimposed on the former structure in 1949, were designed to distinguish higher levels of responsibility and competence.

These—and their opposite numbers outside the classified civil service—are the central interest of this statement.

disagreement with presidential political philosophy, at least so far as administrative judgments and actions are concerned. Apart from the bi-partisan boards and commissions, these men are normally identified with the political party of the president, or are sympathetic to it, although there are exceptions.

There are four distinguishable kinds of top presidential appointees, including:

—Those whom the president selects at the outset to establish immediate and effective control over the government (e.g., cabinet secretaries, agency heads, his own White House staff and executive office personnel).

—Those selected by department and agency heads in order to establish control within their respective organizations (e.g., assistant secretaries, deputies, assistants to, and major line posts in some bureaus and divisions).

—High-level appointees who—though often requiring clearance through political or interest group channels, or both—must have known scientific or professional competence (e.g., the surgeon general, the commissioner of education).

—Those named to residual positions traditionally filled on a partisan patronage basis.

These appointees are regarded primarily as policy-makers and as overseers of policy execution. In practice, however, they usually have substantial responsibilities in line management, often requiring a thorough knowledge of substantive agency programs.

2. *Civilian career executives and professionals,* about 5,500 of them, occupy positions in the three upper grades under the Classification Act (GS-16, GS-17, and G-18), or in the postal field service (grades 18, 19, and 20), or in high posts under Public Law 313 which was enacted to facilitate recruitment of needed scientific or specialized skills. Also included are comparable positions in the Atomic Energy Commission, the Tennessee Valley Authority, the United States Public Health Service, the Veterans Administration Department of Medicine and Surgery, and other agencies outside the Classification Act.

Supergrade personnel are responsible for executing policies established by their superiors. They also play a significant part in formulating policies. They provide the experience, the intimate knowledge, and often the insights on which the 500 presidential appointees rely in discharging their policy-making and managerial responsibilities.

Not all of these 5,500 have risen from the ranks of the career services. There are 500 Classification Act positions lacking standard career protection—the "Schedule C" jobs described elsewhere in this statement. Over half of these 500 positions are filled by career employees from lower civil service ranks, who can fall back to their classified service grades if called upon to do so; the other half of the 500, plus a few others among the 5,500, are regarded as political appointees without tenure.

Most career executives have achieved their present rank and status by dint of demonstrated technical competence and after a lengthy apprenticeship, as in many large and long-established private firms. In the government, about 90 percent have had ten years or more of federal service, and about half were first recruited at middle or lower grades. Only a small percentage has been brought into government from comparable outside posts.

Most top career servants, whether promoted to their positions from within or recruited from outside, have tended to "stay put." For example, two-thirds of a large sample studied recently had worked only in one or two departments or bureaus in their entire public careers although most were long-time federal employees. Hence their experience, lengthy though it may be, lacks breadth.

3. Military flag officers. Nearly 1,300 generals and admirals play a major part in formulating the policies, planning the expenditures, and directing operations for 2.6 million persons on active military duty, and some one million civilians in the defense establishment. Responsible, in turn, to civilian secretariats, they execute day-to-day assignments similar in many ways to those of the so-called "supergrade" civil servants (GS-16, GS-17, and GS-18) and of persons holding positions under Public Law 313.

Ordinarily, flag officers reach their senior positions through promotion from within. Over 90 percent of flag-rank officers in the Navy, two-thirds in the Army, and one-third in the Air Force were first recruited through the service academies, and most have earned one or more university degrees. They have been trained, rotated, and selectively promoted until those judged most capable have reached general officer levels, although seniority has a major influence.

4. Foreign service officers. Over 1,300 including reserve officers, serve in foreign affairs agencies (State Department, Agency for International Development, and the United States Information Agency, for example) at home or in diplomatic posts.[2] They are responsible for the detailed conduct of consular, economic, political, and administrative operations in more than 100 foreign countries.

Recruitment sources vary from agency to agency. About 80 percent of those in the State Department attained their present positions through promotion, although a number were brought in at upper grades as a result of the lateral appointment provisions of the Foreign Service Act of 1946, and the subsequent Wriston Program of 1954. On the other hand, the Agency for International Development (AID) has relied almost exclusively on persons brought in at middle and upper grades. The pattern in the United States Information Agency (USIA) is midway between State and AID.

Variety of assignments for the 8,600

These 8,600 top officials in the political, career civilian, military, and foreign service categories may be described loosely as "the management" of the federal government, although their activities vary widely. Personnel in each of these groups have three distinct kinds of jobs.[3]

1. Line managers (program administrators) constitute about 35 percent of the 8,600. They serve as agency heads, bureau chiefs, office and division directors, and are responsible in each case for a specific line unit and for one or more programs." (For example, the Director of the Division of Timber Management in the Forest Service sells one-fifth of the nation's supply of timber, and thus determines how this substantial federal activity involving sales of $135 million per year shall affect lumber production and related private industries.)

[2] Individuals in this group are those in the Foreign Service, in the Foreign Service Reserve, or in Staff categories at grades comparable to FSO (Foreign Service Officers) 1 and 2, in addition to Career Ambassadors and Career Ministers.

[3] These job categories were developed in a recent study—as yet unpublished—of 424 civilian career supergrade executives made by John Corson of Princeton University and McKinsey and Company.

To keep things running, these line managers have to make many important decisions on the spot. They do this within the framework of general "policy" where this is set by law or by responsible superiors; but many day-to-day decisions deal with new situations and emergencies, and are thus in fact shot through with policy problems. This kind of work has prime significance.

2. *Supporting staff specialists* constitute another 35 percent. They provide managerial services—budget and fiscal, management analysis, personnel, general administration—or serve as deputies or "assistants-to." Although some of them have line responsibility in the sense that they head offices or divisions with large numbers or employees, they differ from "line managers" in that they render their services only internally to their respective agencies and in support of "program" activities. Although the deputies and assistants to line managers make up less than one-third of this category, they often work closely with top administrators and influence agency policies and programs.

3. *Professional staff members* make up the remaining 30 percent of the 8,600. They provide needed professional services, often based on individual contributions in scientific and technical areas. Typically, they are experts in a specialty or profession—legal counsel, economic advisors, or scientists. At these upper levels they are often assisted by professionally trained staffs, usually small, but some perform scientific or technical tasks with little or no supporting staff. (One such "performer," for example, is the Special Assistant for Fisheries and Wildlife in the Department of State. A marine biologist and international fisheries expert, he formulates U.S. fisheries policies and acts as the principal contact point between fishing industry interests and the Department.)

Frustrations and rewards of federal service

According to careful studies of large samples, those who have served and those who are serving at the upper levels of the federal government commonly feel that both the psychological rewards and the disappointments of public service are greater than in most other fields of human endeavor. They report specific frustrations and disappointments that discourage outstanding performance and inhibit willingness to assume responsibility. Frustrations are suffered, of course, by all managers (in and out of government) who take responsibility seriously; and those without frustrations are unlikely to be trying very hard. Nevertheless, key people at the top of the federal service—political and career alike—are concerned that:

—The quality of program management is reduced by the inability to overcome the adverse effects of pressures from Congress, from powerful interest groups, and from other agencies;

—High turnover rates among top political appointees have a damaging effect on the continuity of programs and on full utilization of supporting staffs;

—Too many levels of required approval discourage efforts to improve quality and to weed out substandard performers; and

—Reservoirs of promotable, qualified management talent are inadequate. This they attribute to failure by the government to attract the most highly qualified graduates from leading colleges and universities.

Nonetheless, senior federal executives acknowledge that appealing rewards may attend a career in federal service. They say that:

—Opportunity to rise to the top and to manage a large and vital program is in their eyes greater than in industry;

—A responsible federal position permits the holder to make a worthwhile contribution to his country and to humanity, with resultant recognition and prestige;

—Key people have frequent contacts with stimulating leaders of their respective professions;

—The challenge of new problems and the opportunities for achieving major improvements are present in many government programs; and

—The world-wide scope and diversity of federal programs affords a stimulating and interesting work environment.

The quality of sustained performance by those at the top of the federal service is greatly influenced by the extent to which the underlying causes of these frustrations and disappointments can be identified and eliminated.

7

Influence, Power, and Authority in Organization

Geoffrey Y. Cornog

Large organizations stand as monuments to man's ability to overcome his own limitations in his natural environment. In turn, an important reason for this success is the ability to coordinate the actions and efforts of large numbers of complex human beings. Since coordination requires control of human behavior, an organization is from this point of view a system designed to influence human behavior.

In the traditional theories of organization, organization control is imposed on the various task-oriented units and individuals by means of a hierarchical pyramid of delegated authority from the top down to the line operator at the bottom of the pyramid. The major goal is factored into subgoals and, then, into tasks. These tasks are combined into positions and individuals are assigned to these positions to perform these tasks. In addition, general rules and regulations are established to guide the occupants of these positions. Thus, the task system is seen in the traditional view as coordinated and controlled by the authority system so that, except for the very top, everyone in the organization is supervised by a superior who has authority to control his behavior. It is assumed that the duties, responsibility, and authority of each position are clear and unambiguous.

Within this view of organization, authority was assumed to rest formally, legally, and legitimately in the position to which it was delegated, there to be exercised by the individual occupying the position who enforced his authority through the use of rewards and penalties. Formal authority in this context is seen as the sole way of making things happen in the way you want. The delegation of authority here is seen as a grant of power where power is defined as the ability to determine another's
behavior through the coercive use of penalties. Thus, within the tradi-

tional ideas of organization the term authority is commonly employed with the unspoken assumption that the delegation of authority is a delegation of power, i.e., power to control behavior.

The traditional approach has been under continuous attack at least since the Hawthorne studies in the 1920s, and probably before then. From the simple earlier approach has developed a much more complex view of authority, power, and influence and organization control. The accepted view now is that power and authority are part of a larger thing called influence which is not a simple property of a person but a relation between two people. Thus, influence is defined as a relation among actors in which one actor induces other actors to act in some way they would not otherwise act. Power is then seen as a special instance of influence which depends upon threat or expectation of severe penalties or great losses. That is, power is coercive influence.

Robert Dahl illustrates coercive influence in this way:

> Imagine a continuum representing various degrees of some value that A regards as important—honor, wealth, prestige, popularity. A's present position is at A_o on the continuum. That is, a gain in, say, honor, for A is represented by a move to the right; a loss in honor is represented by a move to the left. Hence one might try to influence A by offering him rewards or threatening him with penalties, or some combination of the two. ... The domain of influence, one might say, runs all the way from one extreme to the other, from A- to A+ and includes all possible combinations. The extreme left portion of the continuum, let us say from A- to A_c, represents the most severe penalties. This is the domain of coercive influence, which is sometimes called power.

COERCION

A- A_c A_o A+

LOSSES   GAINS

Authority, from this point of view, is a kind of influence. It is a relation among actors in a special kind of environment called an organization. In organizations as they operate over time there are many instances where one actor influences another. However, a subset of all of these influence attempts are those designed into the organization system as a means of ensuring role performance. This subset of influence attempts we designate by the term authority and, in organizations, authority and its supports are consciously organized and obvious. Organization as a goal-seeking system requires the coordination of the actions of its members and one method of controlling behavior is through assigning to some individuals the responsibility of influencing organization members.

While power and authority are both types of influence, they are not the same thing. Authority in organization may range from simple influence to coercive influence or power. The only way to determine whether authority reaches the level of power in any organization is to ascertain whether a significant amount of coercion is involved. Thus, in a military organization in wartime, authority may overlap the power-type of influence to the extent that it is influence coerced by strong social sanctions supplemented by the ultimate sanction of the death penalty. However, in a private business organization the ultimate sanction of dismissal may be relatively meaningless, if jobs are plentiful and other social sanctions are minimal.

Of course, organization members are subject to many influences in addition to authority. A member's primary work group attempts to influence his behavior; his professional colleagues or professional organization may attempt to exert influence; and his family or friends outside the organization may attempt to influence his behavior. However, in spite of these many influences, the obvious fact is that organization members do in large part accept the attempts to exert authority and accept control of their behavior. It is logical to ask and important to discuss the question: Just what are the bases of organization member acceptance of management attempts to exert authority over them?

A number of schemes have been suggested for answering this question and categorizing the bases of organization authority. French and Raven suggest five bases of power in small groups which fit our view of authority as a form of influence in organization[1] and which constitute a useful typology.[2] The bases they suggest are: legitimacy, reward, coer-

[1]Robert A. Dahl, *Modern Political Analysis* (Englewood Cliffs, N.J.: Prentice-Hall, Inc., 1963).

[2]J. R. P. French, and B. Raven, "The Bases of Social Power," in D. Cartwright, ed., *Studies in Social Power* (Ann Arbor: University of Michigan, Institute of Social Research, 1959).

cion, reference, and expertise. Authority based on legitimacy, in this scheme, draws on the cultural values the individual has been socialized to accept. The organization is seen as a legitimate part of the social system. It assigns responsibilities to positions in the organization and legitimately assigns circumscribed authority to the individual occupying that position. It is this assignment or delegation that the employee accepts when he joins the organization. This is the "fiction of superior authority" mentioned by C. I. Barnard where the individual accepts authority as depersonalized acts for the good of the organization which, according to his socialized scheme of values, are accepted as legitimate.[3] However, this is seen as a fiction because it does depend on the individual accepting the authority act as legitimate. The significance of this fact of acceptance is that it then follows that the ability to apply legitimate authority varies according to a number of conditions. Thus, the problem of exerting authority becomes much more complex than just issuing a command or an order. The superior must consider these conditions, not the least of which is the subordinate's willingness to cooperate.

Reward authority is just what it says, influence based on rewarding conformity with something of value. The value of the reward and the probability of obtaining the reward determine the strength of authority based on reward. Also, since the reward is based on conforming, the individual must be monitored and the new behavior often will continue only so long as it is monitored or is reinforced. At some point, however, even a minor reward can result in an individual learning an appropriate response so firmly that the response can only be extinguished with great difficulty.

Coercive authority is similar to reward authority and depends upon the importance of the threatened loss, as well as upon its probability. It is significantly different from authority based on reward, however, because it tends to produce frustrated behavior and antagonistic relationships. Moreover, the coercion is effective only for those behaviors that the individual feels the agent can observe. Finally, coercive authority may be best suited to inhibit old behaviors rather than to develop new skills or behaviors. Authority based on coercion is very similar to the traditional

---

[3]C. I. Barnard, *Functions of the Executive* (Cambridge: Harvard University Press, 1938).

concept of authority and may merge into the power end of the influence continuum.

Referent authority is based upon identification where one individual feels a oneness with, and identity with, or an attraction to another person, and the first individual allows himself to be influenced. Referent authority is subtle. In fact, the influence may occur without any overt attempt to influence. In this process the person tends to internalize the desired values of the referent person or group, and he evaluates his own efforts in terms of these values. Referent authority is often significantly related to reward authority because the giving of the rewards tends to increase the influence receiver's attraction to the authority wielder.

Expert authority, the last in the French and Raven typology, is based upon superior knowledge or expertness within a given area and its range usually extends only to that area. Frequently, if an attempt is made to extend influence beyond that area it may undermine the authority of the expert by reducing the level of confidence in the authority wielder. There are a number of reasons why an individual attributes expertness to another. Demonstrated ability, experience, and reputation are some of the reasons.

Accepting the fact that authority exists, and recognizing the diverse bases on which acceptance of authority rests, are both important. However, two other aspects of authority must be recognized to round-off consideration of how authority operates in organizations. Specifically, authority is exerted by someone and authority is exerted through some means. This sounds like a tautology, but the point of the dualites of authority is central.

Given a reciprocal concept of authority, the individual exerting authority is faced with a more complex process than merely giving a simple command. He does have a relation with another actor who, within some limits, is free to disobey. At the same time, he himself is subject to the pressure of authority from his own superior. He has his own conception of the authority relations that exist in both directions, up and down. In addition, he has a perception of the conditions that exist affecting the willingness of the employee to accept any attempt to exert authority. Thus, the individual must make a decision, varying in difficulty over time, whether to exert authority and how to exert it. As with any decision, the objectives must be evaluated, the means compared, and the results estimated. That, in most instances, this process occurs unconsciously does not lessen the significance of the problems of exerting authority in organization.

Emphasizing the means of exercising authority makes the point that there is more than one way to exert authority. Cartwright identifies four broad classes of methods of influencing.[4] Identifying O as the individual exerting influence and P as the individual being influenced, Cartwright lists these classes of methods of influencing: (a) O exerts physical control over P's body; (b) O exerts control over the gains and costs experienced by P; (c) O exerts control over the information available to P; and (d) O uses P's attitudes toward being influenced by O. These are broad classes of methods of influence with more specific means included within each class. However, there is no need for a lengthy discussion of the specific means to make the point that each method varies in its relative effectiveness, in the immediate and long term costs of application of each of the methods.

Clearly, the richness of the subject of power, influence, and authority in organization goes far beyond the sterile, mechanical power model of the traditional organization theorists. For the student of the behavior of human beings in organizations, clarification of his own view of these concepts and care exercised in their use are minimum requirements.

[4]Dorwin Cartwright, "Influence, Leadership, and Control," in James G. March, ed., *Handbook of Organizations* (Chicago: Rand McNally and Co., 1965), pp. 1–47.

8

The Personnel Administrator: His Role and His Role Conflicts

Geoffrey Y. Cornog

"The personnel man is confused. At the center of his confusion, though he does not realize it, is the issue of his role in the organization."[1] This article considers the personnel administrator's role in an organization and the factors that contribute, not only to the confusion in the definition, but also to the conflicts that are inherent in the personnel administrator's role.

Role theory or role analysis is one of the tools of the social scientist that has great promise as a method of increasing the personnel administrator's insight into human behavior in organization as the major focus of personnel administration.[2] With the perspective of role analysis, a description of a personnel administrator's position becomes much more meaningful than the conventional description of duties and responsibilities set forth in a position description.

Reprinted with permission of author and publisher. From Geoffrey Y. Cornog, "All the World a Stage, But Who Writes the Roles?," *Personnel Administration,* November–December 1970, pp. 26–31.

[1]Stanley M. Herman, *The People Specialists* (New York: Alfred A. Knopf, 1968), p. 7.

[2]In addition to the items listed insights were drawn from: Frederick L. Bates, *The Structure of Occupations: A Role Theory Approach* (Raleigh, N.C.: North Carolina State University, Center for Occupational Education, Monograph #2, 1968); Bruce Biddle and E. Thomas (eds.), *Social Role: Readings in Theory and Application* (New York: John Wiley and Sons, 1964); Neal Gross, W. S. Mason, and A. W. McEachern, *Explorations in Role Analysis* (New York: John Wiley and Sons, 1966); G. Ritzer and H. M. Trice, *An Occupation in Conflict* (Ithaca, N.Y.: Cornell University Press, 1969).

Elements of the personnel man's role

Four major elements of the personnel man's role need to be examined to clarify his role in an organization. These elements are: (a) the duties and responsibilities determined by the organization, i.e., the personnel administrator's organization *role prescription;* (b) the organization members who have a work relationship with the personnel administrator, i.e., his *role set;* (c) the interpersonal relations between the personnel man and the members of his role set; and (d) the individual taking the role. These elements are all familiar. However, that very familiarity may obscure some important facts.

The organization role prescription

The organization aspect is much overworked in any discussion of the personnel man and is one that requires clarity, if it is to be kept in perspective. An organization may be viewed as a network of related positions. These positions may be said to be located in "organization space," where each position makes sense only as it relates to other positions. In the common view of organization, each of these positions represents the combination of tasks which can be performed by one employee and which are presumed to be related to the achievement of the goal or goals of the organization. The position or job description spells out these duties and responsibilities and may be called the organization definition of what any person occupying the position should do.

In role theory, there is a *position* located in organization space and occupied by someone. A *role* is defined as the activities performed by the person occupying the position. However, there is a significant addition. The actions that are identified as a role include more than those encompassed in the duties and responsibilities listed in the job description. Role theory includes *role demand,* this means actions or behaviors expected by anyone who is affected by the behavior of another individual. Therefore, from this view point, the duties and responsibilities in the official job description of a position represent the demand made by the organization on the incumbent to behave in certain ways, but it is only one demand among many.

The position description of the Chief, Personnel Branch (from now on he will be called the Personnel Chief) might say that he

> formulates and recommends personnel policies, and establishes and implements personnel activities, techniques, and methods to insure sound, meaningful, and practical personnel administration in keeping with current and advanced concepts and objectives of personnel management.

What this may mean in practice can vary considerably. For example, think of the variation in the resources the agency might furnish the Personnel Chief and the impact of the various levels on his ability to perform his role. His role behavior will be quite different, depending on whether the agency furnishes him a staff of ten professional personnel people or a staff of two. Organizations will, in addition, differ considerably on the coherence of their role demands, on the amount of agreement on these demands, on how important they are considered to be, and on the amount of freedom an individual may have in how he responds to these demands.[3]

These things are often overlooked when professional personnel men speak of their "role" in organization. This fact is particularly important, however, because the variation in organization demands among organizations makes the other three elements of organization role much more significant than we usually realize.

Personnel man's role set

In his day-to-day response to the demands of the organization, the Personnel Chief will relate to many individuals. Management at many levels, other staff officials, employees, employee representatives, Civil Service Commission staff members, other professional personnel col-

[3]Daniel J. Levinson, "Role, Personality, and Social Structure in the Organizational Setting," *Journal of Abnormal and Social Psychology* 58 (1959): 174.

leagues, local government agency people, and private groups may all be included in the contacts and relations that arise from the performance of his role. These many individuals are considered to be his *role set,* because they all have contact with him and have some interest in what he does or does not do, how he does it, what he thinks, and what kind of person he is. The behavior of the Personnel Chief affects these individuals and, because of this, they attempt to influence him to behave in a way that satisfies their *role demands.*

These role demands take many different forms, ranging from the direct order from the Personnel Chief's superior, the Chief, Administrative Division, to the expression on the face of a personnel technician when the Personnel Chief gives him something to do. However, the Personnel Chief must interpret these role demands, which are often confusing. He must understand what behavior is being demanded, evaluate the power of the sender to affect him, and assess how important the demand that is being made is to that sender. For the Personnel Chief who deals with individuals located throughout the agency evaluating role demands can become a very complex problem. For example, the Regional Director, the Deputy Regional Director, and the Chief, Administrative Division, may each be interested in a different mix of personnel program elements while generally supporting the organization role demands. Civil Service Commission staff members may be seeking greater conformity with federal government-wide regulations that conflict with organization demands. Supervisors may aim at making their own life easier by demanding that an employee be upgraded to keep him from quitting, even though there has been no significant change in that employee's duties and responsibilities.

These facts are grist in the mill of organization life for any personnel man. But it is a grist that is often overlooked in discussions of the role of the personnel man. Overlooking it raises several problems.

First, it results in overestimation of the common elements of the role of the personnel man across organizations.

Second, it brings a serious underestimation of the importance of finding out through empirical studies exactly what personnel men do, the problems they face, the characteristic ambiguities and conflicts to which they are subject, and the possibility that certain personality types are better suited to fill the personnel roles than others.

Interpersonal relationships

Interpersonal relationships deserve separate identification from previously described elements of organization role because of their impact on the role demands of the Personnel Chief's role set and his response to the individuals making those demands. Acknowledging the existence of these interpersonal relationships tends to enrich our insight by emphasizing a time dimension that is frequently neglected. It is an important fact that people live and work in organizations over periods of time during which relationships are established, grow, continue, blow up, or decline; and the existence and state of these relationships have a great effect on how we behave toward one another. The Personnel Chief may have a long-standing disagreement with his boss over his share of the division's resources, he may like and get support from the Deputy Regional Director, he may be friends with and visit socially one of the operating branch chiefs, he may feud with a Civil Service Commission staff member, and so on.

All of these interpersonal relations and others, in various dynamic combinations, will affect the role demands on Personnel Chief, the level of influence applied to enforce the role demands, and the nature of the Personnel Chief's response. Frequent interaction over time that has resulted in mutual liking and agreement on important values tends to bring a much more positive response to a role demand. Not that the law, regulation, or rule will be violated, it is just that more effort will probably be expended willingly in the search for a way to respond positively to such a demand. Then, too, this positive response feeds back to the source of the role demands modified.

The individual in the role

The description thus far emphasizes that the Personnel Chief, or any organization member, is confronted with many situations where contradictions, conflict, dilemmas, and ambiguities are present. The individual in the position of Personnel Chief will respond to these situations and, in doing so, will define his complex social reality and his place in it. The result of this process will be his *personal role definition*.[4] The Personnel Chief will perceive the many demands on him through the filtering mechanism that is his view of himself—his basic values, his life goals, his idea of the kind of person he is—and his view of his occupational role generally—his view of the agency, of personnel administration, of the civil service system, and of public administration in a democratic society.

The Personnel Chief's definition of his role from this point of view is the result of the interplay between organization situations on the one hand and the Personnel Chief's individual capacity and characteristic ways of handling his impulses, anxieties, and unconscious processes and his ways of transforming them into conscious thought, feeling, and action, on the other. The result is a set of ideas or beliefs about the role, a *role conception*. Whether he behaves in accord with his role conception will depend on his ability to live up to his conception of the true role of the Personnel Chief. And, of course, he will not always have control over many of the factors that will affect his ability to make his *role behavior* equal his role conception. In any case, when the Personnel Chief actually acts out his role, his actions feed back into the dynamic movement of the life of the total organization, where they influence the behavior of the members of his role set, and the cycle is then complete.

Conflicts and ambiguities in the personnel man's role

The picture drawn thus far presents the organization as a network of interrelated roles (really role behaviors) where the connections between roles are more than lines of formal authority and include expectations and demands.[5] The Personnel Chief in this view receives and responds to role demands from the organization and from the members of his role set who in one way or another are dependent upon him or affected by his behavior. These role relationships are affected also by interpersonal relations established over a period of time. Finally, the Personnel Chief develops his own personal definition of his role, his role conception, and

[4] *Ibid.*, p. 175ff.

[5] Robert L. Kahn, D. M. Wolfe, R. P. Quinn, J. D. Snoek, *Organizational Stress: Studies in Role Conflict and Ambiguity* (New York: John Wiley and Sons, 1964), pp. 388–89.

acts out this conception as best he can in the actual performance of the role.

This way of looking at the personnel man's role enables us to identify and analyze the ambiguities and conflicts that surround the role taking process in organization. Thus, the Personnel Chief must have enough information available to him to enable him to perform his role, and the information available or not available has an effect on the Personnel Chief's needs and his characteristic ways of behaving. The lack of information and its effect are referred to as *role ambiguity*.[6] The lack of information is called objective role ambiguity since it is related to the objective conditions within which the individual must work. The effect refers to the subjective impact of that information, or its absence, on the individual in terms of his needs for information on his objective environment and is called *subjective or experienced role ambiguity*.

Roles in organization will vary considerably in terms of the amount of information that is available to the person occupying the role. Roles at the lower levels are narrow and well defined and consequently have less role ambiguity. Those in the upper reaches characteristically are broad, undefined, and subject the occupant to considerable role ambiguity. The Personnel Chief, for example, as an individual will have his own needs for information about the objective conditions surrounding his role. What is expected of him by others? What behavior on his part will fulfill those expectations? What are the potential consequences for himself, for his role demand senders, and for the organization in general of his performance or nonperformance of his role? What kinds of behavior will be rewarded or punished, what is the nature of the rewards and punishments, and what is the probability of their occurrence? What kinds of behavior satisfy or frustrate his own needs?

These are questions that can be raised about any organization role but the thesis here is (a) that role ambiguity is much greater for the personnel man and (b) that role ambiguity for the personnel man will vary considerably from organization to organization depending on 1) the degree of coherence among the organizationally defined role requirements; 2) the degree of consensus with which these are held; and 3) the degree of choice or range of acceptable alternative behaviors the individual is

[6] *Ibid.*, pp. 21–26.

permitted. Attempts to define *the* role of the personnel man often proceed on the mistaken assumption that the organization role requirements are absolute and allow few alternatives. But the role requirements of the Personnel Chief will be quite different if he is located in a brand new Office of Economic Opportunity staffed largely with individuals unfamiliar with the federal merit system than if he is in the established, specialized Forest Service.

Close to the idea of role ambiguity is that of role conflict. *Role conflict* occurs when two or more role demands are made and when compliance with one makes it impossible to fulfill the other(s). Thus, the conflict in role demands produces opposing forces within the individual and he experiences psychological conflict, the stronger the forces the greater the conflict.[7]

Researchers have identified four types of role conflict: intra-sender, inter-sender, inter-role, and person-role conflicts. The Personnel Chief is often faced with instances of these different conflict situations. The *intra-sender* conflict confronts the Personnel Chief with contradictory demands from the same member of his role set. The Civil Service Commission, for example, sets a high value on assisting management in getting the agency job done while in audits it cites for corrective action variations from accepted procedures. The Personnel Chief faces *inter-sender* conflict when one of the operating division chiefs wants to promote one of his own subordinates, employing the device of a limited and short-term publicity, while the Personnel Technician wants to make a great effort to meet merit-competitive standards in filling the position. *Inter-role* conflict may require the Personnel Chief to choose between the overtime demands of his job and the demands of his role as a husband and a father. Finally, the Personnel Chief may be confronted by a *person-role* conflict where his role requirements violate his own personal needs, values, or capacities. His role may require him to take actions, such as to facilitate and support the formation of an employee organization, that he believes will mean eventual loss to the organization, its employees, or the general public.

All types of role conflict have one thing in common: members of the

---

[7] *Ibid.,* pp. 18–21; cf., Robert K. Merton, "The Role Set: Problems in Sociological Theory," *British Journal of Sociology* 8 (June 1957): 112–18.

role set exert pressures to change the behavior of the role occupant. The effect of these pressures from individuals with varying amounts of power in the organization is to confront the individual with complex demands 1) that result in internal tensions and anxiety with which the individual must cope and 2) that result in external communication barriers, interpersonal tensions, breaks in the authority structure, and other organizational problems.

Implications for defining the personnel man's role

Personnel administration is complex enough in the private firm or organization, but it is more so in the public service. There, in addition to sharing some portion of the personnel function with a widely dispersed management and an outside superpersonnel agent in the form of a civil service commission, the public personnel function ranges from clerical functions through specialist service functions to top management functions. Little wonder that confusion over the personnel man's role is apparent even to the nonpractitioner.

Although the present confusion exists for a reason, this does not mean that confusion cannot be eliminated or greatly reduced. But the fog of confusion is the result of a lack of knowledge about some important questions the answers to which are necessary to clarify the personnel man's role and the significance of that role in modern organizations.

First, personnel is a management function and its delineation depends in large part on the expectations and demands of management. Clearly, to define the role of the personnel man in organization we must find answers to the question: *What is the operating manager's conception of the role of the personnel man in modern organization?*

It is not sufficient to guess what the expectations of management are. This is too close to the story of the blind man describing the elephant by feeling different parts of the elephant. Levels of management must be identified and queried in an organized, i.e., scientific, fashion on what they demand of the personnel man. On the basis of that kind of data we can then evaluate one of the most significant defining forces of the role of the personnel man. Since the personnel function of organizations is shared with management officials, their view of the personnel man's share in that function is critical.

Second, since the ultimate personnel function of organization management is obtaining and maintaining the contributions of employees, the second question to which answers must be found is: *What is the employee's conception of the role of the personnel man in modern organizations?*

As a number of practicing managers have said, probably one of the most important forces in the rise of modern public service unionism has been the failure of public personnel administration to produce the kind of work environment where employee organizations are not necessary. Whether this is an accurate assessment or not isn't critical here. The fact is that employee unions in the public service constitute a major challenge that personnel administration must meet. To meet that challenge we must learn something about the role demands being made on the personnel man by the rank-and-file employees.

Third, we need answers to several questions faced by the personnel man. For example, *What is the role conception of the personnel man himself?* However, as we noted previously there is frequently a difference between the personnel man's role conception or personal role definition and his role behavior or what he actually does. A second question is necessary: *What does the personnel man actually do?* Given a range of organizations and a range of levels of performance, the answers to this question must have a wide base in terms of types of organizations and in levels and jurisdictions in government as well as levels of personnel activity and responsibility.

Finally, two last questions relate to the kinds of forces or pressures to which the personnel man is subject and to which he must respond: *What role conflicts does the personnel man experience on the job?* Probably, this is the most important question of all. The role demands of management and employee meet the role conception of the personnel man in the crucible of the personnel man's response to the pressures contending within him as he faces on the job the day-to-day choices between alternative behaviors. No amount of informed practical experience, informed intuition and informed academic speculation can substitute for empirical data on that vital question, if we are to define the role of the personnel man effectively.

Related to empirical knowledge about the personnel man's role conflicts is the question: *How can the personnel man resolve his role con-*

flicts in a sound manner? It is clear from the present analysis of the role of the personnel man in organization that his role is characterized by role conflict. Our normal tendency and the tendency in organization is to play down and, if possible, ignore conflict. However, as commentators on organization behavior from Mary Parker Follett on have frequently noted, conflict can be constructive.[8] Well managed, conflict can be a positive force in the movement toward innovative solutions to the problems we face. The key is how conflict is managed and resolved.

Conflict can be resolved by a number of alternative methods. Blake, Shepard, and Mouton, for example, present five methods: a) *withdrawing* from the conflict arena; b) *smoothing* over the differences that are the basis of the conflict; c) *compromising* by the search for an intermediate position; d) *forcing* a resolution in a win-lose situation; and e) *confronting* the conflict, employing a *problem-solving* attitude.[9] Burke, in a recent article in this journal, reports research evidence showing the confrontation—problem-solving approach to be the most effective method of managing conflict.[10]

Confrontation and problem-solving as described by Burke is a summary of much of what we have learned about the attitudes and skills related to interpersonal relations and problem-solving in managing human conflict. The attitudes are those that produce an open, honest, "helping" climate for interpersonal relations where extensive communications can take place. The problem-solving skills relate to those of defining the problem, seeking alternative solutions, selecting the best alternative solution, and implementing that solution. Obtaining these attitudes and skills is critical for the personnel man. The "boundary" location of the personnel function will insure a high rate of role conflict since personnel

---

[8]Mary Parker Follett, *Dynamic Administration: Collected Papers* (New York: Harper Bros., 1942), pp. 30–49.

[9]R. R. Blake, H. A. Shepard, and J. S. Mouton, *Managing Intergroup Conflict in Industry* (Houston: Gulf Publishing Co., 1964), p. 210. Ritzer and Trice, *op. cit.,* and Gross, Mason, and McEachern, *op. cit.,* investigate actual decisions made to resolve role conflict situations; the former employed a sample of personnel administrators.

[10]R. J. Burke, "Methods of Resolving Interpersonal Conflict," *Personnel Administration* 32 (July–August 1969): 48–55.

men deal with many different individuals and groups inside and outside of the organization.

Personnel administrators as a professional group claim an expertise in the human or people aspects of the organization. "Know thyself," including the problems you face, must be one of the first requirements of such an expertise. When it comes to the question of "who writes the role," as a profession, personnel administrators must take a more significant part in resolving the confusion over their role in organization.

9

Administrative Decision-Making

William R. Dill

Decision-making is one of the major functions that administrators (or managers or executives) perform. It is accepted by many, in fact, as *the* central activity in management and as a key subject for attention in management training.[1] The proposition seems so obvious today that we tend to forget how recent it is, and it seems so clear that we can easily overlook the different points of view that the "decision-making" label covers.

Approaches to the study of decisions

Our current responsiveness to the phrase stems from three developments since the years just prior to World War II: a major challenge to the focus and purpose of classical theories of organization and administration; extensive research on the factors which influence the way in which individuals and groups make decisions and the enthusiasm with which they accept and carry out decisions; and the application of mathematics

Reprinted with permission of author and Prentice-Hall, Inc., Englewood Cliffs, New Jersey. From William R. Dill, "Administrative Decision-Making," in Sidney Mailick and Edward H. Van Ness, eds., *Concepts and Issues in Administrative Behavior,* © 1962, pp. 29–48.

[1]See G. L. Bach, "Managerial Decision-Making as an Organizing Concept," in F. C. Pierson and others, *The Education of American Businessmen* (New York: McGraw-Hill, 1959); M. H. Jones, *Executive Decision-Making* (Homewood, Ill.: Irwin, 1957); D. W. Miller and M. K. Starr, *Executive Decisions and Operations Research* (Englewood Cliffs, N.J.: Prentice-Hall, 1960).

and statistics to the analysis and solution of military and industrial decision problems.

An important element of the challenge to traditional organization theory was the argument that decisions as much as actions should be a central unit in the analysis of organizational behavior. In his *Functions of the Executive,* Barnard was one of the first to characterize decision-making as "the essential process of organizational action" and to outline how the performance of an organization could be analyzed into an interlocking, hierarchical system of decisions.[2] The initial paragraphs of Simon's *Administrative Behavior* argue that:

> The task of "deciding" pervades the entire administrative organization quite as much as the task of "doing"—indeed, it is integrally tied up with the latter. A general theory of administration must include principles of organization that will insure correct decision-making, just as it must include principles that will insure effective action.[3]

From the arguments in these two books has come much of the impetus for making the decision process a central focus of organization theory—and of research on administrative action.

Concurrent with the work of Barnard and Simon, behavioral scientists like Lewin and Lazarsfeld were beginning to study decision processes outside the administrative setting. Lewin and his associates were particularly interested in the degree to which a group's participation, or lack of participation, in making decisions affected its willingness to accept the outcome.[4] Lazarsfeld, Katona, and others have worked to find factors which influence voting decisions and purchasing decisions by individuals and groups.[5]

---

[2]C. I. Barnard, *The Functions of the Executive* (Cambridge: Harvard, 1938), ch. xiii.

[3]H. A. Simon, *Administrative Behavior* (New York: Macmillan, 1945), p. 1.

[4]See K. Lewin, "Studies in Group Decision," in D. Cartwright and A. Zander, *Group Dynamics* (Evanston: Row, Peterson, 1953), pp. 287–301.

[5]For a summary of some of the studies, see P. F. Lazarsfeld, "Sociological Reflections on Business: Consumers and Managers," in R. A. Dahl, M. Haire, and P. F. Lazarsfeld, *Social Science Research on Business: Product and Potential* (New York: Columbia, 1959), pp. 99–155.

The work of men like Simon and Lewin comes together as psychologists and sociologists turn more and more to groups within governmental, military, and business organizations as "subjects" for their research, and as organization theorists look for data on human behavior to test their general propositions about the administrative process.[6] The objective is a comprehensive theory which will describe—and help us predict—how administrators make decisions under a variety of conditions. There is also concern, though, about finding better ways to make them; for example, some of the research on the effects of "participation" is specifically intended to suggest better ways of organizing superior-subordinate relationships in industry.[7]

The application of mathematics and statistics to decision-making has been even more normative in character. Using such new kinds of quantitative thinking as game theory, information theory, linear programming, and statistical decision theory, men found it possible to formulate rules for making decisions about inventory levels, production scheduling, quality control, long-range resource allocation, and so on.[8] Many of these rules turned out to be much better guides for reaching decisions than management had been using; and given certain clearly stated assumptions about management goals, many could be shown to be the "best possible" (or optimal) guides to decision. A new profession—operations

[6]For important views on the relations between psychology, sociology, economics, political science, and general theories of organization and administration, see Dahl, Haire, and Lazarsfeld, *op. cit.;* J. G. March and H. A. Simon (with H. Guetzkow), *Organizations* (New York: Wiley, 1959); and M. Haire (ed.), *Modern Organization Theory* (New York: Wiley, 1959).

[7]See R. Likert, *New Patterns of Management* (New York: McGraw-Hill, 1961).

[8]The list of basic references is a long one. For a detailed bibliography, see *A Comprehensive Bibliography on Operations Research* (New York: Wiley, 1958). See also I. D. J. Bross, *Design for Decision* (New York: Macmillan, 1953); R. D. Luce and H. Raiffa, *Games and Decisions* (New York: Wiley, 1957); A. Charnes and W. W. Cooper, *Management Models and Industrial Applications of Linear Programming* (New York: Wiley, 1960); C. Holt and others, *Planning, Production, Inventories, and Work Force* (Englewood Cliffs, N.J.: Prentice-Hall, 1960); M. Shubik, *Competition, Oligopoly and the Theory of Games* (New York: Wiley, 1957).

research—has grown up around the search for new ways of deriving improved decision rules for management.[9]

The work of the mathematicians and statisticians, despite its normative intent, has had considerable impact on our understanding of how administrators have been making decisions. In some cases, the optimal mathematical and statistical models give a standard against which the behavior and the performance of human decision makers can be compared.[10] More generally, though, the new quantitative tools that have become available give the descriptive scientist some powerful new ways to express his predictions and explanations of behavior.

The study of decision-making is proceeding in so many directions that we can lose sight of the basic administrative processes that Barnard and Simon were trying to describe and that so many men have been trying to improve.[11] We shall review what administrative decision-making involves and explore the variety of processes included under the label.

What decisions are

What sorts of activity are encompassed in the phrase "administrative decision-making"? At the simplest level, a decision is a choice among alternatives. We present a board of directors with studies of three possible plant sites; they decide which to buy. We make a wage offer to a group of striking employees; they vote whether to accept it or whether to continue on strike. We interview candidates for a job vacancy; a man-

[9]See Miller and Starr, *op. cit.,* for an overview of the impact of operations research on managerial decision-making.

[10]The kinds of studies which W. Edwards described in "The Theory of Decision-Making," *Psychological Bulletin* 51 (1954): 380–417, tend to use models with essentially normative origins as a tool to predict and explain human behavior in simple choice situations. (This study has been reprinted in A. H. Rubenstein and C. J. Haberstruh, (eds.), *Some Theories of Organization* (Homewood, Ill.: The Dorsey Press, 1960), pp. 385–430. Edwards has also written a sequel, "Behavioral Decision Theory," in P. R. Farnsworth and others, (eds.), *Annual Review of Psychology* 12 (Palo Alto: Annual Reviews, Inc., 1961): 473–98.

[11]For one estimate of the variety of things that have been done, see P. Wasserman and F. S. Silander, *Decision-Making: An Annotated Bibliography* (Ithaca: Cornell, 1958).

ager reviews our reports and decides which of the men—if any—is to be offered the job.

An administrative decision usually involves something more complicated than a single choice among a set of alternatives.[12] We make some of our most important "decisions," in effect, by doing nothing. Sometimes we simply do not recognize that we have alternatives from which to choose, and opportunities to act. One purpose of advertising, for example, is to make people aware of decision opportunities that they did not previously know about. Other times we may deliberately avoid making decisions because a commitment or action on our part would be to our eventual disadvantage. Unintentionally or deliberately, we ignore many of the alternatives that the world presents to us. An understanding of when "not to decide," according to Barnard, is an essential mark of the good manager.

When we do make decisions, we are often unaware that a choice or commitment has been made. As Barnard points out, "most executive decisions produce no direct evidence of themselves and ... knowledge of them can only be derived from the cumulation of indirect evidence."[13] Policy discussions at top management levels sometimes end in a vote or in an explicitly stated choice, but more often they do not. Yet from the discussion and from their prior experiences about what such discussion means, individual managers can carry away clear impressions of what "has been decided" and can work within the organization to carry the "decisions" out.

It is easy to pass from discussions to commitments because we are "programmed" to respond in certain ways to the things that we see or hear. The programs which govern our behavior are based on what we have previously experienced, but they may also be shaped in anticipation of things that we expect to experience in the future. Managers have

[12]As examples of how complicated such decisions can look, see R. M. Cyert, H. A. Simon, D. B. Trow, "Observation of a Business Decision," *Journal of Business* 29 (1956): 237–48; R. M. Cyert, W. R. Dill, J. G. March, "The Role of Expectations in Business Decision-Making," *Administrative Science Quarterly* 3 (1958): 307–40; and R. C. Snyder and G. D. Paige, "The United States' Decision to Resist Aggression in Korea; the Application of an Analytical Scheme," *Administrative Science Quarterly* 3 (1958): 341–78.

[13]Barnard, *op. cit.,* p. 193.

programs, for example, which tell them where to go to get supplementary information if an accident occurs in the plant, if a customer sends in an order for a product, or if a new law on minimum wage levels is passed. A call from Dr. Smith that one of his patients is being sent to the hospital for an emergency appendectomy is enough to set in motion a complex series of programs for decision and action within the hospital organization. His patient's chances for survival, in fact, may depend on the extent to which programs for quick and efficient action are available and on the smoothness with which they take effect.

It is surprising how highly programmed most of our behavior is. Programs generally govern the time an executive starts work in the morning; the order in which he tackles such jobs as answering correspondence; the time he allocates to different persons or tasks; the "decision" whether to read—or to ignore—certain incoming reports on company operations; and the manner in which he trains or controls his subordinates. To the extent that such programs for action are appropriate for the environment in which an organization is operating, they lend simplicity and stability to the organization's operations. To the extent that they lead managers to overlook important information or to limit the time and energy that can be devoted to important new tasks, programs for decision-making can handicap an organization's chances for survival and growth.

Administrative decisions are usually hard to interpret as a single choice among alternatives. Most such decisions really consist of a series of choices and commitments that have been made in sequence. Imagine a department head setting a price for a new product. His decision rests on how he expects customers to react and on what he expects competitors to do. But the choice he finally makes depends as well on earlier decisions about how to predict the behavior of customers and competitors, about how soon the new product must start showing a profit, and about how much can be spent to publicize and promote the new product in the marketplace.

A board of directors meeting to decide whether or not to buy a computer does not review all the relevant information before it decides. It commits the company on the basis of recommendations which others have prepared. Concealed in these recommendations are important decisions that staff subordinates or outside consultants have made about what information the board "needs" to see. What the board learns depends on who made the preliminary studies, on how much time and money was set aside to explore alternatives, and on how influential members of the organization feel about the project. The board's decision may be little more than a confirmation of choices and commitments that have already been made. The computer decision, broadly viewed, includes all the work that preceded the directors' meeting, as well as the meeting itself.

Phases of decision-making activity

Any major decision can be viewed in phases, each of which contributes toward the final commitment and its action consequences. These phases, which involve commitments and choices themselves, are concerned with

1) Agenda building: Defining goals and tasks for the organization and assigning priorities for their completion.
2) Search—looking for alternative courses of action and for information that can be used to evaluate them.
3) Commitment—testing proposed "solutions" to choose one for adoption by the organization.
4) Implementation—elaborating and clarifying decisions so that they can be put into effect; motivating members of the organization to help translate decisions into action.
5) Evaluation—testing the results of previous choices and actions to suggest new tasks for the organizational agenda or to facilitate organizational learning.

In studying managerial decisions, we find that action does not move smoothly from phase to phase in the order suggested here. A sample of the kinds of shifts that occur is given in this summary of an actual decision sequence from a small clothing manufacturer:

Agenda: President asks Sales Manager to design a program to promote the sale of a new line of men's underwear.

Search: The Sales Manager gets the Management Committee to suggest and discuss various kinds of promotional campaigns. He talks the problem over with the company salesman. He gets cost accounting data on the new product so that he can estimate how much the company can spend for the campaign.

New agenda: The Sales Manager discovers, in analyzing the cost data, that the underwear costs considerably more to produce that the price he can expect to sell it for. Questions: Are the cost estimates accurate? Can costs be reduced? Should the product be taken off the market?

Commitment: Implicitly, everyone behaves as if he would prefer to check cost data and to find ways of cutting costs or raising prices before taking the product off the market.

Search: The Office Manager and Chief Accountant undertake a check of the cost data. The Production Supervisors make new estimates of manufacturing costs, and explore ways of reducing the costs. The Sales Manager consults with the President and the salesmen about the conditions under which prices could be increased.

Commitment: The Sales Manager and Office Manager agree that the company's cost accounting procedures are badly out-of-date and that certain revisions are necessary.

Implementation: The Chief Accountant is assigned to design new cost accounting procedures for all products in the company line.

Commitment: Several actions are approved to reduce manufacturing costs for the line of underwear; the selling price is increased; and plans for special advertising and promotion (except for development of a counter-top display) are dropped.

Evaluation: The Chief Accountant is judged by the President and Sales Manager to be incapable of improving the cost records system by himself.

Implementation and new agenda: The Sales Manager is given authority to take over the revision of the cost records system. He and the President make the job a top-priority one for the organization.

Search: Production Supervisors meet with the Sales Manager and the Office Manager to analyze the existing system and to suggest needed changes.

Commitment: Ways of collecting, storing, communicating, and testing cost information are agreed upon and are approved by the President.

Implementation: Production Supervisors assign their assistants to collect up-to-date materials cost estimates for the new system. The Chief Industrial Engineer and his assistant work with the Production Supervisors to bring estimates of labor costs up to date. The Chief Accountant works with clerks in the office to put the estimates together and to add appropriate allowances for overhead, selling expenses, and profit margin. The Management Committee discusses questions of measuring or classifying special kinds of costs. The Sales Manager tries to coordinate the efforts of different groups.

New agenda: The requirements of the coming selling season and the signing of a new labor contract create pressures for early completion of the cost review. Some subordinate personnel within the organization feel threatened by the review and are reluctant to cooperate in the project.

Several things should be noted in this example. First, the problem that the organization is working on changes as new information reveals new problems to work on. In some cases, the shift is to an alternative definition of the agenda; for example, the change from the task of designing a promotional campaign to the task of improving cost accounting procedures. In other cases, the shift is to a subproblem that must be solved as part of the task of completing the original agenda; for example, the change from the task of improving cost accounting procedures to the task of getting better estimates of labor cost.

Labeling the phases depends on interpretation of the organization's agenda. The original agenda-setting phase in the example above, for instance, can be viewed as an implementation phase if the agenda is thought of as the more general goal of earning profits within the organization. The labels used in our example are only illustrative ones; other sets of labels would be possible, given a different view of the decision sequence.

It should also be clear that the course of a decision sequence within an organization is seldom clear at the outset. It develops and changes as the various phases are carried through and as different groups, with new information and new points of view, become involved in the decision process.

Patterns of participation in decision-making

Few administrative decisions are the work of a single person or group within an organization. Generally a number of people will be involved, working together or in sequence. Many variables affect the division of activities among members of an organization.

The simplest set of assumptions about how the work should be divided is in "classical" notions about the advantages of pyramidal forms of organization; . . .

The essential argument of classical theory is that as work on a decision becomes more complicated, more comprehensive in scope, and more significant to the organization, responsibility for that work should be shifted upward to higher-level personnel. A secondary argument is that disagreements between men or groups at the same organizational level should be resolved by a common superior at the next higher level. As one author puts it:

> Decisions at the various levels, however, differ as to scope and time element. At the lower levels, the area is limited and definitely delineated for questions of immediacy. Proceeding up the levels of authority, the area is less limited and may include succeeding or sequential events. Finally, at the topmost levels, decisions are very broad and, in the main, involve questions having to do with the future. . . . Lower level decisions are always subject to upper-level approval or veto, but lower-level decision-making reduces the labor of upper-level executives.

Two major types of decisions are to be found: (1) occasional, superior, or formal; (2) routine or habitual. Although both kinds are found at every level, the occasional are characteristic of the superior aspects; the routine, of the inferior.[14]

Evidence on the degree to which such procedures are followed in the day-to-day functioning of real organizations has been presented in a few studies,[15] but more research needs to be done.

Assignment of decision-making responsibility on this basis presumes several conditions not easily met in real organizations. The first of these is that roles in decision-making activity are *assigned to* individuals and groups in some uniform manner and are not simply *assumed by* them as opportunities present themselves. A second condition is that there are effective organizational means for recognizing the complexity and significance of decision problems and for routing them to the appropriate level within the organization. A third condition is that, moving up in an organization, the men are superior to men at lower levels in access to information, in analytic skills for diagnosing problems, and in competence to render decisions and get them carried out. A final condition is that the men at the top of the pyramid have time to deal with the problems that are shifted up to them.

The manager's job description tells him in general terms the limits to his authority and responsibility, but it leaves more to his imagination than the "classical" theorist likes to admit. To perform effectively, men at subordinate levels must assume roles where none have been assigned. To maintain status and to get ahead, they often feel compelled to try to expand their influence in the organization. Both improvisation and aggrandizement, for example, are shown in the behavior of the Sales Manager for the clothing manufacturer. When others in the organization could not verify the accuracy of the cost estimates on the new line of men's underwear, the Sales Manager undertook to check these himself because he needed to have a basis for planning his promotional cam-

[14]R. T. Livingston, *The Engineering of Organization and Management* (New York: McGraw-Hill, 1949), p. 97.

[15]See E. Jacques, *Measurement of Responsibility* (London: Tavistock, 1956); N. H. Martin, "Differential Decisions in the Management of an Industrial Plant," *Journal of Business* 29 (1956): 249–60; and W. R. Dill, "Environment as an Influence on Managerial Autonomy," in J. D. Thompson and others, *Comparative Studies in Administration* (Pittsburgh: University of Pittsburgh, 1959), pp. 131–61.

paign. His later activities in making the primary decisions about redesigning the cost accounting system were seen both by himself and by others in management as an effort to consolidate his position as the "number two" man in the firm. To assume the leadership role, he was taking advantage of the absence of the President for contract negotiations with the union, of the indifference of the Office Manager and the Chief Accountant to the problems that had been discovered, and of his own previous experience with the design of accounting systems in another firm.

The man or the group who recognizes that a problem exists for an organization has an important voice in the way in which the problem is formulated and in the extent to which it is communicated to others in the organization. The outside environment provides information from which an organization can construct an agenda, but it rarely presents an organization with a clearly defined set of "decisions to be made." Even in small organizations, information enters through a variety of channels; and to understand how decision-making activities are divided—or should be divided—among an organization's members, it is necessary to understand the routes by which various kinds of information come to their attention.

Consider the decisions an organization must make about the steps that are taken to insure acceptable levels of product quality in the manufacturing process. According to the classical model, these decisions are the responsibility of the production executives, who work within the general quality control objectives defined by top management. Much of the information that the production men need to define their quality problems comes from their own inspection and control personnel who are stationed along the production line. Other very important information, though, comes from customers who use the product. This information is not available directly to the production executives in many instances, but must be relayed to them by company salesmen. If the salesmen transmit relevant data about customers' experiences to the production executives, the production executives assume the job of deciding how to do a better job of satisfying customers. If, however, the salesmen interpret the information in other ways, it may be handed to the marketing executives as a problem in devising an advertising campaign to overcome customers' resistance to the product.

Even in cases where inputs from the environment define the organization's task clearly, the scope and significance of the task is often still obscure. Research indicates that administrators have difficulty estimating the significance of many of the problems they work on.[16] Under conditions where the dimensions of a problem's potential impact on the organization are not clear, or are estimated inaccurately, the pattern of participation in dealing with the problem will differ from the pattern predicted by classical theory. The pattern may rest on estimates of the problem's scope and significance, but the estimates will be erroneous. Or in the absence of any estimates, the pattern will depend on who formulates the task, who has time to work on it, and who feels interested or obligated enough to make the necessary decisions.

For different kinds of decisions, different amounts of time and different sorts of skills are required of the organization. The importance of a decision and the kinds of strategies that will lead to the selection of a good alternative often pull in different directions, as far as the assignment of responsibility for the decision within the organization is concerned. Decisions about the allocation of capital to various projects, for example, can be improved by the use of sophisticated mathematical and statistical techniques which most senior executives know little or nothing about. If the techniques are to be applied, they frequently have to be applied by young men, fresh from college courses in applied mathematics and advanced financial analysis, to whom the company would not ordinarily entrust investment decisions. Yet in a real sense, by their knowledge of the new methods by which decisions can be made, these younger men can gain a substantial influence on the outcomes which will later govern company operations.

In addition, because of the scarcity of certain skills (knowledge of engineering or economic techniques, for instance) or equipment (such as computers) that are demanded for making many kinds of decisions, tradi-

---

[16]Dill, *op. cit.,* p. 154. See also papers by R. M. Cyert and J. G. March in which they set forth the concept of "organizational slack"—in essence, the notion that the attention of organizations tends to focus on tasks identified as "critical" by the environment, rather than on tasks of equal but less obvious significance. (See "Organizational Factors in the Theory of Oligopoly," *Quarterly Journal of Economics* 70 [1956]: 44–64.)

tional departmental boundaries break down. A company which has a group using statistical methods within the production department to make inventory control decisions will often not be in a position to set up a duplicate group (with duplicate computer equipment) for the sales department to make market forecasts or for the personnel department to set up a wage and salary evaluation system. In many orgnizations, the statistically-oriented group, originally associated with production, will begin to perform similar services for the other departments. We begin, then, to get groups in the organization identified by the kinds of analysis they do rather than by the level of importance or the functional characteristics of the decisions they are working on.

Finally, within most organizations there are informal patterns of influence and authority which often do not square with the pyramidal organization chart. When management anticipates difficulties in getting a decision accepted, considerations of how "important" the decision is or of who is "best able" to develop a satisfactory solution may be overruled by questions of who needs to be involved in the decision in order to facilitate its implementation. Depending on the decision which is to be made, on the situation of the company at the time of the decision, and on the governing philosophy of management about employee participation in decision-making, one of two shifts from the classical model may occur. In some instances, to give added authority and force to a decision that would normally be left to a lower level in the organization, top management may make the choice. This enhances the legitimacy and the urgency of the decision for the people who will have to carry it out. In other cases, people from subordinate levels in the organization participate in decisions which top management would ordinarily make alone. A great deal of research with laboratory groups and real organizations indicates that this step makes the subordinates feel more closely identified with management and with the course of action that is finally chosen, and thus, more willing to carry it out.

The characteristics of decision problems that determine who works on them, then, include more than dimensions of importance, comprehensiveness, and complexity. We have highlighted four others: (1) the initiative of subordinate groups in planning their own job activities; (2) the information from which problems are formulated and the routes by which this information enters the organization; (3) the specialized training, experience, or equipment used to obtain improved decisions and the ways in which such resources are distributed in the organization; and (4) the kinds of people who will be called on to implement decisions once they are made and their expectations regarding participation in making decisions.

The role of computers in decision-making

The question of who makes decisions becomes more complicated as electronic data-processing units begin to make choices for organizations as well to perform calculations for them. There is no longer any doubt that computers will be able to assume many of the decision-making functions that administrators now perform. The discussion now centers around how soon this will happen and where computers will have the strongest initial impact.[17]

As electronic data-processing systems multiply in number and influence, our theories of administrative decision-making will have to be modified to consider the following developments:

1. An increase in the influence of men who know how to use the new equipment and to fit it into company operations. At least temporarily, pending further development of both managers and computers, an organization must have men who can translate managers' instructions into a language the computer understands and who can define for management the limits to what the computer will do.

2. The already well-developed applications of computers to aid human decision-makers, particularly in recording, storing, finding,

[17]For a summary of what has been accomplished in the few years that organizations have had access to large-scale computers, and for some predictions of what lies ahead, see H. A. Simon, *The New Science of Management Decision* (New York: Harper & Bros., 1960); G. P. Schultz and T. Whisler (eds.), *Management, Organization and the Computer* (Glencoe, Illinois: Free Press, 1960); and H. A. Simon, "The Corporation: Will It Be Managed by Men or Machines," in M. Anshen and G. L. Bach (eds.), *Management and Corporation: 1985* (New York: McGraw-Hill, 1960).

and interpreting information, and in preparing analyses for use in reaching decisions.

3. The use of computers to replace human decision-makers, at levels ranging from routine production scheduling or inventory management to such complex decisions as the scheduling of nonrepetitive operations, the long-range allocation of capital funds, or the planning of sales campaigns for new products.

4. The ability of computers to learn from the outcomes of their decisions and to improve the programs which govern their operations without intervention by human operators. A theory of decision-making will have to cover not only the programs initially given to computers, but the rules by which programs modify and improve themselves.

Some issues in the analysis of administrative decisions

What are the important varieties of administrative decision? The answer to this question depends on our purpose in asking it, for there are as many ways of categorizing and labeling decisions as there are reasons for doing so. In this final section, we shall summarize a few of the many dimensions of administrative decision-making and discuss our reasons for interest in them.

One set of dimensions describes the place of a decision or of a decision-sequence in the life history of an organization. Relative to an organization's chances for survival and growth or for attaining more specific objectives, some decisions are clearly more important than others. A major point of many discussions of decision-making, especially in public administration, is that administrators must know what decisions to make as well as how to make them well.[18] The distinction lies, in Selznick's terms, between "routine" decisions, which can be made without changing the character of the organization, and "critical" decisions,

---

[18]H. A. Kissinger, "The Policymaker and the Intellectual," *The Reporter* 20 (March 5, 1959): 30–35; P. Selznick, *Leadership in Administration* (Evanston: Row, Peterson, 1957), chapter 2.

which raise questions about the basic values to which the organization subscribes.

There is no evidence that, other things being equal, "critical" decisions require different patterns of organization or different modes of analysis and choice from "routine" decisions. Often the two kinds of decisions cannot be told apart before their outcomes are known. The difference between what is routine and what is critical, in fact, may rest in the circumstances of the organization vis-a-vis its environment at a particular point in time rather than on the intrinsic characteristics of the decision problem. The importance of the distinction lies in its use by real organizations and in the effects of this use on the order in which they approach different tasks.

Roughly speaking, what Selznick identifies as critical decisions March and Simon identify as planning decisions. As March and Simon point out, there seems to exist a "Gresham's Law" of decision-making; that is, routine activity drives out innovative, planning activity.[19] In their eyes, this results from the tendency for routine decision-making activities to carry more immediate and more explicit time deadlines and for them to be associated with more clearly defined goals and more explicit rewards and penalties. Selznick and Kissinger would add another explanation: the tendency for administrators in our culture to avoid any decisions which threaten to disrupt the customary workings of the organization.

The placement of decisions in the history of an organization also requires some labels for linking decisions with one another. Several dimensions become relevant here. One we have already discussed—the separation of agenda-building, search, commitment, implementation, and evaluation phases in a decision sequence. This corresponds closely to the four-fold breakdown of decision theory which Cyert and March set forth. They name

> . . . four basic subtheories required for a behavioral theory of organizational decision-making: first, the theory of organizational objectives; second, the theory of organizational expectations; third, the theory of organizational choice; fourth, the theory of organizational implementation.[20]

[19]March and Simon, *op. cit.,* p. 185; J. G. March, "Business Decision Making," *Industrial Research* 1 (Spring 1959).

[20]From "Introduction to a Behavioral Theory of Organizational Decision-Making: Organizational Objectives," in Haire, *op. cit.,* p. 78.

A second link between decisions is hierarchical in nature. An administrator decides to put greater emphasis on reducing accidents within his organization. He diverts resources from other kinds of programs, such as those for methods improvement or cost reduction, to the safety campaign. This choice, and the organization's response to it, sets up a series of additional decision problems; decisions on these generate still more problems; and so on. All the problems can be traced back to the original choice which the administrator made.

A particular decision problem in such a hierarchy is located by identifying the prior decisions that give rise to it and by tracing out the subsequent problems that it, in turn, raises.

A third type of sequential link is the one which Thompson and Tuden suggest.[21] They define three essential kinds of issues which can confront decision-makers and which, taken together, make up a total decision problem: issues of choice among alternative courses of action, issues of choice among possible consequences of the different alternatives (in their terms, the question of *causation*), and issues of choice about the desirability of different possible outcomes (the question of *preferences*).

All of these classifications are similar in their emphasis. They assume initial questions of goals, agenda, or preferences in the organization; a move from these considerations toward the discovery of alternatives and the estimation of what will happen if various alternatives are chosen; the choice of a course of action, including in many instances a review of the basis on which the choice was originally supposed to be made; and subsequent steps throughout the organization to realize the administrative commitment.

A weakness of all these schemes is that, although they describe the phases of a closely integrated decision sequence (such as the decisions involved in a computer feasibility study), they do not describe the relations between sequences (e.g., the interaction within a firm between action to find a site for a new plant and action to reorganize the headquarters staff functions).

Describing these relationships may mean considering the contribution of both decision sequences to a more general goal (in the example

---

[21]J. D. Thompson and A. Tuden, "Strategies, Structures, and Processes of Organizational Decision," in Thompson and others, *op. cit.,* pp. 195–216.

of the last paragraph, the contribution, say, to a decision to double the size of the firm's operations within five years). More often, though, the overriding relation between such decision sequences lies in their competition for the time and attention of groups within the organization. Choosing the new plant site may take precedence over reorganizing staff functions, not for logical or strategic reasons, but because it is being pushed by the president, because it can be carried through without hiring an outside consultant, because a group of subordinate executives have decided it is a more interesting project to work on, or because the men who must supply the basic data for the staff reorganization are already overcommitted to other projects.

The fate of a decision sequence depends, then, on the support and interest that the problems it poses generate within the organization; on the degree to which it runs afoul of organizational "bottlenecks" where men, equipment, or monetary resources are tied down to other assignments; and on the programs which exist in the organization for making procedural transfer of activity on the decision sequence from one part of the organization to another.

Closely related to the placement of decisions in the over-all history of the organization are questions about the origins of decision problems. In analyzing and categorizing administrative decisions it is useful to know the route by which information relating to a decision problem enters the organization. As we have already seen, this has an impact both on the way in which the problem is formulated and on the manner in which it is handled by the organization. It is also useful to distinguish those problems which come to the administrative decision-makers pre-formulated, as clearly defined tasks, from those which come as a series of informational inputs, from which the decision-makers must formulate tasks for themselves. In the case of the former, there is less danger that the decision-makers will overlook the problem or will misstate it. There is probably a greater danger, though, that they will react against it, trying either to redefine it or to curtail action on it.

Other ways of classifying administrative decisions relate to the processes used in making the decisions. There are many process categories —from those relating to the cognitive aspects of decision-making to those relating to the interpersonal organizational aspects.

Statistical decision theory, for example, classifies decisions according to the amount of knowledge available about the alternatives, about the consequences that can follow a particular choice, and about the probabilities of given consequences. Most administrative decisions, however, have to be made on the basis of less knowledge than the statistical decision theorists require to apply their decision models.

Simon has drawn a meaningful distinction, between programmed and unprogrammed decisions; that is, between decisions which can be made according to rules, strategies, precedents, or instructions that members of the organization know and can follow, and decisions for which appropriate rules and precedents do not exist. Distinctions are also possible between "well-structured" decisions (for which a rule of choice guaranteeing an optimal solution can be found) and "ill-structured" decisions (for which the best we can do is to look for a satisfactory solution).

In addition to the kinds of analysis that they require, various administrative decisions seem to generate different patterns of organizational action. Thompson and Tuden, for example, define four sorts of decision situations, according to whether there is agreement or disagreement among the prospective decision-makers on their beliefs about causation in the environment or on their preferences about possible outcomes:

		Preferences about possible outcomes	
		Agreement	Disagreement
Beliefs about	Agreement	COMPUTATION	COMPROMISE
causation			
	Disagreement	JUDGMENT	INSPIRATION

Agreement on both causation and preferences makes it possible to reach a decision by straightforward analysis or common sense. Agreement on preferences, but disagreement on causation, leads to judgments by majority rule, often through some sort of voting procedure. Agreement on causation, but disagreement on preferences, requires compromise among the preferences which have been expressed. Disagreement about both causation and preferences, if it does not produce disintegration of the decision-making group or withdrawal from the problem, may result in recourse to "Divine Guidance" or to a charismatic leader (Thompson and Tuden use the example of de Gaulle's 1958 election in France.)[22]

[22]Thompson and Tuden, *op. cit.*, especially pp. 198–204.

Another set of constraints which decision problems impose on organizations applies to the flow of information through the organization before a solution can be reached. Many experiments have explored how organizations with restricted communications among their members manage to handle different kinds of decision problems.[23] If the information relevant to a decision is not easily coded, if it must be relayed to be used, if it must be rewritten or restated as it is relayed, or if a great deal of information has to be processed in a short period of time, the facilities within the organization for transmitting information from one person or group to another become critical factors in organizational performance.

A final set of dimensions pertinent to the analysis of administrative decisions looks ahead to the problems an organization faces in implementing its choices. Two aspects are particularly important here: the degree to which the decision can be stated in operational terms, so that it can be understood and elaborated effectively within the organization; and the degree to which the decision implies disturbance of existing organizational patterns.

Operational, or clearly defined, formulations of a decision are useful when the objective is to obtain specific responses from the organization. A clear formulation tells the implementers what to do; and it reduces any friction that might be caused by a vague, uncertain decision statement. On the other hand, nonoperational statements of decisions are often useful, too. In a situation where the consequences of a decision can be serious, but the possibilities of changing it easily or of reversing it are small, the first response to uncertainty is to delay making a decision. The second, when a commitment becomes necessary, is often to frame the decision in such terms that it can be interpreted by the organization differently at different times. Political party platforms are sometimes regarded as the example, *par excellence,* of nonoperational decisions.

[23]See H. J. Leavitt, "Effects of Certain Communication Patterns on Group Performance," *Journal of Abnormal and Social Psychology* 46 (1951): 38–50; L. S. Christie, "Organization and Information Handling in Task Groups," *Operations Research* 2 (1954): 186–96; H. Guetzkow and W. R. Dill, "Factors in the Organizational Development of Task-Oriented Groups," *Sociometry* 20 (1957): 175–204; M. Glanzer and R. Glaser, "Techniques for the Study of Group Structure and Behavior: II, Empirical Studies of the Effects of Structure in Small Groups," *Psychological Bulletin* 58 (1961): 1–27.

Decisions that imply disturbance of existing patterns of behavior in the organization are important to identify because they are the ones that require most careful planning of the procedures by which a choice is made and carried out. It may be strategic, for example, to conceal much of the preliminary search effort and discussion of alternatives from some members of the organization so that they do not become upset about steps not likely to be carried through. It may be important to give some of those who will have to live with the decision's outcomes a voice in exploring the problem and making the choice. It may be important to compare and evaluate alternatives more carefully and thoroughly so that the choice can be explained and defended for those whom it affects.

Much ambiguity remains in our conception of what an administrative decision is and of how it can be described. Further work is needed to enable us to characterize the dimensions of decision problems, the circumstances that we recognize as choice or commitment, and the relationships that link decisions together in the life history of an organization. It would be premature at this point to try to specify a rigid typology of administrative decisions. Most useful in the short-run, while we proliferate hypotheses about organizational behavior and models for making decisions, will be studies (like those of Snyder and Paige, Thompson and Tuden, and Cyert and March) which begin from an empirical base to spell out theories that apply to particular classes of decisions and inquiries (like those of Simon and his colleagues) into basic aspects of human problem-solving and decision-making behavior.

10

Down the Bureaucracy!

Matthew Dumont

There has been a certain tension among the people of our federal city lately. I am not talking about the black population of the district, which becomes visible to the rest of the world only when its rage boils over. I am referring to the public servants who ooze across the Maryland and Virginia lines each day to manipulate the machinery of government.

It has never been a particularly gleeful population, but in the last year or so it has developed a kind of mass involutional melancholia, a peculiar mixture of depression, anxiety and senescence.

As in similarly depressed communities, the young, the healthy and those with good job prospects have tended to migrate. Among those who have departed are a large proportion of that scarce supply of idealistic and pragmatic people who try to work for social change "within the system." They are leaving because they feel unwanted and ineffectual. Let me describe what they are turning their backs on.

Washington is a malaria swamp covered over with buildings of neofascist design and ringed with military bases.

Do you remember Rastignac shaking his fist at Paris from Goriot's grave site? Washington is a city made for fists to be shaken at. Shaken at, not bloodied on. Federal buildings are especially constructed to be impervious to blood. You can rush headlong into a marble balustrade smearing brains and blood and bile three yards wide. But as the lady does on television, with a smile and a few whisks of a damp cloth, the wonderful material will come up as clean and white and sparkling as before.

Reprinted with permission of author and publisher. From Matthew Dumont, "Down the Bureaucracy," *Trans-action* 12 (October 1970): 10–12, 14. Copyright © October 1970 by TRANS-action, Inc., New Brunswick, New Jersey.

Some people have tried burning themselves into the concrete. That doesn't work either.

And, as you might have guessed, all that urine on the Pentagon was gone within minutes after the armies of the night retreated.

No, you may, individually or en masse, descend upon the Federal Triangle. You may try to impale and exsanguinate yourselves, flay, crucify and castrate yourselves. You may scream shrill cries or sing "Alice's Restaurant" or chant "Om," but it won't help. The buildings were made to last forever and to forever remain shining and white, the summer sun glaring off their walls, stunning the passersby.

Inside, one might spend eternity hearing the sounds of his own footsteps in the corridors of these buildings and never see his sun-cast shadow. If you took all the corridors in all of the federal buildings in Washington and laid them end to end, and inclined one end slightly and started a billiard ball rolling down, by the time it reached the lower end, the ball would have attained such a velocity that it would hurtle on through space while approaching an infinite mass and thereby destroy the universe. This is not likely to happen because such coordination is unheard of among federal agencies. But we will get to that later.

Off the corridors are offices and conference rooms. (There is also a core of mail chutes, telephone lines, elevator shafts, sewer pipes, trash cans and black people, but these are all invisible.) The offices have desks —wooden ones for important people and steel ones for unimportant people. (Otherwise, the distinction is impossible to make unless you could monitor their telephone calls to each other and determine the relative hierarchy depending on whose secretary manages to keep the other party waiting before putting her boss on.)

The offices also contain file cabinets that are filled with paper. The paper is mainly memos—the way people in the federal government communicate to one another. When communication is not necessary, memos "for the record" are written and filed. It has been estimated that the approximate cost in labor and supplies for the typing of a memo is 36¢. The cost in professional time for its preparation is incalculable.

The conference rooms are for conferences. A conference is for the purpose of sharing information among a group of federal officials who have already been apprised of the information to be shared, individually, by memo. Coffee and cigarettes are consumed. By prior arrangement, each participant is, in turn, interrupted by his secretary for an urgent phone call. After the conference additional memos are exchanged.

But let me describe the people who work in the federal government because some mythology must be laid to rest.

They are good people, which is to say that they are no less good than anyone else, which is to say that we are all pretty much cut from the same material and most of it is pretty rotten. I do not wish to be cavalier about the problem of evil, but I will ask you to accept as a premise for this thesis that the differences between the "best of us" and the "worst of us" are no greater than the differences *within* each of us at varying times.

I have been and will be more sober and precise about this issue in other writings, but what I am attempting to convey is a conviction that the great evils of mankind, the genocides and holy wars, the monstrous exploitations and negligences and injustices of societies have less to do with the malice of individuals than with unexamined and unquestioned institutional practices.

I am talking about the Eichmannism—a syndrome wherein individual motives, consciences or goals become irrelevant in the context of organizational behaviors. This can be seen in pure culture in the federal government. There are a host of written rules for behavior for the federal civil servants, but these are rarely salient. It is the unwritten rules, tacit but ever present, subtle but overwhelming, unarticulated but commanding, that determine the behavior of the men and women who buzz out their lives in the spaces defined by the United States government.

These rules are few in number. Rule number one is to *maintain your tenure*. This is at the same time the most significant and the easiest rule to abide by. If you desire to keep a job for several decades and retire from it with an adequate pension, and if you have the capacity to appear at once occupied and inconspicuous, then you can be satisfied as a "fed."

Appearing occupied means walking briskly at all times. It means looking down at your desk rather than up into the distance when thinking. It means always having papers in your hands. Above all, it means, when asked how things are, responding "very hectic" rather than "terrific" or "lousy."

Being inconspicuous means that your competence in appearing occupied should be expressed quietly and without affect. The most intolerable behavior in a civil servant is psychotic behavior. Being psychotic in the federal government is looking people directly in the eye for a moment too long. It is walking around on a weekday without a tie. It is kissing a girl in an elevator. (It doesn't matter whether she is a wife, mistress, secretary or daughter.) It is writing a memo that is excessively detailed, or refusing to write memos. It is laughing too loud or too long at a conference. It is taking a clandestine gulp of wine in a locker room rather than ordering two martinis over lunch. (This explains why there are more suspensions for alcoholism among lower level workers than higher level ones.)

In short, there is no more sensitive indicator of deviant behavior than personnel records of the federal government.

This does not mean that federal officials never vary their behavior. Currently, for example, it is modish to sport sideburns and a moustache. The specter of thousands of civil servants looking like Che Guevara may seem exciting, but it has no more significance than cuffless trousers.

You may or may not wish to follow the fashions, but do not initiate them. In general, follow a golden mean of behavior, that is, do what most people seem to be doing. Do it quietly. And if you are not sure how to behave, take annual leave.

The second rule of behavior in the government, and clearly related to the sustenance of your own tenure, is to *keep the boss from getting embarrassed.* That is the single, most important standard of competence for a federal official. The man who runs interference effectively, who can anticipate and obviate impertinent, urgent or obvious demands from the boss's boss, or from the press, or from the public, or from Congress, will be treasured and rewarded. This is so pervasive a desideratum in a civil servant that the distinction between line and staff activities becomes thin and artificial in the face of it. Your primary function in the hierarchy (after the protection of your own tenure) is the protection of your superior's tenure rather than the fulfillment of assigned responsibilities. (Obvious exceptions to this rule are J. Edgar Hoover and certain elements in the Department of Defense, who, like physicians and priests, respond to a higher authority.)

The third unwritten rule of federal behavior is to *make sure that all appropriated funds are spent by the end of the fiscal year.* Much of the paper that stuffs the orifices of executive desks has to do with justifications for requests for more money. For money to be returned after such justifications are approved is to imply that the requester, his supervisor and Congress itself were improvident in their demands on the taxpayer's money. It would be like a bum asking for a handout for a cup of coffee. A passerby offers a quarter and the bum returns 15¢ saying, "Coffee is only a dime, schmuck."

Contract hustlers, who abound in Washington, know that their halcyon days are in late spring when agencies are frequently panicked at the realization that they have not exhausted their operating funds and may be in the black by the fiscal year's end. Agencies that administer grant-in-aid programs celebrate end-of-fiscal-year parties with Dionysian abandon when instead of having a surplus of funds they cannot pay all of their obligations.

The only effective way to evaluate a federal program is the rapidity with which money is spent. Federal agencies, no less than purveyors of situation comedies, cigarettes and medical care, are dominated by a marketplace mentality which assumes that you have a good product if the demand exceeds the supply.

The fourth unwritten rule of behavior in government is to *keep the program alive.* It is not appropriate to question the original purposes of the program. Nor is it appropriate to ask if the program has any consonance with its original purposes. It is certainly not appropriate to assume that its purposes have been served. It is only appropriate to assume that once a program has been legislated, funded and staffed it must endure. An unstated and probably unconscious blessing of immortality is bestowed upon the titles that clutter organizational charts in federal agencies.

Congress, with its control of funds, is perceived as a nurturant breast with a supply of vital fluids that may at any time run dry and thus starve the program to death. Such a matter must be looked upon with intense ambivalence, a state of mind associated with schizophrenia in the hostile-dependent offspring. And, indeed, Congress is perceived by federal executives with a mixture of adulation and rage, and, indeed, federal programming is schizophrenic. Like the schizophrenic, federal programs have the capacity to assume pseudomorphic identities, having the outline and form of order and direction and vitality but actually being flat, autistic and encrusted with inorganic matter. Like the schizophrenic, federal programs develop a primitive narcissism that is independent of feedback from the environment other than the provision of life-sustaining funds.

Even programs that are conceived with some imagination as relatively bold and aggressive attempts to institutionalize change, such as Model Cities or Comprehensive Community Mental Health Centers or Community Action Programs, become so preoccupied with survival that compromises in the face of real or imagined criticism from Congress very quickly blunt whatever cutting edges the program may have had.

The fifth and final unwritten rule of federal behavior is to *maintain a stable and well-circumscribed constituency.* With so great a concern for survival in the government, it is necessary to have friends outside of it. One's equity within an agency and a program's equity in Congress are a function of equity with vested interests outside. The most visible and articulate vestedness is best to cultivate. Every agency and every department knows this, as does every successful executive. The constituency not only represents survival credits but has the quality of a significant reference group. The values, purposes and rewards of the federal agent must mesh with those of his program's constituents.

It is easy to see how this works between the Defense Department and the military-industrial complex; between Agriculture and the large, industrialized farming interests; between Labor and the unions; between Commerce and big business. It is obvious that the regulatory commissions of government have a friendly, symbiotic relationship with the organizations they were meant to monitor. It is less clear, however, that the good guys in government, the liberals who run the "social programs," have their exclusive constituents as well. The constituents of welfare programs are not welfare recipients, but social workers. The constituents of educational programs are not students, but educators. The constituents of health programs are the providers of health care, not their consumers. The mental health programs of the government are sensitive to the perturbations of mental health professionals and social scientists, not so much to the walking wounded.

In the latter case, for example, to suggest that nonprofessionals should have something to say about the expenditure of millions of research, training and service dollars is to threaten a constituency. And a threatened one is an unfriendly one, which is not good for the program in Congress or for the job possibilities of the executive in the marketplace. As long as the constituency is stable and circumscribed, credits can be counted.

These, then, are the rules of behavior for functionaries in the federal bureaucracy. If they sound familiar, they should. They are not by any means unique to this system. With minor alterations, they serve as the uncodified code of conduct in any organization. They are what sustained every archbureaucrat from Pilate to Eichmann. They explain in large part why the United States government is such a swollen beast, incapable of responding to the unmet needs of so many people.

But only in part. One other feature of the Washington scene must be described before we can say we know enough of it to elaborate a strategy of assault. This has to do with power.

There is a lot of nonsense about power in the government. One sees a black Chrysler with a vinyl top speeding by. A liveried chauffeur, determined and grim, operates the vehicle. In the rear, a gooseneck, high-intensity lamp arched over his shoulder, sits a man studying the *Washington Post.* One is tempted to say, "There goes a man of power."

It is a vain temptation. Power in the government does not reside within gray eminences in black Chryslers. It is a soft, pluralistic business shared by a large number of middle managers. Organizational charts in federal agencies read as if there is a rigid line of authority and control from the top down. It would appear that the secretary of each department with his designated assistants and deputies would control the behavior of the entire establishment. In fact, there is a huge permanent government that watches with covert bemusement as the political appointees at the top come and go, attempting in their turn to control the behavior of the agencies "responsible to them."

This does not mean that there is not a good deal of respect and deference paid by middle managers to their superiors. But, as in many organizations, this deference can have an empty and superficial quality to it that amounts to mockery. In most hospitals, for example, it is not the doctors who determine what happens to patients, but nurses. Nurses may appear as subordinate to physicians as slaves to their masters, but as soon as the doctor has left the ward the nurse does what she wants to do anyway.

Similarly, in federal agencies, it is the great army of middle managers that controls the show. There is not even the built-in accountability of a dead patient for the boss to see.

Power in the government resides less in position and funds than it does in information, which is the medium of exchange. The flow of information is controlled not at the top, but at the middle. There is very little horizontal flow between agencies because of the constant competition for funds, and all vertical flow must be mediated by the GS 14 to GS 17 bureaucrats who make up the permanent government.

This concentration of power in the middle, controlled by masses of managers who subscribe to the unwritten code of behavior described above, is the reason why the national government is essentially unresponsive. It does not respond to the top or the bottom; it does not respond to ideology. It is a great, indestructible mollusk that absorbs kicks and taunts and seductions and does nothing but grow.

But it's worse than that. The government is righteous. The people who man the bastions of the executive branch (like the rest of us) have the capacity to invest their jobs with their personal identities. Because it is theirs, their function must be defended. Their roles become, in the language of psychiatry, ego-syntonic. Their sense of personal integrity, their consciences, their self-esteem begin to grow into the positions they hold. It is as if their very identities partake of the same definition as their organizationally defined function.

Can you imagine trying to fight a revolution against a huge, righteous marshmallow? Even if you had enough troops not to be suffocated by it, the best you can hope for is to eat it. And, as you all know, you become what you eat. And that is the point. For a revolution to be meaningful it must take into account the nature of organizational life. It must assume that the ideologically pure and the ideologically impure are subject to the same Eichmannesque forces. If a revolution harbors the illusion that a region of terror will purify a bureaucracy of scoundrels and exploiters, it will fail. It matters little whether bureaucrats are Royalist or Republican, Czarist or Bolshevik, Conservative or Liberal, or what have you. It is the built-in forces of life in a bureaucracy that result in the bureaucracy being so indifferent to suffering and aspiration.

Does this mean that radical change is not possible? No. It means that intelligence and planning must be used, as well as rhetoric, songs, threats, uniforms and all the other trappings of a "movement." The intelligence and planning might orient themselves around a concept of nonalienated revolution that relies on a strategy of guerrilla administration.

This is not meant to be an exclusive strategy. Social change, radical and otherwise, has to be a pluralistic phenomenon. It needs to allow for foxes as well as hedgehogs. This represents one attempt, then, to approach the Great White Marshmallow in such a way that victories are neither impossible nor terrible.

Assuming that power in the federal government is controlled by a vast cadre of middle managers who are essentially homeostatic, and assuming the softness and purposelessness of the system in which they operate, it is conceivable that a critical mass of change agents working within that system may be effective in achieving increasingly significant ad hoc successes.

This requires a group of people who are prepared to work as civil servants but who have little or no concern with the five unwritten rules of behavior of such service. Specifically, their investment in their own jobs carries a very limited liability. The ultimate sanction, being fired, is no sanction at all. Either because they command credentials which will afford them the security they need wherever they work or because they emerge from a generation that has not been tainted by the depression and so have fewer security needs, they are not afraid of being fired.

While they may like the boss, and one may hope they do, they do not see themselves as primarily concerned with saving him from embarrassment.

Spending the program money by the end of the fiscal year and the related rule—keeping the program alive—are significant to them only insofar as the program's purposes mesh with their social consciences, and then only insofar as the program is demonstrating some fealty to those purposes.

Most important, however, is that this critical mass of change agents *not* abide by the rule of maintaining a stable and circumscribed constituency. This is at the same time a liberating principle of behavior and a major strategy of change. It is precisely by broadening the base of the constituencies of federal programs that they will become more responsible to the needs of more people.

This network of communication and collaboration shares as its purpose the frustration of the bureaucracy. But it is the homeostatic, self-serving and elitist aspects of bureaucratic life that are to be frustrated. And this can only be accomplished through the creative tension that emerges from a constant appreciation of unmet needs.

The network of change agents represents a built-in amplifier of those needs either because the agents are, themselves, among the poor, the colored and the young or because they are advocates of them.

It is not critical that the guerrilla administrators who compromise this network be in a position to command funds or program directions. They must simply have access to information, which, you recall, is the medium of exchange in government.

This network, in order to avoid the same traps as the bureaucracy it is meant to frustrate, should never become solidified or rigidified in structure and function. It may have the form of a floating crap game whose location and participation are fluid and changing, but whose purposes and activities are constant. The contacts should remain informal, non-hierarchical and task-oriented. The tasks chosen should be finite, specific, salient and feasible. The makeup of each task force is an ad hoc, self-selected clustering of individuals whose skills or location or access to information suggests their roles. This network of change agents becomes a reference group, but not a brotherhood. There need not be a preoccupation with loyalty, cordiality or steadfastness. They do not even have to be friendly.

This is a rather dry and unromantic strategy of social change. It does not stir one's heart or glands. Where is the image of Parnell pulling his cap low on his forehead as he points his gallant band to the General Post Office? Or Lenin approaching the borders of a trembling Russia in a sealed train? Or Fidel or Che? Or Spartacus, or Mao? Where are the clasped hands and the eyes squinting into a distant line of troops? Where are the songs, the flags, the legends? Where is the courage? Where is the glory?

Such a revolutionary force has nothing of the triumphal arch in it. Nor has it anything of the gallows. It lives without the hope of victory or the fear of defeat. It will yearn for saints and despair of scoundrels, but it will see as its eternal mission the subversion of those systems that force both saints and scoundrels into a common, faceless repression of the human spirit.

11

Selecting Field Service Areas

James W. Fesler

The basic distribution of administrative authority within each of our governments is functional. In the federal government only the Department of State, the Tennessee Valley Authority, and, to a lesser degree, the Department of the Interior have unique areal responsibilities. In the typical state government there are no major departments concerned with particular sections of the state, nor is there even a department of local government relations. We are so accustomed to this feature of government that it is seldom remarked. Yet area is the very foundation of legislative representation, and outweighs functional specialization in the judicial system. Only in the executive branch is the distribution of authority by function given such preeminence.[1]

Functional specialization underlies not only the primary distribution of authority among administrative departments. It also accounts for the elaborate hierarchy of bureaus, divisions, sections, and units specializing in particular activities. Almost every operating agency, however, recognizes that its job cannot wholly be performed at the capital city. An agricultural program cannot be administered without contact with farmers on their farms. Reclamation and power projects cannot be built and operated without officials at the sites. Compliance with tax laws, price controls, and labor standards cannot be checked by polite correspon-

Reprinted with permission of author and publisher from *Area and Administration* (University, Ala.: University of Alabama Press, 1964), pp. 49–70.

[1]In each of the other branches the claims of functional specialization are recognized, of course, but they are subsidiary to the main emphasis on area. Legislative bodies have functionally specialized committees. Local courts are sometimes specialized, and on collegiate courts there often develops functional specialization in the assignment of the writing of opinions.

dence between the capital and the citizen. A field service that will span the distance from the agency headquarters to the outer bounds of the total governmental area is therefore necessary.

Once the necessity of a field service is recognized, a Pandora's box of troubles is opened. There is the problem of demarcation of field service areas and location of area headquarters. There is the problem of whether and how the field service is to be used to centralize or decentralize authority. Still more complex is the fusing of the areal organization in the field with the functional organization at the capital. All these are being wrestled with constantly by individual agencies intent primarily on effective discharge of their specialized responsibilities. Beyond such intra-agency difficulties lies the challenge to coordinate the activities of all functional agencies as they bear on each section of the country.

Guides to the demarcation of an agency's major field service areas and to its selection of headquarters cities for administration of particular functions or clusters of functions can be formulated in the light of federal agencies' experience.[2] While I shall confine attention to the federal problem, which is the most complex, the guides may be suggestive as well for state and even local governments. A first consideration is the span of control—the limitation on the number of immediate subordinates a superior official can supervise effectively. This limitation cannot be expressed as a universally valid mathematical figure. The limitation will vary with the age of the agency, the clarity of policy, the type of function, the competence of the superior, the adequacy of staff assistance for the superior, the competence of the subordinates, the objectives of the supervision, and other factors. Most federal agencies, mindful of the span of control, have kept their principal subnational areas to less than 20. Should other considerations dictate a larger number of field service areas, these numerous, small areas must generally be placed under the wings of 20 or fewer principal field offices, each having a subnational area that includes several small areas. To facilitate our discussion, I shall use the word

---

[2] I have drawn freely on my "Criteria for Administrative Regions," *Social Forces* 22 (October 1943): 26–32. See also Legislative Reference Service, Library of Congress, *Federal Field Offices* (Senate Doc. No. 22, 78th Cong., 1st Sess., 1943).

"region" to refer to a major subnational field service area, and the word "district" to refer to a subregional field service area.

A second consideration in establishing limits for field service areas is the nature, multiplicity, and grouping of the objects of administration —that is, of the phenomena with which the agency is concerned. It is here that one finds the greatest variety among governmental functions, for the nature, multiplicity, and grouping of tobacco farms is different from the nature, multiplicity, and grouping of banks or oil wells or meat-packing plants or Indians. This consideration draws us back to the concept of the natural area, for it is axiomatic that field service area boundaries ordinarily should not divide the natural areas, which for this purpose are the natural groupings of the objects of administration of the particular agency. Thus, agencies concerned primarily with irrigation, flood control, river navigation, and power development might be expected to establish regions corresponding to the river systems of the country, attempting so far as possible to draw areal boundaries along the ridges of watersheds.

* * *

A third consideration in laying out field service areas is the prospective workload of the field offices. Each area must be of a size to provide a workload appropriate to the most effective organization of a field office staff. Assuming a substantial but limited number of persons available for field duty, if field service areas are few in number, each area can have a large staff with a functional differentiation of duties. But, on the same assumption, if the areas are numerous, one or a few persons will have to perform all the functions of the agency in each area—functions in each of which the jack-of-all trades in a small area can scarcely have the same ability as a specialist performing exclusively a particular function for a large area.

* * *

Furthermore, regardless of the total size of the field staff, it is desirable for each field service area director to represent an equally important part of the field work if the area directors are to receive the same salary and bear the same title. Even where salary is not a consideration, the area directors are jealous of their dignity and resent the greater prestige of other area directors. This consideration, as was revealed in Work

Projects Administration experience, is an important objection to the use of the 48 states as field service regions.[3]

Field service organization for a function, in the fourth place, should take account of the areas and headquarters cities already in use by governments, agencies, and private groups whose work affects that function. A specific conclusion from this consideration is that federal agencies, such as the Public Roads Administration and the Social Security Administration, whose activities revolve about federal grants-in-aid to the states, should ordinarily observe state lines in drawing regional boundaries. This follows naturally from the fact that much of the regional officials' time is spent in working closely with state highway commissions, state welfare departments, and similar state agencies using federal funds. State boundaries may also be respected by federal agencies that make extensive use of statistics either gathered by state governments or compiled by other agencies that use states as their units for compilation of data. Even when statistical information is available on county and metropolitan area bases, the task of adding a number of these figures together to give a total for an administrative region with irregular boundaries is too onerous for a small regional staff.

* * *

A fifth consideration is what, for lack of a better term, may be called administrative convenience. Travel costs and travel convenience play a major role in the selection of field service area boundaries and headquarters. Occasionally an agency will even select its headquarters cities first and then use a yardstick of travel costs from each city to settle the question of area boundaries. Taking the opposite tack, with area boundaries fixed, the selection of area headquarters may well aim at placing each field staff at the point of greatest volume of work within its area. Thus, in the first World War 95 percent of the work of the Pittsburgh Ordnance District was located within 20 miles of Pittsburgh. Although the district covered a much greater territory, the placement of headquarters at any place but Pittsburgh would have been absurd.

[3]Arthur W. Macmahon, John D. Millett, and Gladys Ogden, *The Administration of Federal Work Relief* (Chicago: Public Administration Service, 1941), pp. 198–200.

* * *

Finally, political considerations enter into the selection of boundaries and headquarters in two ways. Claims to patronage are always most insistent from political organizations and leaders whose constituencies embrace the total area within which a prospective appointee will have administrative jurisdiction. Where the 48 states are made field service areas by an agency the requirements of political clearance for area directors are most insistent, as is well illustrated by the controversy over the selection of state directors of the Office of Price Administration in 1942. If direct claims to patronage courtesies are to be avoided, field service areas should be larger than states. No political organization or person short of the National Party Committee and the president has a *prima facie* claim to dictate the appointment of a regional director who administers an area larger than a state. Secondly, political pressure, reflecting in turn the pressures of local interests, severely handicaps the moving of field service area headquarters from one city to another or the complete discontinuance of some offices. Illustrative is the effort of the War Production Board to reduce its district offices from more than 120 to about 70. The official charged with effecting the reduction reports that "experience quickly showed that the political difficulties incident to closing some of the smaller offices were so great that it was probably worth $8,000 or $10,000 a year to keep some of these very small offices in existence, as against the tremendous loss in time and energy which must otherwise be expended by the president and Mr. Nelson [the War Production Board Chairman], as well as this organization, in dealings with congressmen and senators, primarily interested in maintaining the local pride of their constituents."[4] A later effort to economize by closing 23 district offices stimulated protests from 46 senators and representatives, not to mention chambers of commerce and individual businessmen.[5]

* * *

Agencies often go astray in their efforts to discover natural physical,

---

[4]Quoted in Carroll K. Shaw, *Field Organization and Administration of the War Production Board and Predecessor Agencies* (Washington: Civilian Production Administration, 1947), p. 43.

[5]*Ibid.,* p. 44.

economic, or social areas bearing on their functional responsibilities. For example, in trying to locate the objects of administration and to equalize workload, the War Department at one time or another seriously considered gearing the boundaries of its procurement planning districts to the distribution of the male population, or to the distribution of power facilities, or to the distribution of all factories, whether large or small and whether capable or incapable of producing war goods. None of these provided a true index to the geographical distribution and productive capacities of factories for production of war goods.[6]

Finally, agencies often let accidents in the initial stages of regionalization affect the final results. For some reason, administrative regionalists start with the magic number *twelve* as the proper number of regions. This probably dates back to the 1913 decision of Congress to create "not to exceed twelve" Federal Reserve Districts. It is, of course, necessary to start with some concept of the number of regions desired, but this number should not be such a fixed standard that violence is done to the logical grouping of objects of administration.

* * *

The delineation of regional and district boundaries and the selection of headquarters cities create a framework within which other problems of field service areas may be attacked. The most important of these remaining problems are two: First, the vertical distribution of authority between the national area, with headquarters at Washington, and the field service areas administered from regional and district headquarters cities; and second, the coordination within each field service area or each natural area of the several functions being performed by an agency or by several agencies in that area. The first of these problems, vertical distribution of authority, will occupy our attention for the balance of the present discussion. The second, areal coordination of functions, will be the subject of the next lecture.

There are several traps set for those who approach the question of vertical relations in a field organization. It is easy to assume that because a function is legally a federal responsibility, the administration of the

[6]James W. Fesler, "Areas for Industrial Mobilization," *Public Administration Review* 1 (Winter 1941): 149–66.

function must be highly centralized. It is almost as easy to jump to the conclusion that because an agency has established field service areas it recognizes the need for diversity in administration. Neither assumption is sound. Centralized authority for policy-making can be wedded to decentralized administration and devolution of discretionary powers. The wartime price and rationing boards of the Office of Price Administration and the local boards of the Selective Service Administration, both at the local, subdistrict level, are too recent in our memory to let the possibility of decentralized federal administration escape us. On the other hand, the mere creation of field service areas is no guarantee of decentralization. Field organizations have their historical genesis in the need of central governments to carry their regulations and their services to citizens throughout the country. The flow may be entirely from the center to the circumference, with field agents merely executing central orders.

Another trap exists for those who wish to measure the degree of decentralization. The fact that the field service areas carry a substantial part of the workload of the agency does not necessarily mean that authority has been decentralized. A field service area may process a large number of applications from citizens. It may even give final approval or disapproval to most of them. Yet if the processing is done against detailed central instructions as to what factors shall dictate approval and what factors disapproval, the field office may be performing only a routine clerical function wholly devoid of any element of discretion.

Closely related to this snare is the assumption that there is such a thing as absolute centralization or absolute decentralization. It seems evident that what we want is a reasonable balance between centralization and decentralization. Complete centralization of a function runs up against the obvious fact of the diversities in American culture and the need for adapting administration to these diversities. Complete decentralization clashes with the need for consistency in the application of public policies and for reasonably uniform standards of equity for people wherever they may live. The task is one of statesmanship in achieving the proper balance of centralization and decentralization, not one of standing up to be counted either for centralization or for decentralization.

A further complication arises in multi-level field administration. Have we achieved decentralization when authority has been delegated by Washington to, say, three great regions headquartered at New York,

Chicago, and San Francisco? Or must decentralization to be effective be pressed to the district and perhaps county and community levels? Even such a regional agency as the Tennessee Valley Authority has to face the problem of moving authority out of Knoxville to the reservoir areas. This suggests that grass roots administration may embrace too many kinds of grasses if the area involved is as large as a region. Again, I would suggest that the subtle student avoid the "either-or" dichotomy. Wartime rationing experience illustrated the need for capitalizing on all levels of a multi-level field organization, according functions to the several levels with an eye to organization of trade and industry, the intensity of local and regional pressures, and the greater specialized skills in the higher-level field offices.

To some, decentralization means much more than simple devolution of authority down the administrative hierarchy. If the grass roots are to be tapped and the spirit as well as the form of decentralization to be realized, we need to expose the field official very fully to the community of people within his jurisdictional area. Advisory committees of farmers or towns-people or leaders of particular groups may be needed. The field official himself may need to become a part of the community, sharing actively in the work of community councils, civic clubs, and similar groups. Such a concept of decentralization gets away from a narrow, sterile interpretation of the role of the administrator in modern society. At the same time, it calls for a high order of field official, one who can be a part of a community and yet not become a spokesman for local and provincial interests at the expense of the broader goals of the whole people.

The factors that incline an agency to move or not to move discretionary authority to its field areas are legion. As I have elsewhere attempted to isolate these in some detail,[7] I shall here simply review certain features of administrative psychology that block a vigorous policy of decentralization. Agency heads subject to being held responsible for the agency's sins of omission and commission may be reluctant to delegate authority either to heads of functional divisions at Washington or to heads of regions and districts in the field. That this violates elementary ideas of

[7] In Fritz Morstein Marx (ed.), *Elements of Public Administration* (New York: Prentice-Hall, Inc., 1946), pp. 270–76.

sound administration does not diminish its reality as an understandable human trait nor its significance as a bar to decentralization. The tendency, as it relates to the field service, is often nourished by functional divisions at Washington, which resist the decentralization to field service areas of important phases of their functional responsibilities, lest mistakes by field officials weaken the achievement of functional goals.

All this gets mixed up with a chicken-and-egg dilemma revolving about the competence of officials in the field service areas. The centralist tendencies I have noted are strongest in the early months and years of an agency's life, and they recur whenever policies or central organization are in a ferment. This is because a field service cannot avoid chaos in its exercise of discretionary authority unless policy and organization at the center are reasonably clear and stable. Not unnaturally in periods of confusion or reorientation at the center, it seems important not to worse confound the confusion by turning field agents loose without guides to policy and organization. The fact that confusion is common to new agencies means that the field service is initially staffed with men content to plug away at nondiscretionary duties, to serve as "eyes and ears" of the central office, or to promote favorable public relations. By the time the agency has calmed down at the center and the question of delegation of discretionary authority to the field service areas can properly be raised, the agency may be saddled with unimaginative, nonexpert field personnel, and the central functional divisions may have developed a lack of confidence in the readiness of the field service for more substantial responsibilities. In other words, unless the agency delegates discretionary authority to the field at the start, it will not attract able men to its field staff. And if it does not attract able men at the start, it cannot subsequently delegate discretionary authority. The fact that decentralization at the start is impracticable prejudices decentralization later. In addition, by the time an agency has passed its infancy central divisions have already acquired jurisdictional prerogatives from which they resist dislodgment.

Apart from the obstacles to decentralization imposed by the early history of an agency's field service is a problem that is ever with us. This is the contrast between the specialized competence of the Washington office and the more generalized orientation of regional and district offices. The central headquarters can generally slice its functional responsibility more finely than can the field offices. Thus, a business regulatory agency can have at its headquarters separate organization units, each specializing on one of the hundreds of American industries and businesses. Too, it can have specialization by commodity or function within its legal staff. Even its administrative management units will break down such a function as personnel administration into a variety of specialties—from recreation and in-service training to classification and placement. Such specialization by groups of employees cannot be wholly reproduced at regional and district offices. A business regulatory agency clearly cannot place in each field office experts on every industry and business. Even the one or few lawyers in a field office must range up and down the whole gamut of agency activities. So too, the administrative officer has to encompass all phases of administrative management, and certainly cannot employ a specialist on each phase of personnel administration.

The Washington office, then, is a complex of specialties, while the field office is much more generalized in function and personnel. This is most evident at the district level, and perhaps clearer still in the county agent, a generalist in agriculture who contrasts sharply with the thousands of specialists in the United States Department of Agriculture's Washington office and in the state agricultural colleges.

This contrast between specialization at Washington and generalization in the field retards the process of decentralization. Specialists distrust generalists, particularly those generalists that appear at the bottom rather than the top of the organization chart and that receive lower pay than the central specialists. Distrusting field generalists' competence to handle specialized problems, the Washington specialists are reluctant to have final decision-making authority lodged in the field. In addition, the weakness of specialization in the field offices handicaps participation by field offices in the formation of agency policy.

* * *

This is, of course, a caricature, and does not accurately mirror the varying degrees of specialization in the field nor the spread between true professional specialties and off-the-cuff specialties. In addition, it does not recognize the variations among agencies in functional responsibilities. Approaching the specialists' problem with sympathy, for we cannot doubt the values in functional specialization, we can carve out some channels along which decentralization might flow. Specialization is not critically sacrificed if the agency itself has only a single function, and that a function for whose performance specific training and experience are necessary. The field agents, in such a case, can be professionally trained men whom the central specialists will respect and to whom they will be willing to decentralize authority. Similarly, even in multipurpose agencies, the degree of sacrifice of specialization is modified if adequate funds are allotted to permit regional offices to develop specialized staffs. While such regional specialization may fall short of that at Washington, one can approach breakdowns conforming to recognized professions and skills and thus again win at least the grudging respect of Washington specialists. Pushing even this limited specialization down to the district level is almost impossible, and the district director must somehow reconcile himself to a constant flow of instructions and advice from regional and Washington offices. But decentralization to at least the regional level is often quite feasible.

* * *

The simple, albeit unfortunate, course chosen by many agencies is to postpone decentralization until public demand, the impossible workload of the central office, or the insistent pleas of regional and district directors force it. Thus the agency can put off resolution of the problem of adjusting less skilled field personnel to the more demanding tasks they must assume under decentralization. It can at the same time postpone a host of administrative problems. An agency administrator must spend much of his time mediating the puzzling contests between line and staff officials, between policy makers and policy executors, and among operating divisions seeking to nibble at each other's jurisdictions. To all these, which are distressing enough to an agency head, are added still other issues when an agency decentralizes. Should regional directors report to the agency head, to a staff office of field operations, or to a subordinate operating official? Do all instructions to regional directors have to clear through this central point of contact, or can functional line and staff divisions issue orders to the regional directors? Can the functional divisions communicate directly with functional specialists on the regional director's staff, or must they work through the regional directors? Can the regional office be by-passed if Washington wishes to communicate with a district office? Must important field appointments and changes of head-quarters cities be cleared in advance with legislators and other political leaders of the areas involved? Should appointments of functional special-ists in a region be made by the regional director or by the functional division at the center? These are all grist for vigorous debate, with the agency head as the arbiter. And they are so vital, the interests of contest-ing parts of the organization are so much at stake, and we are as yet so far from universally valid answers that the debate is almost continuous. Small wonder that an agency head, harassed by organizational problems of the center, may not be hospitable to decentralization with its myriad problems.

12

The Politics of Impounded Funds

Louis Fisher

During the past three decades, presidents have refused to release funds for such programs as the B-70 bomber, air force groups, antimissile systems, flood control projects, highways, supercarriers, and small watershed projects. By impounding these funds, the president provokes the charge that he is obligated under the Constitution to execute the laws, not hold them in defiance; obligated to interpret appropriation bills not as mere permission to spend but as a mandate to spend as Congress directs. Otherwise, he is said to encroach upon the spending prerogatives of Congress, violate the doctrine of separated powers, and assume a power of item veto neither sanctioned by the Constitution nor granted by Congress.

Several authors advance this line of argument. Stassen (1969), Davis (1964), and Goostree (1962) invoked Supreme Court decisions to demonstrate that presidents lack constitutional authority to impound funds. On the other hand, Kranz (1962) produced legal evidence to show that there is both statutory and constitutional support for the president's impounding of funds. Yet these Court decisions are less germane than the political context within which the president decides to impound funds (Fisher, 1969). As Miller (1965: 533) observed, the president "can and may withhold expenditure of funds to the extent that the political milieu in which he operates permits him to do so." Unfortunately, there is little in the literature on this political aspect. Williams (1955) wrote an excellent study on the interplay between politics and impounded funds from 1941 to 1943. Ramsey (1968) and Jackson (1967) discussed impound-

Reprinted with permission of author and publisher. From *Administrative Science Quarterly* 15, no. 3 (September 1970): 361–77.

ment disputes of the postwar period, but neither attempted a political evaluation. The attempt here is to trace the subject of impounded funds from 1921 to 1970, searching for historical and political factors that help explain why a president resorts to impoundment, and under what conditions his will is likely to prevail over that of Congress.

Source of authority to impound funds

Part of the president's responsibility for controlling the level of expenditures can be traced back to the years following the Civil War, when congressional control over the spending power declined as a result of fragmentation of committees. The House Ways and Means Committee split apart in 1865, retaining jurisdiction over revenue but surrendering responsibilities over appropriations and banking and currency to two newly formed committees. Within a few years the jurisdiction of the House Appropriations Committee splintered, with autonomous spending powers parceled out to separate committees. In the wake of legislative extravagances in the late 1800s, the president, not Congress, played the role of guardian of the public purse (Fisher, 1971).

Antideficiency acts

At the turn of the century, outlays for pension bills, river and harbor projects, the Spanish-American War, and the Panama Canal all converged to produce a series of budget deficits. The Antideficiency Act of 1905 introduced the technique of monthly or other allotments to prevent "undue expenditures in one portion of the year that may require deficiency or additional appropriations to complete the service of the fiscal year ..." (33 Stat. 1257, sec. 4). In the Antideficiency Act of 1906, Congress stipulated that apportionments could be waived or modified in the event of "some extraordinary emergency or unusual circumstances which could not be anticipated at the time of making such apportionment" (34 Stat. 49, sec. 3). This constituted an admission by Congress that regardless of spending patterns anticipated when passing appropriation bills, or even after apportioning funds, conditions might change and necessitate a different course for actual expenditures.

President Taft received funds in 1910 to investigate into more efficient and economical ways of transacting public business (36 Stat. 703), but when his Commission on Economy and Efficiency recommended the adoption of an executive budget two years later, Congress ignored the proposal. The magnitude of federal spending during World War I, coupled with the pressing need for managing the huge debt after the war, finally made budget reform unavoidable. The main thrust of recommendations after 1918 centered on two principles: an increase in executive responsibility, and a decrease in legislative opportunities for extravagance.

* * *

These constraints on legislative additions were not incorporated into the Budget and Accounting Act of 1921, which set forth procedures for the new national budget. Nor was the president protected from insubordination within his own ranks. While section 206 of the act prohibited agency officials from seeking additional funds unless requested to do so by Congress, agencies and bureaus—denied a portion of their request by the president—could make informal overtures to Congress to have their funds restored. Without item-veto authority, presidents developed the art of impoundment in order to maintain control over legislative increases and their own executive officials.

Following the 1921 act, administrative regulations extended the Budget Bureau's control over spending levels. The first budget director, Charles G. Dawes, issued a circular setting forth procedures for establishing reserves and effecting savings. Appropriations from Congress were to be treated as a mere ceiling on expenditures, rather than as a directive to spend the full amount. He ordered each executive department and bureau to determine the portion of appropriations considered indispensable for carrying out activities. The estimated savings would be carried as a General Reserve, with the amount approved by the president for expenditure under an appropriation title representing the *"maximum available for obligation during the fiscal year"* (U.S. Bureau of the Budget, 1921). Since further savings would be attempted during the course of the fiscal year, each bureau was to withhold additional sums from obligation so that these amounts could be added to the General Reserve. As a result of this circular, the allotment technique now had two objectives: to prevent deficiencies, and to effect savings.

Depression policies

Economic collapse in 1929 led to broader presidential authority for reducing expenditures. When deficits appeared in 1931 for the first time in a decade, President Hoover asked for authority to effect savings through reorganization of the executive departments. Earlier efforts by Congress to reduce spending had been thwarted by such influential lobbyists as veterans' groups. "The only way by which we will get results," Senator Reed told his colleagues, "is by putting the power into the hands of somebody who will assume the responsibility and use it . . . if we are to get economies made they have to be made by some one who has the power to make the order and stand by it. Leave it to Congress and we will fiddle around here all summer trying to satisfy every lobbyist, and we will get nowhere" (U.S. Congress, 1932: 9644).

President Hoover received authority to make partial layoffs, reduce compensation for public officials, and consolidate executive agencies in order to effect savings. Funds impounded by this economy act were to be returned to the Treasury Department (47 Stat. 382, Part II, Titles I and IV). Hoover subsequently issued executive orders to regroup and consolidate a total of 58 agencies, but the House disapproved the orders on January 19, 1933, preferring to leave reorganization changes to the new president. In his last two days in office, Hoover signed two more economy measures, authorizing his successor to effect further reorganization and to reduce military spending in accordance with an economy survey ordered by the president (47 Stat. 1519, sec. 16; 47 Stat. 1602, Title II, sec. 4).

* * *

The inability of Congress to control expenditures when faced with lobbying pressures was illustrated again in the late 1930s. On the basis of recommendations by the Committee on Administrative Management (the Brownlow committee), Roosevelt proposed in 1937 that Congress establish general principles by which the president could reorganize the executive branch on a continuing basis. He emphasized that although reorganization could improve efficiency and morale, it was not intended as an instrument for major spending reductions (Rosenman, 1938c: 668; 1941a: 498). Nevertheless, the reorganization proposal gradually acquired a cost-saving reputation. In January 1938, Congressman Woodrum recommended that the president be authorized to reduce any appropriation whenever he determined, by investigation, that such action would help balance the budget or reduce the public debt, and would serve the public interest. One could interpret this either as a generous extension of impoundment authority under the economy acts of 1932 and 1933, or else as item-veto authority. Woodrum explained that his proposal would protect the president from extraneous items attached to appropriation bills, a legislative practice which put the president in a position of "having to swallow things he does not want or approve items he does not want in order to get an appropriation bill passed" (U.S. Congress, 1938a: 355).

Opponents of the Woodrum motion charged that the president could use the authority to dominate Congress and intimidate opposition. Congressman Maverick argued that legislators would hesitate to challenge the president since he "could single out any district or portion of America to have appropriations or not to have appropriations, as he pleased." Congressman Ditter charged that the reorganization bill put the public purse at the disposal of the president and made the civil service the "ready tool of the Executive for political appointments." With Roosevelt's Court-packing proposal cited as an effort to destroy the independence of the judiciary, the reorganization plan was characterized as a companion move to deprive Congress of its vital spending prerogatives (U.S. Congress, 1938b: 387; 1938c: 4630; cf. Wann, 1968: 72–98).

A different version of the reorganization bill finally passed in 1939, stating that continuing deficits made cutbacks desirable and directing the president to effect savings by consolidating or abolishing agencies for more efficient operation. Reorganization would take effect after 60 days unless voted down by concurrent resolution. Of the five purposes identified in the act, spending reduction was listed first. Any appropriation unexpended as a result of this act would be impounded and returned to the Treasury (53 Stat. 561). Roosevelt strengthened his control over the budget by using the reorganization authority to transfer the Budget

Bureau from the Treasury to the newly formed Executive Office of the President (53 Stat. 1423).

War priorities

With war imminent, the leverage for presidential impoundment increased. In his January 1941 budget message, Roosevelt announced that the government had "embarked on a program for the total defense of our democracy." It therefore seemed appropriate, he told Congress, to "defer construction projects that interfere with the defense program by diverting manpower and materials. Further, it is very wise for us to establish a reservoir of post-defense projects to help absorb labor that later will be released by defense industry." He recommended reductions for rivers and harbors and flood-control work, but funds for power and other projects considered essential to national defense should continue (Rosenman, 1941b: 656).

On May 27, 1941, the president declared a state of unlimited national emergency. When the House passed a rivers and harbors bill which he felt might jeopardize the defense effort, he appealed to the Senate to amend the bill "so as to restrict new construction work to projects having important defense values" (U.S. Congress, 1941a: 5807, 5817). Congress refused to delegate to the president the sole right to decide which projects should go forward, but did acknowledge the gravity of the emergency period by following Budget Bureau recommendations on flood control funds and by including in the appropriation bill the provision that flood control projects "shall be prosecuted as speedily as may be consistent with budgetary requirements" (U.S. Congress, 1941b: 6767–68; 55 Stat. 638, sec. 3).

After Pearl Harbor, Roosevelt carried out his policy of withholding allocations from projects which did not have important value for national defense, but the line between national defense and domestic projects was not always clear. When funds totaling $513,000 for a flood control project in Oklahoma were impounded, congressmen and local business groups from the area assailed the decision. The Budget Bureau maintained that the building of levees near Tulsa would divert funds, machinery, and skilled labor from essential war activities. Nature intervened at this point to upset the Bureau's rationale. Heavy rains caused the Arkansas River to overflow its banks in June 1942, flooding an area near Tulsa. The War Production Board (WPB) received notice that a steel mill handling war contracts had to be closed because of the flooding. When the WPB later certified that the Tulsa levees were essential for the war effort, the Budget Bureau released the funds; but scores of other projects were curtailed because of the defense effort. By the end of 1943, impounding of funds for scheduled public works had reached a half billion dollars (Williams, 1955: 12–20, 28).

Some members of Congress tried to reassert legislative authority over spending. In the summer of 1943, the Senate included a section in the Rural Post Roads Act to prohibit the impounding of funds by any agency or official other than the commissioner of public roads. The object of this section, Senator Hayden said, was to bypass the budget director, who had previously impounded large sums of highway funds. Senator McKellar noted that the section would determine "whether the will of the Congress shall be supreme, or whether the will of the Bureau of the Budget shall be supreme" (U.S. Congress, 1943a: 6313). House conferees found the section "wholly objectionable" and recommended that the impounding authority be placed in the hands of the WPB. The Senate receded on this point and Section 9 of the statute authorized the WPB to withhold funds after certifying that the "use of critical material for additional highway construction would impede the conduct of the war" (U.S. Congress, 1943b: 4; 1943c: 7385–86, 7345–46; 57 Stat. 563).

. . .

Subsequent legislation acknowledged the need for presidential discretion on priorities. Congress authorized public works in December 1944 and March 1945 in the "interest of the national security" and for the purpose of providing a reservoir of useful public works in the postwar period, to be initiated "as expeditiously and prosecuted as vigorously as may be consistent with budgetary requirements" (58 Stat. 887, sec. 10; 59 Stat. 11, sec. 2). No project was to be funded or constructed until six months after the end of the war, unless recommended by an authorized defense agency and approved by the president as being "necessary or desirable in the interest of the national defense and security, and the President has notified the Congress to that effect" (59 Stat. 12).

Interservice rivalries

In the period after World War II, congressional strategy for controlling defense spending shifted from the traditional ceiling on spending levels to the setting of floors or minimums. This reversed the usual legislative-executive relationship. As Huntington (1961: 140) noted, the issue in earlier centuries was "whether the legislature could prevent the executive from maintaining forces which the legislature did not want. The issue in the mid-twentieth century is whether the legislature can urge or compel the executive to maintain forces which the executive does not want."

In this contest for control, the president often faces an alliance of legislators and military leaders. While serving as U.S. Senator during the war, Truman (1955: 88) noticed that generals and admirals would take over the service secretaries and the military committees in Congress, especially in defense procurement. Army and navy professionals, he said, "seldom had any idea of the value of money. They did not seem to care what the cost was. . . ." Since career men looked upon elected officials as temporary occupants in office, the president had to take special care to see that they did not try to circumvent his policy. Truman (1956: 165) found that it "often happened in the War and Navy Departments that the generals and the admirals, instead of working for and under the Secretaries, succeeded in having the Secretaries act for and under them."

One of Truman's first steps as president was to advocate a single department of national defense under the direction of a single civilian secretary, thereby strengthening presidential control over the military. The National Security Act of 1947 represented a weak compromise, calling for three separately administered departments of the army, the navy, and the air force, subject only to the "general direction" of a secretary of defense (61 Stat. 495; cf. Truman, 1945: 554–558; 1946: 303). The Act was amended in 1949 to provide for a Department of Defense and the removal of service secretaries as statutory members of the National Security Council. At the same time, Congress recognized the right of service secretaries and members of the Joint Chiefs of Staff to bypass the president and make recommendations to Congress on their own initiative (63 Stat. 580).

The gap between presidential and legislative conceptions of national security became evident in 1948 and 1949. A supplemental appropriation act in 1948 included $822 million more in contract authority for aircraft than President Truman had requested. In this case, the increase did not particularly disturb the Administration, since Defense Secretary Forrestal learned that the House had added a "hooker" extending the time during which the money had to be spent, moving the date from June 30, 1949 to a year later (Millis, 1951: 416–417). Furthermore, the statute also specified that funds were to be released only after the president had determined that the contracts let were necessary for the national defense (62 Stat. 258; cf. Truman, 1948: 272).

Air force groups

More forceful legislation appeared in 1949 when Congress voted to increase the president's air force request from 48 to 58 groups. Truman signed the measure, but announced that he was directing his defense secretary to place the extra funds in reserve. Impounded funds included $577 million in contract authority for aircraft construction, $130 million for maintenance and operations, and lesser amounts for contingencies, special procurement, and research and development. All told, impounded funds came to $735 million (U.S. Congress, 1950a: 27).

Several factors produced this collision between Congress and the president. First, Louis Johnson replaced Forrestal in March 1949 as the new secretary of defense and subjected the military budget to fresh examination. Moreover, even though the Berlin airlift was still in operation, and the Korean war little more than a year off, Johnson was optimistic about the chances for peace. As he later recalled, the "climate on the Hill, the climate of the President's economists and all the rest of the economists, the climate of the world at that moment—the airlift being successful—the climate was, there was going to be peace" (U.S. Congress, 1951a: 2607).

Retrenchment in defense spending became more probable when the Eberstadt task force of the Hoover Commission released its findings on the Pentagon. In December 1948, the task force charged that intense interservice rivalries had hampered defense policy and that military services lacked a "sense of cost consciousness," being "far too prodigal" with government funds. The following April, former President Hoover told Congress that $1.5 billion could be cut from the military budget without threatening national security (The New York Times, 1948; 1949a). Although Secretary Johnson considered the defense budget too small when he presented it in 1949, he concluded that larger appropriations—because of waste within the Defense Department—would be like throwing money "down a rat hole" (U.S. Congress, 1951a: 2607).

Still another factor behind the impounding of air force funds was Truman's fiscal policy of relying on budget surpluses and debt retirement to restrain inflation. Twice in 1947 he vetoed tax-reduction bills, but in 1948, when he again vetoed a tax-reduction bill, Democrats joined with Republicans to override him. With revenue now lost to tax relief, and receipts down as a result of the 1948–49 recession, Truman redoubled his efforts to control expenditures.

By the time Air Force Secretary Stuart Symington testified before Congress in June 1949, he no longer insisted on 70 air force groups as he had in the past. Instead, he now placed his budgetary request in the context of the president's program. The air force recognized, he said, that "armed forces are only one component of our total national strength. We recognize further, the great burden of responsibility on those in positions of highest authority to balance the several components of this strength to meet the needs of the United States; and therefore, we support the President's budget" (U.S. Congress, 1949a: 328).

The Senate joined with the president in opposing air force funds added by the House, and the matter lay deadlocked in conference committee. A motion by the Senate to vote continuing appropriations was rejected by the House. With adjournment close at hand, and military services in need of funds to meet their payrolls, the Senate reluctantly agreed to the 58 groups but on the understanding that "if the money is appropriated it may not be used" by the president (U.S. Congress, 1949b: 14355, 14855). Truman signed the bill, explaining that it was his responsibility to provide a defense structure which would meet the needs of national security without imposing too great a strain on the domestic economy. He was concerned not merely with the additional procurement costs for aircraft but also such related items as extra personnel, higher maintenance and operating costs, and greater replacement expenses. He reminded Congress, moreover, that his defense program was based on a unified strategic concept, and that an expanded air force would necessitate augmented levels for other services. To maintain a balance between national security and a sound economy, he placed the extra air force funds in reserve (Truman, 1949: 538–539).

* * *

Anti-inflation policy

Federal responsibility for economic stability—tacitly admitted during the 1930s and during World War II—received formal acknowledgment with the Employment Act of 1946. Explicit objectives of the Act included the promotion of maximum employment, production, and purchasing power. Though control of inflation was not specifically mentioned (a postwar depression seemed more likely), price stability could be inferred from the goal of maximum purchasing power and the development of policies to "avoid economic fluctuations" [60 Stat. 23, sec. 4(c)]. All postwar presidents interpreted the Act to include federal responsibility for combating inflation. The question was whether this responsibility would fall primarily on Congress or on the president.

Spending controls

Congress tried several techniques in the postwar years to place restrictions on federal spending. As part of the Legislative Reorganization Act of 1946, a joint committee was formed to prepare a legislative budget and prescribe a ceiling on expenditures. The work of the joint committee, consisting of 102 members from the taxing and spending committees of each house, was hampered by friction between the two houses, between taxing and spending committees, and by intraparty wrangling. Moreover, this new procedure conflicted with the established practice of having separate appropriations subcommittees review the president's budget to decide the level of funding. Thus, the legislative budget prematurely set a ceiling before the subcommittees could complete their work, and was abandoned by Congress after three unsuccessful efforts (cf. Leiserson, 1948; Fielder, 1951).

In 1950, instead of handling appropriations by separate bills, the House Appropriations Committee reported out an omnibus appropriation bill. In addition to making selective cuts in the president's budget, the House considered a proposal by Congressman Thomas to authorize the president to cut the budget by an additional $500 million, subject to two legislative guidelines: reductions would not be applied to military programs, and no domestic program could be cut by more than 15 percent. Clarence Cannon, chairman of the House Appropriations Committee, considered this an abdication of legislative responsibility, while Congressman Keefe charged that the prospect of turning over to the president the responsibility for making reductions was "a monstrous display of congressional incompetence, to say the least" (U.S. Congress, 1950b: 6812, 6814). Congressman Taber moved to increase the reduction from $500 million to $600 million, but limited the president to 10 areas in which cuts could be made, and restricted the reductions to either 5 or 10 percent. The Taber–Thomas proposal passed, satisfying economy advocates as well as those who wished to exercise greater congressional responsibility in the spending power (U.S. Congress, 1950c: 6815, 6844).

* * *

The conference committee decided to drop both the Taber-Thomas and Byrd-Bridges admendments and simply direct the president to cut the budget by not less than $550 million without impairing the national defense. President Truman fulfilled the statutory directive by placing $573 million in reserve, including $343 million in appropriations, $119 million in contract authority, and $110 million in authorizations to borrow from the Treasury (64 Stat. 595, sec. 1214; U.S. Congress, 1951b). Congressman Phillips later remarked, it was "an ironic paradox that members of Congress who shudder at the thought of a Constitutional amendment allowing a President to veto individual items in a bill have supported an extra-Constitutional device which in effect gives the President the same veto power but allows the Congress no opportunity to override him" (Phillips, 1951: 255; cf. Nelson, 1953).

Before 1950, the authority to create reserves and to spend less than Congress appropriated had been drawn initially from the Budget Bureau's interpretation of the Budget and Accounting Act, and then later supported in 1933 by Executive Order 6166. The effect of Section 1211 of the 1950 omnibus appropriation act was to amplify this authority in the statutes and the U.S. Code: "In apportioning any appropriation, reserves may be established to provide for contingencies, or to effect savings whenever savings are made possible by or through changes in requirements, greater efficiency of operations, or other developments subsequent to the date on which such appropriation was made available" [64 Stat. 595, sec. 1211: 31 U.S.C. § 665 (c)].

Anti-inflation policy

The meaning of "changes in requirements" and "other developments" has been broadly interpreted to include inflationary pressures. Congressman Mahon explained that President Johnson impounded funds in 1966 when "we had inflationary problems, and a changing condition following the time the appropriations were made, and I assume the President relied upon the portion of the law [the 1950 omnibus appropriation act] to which I have referred" (U.S. Congress, 1967b: 29282).

In signing an agricultural appropriation bill in September 1966, President Johnson noted that Congress had added $312.5 million to his budget request. "During a period," he said, "when we are making every effort to moderate inflationary pressures, this degree of increase is, I believe, most unwise." Instead of vetoing the bill and losing funds he wanted, he decided to reduce expenditures for certain items in the bill "in an attempt to avert expending more in the coming year than provided in the budget" (Johnson, 1966: 980). The president's economic message to Congress, September 8, 1966, estimated that spending must be cut $3 billion to protect the nation's economy. Johnson had already ordered agencies to save $1.5 billion by deferring, stretching out, and otherwise reducing contracts, new orders, and commitments. Whenever possible, appropriations provided in excess of the president's recommendations were to be withheld (Johnson, 1966: 987–988).

Exactly where the economy axe would fall was not known until after the November elections. At that point, the president announced a $5.3 billion reduction in federal programs, permitting more than a $3 billion reduction for the remaining seven months of the fiscal year. The major items affected included a reduction of $1.1 billion in obligations under the highway trust fund, $750 million withheld from housing and urban development, and sizable cutbacks in the Departments of Health, Education, and Welfare, Agriculture, Interior, and in education funds for the Elementary and Secondary Education Act. About half of these reductions represented deferrals rather than outright cancellations (U.S. Congress, 1967c: 13–14; Johnson, 1966: 1406–10).

· · ·

These economic and legal justifications failed to placate localities affected by the cutbacks. Sensitive to criticism from the states, President Johnson released $175 million in highway funds in February 1967, and on the eve of a conference the next month with governors, released another $791 million, including $350 million for highways, $250 million for low-cost housing, and lesser amounts for agricultural loans, flood control projects, and education grants (Johnson, 1967: 219, 357).

· · ·

Congress tried a more stringent method of control in July 1969, setting the spending ceiling for fiscal 1970 at $191.9 billion ($1 billion below Nixon's recommendation), but this time allowing no exemptions. Congress permitted the president some flexibility by authorizing him to raise the ceiling by as much as $2 billion to cover certain "uncontrollable" items: interest on the public debt, farm price supports, Medicare, and other social insurance trust funds. The ceiling could thus range from $191.9 billion to $193.9 billion (PL 91–47). In signing this bill, President Nixon stated that his earlier expenditure estimates for fiscal 1970 appeared to be low by about $2.5 billion, and that congressional action and inaction threatened to add another billion to expenditures. Consequently, he directed the heads of all departments and agencies to reduce spending by $3.5 billion. A few weeks later, when the House persisted in voting more funds than he had requested, he repeated his determination to stay within his budget target of $192.9 billion. Referring to his "obligation under the Constitution and the laws," he said that he would not spend funds in excess of the expenditure ceiling (Nixon, 1969a: 1021; 1969b: 1142).

President Nixon subsequently ordered all federal agencies to reduce new contracts for government construction by 75 percent in an effort to direct resources into the depressed housing market. In dollar terms, this meant deferral of $1.5 billion in contracts and an expected saving of $300 million for fiscal 1970. This announcement was followed by plans to reduce research health grants, defer $215 million in Model Cities funds, and reduce grants for urban renewal (Nixon, 1969c: 1225; The New York Times, 1969, 1970). This opened the president to the charge that he had allowed his anti-inflation policy to fall most heavily on the cities and public services, while at the same time backing such costly projects as the supersonic transport, a manned landing on Mars, revenue sharing, a larger merchant marine fleet, a new manned bomber, and the Safeguard ABM system. Impoundment was used here not simply as an anti-inflation technique but to shift the scale of priorities from one Administration to the next.

The question of priorities came to a head on January 26, 1970, when President Nixon vetoed a Labor-HEW appropriation bill which provided $1.1 billion more than he had requested. After the veto was sustained, Congress agreed to reduce appropriations from $19.7 billion to $19.3 billion. The bill included a provision limiting expenditures to 98 percent of appropriations, specifying that no single appropriation could be cut more than 15 percent. This 2-percent cutback provision represented a further reduction of $347 million. President Nixon signed the bill on March 5 (PL 91–204; U.S. Congress, 1970: S2913). The tables were reversed in June when Nixon's veto of the Hill-Burton hospital construction bill was overridden by Congress, authorizing direct grants more than $300 million in excess of Nixon's fiscal 1971 budget.

While this executive-legislative struggle was in process, two factors were at work to frustrate the spending ceiling for fiscal 1970. Congress reserved for itself the privilege of increasing appropriations and raising the spending ceiling, converting it into what Nixon (1969d: 1758) called a "rubber ceiling." Legislative actions increased the budget by $1.8 billion. Secondly, Nixon announced in his budget message of February 2, 1970, that uncontrollable spending had increased by $4.3 billion—$2.3

billion higher than Congress' allowance. As a result, the "ceiling" starts at $191.9 billion, climbs by $1.8 billion and then again by $4.3 billion, and ends up at $198 billion.

Boundaries of impoundment power

The delegation of budget-making responsibilities to the president in 1921 was merely one step in the decline of legislative spending prerogatives. Since that time, Congress has demonstrated on many occasions its inability to cut expenditures when needed. Though legislators could reach agreement on the need for retrenchment, they were frequently unable, or unwilling, to make specific reductions and offend the affected constituents and interest groups.

When impounding funds to prevent deficiencies or to effect savings, few legislators would contest the president's authority. George H. Mahon (1969), chairman of the House Appropriations Committee, has said that "the weight of experience and practice bears out the general proposition that an appropriation does not constitute a mandate to spend every dollar appropriated. That is a generally accepted concept. It squares with the rule of common sense. I subscribe fully to it. The Congress does not administer the government. . . . I believe it is fundamentally desirable that the Executive have limited powers of impoundment in the interests of good management and constructive economy in public expenditures." The decision to impound becomes more controversial when used for canceling domestic projects which compete with wartime production, delaying weapons systems while awaiting further tests, withholding funds from specific projects as an anti-inflation measure, or when canceling programs altogether.

Because of legal obligations and political constraints, relatively few items in the budget are subject to impoundment. In the 1971 budget presented by President Nixon, the total budget estimate of $200.8 billion for expenditures includes outlays of $138.4 billion considered relatively uncontrollable. These outlays include $46.9 billion for social security, Medicare, and other social insurance trust funds under January 1969 laws; $4.6 billion for social insurance benefit increases recently enacted; $17.8 billion for interest on the public debt, and other amounts to cover military retired pay, veterans benefits, farm price supports, public assistance grants (including Medicaid), postal operations, legislative and judiciary expenses, and other essential programs. Funds already obligated because of contractual and other legal obligations come to $23.7 billion for national defense and $19.6 billion for civilian programs. Thus, out of the total budget, about 69 percent consists of outlays that are relatively uncontrollable (U.S. Bureau of the Budget, 1970a: 44).

The greatest opportunity for impoundment lies with defense spending. Close to half of Defense Department appropriations is in the form of "no-year money." This is money made available until expended, and permits the president to release these funds when he determines that the money can be spent in the most effective manner. In the 1971 budget, no-year money in Defense Department funds includes $17.7 billion for procurement, $7.3 billion for research, development, test, and evaluation, and $1.4 billion for military construction (U.S. Bureau of the Budget, 1970b: 283–307).

In periods of inflation, especially when Congress adds to the president's budget without making commensurate reductions elsewhere, the president's power to impound gains greater legitimacy. Congressional programs also become vulnerable to impoundment when unusual, extraconstitutional procedures are employed, such as committee resolutions. If a particular public works project fails to receive a favorable report from the Corps of Engineers, or if the Budget Bureau excludes the project from the president's program, the Senate or House Committee on Public Works may pass a resolution requesting the Corps to "reexamine" the project. These resolutions are not subject to presidential veto (33 U.S.C. §§ 541, 542, and 701; cf. Maass, 1950). Omnibus bills for rivers and harbors projects further dilute his veto power, forcing the president either to acquiesce or else veto the entire package. Since appropriation bills frequently come late in a legislative session, long after the fiscal year has begun, veto is seldom an option. Thus, the president may prefer to sign the bill and impound funds for certain projects. For example when Congress provided funds in 1959 and 1962 for public works projects that had not been authorized, the Budget Bureau placed the amounts in reserve pending authorization. The projects were subsequently authorized and the funds released (U.S. Department of the Army, 1969).

President Johnson impounded funds for small watershed projects because he objected to the use of so-called committee vetoes. This legislative device requires that Administration actions first receive clearance from an appropriate committee. Johnson considered this procedure contrary to the spirit of separation of powers and objected to its use in legislation for water research grants, military installations, and water resource development. Instead of vetoing a rivers and harbors bill in 1965, he noted his opposition to the committee-veto procedure and asked that it be repealed in the next session. Congress refused and the funds for small watershed projects remained impounded (Johnson, 1964: 862; 1965: 907, 1082–83). On March 27, 1969, President Nixon advised his secretary of agriculture that he would not object to the committee-veto procedure for small watershed projects. A list of 18 projects was submitted to Congress on June 30 for committee approval (U.S. Department of Agriculture, 1969; U.S. Congress, 1969b).

To make a judgment about the political merits of impoundment, it is necessary to study individual impoundment disputes in the light of historical developments, economic conditions, the political situation, and legislative procedures, and then construct a scale of legitimacy for the different types of impoundment. No sweeping generalizations can, or should, be made. This review should make possible a better understanding of the historical process that gave rise to greater executive spending power, and an appreciation of some of the factors that lead up to an executive-legislative impasse and eventual impoundment of funds.

References

Davis, Gerald W.
  1964 "Congressional power to require defense expenditures." Fordham Law Review 33:39–60.
Fielder, Clinton.
  1951 "Reform of the congressional legislative budget." National Tax Journal 4:65–76.
Fisher, Louis.
  1969 "Funds impounded by the president: the constitutional issue." George Washington Law Review 38:124–37.
  1971 President and Congress: Shifting Prerogatives. New York: The Free Press, to be published.

Goostree, Robert E.
  1962 "The power of the president to impound appropriated funds: with special reference to grants-in-aid to segregated activities." American University Law Review 11:32–47.

Huntington, Samuel P.
  1961 The Common Defense. New York: Columbia University Press.

Jackson, John C.
  1967 Presidential Impoundment of Appropriations. Washington: Legislative Reference Service, The Library of Congress.

Johnson, Lyndon B.
  1964 Public Papers of the Presidents, 1964. Washington: Government Printing Office.

  1965 Public Papers of the Presidents, 1965. Washington: Government Printing Office.

  1966 Public Papers of the Presidents, 1966. Washington: Government Printing Office.

  1967 Public Papers of the Presidents, 1967. Washington: Government Printing Office.

Kranz, Harry.
  1962 "A 20th century emancipation proclamation: presidential power permits withholding of federal funds from segregated institutions." American University Law Review 11:48–78.

Leiserson, Avery.
  1948 "Coordination of federal budgetary and appropriations procedures under the legislative reorganization act of 1946." National Tax Journal 1:118–26.

Maass, Arthur A.
  1950 "Congress and water resources." American Political Science Review 44:576–93.

Mahon, George H.
  1969 Letter to Senator Sam J. Ervin, Jr., February 25, 1969. Copy given to author by Mr. Eugene B. Wilhelm, staff assistant, House Committee on Appropriations.

Miller, Arthur Selwyn.
  1965 "Presidential power to impound appropriated funds: an exercise in constitutional decision-making." North Carolina Law Review 43:502–47.

Millis, Walter (ed.).
  1951 The Forrestal Diaries. New York: Viking Press.

Nelson, Dalmas H.
  1953 "The omnibus appropriations act of 1950." Journal of Politics 15:274–88.

New York Times.
  1948   December 17, 18:3.
  1949a   April 12, 1:5.
  1969   September 11, 1:1; September 13, 1:4; September 16, 16:1; October
          2, 28:1.
  1970   January 9, 1:8.
Nixon, Richard M.
  1969a   Weekly Compilation of Presidential Documents. Volume 5, number
          30. Washington: Government Printing Office.
  1969b   Weekly Compilation of Presidential Documents. Volume 5, number
          33. Washington: Government Printing Office.
  1969c   Weekly Compilation of Presidential Documents. Volume 5, number
          36. Washington: Government Printing Office.
  1969d   Weekly Compilation of Presidential Documents. Volume 5, number
          51. Washington: Government Printing Office.
Phillips, John.
  1951   "The hadacol of the budget makers." National Tax Journal 4:255–68.
Ramsey, Mary Louise.
  1968   Impoundment by the Executive Department of Funds which Congress
          had Authorized it to Spend or Obligate. Washington: Legislative Ref-
          erence Service, The Library of Congress.
Rosenman, Samuel I. (comp.).
  1938c   Public Papers and Addresses of Franklin D. Roosevelt. Volume 5,
          1936. New York: Random House.
  1941b   Public Papers and Addresses of Franklin D. Roosevelt. Volume 9,
          1940. New York: Macmillan.
Stassen, John H.
  1969   "Separation of powers and the uncommon defense: the case against
          impounding of weapons system appropriations." Georgetown Law
          Journal 57:1159–1210.
Truman, Harry S.
  1945   Public Papers of the Presidents, 1945. Washington: Government
          Printing Office.
  1948   Public Papers of the Presidents, 1948. Washington: Government
          Printing Office.
  1949   Public Papers of the Presidents, 1949. Washington: Government
          Printing Office.
  1955   Memoirs, Volume One, Year of Decisions. Garden City, N.Y.: Double-
          day.
  1956   Memoirs, Volume Two, Years of Trial and Hope. Garden City, N.Y.:
          Doubleday.

U.S. Bureau of the Budget.
  1921   "First budget regulations." Circular No. 4, July 1, 1921.
  1970a The Budget of the United States Government, 1971. Washington: Government Printing Office.
  1970b The Budget of the United States Government, 1971 - Appendix. Washington: Government Printing Office.

U.S. Congress.
  1932   Congressional Record. May 5, 1932.
  1938a Congressional Record. January 11, 1938.
  1938b Congressional Record. January 12, 1938.
  1938c Congressional Record. April 2, 1938.
  1941a Congressional Record. July 3, 1941.
  1941b Congressional Record. August 5, 1941.
  1943a Congressional Record. June 23, 1943.
  1943b House Report No. 677. 78th Congress, 1st Session.
  1943c Congressional Record. July 7, 1943.
  1949a Senate Committee on Appropriations, Hearings on National Military Establishment Appropriation Bill for 1950. 81st Congress, 1st Session.
  1949b Congressional Record. October 12, 1949.
  1950a House Committee on Appropriations, Hearings on Department of Defense Appropriations for 1951. 81st Congress, 2nd Session.
  1950b Congressional Record. May 10, 1950.
  1950c Congressional Record. May 10, 1950.
  1951a Senate Committees on Armed Services and Foreign Relations, Hearings on Military Situation in the Far East. 82nd Congress, 1st Session.
  1951b House Document No. 182. 82nd Congress, 1st Session.
  1967b Congressional Record. October 18, 1967.
  1967c House Ways and Means Committee, Hearings on Temporary Increase in Debt Ceiling. 90th Congress, 1st Session.
  1969b Senate Committee on Finance. Letter to author from Senator Herman E. Talmadge, July 16, 1969, including list of 18 projects.
  1970   Congressional Record (daily ed.). March 4, 1970.

U.S. Department of Agriculture.
  1969   Department of Agriculture release, No. 1015-69, April 1, 1969.

U.S. Department of the Army.
  1969   Letter from Lt. Gen. F.J. Clarke, Chief of Engineers, to Senator Allen J. Ellender, October 14, 1969. Copy of letter sent to author by Senator Ellender.

Wann, A. J.
   1968   The President as Chief Administrator. Washington: Public Affairs
          Press.
Williams, J. D.
   1955   The Impounding of Funds by the Bureau of the Budget. Indianapolis:
          Bobbs-Merrill.

13

Organizations and Their Environments: The School System as a Focus

Frank K. Gibson

While biologists have long argued that all organisms are selectively modified by their environments, social or organizational Darwinism has but recently become a standard part of the literature of organizational behavior. Using the school system as a focal point, this article attempts a generalized statement of the interaction between an organization and its environment, it also reports on some specific research explicating such interactions, and it closes with some suggestions about future events in this area.

Presently, all serious students of organizational theory recognize that there is a high level of interdependence between all social organizations and their larger societal settings. Systems theorists note that an output of any particular subsystem (social organization) often becomes an input of a larger subsystem (society). For example, such outputs of school systems as students and services become an input of the community or professional subsystems, whose outputs then become inputs for even larger subsystems. Explicitly, systems theorists hold that insofar as an organization is "open," its boundaries are permeable, which means that the input-throughout-output cycle involves flows between the organization and its environment as well as within the organization itself.

A major implication inheres in this formulation. Organizational goals themselves are largely set and modified as a result of relationships between an organization and its environment. A change in either the organization or the environment requires review and possible alteration of goals. In fact, organizational goals must continually be reappraised in order to keep them at least partially congruent with environmental settings.[1]

As organizational and societal life interact more and more, one can anticipate a decreasing autonomy and an increasing interdependence for all large organizations. A concomitant of such interdependence is the fact that internal organizational changes (structures, procedures and goals) will increasingly be externally induced. Those organizations most likely to survive as viable instruments are, then, those most able to adapt to what at times may be a rapidly changing environment.

In a remarkably able treatment of this subject, Emery and Trist[2] propose that any comprehensive understanding of organizational behavior requires a knowledge of each member of the following set, where L indicates some potentially lawful connection and the suffix 1 refers to an organization and the suffix 2 to its environment.

These processes can be described as follows:

$L11$ processes within the organization (the area of internal interdependence);

$L12$ exchanges between the organization and its environment initiated from within the organization;

$L21$ exchanges between the organization and its environment initiated from some point in the environment ($L12$ and $L21$ are referred to as transactional interdependence);

$L22$ processes through which parts of the environment become related to each other.

Emery's and Trist's explanation of the degree to which these various processes and systems are related can be summarized simply. One of the *primary* tasks of education administrators is to relate the total organizational system to its environment; matters internal to the structure are of less concern. While most administrators "know" this subconsciously, the press of day-to-day administrative details may blind them to a continual

---

[1]James S. Thompson and William J. McEwen, "Organizational Goals and Environment," *American Sociological Review* 23 (1958): 23–31. Roland Warren, "The Inter-organizational Field as a Focus for Investigation," *Administrative Science Quarterly* 12 (December 1967): 396–419.

[2]"The Causal Texture of Organizational Environments," *Human Relations* 18 (1965): 21–31.

reassessment of the forms of exchange between the school and its environment.[3]

The Emery and Trist model offers very little that is new or unique in the patterning of organizational interactions with their environment. It does, however, emphasize the nature of relationships that while occurring externally to the organization may have an impact on the organization both in terms of its structure, procedures, and policies.

Perhaps an example may serve to illustrate this point. Assume that a series of organizations become sensitive to the need of building better relationships among their citizenry. These units include a human relations council, a local chapter of the League of Women Voters, a local council of churches, and one of the more prestigious fraternal organizations within the community. Their desire to further the cause of better relationships among people leads them to adopt a program calling for a revision of school district lines so as to change residential patterns that, in their opinion, bring about de facto segregation in the school system. While these groups have little more than a peripheral relationship with the local school system, quite obviously the program that they have adopted will have profound impacts on the school system both in terms of its policy and its internal structure.

The coming together of the social organizations would obviously be found in the L22 cell of the model; the interaction between those units and the school system as the units attempt to get their program adopted is obviously an example of the L21 category.

Figure 1 depicts the various interactions that can occur around a problem common to many school systems today.

Accepting the existence of a high level of interdependence between organizations and their environments, several scholars have attempted to construct models depicting strategies which either are or may be used in relating organizations to their community setting. Thompson and McEwen[4] suggest two basic strategies: 1) competition, and 2) cooperation. Under cooperation three subtypes are listed:

[3]Warren G. Bennis, "Organizational Developments and the Fate of Bureaucracy," Address to meeting of American Psychological Association, Los Angeles, California, September 1964. Bennis postulates that a bureaucratic organization is least likely to cope and survive in a rapidly changing environment.

[4]Thompson and McEwen, *op. cit.*

1) *Bargaining:* To the extent that a second party's support is necessary, that party is in a position to exercise a veto over the final choice of alternative goals and thus actually participates in decisions. I posit this to mean that faced with a decision on how best to meet desegregation demands a school system will actively negotiate with those parts of the community power structure whose support on such matters as increased appropriations or other policy changes is essential.

2) *Cooptation:* This strategy usually takes the form of establishing overlapping memberships between the focal organization (school system) and another organization related to it in simple or complicated ways (P.T.A. or Chamber of Commerce) as a means of arriving at compatible goals.

3) *Coalition:* This refers to a combination or merger of two or more organizations for a common purpose. Illustrative of this technique might be a merger of a school system and a vocational training unit of a state department of labor.[5]

FIGURE 1
Interreactions Between a School System and Its Environment

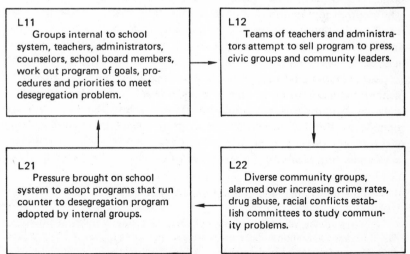

L11
    Groups internal to school system, teachers, administrators, counselors, school board members, work out program of goals, procedures and priorities to meet desegregation problem.
	L12
	    Teams of teachers and administrators attempt to sell program to press, civic groups and community leaders.

L21
    Pressure brought on school system to adopt programs that run counter to desegregation program adopted by internal groups.
	L22
	    Diverse community groups, alarmed over increasing crime rates, drug abuse, racial conflicts establish committees to study community problems.

[5]Examples used are mine, not those of Thompson and McEwen.

Carrying the transactional process one step forward, Litwak and Meyer[6] generate several sets of typologies of administrative styles and of mechanisms which link the school to the community. They offer three modes of community-school contacts as representative of existing patterns of interrelation:

1) *Locked door policy:* Under this policy there is minimal access by the community as far as school programs and policy decisions are concerned. Teachers and administrators in such systems see themselves as professionals who are in a better position to define pupil needs and educational policy than are laymen.

2) *Open door policy:* This policy involves maximal access with professionals, parental groups, and others sharing responsibility for educational policy.

3) *Balanced policy:* In this system situational factors are assessed by school administrators to determine the respective weight to be given to public access (group influence) and professional exclusiveness.[7]

Most school administrators obviously strive for the balanced policy but meet increasing difficulty as competing external groups (the L22 of the Emery-Trist model) individually demand access (L21) while internal groups (L11) stridently stress the prerogatives of professional expertise. The school administrator thus becomes the "man-in-the-middle" between well-organized factions each demanding its share of the policy pie.

The intensity of the interaction between a school and its environment is at least partially a function of the nature of the environment. Studies appear to indicate that community attitudes toward and their impacts on school organizations are differentially related to income, education, nativity, religious affiliation, age, homogeneity, and stability of population. Three of the more interesting of these studies are reported below.

Alford[8] reported on an attempt to consolidate two school districts in California. He found great resistance in District A, which was homoge-

[6]In F. Reiss (ed.), *Schools in a Changing Society* (New York: Free Press, 1965).

[7]For a similar set of community-school administrative styles, see Burton R. Clark, "Interorganizational Patterns in Education," *Administrative Science Quarterly* 10 (September 1955): 224–37.

[8]Robert R. Alford, "School District Reorganization and Community Integration," *Harvard Education Review* 30 (1960): 350–71.

neous ethnically and economically with little class stratification. The school in District A was a symbolic force defining the town's identity and was perhaps its most distinct local institution. In this district, in common with many others in this country, participation in school affairs was a part of local life and tended to bridge what few cleavages did exist in the community. District B was not as homogeneous, and, for this reason, did not resist consolidation nearly as vigorously.

Carter and Sutthoff,[9] in a mail survey of community leaders in 1054 school districts combined with some oral interviews, found that residents of large districts focused on the services provided by schools and tended to rely on public media for information about the school system. Residents of small school districts, on the other hand, focused more sharply on the personal qualities and characteristics of school administrators and teachers, and relied on face-to-face contacts with school officials for school information.

Carter[10] in a sample of 500 urban school districts found a low level of interest in and information about school issues. In general, residents of these districts felt cut off from schools and felt powerless to affect school operations.

The general impact of all environmental studies demonstrates that highly stable homogeneous communities can and probably do have a substantial effect on school operations. Such communities tend to place a high premium on school matters, tend to look upon the school as a focal point of community affairs, and the residents expect to be consulted—formally or informally—on all important changes in procedures or organization. The high level of consensus in such communities can be a force with which school administrators must contend. Urban areas, on the contrary, as a result of their high level of diversity often exhibit extreme levels of dissensus which tend to dilute the ability of any one group to act as an effective force for or against any particular school policy.

As the countermovements from country to city and from city to suburb continue, several factors of grave consequence to school systems

[9] *Communities and Their Schools,* Technical Report, Stanford: Stanford University School of Education, 1960.

[10] *Voters and Their Schools,* Technical Reports, Stanford: Stanford University Institute for Communications Research, 1960.

can be anticipated. School districts covering the central city in an urban area will begin to exhibit certain intracity conflicts as ghetto residents— homogeneous groupings within a heterogeneous population—begin to assume the characteristics of stable nonurban districts. Suburban districts, economically, ethnically, and socially homogeneous will continue to exhibit a high level of consensus on educational matters. Efforts to enlarge school districts could therefore run into very serious obstacles as suburban residents contend against being merged with what they consider to be a group of persons with backgrounds different than their own. Ghetto residents, on the other hand, may also fight against merger for the reason that they may well lose control of the education of their children. While central city non-ghetto residents may not feel strongly about such matters, the existence of two highly motivated groups joined in their opposition to any consolidation of city-suburb school systems, may well spell the defeat of such consolidations. The intense emotions stirred and articulated in the 1968 struggle within the New York City school system may be interpreted as a trend that may be emulated across the nation.

The instability of urban-rural life-styles and the unsettled question of ghetto militancy are but parts of the turbulence that is characteristic of contemporary life in the area of school administration. The rapidity of change, the massive effect of television which brings to the living rooms of practically all citizens dramatic examples of educational experiments has made the life of the school administrator an uneasy one. A television program depicting new programs in mathematics or science can bring a P.T.A. or an industrial group to the door of the superintendent demanding that his school begin such a program. A television commentator who asks, "Does your school have a safe driving program? If not, find out why," can cause a deluge of calls. A militant human relations commission can demand instant faculty desegregation, a temperance group calls for lectures on the evils of drink, a chamber of commerce call for more vocational training in order to make a community more attractive to industry, a large private foundation offers funds—on a matching basis— for an experimental program, a state educational agency decides on the basis of several reasons—at least some of which are political—that certain programs should be added to or taken from a curriculum, and the U.S. Office of Education peers through a door leading to federal funds or federal regulations. Through all this the administrator sits attempting to balance competing interests—a shorthand way of saying he must assess and weigh each of the demands and attempt to ascertain which has the most power behind it.

In their excellent book[11] Cyert and March state that "so long as the environment of the firm is unstable—and predictably unstable—the heart of the theory (of the firm) must be the process of short-run adaptive reactions." Drucker[12] and Gardner[13] echo this concept of rapidity and turbulence of today's environment. It becomes increasingly obvious that rational strategies of planned innovation, long-range planning, and even goal structures are being undermined by unexpected and unpredictable changes. A policy, a structure, a procedure that met the needs of a system a brief time ago becomes untenable as one eruption after another occurs in an organization's setting. The "process of short-run adaptive reactions" is perhaps all that is possible in today's school system.

---

[11]Richard M. Cyert and James G. March (eds.), *A Behavioral Theory of the Firm* (Englewood Cliffs, N.J.: Prentice-Hall, 1963), xxx.

[12]Peter F. Drucker, "The Big Power of Little Ideas," *Harvard Business Review* 42 (May 1964): 6–8.

[13]John W. Gardner, *Self-Renewal* (New York: Harper and Row, 1964), p. 107.

14

Civil Service and Managing Work

Robert T. Golembiewski

Nature seldom allows us to get what we wish without paying her price. This truism is commonly illustrated by the delicate balance in animal life which often cannot be disturbed to satisfy man's wants. (e.g., for fox hunting) without demanding of man in return (e.g., by increases in the rabbit population and in crop damage).

The several civil service systems in this country also illustrate this bittersweet combination of intended and unintended consequences. The argument here will not go to the extreme of one observer, in whose judgment the United States Civil Service Commission was the single greatest obstacle to the successful waging of World War II.[1] Rather, the focus here will be upon several characteristics of our civil service systems that have as presumably unintended consequences an increase in the burdens of managing work. For the most part, the analysis of management problems will derive from the research literature dealing with behavior in organizations, a field of study presently seething with activity.

I. The goal-matrix of our civil service movement

The nature of these unintended consequences is suggested by the matrix of goals, or purposes, underlying our civil service movement. The

Reprinted with permission of author and publisher from *American Political Science Review* 56 (December 1962): 961–74.

[1]John Fisher, "Let's Go Back to the Spoils System," reproduced in part in Dwight Waldo (ed.), *Ideas and Issues in Public Administration* (New York, 1953), pp. 200–201.

primary goal, of course, was the separation of the management of public work from party patronage. Within this overriding goal, Sayre has noted three early subsidiary purposes of our public personnel systems:[2]

1. the guarantee of equal treatment of all employees and all applicants for employment;
2. the application of the logic (or theory) and methods of "scientific management"; and
3. the development of a public career service.

These goals define the field of my present effort. Detailed analysis later will demonstrate the significance for the management of work of the unintended consequences which derive from the ways adopted to achieve these purposes. I take this opportunity to suggest the general nature of these consequences.

Consider first the general tethers on the management of work implicit in the historical pursuit of the three purposes listed. The guarantee of equal treatment, to begin with, has never quite made peace with the managerially convenient notion that unequal contributions demand unequal reward. To take a recent and characteristic example, the teachers' union in Illinois has lately expressed violent opposition to a proposal for merit pay increases based upon performance. This opposition goes deeper than the convenience of seniority or of hours of graduate study as objective criteria for pay increases and far deeper than the blatant protectionism of hacks. However lofty the motives, their effect is clear. In practice, the struggle toward the "equal treatment" goal virtually forced public personnel systems into a monumental preoccupation with technique and mechanics. As Sayre concluded:[3]

> Its main effect has been to move personnel administration, in the words of Gordon Clapp, "into the cold objective atmosphere of tests, scores, weighted indices, and split-digit rankings" so completely that "these technical trappings have become symbols of the merit system."

The management of work pays a stiff price for such technical elegance. Work is notoriously insensitive to such easy capture, and the most

---

[2]Wallace Sayre, "The Triumph of Technique Over Purpose," *Public Administration Review* 8 (Spring 1948): 134–35.

[3]*Ibid.*, p. 134.

subtly contrived managerial rewards and punishments might be frustrated by an awkward distribution of test scores. Moreover, these technical trappings put powerful weapons into the hands of "staff" people. That more than one "line" manager has been stymied by one of these "split-digit rankings" without accepting the results as divinely ordained, moreover, does nothing to lessen the often intense jurisdictional tugs-of-war encouraged by the traditional "line-staff" distinction. These tensions are apt to be increased by the time lag inherent in centralized administrative systems, and public personnel systems are usually operated centrally.

The logic and methods of "scientific management," second, tended to condemn managers to a treadmill even as it aided them. Scientific management was imported from the "practical" world of business where its impact was enormous.[4] But the impact was not one-way. Thus there is no denying the useful revolution in viewing work that the methods of scientific management sparked. However, as recent research particularly demonstrates,[5] the assumptions in the logic (or theory) of scientific management concerning man and his work were mechanistic caricatures. Consequently, the manager tended to be less effective in direct relation to the degree that he patterned his behavior on the logic of the approach. That is, the reasonable methods of scientific management often were guided by an inadequate theory. Consequently, the usefulness of engineering a task with the methods of scientific management must be differentiated sharply from the usefulness of organizing a task's component sequential steps in terms of the theory of scientific management.[6]

The establishment of a public career service, third, also tended to have unintended and unfavorable consequences which counterbalanced the favorable and intended consequences. As Sayre put it,[7]

> Stated in its most positive terms, this objective represents an effort to provide the conditions of work which will attract and hold a public service of optimum talents. In its negative aspects, the goal has been translated into

---

[4]Dwight Waldo, *The Administrative State* (New York, 1948), pp. 47–64.

[5]See my *Behavior and Organization* (Chicago: Rand McNally, 1962), esp. chs. 1—4.

[6]See my "Organizing Work: Techniques and Theories," *Advanced Management—Office Executive,* 1 (June 1962): 26–31.

[7]Sayre, *op. cit.,* pp. 134–35.

an elaborate system of protectionism. In the area of methodology the negative connotations have slowly but surely won the dominant position. ...

Such protectionism, of course, often would bind the manager severely
even as it safeguarded him (and his subordinates) from arbitrary removal.

In sum, then, striving toward the purposes of the civil service movement had its general costs. Three more specific sets of restrictions that
burden the management of work in our civil service systems will concern
us presently.

These costs of our civil service systems, however, must be kept in
perspective. Today we can profit from hindsight and a sophisticated
research literature. The efforts to achieve the separation of civil service
from patronage, in contrast, came before enough was known about the
conceptual and operational problems of the description of organization,
personality, or "position" to preclude an uncomplicated Tinker Toy approach to all three of these elements of personnel administration. That
is, simple assumptions took the place of an understanding of empirical
phenomena which were at least more complex and often essentially
different from the assumptions.

Consequently, the early approach to public personnel administration
is understandable, if inadequate. The compulsions of life could not wait
on the scientific explanation of the universe. However, necessity should
not be suffered to be a virtue, lest the original simplistic assumptions
become too deeply buried under a specialized literature. Students of
public personnel administration, fortunately, have done considerable
self-critical work of late. The determined, if preliminary, efforts since
World War II to outgrow its early biases are a leading feature of the
reorientation currently underway in public administration.[8]

II. Supervisory power and civil service

Perhaps the most rewarding clue to supervisory effectiveness in recent research exploits the "power" concept. "Power" refers, in general,
to the ability to control the job environment. Getting recommendations

[8]The outlines of this reorientation are drawn sharply in O. Glenn Stahl,
Public Personnel Administration (New York, 1956), pp. 577–82.

for promotion accepted, for example, indicates that a supervisor has relatively high power. "Power" thus conceptually complements "authority," which refers to the degree to which the formal organization legitimates a supervisor's control of the job environment. Typically, all supervisors at the same level monitoring similar operations have similar authority; and typically, these supervisors will differ in their power.

Power seems to be related to effective supervisory performance, whether it is exercised upwards, as influence with superiors, or downwards, as control of the specific job site. Pelz, for example, studied some fifty measures of supervisory practices and attitudes without finding any marked correlations with employee morale and attitudes. When the influence of a supervisor with his superior was specified, however, rather sharp differences were observed. High supervisory power was associated with effective performance.[9] Consequently, as Likert concluded, a supervisor must be an effective subordinate as well as an effective superior.[10] Otherwise, reasonably, a supervisor cannot be expected to influence his subordinates consistently.

Similarly, power expressed as control of the job site is associated with effective performance. Likert provides much supporting data. A comparison between the top third and the bottom third of departments (ranked in terms of productivity) is particularly relevant here. Personnel in the "top" departments, in contrast with the "bottom" departments, uniformly attributed greater influence over "what goes on in your department" to these four sources: higher management; plant management; department manager; and the workers themselves. Moreover, the "top" departments also desired that greater influence be exercised by all four sources than did the "bottom" departments. Significantly, the greatest differences between the "top" and "bottom" departments are in the power attributed to department managers (their primary supervisors) and in the power the men desired that department managers exercise.[11] These are reasonable results. A low-power supervisor has little leverage

[9]Donald C. Pelz, "Interaction and Attitudes Between Scientists and Auxiliary Staff," *Administrative Science Quarterly* 4 (December 1959): 321–36, and *ibid.* 4 (March 1960): 410–25.

[10]Rensis Likert, *New Patterns of Management* (New York, 1961), p. 114.

[11]*Ibid.*, pp. 56–57.

for motivating his men *via* his control over the job site. That is, the men have little reason to take him seriously.

If the reasons for the importance of supervisory power to effective performance seem clear enough, our civil service systems do little to ease the burdens of managing work *via* increases in supervisory power. This is particularly lamentable because much evidence suggests that the "power" variable may be influenced substantially by the design of the job, by the organization structure (of which more later), and by training. The supervisor's personality, in short, does not appear to be the crucial (or major) factor in determining power.

Although only empirical research can establish the point definitely, there seems ample evidence of this failure of civil service systems to respond to the need to facilitate the management of work by increasing supervisory power. On the broadest level, the first and third primary goals of the civil service movement certainly do not encourage supervisory power; and (as will be demonstrated) the application of the logic and methods of scientific management has the same effect.

To become more specific, these limitations on supervisory power have many practical impacts. For example, first-line supervisors seem to have less control over hiring and firing than their counterparts in business. The difficulty in business organizations of firing or reductions-in-force need not be underplayed, but the elaborate review procedures and the novel "bumping" arrangements[12] often found in our civil service systems probably admit of less flexibility in public agencies even on the part of officials at relatively high organizational levels. Raw turnover ratios seem to support this position.[13] Similarly, the emphasis upon seniority in promotions and pay increases in the public service plus the failures of supervisory rating of employee performance[14] —both common in our civil service systems—suggest that the environment in public agencies has not been conducive to the general heightening of supervisory power.

Some counterforces are at work, although they do not promise immi-

[12]James E. Drury, *The Displaced Career Executive Program* (Inter-University Case Program, University of Alabama Press, 1952).

[13]Stahl, *op. cit.,* p. 473.

[14]Felix Nigro, *Public Personnel Administration* (New York, 1959), p. 295.

nent change in the present condition of limited encouragement of supervisory power. Thus the federal program for rewarding superior performance permits a modest increase in supervisory power. Even in this case, however, apparently many agencies have preferred to ride very close herd over the recommendations of lower-level supervisors or (in at least one case of which I have personal knowledge) to neglect the immediate supervisor altogether. Thus this program not only died aborning as an opportunity to increase supervisory power, but its administration may even further reduce that power.

All this, be it noted, is not by way of an argument for arbitrary managerial or supervisory action. Just such abuses, of course, supplied motivation for the restraints emphasized above. The stress here, rather, is upon ways of reinforcing formal authority so as to permit greater effectiveness consistent with the policies of an agency. Just as in the case of any delegation, that is, attempts to increase supervisory power imply training and the development of suitable overhead controls. Moreover, "power" in the relevant research does not imply heavy-handed coercive techniques, which most subjects interpret as lack of control of the environment. Evidence such as that reviewed below in the context surrounding footnotes 48–51 supports this point.

The task of inducing high supervisory power, then, is more delicate than a mere reversal of gears toward the "spoils system" or advocacy of an administrative law of the jungle.

III. Job design and civil service

Similarly, our civil service systems tend to limit the potential for increasing managerial effectiveness implicit in job design. The second primary goal noted above is the chief culprit, with strong support from the goal of "equal treatment." Their interaction in increasing managerial burdens can be illustrated in two ways: by considering specific job content, and by considering the place of the job in the broad organization structure.

In its doctrine about simplifying job content, particularly, the logic of scientific management makes difficulties for managing work effectively. As in industry, at low organization levels, the process of routinization often has been carried too far in the public service. The effects of "job enlargement" on employee performance, at least in business concerns,[15] suggest the contribution to effective management that may be gained by adding content to a worker's responsibilities. This may be accomplished by increasing the scope of jobs or by rotating individuals through several jobs.[16] The crucial factor does not seem to be the number of task-elements given to an individual or the complexity of these elements. Patently, a job could become too complex. Rather, the significant point seems to be that various techniques of job enlargement, when they work, work because they increase the worker's control over his job environment.[17] Hence the success of plans for increasing the employee's control over factors which are not in his flow of work, such as that often called "bottom-up management."[18]

The effects of "job enlargement" may be explained in terms of the earlier analysis. In Likert's study, as already noted, employees in high-producing units felt that they themselves exercised and desired more power over their work than did individuals in low-producing units. This is consistent with the favorable effects on output commonly reported in the "job enlargement" literature, while it suggests an apparent paradox. Note that Hi-Pro units ranked themselves *and* three levels of supervisors as higher on "power" than did Lo-Pro units. This might seem curious, but only if one assumes that there is only so much "power" to be had, so that what superiors gain subordinates must lose. The fact seems to be, on the contrary, that a high-power supervisor can afford to (and usually does) allow his subordinates to exercise greater power also.[19] A low-power supervisor is in such an insecure position that he can seldom bring himself to be so generous. The real paradox, then, is that the apparently most straightforward way of adding to one's power is often the most direct way of reducing it. The common mechanical conceptions of organized activity implicit in scientific management discourage such thinking.

[15]Chris Argyris, *Personality and Organization* (New York, 1957), pp. 177–87, summarizes many relevant studies.

[16]*Ibid.,* p. 177.

[17]*Ibid.,* p. 180.

[18]William Given, *Bottom-Up Management* (New York, 1949).

[19]The point has been amply demonstrated in experimental situations. See James G. March, "Influence Measurement in Experimental and Semi-Experimental Groups," *Sociometry* 19 (March 1956): 26–71.

The often marked consequences of job enlargement may be illus-trated briefly. Machine operations in an industrial concern, for example, had been plagued by an array of difficulties: productivity and quality were falling; and tension between operators and inspectors was growing. The crucial factor was that the tool in this particular operation, when dulled to a certain point, would suddenly begin producing pieces which did not meet specifications. Inspectors were not always able to spot such sud-den deteriorations in the product quickly, and operators (inspection not being *their* job) did not always cease work even when the quality was obviously unacceptable. Inspection reports helped little when they did come, the operators marking them down as "ancient history." The solu-tion was easy. Simple gauges were given to operators to make periodic checks on their production, and the operators were allowed to decide when it was necessary to resharpen their cutting tools. The conse-quences: runs of defective products became shorter and less frequent; the nagging tension between inspectors and operators was reduced; and output zoomed.

Examples need not be confined to industrial operations. In a paper-work operation, similarly, a rather simple change increased output by 30 percent and reduced employee turnover by 70 percent.[20]

Although the design of the job could be an important means of reducing the problems of managing work, however, our civil service systems do not encourage the exploitation of such techniques as job enlargement. Consider only one feature which has an inhibiting effect, the very detailed job descriptions common in the public service. That these are an important part of the mechanisms for guaranteeing equal treatment of employees and for developing a career service does little to encourage flexibility in job design. Employee unions and the civil service commission staff can make much of these job descriptions, even in cases in which employees solidly favor changes of a job-enlargement sort. The difficulty is not necessarily avoided by job descriptions which conclude: "or other duties the supervisor may designate." Custom, employee unions, and an overprotective civil service commission can void such open-end descriptions.

[20]Peter F. Drucker, *The Practice of Management* (New York, 1954), pp. 291–92.

Perhaps, however, this leans too heavily on personal (and limited) experience. Some administrators no doubt pay little attention to detailed job descriptions, except for such purposes as convincing the civil service commission that an individual deserves a multi-step promotion. And it may be argued that the significant point is not whether detailed job descriptions exist, but whether strong employee unions exist. Even in such cases, however, the detailed job description is part of the institutional framework within which management and union must function.

In determining the place of the job in the broad organizational pattern, our civil service systems also increase the problems of managing work. Consider two characteristics which tend to dominate patterns of organization in the public service, a limited span of control and organization by function or (at lower levels) by process. These characteristics largely derive from the impact of scientific management upon public personnel administration. Analysis of these two characteristics is particularly useful because it demonstrates, among other features, their tendency to reduce supervisory power.

The analysis of these two characteristics is facilitated by some simplified graphics.[21] Figure 1A presents the orthodox organization of functions (or processes) A, B, C—which may be taken to be any components whose integration is required to perform some administrative task—under the condition of a limited span of control. Figure 1B presents the more unorthodox organization by product (or discrete sub-assembly), which permits a far broader span of control.

The functional model, with modest reservations, can be considered *the* pattern for government organizing. This does not do full justice to the diversity of actual organizational arrangements, admittedly. Various factors—size, pressure of work, geography, and the like—have encouraged significant deviations from the functional model. Thus the Justice Department long ago surrendered the fancy of having every government lawyer in the department. The functional model, however, is commonly encountered in practice and it is certainly the most commonly prescribed model

[21]The parent of this analysis may be found in James C. Worthy, *Big Business and Free Men* (New York, 1959), pp. 90–99.

FIGURE 1A
Functional (Process) Organization with Narrow Span of Control

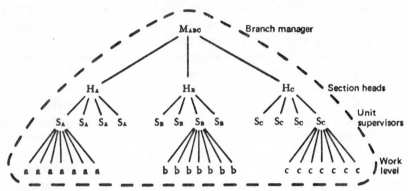

in the literature, as in the Hoover Commission's *Report on the General Management of the Executive Branch.*

The following contrast of the functional model with the product model, then, requires that two points be kept in mind. First, the functional model does not guide all public organizing, but it is nonetheless influential. Second, the product model will not always be a feasible alternative,

FIGURE 1B
Product (Discrete Sub-Assembly) Organization with Broad Span of Control

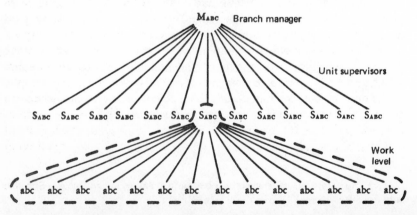

although it often will be. The contrast, that is, has much to recommend it, although hardly everything. Thus, although the analysis may have an either-or flavor, many other factors would serve to soften the contrast in practice and would guide the choice in specific cases of the functional model, the product model, or combinations of the two.

These simple variations in the organization of jobs in larger structures can have profound consequences for the management of work. In general, the type of structure common in most public agencies (see Figure 1A) incurs substantial costs avoided by the less familiar structure in Figure 1B. These costs derive from three features associated with these two patterns of structure: job enlargement; the size of the "managerial entity"; and supervisory power.

First, to point up the obvious, Figure 1B is based upon job enlargement at all levels. Each employee at the work-level in Figure 1B performs all three components of the task, and each supervisor's responsibilities encompass all three. Figure 1A's emphasis upon routinization limits the scope, and perhaps thereby the effectiveness of the management of work. Of course, there are some limits on the functions or processes (A, B, C, . . .) that may be strung together. In general, however, the limits seem to be very broad indeed.[22]

Second, the "managerial entity" is vastly larger in Figure 1A than in Figure 1B. The size of the managerial entity can have profound consequences. It may appear, for instance, that the structure in Figure 1B puts too much strain on the capacities of management, because of the apparently greater demands it imposes upon the supervisors. In reality, however, structures such as that in Figure 1A often imply greater (and different) demands upon management talent. Figure 1B structures reduce in significant ways the management burden carried by M_{ABC} and the supervisors as well. The difficulties faced by M_{ABC} in structures like that in Figure 1A cause considerable problems for supervisors, for example, by tending to reduce their supervisory power. Many of the problems associated with sizeable organizations, more generally, derive not from the aggregate size of the organization, but from the size of its component managerial entities. Thus the manager in our hypothetical organization

---

[22]The point is supported by the example in Drucker, *op. cit.*, p. 291. See also Argyris, *op. cit.*, pp. 177–87.

in Figure 1A directs the work of 99 employees and encounters the difficulties to be enumerated below; the manager in Figure 1B oversees the work of 195 employees, yet significant problems facing the management of work are reduced.

The "managerial entity" concept warrants further analysis. Worthy defines it in these terms:[23]

> The administrative unit can be no smaller than that portion of the organization falling within the jurisdiction of an individual who controls enough elements of the total process to make effective decisions regarding the total process.

A high-level managerial entity might be organized around some total product, for example, water resource development in the Kings River Valley. The processing by each of several competing teams of all categories of mail received by the Government Printing Office, with each team handling all correspondence from writers whose names begin with designated letters of the alphabet, illustrates the kind of discrete sub-assembly around which a low-level managerial entity might be organized.

At whatever level of organization, then, a "managerial entity" contains that parcel of process-components necessary for the performance of some discrete task. The areas enclosed by the heavy dotted lines in the two figures above symbolize "managerial entities." Interpretively, any S_{ABC} in Figure 1B can "get all the way around" our hypothetical administrative task. In Figure 1A, in contrast, only M_{ABC} can do this job. M_{ABC} in Figure 1A has a managerial entity which contains 100 individuals; that of S_{ABC} contains only 15.

Many of the problems in sizeable organizations derive from the failure to restrict the size of the organization's managerial entities. Haire's analogy seems apt in this connection. He suggested the mushrooming problems caused by the growth in the size of organizations *via* the "square-cube law" applied to the story of Jack and the Beanstalk:[24]

> . . . Jack had nothing to fear from the Giant. If he were, as he is pictured, ten times as large as a man and proportioned like one, Jack was perfectly safe.

[23]Worthy, *op. cit.*, pp. 92–93.

[24]Mason Haire (ed.), *Modern Organization Theory* (New York: Wiley, 1959), pp. 273–74.

The Giant's mass would be 10^3 or a thousand times a man's, because he was ten times as big in every dimension. However, the cross section of his leg bones would have increased in only two dimensions, and they would be 10^2 or a hundred times as big as a man's. A human bone simply will not support ten times its normal load, and the Giant, in walking, would break his legs and be helpless.

In a similar way, arithmetic increases in the size of the managerial entity seem to generate exponential increases in the problems of the management of work. Meeting these increases in size within the framework of the type of organization structure in Figure 1A does nothing to reduce these difficulties.

This general position can be elaborated. The size of the managerial entity, in sum, is likely to affect such significant features of administration as: the time lag between the perception of a problem and action on it, which influences supervisory power; the style of supervision; the measurement and the motivation of performance; and the training of subordinates.

Patently, first, decisions will tend to be pushed upward in an organization such as that in Figure 1A; for only M_{ABC} oversees all of the components which require integration. As a result, delegation to supervisors is all but restricted to routine matters, that is, those which involve the single component supervised by any supervisor and only that component.

The separation of decision-making from the action level often has significant costs. Overloading upper levels may make time-pressure a very serious factor, the more so if the stakes are high. A shutdown in any of the sections in Figure 1A might cause output to drop as low as zero. The manager, then, is under great pressure to assure that A, B, and C are integrated, and he is likely to exert that pressure downward. This does not encourage upward communication, in turn, which is difficult enough in the "tall" organization described in Figure 1A. (Notice that Figure 1B, with 69 percent more people, has one less organization level than Figure 1A.) The efforts of the manager to fight the daily battle of integration of the components of his operation and to get the information required for his job, finally, will tend to undercut any efforts by the supervisors to gain high power. The common development of large "staff" units complements this tendency.

In contrast, decisions in Figure 1B organizations would strongly tend to be forced down to the action level, and certainly at least to the level of S_{ABC}. Indeed, M_{ABC} may have no other reasonable alternative, given his broad span of control. Upward communication and supervisory power often will be affected favorably. M_{ABC}, consequently, should be freed from the unremitting pressure of integration implicit in a Figure 1A structure. Downtime at any work station, for example, will not cause difficulty throughout the managerial entity. Output would fall at most by $1/N$. The manager therefore could devote himself to motivating superior performance, to training and counseling, and the like, rather than attempting to eliminate the possibility of error.

These comments on decision-making, second, suggest that the two types of structures encourage different styles of supervision. The structure in Figure 1A encourages "close supervision," i.e., detailed instructions, persistent attempts to direct and observe performance, and the like. The limited span of control, of course, permits this, and the pressure for the integration of the task components may force it. The structure in Figure 1B encourages "general supervision," i.e., monitoring performance in terms of results with considerable freedom for the employee so long as he is performing up to standard. Close supervision of janitors, for example, would require such directions as: "You will sweep from left to right, forty strokes per minute," and correspondingly close checks on performance. General supervision, in contrast, would assume competence and give such instructions as: "Sweep the floors in such time that you are able to get your other work done and so that the floor will reflect x units of light from a refractometer." The refractometer provides the check on performance. Acknowledgedly, this goes a little far. All of the components of general supervision are there, however, especially the measure of performance.

Structures of the type in Figure 1A pay a heavy cost to the degree that they in fact do encourage close supervision. In one study, for example, less than 30 percent of the work teams whose first- or second-level supervisors practiced close supervision had high output. Nearly 70 percent of the work units receiving only general supervision had high output.[25]

[25]Dorwin Cartwright and Alvin Zander (eds.), *Group Dynamics* (Evanston, 1953), esp. pp. 617–19.

The reader may suppose, third, that the manager and supervisors in a Figure 1B organization would face an impossible task in motivating and measuring performance. For general supervision must be based upon performance standards, and what will keep standards high if the supervisor "gets off their backs?" But the several units headed by an S_{ABC}, each performing the same task, obviously set the stage for a relative measure of performance. They are in competition with each other, which tends to keep performance high. This would complement the added contributions to be expected because of the job enlargement practiced in 1B-type structures. At the same time, reduced "line-staff" conflict seems implied by this potential for motivation and measurement, "staff" development being in large part due to top-level management's difficulties in motivating and, especially, measuring performance.

Figure 1A organizations do not offer the same possibilities. One might try to encourage competition within, for example, some S_A unit, or between the S_A units and the S_B units. But competition of that sort, as experimental studies suggest, is not likely to aid performance on most tasks,[26] Since the tasks themselves are not comparable, and may indeed be incommensurable. The point may be driven home by considering this proposition: Assembling all As (or Bs or Cs) in organizationally separate units encourage the restriction of output and invites substantial jurisdictional conflict when the responsibility for an error must be assigned. Much evidence supports this proposition.[27] Responsibility is far more difficult to assign in a 1A-type structure, for at least three inspections would be required to permit accurate assignment of praise or blame, one after each of the component operations. Figure 1B organizations would require only one such inspection. Such considerations, and there are many others, attest to the difficulties of motivating and measuring performance in Figure 1A organizations.

These features of Figure 1B organizations suggest a way out of the objection that public agencies are not guided by "profit" and that therefore performance measurement is difficult. In Figure 1A organizations, in

[26]Robert T. Golembiewski, *The Small Group: An Analysis of Research Concepts and Operations* (University of Chicago Press, 1962), pp. 202–4.

[27]Eliot D. Chapple and Leonard R. Sayles, *The Measure of Management* (New York, 1961), pp. 18–45.

business, the measurement of macroscopic profit does little to determine the often crucial measurement of the effectiveness of constituent units. Hence many business enterprises have approached the type of organization sketched in Figure 1B by establishing "individual profit centers" within (for example) a plant. Their services are then "sold" internally, sometimes with the useful provision that outside purchase is possible if price or quality are not considered appropriate by the "buyer."[28] This encourages self-discipline of both "buyer" and "seller." Comptroller W. J. McNeil worked for years to install arrangements of this sort in the Department of Defense, for the provision of common procurement of goods and services, as a means of economy and of strengthening the secretary's hand.

In any case, fourth, Figure 1B organizations seem to have a definite advantage in the training of subordinates. Patently, S_{ABC} faces training challenges not available to S_A (or S_B or S_C) in the normal course of events. Reasonably, then, organization structures such as that in Figure 1B should tend toward the early elimination of those without management ability, while it would attract the more able. Reasonably, also, high satisfaction and output should characterize Figure 1B organizations. These expectations, indeed, are supported by some research in the Sears, Roebuck chain[29] and elsewhere.[30]

Despite these (and other) advantages of 1B structures, our public personnel systems do not provide a congenial home for them. The dominant emphasis in these systems—and it is no doubt often a necessary emphasis—is negative rather than positive. As one observer with high-level experience in both government and industry noted:[31]

> ... no matter how well briefed on federal service peculiarities the private business executive may be, one of the first things he notices in public

[28]W. H. Mylander, "Management by Executive Committee," *Harvard Business Review* 33 (May 1950): 51–58.

[29]See William F. Whyte, *Man and Organization* (Homewood, III.: Irwin, 1959), pp. 11–16.

[30]Ernest Dale, "Centralization versus Decentralization," *Advanced Management* 21 (June 1956): 15.

[31]Marver Bernstein, *The Job of the Federal Executive* (Washington, D.C.: Brookings Institution, 1958), pp. 34–35.

administration is this emphasis on procedure and routine. This emphasis is admittedly necessary and desirable provided it does not make method an end in itself. When it does, over-organized bewilderment results. The new-comer to top management positions in the federal service frequently feels that the organization and methods set up with the laudable idea of keeping him from doing wrong actually result in making it excessively difficult to do right.

This emphasis, despite its legitimacy, seems to have been overdone at all levels. Overdone or not, it is something to know what it costs to preserve the emphasis in Figure 1A structures.

Generations of organization theorists have labored hard to preserve the fiction of the unity of command in our public affairs, this being the very slender thread by which we demonstrate that the electorate really does control the administration through its election of the president. One may judge the impact of this theory upon supervisory practices from the longevity of the logically consistent but unrealistic notion that "politics" and "administration" are somehow separate. This notion, of course, is the keystone of our civil service systems. Their failure to respect the realities of delegation hardly augurs for better treatment of this matter at lower organization levels. Comfortable as the fiction of unity of command may be to many, multi-line relations exist. We may choose to neglect this datum for various reasons, as the Hoover Commission did in arguing for a structure such as that in Figure 1A.[32] But this neglect may prove embarrassing,[33] and it is very likely that our theoretical simplicism has a high cost. Gaus long ago put the argument for a multi-line view in these convincing terms.[34]

Such a theory ... is the only one which fits the facts of contemporary delegation of wide discretionary power by electorates, constitutions, and legislatures to the administrators [who] must, of necessity, determine some

[32]Hoover Commission, *Report on the General Management of the Executive Branch* (Washington, D.C., 1949), pp. 1, 3–4.

[33]As, e.g., in *Morgan vs. United States,* 298 U.S. 468, where the Secretary of Agriculture was rebuked for deciding a case he had not heard in person.

[34]In Gaus, Leonard D. White, and Marshall E. Dimock, *The Frontiers of Public Administration* (University of Chicago Press, 1940), p. 91.

part of the purpose and a large part of the means whereby it will be achieved in the modern state.

Finally, the accepted pattern of organization in public agencies (as well as in business concerns) is functional. This reflects the historic strength of the model sketched in Figure 1A and suggests the barriers which will restrain attempts to approach the Figure 1B model in organizing.

IV. Job description and civil service

It says worlds, while it avoids an enormous complexity, to note that our civil service systems typically are based upon a duties classification, as opposed to a rank classification. Public personnel specialists have gone in for a duties classification with a sometimes uncritical zeal. As Nigro explains:[35]

> In a duties classification, the beginning point is a detailed analysis of the tasks required in the individual position. In fact, the tendency in the United States has been to make fairly minute investigations of job content.

The emphasis need not be exaggerated, for the specialists have providently refrained from stressing the content of all jobs. The handling of secretarial positions—whose importance is usually measured by secretaries and bosses in terms of what the boss does rather than what the secretary does—is perhaps the most striking illustration of what has been called the "realistic" approach to classification.[36] But the bias of job description in this country has not moved very far from the classic expression it was given, for example, in the 1932 classification plan for Philadelphia. Nigro called this "one of the best books of specifications on record." It listed twenty individual classes of clerks, for each of which specifications had been developed. Specifications also were stated for

[35]Nigro, *op. cit.,* p. 85.

[36]Julius E. Eitington, "Injecting Realism into Classification," *Public Personnel Administration* 15 (March 1952): 31–35.

thirty additional classes of principal and chief clerks in the various city departments.[37]

The inspirations for this emphasis on job description in our public personnel systems seem clear enough. The logic and methods of scientific management—which encouraged the view of organization as a "delicate mechanism" of gear-like "positions" whose drive shaft was the line of command—clearly had their influence. Moreover, position classification provides the bases for equal treatment, general formal policies and procedures regarding recruitment, salary, promotions, and the like. Finally, position classification encourages the attempt to group similar jobs into a reasonable number of classes, sub-classes, and so on. This provided a ladder-like framework upon which a permanent career service could be built.

Despite its contribution to achieving the goals of our civil service movement, the American approach to job description has its unintended costs. Some obvious costs will be considered immediately; subsequent analysis will consider one less obvious set of costs in some detail.

Since one product of position classification was to be a manageable number of classes, first, this required a procrustean neglect of distinguishing job characteristics. The position approach, second, became the victim of its own imprecise terms. Consider the common observation that the "position" is the "universal building block of all organizations."[38] The observation has a certain validity, since all organizations contain positions. It tended to mislead the unwary, however, into supposing that "organization" is only a set of positions. The temptation to think of organization as some massive mechanical structure of positions linked by lines of authority was strong, since it apparently served to simplify the problems of personnel work.

The emphasis upon a duties classification, third, implies a substantial rigidity. Consider the difficulties of dealing with the many positions which have a kind of life cycle, with stages that impose varying demands on the incumbent. Developing an administrative role may be a very delicate task, while playing the role thereafter may be child's play. This phenome-

---

[37]Nigro, *op. cit.,* pp. 98–99.
[38]Leonard D. White, *Introduction to the Study of Public Administration* (New York, 1948), p. 28.

non is difficult to accommodate within the framework of most of our public personnel systems. Some adaptations may be made quickly enough. But often it is necessary to waste a "big" man on a job too small for him or to give a "small" man a job too big for him. Similarly, the emphasis upon a duties classification makes it difficult to utilize positions for training purposes without the stretching of a point or two by the position analyst. The traditional question—What does the incumbent do? —is not appropriate for such positions, for he may, in fact, contribute little toward immediate task performance.

The abortive struggles toward a Senior Civil Service, and then a Career Executive Program, for the federal government, reflect the tenacity of the grip of these two types of inflexibilities.[39] For it was intended that the highly mobile and select corps of administrators in such programs would be used in both of the ways alluded to above, that is, as experienced "firefighters" and as trainees getting the "big picture." The rank-in-job bias in our civil service systems played not a little part in the lack of action.

Fourth and finally, the approach *via* a duties classification taken in this country is not the only available one. Indeed, in public administration, it appears that only Canada and Brazil follow our example closely. Many personnel systems—public and business—emphasize broad and general classes rather than narrow and detailed ones. Some of the spirit claimed for the British civil service, for example, is suggested by this open-end description of the few grades of "scientific officer" in Her Majesty's service:[40]

> It is not possible to define with precision the duties of the various grades but, broadly speaking, the duties of the grades above principal scientific officer include responsibility for the administration and direction of scientific work while the principal scientific officer and lower grades concentrate on the scientific work itself.
>
> But the posts of senior principal scientific officer and above may, with Treasury authority, be created for outstanding individual research workers.

[39]Paul P. Van Riper, "The Senior Civil Service and the Career System," *Public Administration Review* 18 (Summer 1958): 189–200.

[40]Royal Commission on the Civil Service, *Introductory Factual Memorandum on the Civil Service* (London: Her Majesty's Stationery Office, 1953), p. 54.

Not infrequently, on the business side, executives will take the more extreme ground that they will not tolerate even an organization chart at their level, lest if force them into patterns of action which may become inappropriate, just as these patterns develop a vested interest in protecting personnel.

This general approach to job description has its virtues. For example, by all accounts, the British achieve great flexibility, avoid the sometimes gross artificialities of more "precise" efforts, and (one supposes) increase the power of the supervisors whose discretion is obviously emphasized. Their approach also seems to avoid that situation which haunts position analysts and outside observers alike: that an Einstein would have the same grade as any other physicist doing "similar work."

These problems of the American approach are known well enough, although they do not prove the inferiority of a detailed approach to job description in the lower classifications. These problems may have profound consequences for the management of work. At its worst, taking the mechanical aspects of job description too seriously can disrupt the flow of work. Moderation on the part of both "line" and "staff" seems indicated. The decentralization of much personnel work in the federal service suggests that just such a mature moderation has set in.

Other factors encourage a diluted devotion to the methods and theory implicit in the duties classification in this country. Here let us consider only this feature: it is not obvious that the common attempts at precision are precise about all (or most) of the elements of work which are important. This should encourage a healthy skepticism in developing and administering duties classifications. For, first, the technology of duties classification cannot support great precision now, nor is it likely to do so in the immediate future. Second, if a duties classification purports to describe the behaviors required for the effective performance of an organization's work, existing efforts commonly miss many significant possibilities. If it merely codifies existing practices it may not be worthy of vigorous support, for duties classifications are at least implicitly prescriptive.

The specific dimensions which characterize tasks are but imprecisely known. The usual guidelines for classification—level in the hierarchy, formal authority and responsibility, funds administered, and the like —are not sufficient for doing the job tidily. For example, they do not take into account whether Supervisor X is the informal as well as formal leader of his work unit. It is impractical and unjust to treat Supervisor X's job as the same whatever the answer to this question. Moreover, if a job description is prescriptive, a supervisor's socio-emotional performance cannot be overlooked. We may fairly ask of an approach which preaches and seeks precision: Precision about what?

The question remains, what is significant in describing a task? It is a disarming question. Existing research does not suggest that it has an obvious or an uncomplicated answer. Factor analysis, a sophisticated mathematical technique, perhaps offers the most hope of developing a set of dimensions which will permit us to describe jobs precisely. A technical discussion of factor analysis hardly can be attempted here. In general, however, the technique permits an initial judgment as to the number of independent dimensions necessary to account for the variation in some batch of scores (e.g., in rankings by several analysts of jobs in terms of the discretion they require incumbents to exercise). The technique has been utilized, for example, to isolate the various kinds of intellectual abilities measured by intelligence tests. There is no way to solve such problems *a priori.* Factor analysis, in sum, might well complement and direct the enormous amount of observation that normally goes into developing a duties classification and into keeping it current.

Applications of factor analysis to job description suggest the problems which must be met. The technique, for example, has been applied to the ratings of a very large number of characteristics of various jobs. Existing results do not suggest that a synthesis is imminent. A simple manual task, for example, required only a few factors to describe it in one study.[41] Another factor analysis of more complex tasks isolated twenty-three factors.[42] Yet only seven factors were considered necessary to describe the 4,000 jobs listed by the U.S. Employment Service.[43] Thus existing work does not suggest a clear pattern. To further complicate

[41]A. W. Melton, *Apparatus Tests,* AAF Aviation Psychological Program, Research Report No. 4 (Washington, D.C.: Government Printing Office, 1947).

[42]L. L. McQuitty, C. Wrigley, and E. L. Gaier, "An Approach to Isolating Dimensions of Job Success," *Journal of Applied Psychology* 38 (1954): 227–32.

[43]E. J. McCormick, R. H. Finn, and C. D. Scherps, "Patterns of Job Requirements," *Journal of Applied Psychology* 41 (1957): 358–64.

matters, there seem to be "families" of tasks for which individual sets of factor dimensions probably must be developed.[44]

Despite the inconclusiveness of such factor analytical work, two points seem clear. First, the dimensions isolated thus far do not closely resemble the guidelines implicit in much classification work. In fact, the factors need not have any obvious connection with "common-sense" notions.[45] Second, the isolation of such factors is only the initial step. Factor analysis provides a rough map of those things which are important descriptively. Successful prediction, however, is the crucial test. Such validatory work might take such a form: If the task has dimensions a and d, individuals with such-and-such training, proficiency, attitudes, and personality will prove to be high producers.

Even this preliminary factorial work has clear implications for our public personnel systems. Duties classification will have limited usefulness to the degree that task dimensions are not developed and the validatory work referred to above is not undertaken. The interim question of whether the pursuit of precision about characteristics—which may or may not be functionally important in describing the task—is worthwhile probably must remain open. The answer is not obviously in the affirmative. A fundamental reevaluation of the common approach to job description in this country seems required, while we await the scientific explanation which will permit great precision. It would seem useful to attempt to test whether general classification provides savings beyond the reach of the detailed classification.

If detail there must be in job description, many factors could fruitfully be included in the usual duties classification. One such is the style of supervision.

Different jobs seem compatible with different styles of supervision. On the available evidence, general statements under this head must be tentative, largely because we know so little about the dimensions along

---

[44]Launor F. Carter, William Haythorn, and Margaret Howell, "A Further Investigation of the Criteria of Leadership," *Journal of Abnormal and Social Psychology* 45 (1950): 350–58.

[45]The naming of factors is not always an easy task, for any factor normally has "loadings" of several variables. Hence the sometimes exotic designations of factorial structures.

which tasks differ. An example, however, may be hazarded. Provisionally, jobs may be conceived as differing in the degrees to which their performance is programmed and to which their successful performance requires interpersonal cooperation. When a task is unprogrammed and requires high interpersonal cooperation, a permissive supervisory style has seemed most appropriate for these subjects tested. An authoritarian supervisory style will cause the least socio-emotional dislocation on tasks which are highly programmed and require little interpersonal cooperation.[46] These are general relations, indeed, and require much specification of intervening conditions. Similarly, individuals with differing personality characteristics tend to perform most effectively under different supervisory styles.[47] Meeting the needs of employees *via* an appropriate supervisory style probably would serve to increase the power of supervisors, or at least to provide supervisors with a favorable environment in which to seek high power.[48]

The specification of such factors as the supervisory style congenial to a job is particularly important because the logic of scientific management encourages the choice of a generally inappropriate style. Thus close supervision—which is consistent with this theory—seems to be associated with high output in only a minority of cases, as already noted. If one had to make a choice between the two types of supervision, then, it is not crystal clear that one would be well advised to obey the logic of scientific management.

This analysis can be extended. Close supervision, patently, is encouraged by a structure such as that in Figure 1A. Supervisory pressure would seem to be most directly applicable in this model, which in turn might suggest high supervisory power. Things, however, do not seem to happen this way often. Likert reports that the more "unreasonable pressure" reportedly exerted by a supervisor, the less the power attributed to that supervisor.[49] Moreover, evidence suggests that greater supervisory pres-

[46]Robert T. Golembiewski, "Three Styles of Leadership and Their Uses," *Personnel* 38 (July—August 1961): 38–39.

[47]Allen D. Calvin, Frederick K. Hoffman, and Edgar L. Harden, "The Effect of Intelligence and Social Atmosphere on Group Problem-Solving Behavior," *Journal of Social Psychology* 45 (February 1957): 61–74.

[48]Likert, *op. cit.,* pp. 93–94.

[49]Likert, *op. cit.,* pp. 56–57.

sure serves to isolate the supervisor from his men by increasing the danger of communication.[50] In addition, pressure seems inversely related to output. For example, ten of eleven departments in Likert's study which reported little outside pressure to control the pace of work were above-average producers. Nine of ten departments reporting great pressure were below-average producers.[51] Reasonably, then, job descriptions might well profit from the specification of such job-relevant factors as the style of supervision.

This discussion of two approaches to job description—through those factors normally included, and through those factors which are often neglected—permits of simple summary. There seem to be very substantial costs of commission and omission in the job descriptions common in our civil service systems. These costs complicate the management of work, however nicely the systems fit the three core goals underlying the American approach to public personnel administration.

V. Summary

Our federal Civil Service Commission has been accustomed to serve more than one master. As one commentator noted:[52]

> "For whom does the Civil Service Commission work?" We used to reply, "Well, we think it works first for its congressional committees, second for the status employees, third for the American Legion in support of veterans' preference laws, fourth for civil service employees' unions, and possibly fifth for the President." Since the end of World War II, the President has moved up in this list but it is difficult to tell just how far.

The analysis above, in essence, argues that yet another master requires service, the development of a work environment within which a professional manager can do his most effective job. Substantial revisions in traditional thinking and technique about our civil service systems will be required to that end.

---

[50] *Ibid.,* p. 45.

[51] *Ibid.,* p. 20.

[52] Bernstein, *op. cit.,* p. 76.

15

Organization Development in Public Agencies: Perspectives on Theory and Practice*

Robert T. Golembiewski

The special genius of each age is reflected in distinctive ways of organizing work. If the preceding age stressed stability and consistency, roughly, the emphasis today is on organizing for change and variability. The specific implications are diverse and still obscure, but the general point is overwhelming. John W. Gardner reflects both the certainty and the caution. "What may be most in need of innovation is the corporation itself," he notes. "Perhaps what every corporation (and every other organization) needs is a department of continuous renewal that could view the whole organization as a system in need of continuing innovation."[1]

The major recent response to the need for planned organizational change is the burgeoning emphasis on organization development, or OD. Three themes constitute the core of typical OD concepts. As Winn explains:[2]

> The term "organization development" ... implies a normative, re-education strategy intended to affect systems of beliefs, values and attitudes within the organization so that it can adapt better to the accelerated rate of change in technology, in our industrial environment and society in general. It also includes formal organizational restructuring which is frequently initiated, facilitated and reinforced by the normative and behavioral changes.

Changing attitudes or values, modifying behavior, and inducing change in structure and policies, then, are the three core-objectives of OD pro-

Reprinted with permission of author and publisher. From *Public Administration Review* 29 (July-August 1969): 367-77.

*This article is adapted from a paper prepared for delivery at the Annual Meeting of the Southern Political Science Association, held November 6-7, 1968, in Gatlinburg, Tennessee.

grams. In contrast, the reorganization literature in political science is concept-oriented and gives little attention to changes in attitudes and behavior necessary to implement its guiding concept.

This article provides a variety of perspectives on the characteristics of OD programs, and also summarizes experience from a number of OD efforts in public agencies at federal and local levels. Not all these agencies can be identified here, unfortunately, but the data-base consists of seven cases. No attempt will be made to evaluate the effectiveness of any particular OD application; and even less is the purpose here to assess the specific technology of OD programs such as the use of sensitivity training.[3]

The motivation of this piece derives from the following propositions. First, government agencies have begun experimenting with various OD approaches, if less bullishly than business and service organizations. Second, the public sector has a variety of distinctive features that provide special challenges to achieving typical OD objectives. Third, these distinctive features have received inadequate attention in the literature and in the design of OD programs in public agencies. Fourth, applications of OD programs in public agencies probably will become more common. The need to tailor OD programs in public agencies more closely to the distinctive constraints of their environment should consequently increase sharply. Finally, students of public administration can play useful and distinct roles in such OD programs, providing they develop appropriate competencies.

A typical OD program: and the underlying network of findings and hypotheses

Despite their variety, OD programs rest on similar conceptual foundations. These foundations are a mixed bag, including relatively "hard" empirical findings and plausible hypotheses. These foundations of OD programs also prescribe how organizations ought to be so as to be effective, "healthy," or morally acceptable.

Figure 1 simplifies the web of findings/hypotheses/values that underlies the typical OD program. The figure focuses strictly on the "frontload" of OD programs; that is, on how sensitivity training or related techniques can induce greater openness, trust, and shared responsibility. Based on such social and psychological preparation, OD programs can flower diversely. For example, early exposure to sensitivity training might encourage greater openness in an organization, which in turn might highlight critical needs for changes in policies, procedures, structure, or technology. An OD program then would be appropriately expanded to meet such needs, as by additions of training programs, etc.[4]

FIGURE 1
A Simplified Model of Findings/Hypotheses Underlying the Typical OD Program

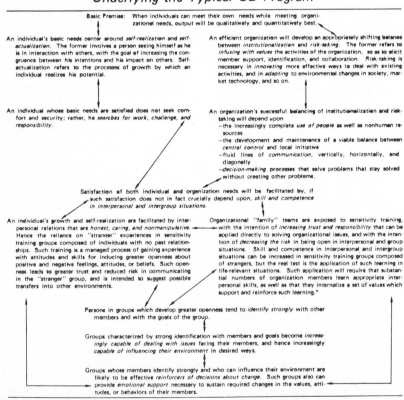

A typical OD program: major objectives

The findings/hypotheses/values underlying OD programs imply several common objectives. Overall, the goal is to release the human potential within an organization. Specifically, a typical OD program emphasizes major objectives such as these:[5]

1. To create an open, problem-solving climate throughout the organization.
2. To supplement the authority associated with role or status with the authority of knowledge and competence.
3. To locate decision-making and problem-solving responsibilities as close to the information sources as possible.
4. To build trust among individuals and groups throughout the organization.
5. To make competition more relevant to work goals and to maximize collaborative efforts.
6. To develop a reward system which recognizes both the achievement of the organization's mission (profits or service) and organization development (growth of people).
7. To increase the sense of "ownership" of organization objectives throughout the work force.
8. To help managers to manage according to relevant objectives rather than according to "past practices" or according to objectives which do not make sense for one's area of responsibility.
9. To increase self-control and self-direction for people within the organization.

Basically, the organization is seen "as a system in need of continuing innovation," and an OD program begins by stressing the development of attitudes, behaviors, and skills that will support such continuing innovation.

The list of OD objectives does double duty here. In addition to providing additional content for the concept "organization development," the list of objectives helps highlight some of the special difficulties facing OD programs in public (and especially federal) agencies. The discussion below focuses on one major question: What specific properties of public agencies make it especially difficult to approach specific objectives such as those above? Evidence comes primarily from seven OD programs at the federal and local levels in which this author has participated.

Character of the institutional environment: constraints on approaching OD objectives

Public agencies present some distinctive challenges to OD programs, as compared with business organizations where most experience with OD programs has been accumulated. Four properties of the public institutional environment particularly complicate achieving the common goals of OD programs.

Multiple access

1. As compared to even the largest of international businesses, the public environment in this country is characterized by what might be called, following David Truman, unusual opportunities for *multiple access to multiple authoritative decision makers*. Multiple access is, in intention if not always in effect, a major way of helping to assure that public business gets looked at from a variety of perspectives. Hence the purpose here is to look at the effects of multiple access rather than to deprecate it. Figure 2 details some major points of multiple access relevant to OD programs in four interacting "systems": the executive, legislative, "special interests," and mass media systems.

Multiple access has its attractive features in beginning OD programs in public agencies. For example, one large OD program was inaugurated in an economical way: a top departmental career official sponsoring an OD program had developed a relation of deep trust with the chairman and the professional staff of a congressional appropriations subcommittee, and that relation quickly, even mercurially, triumphed over lukewarm support or even opposition from the department head, the Bureau of the Budget, and the U.S. Civil Service Commission.

But multiple access can cut two ways. Funds for that very OD program "became unavailable" after its inception, despite strong support from both career and political officers at the top levels. In short, the

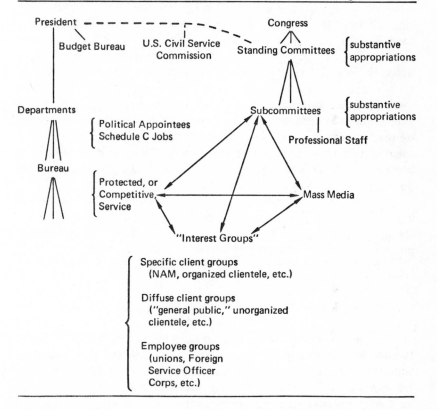

FIGURE 2
Some Critical Publics Relevant to Federal OD Programs

successful counterattack was launched by agency personnel in the pro-
tected/competitive service, an interest group representing these employees, members of a concerned substantive committee of Congress,
and the media. The two themes of the counterattack were common to
several reactions against OD programs of which I know. First, ordinary
decency required allowing the dedicated civil servants affected to complete their careers in peace and in the traditional ways, rather than being
subjected to an unwanted program that was seen as having problematic
value.[6] Second, the use of sensitivity training in the OD program was

disparaged as violating the privacy of organization members, or worse.[7]

Viewed from the perspective of top-level political and career officials intent on inaugurating a public OD program, the "iron quadrangle" in Figure 2 inspires substantial pessimism about a fair trial, in the general case. Specific conditions may raise or lower the odds, since the several links in the counterattacking forces above can be variously strong or weak. For example, a public agency may have a very positive constitutional image, which gives its top officials an important edge in presenting their case to congressional committees, the mass media, or the general public. Similarly, top political and career officials can induce—or capitalize on—organized clientele opposition to policies and procedures and use it to force changes at the protected levels. Or political resources and professional skills may provide agency executives with substantial power to control their environment.[8]

Whether the iron quadrangle is more or less integral, the design and implementation of OD programs in public agencies has given that constellation short shift. Perhaps this is because most experience with OD programs has been gained in business organizations, where nothing even remotely like the iron quadrangle exists at managerial levels.

Greater variety

2. Again as compared to business organizations, the public arena involves in all OD programs a greater variety of individuals and groups with *different and often mutually exclusive sets of interests, reward structures, and values.* In the cast outlined above, for example, the appropriations subcommittee was interested in improved operations and reduced costs. But the substantive subcommittee was concerned more with safeguarding program and personnel with which they had developed a strong identification. And never the twain did meet. Role conflicts between legislators and administrators also seem to have been significant. For example, one congressman explained his opposition to an OD program in these terms: "Improvement of efficiency is O.K., but messing with people's attitudes sounds subversive to my constituents." The agency's top administrators felt no such constituency pressure, and their view was that attitudes toward work had to be changed.

Such incongruencies of expectations, rewards, and values also occur in business organizations, of course, as in labor-management issues. In my experience, however, they occur there in less intense and exotic forms.

A conclusion need not be forced. All OD programs have to stress the development of viable "interfaces," that is, relations between individuals or groups with different values and interests. This problem is enormously complicated in public agencies undertaking OD programs, and has received little explicit attention in concept or in practice. For example, in no case that I know of has the development of an explicit interface between legislative and administrative interests been attempted as part of an OD program, apparently in part because of the constitutional separation of powers.

The failure to build such interfaces was a major contributor to the death of a major recent urban OD program. Departmental officers rejected the idea of attempting to build an explicit interface between a substantive subcommittee, an appropriations subcommittee, and the agency as part of an OD program. Tradition, jealousy over prerogatives, and separation of powers were blamed, and with good reason. But it also seemed that departmental officials preferred things as they were. The lack of integration between subcommittees, perhaps, provided alternative routes of access and gave departmental officials some room to operate.

Command linkages

3. The "line of command" within public agencies, as compared to business and service organizations, is more likely to be characterized by *competing identifications and affiliations.* Again the difference is one of degree, but it approaches one of a kind. Consider only one aspect of the integrity of command linkages common in business organizations. In them, typically, "management" is separated from "labor" only very far down the hierarchy, at or near the level of the first-line supervisor. Moreover, the common identification of all levels of management often is stressed. "Management," moreover, commonly does not enjoy the kind of job security that can come from union contracts. One of the effects of such carrots and sticks, without question, is the more facile implementation of policy changes at all levels of organization.

Hierarchy has its effects in public agencies as well as businesses, but the line of command seems less integral in the former. Thus a unique family of identifications alternative to the hierarchy exists at levels both low and high in public agencies, the apparent underlying motivation being to maximize the probability that evil will not occur, or at least will be found out. That is, the chain of command at the federal level is subject to strong fragmenting forces even up to the highest levels, where political and career strata blend into one another. For example, the ideal of a wall-to-wall civil service is approached closely in practice, and it provides a strong countervailing identification to the executive chain of command. Career officials are "out of politics," but their commitments to programs may be so strong as to inhibit or even thwart executive direction.[9]

That the public institutional environment permits (indeed, encourages) a fragmenting of the management hierarchy at points well up in the higher levels may be illustrated in three ways. First, the "neutrality" of civil servants has been a major defensive issue in at least two federal OD programs in which I have participated, the OD efforts having been painted by many career people as sophisticated but lustful raids on a chaste protected service. Second, Congress is an old hand at creating similar countervailing identifications so as to enhance its control over administration,[10] for which the Constitution and tradition provide a solid rationale. Third, the executive has also played the game, sometimes unwittingly. Consider the presidential-inspired Federal Executive Boards. Basically, these Boards were intended to be a horizontal link between field units of federal agencies and vertically between the presidency and top career field officialdom. The FEB's provide career field managers with a potential way to supplement or even bypass departmental reporting relations, both career employees and political appointees. Indeed, President Kennedy may have intended them as just such a bypass around "the feudal barons of the permanent government" whom he saw as obstacles to change.[11]

A conclusion flows easily. Congress often encourages slack in the executive chain of command to facilitate its oversight of the president and his major appointees; and the executive as well as the protected service itself often uses the same strategy. The integrity of the executive chain of command suffers. Although the consequences are mixed, public executives are limited in initiating[12] (for example) OD programs. Witness the furor over the mere handful of Schedule C jobs removed from the protected service during Eisenhower's first term to permit greater executive leverage. Any corporation president would have an immensely broader field to act upon. The motivation to avoid "spoils politics" is recognized, but managerial rigidity is the other side of the coin. Herbert Kaufman concludes that although extensions of the civil service were intended to provide upper-level political administrators with capable help, the latter have often been driven to "pray for deliverance from their guardians."[13]

Weak linkages

4. Exacerbating the point above, the *linkages between political and career levels* are weak as a consequence of a variety of features of the public institutional environment.[14] This slippage between managerial levels significantly complicates beginning and implementing OD programs, and severely challenges the linkage of executive management with operating management.

The generalization concerning weak linkages in the managerial chain of command is meant to apply in four distinct senses. First, political and career levels often are weakly linked due to the brief tenure of the former. Second, the job of linking the political leadership and the permanent bureaucracy must be handled by a tiny group of executives—political appointees and occupants of Schedule C jobs—who owe diverse allegiance to the chief executive. Third, there is reason to suspect significant slippage between the top career officialdom and lower levels. For example, what lower-level careerists see as necessary protections of tenure, top career officials perceive as cumbersome limitations on managerial flexibility. Fourth, the executive often weakens its own managerial linkages, as it seeks sometimes-unreconcilable political and administrative goals. Thus the unionization of public employees which has been encouraged by presidential executive order hardly discourages labor unions looking for new fields to conquer. But one of the groups of federal employees to organize were inspectors in the U.S. Civil Service Commission who, if anybody, would be seen as "management" in most business organizations.

OD programs consequently must face the issue of somehow interfacing political and career linkages which powerful forces—Constitutional, political, and historic—tend to pull apart. Consider only one dilemma facing OD programs. The general rule of thumb is that OD programs should begin "at the top" of organizational hierarchies, or as close to the top as possible. The rationale is obvious: that is where the power usually is in business organizations. Respecting this rule of thumb in public agencies raises a multidimensional dilemma. Basically, "the top" in public agencies is more complex than in most businesses. Initiating an OD program at the level of the political leadership maximizes formal executive support, but it may also raise complex problems. Support of the OD program is problematic because of frequent personnel changes at that level,[15] because of possible well-entrenched resistance from the permanent service, because legislators may fear that any strengthening of the executive chain of command would only mean fewer points of access and sources of information, and because employee associations may resist executive direction. Relying more on support from those in the competitive/protected service maximizes the chances of permanent support, and it may raise congressional and CSC trust in the program. But this approach may encourage executive resistance from such vantage points as the Bureau of the Budget.

The OD specialist faces real dilemmas, then, in choosing the "top" of the hierarchy at which to direct his interventions. I have participated in change programs that have taken both approaches to seeking a power base, and they show only that avoiding Scylla seems to imply meeting Charybdis. The ideal is to appeal to both the political officialdom and to the permanent service, of course, but that is a demanding ideal indeed.

In summary, four properties of the institutional environment of public agencies complicate attaining the objectives of typical OD programs. Consider the objective of building trust among individuals and groups throughout the organization. Technically, viable interfaces should be created between political officials, the permanent bureaucracy, congressional committees and their staffs, and so on and on. Practically, this is a very tall order, especially because the critical publics tend to have mutually exclusive interests, values, and reward systems. Indeed, although it is easy to caricature the point, Congress has a definite interest in cultivating a certain level of distrust within and between government agencies so as to encourage a flow of information. This may seem a primitive approach but, in the absence of valid and reliable measures of performance, it may be a necessary approach. No OD program in a business organization will face such an array of hurdles, that much is certain.

Character of the habit background: constraints on approaching OD objectives

The "habit background" of public agencies also implies serious obstacles to approaching OD objectives. Five aspects of this habit background are considered below by way of illustrating their impact on OD objectives. These five aspects do not comprise an exclusive list, and they are conceived of only as general patterns and behaviors which give a definite flavor to the broad institutional environment sketched above.

Patterns of delegation

"Habit background" is perhaps better illustrated than defined. First, in my experience, public officials tend to favor patterns of delegation that maximize their sources of information and minimize the control exercised by subordinates. Specifically, the goal is to have decisions brought to their level for action or review. The most common concrete concomitants of the tendency are functional specialization and a narrow span of control, one of whose major consequences is a large number of replicative levels of review.[16]

"Layering" of multiple levels of review is not unique to public administration, indeed it inheres in generally accepted organization theory; but it is supported by forces more or less unique to public agencies that have been powerful enough to substantially curtail innovation of ways to centralize policy and to decentralize operations.[17] The protection of the "public interest" is one such unique factor, for example. The rationale is familiar. Political officials of short tenure often cannot rely on established relations of confidence with personnel at lower levels, nor do they exercise as much control over career rewards and punishments as in common in business organizations or in the military. However, the legislature will hold the political officials responsible. Consequently, political officials seek to maximize information sources and minimize the control exercisable by subordinates. This tendency is reinforced by law and tradition so that it permeates down the hierarchy throughout the permanent bureaucracy. The tendency is often referred to as "keeping short lines of command."

Keeping chains of command short implies constraints on approaching OD objectives in public organizations, based on my experience as well as the logic of the situation. Consider only two of the OD objectives above—three and nine:

—to locate decision-making and problem-solving responsibilities as close to the information sources as possible; and
—to increase self-control and self-direction for people within the organization.

To the degree that the rough distinction above is accurate, public agencies will experience difficulties in approaching both objectives. The prevailing habit pattern in public agencies patently constitutes a tide to swim against in these two particulars, although there are outstanding exceptions to this generalization.

Legal habit

Second, and again only as a description of what exists, legal patterns make approaching OD objectives severely more difficult in public agencies than in business organizations.[18] The point applies in two major senses. Thus patterns of administrative delegation are often specified in minute detail in legislation, basically so as to facilitate oversight by the legislature. To be sure, we are a considerable distance beyond the first Morgan case, which seemed to argue that only administrative actions personally taken by, or under the direct supervision of, a department head were constitutionally defensible. But flexibility in delegation is still a major problem. Perhaps more important, a corpus of law and standard practice exists which also makes it difficult to achieve OD objectives. For example, considering only those employees on the General Schedule, salary and duties are tied to a position classification system whose underlying model emphasizes transdepartmental uniformity and compensation for individual work.[19]

This legal habit background complicates approaching OD values. Thus efforts to achieve OD objective three above may run afoul of the possibility that relocating responsibilities in one agency is considered to have systemwide implications, with consequences that complicate the making of local adjustments. As one official noted of an OD effort in such straits: "I feel like I have to raise the whole civil service by my bootstraps." Relatedly, OD objective two above seeks:

—to supplement the authority associated with role or status with the authority of knowledge and competence.

This is hard to do to the degree that a pattern of delegation is specified in law. The same point applies to any rigidities due to the duties classification common in public agencies in the United States, and especially to the concepts for assigning authority and for organizing work underlying the duties classification. Job enlargement begun as part of OD programs has run afoul of such concepts, for example.

At the bread-and-butter level, existing legal patterns also inhibit approaching OD objectives. Consider objective six which proposes:

—to develop a reward system which recognizes both the achievement of the organization's mission and organization development.

Existing law and practice severely limit the search for such a reward system. Thus rewards for exceptional performance—in money payments or in higher-than-normal GS levels for personnel in the civil service—are now possible, but they still are exceptional in practice. Equal pay for equal work, in sum, still practically means that exceptional work is not rewarded exceptionally. Management in business organizations typically has far greater control over reward systems, and especially at managerial levels. More of a problem, neither existing law nor practice promise much in the way of support for various group compensation plans. Experiments in industry with some such plans have yielded attractive results.

Need for security

Third, the need for security or even secrecy in public agencies as against business organizations is more likely to be strong enough to present obstacles to approaching OD objectives. Military and defense agencies come to mind first, but they hardly exhaust the list. The "need for security" as used here can concern national security, it can be induced by a general anxiety born of a need to make significant decisions whose results will not be manifest for a very long time, or it can derive from felt needs for protection from such outside forces as a congressman with fire in his eye.[20] The need can also be real, exaggerated, or even imagined in various combinations.

Consider one case, which seemed to reflect some of all of these components. Agency personnel were exposed to sensitivity training, one of whose major purposes is to increase skills in being open about both positive and negative emotions or reactions. The training staff provided several settings in which these intentions might be approached, one of which was a "park bench." During one week of sensitivity training some time was set aside each evening for a meeting of all participants in a large room which was the locus of the "park bench." But agency personnel seldom used the arena, although there was a good deal of nervous laughter from the periphery of the "park." After some three abortive tries of an hour each, one participant approached me. "I see the point of the thing," he said, "but a park bench is all wrong." Suddenly, the dawn came. "Park benches" were seen as stereotypic sites for sexual assignations and/or for exchanging secrets with enemy agents. Without doubt, some participants thought the "park bench" a silly notion, and hence did not participate. For most participants, however, the symbolism was so compelling that they could not use the "park bench." Moreover, many agency personnel were so closed, distrustful, and fearful of taking a risk that they could not talk about their guiding symbolism, even if they were aware of it.

This greater need for security cannot be established concretely, to be sure, and all that may be said definitely is that to the degree this need exists so are OD objectives more difficult to reach. Consider only OD objective one above:

—to create an open, problem-solving climate throughout the organization.

An open climate and a great need for security or for secrecy do not mix well.

Procedural regularity and caution

Fourth, for a variety of reasons, government personnel are rather more likely to stress procedural regularity and caution. Perhaps better said, even if agency personnel are convinced that certain heuristics provide solutions that are "good enough," this conviction may conflict with other (and especially congressional) needs for external control. For example, sample checking of vouchers was widely accepted as an efficient enough administrative approach long before relevant publics in Congress and the General Accounting Office recognized it as appropriate for their control purposes.

Good reasons support this bias toward procedural regularity and caution in public agencies of course, and so much the worse for OD objectives. For example, the bias patently runs against the grain of OD objective eight above, which seeks:

—to help managers to manage according to relevant objectives rather than according to "past practices" or according to objectives that do not make sense for one's area of responsibility.

The underlying rub, of course, is that a "past practice" making little or no sense administratively may seem an utter necessity from the legislative point of view. To be sure, the dictum "where you sit determines what you see" applies to all organizations. But the needs and identifications of administrators and legislators are likely to differ more than is the case for (let us say) the executives and middle managers of a business organization.

"Professional manager"

Fifth, the concept "professional manager" is less developed in the public versus the business arena, in rough but useful contrast. The relative incidence of business schools and schools of public administration suggests the conclusion,[21] as do the Jacksonian notions deep at the roots of our basic public personnel policies. For example, the "career system" notion has been a difficult one to develop in this country at the federal level. No small part of the difficulty derives from the value we place on an "open service" with lateral entry. Hence the tendency of our public personnel policies to emphasize hiring for a specific position rather than for long-run potential.

Derivations from these taproots have had profound impact. For example, to simplify a little, massive federal attention to training was long delayed by the wrigglesworthian legislative notion that, since the federal service was hiring people who already had the abilities to do the specific job for which they were hired, there was little need to spend money on training.[22] The relative attractiveness of public employment at the federal level at least through World War II provided the proverbial finger in the dike, but conditions changed much faster than did public policy. Instructively, also, the system of regional executive development centers manned by the U.S. Civil Service Commission began as late as 1964, and then only with a miniscule budget and against substantial congressional opposition. Roughly, business has a 10–20 year lead over government in acting on the need for training. Not very long ago, in contrast, the federal government was considered *the* model employer.

The relatively lesser stress on the "public professional manager" implies significant problems for approaching OD objectives. Thus OD objective seven proposes:

> —to increase the sense of "ownership" of organization objectives throughout the work force.

No sharp contrast is appropriate. But a definite bias of public personnel policy limits such a sense of identification with, and commitment to, public agencies. If there is one thing most civil services reformers did not want, it was a public work force who "owned" the objectives of their agency. The only "owner" was the public; the model employee was a politically neutral technician who repressed his own values in return for guaranteed tenure. Only thus could an elite and unresponsive bureaucracy be avoided, goes a major theme shot through our public personnel policies and institutions.

Conclusion

The body of this paper can be summarized tersely. Organization

Development programs are appearing with increasing frequency in both business and public agencies. Moreover, applications of OD programs in government agencies face some unique problems. However, these unique problems tend to go unrecognized or underrecognized by OD teams in part because students of public administration have tended to be underrepresented on such teams. Hence this paper.

Some derivative implications seem appropriate, in addition. First, "poaching" in the public sector by OD teams composed basically of psychologists and sociologists will continue to grow, if only because (as William F. Whyte noted in another connection) such poaching is necessary. Second, students of public administration can play a useful and partially distinct role in such OD programs. But, third, students of public administration are likely to play such a role only as substantial numbers of them develop competencies that complement their special interests in public administration. Such competency enlargement for "change-agents" or organization consultants is provided by the NTL Institute of Applied Behavioral Science and by such univeristy-based programs as those at UCLA and Boston University.

Notes

1. John W. Gardner, *Self-Renewal* (New York: Harper & Row, 1965).
2. Alexander Winn, "The Laboratory Approach to Organization Development: A Tentative Model of Planned Change," paper read at the Annual Conference, British Psychological Society, Oxford, September 1968, p. 1. More broadly, see Edgar H. Schein and Warren G. Bennis, *Personal and Organization Change Through Group Methods: The Laboratory Method* (New York: Wiley, 1965); and Warren G. Bennis, *Changing Organizations* (New York: McGraw-Hill, 1966).
3. For an overview of the technique, see Robert T. Golembiewski, "The Laboratory Approach to Organization Development: The Schema of A Method," *Public Administration Review* 27 (September 1967): 211–20.
4. Sheldon Davis, "An Organic Problem-Solving Method of Organizational Change," *Journal of Applied Behavioral Science* 3 (January 1967): 3–21.
5. NTL Institute, "What Is OD?" *News and Reports* 2 (June 1968): 1.
6. The theme also appeared in mass-circulation news stories and editorials which argued against Project ACORD in the U.S. Department of State, for

example. Stewart Alsop, "Let the Poor Old Foreign Service Alone," *Saturday Evening Post* (June 1966): 14.

7. For example, sensitivity training has been criticized as "amateur group therapy." For an incisive distinction between training and therapy, see Chris Argyris, "Conditions for Competence Acquisition and Therapy," *Journal of Applied Behavioral Science* 4 (June 1968): 147–78.

8. See, generally, Francis E. Rourke, *Bureaucracy, Politics, and Public Policy* (Boston: Little, Brown, 1969).

9. For a sensitive summary of the programmatic commitments of career personnel, see John J. Corson and R. Shale Paul, *Men Near the Top* (Baltimore: John Hopkins Press, 1966), pp. 23–51.

10. Joseph P. Harris, *Congressional Control of Administration* (Washington, D.C.: The Brookings Institution, 1964).

11. Arthur Schlesinger, *A Thousand Days* (Boston: Houghton Mifflin, 1965), p. 681.

12. President Truman expressed the point directly in contemplating the problems that General Eisenhower would experience as President Eisenhower, without the discipline and definite career patterns and established ways of doing things he knew in the military. "He'll sit here," Truman predicted, "and he'll say, 'Do this!' 'Do that!' *And nothing will happen.* Poor Ike—it won't be a bit like the Army. He'll find it very frustrating." (Richard E. Neustadt, *Presidential Power* [New York: Wiley, 1960], p. 9. His emphases.)

13. Herbert Kaufman, "The Rise of A New Politics," p. 58, in Wallace S. Sayre (ed.), *The Federal Government Service* (Englewood Cliffs, N.J.: Prentice-Hall, 1965).

14. Dean E. Mann, "The Selection of Federal Political Executives," *American Political Science Review* 58 (March 1964): 81–99.

15. One ambitious OD program, for example, was unable to overcome the rumor that several political appointees were negotiating terms of private employment. Agency personnel were encouraged to inaction, since these officials would "soon be riding their OD hobbyhorse" someplace else. These officials did leave. But all claim that the stories were seeded by career personnel who opposed the OD program, and that it was only the intensity of such "dirty fighting" that encouraged the political appointees to seek private employ after the rumors began.

16. Before a reorganization inspired by an OD program in the Department of State, some review layers were so numerous that "it could take as long as six months for an important problem to reach the Deputy Under Secretary. Now it takes an average of two days" (Alfred J. Marrow, "Managerial Revolution in the State Department," *Personnel* [December 1966]: 13).

17. Such innovation has been the major trend in large businesses over the last three or four decades. See Robert T. Golembiewski, *Men, Management, and Morality* (New York: McGraw-Hill, 1965); and *Organizing Men and Power* (Chicago: Rand McNally, 1967). Strong pressures for just such innovation

are now being widely felt in public administration. Aaron Wildavsky provides a case in point in his "Black Rebellion and White Reaction," *The Public Interest,* No. 11 (Spring 1968): especially pp. 9–12.

18. A very useful discussion of the antimanagerial thrust of much legislation is provided by Harris, *Congressional Oversight of Administration.*

19. Robert T. Golembiewski, "Civil Service and Managing Work," *American Political Science Review* 56 (December 1962): 961–74.

20. Great needs for "security" as here broadly defined can rigidify an organization and curb the effectiveness of its members. To the point, see Chris Argyris, "Some Causes of Organizational Ineffectiveness Within the Department of State," Center for International System Research, *Occasional Papers,* No. 2 (1967).

21. Revealingly, it was not until 1946 that Cornell developed the first two-year master of public administration program comparable to the MBA long given by schools of commerce or business administration.

22. Paul P. Van Riper, *History of the United States Civil Service* (Evanston, Ill.: Row, Peterson, 1958), pp. 429–34.

16

The Many American Governments and Outdoor Recreation

Morton Grodzins

Recreation in the United States is a chaos of activity. It is no less a chaos of private and public responsibilities.

* * *

Facilities and services for this infinite variety of recreation activities are provided by an equally inchoate collection of private, semi-public, and public bodies. The industrial society begets industrialized recreation. Just as the automobile culture produces driving as a favorite "outdoor recreation," so the development and promotion of outboard motors have produced a new impetus to boating, and so the technical development of portable oxygen-supplying equipment has spawned a new and rapidly growing breed of underwater creatures. Television has taken people out of movies; aircraft have made skiing in Aspen (or Kitzbühel) easy.

The recreation industry is big business. Dollar estimates of exactly how big it is vary enormously. Using a restricted definition (excluding such items as liquor, soft drinks, tobacco, sports clothes, and recreation transportation), an authoritative study for 1952 showed recreation costs of $11 billion. Adding only vacation travel would bring this figure (in 1960) to well over $23 billion, almost twice as much as Americans spent that year for clothing, accessories, and jewelry. If such items as liquor consumption are added, the figure easily exceeds $40 billion, roughly double all public costs for primary, secondary, and higher education.[1]

Reprinted from *Trends in American Living and Outdoor Recreation* (Washington, D.C.: Government Printing Office, 1962), pp. 62, 63–68.

[1] J. Frederick Dewhurst and Associates, "America's Needs and Resources, A New Survey," (New York: The Twentieth Century Fund, 1955), ch. 2. See also Marion Clawson, "The Crisis in Outdoor Recreation," *American Forests,* March 1959, p. 5, Resources for the Future, reprint No. 13.

The principal suppliers of recreation commodities and services are the vast complex.

There is great overlap of the private and public in the American culture, including the recreation sector. One facet is reciprocal dependence: the sale of fishing gear (almost $160 million in 1952[2]) is largely dependent upon public waters, not only the oceans, the Great Lakes and the Gulf of Mexico, but also the streams (81,000 miles) and lakes (2.7 million acres) of the Forest Service and the reservoirs built by the Tennessee Valley Authority, the Army Corps of Engineers, and the Bureau of Reclamation. This is not to mention the seeding of streams and other waters by federal and state agencies. (In the spring of 1961 Colorado put 2,515,926 fish into its streams.[3]) Most private recreation camps are adjacent to public parks or water, and many operate on public land, as at TVA reservoirs and in national forests. There would be far fewer horses rented, and a corresponding decrease in the sale of riding boots and clothes, without public bridle paths. The boating industry is similarly dependent upon public waters, docks, and launching areas.

A second aspect of the public-private overlap results from enlightened self-interest. Most of the nation's large timber growers allow their lands to be used for some forms of public recreation. At least 60,000,-000 acres are involved.[4] Hunting, fishing, hiking, picnicking, among other activities, are invited. Some companies have full-fledged park and recreation programs.

A third manifestation of the overlap is the familiar group pressure on public policy. The boating industry participated in drawing up the Federal Boating Act of 1958 and a complementary draft statute, recommended for passage by the states. The Izaak Walton League, the motorboat industry, wilderness adherents, and fishing buffs (not always without conflict among themselves or without opposition from mining, grazing, and lumbering interests) attempt to mold public policy at innumerable points in the process of administrative-legislative decision-making. The chains of

[2]Laurence I. Hewes, Jr., "The Demand for Outdoor Recreation—Implications for Natural Resource Allocation," speech presented Aug. 24, 1960, before the Western Resources Conference, Boulder, Colo.

[3]Personal communication from Colorado Game and Fish Department.

[4]"Public Recreation in Private Forests," *American Forests,* April 1958, p. 72.

influence are often circular. The U.S. Fish and Wildlife Service, for example, seeks support for its program from state fish and game commissions, which in turn depend on business and sportsmen's groups organized to promote hunting, fishing, and wildlife management. It is difficult in such cases to determine who is influencing whom. Federal and state programs could not exist without the legislative lobbying of private groups; but the success and implementation of those lobbying activities are in turn dependent upon federal administrative officers and their state counterparts. Influence is symbiotic, and the result is a typical confusion of public and private spheres of responsibility.

The confusion becomes extreme when private groups perform what "a priori" appear to be public services. This is a final manifestation of the public-private overlap. Private acquisition of public recreation lands is a good example. The Trustees of Reservations in Massachusetts (an organization that receives no financial support from any government) spend privately donated funds for parks and forests or acquire such lands by gift. As a public agency might, the trustees base their acquisition program on a statewide survey of scenic sites. Land once acquired is either maintained for public use or, the more usual practice, given to the state or a local government for recreation purposes. A number of states have similar organizations, one of the oldest being the Society for the Protection of New Hampshire Forests. California's Save-the-Redwoods League has had an important role in establishing the state park system, not least of all through its purchase by private subscription of prime park land. Even where formal groups for land purchase do not exist, an analogous function is performed in many states by community trusts and private philanthropies. They purchase parkland that may come on the market at a time when government funds for this purpose are not available. The land is subsequently resold to public agencies, thus freeing the private funds for another cycle of land purchase and transfer.

Land purchases are only one sample of private organizations doing the public's business. Often a community park will be improved by action of private groups. The Rotary Club will install lighting and picnic benches, and the Lions will provide funds for the community swimming pool. In larger communities, the private contribution to public recreation is more likely to take the form of camps for the underprivileged operated by civic, church, and other welfare-oriented organizations. Thousands of such programs exist. If they didn't, public programs would almost certainly take their place.

The substitution of private for public programs is found in other areas of recreation work. The National Recreation Association, a private organization, carries on an extensive consultation service, aiding local governments and other public bodies to establish and improve recreation programs. The association has also assisted state boards of education in the development of school recreation programs and has supervised the training of state and local recreation workers. Very similar services are offered by a number of state governments as well as by the National Park Service.

The welter of private and semipublic sources of recreation facilities and services is matched by a diverse group of governmental units. As a task force of the Second Hoover Commission noted, the concern of the federal government with recreation resources and activities has been incidental to other functions. Recreation has been a byproduct of the objectives of conserving forest, water, and land resources and of effectively utilizing manpower during wartime. Nevertheless, the federal government now operates an extensive network of recreation programs. No fewer than 10 agencies (see Table) are represented in the Federal Inter-Agency Committee on Recreation. All of these, except the Public Housing Administration, have important responsibilities for providing facilities for outdoor recreation. But the members of the Inter-Agency Committee on Recreation by no means exhaust the list of federal bureaus concerned with recreation. For example, the General Services Administration has a key role in the final transfer of surplus federal properties to states and localities for recreation purposes. In the nation's newest outdoor recreation program, the Urban Renewal Administration (Housing and Home Finance Agency) is charged with carrying out provisions of Title VII of the Housing Act of 1961, which provides grants to assist in the acquisition of open-space land in urban areas. The extensive system of dams constructed by the Tennessee Valley Authority provides the major source of recreation opportunities in what was previously a lake-poor region of the nation. The Soil Conservation Service (U.S. Department of Agriculture) has developed a number of recreation areas as a part of its land utilization projects (in 1954 these areas were transferred to the Forest Service). The SCS has also made important contributions to the preservation of wildlife in agricultural lands and privately owned forests, through its 2,900 soil conservation districts of the country, and to the development of facilities for recreation through its small watersheds program. The Coast and Geodetic Survey provides maps, charts, and tidetables to boaters, among other recreation services. Even the Department of State, through the Under Secretary's Special Assistant for Fisheries and Wildlife, contributes to recreation. These are only samples of a very long list.

The Federal Inter-Agency Committee on Recreation works under a general policy statement that declares "recreation is a human need which is essential at all times to the well being of the people"; and "the national welfare is promoted by providing opportunities for wholesome and adequate recreation." Legislative authorizations are often far less clear-cut, and administrative practices have often subordinated recreation to other purposes.

The Corps of Engineers, for example, constructs reservoirs primarily for flood control, navigation, and power development. No authorization existed at all for the development of recreation activities at reservoirs until 1944. Even under that authorization, recreation became, at best, a secondary or tertiary purpose of the reservoirs. Recreation specialists have often criticized the Corps of Engineers (as well as the Bureau of Reclamation) for their failure to provide sufficient recreation land at reservoir sites.[5] The Bureau of Land Management, the federal government's largest landholder, similarly recognizes recreation as only one of a number of purposes it must fulfill. The Bureau's large-scale disposal of the public domain for commercial purposes has been opposed in recent years by many recreation and conservation leaders. Soon after assuming office in 1961, Secretary of the Interior Udall declared a moratorium on BLM land disposals for commercial use, awaiting completion of a classifi-

---

[5]Since the paragraph was written, the Corps of Engineers has evolved new policies placing "major emphasis on comprehensive planning. . . . Recreation is . . . dealt with in the same manner as any other use of water resources." In addition, "steps have been taken . . . to assure that adequate lands are acquired to meet the needs for future recreation use and development in accordance with the policy of the administration. . . ." (Personal communication from Office of Assistant Secretary of the Army, "Financial Management," August 25, 1961.)

Agencies in Federal Inter-Agency Committee on Recreation

National Park Service, U.S. Department of the Interior.
Administration of the national parks, monuments, historical sites and other areas which comprise the national park system and national recreation areas; planning of recreation facilities at Bureau of Reclamation reservoir sites; cooperation with federal and state and local agencies in planning for their park, parkway, and recreation-area programs.

Forest Service, U.S. Department of Agriculture.
Recreation in the 186 million acres of national forest system, including national grasslands. Also research in forest recreation.

Fish and Wildlife Service, U.S. Department of the Interior.
Recreation on national wildlife refuges and federal fish and culture stations. Administers program of grants to state agencies for conservation and fish and game management.

Corps of Engineers, U.S. Department of the Army.
Recreation in navigation and flood control project areas under jurisdiction of the corps. Other aids to recreation through beach erosion control and other related programs.

Bureau of Reclamation, U.S. Department of the Interior.
Recreation at reservoir sites of the Bureau. For most reclamation reservoirs a master and development plan for recreation is prepared by the National Park Service.

Bureau of Land Management, U.S. Department of the Interior.
Recreation in the public lands of United States. Conveys land to state and local governments for recreation purposes.

Federal Extension Service, U.S. Department of Agriculture.
Rural community recreation through state agricultural college and county extension services.

Public Health Service, U.S. Department of Health, Education, and Welfare.
Public health, including enviornmental sanitation and control of stream pollution, in recreation areas.

Office of Education, U.S. Department of Health, Education, and Welfare.
School and community recreation; outdoor education and school camping.

Public Housing Administration, Housing and Home Finance Agency.
Concerned that local housing authorities which own projects in federally assisted low-rent housing program obtain the same community services (including recreation) for their tenants as are available to other residents in the community. Indoor community activities space and outdoor play areas may be provided on the project.

Source: Release (undated) of Federal Inter-Agency Committee on Recreation, supplemented by data from agencies.

cation study and, presumably, the allocation of prime land for recreation.[6]

Substantially all of the national forests and grasslands (186 million acres) are open to the public and used for hunting, fishing, and hiking. Wilderness areas, comprising more than 14 million acres, are operated to preserve their primitive condition, and in these areas all other uses are subordinate. Wilderness areas, a relatively tiny fraction of the national forests, are set aside for exclusive recreation use (estimates range from one-tenth of 1 percent to 2.5 percent). Over the rest of the national forests, management is based on multiple-use principles. Some types of recreation use are compatible with some types of commercial use on a given area of forest land. But full development of one purpose must, in most cases, result in decreased utilization for the other. The sharpness of the conflict has tended to increase with the upsurge of both recreation and commercial lumbering on forest lands during the postwar years. The difficulty was by no means solved by the 1960 congressional legislation which established outdoor recreation on the same plane as "range, timber, watershed, and wildlife and fish purposes" in the Forest Service's program. Such legislation simply transfers struggle for actual land-use priority (in the large number of cases where equal intensity of commercial and recreation use is not possible) from the legislative to the administrative arena. Commercial pressures on the Forest Service are immense and well organized. Large gains in the recreation use of the national forests depend upon concerted public efforts in support of that use. Steps in the direction are the Forest Service's "Operation Outdoors," a 5-year program of recreation development begun in 1957, and a program for the national forests which lays great stress on recreation.[7]

[6]The text of Secretary Udall's moratorium notice is given in the *Federal Register,* Feb. 16, 1961, p. 1382.

[7]For discussion of actual and potential conflicts in multiple-use administration of national forests, see Evan W. Kelley, "Problems of Land Management and Administration Arising from Associated Uses of Land for the Various Services which the Public Seeks from the National Forests," *Proceedings of the Western Farm Economics Association,* 1938; Marion Clawson and Burnell Held, "The Federal Lands: Their Use and Management," (Baltimore: The Johns Hopkins Press, 1957), chs. 2 and 3. I have also profited from reading an unpublished paper by Prof. Michael McCloskey of the University of Oregon.

The Fish and Wildlife Service is primarily concerned with increasing and protecting fish and wildlife resources and enforcing federal game laws. "Incident to these responsibilities," according to an official policy statement, "the Service has recognized the necessity and desirability of providing, when not inconsistent with these primary objectives, the optimum of its facilities and services for recreation use."[8] Again recreation is not the primary legislated function. The several hundred national wildlife refuges make a direct contribution to recreation through the production and protection of wildlife, particularly migratory waterfowl. Facilities in the refuges are also provided for fishing, camping, boating, picnicking, and nature study. Furthermore, in this case the powerful, well-organized citizens' groups devoted to hunting, fishing, and wildlife preservation have produced an overall fish and wildlife program that substantially serves recreation purposes. The task has been easier because of the longrun compatibility between hunting and fishing, on the one hand, and production and management of fish and game, on the other. A powerful lever for sportsmen is the fact that their hunting and fishing license fees (plus taxes on their equipment) substantially pay for state fish and wildlife programs.

Of all federal agencies related to recreation, the National Park Service is most clearly focused on recreation. But even its mission contains ambiguities. It is charged with the conservation of "scenery and . . . natural and historical objects and wildlife," as well as with providing "for the enjoyment of same in such manner and by such means as will leave them unimpaired for the enjoyment of future generations." Park areas must be preserved if they are to be enjoyed. Yet at any particular moment enjoyment of resources can conflict with their conservation, as when very large numbers of those coming to enjoy may, by their very overuse, threaten the natural scene with destruction. The Park Service in 1956 moved to solve this dilemma by its Mission 66 program, a 10-year effort

[8]Federal Inter-Agency Committee on Recreation, "The Role of the Federal Government in the Field of Public Recreation," mimeographed, rev. ed. (Washington, D.C., 1956), p. 21. (This report is hereafter cited as "The Role of the Federal Government.") The Fish and Wildlife Service also has important responsibilities in recreation planning for reservoirs of the Bureau of Reclamation and the Corps of Engineers.

to meet rising demand for park use by increased facilities and staffs and, in the process, to provide for the protection of natural and historic areas. The Park Service has been actively supported through the years by a large number of citizen groups, including the National Parks Association.

The states and localities present equally complicated patterns of organization for recreation purposes. Each state has at least 1 park agency (Massachusetts has 10). Agencies charged with park and recreation responsibilities range from rudimentary, part-time custodial commissions to highly professional, large-scale staffs doing specialized tasks, as in California, New York, Pennsylvania, Michigan, and Indiana. Only about 12 states have unified recreation agencies whose responsibilities include both wildlife management (essentially programs for hunting and fishing) and park management for general recreation purposes. The largest number of states have separate administrative organizations for these purposes, each usually with its own governing commission, and almost uniformly the fish and wildlife program is supported by larger budgets, larger and more professional staffs, and better organized citizen support. Other independent agencies in most states perform peripheral recreation services. The maintenance of state forests is undertaken by a forestry commission in almost every state. Roadside parks are usually the responsibility of the highway department. Historical landmarks are frequently administered by a private historical society. A water resources bureau in some states controls lakes or reservoirs which are the source of water for communities, agriculture, and industry.[9]

Competition and cross-purposes among public bodies sometimes exist as they do among private suppliers of recreation. Roads for tourists are the enemy of wilderness areas. The management of fish and game for sportsmen may conflict with the development of intensive-use park areas. Demands for water purity for household use may limit or prohibit recreation use of lakes and reservoirs. And private business may of course interfere with public pleasure. The lumbering industry has often opposed significant increases in the exclusive recreation use of national forest land (as in the designation of new wilderness areas). In Arizona a

[9]"Directory of State Outdoor Recreation Administration," a Commission staff project based on an American Political Science Association study, ORRRC Study Report 14.

state park system was opposed for many years by livestock interest which feared reduction of grazing areas. When a State Parks Board was finally established in 1957, the livestock industry effectively curtailed its scope of action through two provisions in the law: no fewer than two of the seven board members must represent the livestock industry, and no park of more than 100 acres can be established without special legislative action.[10] In its first 3 years of operation, the State Parks Board acquired 14 acres of parkland.

On the local plane, virtually every city with 10,000 people or more, and many smaller ones, have park and recreation departments. The largest cities almost uniformly have well-developed recreation programs, and city facilities may include parks, golf courses, tennis courts, amphitheatres, bridle paths, zoos, museums, arboretums, outside-the-city camps, stadia, scenic drives, and beaches and boat harbors. Special programs are offered for the young, old, indigent, potentially delinquent, and non-English speaking, as well as for special skill groups in areas ranging from archery and bowling to boatbuilding and flying high-powered model airplanes. The smaller the city, the more likely that private groups (Boy Scouts, YMCA, Rotary) are chiefly responsible for public recreation, and the more certain, too, that facilities will be fewer in number, the bare minimum being a picnic area, a Little League ball park, or a swimming pool.

County recreation programs vary even more widely, from none at all in perhaps one-half the nation's 3,000 counties to elaborate undertakings in a few places such as Kern County, Calif., Westchester County, N.Y., and Douglas County, Ore. Where programs are rudimentary they are likely to be operated by nonprofit groups, financed in some cases through informal community fund-raising and in others through community chests or united funds. The trend almost everywhere is toward formal, publicly financed agencies. Twenty-four of Oregon's 36 counties, for example, have some type of recreation program.[11] Many counties have developed recreation facilities jointly with schools or with schools and cities. Counties in highly urbanized areas have been especially active in

---

[10]*Ibid.*, ch. on Arizona.

[11]Clayton E. Anderson, "Cooperation Helps to Build Parks in Oregon Counties," *The County Officer*, May 1961, p. 146.

recreation, and some urban counties have taken the lead in establishing joint programs with cities or adjoining counties. The Huron-Clinton Metropolitan Authority, for example, is a five-county, special tax-levying government, providing a wide range of park and recreation facilities for the Detroit Metropolitan area. The Metropolitan Park District of Boston, the East Bay Regional Park District of California (serving Oakland, Berkeley, and other cities in two counties), and Cleveland's Metropolitan Park District are other examples of cross-county and county-city recreation areas.

Still other public agencies and facilities for recreation abound. Data on municipal and county forests are inexact, but holdings are extensive and growing. The town forest is common in Europe, and the first such forest in the United States was planted in Newington, N.H., in 1710. There are today at least 3,600 community forests in 40 states, most of them in the Northeast (especially New York, Pennsylvania, and New England), in the Great Lakes region, and on the Pacific Coast. Michigan, New York, and Wisconsin have the most community forests. Over the country, the forests range in size from an acre or 2 to the 83,000 acres owned by Seattle. Ownership is vested variously in towns, townships, cities, counties, schools, hospitals, and churches. Many community forests are used to produce income, but recreation is an important function in most states. An important recreation resource of Chicago, for example, is the land of the Forest Preserve District of Cook County. The district owns more than 45,000 acres, principally strung out in irregular strips along major water courses on the outskirts of Chicago. Facilities include golf courses, swimming pools, and picnic areas, as well as large wildlife areas. A half million people use the forest preserves on a peak summer day. In Wisconsin, more than 350 county and town forests include over 2.2 million acres, an area greater than the state's combined acreage of national and state recreation land.

The virtues of chaos

Those with a reformist bent or a directive to recommend policy are likely to look aghast at the chaos of services and facilities that exist for recreation purposes in the United States. There is no neatness in the situation. Responsibilities overlap. Concern and effort are widely shared and appear to be poorly coordinated. It is difficult even to describe who is accountable for what or to understand where one government's responsibility begins and another's ends. If for no other reason than to aid his understanding—to bring some order out of apparent disorder—the observer is tempted to recommend that the system be made more simple and therefore more rational. He who recommends policy is by nature a neatener. The first progress report of the Outdoor Recreation Resources Review Commission comes to this sort of conclusion:

> There are a proliferation of policies, a multitude of agencies, ten score activities, and an interest group or clientele for each activity . . . it is this very overabundance of concern and fragmentation of responsibility that complicate, and in part even create, "the outdoor recreation problem."[12]

The opposite view in fact recommends itself. "Overabundance of concern" does not in any sense create the outdoor recreation "problem"; that concern rather is the best route to solving the problem, however it may be defined. Nor is "fragmentation of responsibility" a source of difficulty. Rather it is the desirable method by which American governments characteristically carry out almost all of their functional tasks.

Why does lack of neatness recommend itself?

First of all, the overlapping concern of many governments in a single problem in no way prohibits, indeed it invites, the establishment of general goals by the central government. It also invites central authorities, usually through grants of money, to stimulate activity by the smaller governments. These are functions of the American national government in virtually every major domestic public program. The central government has carried out these tasks since the beginning of the Union and even before the Union, as in the allocation of public lands for education in the Northwest Ordinance of 1785. In recreation, as in other programs, the goal-setting and stimulating roles do not mean that the central government's program becomes an exclusive program. Typically, it leaves room for a vast proliferation of ancillary, if not competing, programs in

[12] *A Progress Report to the President and to the Congress by the Outdoor Recreation Resources Review Commission* (Washington: Government Printing Office, 1961), p. 62.

the same area. This is a nation rarely possessing a single goal in a given field. We specialize in goals.

Second, the existence of many governments operating freely in a single program area preserves a desirable openness in the system. There is no single source of initiative, rather there are many. There is no single standard for determining what is desirable, and no single set of officials with the power to define the desirable and undesirable. Power, as well as function, is dispersed.

Third, a system of many power centers is well suited to meet the infinite variety of expressed needs. It responds quickly (sometimes too quickly) to citizen demand. Because there are many points for decision, citizens and citizen groups have multiple opportunities to influence decision-makers. If a group does not get satisfaction at one place, it can try another. And if the second is unresponsive, there may exist a third or a fourth. This openness in the system for making government decisions is particularly appropriate for recreation because it is not a single but many things. The very diversity of activities that are labeled "recreation" makes it unwise to vest any single set of public officials with the power to make decisions concerning them all. Even for a single recreation need, exclusive responsibility is both difficult to achieve and unwise if achievable. Many points of public power, with different degrees of accommodation to different sorts of recreation demand, mean, in the end, that no reasonably wide-spread recreation need will be unfulfilled.

Fourth, many governments operating in recreation, even if they do roughly the same thing, are effective in meeting the growing pressure on recreation resources. Parks, like roads, seem to play the role of food in the old Malthusian calculus: rather than relieving the pressures of population on them, new resources produce new use. There is little chance in the foreseeable future of providing too much recreation land, especially since recreation, as a political issue, does not sustain widespread public attention. One recreation area frequently substitutes for another, and development of new recreation facilities by states and localities directly relieves pressure on areas under federal management, and vice versa. All this argues for more duplication of effort, not less.

Many governments doing one job may appear inefficient and wasteful. Neither charge, except for units of small population, has been effectively demonstrated. The situation does lack neatness and thus is difficult to comprehend fully. In healthy institutions, ambiguities of this sort must be tolerated. In government, as in family life, business, and educational institutions, the absence of complete direction from above disperses initiative and releases energies. It should be preserved. Hierarchy, order, and the delegation of neatly packaged responsibilities are not adequate substitutes. No function of American government—not even so-called local functions such as education or so-called national functions such as foreign affairs—are so packaged. Lack of neatness in the allocation of government functions is a good thing.

17

Various Vehicles for Legislative Control of Administration

Joseph Harris

Of the various appropriation riders placing restrictions and limitations on personnel administration, the original Whitten Amendment, adopted in 1950 after the outbreak of hostilities in Korea, has attracted most attention. No other rider illustrates so well the difficulties and unfortunate effects that flow from detailed legislative limitations and restrictions on personnel, however laudable their objectives. Intended to accomplish several different purposes during the emergency, the amendment included various detailed restrictions, some of which were still in effect as of 1961—still hampering personnel administration, although the departments have found ways of operating under the restrictions.

Many members of Congress feared in 1950 that the Korean War would result in permanent increases in personnel, indiscriminate upgrading of positions, and unduly rapid promotion of employees. As a safeguard against these assumed dangers and to encourage the transfer of federal employees from nondefense to defense agencies, the Whitten Amendment was adopted as a rider to the Supplemental Appropriation Act for 1951 (64 Stat. 1066). It provided that the number of permanent employees of covered departments and agencies could not exceed the number on September 1, 1950, banned permanent transfers, promotions, and reinstatements during the emergency period, and directed the departments, as far as possible, to make only temporary new appointments.

To clarify the appointment situation, it was necessary for the presi-

Reprinted with permission of author and publisher from *Congressional Control of Administration* (Washington, D.C.: Brookings Institution, 1964), pp. 195–97, 233–36.

dent to issue an executive order (No. 10180) in November 1950, directing that all appointments thereafter, with certain exceptions, should be temporary. The effect of the ban on permanent appointments, according to a 1953 report of the Senate civil service committee, was to handicap the government in recruiting personnel in certain professional categories, including scientists and engineers, in competition with private industry. The report also pointed out that the government would be faced at the end of the emergency with the necessity of going through another expensive reconversion program.[1]

The amendment had also been intended to facilitate the war effort by encouraging transfers from nondefense to defense agencies, but the ban on permanent transfers had the opposite effect. (This ban was later rescinded.) The provision that gave transferred employees the right to return to their former jobs and forbade the departments to fill these positions except with temporary appointees gave rise to serious administrative difficulties.

In 1951 the act was amended to require a minimum period of service of one year in grade before an employee was eligible to be promoted to the next higher grade. Although this rule appeared simple and easily enforceable, and obviously was enacted to curb reported administrative abuses, in practice it proved to be difficult to administer, as is often the case with such legislation. In some cases two-step promotions are the standard practice, there being no classifications at the intermediate grades. In many other situations the inflexible rule greatly hampered good administration by preventing departments from promoting the best-qualified persons to vacant positions. After these and similar problems were pointed out, a long and complex section was added to the rule authorizing the Civil Service Commission to make exceptions under certain conditions. The loophole thus provided made the difference between tolerable and intolerable legislation.

The Whitten Amendment required all departments and agencies annually (1) to review all positions which had been created or placed at a higher grade during the preceding year, (2) to abolish positions found to be unnecessary, (3) to readjust those retained, and (4) to report the results

---

[1] *Analysis of the Whitten Amendment,* Senate Document No. 35, 83d Cong., 1st sess. (March 1953), pp. 2–3.

of the survey to the House and Senate civil service and appropriations committees. Although the required annual classification survey might appear to be reasonable and salutary, in actual operation it proved to be expensive and of little value. Some agencies and departments, having insufficient staff to conduct the survey without neglecting more urgent work, made only perfunctory studies. According to the Senate civil service committee's 1953 analysis, the requirement had created "unnecessary cost, red tape, and administrative inconvenience. It has put into law what is properly an administrative problem."[2]

Experience indicates that the imposition of arbitrary restrictions and limitations on personnel administration is undesirable and has harmful effects on departmental administration. The expected economies are seldom produced; on the contrary, such legislation has often made government operations more expensive. As we have seen in the above discussion, the restrictions and limitations of the Jensen and Whitten riders created serious administrative difficulties, necessitated extra records and controls, increased red tape, and resulted in excessive centralization. As Arthur S. Flemming testified before the Senate Civil Service Committee in 1951, "the end result of such riders can be nothing more or less than to tie personnel administration up in a knot."[3]

* * *

Another legislative device which enables committees to review proposed executive actions is the requirement of advance reports, without mention of a veto power. Such reports are customarily required from thirty to ninety days before the action may be taken, but under some acts the committees may reduce the waiting period by earlier approval of the proposed action. The effect of the requirement is the same though a formal veto power were granted, since the advance report puts a committee on notice and enables it to inquire into proposed actions or plans. If the action is questioned by a member of the committee or its staff, or by

[2] *Ibid.,* p. 14.

[3] *Bills to Implement Recommendations of the Commission on Organization of the Executive Branch of the Government,* Hearings Before Subcommittees of the Senate ... Civil Service Committee on S.1135, S.1148, and S.1160, 82d Cong., 1st sess. (August and September 1951), p. 15.

other members of Congress, the department will usually be asked to supply additional information, and the committee may conduct hearings. If the committee objects to the proposed action, the departments invariably suspend action or modify the plans to meet the wishes of the committee.

The first such statutory requirement of advance reports of executive decisions appears to have been an appropriations rider of 1927, which provided that tax refunds in excess of $75,000 must be reported to the Joint Committee on Internal Revenue Taxation sixty days before being paid. This rider was passed as a result of criticisms and charges of irregularities in connection with the large refunds which were paid in the years following World War I when Andrew Mellon was Secretary of the Treasury. As of 1961, the provision was still in effect, although the act has been revised to reduce the waiting period to thirty days, and to increase the minimum refund required to be reported to $100,000.

In an average year there are approximately 250 tax refunds of more than $100,000, each of which under law must be reported to the Joint Committee on Internal Revenue Taxation thirty days before they are paid. The total averages about $250 million annually, or slightly less than 10 percent of all tax refunds.[4] In practice, the Internal Revenue Service does not pay these refunds until they have been cleared by the committee staff, and the thirty-day waiting period is extended when necessary to permit the staff to complete its examination. Although the committee and its staff are not authorized to disallow payments, Internal Revenue accepts their ruling as binding upon it, and will not pay—except on a court order—when there has been objection.

To pre-audit the refunds the committee utilizes a staff consisting of four attorneys, whose offices are located in the Internal Revenue building. Their examination is concerned primarily with the accuracy of Internal Revenue's tax determination, whether the evidence submitted in support of a claim is sufficient and in correct form, and whether correct interpretations have been made of the tax laws. Although comparatively few disallowances result from the examination, the staff often raises questions or takes exceptions that lead to revision of the determinations.

[4]Information supplied to the author by the Internal Revenue Service.

If agreement is not reached between the committee staff and Internal Revenue, the case is referred to the chief counsel of the Joint Committee, who reviews the case and may hold a hearing to permit Internal Revenue to present oral argument. His decision may be appealed to the Joint Committee, though this is rarely done.

The requirement of advance reporting of large tax refunds to the committee was established following serious charges of irregularities in the years before the Internal Revenue Service had established the thorough internal checks and reviews that are used today. It is questionable whether the external pre-audit of large tax refunds by the committee's staff is still needed. It may also be questioned whether this form of examination, limited to large refund cases—which make up only a miniscule fraction of the millions of all types of tax cases each year, which involve some hundreds of millions of dollars—adequately meets the needs of Congress for a check on the administration of the tax laws.

Although it is understandable why this particular type of tax case was originally subjected to congressional scrutiny, the reasons are not applicable today. An independent check of the administration and interpretation of the tax laws is undoubtedly a proper function of a legislative body. However, the examination conducted by the legislative staff should not be limited to large refund cases, which are in no respect a good sample of the tax determinations made by the Internal Revenue Service, but should include a sample of the various types of tax cases, and the examination should be conducted as a post-audit rather than as a pre-audit. The comptroller general, it should be noted, is not authorized to examine the determination of tax cases or to interpret tax laws, but does audit Internal Revenue accounts.

In defense of the present procedure, it may be said that the pre-audit of all large tax refund cases prior to payment provides an added precaution against errors and incorrect interpretations of the law, thus avoiding excess payments. On the other hand, because of the external pre-audit, the Internal Revenue Service has instituted more elaborate checks and reviews of such cases than would otherwise be used, and a voluminous record and report is prepared for each case. These additional checks and reviews involve added administrative expense and delays. Payment on the tax refunds which come under the scrutiny of the Joint Committee staff are delayed, on the average, a year and a half, involving an annual interest charge of over $40 million. In a recent year the interest charges on tax refunds audited by the Joint Committee staff averaged 9 percent, while the interest charges on other refunds averaged only 0.6 percent.[5] Thus, the savings that may be attributed to the refund audit by the committee staff and to the additional checks made by Internal Revenue in handling these cases would appear to be more than offset by the added interest charges and administrative expense. (It may be noted, however, that not all of the increased time in handling large tax refunds is the result of the committee staff's pre-audit, for in any event more elaborate checks and reviews would be used for large tax refunds than for small ones, most of which are paid out prior to the audit.)

A review of the experience during some thirty-five years of advance reports to Congress of large tax refunds is significant to this study because it shows that advance reporting has substantially the same effect as a committee's formal veto of executive decisions. The Internal Revenue Service accepts the determinations of the Joint Committee staff, though not legally bound to do so, and will not pay refunds to which exception has been taken. It is also significant that the Joint Committee has delegated the examination and determinations almost wholly to its staff. In a recent three-year period only one case was referred back to the Joint Committee.[6] Congressional committee oversight has in this case become largely staff oversight. And the staff's present examination, in being concerned only with the accuracy with which large tax refunds are determined, bypasses the more important and proper legislative function of checking the administration of the tax laws to ascertain whether they are being correctly interpreted, the taxes properly assessed and collected, and adequate internal checks utilized—the kind of check that would enable the Joint Committee to hold the executive officers accountable.

[5]Information supplied by the Internal Revenue Service.

[6]Interview with Russell C. Harrington, Commissioner of Internal Revenue, August 1958.

18

What is
a PPBS System?

Harry P. Hatry and
John F. Cotton

PPB is a system aimed at helping management make better decisions on the allocation of resources among alternative ways to attain
government objectives. Its essence is the development and presentation
of information as to the full implications, the costs and benefits, of the
major alternative courses of action relevant to major resource allocation
decisions. It is not, of course, intended as a cure for all types of government administrative problems. Such problems as budget implementation, manpower selection, the assessment of the work-efficiency of
operating units, and cost control of current operations are generally
considered to be outside the purview of PPBS. Cost accounting and
non-fiscal performance reporting systems are very important in providing
basic data required for PPBS analyses (as well as for fiscal accounting
and management control purposes). However, such systems are usually
considered complementary to PPBS rather than being directly part of it,
and they will not be discussed at length in this paper.

PPBS should not be confused with efforts to reduce public spending;
it is neutral on the issue of cost reduction. But its objective is to provide
information on the benefits obtainable at different funding levels, and, for
any given level of funding, it seeks the most efficient allocation of resources.

Reprinted from Harry P. Hatry and John F. Cotton, *Program Planning for
State, County, City* (Washington, D.C.: The George Washington University, January 1967), pp. 14–28.

A great deal has been published about PPBS recently.[1] *There is, however, little new in the individual concepts of PPBS.*[2] *What is new is the combination of a number of these concepts into a package and the systematic application of the package in total to government planning.* The primary distinctive characteristics of a PPB system are:

1. It focuses on identifying the fundamental objectives of the government and then relating all activities of these (regardless of organizational placement).
2. Future year implications are explicitly identified.
3. All pertinent costs are considered.
4. Systematic analysis of alternatives is performed. This is the crux of PPBS. It involves (a) identification of the governmental objectives, (b) explicit, systematic identification of alternative ways of carrying out the objectives, (c) estimation of the total cost implica-

---

[1]See, for example David Novick, (ed.), *Program Budgeting, Program Analysis, and the Federal Budget* (Harvard University Press, 1965), and Committee for Economic Development, *Budgeting for National Objectives*, 1966. In the governmental sector, the U.S. Bureau of the Budget has issued the following implementing bulletins: U.S. Bureau of the Budget, Bulletin No. 66-3, *Planning-Programming-Budgeting*, October 12, 1965, and Supplement to Bulletin No. 66-3, *Planning-Programming-Budgeting*, February 21, 1966. In addition, at least two states, thus far, have issued formal documents calling for the introduction of PPB in their governments. "Guidelines for Integrated Planning-Programming-Budgeting," New York State Division and Office for Regional Development, March, 1966: "Programming and Budgeting System," Governor's Directive, State of California, May 16, 1966; and "Conversions to the Programming and Budgeting System," Department of Finance Management Memorandum 66-14, State of California, May 17, 1966.

[2]The principles of marginal analysis which are at the core of the analytics of PPBS have been epostulated for decades. Cost-benefit (cost-effectiveness, or systems analysis) have been practiced in one form or another for many years; in the current, formal sense, however, one of the early references is R. N. McKean, *Efficiency in Government Through Systems Analysis* (Wiley, 1958). As for the "program," rather than object-class, orientation, the concepts of program and performance budgeting have been debated since at least 1949, when the first Hoover Commission recommendations were issued. For an excellent review of some of the ancestry of PPB from a budgeting standpoint, see Allan Schick, "The Road to PPB, the Stages of Budget Reform," *Public Administration Review* 26 (December 1966).

tions of each alternative, and (d) estimation of the expected results of each alternative.

The main contribution of PPBS lies in the planning process, i.e., the process of making program policy decisions that lead to a specific budget and specific multi-year plans. The budget is the detailed short term resource plan for implementing the program decisions.[3] PPBS does not replace the need for careful budget analysis to assure that approved programs will be carried out in an efficient and cost-conscious manner, nor does it remove the need for the preparation of detailed, line-item, type of information to support budget submissions. The analysis process, however, should provide a governmental decision-maker with a considerably improved understanding of the issues and the alternatives open to him; the resulting program plan and its implementing budget should thereby also be considerably improved.

Individual PPBS characteristics

Each of the four characteristics of PPBS indicated above is discussed in some detail in the following paragraphs. The fourth characteristic, systematic analysis of program alternatives, is the key to PPBS.

Focus on fundamental government objectives

In using PPBS, emphasis is placed on identifying the major objectives of the government. (For the purposes of this paper the terms "aims," "purposes," "missions," "goals" are synonymous with "objectives.") Proposed individual activities are evaluated with respect to their contribution to each objective. Activities relevant to a government objective are evaluated together—regardless of which organizational units may be responsible for the funds.

[3]As usual when a relatively new field is being discussed, terminology is a problem, particularly where the field has already begun to develop its own jargon. We will attempt to explain, as they arise, terms used in a way peculiar to the PPB field. The term "program," for example, is used in this paper to refer to an integrated activity, or set of activities, including the combination of personnel, equipment, facilities, etc., which together constitute an identifiable means to some governmental purpose. Programs are the elements about which objective-oriented decisions are made.

Current practice in most governments is to make many program decisions during the budgetary process. Conventional budgeting classifies expenditures under such headings as personal services, materials and supplies, and equipment, with emphasis placed on identifying these classes of expenditures by organizational units.

A number of state and local governments have made initial efforts to translate their budgets into program terms by adopting "program" or "performance" budgets.[4] These initial attempts have directed attention to activities rather than objects, and represent considerable progress. For the most part, however, they have not gone far enough in identifying their government's major objectives and in categorizing the activities accordingly. The categories used in these budgets have tended to stay within existing organizational lines; this greatly inhibits consideration of interrelated programs of different organizational units.

Identification of specific government objectives and establishment of appropriate categories (which cut across departmental lines where needed) are major initial steps in instituting a PPB system. One example of such a set of categories (a "program structure," in PPBS language) is shown in Exhibit 1, which attempts to relate all government activities to the needs of the individual citizen.

No program structure can be perfect in establishing program groupings that are completely independent of each other; inevitably some activities will contribute to more than one program grouping.

> For example, the amount of education provided by a government yields such direct investment returns as increased earning potential and increased personal satisfaction (the latter clearly being very difficult to quantify but certainly important). But the amount of education also has potential indirect effects (both immediate and in the future) upon the need for law enforcement, recreational facilities, health service utilization, etc. On the one hand

[4]The term "program budgeting" is used throughout this paper to refer only to budgets which emphasize categorizations by programs, functions, or activities rather than by objects of expenditures—e.g., personal services, materials and supplies, equipment, etc. Unfortunately some writers have used the term to encompass all aspects of PPBS, which leads to some confusion between the terms "program budgeting" and "PPBS." PPBS, in addition to its emphasis on programs, which it has in common with program budgeting, also entails the three other characteristics; program budgeting has *not* included these other characteristics.

EXHIBIT 1
Illustrative PPBS Program Structure[a]

I. *Personal Safety*

   A. Law Enforcement
   B. Traffic Safety
   C. Fire Prevention and Control
   D. Safety From Animals
   E. Protection and Control of Disasters Natural and Man-made
   F. Prevention of Other Accidents

II. *Health*

   A. Physical Health
   B. Mental Health
   C. Drug and Alcohol Addiction, Prevention and Control

III. *Intellectual Development and Personal Enrichment*

   A. Preschool Education
   B. Primary Education
   C. Secondary Education
   D. Higher Education
   E. Adult Education

IV. *Satisfactory Home/Community Environment*

   A. Comprehensive Community Planning
   B. Homes for the Dependent
   C. Housing (other than that in A and B)
   D. Water Supply
   E. Solid Waste Disposal
   F. Air Pollution Control
   G. Pest Control
   H. Noise Abatement
   I. Local Beautification
   J. Intra-Community Relations
   K. Homemaking Aid/Information

V. *Economic Satisfaction & Satisfactory Work Opportunities for the Individual*

   A. Financial Assistance to the Needy
   B. Increased Job Opportunity
   C. Protection of an Individual as an Employee
   D. Aid to the Individual as a Businessman
   E. Protection of the Individual as a Consumer of Goods and Services
   F. Judicial Activities for Protection of Consumers and Businessmen, alike

VI. *Leisure-Time Opportunities*

   A. Outdoor
   B. Indoor
   C. Recreational Activities for Senior Citizens
   D. Cultural Activities

VII. *Transportation-Communication-Location*

   A. Motor Vehicle
   B. Urban Transit Systems
   C. Pedestrian
   D. Water Transport
   E. Air Transport
   F. Location Programs
   G. Communications Substitutes for Transportation

VIII. *General Support*

   A. General Government Management
   B. Financial
   C. Purchasing and Property Mgt.
   D. Personnel Services
   E. Unassignable EDP
   F. Legislative
   G. Legal
   H. Elections

---

[a]The focus of this categorization is the individual citizen—his needs and wants. Two category levels are shown (one represented by the roman numerals, the other by the capital letters. For a complete program structure, however, more levels are needed to display the applicable individual government activities. ... Furthermore, the descriptions of each category (not shown here), including statements of major objectives, are an indispensible part of program structure preparation. ...

a government might be interested in evaluating its whole educational program. A program structure having an "Education" grouping would be most useful for this problem. At another time, however, the government might wish to evaluate its public safety program. Education might be one of the ingredients that would need to be considered as part of the public safety package.

As a practical matter, for a government's formal program structure, a single structure should be chosen. The choice will be a compromise. Fortunately, there are probably many satisfactory program structures which could be used for any given organization. Though it is desirable to have a fairly stable formal program structure, when dealing with a specific problem the analysis must often consider elements of different program categories as is indicated in the above example on education. The existence of a formal program structure should not inhibit the specific program analyses; any programs pertinent to the particular problem should be considered regardless of their location in the program structure.

Provision can, however, be made for various special compilations. Thus, in preparing a program structure, consideration might be given to the identification of programs by age, race, income level, geographical location, type of disability, whether programs are preventive or curative, etc. Through appropriate coding of the elements of the program structure, various such groupings could be compiled as the need arises. In addition, an activity that is considered very important to more than one program grouping might also be shown as a "non-add" program element in the other groupings. (That is, such entries should be identified so as to avoid double-counting when computing totals.)

The governmental objectives to which the program groupings are related should be identified as specifically as possible. Preferably these objectives should be stated in terms that permit quantitative measurements. However, it will be misleading if significant objectives are ignored because they seemingly can only be described qualitatively.

For example, to state the objectives of "Law Enforcement" (program category I.A. of Exhibit 1) as "to control crime" is too general to be of use. A much better statement would be "to reduce the incidence of major types of crime," because it permits quantification and measurement and is certainly an important governmental objective. Actual crime rates can be measured and future crime rates estimated for each mix of law enforcement programs evaluated. Such objectives as "to increase the number of arrests made per officer," or "to have a ratio of X officers per 1,000 people," though perhaps measures of efficiency and of the size of the police department, are not ends in themselves and would not be satisfactory for law enforcement activities.

A financial plan presented in terms of an objective-oriented program structure is valuable simply because it improves the decision-makers' perspective of their activities. A well-designed program structure suggests how various activities can substitute for, or complement, each other to further the government's objectives. Perhaps one of the more valuable contributions of a program structure to decision-making is that, by displaying different approaches to particular objectives, it encourages comparative evaluation of the different approaches and perhaps suggests the need for new alternatives. The mere process of establishing a set of program categories is itself enlightening and informative for persons instituting a PPB system.

Explicitly identifying the principal governmental objectives and the programs or activities which contribute to each objective insures that appropriate governmental effort is directed towards these objectives and forms a basis for the evaluation of the alternative means to accomplish them.

Explicit identification of future year implications

Many, if not all, decisions on allocation of resources have future implications and therefore imply future commitments. Also, balance is needed between funds applied to current operations and those used for investment in activities and facilities that support operations in future periods. It is highly desirable to be sure that current decisions can lead to orderly, balanced, and efficient activities in subsequent years.

For example:

—The decision to fund road or building construction in the next budget implies that maintenance will be required in future years.

—The decision to fund elimination of grade crossing on highways should reduce traffic accidents and lower the costs resulting from traffic accidents in current and subsequent years.

—The decision to station patrolmen at grade crossings this year to control traffic flows means that these same funds are not available for the installation of traffic lights that could control traffic flows in future years.

Estimates of future expenditures and outputs are necessary for making current decisions. Therefore, an integral part of the PPBS concept is the estimation of the time-phased expenditure requirements and outputs of each program for each alternative mix of programs being considered. These estimates are part of the analysis process.

Based upon the decisions made, a formal "multi-year program and financial plan" can be prepared. This consists of two interrelated parts: the multi-year financial plan and the corresponding multi-year program (or "output") plan. Though discussed separately in the following paragraphs, these two plans are closely related, the first displaying the estimated costs of the plan and the second indicating what is expected to be achieved from the planned expenditure.

Multi-year financial plan. This plan displays for each element of the program structure the projected costs corresponding to the decisions made. . . . Typically, dollars are considered as the scarce resource that is to be budgeted and programmed. "Dollars" are therefore the main interest both in budgets and in PPBS. For PPBS, this is based upon the belief that dollars are the single best measure of scarce resources. However, it should be recognized that other types of resources such as skilled manpower and land may become major constraints in certain problems. The present federal government systems contain, in addition to the program and financial plan, separate tables that show the estimated number of personnel required by the plan for each year of the plan; these manpower estimates are also kept according to program. A state or local government may also feel it desirable to have such tables.

In the current federal PPB systems, five years, including the budget year, has generally been selected as the time period for the formal, multi-year financial plans. Information on prior years may also be shown for reference purposes. Different issues, however, may require different planning horizons. For example, certain transportation decisions—e.g. in highway construction—are likely to require considerably more than a five-year look because of the lead times involved in planning, engineering, and construction and the length of life of the roadbed; other decisions may have little impact beyond two or three years. Therefore, for individual program analyses (from which the formal multi-year financial plan is developed), the length of time to be considered should be decided on an individual basis.

Cost estimates for future years need not be as detailed or as precise as those for budget presentation. As to detail, in the multi-year financial plan such a classification as object class would not be necessary (though object-class data probably would be used to develop the cost factors needed for estimating the future costs). Such detail is not likely to be needed for program choice. Less precision is also to be expected for the future year cost estimates. As extension of the period into the future increases, the uncertainty of the estimates increases also. In the Department of Defense system, "rough" cost estimates for the future years and for the budget year are used during the program analysis process. Decisions are made based upon these estimates. These decisions are then used as guidance for the preparation of the budget. The preparation of estimates for the budget, however, involves the use of considerable detail and an attempt at preciseness. The planning/programming process and the budget document preparation process have been kept somewhat distinct. This separation permits the planners to avoid budget detail and preciseness in the preparation of analyses and the multi-year financial plan.

In summary, the multi-year financial plan displays the costs of the planned programs over a number of years. It gives a picture of total, time-phased, program costs and thereby permits an improved perspective on the financial implications of the decisions.

Multi-year output plan. This plan, corresponding to the financial plan, is needed to indicate what the expected products implied by the decisions are. The outputs are the major services and goods produced by the programs, defined in quantitative terms.

The needed measures of output should indicate the magnitude of each program and, if possible, the quality level if not implied by the measure of magnitude. For example, the following measures indicate program magnitudes. If used in a multi-year output plan, values would have to be estimated for each year included in the plan.

—Health Programs: number of hospitals; number of patients capacity.

—Highways: number of miles; number of new miles added.

—Fire Control: number of fire stations; number of firemen per population.

—Manpower Development Training Programs: capacity—number of trainees; number of man-months of training.

—Welfare Programs: number of persons serviced; number of dollars distributed.

Though useful in indicating the magnitude of the planned programs, these measures for the most part fail to relate the programs to government objectives. Additional measures, therefore, are highly desirable. For example, the following would be desirable:

—Health Programs: mortality rates; average number of days lost for health reasons per capita.

—Highways: average trip time between various points at various times of the day; accident and death rates.

—Fire Control: number of lives lost in fires; number of dollars of property damage—perhaps expressed as the damage per dollar of total property value.

—Manpower Development Training Programs: number of persons placed in appropriate jobs; unemployment rates.

—Welfare Programs: number of families with total resources from all sources that are below "poverty level."

Numerical values for each year for many of these measures, particularly the latter group, will be difficult to estimate. Ideally, these measures and their values would be obtained from the individual program analyses, two of whose main tasks are the selection of evaluation criteria (i.e., "measures of effectiveness") and their measurement for each alternative. However, such measures of effectiveness, taken out of context of the individual program analyses, may be misleading. (For example, attempts may be made in the evaluation of illness-prevention programs to translate lost time due to illness into dollar terms. Because of the controversial nature of the procedures for applying dollar values to lost time, it is highly desirable to examine the assumptions in order to interpret the results.)

As a practical matter, the formal multi-year output plan is likely, at least initially, to consist primarily of program magnitude measures. (The

Department of Defense still displays in its multi-year "output" plan the number of ships, aircraft, and missiles available, not, for example, a measure of the number of enemy targets that can be destroyed.) Management will need to examine the individual program analyses to obtain a full perspective as to the planned program accomplishment.

Currently many state and local governments include selected workload statistics in their budget submissions. Some of these will be appropriate for inclusion in the multi-year output plans; others will not. Such statistics as number of reports prepared, number of fines levied, and amounts of drugs administered have little value as significant indicators of a program's size or contribution to government objectives and should be excluded. Also, work-performance efficiency indicators such as cost per square foot of road and the number of welfare cases handled per welfare worker, though useful for the evaluation and control of current operations and in the preparation of cost and output projections, are not in themselves usually appropriate for output plans, because they are "means" and not "end" oriented. A cost accountant or measurement specialist can measure the cost or effort required to perform a task without probing into the purpose of the work or its relationship to governmental objectives.

The length of the time period included in the output plan usually has been the same as that used in the multi-year financial plan—five years in the federal agencies. . . .

It should be kept in mind that both the multi-year output plan and the financial plan are very limited in their ability to present a full perspective on any individual issues. For the necessary perspective, individual program analysis will be needed.

Consideration of all pertinent costs

For each program category of the program structure, the cost estimates should represent estimates of all costs pertinent to the program. All appropriate costs should be considered regardless of what fund, what government organization unit, or what source of revenue is involved (though such considerations may cause certain constraints on the eventual decisions). Consideration should be given to both direct and indirect costs and to both current and future cost implications. For example:

—A highway program would probably need to include not only the initial land acquisition and construction costs but also such cost elements as highway maintenance, lighting, marking, and traffic controls, highway police patrols, administration, etc.

—A law enforcement program would probably need to include the costs of: salaries and benefits for policemen, procurement and maintenance of vehicles and equipment, training facilities, laboratories, supporting personnel and their overhead, etc.

—State and local governments sometimes include employee benefit costs in a separate category in their budgets. In PPBS, these costs should be applied against the individual programs in which they originate (as is done where a local government has a special fund for a particular activity).

—State and local governments typically consider capital and operating costs separately (sometimes such budgets are even reviewed at different times). For proper program analysis, both types of costs need to be considered as part of total program costs.

All governments will have a problem with regard to showing costs for activities and facilities that provide joint services to more than one program. In general, current PPB systems display such jointly used activities as separate programs rather than attempting to allocate the costs to each of the supported programs. For specific program analyses, however, it is necessary to estimate for each alternative under consideration the effects on these support activities.

The need to cost out numerous program options, each for several years into the future, is highly likely to create a requirement for increased government cost analysis capabilities. Cost factors and relationships that permit reasonably rapid costing of alternatives need to be developed. For example, for law enforcement programs such cost factors as the following might be required:

—Salary and benefits cost per policeman
—Training cost per new recruit
—Equipment cost per policeman
—Vehicle maintenance and operating cost per police car

—Support cost per policeman

The nature and sources of revenues associated with each program will frequently be of considerable significance. For each program the multi-year financial plans probably should display—or at least have available in the backup detail—total program costs, projections of the appropriate offsetting revenue, and net program costs.

Systematic analysis of the program alternatives

The cornerstone of PPBS is the systematic identification and analysis of alternative ways to achieve government objectives. It is this process that leads to the selection of the multi-year plans discussed above. The three characteristics already discussed also apply to the analysis process. The analysis should culminate in what is probably the key output of a PPB system, clearly written summary analysis documents describing the various alternatives and the main costs and benefits relative to government objectives.

Certainly considerable planning activity takes place today in state and local governments. Numerous studies are generated that often look many years into the future, and such material will continue to be useful with PPBS. However, two principal deficiencies appear to be present in the current planning process. First, the studies have concentrated on the physical requirements for an activity (such as roads, schools, hospitals, etc.) without carefully developing and evaluating alternatives by comparisons of costs and benefits. Second, the studies appear to be of an ad hoc variety without any provision for continuing systematic review and analysis.

Current justification material for budgets and other proposals is often quite extensive and provides considerable information. Such materials are certainly useful for describing specific budget funding requests, but they generally have major failings as analysis documents. They (and this applies as well to supporting material for "program" and "performance" budgets) seldom discuss alternatives sufficiently; comparison with the prior year's budget is insufficient for this purpose. The justifications provide no objective basis for evaluating the cost-benefit relationship of the proposed activities, and they seldom explore the costs and benefits of varying the size of the proposed activity or of other major ways of performing the objectives.

Proposals are too often based on the assumption of a rigid funding constraint. Even if there truly is a rigid ceiling for the budget year, this ceiling is likely to be subject to negotiations for the other years of the planning horizon. Decisions as to the appropriate program funding levels should not be made without considering jointly the costs and benefits at various funding levels. (The "marginal" returns at a pre-specified funding level may be sufficiently attractive relative to the "marginal" costs so that the government would find it worthwhile to attempt to seek a higher funding level such as by seeking revision of certain tax rates.)

In PPBS, analysis can take many different forms and can be done at many levels of refinement. However, it is useful to distinguish two levels —the less refined, less rigorous analysis, and the "in-depth" analysis. Each is briefly described below, and then considerations applicable to both are discussed.

Less "rigorous" analysis. This level of analysis is very likely, at least initially, to be the most prevalent. Even where in-depth studies are not attempted or prove of slight use, a considerably improved understanding of program alternatives can be achieved through less rigorous, less refined analysis. A great deal can be achieved for resource allocation problems through the identification and documentation of the following elements:

1. The real objectives;
2. The major feasible alternatives;
3. For each alternative, the best available estimates of the total program costs for each year considered;
4. For each alternative, the best available estimates of the benefits (and/or "penalties") relevant to the objectives for each year considered (at this level of analysis these estimates might be largely qualitative);
5. The major assumptions and uncertainties associated with the alternatives;
6. The impact of proposed programs on other programs, other agencies, other levels of government, and on private organizations.

Although these elements are also essential for in-depth studies, their investigation even without the more rigorous analytical tools can provide considerable illumination.

Much of the real gain from existing PPB systems has probably been derived from the "dialogue"—the questioning and response—among the decision makers, the proposal makers, and the program analysts. Much of the relevant analytical work done thus far in government PPB systems has resulted not from the in-depth analyses performed by specialists, but from penetrating questioning and the improved perspective obtained on the issues by applying this less rigorous level of analysis. The visibility of relevant information provided by the PPB system has been the key element.[5]

"In-depth" analysis. A fully implemented PPB system should provide for the preparation of in-depth studies, often referred to as cost-benefit studies—also sometimes called cost-effectiveness or cost-utility analyses.[6] These studies draw heavily upon the analytical tools of the professional disciplines, including mathematics, economics, operations research, engineering, and the computer sciences. They also seek the six information elements listed above, but with a much closer examination. The studies attempt to identify, quantitatively to the extent possible, the cost and benefit implications of the range of feasible alternatives. Satisfactory published examples of cost-benefit analysis are hard to find; however, the interested reader can sample various interesting facets of the approach in the works cited below.[7]

[5]For example, Robert A. Levine, of the Office of Economic Opportunity, Research Division, suggests this in his paper "Systems Analysis in the War on Poverty," presented to the Operations Research Society of America, May 19, 1966.

[6]Some writers prefer to attempt distinctions between these terms; the present author prefers to consider them as interchangeable.

[7]McKean, op. cit.; C. J. Hitch and R. N. McKean, The Economics of Defense in the Nuclear Age (Harvard University Press, 1960); Robert Dorfman (ed.), Measuring the Benefits of Government Investments (Brookings Institution, 1965); Werner Z. Hirsch, "Cost Functions of an Urban Government Service: Refuse Collection," Review of Economics and Statistics 47 (February 1965): 87–92; Dorothy P. Rice, Estimating the Cost of Illness (Health Economic Series, No. 6), U.S. Public Health Service, 1966; F. H. Trinkl, "An Integrated Planning-Programming-Budgeting System for State and Local Governments" mimeographed (State and Local Finances Project, George Washington University, July 1966).

Cost-benefit analysis is sometimes considered to be restricted to factors that can be quantified, but such restriction lessens the usefulness of the analysis. Significant non-quantifiable program effects should also be discussed. Also, as illustrated in Section II above, the evaluation criteria chosen often will not be expressed in dollar units, and generally more than one criterion will be pertinent when considering a given program area.

Cost-benefit analyses can seldom provide complete answers. They are intended primarily to provide information to decision-makers concerning the major trade-offs and implications existing among the alternatives considered. This information would then be available for use by decision-makers, along with any other information available—e.g., that pertaining to political, psychological, and other factors which may not have been included in the cost-benefit study.

There are currently some severe limitations on the undertaking of meaningful in-depth cost-benefit analyses for state and local government problems. Important among them are:

1. Problems in defining the real objectives.
2. The presence of multiple, incommensurable benefits—some of which may apply to other missions as well as the one being considered.
3. Problems in obtaining accurate data pertinent to the analysis—including information as to what effect each alternative program will have on the objectives as well as data describing where we are today.
4. Difficulties in considering a time stream of costs and benefits, rather than the simpler evaluation of costs and benefits for a single point in time.

In addition, state and local governments may find it difficult to find and fund staff with the appropriate backgrounds to perform the in-depth analyses. The use of outside consultants or firms on contract is a partial, but not fully satisfactory, solution.

However, even when the conceptual and informational bases for cost-benefit analyses are not wholly adequate, the exercise of performing analyses with the imperfect tools that are available can frequently help in the decision-making process by providing information to sharpen the judgment of decision-makers.

In-depth analyses typically take many weeks. Even the largest of organizations have to be selective in choosing subjects for such efforts. For each major program area (such as "Personal Safety," "Health," etc., if a jurisdiction used the program structure of Exhibit 1), a program analysis document probably should be prepared each year (even if the jurisdiction has a biennial budget). This document should contain the results of any pertinent cost-benefit analyses. However, as just indicated, it is unlikely that more than one, or two, of the major issues covered in the document can be supported by in-depth analysis.

Because of the considerable number of interrelationships among major program areas, a given cost-benefit analysis may well involve more than one program area and therefore may support more than one major program area.

Other analysis considerations. A number of considerations are applicable to both in-depth and less rigorous analysis, as follows:

1. A significant product that many persons feel results from the program analysis process (whether at the in-depth or the less rigorous level) is the identification of *new* alternatives that perhaps combine some of the better features of other proposed alternatives but with fewer disadvantages.

2. The analysis process should not ignore the political and legislative limitations that are pertinent. The analysis should seek to optimize resource allocation within these constraints. However, analysis also should be used to indicate the potential penalties arising from them. This will provide information to government decision-makers, suggesting how worthwhile it might be to try to overcome these constraints. For example, state and local governments are forced into specific limitations as to the uses to which certain types of revenues can be applied along with upper limits as to the amounts that will be available. (This occurs both with federal grants as well as locally legislated revenues.) In the short run these may indeed be firm constraints. However, if the analysis indicates good reason for changing these limitations, the government can attempt to get them revised so that the constraints do not remain indefinitely. Also, if the need appears substantial, it may be possible to find ways, even in the short run, to alleviate the restrictions.

3. Program analysis, at any level, is not easy. It makes severe de-

mands for data on costs, benefits, and various planning factors (such as the social and economic profile statistics pertinent to the government's problems). In many cases such data will be nonexistent, or at least very difficult to obtain. Certain benefit measures that might be sought such as the increase in "personal satisfaction" from various magnitudes of various programs, or the measuring of the quality of such program areas as recreation, will also be difficult, or even impossible, to measure directly. In such instances the analysts' ingenuity in coming up with satisfactory substitutes will be tested or such measurement will be left explicitly to the judgment or intuition of the decision-makers.

4. Government decision makers implicitly, if not explicitly, compare programs of one major program area to those of another. (For example, expenditures on health programs by implication are traded off against expenditures for personal safety, recreation, etc.) Since it will be very difficult, if not impossible, to develop measures which permit fully satisfactory direct quantitative comparisons of health and, say, recreation programs, analysis will have to yield at this point to the judgments of the decision-maker. Nevertheless, analysis can develop considerable information on the costs and benefits of *each* of the program areas (i.e., health and recreation). This should place the decision-makers in a considerably improved position to apply judgments to the relative worths in meeting governmental needs.

5. The results of the analyses should be clearly documented for the decision makers. The documentation could be in the form of program change proposals, program memoranda, or special reports. . . .

6. An often held notion that cost-benefit analysis (and program analysis in general) should provide *clear-cut solutions* to problems is most unfortunate. When such expectations cannot be fulfilled, as generally is the case, cost-benefit analysis is condemned. Instead, it should be judged on its real, though more limited, merits—that of providing *significant information* relevant to the needed decisions, which information would not otherwise be provided. Cost-benefit analysis, properly undertaken, should be able to perform this function even if it does not cover all aspects of the problem.

19

The Fateful Process
of Mr. A Talking to Mr. B

Wendell Johnson

It is a source of never-ending astonishment to me that there are so few men who possess in high degree the peculiar pattern of abilities required for administrative success. There are hundreds who can "meet people well" for every one who can gain the confidence, goodwill, and deep esteem of his fellows. There are thousands who can speak fluently and pleasantly for every one who can make statements of clear significance. There are tens of thousands who are cunning and clever for every one who is wise and creative.

Why is this so? The two stock answers which I have heard so often in so many different contexts are: (1) administrators are born, and (2) administrators are made.

The trouble with the first explanation—entirely apart from the fact that it contradicts the second—is that those who insist that only God can make a chairman of the board usually think themselves into unimaginative acceptance of men as they find them. Hence any attempt at improving men for leadership is automatically ruled out.

Meanwhile, those who contend that administrators can be tailor-made are far from omniscient in their varied approaches to the practical job of transforming bright young men into the inspired leaders without which our national economy could not long survive. Nevertheless, it is in the self-acknowledged but earnest fumblings of those who would seek out and train our future executives and administrators that we may find our finest hopes and possibilities.

Reprinted with permission of author and publisher. From *Harvard Business Review* 31 (January–February 1953): 49–56. © 1952 by the President and Fellows of Harvard College. All rights reserved.

This article does not propose to wrap up the problem of what will make men better administrators. Such an attempt would be presumptuous and foolhardy on anyone's part; there are too many side issues, too many far-reaching ramifications. Rather, this is simply an exploration into one of the relatively uncharted areas of the subject, made with the thought that the observations presented may help others to find their way a little better. At the same time, the objective of our exploration can perhaps be described as an oasis of insight in what otherwise is a rather frightening expanse of doubt and confusion.

The ability to respond to and with symbols would seem to be the single most important attribute of great administrators. Adroitness in reading and listening, in speaking and writing, in figuring, in drawing designs and diagrams, in smoothing the skin to conceal and wrinkling it to express inner feelings, and in making the pictures inside the head by means of which thinking, imagining, pondering, and evaluating are carried on—these are the fundamental skills without which no man may adequately exercise administrative responsibilities.

Many of the more significant aspects of these administrative prerequisites may be brought into focus by means of a consideration of what is probably the most fateful of all human functions, and certainly the one function indispensable to our economic life: communication. So let us go on, now, to look at the process of communication and to try to understand the difficulties and disorders that beset us in our efforts to communicate with one another.

The process diagramed

Several years ago I spent five weeks as a member of a group of university professors who had the job of setting up a project concerned with the study of speech. In the course of this academic exploring party we spent a major part of our time talking—or at least making noises—about "communication." By the second or third day it had become plain, and each day thereafter it became plainer, that we had no common and clear notion of just what the word "communication" meant.

After several days of deepening bewilderment, I recalled an old saying: "If you can't diagram it, you don't understand it." The next day I made a modest attempt to bring order out of the chaos—for myself, at least—by drawing on the blackboard a simple diagram representing what seemed to me to be the main steps in the curious process of Mr. A talking to Mr. B. Then I tried to discuss communication by describing what goes on at each step—and what might go wrong. Since sketching that first diagram on the blackboard eight or nine years ago, I have refined and elaborated it, and I have tried from time to time, as I shall again here, to discuss the process of communication in terms of it (see Exhibit 1).[1]

Inside Mr. A

What appears to take place when Mr. A talks to Mr. B is that first of all, at Stage 1, some event occurs which is external to Mr. A's eyes, ears, taste buds, or other sensory organs. This event arouses the sensory stimulation that occurs at Stage 2. The dotted lines are intended to represent the fact that the process of communication takes place in a "field of reality," a context of energy manifestations external to the communication process and in major part external to both the speaker and the listener.

The importance of this fact is evident in relation to Stage 2 (or Stage 2'). The small size of the "opening" to Stage 2 in relation to the magnitude of the "channel" of Stage 1 represents the fact that our sensory receptors are capable of responding only to relatively small segments of the total ranges of energy radiations.

---

[1]The diagram, with a discussion of it, was first published in my book *People in Quandaries* (New York: Harper & Brothers, 1946), chapter 18, "The Urgency of Paradise." I developed it further in *The Communication of Ideas,* ed. Lyman Bryson (New York: Harper & Brothers, 1948), chapter 5, "Speech and Personality." It was also reproduced in *Mass Communications,* ed. Wilbur Schramm (Urbana: University of Illinois Press, 1949), pp. 261–74. The most recent statement is to be found in my article, "The Spoken Word and the Great Unsaid," *Quarterly Journal of Speech,* December 1951, pp. 419–29. The form of the diagram reproduced here, together with a substantial portion of the text, are used by permission of the *Quarterly Journal of Speech.*

Sensory limitations

The wave lengths to which the eye responds are but a small part of the total spectrum of such wave lengths. We register as sound only a narrow band of the full range of air vibrations. Noiseless dog whistles, "electronic eyes," and radar mechanisms—to say nothing of homing pigeons—underscore the primitive character of man's sensory equipment. Indeed, we seem little more than barely capable of tasting and smelling, and the narrowness of the temperature range we can tolerate is downright sobering to anyone dispassionately concerned with the efficiency of survival mechanisms.

The situation with regard to the normal individual may appear to be

EXHIBIT 1
The Process of Communication

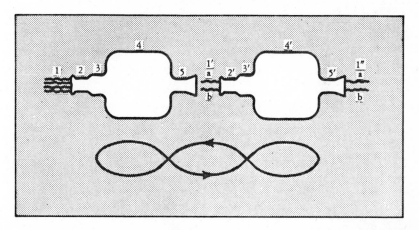

KEY: Stage 1, event, or source of stimulation, external to the sensory end organs of the speaker; Stage 2, sensory stimulation; Stage 3, pre-verbal neurophysiological state; Stage 4, transformation of pre-verbal into symbolic forms; Stage 5, verbal formulations in "final draft" for overt expression; Stage 1', transformation of verbal formulations into (a) air waves and (b) light waves, which serve as sources of stimulation for the listener (who may be either the speaker himself or another person); Stages 2' through 1" correspond, in the listener, to Stages 2 through 1'. The arrowed loops represent the functional interrelationships of the stages in the process as a whole.

sufficiently dismal; let us not forget, however, how few of us are wholly normal in sensory acuity. We are familiar with the blind and partially sighted, the deaf and hard of hearing; we notice less the equally if not more numerous individuals who cannot taste the difference between peaches and strawberries, who cannot smell a distraught civet cat or feel a fly bite.

All in all, the degree to which we can know directly, through sensory avenues, the world outside (and this includes the world outside the sensory receptors but inside the body) is impressively restricted.

Any speaker is correspondingly limited in his physical ability to know what he is talking about. Relatively sophisticated listeners are likely to judge a speaker's dependability as a communicating agent by the degree to which he discloses his awareness of this limitation. The executive who demonstrates a realistic awareness of his own ignorance will in the long run acquire among his peers and subordinates a far better reputation for good judgment than the one who reveals his limitations by refusing to acknowledge them.

Pre-verbal state

Once a sensory receptor has been stimulated, nerve currents travel quickly into the spinal cord and normally up through the base of the brain to the higher reaches of the cortex, out again along return tracts to the muscles and glands. The contractions and secretions they cause bring about new sensory stimulations which are "fed back" into the cord and brain and effect still further changes. The resulting reverberations of stimulation and response define what we may call a pre-verbal state of affairs within the organism. This state is represented at Stage 3 of the diagram.

Two statements about this pre-verbal state are fundamental: (1) we need to realize that our direct knowledge of this state is slight; (2) at the same time we are justified in assuming that it does occur.

No one has ever trudged through the spinal cord and brain with gun and camera, at least not while the owner of those organs was alive. Nevertheless, we are reasonably sure of certain facts about the nervous system. Observations have been reported by neurosurgeons, electroencephalographers, nerve physiologists, and anatomists. Thousands of laboratory animals have been sacrificed on the altars of scientific inquiry. We know that there are nerve currents, that they travel at known rates of speed, exhibit certain electrical properties, and are functionally related to specified kinds and loci of stimulation and to specified kinds of loci of response.

Thus, though our factual information is meager as yet, certainly it is sufficient to demonstrate that the nervous system is not merely a hypothetical construct. We can say with practical assurance that stimulation of our sensory end organs is normally followed by the transmission of nerve currents into the central nervous system, with a consequent reverberation effect, as described above, and the resulting state of affairs within the organism.

Two specific observations about this state of affairs are crucial: (1) it is truly pre-verbal, or silent; (2) it is this noiseless bodily state that gets transformed into words (or other symbols). Therefore—and these next few words should be read at a snail's pace and pondered long and fretfully—besides talking always to ourselves (although others may be listening more or less too), and whatever else we may also be striving to symbolize, *we inevitably talk about ourselves.*

The individual's filter

What the speaker—whether he be a junior executive or the general manager—directly symbolizes, *what he turns into words,* are physiological or electrochemical goings-on inside his own body. His organism, in this sense, operates constantly as a kind of filter through which facts (in the sense of things that arouse sensory impulses) must pass before they can become known to him and before they can be *communicated* by him to others in some symbolic form, such as standard English speech.

It follows, to present a single, seemingly trivial, but quite representative example, that when the junior executive says to the general manager, "It's certainly a fine day," he is exhibiting an elaborate variety of confusion; indeed, he appears literally not to know what he is talking about. In the meantime, he is talking about himself—or at least about the weather only as "filtered" by himself. He is symbolizing an inner state, first of all. In this he is the brother of all of us who speak.

I do not mean to imply that we talk solely about our inner states. We often talk about the world outside; but when we do, we filter it through our inner states. To the degree that our individual filters are standardized and alike, we will agree in the statements we make about the world outside—allowing, of course, for differences in time, place, observational set, equipment, sensory acuity, perceptive skill, and manner of making verbal reports.

The existence of the filter at Stage 3 of the process of communication is the basic fact. We may differ in our manner of appreciating and interpreting the significance of the filter, and in so doing make ourselves interesting to each other. But when the administrator—when anyone at all—simply never learns that the filter is there, or forgets or disregards it, he becomes, as a speaker, a threat to his own sanity and a potential or actual menace in a public sense.

Self-projection

Because the filter is there in each of us, self-projection is a basic bodily process that operates not only in all our speaking but in other kinds of communicative behavior. To claim to speak literally, then, a person must always say "as I see it," or "as I interpret the facts," or "as I filter the world" if you please, or simply "to me."

An administrator whose language becomes too "is"-y tends to persuade himself that what he says the facts are is the same thing as the facts, and under the numbing spell of this illusion he may become quite incapable of evaluating his own judgments. If he is aware of projection, he must make clear, first of all to himself, that he is not speaking about reality in some utterly impersonal or disembodied and "revealed" sense, but only about reality as the prism of his own nervous system projects it upon the gray screen of his own language—and he must realize that this projection, however trustworthy or untrustworthy, must still be received, filtered, and reprojected by each of his listeners.

Sufficient contemplation of this curious engineering scheme renders one sensitive to the hazards involved in its use. As with any other possibility of miracle, one is well advised not to expect too much of it.

Patterns and symbols

Stage 4, the first stage of symbolization, is represented in our diagram as a great enlargement in the tunnel through which "the world" passes from Stage 1 to Stage 1'. The words ultimately selected for utterance (at Stage 5) are a very small part of the lush abundance of possible verbalizations from which they are abstracted. Moreover, the bulge is intended to suggest that the state of affairs at Stage 3 becomes in a peculiarly human way much more significant by virtue of its symbolization at Stage 4.

At Stage 4 the individual's symbolic system and the pattern of evaluation reflected in its use come into play. The evaluative processes represented at this stage have been the object of much and varied study and speculation:

Freud—Here, it would appear, was the location of Freud's chief preoccupations, as he attempted to explain them in terms of the so-called unconscious depths of the person, the struggle between the Id and the Super-Ego from which the Ego evolves, the ceaseless brewing of dream-stuff, wish and counterwish, the fabulous symbolism of the drama that we call the human personality.[2] Indeed, at this stage there is more than meets the eye—incredibly more so far as we may dimly but compellingly surmise.

Korzybski—Here, too, were the major preoccupations of the founder of general semantics, Alfred Korzybski: the symbol; the creation of symbols and of systems of symbols; the appalling distortions of experience wrought by the culturally imposed semantic crippling of the young through the witless and artful indoctrination of each new generation by the fateful words of the elders—the words which are the carriers of prejudice, unreasoning aspiration, delusional absolutes, and the resulting attitudes of self-abandonment. But also here we find the unencompassable promise of all that *human* can suggest, and this Korzybski

---

[2] Sigmund Freud, *A General Introduction to Psychoanalysis,* trans. Joan Riviere (New York: Liveright Publishing, 1935).

called upon all men to see, to cherish, and to cultivate with fierce tenderness.[3]

Pavlov—The father of the modern science of behavior, Pavlov, also busied himself with ingenious explanations of occurrences at what we have called Stage 4.[4] In human beings, at least, the learning processes, as well as the drives and goals that power and direct them, appear to function at this stage of incipient symbolization.

It seems useful to conjecture that perhaps the general *patterns* of symbolic conditioning are formed at Stage 4, in contrast to the conditioning of specific symbolic responses (i.e., particular statements) produced at Stage 5. We may put it this way: at Stage 4 the syllogism, for example, as a *pattern* or *form* of possible symbolic response, is laid down, while at Stage 5 there occur the specific verbal responses patterned in this syllogistic mold.

Again, at Stage 4 we find the general form, "X affects Y"; at Stage 5 we see its specific progeny in such statements as "John loves Mary," "germs cause disease," "clothes make the man," and so on. In this relationship between general forms or patterns at Stage 4 we find the substantial sense of the proposition that our language does our thinking for us.

In fact, one of the grave disorders that we may usefully locate at Stage 4 consists in a lack of awareness of the influence on one's overt speech of the general symbolic forms operating at Stage 4. The more the individual knows about these forms, the more different forms he knows —or originates—and the more adroit he is in the selective and systematic use of them in patterning specific statements at Stage 5, the more control he exercises over "the language that does his thinking for him." The degree of such control exercised over the verbal responses at Stage 5 represents one of the important dimensions along which speakers range themselves, all the way from the naïveté of the irresponsible robot—or

---

[3]Alfred Korzybski, *Science and Sanity: An Introduction to Non-Aristotelian Systems and General Semantics* 3rd ed. (Lancaster, Pa.: Science Press, 1948).

[4]I. P. Pavlov, *Conditioned Reflexes: An Investigation of the Physiological Activity of the Cerebral Cortex,* trans. and ed. G. V. Anrep (London: Oxford University Press, 1927).

compulsive schizophrenic patient—to the culture-shaping symbolic sophistication of the creative genius.

(Generally speaking, most of the disorders of abstracting described and emphasized by the general semanticists are to be most usefully thought of as operating chiefly at Stage 4. These disorders include those involving identification or lack of effective discrimination for purposes of sound evaluation.[5])

The final draft

The fact has been mentioned, and should be emphasized, that the "final draft" formulated at Stage 5, the words that come to be spoken, represents as a rule a highly condensed abstract of all that might have been spoken. What enters into this final draft is determined, in a positive sense, by the speaker's available knowledge of fact and relationship, his vocabulary, and his flexibility in using it, his purposes, and (to use the term in a broad sense) his habits. What enters into it is determined negatively by the repressions, inhibitions, taboos, semantic blockages, and ignorances, as well as the limiting symbolic forms, operating at Stage 4.

Mr. A to Mr. B

As the communication process moves from Stage 5 to Stage 1', it undergoes another of the incredible transformations which give it a unique and altogether remarkable character: the words, phrases, and sentences at Stage 5 are changed into air waves (and light waves) at Stage 1'. At close quarters, Mr. A may at times pat the listener's shoulder, tug at his coat lapels, or in some other way try to inject his meaning into Mr. B by hand, as it were, but this transmission of meaning through mechanical pressure may be disregarded for present purposes.

[5]See Alfred Korzybski, *op. cit.,* and Wendell Johnson, *People in Quandaries,* particularly chapters 5 through 10.

Inefficiency of air waves

In general, it seems a valid observation that we place an unwarranted trust in spoken words, partly because we disregard, or do not appreciate, the inefficiency of air waves as carriers of information and evaluation. The reasons for this inefficiency lie both in the speaker and in the listener, of course, as well as in the air waves themselves. What the listener ends up with is necessarily a highly abstracted version of what the speaker intends to convey.

The speaker who sufficiently understands this—the wise administrator—expects to be misunderstood and, as a matter of fact, predicts quite well the particular misunderstandings with which he will need to contend. Consequently, he is able not only to forestall confusion to some extent but also to give himself a chance to meet misunderstanding with the poise essential to an intelligent handling of the relationships arising out of it. A minimal requirement for the handling of such relationships is that either the speaker or the listener (or, better, both) recognize that the fault lies not so much in either one of them as in the process of communication itself—including particularly the fragile and tenuous air waves, whose cargo of meaning, whether too light to be retained or too heavy to be borne, is so often lost in transit.

Such an executive takes sufficiently into account the fact that words, whether spoken or written, are not foolproof. He will do all he can, within reason, to find out how his statements, his letters and press releases, his instructions to subordinates, and so on are received and interpreted. He will not take for granted that anyone else thinks he means what he himself thinks he means. And when he discovers the misunderstandings and confusions he has learned to expect, he reacts with disarming and constructive forbearance to the resentments and disturbed human relationships that he recognizes as being due, not to men, but to the far from perfect communications by means of which men try to work and live together.

Inside Mr. B

The air waves (and light waves) that arrive at Stage 2'—that is, at the ears and eyes of the listener—serve to trigger the complex abstracting process which we have just examined, except that now it moves from 2' through 5' instead of 2 through 5. That is, the various stages sketched in the speaker are now repeated in the listener. To understand speech, or the communication process in general, is to be aware of the various functions and the disorders operating at each stage in the process—and to be conscious of the complex pattern of relationships among the various stages, as represented schematically by the double-arrowed loops in the diagram.

Effect of feedback

Always important, these relationships become particularly significant when the speaker and listener are one and the same individual. And this, of course, is always the case, even when there are other listeners. The speaker is always affected by "feedback": he hears himself. What is significant is precisely the degree to which he is affected by feedback. It may, in fact, be ventured as a basic principle that the speaker's responsiveness to feedback—or, particularly important, the *administrator's* responsiveness to feedback—is crucial in determining the soundness of his spoken evaluations. It is crucial, also, in determining his effectiveness in maintaining good working relationships with his associates.

Applications to problems

This view of the process of Mr. A speaking to Mr. B may be applied to any one of a great many specific problems and purposes. The diagram can be used especially well as a means of directing attention to the disorders of communication, such as those encountered daily in the world of trade and industry.

Preventing troubles

In this connection, let me call attention to the fact that Professor Irving Lee of the School of Speech at Northwestern University has written a book on *How to Talk with People*,[6] which is of particular interest to anyone concerned with such disorders. Its subtitle describes it as "a program for preventing troubles that come when people talk together." The sorts of troubles with which Professor Lee is concerned in this book are among those of greatest interest and importance to personnel managers and business administrators and executives generally, and there would seem to be no better way to make my diagram take on a very practical kind of meaning than to sketch briefly what Professor Lee did and what he found in his studies of men in the world of business trying to communicate with one another.

Over a period of nearly ten years Professor Lee listened to the deliberations of more than 200 boards of directors, committees, organization staffs, and other similar groups. He made notes of the troubles he observed, and in some cases he was able to get the groups to try out his suggestions for reducing such troubles as they were having; and as they tried out his suggestions, he observed what happened and took more notes.

Among the many problems he describes in *How to Talk with People*, there are three of special interest, which can be summarized thus:

(1) First of all, misunderstanding results when one man assumes that another uses words just as he does. Professor Quine of Harvard once referred to this as "the uncritical assumption of mutual understanding." It is beyond question, one of our most serious obstacles to effective thinking and communication. Professor Lee suggests a remedy, deceptively simple but profoundly revolutionary: better habits of listening. We must learn, he says, not only how to define our own terms but also how to ask others what they are talking about. He is advising us to pay as much attention to the righthand side of our diagram as to the lefthand side of it.

(2) Another problem is represented by the person who takes it for granted that anyone who does not feel the way he does about something is a fool. "What is important here," says Lee, "is not that men disagree, but that they become disagreeable about it." The fact is, of course, that the very disagreeable disagreer is more or less sick, from a psychological and semantic point of view. Such a person is indulging in "unconscious projection." As we observed in considering the amazing transformation of the physiological goings-on at Stage 3 into words or other symbols at Stage 4, the only way we can talk about the world outside is to filter it through our

[6]Irving Lee, *How to Talk with People* (New York: Harper & Brothers, 1952).

private inner states. The disagreeable disagreer is one who has never learned that he possesses such a filter, or has forgotten it, or is so desperate, demoralized, drunk, or distracted as not to care about it.

A trained consciousness of the projection process would seem to be essential in any very effective approach to this problem. The kind of training called for may be indicated by the suggestion to any administrator who is inclined to try it out that he qualify any important statements he makes, with which others may disagree, by such phrases as "to my way of thinking," "to one with my particular background," "as I see it," and the like.

(3) One more source of trouble is found in the executive who thinks a meeting should be "as workmanlike as a belt line." He has such a business-only attitude that he simply leaves out of account the fact that "people like to get things off their chests almost as much as they like to solve problems." Professor Lee's sensible recommendation is this: "If people in a group want to interrupt serious discussion with some diversion or personal expression —let them. Then bring them back to the agenda. Committees work best when the talk swings between the personal and the purposeful."

Constructive factors

Professor Lee saw something, however, in addition to the "troubles that come when people talk together." He has this heartening and important observation to report:

In sixteen groups we saw illustrations of men and women talking together, spontaneously, cooperatively, constructively. There was team-play and team-work. We tried to isolate some of the factors we found there: (1) The leader did not try to tell the others what to do or how to think; he was thinking along with them. (2) No one presumed to know it all; one might be eager and vigorous in his manner of talking, but he was amenable and attentive when others spoke. (3) The people thought of the accomplishments of the group rather than of their individual exploits.

This can happen—and where it does not happen, something is amiss. The diagram presented in Exhibit 1, along with the description of the process of communication fashioned in terms of it, is designed to help us figure out what might be at fault when such harmony is not to be found. And it is intended to provide essential leads to better and more fruitful communication in business and industry, and under all other circumstances as well.

Conclusion

Mr. A talking to Mr. B is a deceptively simple affair, and we take it for granted to a fantastic and tragic degree. It would surely be true that our lives would be longer and richer if only we were to spend a greater share of them in the tranquil hush of thoughtful listening. We are a noisy lot; and of what gets said among us, far more goes unheard and un-heeded than seems possible. We have yet to learn on a grand scale how to use the wonders of speaking and listening in our own best interests and for the good of all our fellows. It is the finest art still to be mastered by men.

20

Decentralization for What?

Irving Kristol

The major story on page 1 of the *New York Times* for November 17, 1967, reported that the Model Cities Program was getting under way:

> The Administration made public today a list of 63 cities ... that will take part in the first phase of the model cities program. .... The winners will share $11-million in planning money appropriated by Congress last year. The exact amount of each grant will be worked out in negotiations between federal and local officials. After the cities have drawn up detailed plans and submitted them to Washington, they will become eligible for $300-million appropriated last month to carry out the rebuilding process.

At first glance, this looks all too familiar—a recipe for bureaucratic nightmare, after the fashion of the older urban renewal program, now generally thought to be something less than a success. You will have a small group of experts in the sixty-three cities—men who will, for the occasion, be presumed to be highly knowledgeable about slum life, slum people, slum buildings, slum real estate, etc.—trying to come up with a blueprint they can sell to their local constituencies and to their Washington overseers. You will have a smaller group of presumed experts in Washington, working desperately to make sense of the detailed plans submitted to them, hoping against hope that the plans will actually be carried out as intended, worrying endlessly (and legitimately) about whether the reports they are receiving "from the field" have any connection with what is really happening. Very few of the experts will, of course, be expert enough to avoid major miscalculations. And even if they were, there would still be the delays imposed by bureaucratic red tape to throw

Reprinted with permission of author and publisher. From *The Public Interest* No. 11 (Spring 1968): 17–25, © 1968 by National Affairs, Inc.

their calculations into disarray. In short: a typical social welfare program that threatens to metamorphose into one controversial shambles after another.

Only, in this case, there is something new. The men who devised the Model Cities program were alert to the problems of bureaucratic mismanagement. They therefore wrote into the law a provision for "popular participation" in this bold new venture into city planning. To get its allotted funds, each of these sixty-three cities has to demonstrate to Washington's satisfaction that citizens' governing boards in the affected neighborhoods "participated actively in planning and carrying out" the program. These boards are now being formed via popular election. In Atlanta, a white neighborhood has elected a couple of Ku Klux Klansmen. In Detroit, in a half-Negro, half-white neighborhood, the board is all-Negro. Officials in Washington are reported to be very upset at the way things are going.

Which leads one to contemplate the possibility that there is more than one kind of bureaucratic nightmare—and that the worst kind may yet turn out to be of the "anti-bureaucratic" variety.

 ## The right problem at the wrong time

Americans have never taken questions of public administration too seriously. To do so is to suggest that there may be inherent limitations on the execution of the popular will (and our democratic ideology discourages such a notion) or that the natural capacities of the average American may be inadequate to the detailed tasks of government (a national heresy since the days of Andrew Jackson). But the experience of liberals during the Kennedy administration was a critical one. Whereas they had previously scoffed at criticisms of "bureaucracy"—by conservatives in general, and businessmen in particular—they soon discovered that there really was such a thing and that its power to thwart or distort social programs was never to be underestimated. Just as most intellectuals only get interested in education when their children start going to school, so the liberal intellectuals around John F. Kennedy suddenly found themselves getting interested in public administration when they discovered that their good ideas and fine intentions got mangled on the way to achieving reality.

The simple fact, they learned, is that the number of programs the political and sociological imagination is capable of inventing always exceeds the number of available people who can realize these programs *as intended.* You always end up with programs being carried out by a bureaucratic hierarchy that understands them only imperfectly and possibly may not even be much interested in them at all.

So it became proper for liberals to talk about the problems of "bureaucracy" and of "centralization," and many started doing so. As a matter of fact "decentralization" has in general become a very fashionable idea. Thus, where political scientists used to argue that municipal government was incapable of coping with the problems of the city and that larger, more comprehensive metropolitan governments were needed, this argument has suddenly been reversed. In his recent presidential address to the American Political Science Association, Robert Dahl pointed out that the population of New York City is about the same as that of Sweden, and that New York is "badly in need of being broken up into smaller units for purposes of local government." Indeed, Professor Dahl took a dim view of any unit of local government that encompasses more than 200,000 souls.

So far, so good. We have become keenly aware—and it's about time, too—of the deficiencies of overly centralized planning and overly centralized government. We are all decentralists now. But, unfortunately, liberal intellectuals do seem to have an uncanny knack for focusing on the right problem at the wrong time, and in the wrong way. They have opted for decentralization with the same kind of enthusiastic abstractness they once brought to centralization. They have slighted, when they have not entirely ignored, the supreme political consideration—circumstance. For, as Edmund Burke long ago observed, "Circumstances . . . give in reality to every political principle its distinguishing colour and discriminating effect. The circumstances are what render every civil and political scheme beneficial or noxious. . . ."

I shall have something to say later about the most significant "circumstance" that today affects (or should affect) our efforts at decentralization. But, first of all, it is worth taking a look at the way the *idea* of decentralization became the *ideology* of decentralization.

Populism and neo-populism

We have, during this past decade, witnessed a mounting anxiety about the fate of democracy in a mass, industrialized society. We have simultaneously witnessed a sharp upsurge of populism in American feeling—both on the left and (to a somewhat lesser extent) on the right. A "credibility gap" has emerged which separates the citizen, not merely from any particular administration, but from government itself. As a result, the need for "visible government" (in Mayor Lindsay's phrase) and the importance of "participation" (in just about everyone's phrase) has become widely accepted among social critics and social reformers. The vision of the American people regaining a lost political heritage through a revival of "the town meeting" within our large urban centers has become exceedingly attractive. And, since there is no blinking the fact that ours is a complex and interdependent society, the constituency for such "town meetings" is frequently redefined along "functional" lines, so as to transcend mere locality and encompass all those involved with one governmental program or another. Has not Sargeant Shriver roundly announced that "welfare without representation is tyranny"?

At about the same time, various sociologists, psychologists, anthropologists, and social theorists came to the conclusion that conventional populism was not enough. The people had not merely to be "involved" or "consulted" so as to gain their active consent. The people had to "participate" in their democracy in a very special way—i.e., through "social conflict." What these social critics had in mind was no reconstituted New England town meeting of any kind: *that* was a vehicle for consensus. Rather, they entertained images of mass picketing, rent strikes, organized boycotts of local merchants, harassment of all official bureaucracies, etc. Activities such as these, it was insisted, were necessary to the mental health and spiritual uplift of the people, and especially the poor and dispossessed among them.

Just where this particular ideology came from, and how it achieved its popularity, is an interesting question but, for our purposes, an irrelevant one. (Obviously, it had more to do with an initial animus against the status quo than with any ripe sagacity about the difficulties of public administration in a large democracy.) In any event, it came to be accepted by many eminent authorities and respectable institutions. The Ford Foundation has been a leader in stimulating this novel version of populism. A group of scholars at the Columbia School of Social Work has also played a notable role in sponsoring a neo-populist rebellion against "the welfare establishment." The New Left has made it clear that, in its eyes, "participatory democracy" was essentially connected with the class struggle. And black nationalism in the ghettos has learned to insist that true democracy is essentially connected with race conflict, and indeed is quite simply Black Power.

The whole business has by now become a thoroughly confusing tragi-comedy of errors. And no group has been more confused than our governing authorities. Congressmen who voted for Community Action Programs and all sorts of "maximum participation" clauses, thinking they were striking a blow against "bureaucrats" and in favor of "the grass roots," are beginning to wonder what they have wrought. In desperation, they resort to the only kind of defensive action they can think of: indiscriminately cutting the budget for social services.

The schools of New York

Meanwhile, the impulse to decentralization, oblivious to its own ideological muddle and blind to circumstance, gathers momentum. The most sensational venture of the "new decentralization" is the Ford Foundation's program for turning over New York's public schools to locally elected school boards. This is not the occasion to go into a detailed critique of the Ford plan. Suffice it to say that in my opinion—and it is not mine alone—Ford's plan will drive white parents out of integrated (i.e., mixed) neighborhoods, white children out of public schools, and white teachers out of the city altogether. It will have the same effect on many middle-class Negroes. In addition, it will certainly result in inferior education for Negro children in the central city, as experienced white teachers move (or are moved) elsewhere. All this will be accomplished in the name of "decentralization" and "neighborhood self-government"—which, in reality, will mean school boards that polarize and intensify all latent racial and political conflicts in any particular section of the city.

It is conceivable—let us even say it is probable—that, had the Ford program been introduced fifteen or twenty years ago, it would have represented an improvement. At that time, the politics of the Negro community centered around the demand for "integration," and Negro leaders would have had considerable latitude in negotiating with whites over the manner and matter of education. This is no longer true. The dominant political ethos of the Negro community is now black nationalism.[1] So far as one can see, this ethos will become stronger rather than weaker in the troubled years that lie immediately ahead. This being the case, the popularly elected school boards are going to be forums for conflict and hostility rather than cooperation and communality. They are going to be weak and turbulent authorities, not strong and resolute centers of direction. (Indeed, where such school boards already exist, on an advisory basis, this is precisely what is happening.) And if, after the initial turmoil and chaos, they should become strong and resolute, they are very likely to behave in a thoroughly racist way.

Decentralization confused with democracy

To criticisms of this kind, which have been directed against its plan for reorganizing public education in New York, the Ford Foundation has only one strong rejoinder: the present system doesn't work. It would be more accurate and more candid to say that the system "works" no less well than it ever did, but that it has not been able to cope with lower-class Negroes as it previously coped with, say, lower-class Italians. (Essentially the same thing can be said about our welfare system.) Still, it is clear enough that New York's public education system, even when and where it works, is very efficient in enforcing petty regulations, extremely inefficient in coping with new problems or new opportunities. There is indeed, then, *in the abstract,* a valid case for decentralization. But, even in the abstract, what kind of decentralization?

[1] I am not saying that the majority of Negroes are, or ever will be, black nationalists—except perhaps in a highly attentuated and rather passive way. But it seems clear that no Negro group will be able to *oppose* black nationalism without committing political suicide. The anti-nationalists are already in the process of being transformed into "moderate" nationalists.

It is always a good idea, when reforming an institution or a program, to take guidance, not only from general principles or preconceived opinions, but from comparable institutions and programs that do seem to work. Now, not all of education in New York City is out of popular favor. The affluent private schools, on the whole, are well regarded by parents, students, and teachers. So are the anything-but-affluent parochial schools, which the majority of Negro parents would be delighted to send their children to, were there room for them What is it that makes these schools acceptable at the least, desirable at the best?

The answer has nothing to do with these schools being run on principles of local democracy which they are not. It has everything to do with these schools being run on principles of *delegated authority*. Specifically, the reason these schools "work" better is that they are governed by headmasters who have considerable managerial power, managerial discretion, managerial immunity to outside pressures (*including* parental pressures). From what I have seen of public school principals in New York City, they compare favorably enough to private school headmasters. What they lack is any kind of real power to do a good job.

I am not unaware of the difficulties involved in conceding to them this power. Indeed, the difficulties are just about identical with those the Ford Foundation program is likely to encounter, but with the tumult swirling around the choice of principal instead of the school board. In any case, I am not here interested in arguing the case for one particular kind of educational reform as against another. I wish only to stress a significant, and frequently misconceived, point: decentralization is one thing, democracy is another. The government of Sweden is far more decentralized than the government of New York City, but it is not thereby more democratic. Indeed, the Swedish government is probably *less* democratic than is New York's—and better governed.

Or, to put it another way: *decentralization, if it is to work, must create stronger local authorities, not weaker ones. Effective decentralization does not diffuse authority; it takes the power that is diffused throughout a large bureaucracy and concentrates it into new nuclei of authority.* Before we commit ourselves to any scheme of decentralization, we ought to make certain that this particular reconstitution of authority is what we really want. And I find it instructive to note that many of those who favor radical decentralization of education in our northern urban regions are simultaneously demanding the extension of federal bureaucratic controls over education in the South.

The most important circumstance

In the United States today, the key "circumstance" that ought to affect one's attitude toward decentralization is the relationship between black and white—the present racial tensions we dare not ignore, the future integration we dare not despair of. Every reforming enterprise must, first of all and above all, take its bearings from this circumstance. It is always useful to inquire to what extent we can decentralize our cumbersome service bureaucracies (in education, welfare, housing, perhaps even policing). But it is even more useful to inquire to what extent we can decentralize our services *without fractioning our heterogeneous political community.* I am not saying that, under present circumstances, such decentralization is always undesirable. I am saying simply that we must always ask *whether* it is, in the light of these circumstances.

Indeed, were it not for the racial heterogeneity of this nation, the organization of our social services would be a relatively superficial problem. Politicians, of course, might kick up a big fuss about one thing or another. But whichever way the issue were resolved, it wouldn't make all that amount of difference. Take education, for instance. To begin with, were it not for the race issue, it might not be widely regarded as a "problem" at all. (In the all-white neighborhoods of Brooklyn, Queens, and Staten Island there isn't even as much dissatisfaction with the New York public school system as, in my opinion, there ought to be.) Second, if one wished to experiment with various forms of "decentralization," one easily could—whatever controversies they engendered would not be more damaging than, say, present controversies in smaller communities over local school board issues. (In these controversies, feelings run high —but only temporarily.) Third, one could even contemplate experimenting with quite radical reforms that go beyond "decentralization"—such as extending "consumer sovereignty" to the educational sector by abolishing "free" schools and distributing educational expenditures (in either cash or vouchers) to parents, who could then shop for schools as they please. The important thing is that, whatever was tried or not tried, whatever worked or didn't work, would not seriously affect the shape of the American republic or its ultimate destiny.

But we *are* a racially heterogeneous nation. And we *are* committed to creating a racially integrated society.[2] This fact and this commitment are—and ought to be—dominant in our minds. It is therefore of great importance that the major impulses toward "decentralization" now come from the white segregationists in the South and the black nationalists (together with their white, radical allies) in the North. Should these impulses prevail, the task of molding this country into one nation will be made infinitely more difficult, and perhaps impossible. The statesman's responsibility is to resist these impulses where he can, to "contain" them where he cannot resist. "Decentralization," in practice, has come too often to mean the hasty "appeasement" of these tendencies.

The school as scapegoat

There are two further—and not unimportant points—to be made:

1. "Decentralization" is not likely to solve any of the problems of education in our northern ghettos.

[2]One of the arguments of those who propose decentralization along racial lines is that "integration" is turning out to be a will-o'-the-wisp, anyway. I think these people have an erroneous and highly utopian notion of integration. Yes, of course the proportion of all-Negro or predominantly Negro schools is increasing in our central cities, as the Negro population of these cities grows. That is inevitable. But I would argue that this is a stage in the process of integration, rather than some kind of contrary tendency. The Irish, the Italians, and the Jews also flooded their local schools, in their time. Integration doesn't mean instant assimilation. It doesn't mean—has never meant in America—that a new ethnic group is going to be warmly welcomed into the bosom of the old. It means, to begin with, the establishment of a checkerboard pattern of ethnic neighborhoods—and many Negro "neighborhoods" are now emerging in different sections of New York City, for instance. (We mindlessly persist in calling them all "ghettos," but many people who live there don't think of them as such. After all, even in Bedford-Stuyvesant some 15 percent of the residents are homeowners.) Every day, and in almost every way, New York City is becoming much more "mixed up" racially than it used to be. Decentralization can freeze the pattern and reconvert neighborhoods back into ghettos.

The sociological evidence seems to be conclusive that the schools themselves have only a partial—maybe only marginal—impact on broad educational achievements. What we glibly call the "problem of education in the ghetto" is probably little more than an aspect of the problem of poverty. Though a devoted, imaginative, and inspiring teacher can always make a difference, in any school, any time, there's not much point in asserting that what the ghetto needs is masses of such teachers: they just don't exist in the mass. Nor is there any evidence that changes in the curriculum matter much; or new school buildings as against old; or even smaller classes as against larger ones. What does count is the environment, as established by home and community. The basic fact is that middle-class Negroes, living in middle-class neighborhoods (whether integrated or not), do *not* have a "crisis in education." Centering one's attention on the schools is an effective way of distracting one's attention from the far more important realities of poverty and discrimination.

One can understand why residents of the slums should be tempted to make the schools scapegoats for all of their frustrations. One can even understand—though with less tolerance—why government officials should join in this witch hunt, denouncing the schools for failing to achieve what no schools can achieve. But it is less easy to understand why social scientists in general should wish to participate in this demagogic campaign. Perhaps they do so for the same reason right-wing groups also tend to make the school a center of controversy: they feel impotent to engender controversy about anything else.

2. It is an accidental fact, but an important one, that *our large and cumbersome bureaucracies, in such fields as education, welfare, and in the civil service generally, happen to play a crucial role in integrating large numbers of middle-class Negroes into American society.* These bureaucracies are, in truth, the best-integrated sectors of American society. To this end, they "work" exceedingly well. Decentralization of these bureaucracies will almost certainly mean disintegrating them. We shall end up with only Negro teachers in Negro schools, only Negro police in Negro neighborhoods, only Negro social workers handling Negro clients, etc. That, in my view, would be a major step backward. And I take it as a terrible irony that the idea of "separate but equal" should, fourteen years after the Supreme Court's *Brown* decision, become so dear to the progressive heart and mind.

Even among the various racial and ethnic minorities themselves, decentralization is already furthering conflict. In New York City, the anti-poverty program is pitting Negroes against Puerto Ricans in open hostility, with each side claiming that the results of local elections to the governing boards of various agencies are "unrepresentative." And, indeed, since so few people take part in these elections, the consequences are bound to be haphazard. The city is trying to cope with this problem by issuing directives that set "correct" numerical ratios, according to race, creed, and color. Since neighborhoods are always changing their ethnic complexion, these directives are subject to constant, and mathematically refined, revisions.

Nor is that all. If this kind of apportionment is to continue, someone will have to decide *who* is black, white, or in-between. This is less simple than would appear at first sight. A group of Negro employees of New York's Community Development Agency have opposed a Negro candidate for the post of commissioner on the grounds he is "not really black." The group informed both the city authorities and the press that it reserved the right to define blackness.

I began this essay by suggesting that, at this time and this place, bureaucratic nightmares might not be the worst imaginable nightmares. I also believe that, if by some miracle these bureaucracies did not now exist, we should have to invent them, as an indispensable mechanism of racial integration. Come to think of it, if we *did* invent them, and gave them a fancy over-all title (Office for Professional Equality?), we should probably flatter ourselves on having taken a great stride forward to the Great Society.

Decentralizing these bureaucracies remains a valid and important long-term objective. But in these times, under these circumstances, it is precisely the wrong objective.

21

An Experiment in Management: Putting Theory Y to the Test

Arthur H. Kuriloff

For some time now, Douglas McGregor, Professor of Industrial Management at M.I.T., has been insisting that most organizations today are managed on principles that run counter to what we now know about human behavior. There's no doubt that McGregor's views, which he explained at length in his book, *The Human Side of Enterprise,* published by McGraw-Hill in 1960, have created considerable stir among serious students of management. But whether they have had any real impact on the way our business organizations are actually run is, of course, quite another question, and a pertinent one.

My guess is, though, that many practicing managers who haven't yet got around to reading McGregor's book, much less acting upon it, are at least aware that it discusses two sharply divergent concepts of management, which McGregor calls Theory *X* and Theory *Y.* Theory *X* is the conventional approach to management, which, McGregor says, is based on hidebound traditional assumptions about human behavior.

This author's Theory *Y,* by contrast, derives from the findings of modern behavioral science research—in other words, it is based on how people actually do behave in the work situation, not on how managers think they will or should behave. If companies want to get the best out of their people, McGregor asserts, they should operate in accordance with the principles of Theory *Y, not* Theory *X.*

Now one of the difficulties of McGregor's position is that Theory *X,* whatever its shortcomings, manifestly works up to a point. Obviously, if it did not, business would be at a complete standstill, a state of affairs we

Reprinted with permission of author and the American Management Association. From *Personnel* 40 (November-December 1963): 8–17.

have hardly reached yet. Theory *Y,* on the other hand, is still little more than a theory—and a theory, moreover, that turns most of our time-honored ideas about the management of people inside out. It may indeed conceptualize a far more effective way of managing than Theory *X*—but where's the proof?

For all I know, there are many organizations that are now quietly experimenting with Theory *Y,* but if so, they are not talking about it. Shortly after McGregor's book appeared, though, my company, Non-Linear Systems, Inc., decided to make the switch. In this article I shall describe how we went about converting Theory *Y* into practice and what results we have achieved. Before doing so, however, perhaps it would be advisable for me to place both Theory *X* and Theory *Y* in their conceptual framework, so that we can more clearly see their differences.

As I have said, Theory *X* management, the conventional approach, springs from certain assumptions about human behavior in the work situation—assumptions that are frozen in our culture. According to McGregor, these assumptions are:

1. Human beings are inherently lazy and will shun work if they can.
2. People must be directed, controlled, and motivated by fear of punishment or deprivation to impel them to work as the company requires.
3. The average human being prefers to be directed, wishes to avoid responsibility, has relatively little ambition, and wants security above all.

These negative assumptions underlie the philosophy of the assembly line and the robotization of human existence—an evolution clearly forseen by Thoreau over a century ago. Even then, Thoreau pointed out, most men led "lives of quiet desperation." We have gone much further along the road to depersonalization since Thoreau's day, and the quiet desperation we now see so clearly all around us is surely due in great part to the assembly line, to the mechanization of *people* as well as of processes.

The organizational structure that develops from the assumptions of Theory *X* is the customary pyramid—multilayered, complex. As we all know, it is clogged with communication blocks and distortions as orders and information limp up and down the organizational ladder.

If we were to invert the pyramid and balance it on its point, we would have a condition of instability not uncommon in reality. Moving through the layers to the apex, we pass through sections of decreasing area, with the managers at each level feeling with increasing intensity the pressures in supporting the organization above them. If we were further to imagine the individual managers loosely linked together by elastic bands across and between tiers, we would then find them in violent random motion, like the dance of Brownian particles. The frenetic movements of the dance are aimed at keeping the organization from toppling and falling apart with a crash.

This, then, is the traditional organization, based, as I have said, on no more than time-honored beliefs about human behavior. Now let's take a look at the assumptions of Theory *Y,* which, as I have also stressed, derive from the facts of life that have been uncovered by objective behavioral research. According to McGregor, these assumptions (which are constantly being reinforced by new data as psychological and motivational research accumulates) are:

1. The expenditure of physical and mental effort in work is as natural as play or rest.
2. External control and the threat of punishment are not the only means of inducing people to work toward organizational goals. Man will exercise self-direction and self-control in the service of objectives to which he is committed.
3. Commitment to objectives is a function of the rewards associated with their achievement.
4. The average human being learns, under proper conditions, not only to accept but also to seek responsibility.
5. The capacity of exercising a relatively high degree of imagination, ingenuity, and creativity in solving organizational problems is widely, not narrowly, distributed in the population.
6. Under the conditions of modern industrial life, the intellectual potentialities of the average human being are only partially utilized.

The psychological foundations on which these assumptions rest include the well-known formulation of human need developed by A. H. Maslow of Brandeis University. According to Maslow, man is a creature of ever-expanding wants. Once his basic needs have been satisfied, others take their place. Thus, man's needs may be ordered in a hierarchy, starting with his basic biological requirements and proceeding through a series of levels, each more intangible than the preceding one. To satisfy his needs, man expends energy; but once a need has been fairly well fulfilled, it no longer acts as a motivating force and man's efforts are then directed toward satisfying the need of the next level in the hierarchy. In this hierarchy of needs, Maslow has identified five levels:

1. *Physiological needs.* These are the needs for food, water, air, shelter, rest, exercise, and others required to satisfy the biological demands of the human organism.
2. *Safety needs.* These are needs to be free from fear of deprivation, danger, and threat, on the job and off.
3. *Social needs.* These are the needs people have for gregariousness and social interaction. Men like to group together for many purposes of life. They need to associate, to belong, to accept and be accepted, to love and to be loved.
4. *Ego needs.* These are the needs for reputation, self-respect, and self-esteem. Men need to feel competent and knowledgeable. They need respect, recognition, and status.
5. *Self-actualization needs.* The needs for the realization of individual potential, the liberation of creative talents, the widest possible use of abilities and aptitudes—in short, for personal fulfillment.

It should be noted, however, that these needs overlap and are interdependent. A higher, less tangible need emerges before the lower one is fully satisfied. Thus, Maslow has estimated that, in our society, the average citizen is about 85 percent satisfied in his physiological needs, 70 percent in his safety needs, 50 percent in his social needs, and 40 percent in his ego needs, but only 10 percent in his self-actualization needs.

Since we live in an economy where the basic human needs are reasonably well taken care of, more and more people today tend to be motivated by the intangible rewards offered by the higher levels in the needs hierarchy. It is these motivating forces that Theory *Y* management proposes to tap. In other words, Theory *Y* management aims at integrating individual goals with those of the organization—at making the job the principal means through which each employee can enlarge his competence, self-control, and sense of accomplishment. In such an atmosphere, Theory *Y* holds, employees are likely to identify with the goals of the organization because the organization identifies with their goals. In effect, the organization is propelled by the motivation of its various members, whose individual contributions combine to achieve the over-all goals of the enterprise.

This self-propelled, self-disciplining kind of organization is what we have been aiming for in our experiment in management at Non-Linear Systems. Our company develops and sells precision electronic instruments and we have been in business for 11 years. When we started our experiment three years ago, we had a work-force of about 225 employees. Today we have 350.

We began by adopting a horizontal form of organization. We have an executive council of eight members, which establishes basic strategy and initiates action toward its accomplishment. This council is headed by our president. Working with him are seven vice presidents. Each council member is responsible for one of the eight areas of operation identified by Drucker as fundamental to the attainment of goals in any business: innovation, market standing, profitability, productivity, physical and financial resources, manager performance and development, worker attitude and performance, and public responsibility.

Horizontal responsibility

Each vice president is responsible for the functioning of his area of operations throughout the organization. Thus, our vice president for productivity works to improve output per unit in every phase of the company's operations, whether it be the number of hours required to assemble an instrument, the streamlining of paper work, the elimination of waste motions in shipping, or determining the optimum number of personnel in a department or group. Similarly, the vice president for manager performance and development is concerned with training employees to understand company objectives, establishing courses for improving skills at all levels, developing improved hiring techniques, assessing performance throughout the company and, in general, making sure that there is a continual reservoir of knowledgeable and skilled people to assume the posts of increasing responsibility that open up as the company grows.

The executive council divorces itself from day-to-day tactical activities. These are the duties of some 30 department managers. All the departments are on a single level, just below the executive council. The department managers report to the executive council as a whole and not to individual members, and so executive-manager relationships follow functional lines. Any department head may seek out the member of the executive council who is concerned with the area central to the problem in question. Since areas often overlap and cannot be sharply delineated, members of the council often act by mutual consent; frequently they substitute for one another. Over the past three years our managers and indeed, most of the employees, have learned where to go for counsel. They are not all perturbed at finding themselves talking to two or three vice presidents either singly or at the same time, to cover all areas involved in the problem. Implicit in this conduct of the company's affairs is an atmosphere of mutual trust and acceptance.

Emphasis on teaching

In accordance with the Theory *Y* philosophy we regard management as basically an affair of teaching and training, not one of directing and controlling. We do control, of course, but we control the process, not the people. To understand how we are trying to achieve this kind of control we might look at our company in terms of Theory *Y* and Maslow's formulation of human needs.

Physiological needs in our society can be taken care of by money. Hence we decided to pay a minimum salary at least sufficient to provide for food, shelter, and other physical necessities and leave a little over, if possible. At the beginning of 1961, therefore, we established a minimum wage of $100 a week.* Simultaneously, we did away with time clocks. Time clocks are an offense to human dignity and imply mistrust of people. We also abandoned the practice of docking employees when they are out ill. Nevertheless, our absentee rate for the past year has been 2.8 percent less than half the prevailing rate in similar businesses in our community.

*This rate is approximately 60 cents more, on a equivalent hourly basis, or $24 per week, than comparable rates paid in the community.

To provide for safety needs we strive for an unconstraint coupled with a consistent managerial approach. Our objective is to achieve a calm, unharried atmosphere that induces rational, creative behavior throughout our operations. We try, as a company, to maintain steady employment. When sales are low, we stockpile finished products; when orders come pouring in, we do not hire at an accelerated pace. We prefer to ask our customers to bear with us for a little longer delivery than usual. In this way we avoid those cyclical hiring and firing peaks that cause employees to feel insecure and uncertain about their jobs. We have made this policy widely known throughout the company. We believe that it is well understood and has effectively contributed toward satisfying our employees' safety needs.

For the fulfillment of social needs we use the small group approach wherever we can. Gregariousness, affiliation, belonging—all these needs are served in the group. The individual members exchange information and gossip; they help and teach each other. Hence, we have discarded our assembly lines and reorganized the people who had been manning them into a number of seven-man teams. This we did in 1960, heading each team with a competent technician, whom we called Assistant Assembly Manager. Under his tutelage, the groups were asked to build complete instruments. This they have since learned to do and do well.

Self-paced teams

Today these teams complete instruments from kits of parts, electronic components, and hardware. They insert components on the printed circuit boards, solder and fabricate wiring harnesses. They bolt the hardware together. They complete the subassemblies, testing as they go. They run-in and calibrate finished instruments. There is no formal planning. By mutual agreement the team members decide who will do what and in what sequence. They pace themselves at their own rhythm. They know each other's strengths and generally do a far better job of planning than if directed by some external authority. As a result productivity in man-hours per instrument has steadily improved. Today it is 30 percent better than at any period in the company's history.

The group method, we have found, is an ideal way also to provide for the ego needs. Within the group a man is recognized for his excellences. He attains status by virtue of his demonstrated abilities. Since everyone has skills of one kind or another, each member of the group is deferred to in the area of his special competence. He is given the chance to achieve and to be acknowledged for his achievement. No one is pushed around. Each man can speak up and be listened to. He develops pride in his product and the company as he perfects his skills.

In these small groups we very often see one member teaching another some special technique or skill. This appears to us the highest accolade one can give—to defer to the expertise of another. The result has been a noticeable improvement in the quality of our products, which has steadily decreased the number of complaints from the field. These are now 70 percent fewer than they were three years ago.

When it comes to satisfying the highest area of human needs, self-actualization, we are dealing with the factor that holds the greatest potential for organizational growth and improvement. As I have said, we believe that the prime job of management is teaching and training, and so we endeavor to release dormant creativity by encouraging employees to improve their skills. We regularly conduct numerous classes and training groups. These cover a variety of subjects and are held both on and off company time.

Almost all of our training courses are completely voluntary. Some are led by trainers from within the company, some by specialists brought in from outside: Sometimes we have a senior engineer teaching a class of young engineers logic circuitry theory at night, an electronic technician teaching basic electricity to a group of men and women assemblers during the lunch period, and another group learning the elements of selling from an outside consultant in the morning.

Our training goes on at many levels. We have a number of small groups taking management training on a continuing basis. Some of these are "family" groups, some "cousins," and some "strangers" groups; that is to say, some groups are all from one department, some are made up of people holding the same positions but coming from different departments, while others are made up of people from a variety of departments and job levels. The training, though, is the same for all—the fundamentals of Theory *Y* management.

On the lookout for talent

Inherent in our management approach is a restless and never-ceasing search for talent. We continually assess performance. We do not use a formal procedure—evaluation in our book is a subjective process performed by our managers at all levels. In this process, we have come to rely heavily on insight and feeling. Not that we disparage objective testing—we employ an outside testing service, for example, to help us compile an inventory of employee aptitudes. However, in the final say, we have learned to trust our own observations and judgments.

We often move employees from one position to another in order to better match aptitudes and talents to job requirements. People may themselves request transfers to other kinds of work. We also dip into our reservoir of trained personnel when promotions open up. Of the 16 assistant managers in our instrument assembly department two years ago, not one remains in his original post. All have been moved up to more responsible positions calling for greater skills or more specialized knowledge.

From start to finish

We also try to arrange work so employees can obtain "closure," that is, the completion of a whole job. Seeing the whole job is a fundamental element of Theory Y. In the assembly-line approach of Theory X, by contrast, all the worker can see is the minute segment that's in front of him. A complete job is likely to engage a variety of aptitudes and skills. By providing closure—engaging the whole man, as it were, in the job— self-actualization becomes a vital motivating force. In this fashion we strive to create an operating climate that is conducive to commitment to work. The satisfaction of doing a whole job and a genuine commitment to work tend to produce a healthier employee—therefore a healthier organization.

To illustrate these ideas more specifically, let's take a look at a typical operation—our materials department. This department is responsible for all our purchasing. It is headed by a department manager and is subdivided into three groups, which act in parallel. Each group is headed by an assistant department manager. Working with him are an administrative assistant, a stockroom clerk, and a receiving inspection technician.

Since our executive council sets a limit on the total amount of dollars that can be tied up in the stockroom, the groups have to plan very carefully to insure that their purchases keep within the prescribed bounds. They must be alert to our constantly changing product mix and take particular account of long-lead procurement items. To guide their planning they receive data from the weekly meetings of the managers of our production departments and the distribution department. The latter is in daily touch with our marketing offices around the country, and so provides vital information on sales and sales prospects. The information given to managers of the materials department enables them to assess current and prospective changes in our product mix. They adjust their purchasing schedules accordingly, taking calculated risks where their judgment so dictates.

We buy about 2,500 different items. Each materials group buys about one-third of this number. Their planning task is therefore a formidable one and requires continuous attention to avoid critical shortages. The groups buy parts, components, and raw stock. They inspect the incoming materials to make sure that what they have bought is up to specification. They stock these materials. They assemble individual kits of the parts, components, and hardware required for the manufacture of each instrument, and they deliver these kits on demand to the instrument assembly department. Finally, in the act that provides closure to their part of the company's operations, they write the checks to pay for what they have bought.

The structure of our organization is such as to encourage meetings of many kinds for the exchange of information. Since there is only a limited chain of command, we get along with very few formal memos. Employees are advised to seek whatever information they need from those best able to give it. In fact, we have thrown out the classic injunction, "Write it, don't say it," and substituted, "Say it, don't write it," in its stead. As a result, we have no need for the informal organization that arises *sub rosa* in the conventionally run company and usually gets things done regardless of how the organization chart indicates they should be done.

By "saying it" instead of "writing it" we have opened up numerous channels of communication instead of confining ourselves to one medium in which many people have limited capability anyway. When people talk face-to-face, their understanding is almost invariably improved—tone, inflection, facial expression, and all such nuances reinforce the message that is being transmitted. Above all, there is a fair guarantee that the message has actually been received. In this way we aim at minimizing error.

Fallibility expected

Error, however, does creep in, as it does in any organization composed of human beings. The Theory Y philosophy accepts human error so long as it is within reasonable bounds. Growth, creativity, and productivity must involve mistakes from time to time and their correction. In most companies, memos are frequently written as a protection against error. We believe that where there is mutual trust there is no need for protective paper. Mutual trust is mutually reinforcing. We still have a great distance to go, but I believe we have made notable progress in improving openness and trust throughout the organization since our experiment in management began three years ago.

I realize that what I have written here may sound somewhat pious. Nevertheless, Theory Y suggests, to our minds, a return to the rugged, inner-directed qualities that drove our forefathers to hew civilization out of the wilderness. The calculated democratization of our enterprise represents, we think, an organic situation in which individual growth is encouraged and stimulated and in turn contributes to the continued growth of the enterprise as a whole.

At all events, in these past three years we have witnessed significant improvements in our capabilities. We have multiplied our product line fourfold, with no more than minor dips in our steadily improving productive effectiveness. We have probed and tested new ways of doing things. It's true that we have made mistakes along the way, but we have corrected them. We expect to make mistakes and correct them in the future. But at this point we feel that we are well launched on an exciting experiment that ultimately will not only pay off in larger profits for the company but will also contribute in some small measure toward the betterment of our industrial society.

The long-range view

After analyzing both the theory and practice of his Theory *Y* in *The Human Side of Enterprise,* Douglas McGregor considers it in the broader context of the next half century, which he believes, "will bring the most dramatic social changes in human history." He concludes: "It is not important that management accept the assumptions of Theory *Y*. These are one man's interpretations of current social science knowledge, and they will be modified—possibly supplanted—by new knowledge within a short time. It *is* important that management abandon limiting assumptions like those of Theory *X*, so that future inventions with respect to the human side of enterprise will be more than minor changes in already obsolescent conceptions of organized human effort."

22

Behavioral Theory vs. Reality

James A. Lee

Most behavioral theorists have "known" for years how an organization and its management style should be changed to bring about tremendous improvement in morale and productivity. Executives, managers, and administrators who have been exposed to Modern Human Resource Management theories appear, at least to the theorist, to have adopted their "findings" almost not at all.

And the question is: Why?

The purpose of this article is to answer this question. The reasons, in my view, are quite simple and straightforward. But because of the approaches of many behavioral theorists and training consultants, most managers have been placed in such a defensive position that to argue effectively against Modern Human Resource Management would be tantamount to shooting Smokey the Bear for sport.

A typical example of apparent management rejection, as it appears to some behavioral theorists, is in the introductory chapter of a recent book containing excerpts from the writings of most Modern Human Resource Management theorists:

> Recently one of the authors of this book proposed a management development program to a major American corporation. Human behavior in organizations was to be the subject of the first week, new decision-making tools the second, and business and society relationships the third. The latter two weeks were accepted, the first rejected rather strongly—with an oath about having had enough human relations! Of course, this may reflect one chief

executive's opinion, but it does seem symptomatic of the suspicion and perhaps cynicism that characterizes management's view on the subject of human relations. "Not useful," "too fuzzy," "theoretical," "soft," "not operational" are all responses we have received to pleas for consideration of behavior.[1]

One must admit that the reasons just given are not pieces of a carefully prepared rationale. Because they appear flippant and somewhat unrelated, however, they cannot be brushed aside as evidence of simply a bad decision by a single unenlightened executive.

I propose to provide here a useful rationale that will account for the rates at which Modern Human Resource Management theories can be found in application. My purpose is not to provide executives with a better list of reasons for rejecting proposals for Modern Human Resource Management training. I believe, however, that if *real* causes of the resistance are not carefully analyzed, there is little chance for increasing the use of what is known today about organizational behavior motivation.

MHRM theories

At the outset, my definition of Modern Human Resource Management should be explained in some detail. By MHRM, I refer primarily to the overlapping theories and concepts of behavioral theorists such as Douglas McGregor, Frederick Herzberg, Chris Argyris, Rensis Likert, Robert Blake with Jane S. Mouton, and Abraham Maslow. Consider:

—McGregor described two sets of contrasting assumptions about man and his attitudes toward his work. The Theory *X* assumptions (man is lazy, needs watching and prodding), and Theory *Y* assumptions (workers seek responsibility and are capable of self-control) are now part of management jargon.

—Herzberg's work, focusing on worker motivation, pointed up "hy-

[1]David R. Hampton, Charles E. Summer, and Ross A. Webber, *Organizational Behavior and the Practice of Management* (Glenview, Illinois: Scott, Foresman, 1968), p. 5; see also *Studies in Personnel Policy No. 216* (New York: National Industrial Conference Board, 1969), for results of a survey of opinions of management in over 300 companies regarding the impact of various behavioral theorists.

giene" factors (working conditions, fringe benefits, and so on) as essential but not motivators, and the real motivators (responsibility, achievement, and so forth) as the key to improving worker performance.

—Argyris' theories are concerned with the effects of organizational life on individual motivation. He has developed organizational structures and control systems designed to help build consistency between organizational and individual goals.

—Likert has developed four organizational model systems. His System 1 could be said to be a Theory *X* type, and his System 4 manager, a group consensus seeker, is not far from holding Theory *Y* assumptions. Likert has also proposed a human-assets inventory approach involving the management of people with at least the same care and concern as the management of land and other material resources.

—Blake and Mouton provided the theory that integrated the work of McGregor, Likert, and others. Their 9,9 manager (people and output oriented) is similar to a System 4 or Theory Y manager, while at the opposite corner of their grid is a 9,1 manager who is primarily concerned with output but not particularly concerned with people.

—Maslow, a theoretical psychologist and father of the "need hierarchy" concept (a dynamic model of Aristotle's soul hierarchy), has suggested that efforts to motivate workers must be consistent with the theory that a satisfied need does not offer opportunities for motivation. Higher order needs must be acknowledged as motivators as lower order needs are fulfilled.

Modern Human Resource Management as used here, then, is an abbreviated summary of these theories which, in general, hold that (a) managers should trust their subordinates to be more responsible in the performance of their jobs; (b) managers should permit the subordinate to participate in the making of his own job; and (c) managers should replace much of the mechanistic structure, characteristic of most institutions, with an organic approach to organization.

Before beginning with an analysis of the resistance to wholesale adoption of MHRM approaches, let me point out that over the years managers *have* changed in the way they approach human resource management. Their changes have been necessarily integral with the cultural changes in Western societies (more on this later). For training directors, consultants, theorists, or anyone who would contemplate influencing an

Reasons for Resistance to MHRM

From sociology and anthropology[a]

O A society is a semistationary integrated unit.
O The introduction of a new element affects other elements.
O Many elements in the culture must be changed to accommodate the new element.
O This reordering process is a very slow one.

From industrial case analysis[b]

O Most behavioral science is focused on human motivation and group behavior without fully accounting for the technical environment which circumscribes, even determines, the roles the actors will play.
O Such abstractions as motivation, interaction, and authority do not take place in a technical vacuum.

From research in industrial administration[c]

O The link between technology and organization persists in spite of, rather than because of, conscious behavior or deliberate policy.
O Therefore, analysis of situational demands is necessary before organization appraising is attempted.
O This analysis would also lead to an increased understanding of the personal qualities and skills required in different industrial situations.

From social psychology[d]

O Perception is functionally selective.
O Beliefs and culturally acquired attitudes about leaders and followers play a significant role in determining the nature of this selectivity and tend to determine the meaning of these perceptions.
O The new data available to an individual but contradictory to his beliefs and attitudes may not be fully perceived or may be assimilated in such a way that the basic beliefs are not changed (lip service to MHRM, for example).

From applied behavioral science[e]

O A person's leadership style reflects the individual's motivational and need structure.
O It takes several years of intensive psychotherapy to effect lasting changes in this structure.
O A few hours of lectures and role-playing are not the equivalent of intensive psychotherapy.

From experimental application in industry
(representative examples only)

* * *

O The Ohio State University Studies indicated that human relations training (with role-playing, group discussion, etc.) had no measurable effect on plant behavior after return to work. "The results clearly indicated that the foreman is more responsible to the day-to-day climate (subculture) in which he operates than to any special course of training he may have been given." (Parentheses added.) f
O A Southern California company that had experimented with a number of MHRM techniques reversed its style, letting go senior executives in the process. Financial difficulties were blamed for dropping the experiment. g . . .

[a]William F. Ogburn and Meyer F. Nimkoff, *Sociology* (New York: Houghton Mifflin, 1946), pp. 880-82.
[b]Robert H. Guest, *Organizational Change: The Effect of Successful Leadership* (New York: Irwin-Dorsey Press, 1963), p. 74.
[c]Joan Woodward et al., *Industrial Organization: Theory and Practice* (London: Oxford University Press, 1965), p. 74.
[d]David Krech and Richard S. Crutchfield, *Theory and Problems of Social Psychology* (New York: McGraw-Hill, 1948), pp. 190-92.
[e]Fred A. Fiedler, *A Theory of Leadership Effectiveness* (Urbana: University of Illinois, 1967), p. 248.
[f]Edwin A. Fleishman, Edwin F. Harris, and Harold E. Burtt, *Leadership and Supervision in Industry: An Evaluation of a Supervisory Training Program*, Monograph No. 33 (Columbus , Ohio: Bureau of Educational Research, Ohio State University, 1955), p. 94.
[g]*Business Week,* March 20, 1965, pp. 93-94; see also Vance Packard, "A Chance for Everyone to Grow," *Reader's Digest,* November 1963 , pp. 114-18.

organization's management to adopt MHRM applications, however, I suggest beginning with a quick review of the list of obvious possible reasons for resistance shown in the accompanying ruled insert.

It should be noted here that top management's willingness to experiment is to be commended, even though many such organizational experiments fail or offer questionable results. The risks can be quite high compared with experiments using college sophomores or tiny work-force units.

All of the accompanying rationales shown in the ruled insert suggest or point directly to the need for a system approach as the only useful avenue for further exploration and application. Since managerial behavioral change is primarily a function of cultural change, it is implicit that subordinates must change integrally with superiors and that this subsystem is part of a subculture which must change and which is part of a total culture which must also change.

All MHRM theory I have ever seen or heard is addressed to only one element (management) in the culture, as though it were independent. (Where is the Theory Y for nonmanagers—"Trust your boss to do the right thing"—or for the engineer—"Trust the worker to have useful ideas of his own"—and what behavioral scientist is writing to the union leaders urging them to trust corporate management to be fair and honest?)

Cultural changes

The first step in the analysis requires that one accept an anthropologist's view of a culture or subculture as an integrated unit. If we hold this point of view, we can eventually arrive at the conclusion that most MHRM theories are only *descriptions* of cultural changes taking place in institutional subcultures in certain Western societies. Once seen in this light, the varying rate of adoption of techniques springing from these theories begins to make sense.

Cultural or societal change in Western countries is usually uneven. The factors influencing this change are not present to the same degree everywhere in the culture at the same time. Therefore, there are a few subcultures or semiencapsulated groups changing less slowly than others. The general *direction* of this change appears to be more or less the same, however, and there is enough evidence available for me to describe certain aspects of it in terms of moving either *toward* or *away from*.

Toward:

—More autonomy for individuals in institutional settings.

—Greater demand for information affecting autonomy, health, and security, and increased ability to get this information.

—Wider participation in institutional planning and decision making.

—Greater dependence upon individual's judgment in institutional task performances.

—More widespread recognition of the potential power of the non-manager to effect institutional goal attainment.

—More response to the law of the situation.

—More self-evaluation with the implicit discipline of the task.

—More organic organizational structures.

Away from:

—Elitism (blood, class, or technical).

—Mechanistic organizational structures.

—Sacredness of management rights and institutional policies and procedures.

—Formal discipline based upon position authority.

There can be no isolated cause of these directional changes, of course. However, the causal whole can be described by my listing its most important elements: technological, economic, family, and educational.

Technological changes.   In the past 70 years in the United States, few work tasks have not been changed radically. The nature of individual tasks in certain industries (electronics, space, R&D, chemical) has resulted in altered behavior that has begun to produce changes in attitudes toward work performance and the roles of superiors. The increased proportion of complicated work cannot be supervised in the same manner as could the simple tasks of a previous period.

Certain technologies have severely altered intra-institutional worker density and the nature of worker controls. (Compare a machine-paced mass production work environment with that of a modern refinery or chemical processing operation.)

Communication and transportation changes have made available more information and opportunity for escape from immediate subcultures.

Economic changes. Increased affluence, partly a function of technological changes, has altered the early need of the young to work. It has made possible educational gain throughout society. The family has been radically altered (see next part) due to a combination of technological and economic changes. Increased independence and mobility of individual members of society is due at least in part to increased affluence.

The family. There can be little doubt that the family is the most powerful single environmental force in shaping the personality structure, social response patterns, values, and attitudes toward work, authority, and autonomy.

There is also little doubt that this root social institution is changing. The increased absence of both parents from their young for longer periods (divorces, separations, and work), the reduced need for interdependence for economic survival, the increased freedom from drudgery in the home, and the relatively private use of leisure time cannot help but change the family. Moreover, since many parents have the knowledge and time to consciously raise their children according to some philosophy (Spock, Freud, the Existentialists, la Leche, and others), it is unreasonable to expect the family to remain stable.

Because the family is the nuclear social unit, roles and power relations changes can be seen reflected in the larger institutions in the society. The mother (traditional roles: suckle, teach, comfort) has begun a new role with a new "authority" in relation to the father (decide, discipline, direct) whose position of authority has been diluted. The children (learn, work, obey) who have more knowledge and better education, are needed very little for the family's economic survival and are gaining autonomy and power in the family earlier. These changes also appear in larger social roles and relationships comparable to those of the family: government (suckle, teach, comfort), business, (decide, discipline, direct), and workers (learn, work, obey).

The results of family changes reflected in the wider culture are obvious: the power relationships between government, business, and labor are mirror images of the changes that have taken place in the individual family. For a long-range prediction of major institutional power relationships, one should now observe the family carefully.

For example, when the children begin to take greater license with the mother, one should expect (a few years later) the unions of government employees to begin to exert greater pressure on the government.

Other results should also be obvious: attitudes toward work, drudgery, authority, and autonomy affect employee motivation. And as these changes reach the organizational setting through workers, the pressures thus generated change managerial behavior.

Educational changes. Teaching philosophies and methods have focused more on the individual. During a child's most formative period, his teachers are more often women than men. Democratic approaches to school administration and classroom activities have altered individual role conceptions. A greater proportion of the population is educated at all levels.[2] People are more interested in information now that more of them know how to use it.

All these important elements are obviously interrelated. They are abstracted here only for the purpose of elaborating on the causes of the cultural changes that affect behavior in organizational settings. Another thing is obvious: *the manager does not have much direct control over these changes.*

Which of the causal factors are within the manager's control?

Education of the work force can be effected (directly but only slightly) by two methods: (1) tuition refund and training programs, and (2) changes in the work technology (through product or production method changes) that will force a replacement of some of the workforce population.

Technology of the work can be affected by changes in products or

---

[2]In 1920, 17 percent finished high school compared with 80 percent today, and over half of our high school graduates enter college, compared with 20 percent in 1940.

methods of production. These changes, however, are not conscious managerial choices for MHRM purposes but are dependent on many factors (e.g., markets and economics).

The *family,* of course, is almost completely outside the direct control of management. If at all, management indirectly affects this institution through the hiring of more wives and mothers.

Another indirect effect has been the reduction of family worry over financial catastrophe through health and life insurance plans. The role of the wife-mother has been altered, therefore, because in lower- and middle-class families in Western countries, she was often the primary force influencing the "saving for the rainy day" behavior. Today's increased affluence is also outside any immediate control by the manager. Only through the overall increases in national productivity does the manager influence the standard of living which in turn alters the social institutional environments.

"Vanguard" institutions

A few institutional populations are affected more than others by these cultural changes. Roughly, in order of their change rate, they are:

—Research and development institutions.

—Many government departments.

—Certain quarters of the space, aeronautics, electronics, and chemical industries.

—Certain quarters of the utility industries.

One can hardly miss the government thread running through most of the list, although given the government's increased role in the protection of the individual over the past 50 years (labor legislation, civil liberties, individual rights, and so on), this is hardly surprising.

Behavioral scientists will appear to have had more success with their management seminars in the institutions just listed. Failures occur more often in industries whose success depends little on the coordinated efforts of affluent professionals and highly educated technicians who are in the forefront of cultural change in our society.

Therefore, the adoption of Modern Human Resource Management will necessarily be slow simply because manpower management style is almost completely intertwined in the system of cultural values. These values are in turn a function of technological, economic, family, and educational changes that alter behavior.

As the economic, family, and educational changes have an impact on behavior, of course, so will they change the manpower management styles, with or without much help from seminars offered by behavioral scientists. These cultural values will change not as a direct result of these scientists' findings.

Rather, quite the opposite is closer to the truth: as the culture changes, so will the scientists, their findings, and their seminars. The history of management theory is replete with subculturally and self-referenced contributors. Consider:

—*Niccolo Machiavelli* (1469–1527) who was exiled by a conquering family before writing *The Prince,* which was designed to show how power should be gained and held.

—*Adam Smith* (1723–1790) who was professor of moral philosophy for eight years before publishing *The Theory of Moral Sentiments,* and worked 2 1/2 years as private tutor to the stepson of the Chancellor of the Exchequer, Charles Townshend, before writing *Wealth of Nations.*

—*Thomas Alva Edison* (1847–1931), the inventor's inventor, who on several occasions devised machines for the specific purpose of replacing troublesome workers.

—*Frederick W. Taylor* (1856–1915), a laborer and shop worker of unusual intelligence, who devoted his life to efficiency in shop methods and tooling.

—*Mary Parker Follett* (1868–1938), primarily associated with social work institutions, who emphasized the role of the group in satisfying needs, in realizing individual potential, and in decision making.

—*James David Mooney* (1884–1957), author of *Principles of Organization* in 1926, who was an engineer, a vice president of General Motors, and a 20-year reserve military officer, and who emphasized the need for all organizations to be hierarchical.

* * *

The vast majority of the behavioral theorists today are professors, whose strong autonomy needs and antiauthoritarian bias govern much of their research approach and ideal model-building.[3] They bounce their theories off other faculty members and students, who are well known to have similar needs and biases; they use students for subjects for some of their studies, and they arrive at a recommended work environment in the image of the ideal university.

Among the theorists, Douglas McGregor (if not his zealous followers) must be considered an exception. On the eve of his retirement as President of Antioch, he wrote:

"Before coming to Antioch I had observed and worked with top executives as an adviser in a number of organizations. I thought I knew how they felt about their responsibilities and what led them to behave as they did. I even thought that I could create a role for myself which would enable me to avoid some of the difficulties they encountered.

"I was wrong! It took the direct experience of becoming a line executive and meeting personally the problems involved to teach me what no amount of observation of other people could have taught.

"I believed, for example, that a leader could operate successfully as a kind of adviser to his organization, I thought I could avoid being a 'boss' ... but I couldn't have been more wrong."[4]

Most MHRM theories, then, are self- and subculturally referenced. They have been given to us in some detail. Most, however, are descriptions of what is fairly standard practice in a few small subcultures in the vanguard of cultural changes in most Western societies. Theorist-consultants have studied attempts to produce change in a few socio-industrial subcultures. They have reported all the temporary successes and few, if any, of the failures.

The southern California company mentioned earlier in the ruled insert, which used everything from T-groups to complete self-determination of production process and control, was described by Vance Packard as "a chance for everyone to grow," and was the subject of several

---

[3]See Peter P. Gil and Warren G. Bennis, "Science and Management: Two Cultures," *Journal of Applied Behavioral Sciences* 4, no. 1 (1968), in which case analyses of a group of behavioral scientists and industrial managers were compared, yielding an easy identification of the effects of the scientists' antiauthoritarian bias.

[4]*Antioch Notes,* 31, no. 9.

evangelistically designed cases registered with the Harvard Case Clearing House.[5] No follow-up cases have been prepared telling the rest of the story, which was available as early as 1965. (One of the MHRM-oriented "let-go" vice presidents visited the Harvard Business School at that time, looking for a job.) Yet these cases are still being used by organizational behavior faculty in business schools!

The major chemical company (also cited in the ruled insert), with the organizational development department that was hailed in business news media, was similarly the subject of business cases, but follow-up studies and cases marking the elimination of the department are conspicuously lacking.

Managerial approach

If the managers and the theorists are not directly responsible for cultural change, then what value is there in all the research and theory? Considerable, in my opinion, if a reasonable change rate (with limits that we do not yet know how to alter significantly in specific operational environments) can be accepted.

Here, then, is an eight-step approach for managers that would make maximum use, however meager the actual results, of our knowledge of human behavior in organizations.

First, avoid all theory suggesting that managers alone can, by conscious design, change enough to become the major direct change agent of organizational behavior. If managerial tasks can be altered to produce behavior in the desired direction, it is worth a try.

Consider this example: if a manager seems to avoid utilizing known or suspected talent under his supervision, *ask* him what his people think about a certain problem. This can be done only after he has been assured that the better his people are, the better he is.

Here is another example: if a particular manager needs to learn to delegate more of his work but glues himself to his operation, his superior

[5]"A Chance for Everyone to Grow," *Reader's Digest,* November 1963, pp. 114–18.

officer can give him specific tasks that take him physically away from his operation before sending him to management seminars on "how to delegate."

Second, if a major organizational change is needed, top management should double a behavioral scientist's estimate of the time required and triple its own. Subcultures change more slowly than everybody realizes.

For example, a large U.S. corporation with a holding company history and style figured that a new president and a few new staff vice presidential appointments at corporate headquarters would lead to integration in a few years. When integration failed to take place, corporate management was so disappointed that it replaced this president with one who left the new cadre of corporate headquarters vice presidents to quit or find some busy work.

Another major American corporation utilized the most well-known behavioral scientist consultants available and an internal team of organizational development people in an effort to integrate an old holding company. They made good progress, but not fast enough to satisfy the board. Every time the president would make an effort to accelerate the integrative process, flak from within the system would undermine his position. A bad year for earnings now and then further undermined his efforts because in some quarters it was attributed to his change program. He is still suffering from poor judgment of the *rate* at which he could produce change.

Third, determine the need for organizational changes in terms of performance in relation to company objectives—and not because of measured attitudes, fashions, or the opinions of behavioral scientists. Look for *behavioral* changes necessary to achieve the organizational changes, which, in turn, will enable the company to attain its organizational objectives. Begin with organizational and individual incentives to change behavior through fairly straightforward but well-publicized policy changes and reward system changes.

For example, a division of a major mining company needed to adapt to closure threats from the U.S. Bureau of Mines because of its accident record. All supervisory and middle-management personnel job descriptions were rewritten to incorporate accident prevention responsibilities, performance appraisal forms were rewritten to conform, and supervisory management training programs were launched to teach accident prevention techniques.

The evidence that these took top management initiation and support was unmistakable. The accident frequency, severity, and compensation per each $100 of payroll were cut by some 90% within three years. The division's cost per ton mined was the best of all its domestic operations.

Fourth, study the organization to determine if integration efforts have resulted in a single management cadre over several different technologies. Specifically, mines, mills, smelters, and fabricating units require different types of managements, attract different kinds of people, and usually require different policies. Attempts to integrate them on a management and policy basis can produce unnecessary problems.

For example, a large light-metal mining and processing division of a major corporation is certain its productivity can be increased. It has been studied to death by top MHRM people who have ignored the varieties of technologies (and subcultures) under one roof. Its single union has as much trouble with influence as does management. The executive style (because of historical promotional streams) represents mostly only one of the three technologies, as does the corporate headquarters management.

No one in management or among the MHRM people is considering any short- or long-range plan that recognizes the differences in the subcultures formed by the technologies of a mill, smelter, or fabricating unit. The company, given its locked-in capital investment, would probably be better off to have three separate, relatively autonomous managements with three sets of local policies and a plan for replacing, over time, the one union with two or three unions.

Conglomerates should study their organizations to determine if acquisitions have resulted in a single management cadre with a single policy system over several different technologies. Remember, different tasks attract different people who glue themselves together and respond as groups with needs for different policies and incentives.

Fifth, do not attempt significant change unless most top people are prepared to introduce adequate tension along with a powerful change agent or two.

This point is illustrated by the experience of a machinery manufacturer's president who attempted to bull his way through a difficult labor negotiations year representing a major change in the corporate labor relations approach. Most top people nodded approval, but, when the chips were down, they undermined the whole strategy by subtle foot-dragging so as to avoid the production of tension below them.

The president should have taken more care to look behind their apparent agreement with the strategy. He could have done this by discussing in detail, and in advance, the course of negotiations as each projected stage produced probable alternatives to be faced in carrying out the planned strategy.

If too many such alternatives were to emerge, he could have dropped his plan. It also follows that perceived radical shifts in strategy would be tested thoroughly by the top people because they had, at least instinctively, a good feel for an impractical change rate.

Sixth, determine, with the help of behavioral scientists if necessary, a readiness for change diagnosis. This should include an assessment of rate readiness as well as a priority of changes in order of the likelihood of success.

Thus, if a company needs to begin in earnest to integrate blacks into supervisory or management cadres, it should have a long-range plan devised with the help of social scientists. Be wary of any short-range plan that promises to achieve real integration objectives. (Also beware of any plan that looks like it will have blacks "sitting near the door.")

If a readiness diagnosis indicates that rank-and-file supervisors will openly resist the plan, hold off the plan while a readiness program is undertaken. Get social scientists' help with the readiness program and with the plan to follow. Remember, though, that both of you likely will err in the direction of impatience.

Seventh, ask a behavioral science consultant, in specific terms, *how* any proposed change in managerial behavior or style will be accomplished. Whether his choice is T-groups, role playing, or ignorance removal, ask him to include follow-up studies at least six months after the training period to test the program's effectiveness.

Eighth, remember that there is scant evidence that attitudes can be changed, and then behavior. There is a mountain of evidence that "belief is shown in the willingness to act." Strive for changes in behavior. The attitudes will follow for behavioral scientists to come around and measure.

In summary

In this article, I have attempted to point out why there are differential rates of the application of Modern Human Resource Management techniques, and that these rates are relatively unrelated to the direct efforts of behavioral science theorists. Managerial style or behavior has been shown to be integral to social subsystems and, therefore, cannot be changed in a vacuum. Managers, as integrated parts of subcultures, change their behavior primarily in response to changes in their subculture (work environment), after which measurable changes in their attitudes and values take place.

Attention, then, must be focused on the *total* system in which they operate before any changes should be attempted. This examination must be done with the full knowledge that technological, educational, economic, and family elements are responsible for altering behavior that produces managerial style changes.

If an obvious gap indicates the need for managerial changes, search for means of focusing on a task that can result in the desired managerial behavior changes. Examine thoroughly the evidence that such a gap, when closed, will help the organization achieve its objectives.

I have also pointed out that most behavioral scientists are more observers and describers of cultural, and therefore managerial, change than causes of it. By my revised version of the Hindustani fable of "The Blind Men and the Elephant" I am suggesting, as did Douglas McGregor, that there is still a sizable gap between observing and doing.

23

Good Judgment
Wayne A. R. Leys

The connection between ethics and policy decisions is not very clearly understood. If you make a few inquiries, you will find some people who entertain clear and straight-forward ideas about ethical duties, and they may have definite notions about policies; but they can't tell you how you get from ethics to policy or vice versa.

Suppose that you start with a moral commandment, such as, "Thou shalt not steal," or a philosophical phrase like "The greatest happiness of the greatest number." No one seems to experience much difficulty in talking about such things. The trouble begins when you try to apply the ethical formula to the policy problems of government, of business, or of family. You may not be able to find a moment of decision when anyone clearly faces an alternative that could be called "stealing" or is aware that what he was doing had an effect upon happiness. A policy may be the work of many hands. Even when responsibility is consciously shouldered by one person, the basis of his choice is often a hunch, "an intuition of experience which outruns analyses and sums up many unnamed and tangled impressions which lie beneath consciousness."

Honest thinkers, discovering that some policy makers have "played by ear," begin to suspect that all high principles are after-thoughts. A Viennese cynic whom I met last year held this opinion and, rather appropriately, mispronounced the word "ethics." He kept saying "attics." Attics are high places where we store things that we don't use anymore, things that we haven't enough nerve to throw away.

Reprinted with permission of author and Prentice-Hall, Inc., Englewood Cliffs, New Jersey. From Wayne A. R. Leys, *Ethics for Policy Decisions*, © 1952, pp. 3–11.

You will recognize a common variety of cynicism in these sarcastic remarks. They are the sort of comment that some readers will expect in this book. Cynical remarks are entertaining and in some situations they are about all that can be said. But no one needs to have a book written to tell him that the world is not run consistently by the Golden Rule.

It is not the purpose of this book to prove that villains are villainous. It is rather to learn whether anything can be done to make the standards of ethics more applicable to the controversial issues of public and private life. Can problems of policy be analyzed in such a way that fewer of them have to be settled by hunch and more of them can be enlightened by moral principle? Is it possible to articulate what we mean by wisdom and good judgment? Can more of our deliberations achieve the level of philosophy?

The task is formidable in view of the quickening tempo of life. In recent decades we have lost rather than gained hours for reflection. Our moments of decision are a bottleneck for all kinds of knowledge. Much of the progress in the arts and sciences has been nullified by the shortening of time for deliberation. Hence, ethics will not be a successful guide in action, unless its insights can be mobilized quickly under exciting and distracting circumstances.

What is ethics and what is policy?

The study of standards for decision-making is the part of philosophy that has been called *ethics*. Ethics has been a subject for systematic investigation for about twenty-five hundred years. In that time the philosophers have worked out formulas of justice, loyalty, and happiness that should help policy-makers avoid reliance on blind hunch.

The word "philosophy" originally meant "the love of wisdom," and the philosophers have conceived of their task as the discovery of very general principles of wisdom. They have tried to say what would determine right conduct in all times and places. They have tried to identify what is always good.

A completely general wisdom may seem to compete with the specialized and local wisdom that men of action call "good policy." In fact, ethics and policy are contrasted by many writers, who look down on the policy arts as mere technologies or, at best, applied social sciences. The policy subjects are supposed to serve the man of action by telling him how to get a certain result, whether the result is good by philosophical standards or not. The policy arts include business and public administration, law, social work, pedagogy, psychiatry, vocational guidance, military science, and pastoral theology. These disciplines have voluminous literatures; they deliver to the man who has a problem those encapsulated research findings that will prevent ill-advised action in his particular kind of work. Such fact-oriented guidance is often contrasted with the general and supposedly vague value-principles of ethics.

When we get down to cases, the contrast between ethics and policy is not so sharp. The policy arts reach for general standards of conduct, although they do not employ the vocabulary of traditional ethics. In their attack upon the causes of bad judgment, the students of administration, engineering, and law become concerned about occupational biases. They see the need for "principles," for "orientation," for "the quality of philosophy" that will enable their practitioners to see "broad policy issues" and "call up from the depths of their minds those things superficially impertinent which once grasped may be the fundamental pertinences."

Although philosophers might make poor policy-makers and although policy-makers are seldom philosophers, it is the thesis of this book that good judgment in policy matters requires philosophical viewpoints. Ethics and policy are not opposites, unless one chooses to employ these words to mean "noble principles" and "unprincipled expediency," respectively. By a policy decision we mean a choice that "lays down a policy," that creates a precedent or that determines a course of action; in a word, it is a decision that is intended to affect more than one action. It may be intended to affect future decisions or it may influence the choices of other people. This definition will be refined in Chapter 12, but the reference to future and distant action is enough to explain why specialized vocational training, if it produces any narrowness of mind, may need to be supplemented by philosophy.

Throughout this book we shall be commenting on policy discussions in which specialists were blind to facts and purposes that were obvious to persons who had a different kind of training or experience. These

discussions will reveal the need for a more general wisdom to complement, if not to refute, the more specialized wisdom of the professions.

A neat illustration of occupational bias is supplied by two Philadel-
phians, a lawyer and a forester. During a congressional investigation in
1910, George Wharton Pepper, the lawyer, served as counsel for Gifford
Pinchot, the forester. Pinchot had been chief United States Forester, a
position from which he was discharged after he publicly accused President Taft of permitting the Secretary of Interior to sell Alaska coal lands
contrary to the public interest. A congressional committee held pro-
tracted hearings on the charges and counter-charges.

In 1944 Mr. Pepper published his memoirs, and took the occasion
to criticize the behavior of his client, Pinchot. He thought Pinchot had
made a poor witness and had been reckless in his statements to the
press.

In 1947 Pinchot's memoirs were published, and they contained
some comments upon Pepper's complaint.

> George Pepper was really able, unusually able, within his limitations, and in
> an ordinary case would doubtless have done an excellent job. But this was
> not an ordinary case, and George couldn't adjust himself to the central fact
> that the judge before whom this issue was being tried was not the Commit-
> tee, with Knute Nelson at its head, but the whole people of the United States.
>
> The newspaper men at the press table were never part of the audience
> to which George spoke. After he made an important point and got it in the
> record, it never occurred to him that a minute or two would be well spent
> in getting that point to the general public through the press.
>
> Again and again I had to supplement George's failure to connect with the
> larger audience by making a public statement of my own, and again and
> again George, horror-stricken, threatened to resign. From his point of view
> that wasn't cricket. From my point of view it was the indispensable essence
> of the whole affair.
>
> The trouble with George was that he had lived too much with courts and
> lawyers, and not enough with the world of men.
>
> All the rest of us knew that the majority of the Committee, with its
> carefully selected standpat membership, would report in favor of Ballinger
> (and according to his reminiscences, Pepper knew it too). What we were
> after, therefore, was the verdict of the larger jury, and that, in spite of
> Pepper, in the end we got.
>
> There could have been no greater contrast than between Brandeis' view
> of what this whole conflict was about, and George Pepper's. And it was
> never more clearly shown than when Brandeis, by almost incredible skill

and persistence, and with the courageous and patriotic help of young Kerby ... uncovered the Lawler letter and the Wickersham misdating. To Pepper it was lese majesty of the deepest dye, and he couldn't stand it.

After Brandeis had brought Taft into the case, Pepper evaporated. He didn't resign; he just simply, for all practical purposes, wasn't there any more. His rigid conformist mind was out of its depth in water in which it couldn't swim—and if that is a mixed metaphor, you'll get what I mean anyhow.

Pinchot has portrayed a lawyer trying to handle a political problem as if it were a legal case, primarily concerned with proving who said and did what and what was in accordance with law. Pinchot thought Pepper failed to appreciate the political problem of arousing the public to demand from the indifferent Taft administration action to conserve natural resources.

Attorneys have been criticized as policy-makers on many other occasions. Parkinson, the insurance executive, for example, bitterly recalled how lawyers had "perfected" the warranties of insurance contracts until no dishonest claims could be collected in court; but they did this legal job so well that many honest claims could not be collected, either, and that aroused a storm of public indignation and some punitive legislation.

Yet, the legal mind, for all its shortcomings, avoids bad judgment in situations where insurance men, foresters, physicians, and other specialists go wrong. Laymen who do not consult lawyers are often oblivious of other people's rights until the are served with a notice of a damage suit. People who are eager to work out a contract usually need a lawyer to remind them of the possibility that one of the contracting parties may die, and that some provision should be made for that contingency.

Every profession, however, has blind spots peculiar to it. The blind spots of engineers, for example, are usually different from those of lawyers. In responding to the opportunities for more efficiency, the engineers sometimes forget about the feelings of human machines. Or, confronted with a non-mechanical problem, they do what Henry Stimson disliked in President Hoover: They calculate all their moves as they would in building a bridge. Stimson thought Hoover missed his chances for effective action and depressed the whole government by his somber planning conferences, which the Secretary of State likened to "sitting in a bath of ink."

The opposite extreme is exemplified by advertising and public relations men, as well as some professional politicians who "tend to believe that words can accomplish anything" and want to rush into the promotion of schemes that need engineering. They seem to have the kind of faith that A. K. Rogers attributed to Kingsley: "Let us get enthusiastically together and do something for the glory of God, and matters of theory will look after themselves!"

The incomplete insights of specialists made the poet, Auden, wonder if "Brokers see the Ding-an-sich as Real Estate," or in the case of a politician, dreaming about his sweetheart, "Does he multiply her face into a crowd?" A contemporary administrator has stated, more prosaically, that the tendency to apply the criteria of one specialty "produces dogmatism, prejudice, and narrow-mindedness, particularly toward other large fields." The philosopher, Hegel, if he were alive today, would undoubtedly see occupational insights and biases as parts of the human comedy, each having an urge to be the whole of wisdom, idolatrously worshipping its limited self as if it were the whole of what is valuable and important.

The wisdom of specialists is an improvement upon the blind hunch when the action that is needed lies within the field for which the specialist was educated. If, however, the expert ventures beyond his competence, or has to collaborate with other professions, he needs more general principles. Without them he may sometimes be compared with a man who, by running very fast, succeeds in jumping aboard the wrong train.

How to read philosophy

Is there such a thing as philosophical wisdom, a correction of occupational biases and other prejudices? When wisdom-seekers read the history of moral philosophy they are often discouraged. They may, like Mencken, conclude that philosophy is all ancient nonsense, trying to prove that it is a waste of time to hunt for facts. They read the interminable "refutation of the refutation." Although they are looking for guidance in a situation that does not permit complete factual knowledge, they are offended by the philosopher's high and mighty disdain for any particular set of facts.

Let the wisdom-seeker read a few representative treatises: *The Gorgias* by Plato, *The Nichomachean Ethics* by Aristotle, *The Discourses* of Epictetus, *The Leviathan* by Hobbes, *The Principles of Morals and Legislation* by Bentham, *The Critique of Practical Reason* by Kant, *Ethics* by Dewey and Tufts, *Ethics* by Nicolai Hartmann, and *Principia Ethica* by Moore.

Unfortunately, the reader may find that some, at least, of the philosophers have become specialists, speaking in a technical jargon and, worse yet, taking in one another's washing, just as lawyers and economists are wont to do. Philosophical opinions often do not transcend partisanship; they only add to the confusing conflict of opinions.

In the chapters that follow, ethics will be presented as more than a collection of opinions. The disillusioned reader usually has paid too much attention to the dated opinions, and has, therefore, missed the point of philosophical inquiry. He has looked for answers that someone else prepared for the reader. He tries to read philosophy as one reads a handbook in chemistry. But the point of moral philosophy is to discover whether the right question is being asked. Dogmatic assertions in philosophy often have the potential effect of a question. At least, it will be the assumption of this book that philosophy is read profitably as a series of questions. As William James said,

> Philosophic study means the habit of always seeing an alternative, of not taking the usual for granted, of making conventionalities fluid again, of imagining foreign states of mind.

Those who derive more than historical information from other men's philosophies are jolted out of their prejudices, sometimes by a phrase, sometimes by a query, but always by words that have the effect of a question. Thus, intelligent men who sometimes assert that great wisdom is contained in some asinine little slogan or brochure that, to everyone else, is devoid of meaning, do so because for them it chanced to be a rescuer from the vicious circle of their own inadequate thoughts.

The next nine chapters will explore the systems of ethics that have meant the most to western civilization. We shall focus attention upon the different sets of questions that these systems articulated. It is our contention that these contrasting inquiries are the most communicable part of wisdom. For that reason, we shall not be much troubled by the clashing opinions that the philosophers asserted. Some of the *religious moralists,* for example, have enjoined upon deliberators respect for certain rights that, in their view, are commanded by the law of God. The *Utilitarians* have been very suspicious of theological revelations and have urged decision makers to bear in mind that the happiness of the greatest number is the good to be achieved. Nevertheless, however parochial or wrong-headed the God-fearing and the happiness-seeking philosophers may have adjudged one another, we can still learn something from them.

The religious moralist is usually a "casuist," a student of cases, and he is occupied with questions like these:

What authoritative rules bear upon this case?

What relevant precedents, accepted principles, and agreements can be cited?

If there is a conflict of citations, how may the authoritative precedents be distinguished?

The Utilitarian is busy with other questions:

What are the alternatives and what are their consequences of happiness and misery?

How do the alternatives compare in advantages and disadvantages?

Have remote consequences been considered as well as the immediate ones? Have they been evaluated by considering the relative intensity, duration, and extent of the satisfactions that are involved?

If one asks these questions and does not presume that one already knows the proper answer, there is no reason why one cannot be enlightened by the questions of both the casuist *and* the Utilitarian.

Whereas philosophy as a set of questionable answers is often at odds with science and the policy arts, philosophy as a set of answerable questions is an organizer of practical thought, as recent philosophers have tended to realize. In his role as interrogator, the philosopher does not ask all kinds of questions indiscriminately. Some inquiries send men into blind alleys, and others have a very limited relevance that is easily exaggerated. The philosophically minded person has some awareness of the services that a given question can perform in revealing the best possible choices.

The key questions articulated by the other philosophers bring to mind considerations that are not entirely overlooked by the casuist and the Utilitarian, but for *some* purposes they are much better than the questions previously mentioned.

Epictetus: What is not within my power?

Hobbes: What are the important motives, and have we overlooked any of them in thinking about our dealings with others?

Plato: With what general principles are our intentions consistent?

Kant: Would we be willing to make this rule universal?

Aristotle: What would be the undesirable extremes in this situation?

Hegel: How is this choice related to larger institutional trends? What loyalty is served?

Marx: What are the class interests in this choice?

Dewey: Exactly what is the problem? What will satisfactorily terminate the conflict?

Semanticists: What part of our discussion is satisfying emotional needs and what part refers to fact?

Ethics, as a discipline of questions, should unparalyze the mind at the moment of action. It suggests the unremembered or unperceived angles that may need investigation. If there is a logic of practical judgment, it is a logic of questions. It does not supply factual information, but is a reminder of the kind of facts that may need investigating. Like Sam Goldwyn, ethics says: "For your information, let me ask you a question!"

24

The Science
of Muddling Through

Charles E. Lindblom

Suppose an administrator is given responsibility for formulating policy with respect to inflation. He might start by trying to list all related values in order of importance, e.g., full employment, reasonable business profit, protection of small savings, prevention of a stock market crash. Then all possible policy outcomes could be rated as more or less efficient in attaining a maximum of these values. This would of course require a prodigious inquiry into values held by members of society and an equally prodigious set of calculations on how much of each value is equal to how much of each other value. He could then proceed to outline all possible policy alternatives. In a third step, he would undertake systematic comparison of his multitude of alternatives to determine which attains the greatest amount of values.

In comparing policies, he would take advantage of any theory available that generalized about classes of policies. In considering inflation, for example, he would compare all policies in the light of the theory of prices. Since no alternatives are beyond his investigation, he would consider strict central control and the abolition of all prices and markets on the one hand and elimination of all public controls with reliance completely on the free market on the other, both in the light of whatever theoretical generalizations he could find on such hypothetical economies.

Finally, he would try to make the choice that would in fact maximize his values.

An alternative line of attack would be to set as his principal objective,

Reprinted with permission of author and publisher. From *Public Administration Review* 19 (Spring 1959): 79–88.

either explicitly or without conscious thought, the relatively simple goal of keeping prices level. This objective might be compromised or complicated by only a few other goals, such as full employment. He would in fact disregard most other social values as beyond his present interest, and he would for the moment not even attempt to rank the few values that he regarded as immediately relevant. Were he pressed, he would quickly admit that he was ignoring many related values and many possible important consequences of his policies.

As a second step, he would outline those relatively few policy alternatives that occurred to him. He would then compare them. In comparing his limited number of alternatives, most of them familiar from past controversies, he would not ordinarily find a body of theory precise enough to carry him through a comparison of their respective consequences. Instead he would rely heavily on the record of past experience with small policy steps to predict the consequences of similar steps extended into the future.

Moreover, he would find that the policy alternatives combined objectives or values in different ways. For example, one policy might offer price level stability at the cost of some risk of unemployment; another might offer less price stability but also less risk of unemployment. Hence, the next step in his approach—the final selection—would combine into one the choice among values and the choice among instruments for reaching values. It would not, as in the first method of policy-making, approximate a more mechanical process of choosing the means that best satisfied goals that were previously clarified and ranked. Because practitioners of the second approach expect to achieve their goals only partially, they would expect to repeat endlessly the sequence just described, as conditions and aspirations changed and as accuracy of prediction improved.

By root or by branch

For complex problems, the first of these two approaches is of course impossible. Although such an approach can be described, it cannot be practiced except for relatively simple problems and even then only in a somewhat modified form. It assumes intellectual capacities and sources of information that men simply do not possess, and it is even more absurd as an approach to policy when the time and money that can be allocated to a policy problem is limited, as is always the case. Of particular importance to public administrators is the fact that public agencies are in effect usually instructed not to practice the first method. That is to say, their prescribed functions and constraints—the politically or legally possible —restrict their attention to relatively few values and relatively few alternative policies among the countless alternatives that might be imagined. It is the second method that is practiced.

Curiously, however, the literatures of decision-making, policy formulation, planning, and public administration formalize the first approach rather than the second, leaving public administrators who handle complex decisions in the position of practicing what few preach. For emphasis I run some risk of overstatement. True enough, the literature is well aware of limits on man's capacities and of the inevitability that policies will be approached in some such style as the second. But attempts to formalize rational policy formulation—to lay out explicitly the necessary steps in the process—usually describe the first approach and not the second.[1]

The common tendency to describe policy formulation even for complex problems as though it followed the first approach has been strengthened by the attention given to, and successes enjoyed by, operations research, statistical decision theory, and systems analysis. The hallmarks of these procedures, typical of the first approach, are clarity of objective, explicitness of evaluation, a high degree of comprehensiveness of overview, and wherever possible, quantification of values for mathematical analysis. But these advanced procedures remain largely the appropriate techniques of relatively small-scale problem-solving where the total number of variables to be considered is small and value problems restricted. Charles Hitch, head of the Economics Division of RAND Corporation, one of the leading centers for application of these techniques, has written:

> I would make the empirical generalization from my experience at RAND and elsewhere that operations research is the art of sub-optimizing, i.e., of solv-

[1] James G. March and Herbert A. Simon similarly characterize the literature. They also take some important steps, as have Simon's recent articles, to describe a less heroic model of policy-making. See *Organizations* (John Wiley and Sons, 1958), p. 137.

ing some lower-level problems, and that difficulties increase and our special competence diminishes by an order of magnitude with every level of decision-making we attempt to ascend. The sort of simple explicit model which operations researchers are so proficient in using can certainly reflect most of the significant factors influencing traffic control on the George Washington Bridge, but the proportion of the relevant reality which we can represent by any such model or models in studying, say, a major foreign-policy decision, appears to be almost trivial.[2]

Accordingly, I propose in this paper to clarify and formalize the second method, much neglected in the literature. This might be described as the method of *successive limited comparisons.* I will contrast it with the first approach, which might be called the rational-comprehensive method.[3] More impressionistically and briefly—and therefore generally used in this article—they could be characterized as the branch method and root method, the former continually building out from the current situation, step-by-step and by small degrees; the latter starting from fundamentals anew each time, building on the past only as experience is embodied in a theory, and always prepared to start completely from the ground up.

Let us put the characteristics of the two methods side by side in simplest terms.

Assuming that the root method is familiar and understandable, we proceed directly to clarification of its alternative by contrast. In explaining the second, we shall be describing how most administrators do in fact approach complex questions, for the root method, the "best" way as a blueprint or model, is in fact not workable for complex policy questions,

[2]"Operations Research and National Planning—A Dissent," *Operations Research* 5 (October 1957): 718. Hitch's dissent is from particular points made in the article to which his paper is a reply; his claim that operations research is for low-level problems is widely accepted.

For examples of the kind of problems to which operations research is applied, see C. W. Churchman, R. L. Ackoff and E. L. Arnoff, *Introduction to Operations Research* (John Wiley and Sons, 1957); and J. F. McCloskey and J. M. Coppinger (eds.), *Operations Research for Management,* Vol. II (The Johns Hopkins Press, 1956).

[3]I am assuming that administrators often make policy and advise in the making of policy and am treating decision-making and policy-making as synonymous for purposes of this paper.

Rational-Comprehensive (Root)	Successive Limited Comparisons (Branch)
1a. Clarification of values or objectives distinct from and usually prerequisite to empirical analysis of alternative policies.	1b. Selection of value goals and empirical analysis of the needed action are not distinct from one another but are closely intertwined.
2a. Policy-formulation is therefore approached through means-end analysis: First the ends are isolated, then the means to achieve them are sought.	2b. Since means and ends are not distinct, means-end analysis is often inappropriate or limited.
3a. The test of a "good" policy is that it can be shown to be the most appropriate means to desired ends.	3b. The test of a "good" policy is typically that various analysts find themselves directly agreeing on a policy (without their agreeing that it is the most appropriate means to an agreed objective).
4a. Analysis is comprehensive; every important relevant factor is taken into account.	4b. Analysis is drastically limited: i) Important possible outcomes are neglected. ii) Important alternative potential policies are neglected. iii) Important affected values are neglected.
5a. Theory is often heavily relied upon.	5b. A succession of comparisons greatly reduces or eliminates reliance on theory.

and administrators are forced to use the method of successive limited comparisons.

Intertwining evaluation and empirical analysis (1b)

The quickest way to understand how values are handled in the method of successive limited comparisons is to see how the root method often breaks down in *its* handling of values or objectives. The idea that values should be clarified, and in advance of the examination of alternative policies, is appealing. But what happens when we attempt it for complex social problems? The first difficulty is that on many critical values or objectives, citizens disagree, congressmen disagree, and public administrators disagree. Even where a fairly specific objective is prescribed for the administrator, there remains considerable room for disagreement on sub-objectives. Consider, for example, the conflict with respect to locating public housing, described in Meyerson and Banfield's study of the Chicago Housing Authority[4]—disagreement which occurred despite the clear objective of providing a certain number of public housing units in the city. Similarly conflicting are objectives in highway location, traffic control, minimum wage administration, development of tourist facilities in national parks, or insect control.

Administrators cannot escape these conflicts by ascertaining the majority's preference, for preferences have not been registered on most issues; indeed, there often *are* no preferences in the absence of public discussion sufficient to bring an issue to the attention of the electorate. Furthermore, there is a question of whether intensity of feeling should be considered as well as the number of persons preferring each alternative. By the impossibility of doing otherwise, administrators often are reduced to deciding policy without clarifying objectives first.

Even when an administrator resolves to follow his own values as a criterion for decisions, he often will not know how to rank them when they conflict with one another, as they usually do. Suppose, for example, that an administrator must relocate tenants living in tenements scheduled for destruction. One objective is to empty the buildings fairly promptly, another is to find suitable accommodations for persons displaced, another is to avoid friction with residents in other areas in which a large influx would be unwelcome, another is to deal with all concerned through persuasion if possible, and so on.

How does one state even to himself the relative importance of these partially conflicting values? A simple ranking of them is not enough; one needs ideally to know how much of one value is worth sacrificing for some of another value. The answer is that typically the administrator chooses—and must choose—directly among policies in which these values are combined in different ways. He cannot first clarify his values and then choose among policies.

[4]Martin Meyerson and Edward C. Banfield, *Politics, Planning and the Public Interest* (The Free Press, 1955).

A more subtle third point underlies both the first two. Social objectives do not always have the same relative values. One objective may be highly prized in one circumstance, another in another circumstance. If, for example, an administrator values highly both the dispatch with which his agency can carry through its projects *and* good public relations, it matters little which of the two possibly conflicting values he favors in some abstract or general sense. Policy questions arise in forms which put to administrators such a question as: Given the degree to which we are or are not already achieving the values of dispatch and the values of good public relations, is it worth sacrificing a little speed for a happier clientele, or is it better to risk offending the clientele so that we can get on with our work? The answer to such a question varies with circumstances.

The value problem is, as the example shows, always a problem of adjustments at a margin. But there is no practicable way to state marginal objectives or values except in terms of particular policies. That one value is preferred to another in one decision situation does not mean that it will be preferred in another decision situation in which it can be had only at great sacrifice of another value. Attempts to rank or order values in general and abstract terms so that they do not shift from decision to decision end up by ignoring the relevant marginal preferences. The significance of this third point thus goes very far. Even if all administrators had at hand an agreed set of values, objectives, and constraints, and an agreed ranking of these values, objectives, and constraints, their marginal values in actual choice situations would be impossible to formulate.

Unable consequently to formulate the relevant values first and then choose among policies to achieve them, administrators must choose directly among alternative policies that offer different marginal combinations of values. Somewhat paradoxically, the only practicable way to disclose one's relevant marginal values even to oneself is to describe the policy one chooses to achieve them. Except roughly and vaguely, I know of no way to describe—or even to understand—what my relative evaluations are for, say, freedom and security, speed and accuracy in governmental decisions, or low taxes and better schools than to describe my preferences among specific policy choices that might be made between the alternatives in each of the pairs.

In summary, two aspects of the process by which values are actually handled can be distinguished. The first is clear: evaluation and empirical analysis are intertwined; that is, one chooses among values and among policies at one and the same time. Put a little more elaborately, one simultaneously chooses a policy to attain certain objectives and chooses the objectives themselves. The second aspect is related but distinct: the administrator focuses his attention on marginal or incremental values. Whether he is aware of it or not, he does not find general formulations of objectives very helpful and in fact makes specific marginal or incremental comparisons. Two policies, X and Y, confront him. Both promise the same degree of attainment of objectives *a, b, c, d,* and *e.* But X promises him somewhat more of *f* than does Y, while Y promises him somewhat more of *g* than does X. In choosing between them, he is in fact offered the alternative of a marginal or incremental amount of *f* at the expense of a marginal or incremental amount of *g.* The only values that are relevant to his choice are these increments by which the two policies differ; and, when he finally chooses between the two marginal values, he does so by making a choice between policies.[5]

As to whether the attempt to clarify objectives in advance of policy selection is more or less rational than the close intertwining of marginal evaluation and empirical analysis, the principal difference established is that for complex problems the first is impossible and irrelevant, and the second is both possible and relevant. The second is possible because the administrator need not try to analyze any values except the values by which alternative policies differ and need not be concerned with them except as they differ marginally. His need for information on values or objectives is drastically reduced as compared with the root method; and his capacity for grasping, comprehending, and relating values to one another is not strained beyond the breaking point.

Relations between means and ends (2b)

Decision-making is ordinarily formalized as a means-ends relationship: means are conceived to be evaluated and chosen in the light of ends finally selected independently of and prior to the choice of means. This

[5]The line of argument is, of course, an extension of the theory of market choice, especially the theory of consumer choice, to public policy choices.

is the means-ends relationship of the root method. But it follows from all that has just been said that such a means-ends relationship is possible only to the extent that values are agreed upon, are reconcilable, and are stable at the margin. Typically, therefore, such a means-ends relationship is absent from the branch method, where means and ends are simultaneously chosen.

Yet any departure from the means-ends relationship of the root method will strike some readers as inconceivable. For it will appear to them that only in such a relationship is it possible to determine whether one policy choice is better or worse than another. How can an administrator know whether he has made a wise or foolish decision if he is without prior values or objectives by which to judge his decisions? The answer to this question calls up the third distinctive difference between root and branch methods: how to decide the best policy.

The test of "good" policy (3b)

In the root method, a decision is "correct," "good," or "rational" if it can be shown to attain some specified objective, where the objective can be specified without simply describing the decision itself. Where objectives are defined only through the marginal or incremental approach to values described above, it is still sometimes possible to test whether a policy does in fact attain the desired objectives; but a precise statement of the objectives takes the form of a description of the policy chosen or some alternative to it. To show that a policy is mistaken one cannot offer an abstract argument that important objectives are not achieved; one must instead argue that another policy is more to be preferred.

So far, the departure from customary ways of looking at problem-solving is not troublesome, for many administrators will be quick to agree that the most effective discussion of the correctness of policy does take the form of comparison with other policies that might have been chosen. But what of the situation in which administrators cannot agree on values or objectives, either abstractly or in marginal terms? What then is the test of "good" policy? For the root method, there is no test. Agreement on objectives failing, there is no standard of "correctness." For the method of successive limited comparisons, the test is agreement on policy itself, which remains possible even when agreement on values is not.

It has been suggested that continuing agreement in Congress on the desirability of extending old age insurance stems from liberal desires to strengthen the welfare programs of the federal government and from conservative desires to reduce union demands for private pension plans. If so, this is an excellent demonstration of the ease with which individuals of different ideologies often can agree on concrete policy. Labor mediators report a similar phenomenon: the contestants cannot agree on criteria for settling their disputes but can agree on specific proposals. Similarly, when one administrator's objective turns out to be another's means, they often can agree on policy.

Agreement on policy thus becomes the only practicable test of the policy's correctness. And for one administrator to seek to win the other over to agreement on ends as well would accomplish nothing and create quite unnecessary controversy.

If agreement directly on policy as a test for "best" policy seems a poor substitute for testing the policy against its objectives, it ought to be remembered that objectives themselves have no ultimate validity other than they are agreed upon. Hence agreement is the test of "best" policy in both methods. But where the root method requires agreement on what elements in the decision constitute objectives and on which of these objectives should be sought, the branch method falls back on agreement wherever it can be found.

In an important sense, therefore, it is not irrational for an administrator to defend a policy as good without being able to specify what it is good for.

Non-comprehensive analysis (4b)

Ideally, rational-comprehensive analysis leaves out nothing important. But it is impossible to take everything important into consideration unless "important" is so narrowly defined that analysis is in fact quite limited. Limits on human intellectual capacities and on available information set definite limits to man's capacity to be comprehensive. In actual fact, therefore, no one can practice the rational-comprehensive method for really complex problems, and every administrator faced with a sufficiently complex problem must find ways drastically to simplify.

An administrator assisting in the formulation of agricultural economic policy cannot in the first place be competent on all possible policies. He cannot even comprehend one policy entirely. In planning a soil bank program, he cannot successfully anticipate the impact of higher or lower farm income on, say, urbanization—the possible consequent loosening of family ties, possible consequent eventual need for revisions in social security and further implications for tax problems arising out of new federal responsibilities for social security and municipal responsibilities for urban services. Nor, to follow another line of repercussions, can he work through the soil bank program's effects on prices for agricultural products in foreign markets and consequent implications for foreign markets and consequent implications for foreign relations, including those arising out of economic rivalry between the United States and the U.S.S.R.

In the method of successive limited comparisons, simplification is systematically achieved in two principal ways. First, it is achieved through limitation of policy comparisons to those policies that differ in relatively small degree from policies presently in effect. Such a limitation immediately reduces the number of alternatives to be investigated and also drastically simplifies the character of the investigation of each. For it is not necessary to undertake fundamental inquiry into an alternative and its consequences; it is necessary only to study those respects in which the proposed alternative and its consequences differ from the status quo. The empirical comparison of marginal differences among alternative policies that differ only marginally is, of course, a counterpart of the incremental or marginal comparison of values discussed above.[6]

Relevance as well as realism

It is a matter of common observation that in Western democracies

[6]A more precise definition of incremental policies and a discussion of whether a change that appears "small" to one observer might be seen differently by another is to be found in my "Policy Analysis," *American Economic Review* 48 (June 1958): 298.

public administrators and policy analysts in general do largely limit their analyses to incremental or marginal differences in policies that are chosen to differ only incrementally. They do not do so, however, solely because they desperately need some way to simplify their problems; they also do so in order to be relevant. Democracies change their policies almost entirely through incremental adjustments. Policy does not move in leaps and bounds.

The incremental character of political change in the United States has often been remarked. The two major political parties agree on fundamentals; they offer alternative policies to the voters only on relatively small points of difference. Both parties favor full employment, but they define it somewhat differently; both favor the development of water power resources, but in slightly different ways; and both favor unemployment compensation, but not the same level of benefits. Similarly, shifts of policy within a party take place largely through a series of relatively small changes, as can be seen in their only gradual acceptance of the idea of governmental responsibility for support of the unemployed, a change in party positions beginning in the early 1930's and culminating in a sense in the Employment Act of 1946.

Party behavior is in turn rooted in public attitudes, and political theorists cannot conceive of democracy's surviving in the United States in the absence of fundamental agreement on potentially disruptive issues, with consequent limitation of policy debates to relatively small differences in policy.

Since the policies ignored by the administrator are politically impossible and so irrelevant, the simplification of analysis achieved by concentrating on policies that differ only incrementally is not a capricious kind of simplification. In addition, it can be argued that, given the limits on knowledge within which policy-makers are confined, simplifying by limiting the focus to small variations from present policy makes the most of available knowledge. Because policies being considered are like present and past policies, the administrator can obtain information and claim some insight. Non-incremental policy proposals are therefore typically not only politically irrelevant but also unpredictable in their consequences.

The second method of simplification of analysis is the practice of ignoring important possible consequences of possible policies, as well as the values attached to the neglected consequences. If this appears to disclose a shocking shortcoming of successive limited comparisons, it can be replied that, even if the exclusions are random, policies may nevertheless be more intelligently formulated than through futile attempts to achieve a comprehensiveness beyond human capacity. Actually, however, the exclusions, seeming arbitrary or random from one point of view, need be neither.

Achieving a degree of comprehensiveness

Suppose that each value neglected by one policy-making agency were a major concern of at least one other agency. In that case, a helpful division of labor would be achieved, and no agency need find its task beyond its capacities. The shortcomings of such a system would be that one agency might destroy a value either before another agency could be activated to safeguard it or in spite of another agency's efforts. But the possibility that important values may be lost is present in any form of organization, even where agencies attempt to comprehend in planning more than is humanly possible.

The virtue of such a hypothetical division of labor is that every important interest or value has its watchdog. And these watchdogs can protect the interests in their jurisdiction in two quite different ways: first, by redressing damages done by other agencies; and, second, by anticipating and heading off injury before it occurs.

In a society like that of the United States in which individuals are free to combine to pursue almost any possible common interest they might have and in which government agencies are sensitive to the pressures of these groups, the system described is approximated. Almost every interest has its watchdog. Without claiming that every interest has a sufficiently powerful watchdog, it can be argued that our system often can assure a more comprehensive regard for the value of the whole society than any attempt at intellectual comprehensiveness.

In the United States, for example, no part of government attempts a comprehensive overview of policy on income distribution. A policy nevertheless evolves, and one responding to a wide variety of interests. A process of mutual adjustment among farm groups, labor unions, municipalities and school boards, tax authorities, and government agencies with responsibilities in the fields of housing, health, highways, national parks, fire, and police accomplishes a distribution of income in which particular income problems neglected at one point in the decision processes become central at another point.

Mutual adjustment is more pervasive than the explicit forms it takes in negotiation between groups; it persists through the mutual impacts of groups upon each other even where they are not in communication. For all the imperfections and latent dangers in this ubiquitous process of mutual adjustment, it will often accomplish an adaptation of policies to a wider range of interests than could be done by one group centrally.

Note, too, how the incremental pattern of policy-making fits with the multiple pressure pattern. For when decisions are only incremental—closely related to known policies, it is easier for one group to anticipate the kind of moves another might make and easier too for it to make correction for injury already accomplished.[7]

Even partisanship and narrowness, to use pejorative terms, will sometimes be assets to rational decision-making, for they can doubly insure that what one agency neglects, another will not; they specialize personnel to distinct points of view. The claim is valid that effective rational coordination of the federal administration, if possible to achieve at all, would require an agreed set of values[8]—if "rational" is defined as the practice of the root method of decision-making. But a high degree of administrative coordination occurs as each agency adjusts its policies to the concerns of the other agencies in the process of fragmented decision-making I have just described.

For all the apparent shortcomings of the incremental approach to policy alternatives with its arbitrary exclusion coupled with fragmentation, when compared to the root method, the branch method often looks far superior. In the root method, the inevitable exclusion of factors is accidental, unsystematic, and not defensible by any argument so far developed, while in the branch method the exclusions are deliberate,

[7]The link between the practice of the method of successive limited comparisons and mutual adjustment of interests in a highly fragmented decision-making process adds a new facet to pluralist theories of government and administration.

[8]Herbert Simon, Donald W. Smithburg, and Victor A. Thompson, *Public Administration* (Alfred A. Knopf, 1950), p. 434.

systematic, and defensible. Ideally, of course, the root method does not exclude; in practice it must.

Nor does the branch method necessarily neglect long-run considerations and objectives. It is clear that important values must be omitted in considering policy, and sometimes the only way long-run objectives can be given adequate attention is through the neglect of short-run considerations. But the values omitted can be either long-run or short-run.

Succession of comparisons (5b)

The final distinctive element in the branch method is that the comparisons, together with the policy choice, proceed in a chronological series. Policy is not made once and for all; it is made and re-made endlessly. Policy-making is a process of successive approximation to some desired objectives in which what is desired itself continues to change under reconsideration.

Making policy is at best a very rough process. Neither social scientists, nor politicians, nor public administrators yet know enough about the social world to avoid repeated error in predicting the consequences of policy moves. A wise policy-maker consequently expects that his policies will achieve only part of what he hopes and at the same time will produce unanticipated consequences he would have preferred to avoid. If he proceeds through a *succession* of incremental changes, he avoids serious lasting mistakes in several ways.

In the first place, past sequences of policy steps have given him knowledge about the probable consequences of further similar steps. Second, he need not attempt big jumps toward his goals that would require predictions beyond his or anyone else's knowledge, because he never expects his policy to be a final resolution of a problem. His decision is only one step, one that if successful can quickly be followed by another. Third, he is in effect able to test his previous predictions as he moves on to each further step. Lastly, he often can remedy a past error fairly quickly—more quickly than if policy proceeded through more distinct steps widely spaced in time.

Compare this comparative analysis of incremental changes with the aspiration to employ theory in the root method. Man cannot think without classifying, without subsuming one experience under a more general category of experiences. The attempt to push categorization as far as possible and to find general propositions which can be applied to specific situations is what I refer to with the word "theory." Where root analysis often leans heavily on theory in this sense, the branch method does not.

The assumption of root analysis is that theory is the most systematic and economical way to bring relevant knowledge to bear on a specific problem. Granting the assumption, an unhappy fact is that we do not have adequate theory to apply to problems in any policy area, although theory is more adequate in some areas—monetary policy, for example—than in others. Comparative analysis, as in the branch method, is sometimes a systematic alternative to theory.

Suppose an administrator must choose among a small group of policies that differ only incrementally from each other and from present policy. He might aspire to "understand" each of the alternatives—for example, to know all the consequences of each aspect of each policy. If so, he would indeed require theory. In fact, however, he would usually decide that, *for policy-making purposes,* he need know, as explained above, only the consequences of each of those aspects of the policies in which they differed from one another. For this much more modest aspiration, he requires no theory (although it might be helpful, if available), for he can proceed to isolate probable differences by examining the differences in consequences associated with past differences in policies, a feasible program because he can take his observations from a long sequence of incremental changes.

For example, without a more comprehensive social theory about juvenile delinquency than scholars have yet produced, one cannot possibly understand the ways in which a variety of public policies—say on education, housing, recreation, employment, race relations, and policing—might encourage or discourage delinquency. And one needs such an understanding if he undertakes the comprehensive overview of the problem prescribed in the models of the root method. If, however, one merely wants to mobilize knowledge sufficient to assist in a choice among a small group of similar policies—alternative policies on juvenile court procedures, for example—he can do so by comparative analysis of the results of similar past policy moves.

Theorists and practitioners

This difference explains—in some cases at least—why the administrator often feels that the outside expert or academic problem-solver is sometimes not helpful and why they in turn often urge more theory on him. And it explains why an administrator often feels more confident when "flying by the seat of his pants" than when following the advice of theorists. Theorists often ask the administrator to go the long way round to the solution of his problems, in effect ask him to follow the best canons of the scientific method, when the administrator knows that the best available theory will work less well than more modest incremental comparisons. Theorists do not realize that the administrator is often in fact practicing a systematic method. It would be foolish to push this explanation too far, for sometimes practical decision-makers are pursuing neither a theoretical approach nor successive comparisons, nor any other systematic method.

It may be worth emphasizing that theory is sometimes of extremely limited helpfulness in policy-making for at least two rather different reasons. It is greedy for facts; it can be constructed only through a great collection of observations. And it is typically insufficiently precise for application to a policy process that moves through small changes. In contrast, the comparative method both economizes on the need for facts and directs the analyst's attention to just those facts that are relevant to the fine choices faced by the decision-maker.

With respect to precision of theory, economic theory serves as an example. It predicts that an economy without money or prices would in certain specified ways misallocate resources, but this finding pertains to an alternative far removed from the kind of policies on which administrators need help. On the other hand, it is not precise enough to predict the consequences of policies restricting business mergers, and this is the kind of issue on which the administrators need help. Only in relatively restricted areas does economic theory achieve sufficient precision to go far in resolving policy questions; its helpfulness in policy-making is always so limited that it requires supplementation through comparative analysis.

Successive comparison as a system

Successive limited comparisons is, then, indeed a method or system; it is not a failure of method for which administrators ought to apologize. Nonetheless, its imperfections, which have not been explored in this paper, are many. For example, the method is without a built-in safeguard for all relevant values, and it also may lead the decision-maker to overlook excellent policies for no other reason than that they are not suggested by the chain of successive policy steps leading up to the present. Hence, it ought to be said that under this method, as well as under some of the most sophisticated variants of the root method—operations research, for example—policies will continue to be as foolish as they are wise.

Why then bother to describe the method in all the above detail? Because it is in fact a common method of policy formulation, and is, for complex problems, the principal reliance of administrators as well as of other policy analysts.[9] And because it will be superior to any other decision-making method available for complex problems in many circumstances, certainly superior to a futile attempt at superhuman comprehensiveness. The reaction of the public administrator to the exposition of method doubtless will be less a discovery of a new method than a better acquaintance with an old. But by becoming more conscious of their practice of this method, administrators might practice it with more skill

[9]Elsewhere I have explored this same method of policy formulation as practiced by academic analysts of policy ("Policy Analysis," *American Economic Review* 48 [June, 1958]: 298). Although it has been here presented as a method for public administrators, it is no less necessary to analysts more removed from immediate policy questions, despite their tendencies to describe their own analytical efforts as though they were the rational-comprehensive method with an especially heavy use of theory. Similarly, this same method is inevitably resorted to in personal problem-solving, where means and ends are sometimes impossible to separate, where aspirations or objectives undergo constant development, and where drastic simplification of the complexity of the real world is urgent if problems are to be solved in the time that can be given to them. To an economist accustomed to dealing with the marginal or incremental concept in market processes, the central idea in the method is that both evaluation and empirical analysis are incremental. Accordingly I have referred to the method elsewhere as "the incremental method."

and know when to extend or constrict its use. (That they sometimes practice it effectively and sometimes not may explain the extremes of opinion on "muddling through," which is both praised as a highly sophisticated form of problem-solving and denounced as no method at all. For I suspect that in so far as there is a system in what is known as "muddling through," this method is it.)

One of the noteworthy incidental consequences of clarification of the method is the light it throws on the suspicion an administrator sometimes entertains that a consultant or adviser is not speaking relevantly and responsibly when in fact by all ordinary objective evidence he is. The trouble lies in the fact that most of us approach policy problems within a framework given by our view of a chain of successive policy choices made up to the present. One's thinking about appropriate policies with respect, say, to urban traffic control is greatly influenced by one's knowledge of the incremental steps taken up to the present. An administrator enjoys an intimate knowledge of his past sequences that "outsiders" do not share, and his thinking and that of the "outsider" will consequently be different in ways that may puzzle both. Both may appear to be talking intelligently, yet each may find the other unsatisfactory. The relevance of the policy chain of succession is even more clear when an American tries to discuss, say, antitrust policy with a Swiss, for the chains of policy in the two countries are strikingly different and the two individuals consequently have organized their knowledge in quite different ways.

If this phenomenon is a barrier to communication, an understanding of it promises an enrichment of intellectual interaction in policy formulation. Once the source of difference is understood, it will sometimes be stimulating for an administrator to seek out a policy analyst whose recent experience is with a policy chain different from his own.

This raises again a question only briefly discussed above on the merits of like-mindedness among government administrators. While much of organization theory argues the virtues of common values and agreed organizational objectives, for complex problems in which the root method is inapplicable, agencies will want among their own personnel two types of diversification: administrators whose thinking is organized by reference to policy chains other than those familiar to most members of the organization and, even more commonly, administrators whose professional or personal values or interests create diversity of view (perhaps coming from different specialties, social classes, geographical areas) so that, even within a single agency, decision-making can be fragmented and parts of the agency can serve as watchdogs for other parts.

25

Delegation:
Anticipated and
Unanticipated Consequences

James G. March and
Herbert Simon

The Selznick model. Where Merton emphasizes rules as a response to the demand for control, Selznick (1949) emphasizes the delegation of authority. Like Merton, however, Selznick wishes to show how the use of a control technique (i.e., delegation) brings about a series of unanticipated consequences. Also, like Merton, Selznick shows how these consequences stem from the problems of maintaining highly interrelated systems of interpersonal relations.

Selznick's model starts with the demand for control made by the top hierarchy. As a result of this demand, an increased *delegation of authority* (3.14) is instituted [3.14:3.1].

Delegation, however, has several immediate consequences. As intended, it increases the *amount of training in specialized competences* (3.15) [3.15:3.14]. Restriction of attention to a relatively small number of problems increases experience within these limited areas and improves the employee's ability to deal with these problems. Operating through this mechanism, delegation tends to decrease the *difference between organizational goals and achievement* (3.16) [3.16:3.15], and thus to stimulate more delegation [3.14:3.16]. At the same time, however, delegation results in departmentalization and an increase in the *bifurcation of interests* (3.17) among the subunits in the organization [3.17:3.14]. The maintenance needs of the subunits dictate a commitment to the subunit goals over and above their contribution to the total organizational program. Many individual needs depend on the continued success and even expansion of the subunit. As in the previous example, the activities

Reprinted with permission of authors and publisher. From *Organizations* (New York: John Wiley, 1958), pp. 40–44.

originally evaluated in terms of the organization goals are seen to have additional important ramifications for the subunits.

Bifurcation of interests is also stimulated by the specialized training that delegation (intendedly) produces. Training results in increased competence and, therefore, in increased *costs of changing personnel* (3.18) [3.18:3.15] and this results, in turn, in further differentiation of subunit goals [3.17:3.18].

The bifurcation within the organization leads to increased *conflict among organizational subunits* (3.19) [3.19:3.17]. As a consequence, the *content of decisions* (3.20) made within the organization depends increasingly upon considerations of internal strategy, particularly if there is little *internalization of organizational goals by participants* (3.21) [3.20:3.19, 3.21]. As a result there is an increase in the difference between organizational goals and achievement [3.16:3.20] and this results in an increase in delegation [3.14:3.16]. . . .

This effect on daily decisions is accentuated by two other mechanisms in Selznick's system. The struggle for internal control not only affects directly the content of decisions, but also causes greater *elaboration of subunit ideologies* (3.22) [3.22:3.19]. Each subunit seeks success by fitting its policy into the official doctrine of the large organization to legitimize its demands. Such a tactic increases the *internalization of subgoals by participants* (3.23) within subunits [3.23:3.22].

At the same time, the internalization of subgoals is reinforced by a feedback from the daily decisions it influences. The necessity for making daily decisions creates a system of precedents. Decisions depend primarily on the operational criteria provided by the organization, and, among these criteria, subunit goals are of considerable importance [3.20:3.23]. Precedents tend to become habitual responses to the situations for which they are defined as relevant and thus to reinforce the internalization of subunit goals [3.23:3.20]. Obviously, internalization of subgoals is partially dependent on the *operationality of organizational goals* (3.24). By operationality of goals, we mean the extent to which it is possible to observe and test how well goals are being achieved. Variations in the operationality of organizational goals affect the content of daily decisions [3.20:3.24] and thus the extent of subunit goal internalization.

From this it is clear that delegation has both functional and dysfunctional consequences for the achievement of organizational goals. It contributes both to their realization and to their deflection. Surprisingly, the theory postulates that both increases and decreases in goal achievement cause an increase in delegation. Why does not normal learning occur

FIGURE 3.3
The Simplified Selznick Model

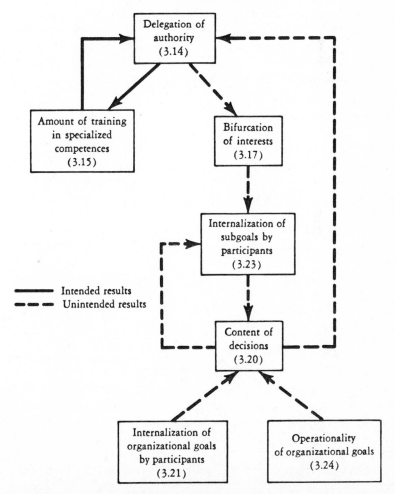

here? The answer seems to be that when goals are not achieved, delegation is—within the framework of the "machine" model—the correct response, and the model does not consider alternatives to simple delegation. On the other hand, the model offers explicitly at least two "dampers" that limit the operation of the dysfunctional mechanisms. As is indicated in Figure 3.3, where the skeleton of the Selznick model is outlined, there are two (not entirely independent) variables treated as independent but potentially amenable to organizational control, each of which restrains the runaway features of daily decision-making. By suitable changes in the extent to which organizational goals are operational or in the internalization of organizational goals by participants, some of the dysfunctional effects of delegation can be reduced.

26

Participation, Poverty, and Administration

S. M. Miller and
Martin Rein

Three fateful words—"maximum feasible participation"—have ushered in a new era in American policy and administration. Surprisingly, their entry was preceded neither by a historical legacy, a searching analysis, nor an active constituency. While the congressional hearings on the Economic Opportunity Act of 1964 reviewed many issues, what later proved to be the most embattled aspect of the legislation—the call for maximum feasible participation of the poor in the planning and conduct of the community action program—was accepted without contention and indeed without understanding.

Those who helped draw up the Economic Opportunity Act disagree on what was intended by the three words.[1] A program of maximum participation proved to be politically unfeasible, while the very concept of participation displayed a brilliant ambiguity. We are less concerned in this article with the development of the phrase than with the evolving purposes to which it has been put in practice.

Maximum feasible participation emerged unclear, unexamined, and unununderstood. Because it served many agendas, it enjoyed a vitality which permitted it to grow in this uncertain terrain. The conflict among the agendas was unanticipated or veiled. As conflict erupted in community action programs and the national racial scene changed, purposes shifted. Old purposes did not die; they were partially supplanted by new

Reprinted with permission of authors and publisher. From *Public Administration Review* (January-February 1969): 15–25.

[1]Adam Yarmolinsky and Leonard Duhl in James L. Sundquist (ed.), *On Fighting Poverty: Perspectives from Experiences,* Vol. II, Perspectives in Poverty Series (New York: Basic Books, 1969).

objectives. To some extent, old and new objectives fluctuate in ascendancy.

"Max feas," as the term came to be known, blossomed because it enabled the civil rights movement and the black revolution to find new forms for growth. Consequently, the development of participation is highly influenced by the shift in focuses of the effort to improve the situation of blacks in the United States. Yet, despite this origin and commitment, maximum feasible participation has become an important issue for many activities removed from the racial equality struggle. Its impact is not only exhibited in poverty programs, but is extended to a host of other activities in society.

Public agencies are being deeply shaken by the call for participation. It will not be an easy road to incorporate this new demand into the typical bureaucracy. Efficiency and participation do not necessarily converge. Nevertheless, our feeling is that the change will be positive and lasting but ripped by relentless tensions and difficulties.

To understand maximum feasible participation, we find it necessary to discuss the background which led up to it; we follow that with an analysis of the shifting concerns in the actual operation of maximum feasible participation.[2] We then explore some specific problems that it raises for public administrators. Finally, we offer our judgment on what its future may be.

What led to it?

Nearing the end of the 1960's, it is difficult to recapture the texture of thinking at the beginning of the decade. Then it was believed that the poor were, in the vision of Gunnar Myrdal, listlessly powerless, inert and apathetic, politically incompetent; in short, the most backward poor in the world. This description is a far cry from the turmoil and tension produced by the poor, especially the black poor, today! Many believed that public resources for the poor were both adequate and available;

[2] A fuller analysis is in Martin Rein and S. M. Miller, *University of Connecticut Law Review*, January 1969.

poverty existed because the poor were unmotivated or had not learned how to use them or felt so distant from public and voluntary services that they would not frequent them. Poverty, then, resulted from the inadequacies of the poor, rather than the conduct of society. Many still staunchly defend this formulation, but it no longer enjoys the preeminent position that it had in intellectual analysis in the early 1960's. It may, however, continue to play an important role in political decision-making today.

It was easy, then, for the President's Committee on Juvenile Delinquency and Youth Crime, which developed a community program in 1962, to believe in "sociotherapy" as a needed approach to working with the poor. The experience of Richard Boone of the Committee's staff in planning self-help activities for a projected domestic peace corps was also influential. Sociotherapy was based on the assumption that the poor were uninvolved. Alienated from the institutions of society, they would only begin to link themselves with these facilities when they felt accepted and involved. Thus, involvement and participation became ways of motivating the poor to reexamine and change their opinions about these institutions. At the same time, participation would improve the competence of low-income communities in dealing with their problems. Improvement and competence, skill and positive outlook, would lead to the containment of delinquency and social disturbance.[3]

The President's Committee staff had an important role in the drawing up of the community action part of the Economic Opportunity Act. Their activity and the strong support of Senator Robert Kennedy, whose close friend, David Hackett, led the President's Committee staff, were important in gaining a community action provision in the Act. Indeed, Boone is cited by Adam Yarmolinsky as the consistent advocate in the task force of the participation of the poor.[4]

A second major support group for maximum feasible participation envisaged it as primarily a way of providing jobs. Since the Economic Opportunity Act itself was deficient in providing jobs, the notion was that maximum feasible participation meant that the poor should be employed

---

[3]The discussion of the President's Committee is based on the analysis in Peter Marris and Martin Rein, *Dilemmas of Social Reform* (New York: Atherton Press), pp. 20–24.

[4]Yarmolinsky, *op. cit.*

in various capacities.[5] A poverty program should not only increase jobs for middle-class professionals, but should open up employment opportunities for unskilled, low-educated people who lived in the areas. The poor would provide services to other poor people and would thereby become employed and nonpoor. Similarly, the employment deficiency in the original OEO set of programs led to converting training programs like the Job Corps and particularly the Neighborhood Youth Corps into low-level employment programs rather than strictly training programs. Indeed, it was frequently difficult to find the training component in some of these programs. Thus, the inadequacy of the basic law in providing income and jobs was partially overcome by defining participation as job opportunities within the war on poverty itself. Thus, the "nonprofessional job slot" became popular as a way for the poor to participate in the poverty programs through employment.

A third group supported maximum feasible participation because it could legitimate the poverty program.[6] The notion was that the poor were very alienated and angry about programs today. Unless they were involved in them and had some feeling that the programs would not be harming them, they would not be effectively using the services that were provided. This view was similar to sociotherapy but went further. "Maximum feasible participation" was supported because it could be a way of developing a constituency among the poor for the programs. This group saw participation in political terms rather than only in terms of its effects on the delivery of service. Also, aggressive social action was a way of getting change in recalcitrant bureaucracies.

Another variant of this perspective was to see participation as a way of transferring power to the poor in low-income areas. We will return to this perspective below.

Its course

What happened when participation was implemented? Simply put,

---

[5]Daniel P. Moynihan, "What Is Community Action?" *Public Interest* 5 (Fall 1966): 3–8.

[6]See Sanford Kravitz and Leonard Duhl in Daniel P. Moynihan (ed.), *On Understanding Poverty: Perspectives from the Social Sciences,* Vol. I, Perspectives in Poverty Series (New York: Basic Books, 1969).

the concerns with sociotherapy and jobs were transmuted into activities aimed at the transfer of power. A movement for personal self-help escalated into a political movement. As Sumner Rosen has said, the feasible was dropped from maximum feasible participation and the participation was defined as control.[7]

While those who administered the programs frequently thought of the involvement of the poor in sociotherapeutic terms, the poor themselves—and that means the black poor, since they were the dominant poverty group in the big cities—thought of participation as control over the programs. As one Roxbury mother said, "The president wants us to run these programs." The original sociotherapeutic intent of the program was not germane to the people in the community. The civil rights struggles also contributed to this politicalization of participation as anger replaced apathy and the will to command power overwhelmed powerlessness. Therapy was the concern of the outsiders, not that of the poor. The insurgence of black communities swept away the emphasis on the deficiencies of the poor and indicted the inadequacies of the agencies servicing them and the manipulations of city hall.

The struggle over who should run the local community action program led to acrimonious political hassles. In many cities in the beginning days, black leaders and organizations debated with the mayor and prevented him from taking over the programs. Democratic mayors viewed themselves as under attack from programs passed by a Democratic president and Congress. City hall protests to the White House and the lack of success of a poverty program doomed to failure because of its limited mandate to provide jobs or income led to efforts to move away from maximum feasible participation.[8] Shortly after the opening of the war on poverty, Office of Economic Opportunity Director Sargent Shriver was harassed by demands that maximum feasible participation be contained. (The expansion of the war in Vietnam and the containment of the war on

[7]Sumner Rosen, "Better Mousetraps: Reflections on Economic Development in the Ghetto," *Social Policy Papers* (New York: New Careers Development Center, New York University, 1968), p. 2.

[8]See S. M. Miller and Martin Rein, "The War on Poverty—Perspectives and Prospects," in Ben B. Seligman, *Poverty as a Public Issue* (New York: Free Press, 1965).

poverty at home went hand in hand. Vietnam drained resources away from the home programs; less resources meant less success at home; less success at home meant more conflict among those vying for control over the program.)

In many, if not most, community action programs, the ability to effectively administer the community agencies was very low. They were new agencies with new kinds of personnel. Produced under crash pressure, they operated under crisis conditions. Old established agencies felt rejected and frequently would not collaborate. Typical of the resistance was the poverty program in one city which found it difficult to get checks issued on time by the controller's office except by those divisions of the program which knew how to negotiate with this office. Nevertheless, these new institutions developed. City hall and black town battled over control, with city hall gaining important, though incomplete, victories in most cities.

The implied OEO formula that one-third of the board members should be elected by the residents of the area meant representation of the poor but not control by the poor. The term "poor" is misleading since the representatives were of the poverty neighborhood, but not necessarily poor. But "poor" meant black. This latter point is important because the struggle over participation was in large part a struggle over civil rights. Fed by and feeding the participation emphasis in poverty programs, the civil rights movement swung to "power." The struggle over maximum feasible participation must be understood against the struggle over emerging Negro rights, although it has broader implications as well.

San Francisco and Oakland across the bay offer instructive examples of participation in community action. In San Francisco black leaders succeeded in early 1965 in taking over control of the poverty program. The emphasis in the Western Addition section was in first building a political base for black control. Plans were to have a part-time community organizer for almost every block and a full-time organizer for every eight blocks.[9] In developing this program, few services were actually provided residents. In the political struggle within the black community and between it and city hall, the original black leaders lost out. And, as in

[9]Wilfred T. Ussery et al., "The Area Development Plan of the Western Addition Target Area," Western Addition Area Action Board, mimeo.

Philadelphia, a program that had become dominated by black independents was pulled back to city hall influence, though not with total city hall control.[10]

The Oakland community action program grew out of the executive coalition of public and voluntary agency officials that was the Interagency Project Committee. Before the beginning of the poverty program, this had evolved into the Oakland Economic Development Council (OEDC) with the benefit of a Ford Foundation area project grant.[11] Designated as the official community action agency of Oakland, participation of the black and brown Spanish-speaking ethnic groups expanded. Eventually, black leaders, rather than city hall types, dominated the board. In conflict with the mayor and city council, the poverty agency in 1967 voted to become independent of the city government. It has and still receives OEO funds. Thus, OEDC has had the unusual history of evolving from a largely white establishment organization to a largely black organization with some important, though limited, service functions.

In both cities, as elsewhere, a vital question is, who are the legitimate representatives of the black poor? Bickering over access to position is endemic. Also, the quality of services performed is questionable. For some black leaders, service is less important than power. Technical competence is superseded by political prowess. But in the long run, we believe that power without service is unstable.

Spillover effects

Maximum feasible participation has had spillover effects in many areas other than poverty-community action areas. It has fed the concept of black power, which is now being significantly translated into economic power. The community corporation model evolved out of community action experience and the effort to invent new administrative devices

---

[10]James Cunningham, "The Struggle of the American Urbident for Freedom and Power," a report to the Ford Foundation, August 1967, chapter two. Also, Natalie Becker and Marjorie Myhill, "Power and Participation in the San Francisco Community Action Program 1964–67," preliminary draft report to the Office of Economic Opportunity, Grant Number CG–8835A, July 1968.

[11]See Marris and Rein, *op. cit.,* pp. 122–23.

which would combine participation and responsibility. The poverty program emphasis on participation influenced student demands and supported the spread of the issue of participation and involvement in all kinds of bureaucracies, including the university. New legislation, e.g., model cities, requires the participation of users of services of the residents of areas affected by policy decisions.

We believe that the vision of new forms of participation and involvement will have great impact for many years to come. That does not mean that participation will be easy or facile. But we think it is an idea whose time has come. The issues now become how to effectively develop and build on it rather than rejecting it without attempting to transcend the difficulties it produces.

Problems raised for administrators

We have briefly discussed various perspectives which led to the development of maximum feasible participation and some difficulties which it encounters in practice. In the following sections, we turn to the question of how maximum feasible participation in its many different forms affect administrators.

The theme of participation confronts administrators in two basic ways—one is that it focuses attention upon the poor, a group largely neglected by many public bureaucracies; second, it emphasizes degrees of citizen involvement which have not been typical in public bureaucracies. (Some contend that middle-class people have always had these involvements, but we suspect that, except in the field of education, citizens generally have not been as heavily involved in public bureaucracies as some forms of participation demand.)

From these general observations we turn to four specific areas in which participation affects administration:

1. *Personnel,* especially the creation of new categories of manpower and the reassessment of standards of entry and promotion.
2. *Professional discretion,* including the efforts to limit discretion by making more effective use of review machinery or creating new mechanisms whereby the aggrieved and neglected service user can find redress.

3. *Policy development,* as the outcome of the interplay between boards and administrators is being reassessed. In earlier years, the teachers of public administration discovered that administrators were more than passive implementers of policies reached by independent boards. Today, service users want to be involved in setting policies and the hiring of the key administrator.
4. New mechanisms of *accountability* are developing. The theory that bureaucracy is accountable to elected representatives who are responsible to the people has worked imperfectly. More direct mechanisms of citizen accountability is being sought, taking such forms as decentralization and community control.

Personnel

The call for involvement in the form of nonprofessionals means that recruiting activities of agencies will have to be drastically changed.[12] The new expectation is that agencies will make a strenuous effort to bring into their employ not only black people, but unskilled and low-educated blacks.

Since the expectation is that many such people should be brought in, it will become necessary to change job classifications and requirements so that it becomes possible to employ them in large numbers. Old jobs will have to be reconstructed so that people with low skills can perform them. New kinds of jobs will have to be structured which fit the social service demands for various kinds of bridge and linking activities which nonprofessionals can provide particularly well.

In order to increase the number of employees from poverty areas, there will have to be continuing pressure for restructuring jobs. As a general rule, more and more administrators will have to face the necessity of restructuring if jobs continually have to be refilled more than once or twice a year or if they are unable to find people qualified for jobs in less than three or six months.

[12]See Frank Riessman and Hermine Popper (eds.), *Up From Poverty* (New York: Harper and Row, 1968), and Frank Riessman and Arthur Pearl, *New Careers for the Poor* (New York: Free Press, 1965).

In general, it will be important to cut down the commitment to credentialism and to emphasize the possibilities of performance after training of individuals.[13]

These new workers represent a challenge to the orthodox and traditional legitimacy of the agency. They will not behave in the same way as other workers because they come in as a result of the feeling that there is something wrong with the agency—wrong because the agency has had few black workers or, more fundamentally, because the agency has not been helping poor people.

New kinds of employees mean new behavior on the job. Coworkers and supervisors will have to cope with different kinds of behavior than they expect from other workers. There will be less tendency toward docility among these new workers because, to some extent, they have an outside constituency unlike other workers on the job. They apply for the job not on the basis of individual test performance or education, but because they represent a people who now feel they have claim to jobs.

As workers with different styles than traditional civil service workers, supervisors will have to learn how to deal with them,[14] just as the new workers will have to learn how to deal with supervisors. This situation will be very strainful, because many new workers immediately begin to feel that they can perform the job as well as professionals, particularly in agencies which deal primarily with the poor. Furthermore, there will be an expectation of collegiality, rather than hierarchy. They will not accept so easily the notion that they have superiors whom they must look up to because they have infinite wisdom of an incomparable kind.

Training will assume greater importance. But the training has to be relevant to the people who will be performing these jobs. A good deal of attention will have to be paid to developing training which is appropriate for these workers. Traditional training procedures are likely to be inadequate. It will be important not only to train new workers, but to train the supervisors and coworkers to learn how to work effectively with them.

[13]S. M. Miller and Frank Riessman, *Social Class and Social Policy* (New York: Basic Books, 1968), chapter five, "The Credentials Trap."

[14]The strikes of civil service workers in many cities may indicate that a widespread change in outlook is sweeping through the ranks of the public service in an affluent era.

Training can become a substitute for change, as is well known. Consequently, administrators must concentrate on getting actual changes in behavior.

Because of background, style, and independence, it will be more important than ever before to have a due process structure within the agency that will process grievances. Administrators with foresight will establish such procedure early, rather than being overrun later by events. The typical grievance machinery may be ineffective. To achieve legitimacy, coworkers may have to be included in a grievance board.

An expectation of many new nonprofessionals is that they will be upgraded rapidly. The break between nonprofessionals and professionals will become more and more difficult to maintain. Agencies will have to provide procedures and possibilities for rapid upgrading for the people who are coming in at low-level jobs. The present procedures leave the initiative for advancement largely with the worker. We must begin to rethink the way that people learn and grow on a job and develop into higher responsibilities. We cannot expect orthodox examinations nor traditional educational credentials to be adequate ways of offering quick promotion routes for those who come in as nonprofessionals. There is a growing expectation of swift improvement in job level; for this to occur, education and testing cannot be relied upon.

These changes will provoke difficulties for agencies. They may reopen the possibilities of nepotism and individual preference. We will have to develop some creative ways of overcoming these dangers and at the same time not wipe out the possibilities of rapid advancement for those who have ability but who don't meet the usual criteria of promotion —largely based on testing and education.

The non-professional is not just another employee with a different job classification. He represents a whole new set of issues for the administrator of social service and governmental agencies.

Professional discretion: issues of rights and grievances

The theme of participation applies when people have rights as citizens. They are not only the clients of agencies; they are the constituency of the agency. They expect to be treated in humanitarian and dignified ways by the agency. They have a claim to service, not only a privilege dispensed to them by experts or their betters. This formulation means, then, that it is important for an agency to begin to respect and formulate the rights of the people with whom they work. There will be a need for a code which indicates on what basis individuals can get services, the provisions for exclusion, and ways of making claims for service if it is refused. There will be the necessity, consequently, for grievance procedures to deal with those who feel that they have not been adequately treated by the public bureaucracy. Rights are meaningless unless there are ways of enforcing them. A grievance procedure is one of the channels by which this is done.

In recent months, the device of the ombudsman has grown up, perhaps more in name than in actuality in this country. This is a Scandinavian office which has the authority to raise questions about an agency's performance. People with complaints can bring them to the ombudsman. With public disclosure, and sometimes pressure, he is able to get changes in administrative practices.

The European ombudsman is independent of the bureaucracy which he monitors. Our feeling is that a grievance procedure, especially on rights, is likely to require relying, at least at some stage, on people external to the bureaucracy. The effectiveness of grievance procedure depends on its legitimacy. This means that the officials must be able to claim the respect of those who appeal to it.

An effective grievance procedure requires that people usually get decent treatment. Grievance procedures are for the atypical, not the routine case. Otherwise, the procedures would be overwhelmed by activity. Therefore, agencies will now have to reconsider their activities to make sure that the way they treat individuals is dignified and humane. Discourtesy and indifference are legitimate bases for grievance. For example, the practice of long waits in unattractive surroundings for people who come to public bureaucracies will have to change. If service is not a privilege but a right, individuals can demand more humane treatment.

The expression of rights will frequently, as in the case of welfare, lead to the formation of citizen groups who attempt to represent the people who are in contact with the agency. Administrators and their staff will have to learn new ways of accommodating to these pressures. The traditional impermeability between the professional, on one hand, and the client, on the other, is disappearing. The nonprofessional, for example, may side with the client more than with the agency. The notion that the professional disburses privileges is challenged by the substitute view that individuals have a claim on professional services. And the claim extends to the point of raising questions about the relevance of what the professional does with the problems of the client-citizen.

Citizen involvement in the development of policy

The increasing use of professionals and the redefinition of administration as a professional field have fed the notion that planning is politics-free. What we have seen in the last years is criticism, both theoretical and practical, of this perspective. To a degree, then, we are viewing again the death of neutrality in planning. The call for advocacy planning signifies the recognition that any plan is fraught with dangers and benefits for various groups; that no plan can maximize all values; that choice means neglecting the values of some and partially fulfilling the values of others. As a consequence, different interest groups have different kinds of needs in planning.[15]

Policy involvement in community action planning is propelled by the contention that citizens—read poor citizens—should have a focal role in developing plans which affect them. The call for participation in planning has occurred before. But, as in the urban renewal activities of the late '50's and the early '60's, it was a token act or recruited only high-educated and important white groups. The demand for policy involvement today is different because leaders of the black and the poor recognize the importance of policy involvement and are organizing to see that it becomes reality.

Establishing citizen boards without importance and authority will not abate the agitation about participation in planning. The role of planning agencies is itself in debate. The very plans that they produce is subjected to strenuous criticism by neighborhood groups and residents. Profes-

[15]Paul Davidoff, "Advocacy and Pluralism in Planning," *Journal of the American Institute of Planners* (November 1965): 331–38.

sionals are not accepted as having sole authority to make plans. Indeed, frequently their expertise is challenged as inadequate, since people in the neighborhood contend that they know their problems better than anyone else. They do not accept Spiro Agnew's dictum that the experts know more about slums than slum-dwellers.

What we are seeing, then, is a strong attack upon professionalism. Part of this onslaught is know-nothingism. The positive part of the criticism requires that professionals and administrators realign themselves so that they can learn how to work more effectively with grassroots groups who want to be included in those decisions hopefully called "the planning process." Grave difficulties will ensue. Agitation and controversy may bar action, but realistic involvement of the poor cannot be avoided, at least in big cities with large black populations. It becomes important, then, for administrators to be able to establish the kinds of structures which bring in the poor, which legitimate their activities and which result in useful plans and policies. Providing counsel for the people in the neighborhood so that they can be more informed in their recommendations and comments is important.

Winning the confidence of neighborhood representatives is crucial. Promulgating plans and then at the last minute asking for ratification will not be very successful. Bringing in representatives at an early point in the planning may be much more significant. Making residents aware of the issues involved in planning will be more effective than insisting that these are professional decisions which cannot be discussed by untrained persons. Hiring people who are informed or are racially or ethnically like the groups that are clamoring for representation will be significant.

At the same time, it will frequently happen that militant groups that are not very representative and lack widespread support will assert their claims as the authentic voices of the community. The agency will have to develop a wide range of contacts within the low-income community, moving to pay attention to the community, not only at the time of a particular decision but on a continuous basis. It must know its communities so it will be able to work effectively with and within them.

The theme of maximum feasible participation has encouraged the development of organizations in poverty areas at the same time that black consciousness has also stirred organization and action. Many of the new organizations (and many of the old) are militant and aggressive.

Confrontation and disruption are important tactics in their arsenal. They do not accept traditional limits on protest—demonstration, but not disruption. They feel that they have a right to make their feelings and positions known in compelling fashion.

One response to such militancy is stiff-backed resistance as a matter of principle. Such resistance is sometimes called for. It is difficult to maintain, however, if the community organization has considerable support and if its operation is important to the activities of the agency.

Many companies in the '30's followed the policy of strong and unyielding resistance to union pressure to modify company practice. "Managerial prerogatives" and "basic principle" were involved, it was contended. Intransigence frequently facilitated the unionization of the plant. Later, managements learned that they could live with "interference" with their prerogatives. Indeed, what in one period was looked upon as interference, e.g., company policy on pension, became, in another period, a major joint union-management activity.

If intransigence is one extreme reaction, panic is the other. Some agency leaders when under attack are indecisive and vacillating, clutching to straws of accommodation and support, unable to perceive accurately the situation they face.

We do not propose to outline a defense strategy for organizations confronting aggressive social action. The major point is to have continuing contact with the aggrieved community or group. A far-sighted agency will initiate such contact *before* disputes arise, instead of hoping that they will not be pulled into the arena of combat. Since few public agencies can hope to continue to be spectators in the struggle for racial equality, most should open up channels to black leaders before they are compelled to.

There are no magical solutions to the social action-confrontation strategy. Ossified administrations may be only movable by the fire of social action; flexible and adaptive administrations will be in constant and knowing contact with black communities.

Accountability: community control

In the preceding sections we have talked about an agency which is still a typical agency, but with new kinds of responsibilities and expectations placed on it in terms of community involvement. But some agencies will be moving in new directions in which the community now is the focus of authority and the professionals and administrators are responsible to some community board. This is happening in terms of community corporations and is beginning to happen on some limited scale in decentralized school districts, e.g., New York City and Boston, in which local neighborhoods are gaining authority to make and affect decisions.

We expect the expansion of new institutional forms which vest authority in neighborhood groups and representatives. This change is an important part of the transfer of power which is occurring in large cities. Three intersecting forces are speeding this change. One is the demographic shift in large cities so that the Negro, Puerto Rican, or Mexican-American population grows in absolute and relative numbers. The expanding groups want representation which more closely approximates their numerical significance. A second pressure for change is built on dissatisfactions with the operation of existing public and quasi-public agencies—the charge is that they are not doing an adequate job, especially in serving the poor and the discriminated. Schools are particularly attacked, but they are not the only organizations criticized for their deficiencies. The third source of agitation is the strong interest in self-determination, autonomy, or "power." In many black communities, there is high interest in controlling the institutions which directly affect the citizens. The demands for black separation support this pressure.

The demand is not only for decentralized offices, as in multiservice centers which bring together a variety of social services in one accessible building that is in the neighborhood where its users live, rather than in a downtown location. It is control and authority over these offices and services which is basic to the transfer of power. Obviously, there is a transfer of power when black officials are elected to office or when black administrators replace white. But these changes in faces are not the same as a change in which a community-based organization has authority. It is one thing to have a few Negroes on a citywide school board; it is another to have a school board in a Negro neighborhood with wide authority to make decisions about school activities.

Not all transfers of power involve decentralization. But that is now the most likely institutionalized form of the shift in power. (The most common manifestation of the transfer of power will be that of traditional ethnic politics—more blacks will be in important positions, elected and appointive, in city hall.)

The first major issue of decentralization is who represents the community. Elections have been used, but without issues the turnouts have not been great. Small, organized groups can easily win out. How to construct useful representation devices in this beginning period requires more ingenuity than has been displayed.

Ambiguity in defining the limits of authority of the decentralized body has been one of the major ways of reaching agreement between conflicting groups who oppose or support decentralization. The New York City Ocean Hill-Brownsville-American Federation of Teachers fight in 1968 demonstrates that ambiguity is unlikely to be a permanent cover. It is important that early, prior to the actual act of decentralization, at least some of the rules of the game be specified.[16] Certainly employee rights, obligations, and protections should be stated; due process procedures strengthened and clarified. The boundaries of a local board's authority should be delineated, especially in regard to budget and personnel.

At the same time that specification occurs, flexibility should be fostered. Experimentation should be possible or else the rigidities of the past would be compounded. The tension between clarity and experimentation can be great, but some awareness of both needs is desperately needed.

Some administrations should be anticipating difficulties and preparing ways of dealing with them. Too much administrative practice in cities consists of hoping that time will erase problems rather than making problems disappear by anticipating them.

The turn to strong decentralization means that many professionals will find themselves in difficult and disturbing job situations. In many decentralized services the boundary between professional and community (or board) decision will be unclear. Professional decision-making endeavors will be intruded on; community boards with low-educated members may be exercising authority and power over high-educated

[16]See the criticisms of the New York City Board of Education in New York Civil Liberties Union, "The Burden of Blame: A Report on the Ocean Hill-Brownsville School Controversy," 1968.

professionals and administrators. Not only will status relations be jangled; professional domains will be challenged.

Not all of these challenges to professionals are unhealthy. To a considerable extent professionalism has been guild-like, building employment preserves rather than contributing to knowledge or effective action. Professionalism has led to the effort to depoliticize some decisions which are clearly political decisions (e.g., urban redevelopment).

Nonetheless, professionalism has important consequences of not only building competent analysis, but of fostering broader and independent views, less susceptible to fads, political and otherwise, of the day.

Professionalism is under attack on many fronts—from within as well as from without. Even the American Medical Association has been forced to recognize the challenges of the Medical Committee on Human Rights and dissident medical students. Few professions escape charges from some members of "irrelevance" to the issues of the day.

Decentralization will deepen many of these tensions. But decentralization may be one of the routes by which some professions and professionals regain direction and a feeling of relevance. We anticipate conflict in redefining boundaries between what are appropriate decisions best left to professions and what are decisions affecting professionals that should be made by community boards. It might be useful for administrators and professionals to begin now to examine what they should expect of community boards in terms of their prerogatives and what community boards can expect of them.

The theme of participation involves more than the transfer of power; for some, it points to the importance of the *transformation of power*. What is questioned is the extent to which behavior should be regulated. The issue of power transformation is raised when the relations between the governed and the governors are challenged, rather than contesting who should be the governors.[17]

In a society where power is embraced and relished on one hand, and its widespread dispersion heralded on the other, it is difficult to develop a realistic view of the possibilities of transforming power relationships.

---

[17]S. M. Miller, "The Future of Maximum Feasible Participation," a speech given to the Alumni Association of the Columbia University School of Social Work, May 1968.

But the widespread disturbance about "power" means that participation is a social shorthand for symbolizing discomfort and dissatisfaction about power relationships. Consequently, the issue of participation—in its many forms—is not a foible of the '60's, but a fissure in our society.

Is participation viable?

The answer to the question must depend in part on the standards of viability we accept. Obviously, there has already been a great deal of disturbance and traditional modes of behavior of administrators and professionals are indicted and upset. This unrest will continue. The issues which participation raises today are primarily in terms of the neglected and discriminated groups in the society. These are groups fighting for inclusion, for social honor, and for individual respect. Established practice in public bureaucracies has not been adequate. The pressure for change from these groups will continue, for their standards of effective participation are different from those of most administrators and professionals.

Other enduring issues than the ending of discrimination and exclusion are at stake. These are the issues of the humanization and democratizing of bureaucracy, issues which affect not only the poor and discriminated but all groups in society. The objective is not the elimination of bureaucracy and organization but the discovery and inventing of ways of overcoming their dysfunctions and disturbing qualities. The new inventions and the political pressures behind them will frequently prove to be inadequate. But it seems to us that our society is enmeshed in the right kind of struggle. We are attempting to try to develop new institutional practices leading to greater humanization in the treatment of individuals—which requires to some extent their employment and certainly the development of their rights *vis-a-vis* the bureaucracies. The effort is coupled with the objective of achieving more democracy in the large-scale organizations which make important decisions affecting individuals' lives; the new expectation is that these organizations should be subjected to greater citizen influence. The demands are about the relevance, quality, control, and direction of bureaucracy. We do not endorse all the demands upon bureaucracy involved in the concept of maximum feasible participation, but we do embrace the issues which have been raised. They are crucial issues. We should have new expectations about the effects of bureaucracies on people. These new expectations are that greater humanity of treatment and deeper democracy in the formulation and execution of policy be demonstrated in practice.

The challenge to administrators is great. Traditional practices will be upset. Calumnies will be perpetrated in the name of participation. But we have to see this upheaval as part of the historic process of attempting to change the ways bureaucracies operate. We have to learn to deal with, rather than wholly reject, these pressures. We have entered into a new era in which there are now public broadsides about the dissatisfactions with bureaucracy—dissatisfactions which affect people on the political right who are concerned about the intrusion of public agencies into private lives and people of the New Left who are concerned about the absence of participation in decision making.

The next years will not be a happy time to be an administrator or a professional in these agencies. But there will not be many other places more significant in the effort to democratize a society which has grown large and unwieldy.

It may not always be possible to bring together without conflict ideals of efficiency, humanity, and democracy. But we cannot surrender to efficiency as the highest social value.

27

The Constitution
and Public Administration

John D. Millett

Our system of government in the United States rests upon constitutional prescription. One legacy of our Western political heritage is a high regard for law. Indeed, we are convinced that freedom is possible only under law. Nor is law simply a matter of defining the relationships of man to man in society. We have given law an even greater task: to define the relationship of government to man.[1] To this end constitutionalism provides the means. The central role of constitutionalism, or of constitutional democracy, in establishing the essential framework of government is one of the great themes in the political development of Western society.[2]

When the federal Constitution of 1787 was written, two goals were foremost in the political thinking of the day. One was to provide an effective means of common political effort by the thirteen states which had so recently acquired independence from Great Britain. The other objective was to establish a central government, even as they had undertaken to do in each of the thirteen states, which would be limited in scope and safe for men's liberties. The governments established in the first decade of independence reflected the political ideas current in eighteenth-century America. These governments reflected too the conditions of society with which the men of that day were familiar.

[1]Cf. Edwin W. Patterson, *Jurisprudence: Men and Ideas of the Law* (Brooklyn, N.Y.: Foundation Press, 1953).

[2]Cf. Frederick Watkins, *The Political Tradition of the West* (Cambridge, Mass.: Harvard University Press, 1948), especially chap. 6.

American constitutionalism has been primarily concerned with [detailing organs] of decision-making as a part of the system of government. These constitutions have little to say about the structure of political power or the operation of political parties. And they have little to say about bureaucracy. These omissions are noteworthy. Little has been done in the intervening years, however, to enlarge the scope of our formal constitutional documents. Tradition, common practices and understandings, and occasional legal enactments have rounded out the governmental system as a whole. Our "living Constitution," as Howard Lee McBain termed it, has seemed to meet the needs left unresolved or not foreseen by the Founding Fathers.

* * *

It is revealing of the political thinking and of the rudimentary governmental needs of the day that the federal Constitution should have so little to say on the subject of public administration. Indeed, it is fair to say that our federal Constitution assumes the existence of a bureaucracy rather than provides for it. Such mention as does occur of the subject is entirely indirect or oblique.

In defining the powers of the president in Article II, Section 2, the Constitution says that "he may require the opinion, in writing, of the principal officer in each of the executive departments, upon any subject relating to the duties of their respective offices." Farther along in the same section the Constitution sets forth the appointive power of the president in these words: ". . . and he shall nominate, and, by and with the [advice and] consent of the Senate, shall appoint ambassadors, other public ministers and consuls, judges of the Supreme Court, and all other officers of the United States whose appointments are not herein otherwise provided for, and which shall be established by law; but the Congress may by law vest the appointment of such inferior officers, as they think proper, in the president alone, in the courts of law, or in the heads of departments."

Two aspects of these provisions just quoted from Article II of the Constitution should be particularly noted. For one thing, the article does not specifically mention the creation of either "executive departments" or "departments." It simply implies that such agencies will be set up by referring to their heads whom the president may consult in writing, and in whom the Congress may by law vest the power to appoint "inferior officers." Neither of these references to administrative agencies is very explicit. Why does one reference use the expression "executive department" and the other merely the single word "department"? Is there some distinction implied by this differing terminology or is it simply an accident of phraseology? Is there a suggestion here that all administrative agencies must be labeled either executive departments or departments? Is there any particular implication for administrative organization contained in these oblique references? No one can answer such questions as these. There is no authoritative source for providing the answers except continued practice as reflected in legal enactments, presidential attitudes, court decisions, and general acceptance.

A second aspect of this constitutional language is again an indirect one. The words refer to "all other officers of the United States . . . which shall be established by law." Here is the strong implication that officers of the United States must be provided for by law, that is, by enactment of the legislature. In an article which is concerned to set forth the power of the executive the wording appears to suggest that the president shall not create "officers of the United States." Only the legislative process, in which to be sure the executive participates, is capable of establishing such positions.

Yet Article I of the federal Constitution which provides for the legislative power says nothing specifically about administrative agencies. The important section of Article I is, of course, Section 8 enumerating the scope of the legislative authority of the federal government. This section refers to subjects, not to agencies. It speaks of the collection of taxes, the coinage of money, the establishment of post offices, the issuance of patents and copyrights, the support of armies, and the maintenance of a navy. There are other items as well, terminating in a clause which authorizes the Congress to make all laws "necessary and proper for carrying into execution the foregoing powers, and all other powers vested by this Constitution in the government of the United States, or in any department or officer thereof." Here again, instead of any direct provision therefor, is an assumption that administrative agencies will have to be created for the operation of the federal government.

In their eloquent defense of the Constitution, the authors of the collection of papers known as *The Federalist* had little to say about public administration. In essay no. 72, Hamilton commented upon the administrative role of the president, but he appeared to be more concerned about "the stability of the system of administration," which he connected with the term of the president in office, than with the constitutional status of administrative agencies. In a subsequent essay, no. 84, Hamilton enumerated the "principal departments of the administration under the present government" and expressed the opinion that these same agencies would be required under the new government. Yet his major preoccupation appeared to be the practical problem of prospective cost in operating the new central government established by the federal Constitution.

It would be erroneous to assume that the men who framed the Constitution of 1787 were ignorant of administrative problems or belittled the importance of public administration. To be sure, the administrative agencies set up under the Articles of Confederation were few and rudimentary. The authority of the central government was limited. Society was largely commercial and agrarian; population was sparse and scattered the length of the Atlantic seaboard from Maine to Georgia. Overland transportation was slow, dependent upon few roads and upon horse- or oxen-drawn vehicles. Communication was likewise slow. Even in the states governmental services were not extensive. There was little need for or disposition toward governmental administration in eighteenth-century America.

Yet such evidence as is to be found in the federal Constitution itself and in other contemporary documents suggests the conclusion that in 1787 the necessity for public administration as a feature of government was taken for granted. Administrative agencies were in existence at the time. Their continuance, perhaps their expansion, was assumed. Perhaps the menace of a politically irresponsible bureaucracy seemed somewhat remote at that time, but the danger was undoubtedly known to men well-read in the political thinking of their own age and of earlier times.

The governmental challenge of 1787 was not administrative. The basic problem was to establish an effective national government for a newborn nation, to provide organs of decision making competent to meet the needs of the day and even to cope with the developments of the future. One of the tasks of this framework of government was to provide adequate and effective supervision for the administrative agencies of government. This concern was certainly present in the provisions for an executive branch in the new federal government modeled in large measure from the executive branches already existing in the state governments of that day. The constitutions as written were thought to provide the organs of decision-making necessary to operate a government, including the establishment and supervision of a bureaucracy.

Some understanding of the attitude of the Founding Fathers is to be obtained from one of the celebrated cases decided by the Supreme Court of the United States with John Marshall as Chief Justice. In the case of *McCulloch v. Maryland,* the authority of the federal legislature to charter a national bank was challenged.[3] In so far as the specific issue was concerned Marshall found his guidance in the last clause of Section 8 of Article I empowering the Congress to make all laws necessary and proper for carrying into execution the other authority set forth in the Constitution. In the eyes of Marshall, the national bank was not just a private agency chartered by the federal legislature. It was an administrative agency necessary for the performance of duties constitutionally specified as coming within the competence of the Congress. Thus was acknowledged the implied assumption of the federal Constitution that administrative agencies would be created by law as deemed necessary and in such form as the legislature and executive might deem appropriate.

Beyond the immediate issue Marshall saw an even more fundamental proposition. The Chief Justice characterized the Constitution of the United States as "intended to endure for ages to come, and, consequently, to be adapted to the various *crises* of human affairs." He thus implied that the Constitution as fundamental law was expected to grow, to take on new meaning with changing circumstances, while the original words remained unchanged and the great principles of governmental framework continued to function unimpaired. All the administrative problems of a later day did not have to be specifically anticipated by the federal Constitution in order for that document to provide the essential elements of a government adequate to cope with the bureaucracy of our own day.

---

[3] *McCulloch v. Maryland,* 4 Wheat. 316 (1819).

* * *

For the most part federal and state constitutions are concerned with establishing a framework of governmental organs for decision-making. This framework is usually described as a system for the separation of power. In eighteenth-century political thought government was conceived as having three somewhat different, if interrelated, elements. The federal Constitution of 1787 spoke of "all legislative powers," "the executive power," and "the judicial power." The classical statement of the prevailing idea of the time was contained in the Massachusetts Constitution of 1780 which declared: "In the government of this commonwealth the legislative department shall never exercise the executive and judicial powers or either of them; the executive shall never exercise the legislative and judicial powers or either of them; the judicial shall never exercise the legislative and executive powers or either of them: to the end it may be a government of laws and not of men." To be sure, in practice, the separation of governmental power into legislative, executive, and judicial component parts is not absolute. Our constitutions provide for a comingling of power, such as executive participation in the enactment of laws, and legislative participation in the appointment of administrative officials.

The structure of American government recognizes nonetheless three different sets of institutions exercising governmental power. The legislative is one institution, very different in its selection, numbers, procedure, and authority from the other two institutions. Similarly, the executive and judicial institutions are quite different in their characteristics from any of the other two. The separation of power in our constitutional democracy is a separation of organs possessing decision-making authority.

There are other characteristics of the American scheme of government which must be mentioned in passing. A bill of rights and other provisions clearly indicate that government is not all-powerful but limited both in the substance of what it may do and in the procedure for exercising its authority. The nature of these limitations has been referred to in the preceding chapter. In addition, ours is a federal scheme of government, comprising a central government for the nation as a whole and forty-nine constituent governments, each of which possesses the residual power not vested in the central instrument and not specifically prohibited. We shall have something more to say about this federal system and its administrative implications in the next chapter.

Our American constitutions are concerned to set forth a basic framework of government which is conceived to be adequate to the governmental needs of man in society and at the same time protective of his individual liberties. The kind of structure thought proper for this purpose two hundred years ago and still functioning today embodies the existence of a legislature, an executive, and a judiciary. Each is a distinct entity, different from the other and independent in its status. No one branch is thought of as inherently superior to another; no one branch is expected to be dependent for its authority or its existence upon another. Each is thought of as exercising a different part of the sum total of governmental power. All three are essential to the existence and operation of government.

If the legislature, executive, and judiciary encompass the substance of governmental power, what then is the constitutional position of administration? We cannot turn to our constitutions themselves for a clear and definite answer to this question. The fact is that our constitutions do not undertake to provide any answer. The explanation must be something more than the meager administrative activity of the eighteenth century, as we have already commented. It appears that those who wrote our constitutions assumed that there was no problem to worry about, that any question about the constitutional status of administrative agencies could be answered readily and easily enough if only an adequate basic framework of government was brought into existence. It is subsequent students of government, and even political leaders and judges, who have had reason to ponder the issue with the growth of the modern administrative state.

_____

Ideas of constitutional status

In *The Federalist,* no. 72, Alexander Hamilton began:

> The administration of government, in its largest sense, comprehends all the operations of the body politic, whether legislative, executive, or judiciary; but in its most usual and perhaps in its most precise signification, it is limited to executive details, and falls peculiarly within the province of the executive

department. The actual conduct of foreign negotiations, the preparatory plans of finance, the application and disbursement of the public moneys in conformity to the general appropriations of the legislature, the arrangement of the army and navy, the direction of the operations of war—these, and other matters of a like nature, constitute what seems to be most properly understood by the administration of government. The persons, therefore, to whose immediate management these different matters are committed, ought to be considered as the assistants or deputies of the chief magistrate, and on this account, they ought to derive their offices from his appointment, at least from his nomination, and ought to be subject to his superintendence.

In writing about that initial and formative period when the federal government was just starting, Leonard D. White has pointed out that much administrative authority was vested directly in the chief executive by law.[4] Except for the Treasury Department, the president was authorized to prescribe the duties of the heads of departments. Department heads, moreover, were expected to act in accordance with the president's instructions. In addition, many details were left to the chief executive, such as signing patents and approving contracts for the construction of lighthouses. Certainly, in the early days of the Republic, the president was by law made a principal administrative officer of the federal government. In turn, the chief executive was inclined to look upon department heads as his assistants, helping him in the exercise of the executive power.

At the same time, as secretary of the treasury, Hamilton went far beyond the inclination of the president in formulating public policy for congressional enactment. Indeed, Hamilton appeared determined to make his position that of a legislative leader, and to a very real degree the president became an impartial chief magistrate and Hamilton a kind of prime minister. When Jefferson became president, the situation was quite different. The president himself was the party leader. More than this, Jefferson was concerned to slow up the process of building a strong administrative organization in the hands of the central government. The very fact that Jefferson had a determined view about the desirable course of political events made the presidency itself a different kind of

---

[4]Leonard D. White, *The Federalists* (New York: Macmillan, 1948), especially pp. 17–20, and chap. 3.

office from what it had been under Washington and then under Adams. In a sense, Jefferson made the presidency more important politically and less important administratively than it had been under Washington.[5]

In any event, it early became an accepted practice to look upon administration and executive power as one and the same. To this very day, there is a disposition in many quarters to speak of the executive branch of government as encompassing all, or almost all, administrative agencies. Thus in 1947 and again in 1953, Congress in passing legislation to create a special agency to study administrative organization labeled the body "The Commission on Organization of the Executive Branch." In 1937, the President's Committee on Administrative Management had no doubt when asserting: "The president is chief executive and administrator within the federal system and service."[6]

Yet a somewhat different position has been declared from time to time. Under President Jackson a dispute arose between the post-master general, Amos Kendall, and the Congress over a claim rendered by one Stokes as a contractor for carrying mail. Both the post-master general and the president believed the claim to be fraudulent. Congress by law directed the solicitor of the treasury to settle the claim and the postmaster general then to pay the claim so established. Kendall finally credited Stokes with part of the claim but not all of it. He was sued for the balance. Kendall argued that as head of a department he was subject to the direction and control of the president, and that even in the light of statutory enactment he was not obliged to act contrary to instructions from the president. The Supreme Court of the United States refused to accept this reasoning. To accede to Kendall's argument, the Court declared,[7]

> ... would be vesting in the president a dispensing power, which has no countenance for its support, in any part of the Constitution; and is asserting

---

[5]Cf. Lynton K. Caldwell, *The Administrative Theories of Hamilton and Jefferson: Their Contribution to Thought on Public Administration* (Chicago: University of Chicago Press, 1944). See also Leonard D. White, *The Jeffersonians* (New York: Macmillan, 1951).

[6]President's Committee on Administrative Management, *Report with Special Studies* (Washington: Government Printing Office, 1937), p. 2.

[7]*Kendall v. Stokes,* 12 Pet. 610 (1838).

> a principle, which, if carried out in its results, to all cases falling within it, would be clothing the president with a power entirely to control the legislation of Congress, and paralyze the administration of justice. [The Court went on to say] . . . it would be an alarming doctrine, that Congress cannot impose upon any executive officer any duty they may think proper, which is not repugnant to any rights secured and protected by the Constitution; and in such cases, the duty and responsibility grow out of and are subject to the control of the law, and not to the direction of the president. [The Court added] The law is supreme in the United States and is binding upon administrative officers. Apart from the Constitution itself, this emanates primarily from statutory enactment, which originates in the legislature.

Within a two-year span President Pierce received two somewhat different opinions on this same matter from his attorney general, Caleb Cushing. In his first opinion the attorney general declared that heads of departments had a responsibility to Congress. He pointed out that they were created by law and that most of their duties were prescribed by law. The legislature might at all times call upon department heads for information or explanation in matters of official duty and might "as it sees fit interpose by legislation concerning them, when required by the interests of the government."[8] A year later the attorney general declared that no head of a department could lawfully perform an official act against the will of the president. If this were not so, the attorney general said, "Congress might by statute so divide and transfer the executive power as utterly to subvert the government."[9]

Many years later, speaking of the Federal Trade Commission, the Supreme Court called it "an administrative body created by Congress to carry into effect legislative policies embodied in the statute in accordance with the legislative standard therein prescribed, and to perform other specified duties as a legislative or as a judicial aid. Such a body cannot in any proper sense be characterized as an arm or an eye of the executive."[10] It also spoke of the Commission as "charged with no policy except the policy of the law," and accepted the proposition that a Commission member was an "officer who occupies no place in the executive

---

[8] 6 Opinions of the Attorney General 326 (1854).
[9] 7 Opinions of the Attorney General 453 (1855).
[10] *Humphrey's Executor v. United States,* 295 U.S. 602 (1935).

department and who exercises no part of the executive power vested by the Constitution in the president."

These opinions express conflicting legal conceptions about the status of administrative agencies in our scheme of government. At the least they indicate some confusion in fixing the respective relationship of legislature and executive to administrative agencies. The legislature has a certain role to perform. The chief executive still another. A line of demarcation in the scope of these respective branches of government has not been easy to formulate in terms of a clear and consistent doctrine of constitutional status.

Thirty years ago a distinguished political scientist, W. F. Willoughby, thought that the solution to the problem of the constitutional status of administrative agencies lay in drawing a sharp distinction between executive power and administrative power.[11] Willoughby declared that the executive power was that of "representing the government as a whole and of seeing that all its laws are properly complied with by its several parts." On the other hand, "the administrative function, that is, the function of direction, supervision, and control of the administrative activities of the government, resides in the legislative branch."[12] Willoughby likened the authority of the legislature to that of a board of directors in a business corporation. Impressed as he was by the extent of the authority exercised by the legislature over administrative activities, organization, procedure, and expenditure, Willoughby could see no other interpretation of constitutional status which would fit the stubborn facts of actual practice.

Accordingly, Willoughby was led to declare that constitutionally the president "possesses no administrative authority."[13] Instead, he argued that in relation to the heads of administrative agencies the power of the president was limited only to making sure that the orders given them by law were "duly enforced." Willoughby then went on to advocate that as a matter of administrative efficiency the legislature should by law confer upon the chief executive the powers of a "general manager." He wanted

[11]W. F. Willoughby, *Principles of Public Administration* (Washington, D.C.: Brookings Institution, 1927), chaps. 2 and 3.

[12]*Ibid.,* p. 11.

[13]*Ibid.,* p. 36.

the legislature to provide by law that "the line of administrative authority" should run from agency heads to the chief executive to the legislature and not directly from agencies to legislature. The president as general manager should control institutional services, such as care of plant, procurement and distribution of supplies, and the keeping of accounts. The president should prepare the budget. But in all these activities the chief executive would be "strictly a subordinate of the legislature, the agent through which the latter exercises the powers of general administration."[14]

A different position holds that all administrative agencies are themselves simply subordinate elements of the executive branch of the government. Did not the federal Constitution refer to heads of "executive departments"? Has not the legislature itself enacted laws which in effect equate the executive branch with the sum total of all administrative activity? And in a tripartite structure of government where would one expect to find administrative agencies except as a part of the executive branch? Arguments such as these have been put forth to maintain that executive and administration are synonymous in our scheme of government.

This position was advocated by the President's Committee on Administrative Management in 1937.[15] It is said that the work of the executive branch was badly organized and declared: "The whole executive branch of the government should be overhauled and the present 100 agencies reorganized under a few large departments in which every executive activity would find its place."[16] Subsequently the Committee asserted that the Constitution "places in the president, and in the president alone, the whole executive power of the government of the United States."[17] The Committee then acknowledged that the administrative organization to carry out "the executive power" rested upon statutory law. It proceeded to characterize the structure of the executive branch, meaning the structure of administrative agencies, as inefficient, as a "poor instrument for rendering public service," and as thwarting democratic control.[18]

[14] *Ibid.*, p. 49.
[15] President's Committee on Administrative Management, *op. cit.*, p. 2.
[16] *Ibid.*, p. 4.
[17] *Ibid.*, p. 31.
[18] *Ibid.*, pp. 32–33.

Without making its position entirely explicit, the President's Committee, as the above expressions of point of view indicate, conceived of the executive branch not just as the president but rather as the sum total of administrative activities. Yet the Committee realized also that the reforms it was advocating could not be accomplished by the president alone. It urged that Congress be satisfied to determine "the broad outlines of reorganization" by creating executive departments and by adopting "the general policy that all administrative operating agencies be brought within these large executive departments."[19] But the Committee seemed also to anticipate that this proposal might not be entirely acceptable to the Congress.

Confronted with the inescapable fact that the Congress created by law all "executive departments" as well as other administrative agencies, and realizing that the success of its own recommendation depended upon legislative enactment, the President's Committee faced a crucial dilemma. On the one hand, the Committee was committed to the proposition that the executive branch of the federal government embraced all administrative activities. On the other hand, the Committee confronted the necessity of congressional action in order to carry out its proposals. The Committee then proceeded to develop a surprising constitutional doctrine, the doctrine of "accountability of the executive to the Congress."[20] Just where it found this doctrine or how it arrived at such a proposition, the Committee did not say. It opened its discussion with these words:

> Under the American system the executive power is balanced and made safe by freedom of speech by elections, by the protection of civil rights under an independent judiciary, by the making of laws which determine policies including especially appropriations and tax measures, by an independent elective Congress, and by the establishment of executive accountability.

The Committee went on to assert that the preservation of the principle of the "full accountability of the executive to the Congress is an

[19] *Ibid.*, p. 49.
[20] *Ibid.*

essential part of our republican system."[21] It suggested first that account-ability would be achieved through proper executive coordination of ad-ministrative activities. The Committee then spoke of the importance of the legislature and of the work done by committees in considering pend-ing bills and in conducting investigations. "It is with full realization of the necessity of continuing and preserving this important function of the Congress and its committees that we suggest the necessity for improving the machinery of holding the executive branch more effectively account-able to the Congress."[22] The Committee said that "detailed legislative requirements" on organization and operation of the administrative ma-chinery absolved the head of a department and then the president from his executive responsibility. The President's Committee saw as a solu-tion: "The executive then should be held to account through an indepen-dent audit made by an independent auditor who will report promptly to the Congress his criticisms and exceptions of the actions of the execu-tive."[23]

Apart from the prescription, we may note two major aspects of the position put forth by the President's Committee on Administrative Man-agement. First, the Committee appeared to equate the president and all administrative agencies as together constituting the executive branch of government. Secondly, the Committee announced a new constitutional doctrine of presidential accountability to the Congress for the conduct of administrative agencies. These two propositions entail governmental complexities which neither the President's Committee in 1937 nor oth-ers have been able to resolve.

Some political scientists have taken positions similar to that of the President's Committee on Administrative Management but have argued in terms of preferable practice rather than of constitutional prescription. Thus, one writer has set forth his "working bias" in these terms: "An administrative agency should be responsible to the legislature, but only through the chief executive, and primarily for broad issues of public

[21] *Ibid.*
[22] *Ibid.*
[23] *Ibid.,* p. 50.

policy and general administrative performance."[24] The author goes on to point out that administrative agencies "must be answerable in some sense to *both* the chief executive and the legislature."[25] He then poses the issue as whether this dual responsibility shall be structured in terms of an agency being directly and separately responsible to the legislature and the chief executive, or shall an agency be responsible to the legislature through the chief executive? This question is then answered by this particular student of government in terms of the second arrangement being the preferable practice.

The arguments in favor of indirect responsibility are both political and technical in nature. If administrative agencies are responsible to the legislature only through the chief executive, then there is one rather than two sources of official communication and command. Conflicting instructions may be avoided, and administrative action be sure and certain rather than confused and contradictory. Coordination of agencies having common concerns is more readily achieved if there is only one source of command. The executive is better equipped than the legislature for the supervision of administrative agencies. The executive can present balanced and consistent programs to the legislature for consideration, and legislative action can be better informed and clearly focused on major issues.[26]

Opposed to this line of reasoning are two major arguments. One is that since the legislature must set forth the broad outlines of public policy to be carried out by administrative agencies, this necessarily entails some degree of supervision over them. The other is that if legislative responsibility is to be exercised through the executive, does this not make the executive subordinate to the legislature, contrary to the framework of government established by our constitutions?

The various ideas and concepts just cited illustrate an important confusion in the constitutional prescription of American government. Unquestionably those who drafted the federal Constitution and our state constitutions intended to provide an adequate arrangement for the su-

---

[24]Arthur Maass, *Muddy Waters* (Cambridge, Mass.: Harvard University Press, 1951), p. 8.

[25]*Ibid.,* p. 9.

[26]*Ibid.,* pp. 9–11.

pervision of bureaucracy. No one contemplated the possibility of a politically irresponsible administrative apparatus. Rather, it was thought that the scheme of government set up for decision making would be competent to supervise the bureaucracy and ensure its behavior in accordance with instructions from the legislature and executive. How this arrangement would work in practice seems to have given little concern to those who wrote our constitutional documents.

* * *

We cannot look to constitutional doctrine to find an answer to the question: How do we keep the bureaucracy politically responsible in America? Rather we must look to practice. And in practice, as we shall observe, all three branches of government, legislative, executive, and judicial, have major roles to play in maintaining politically responsible behavior. Each such role is different; each operates directly upon administrative agencies. In a sense, administrative agencies are responsible in varying ways to all three branches of government.

We may reasonably think of the bureaucracy in our system of government as being a kind of separate element, apart from the three basic organs of decision making in our governmental structure but subordinate to all three. Yet such an interpretation of status is not founded in constitutional prescription. It is founded in the political practice of American government. It is that practice which points the way in the quest for responsible performance of the bureaucracy.

28

To ... Provide
for the Common Defense

J. Malcolm Moore

A constitutional mini-crisis manufactured in the House Armed Services Committee in 1961 threatened so many other military policy makers into reaction that a rare opportunity emerged—an opportunity to dissect United States military policy-making and to examine *who* does *what* and *how* they do it. *How* decisions are made and *who* makes them regularly determine *what* they are. The RS-70 aircraft was the center of this unusual dispute which spotlighted military policy-making routines.

In terms of money spent and personnel employed, to say nothing of national survival, decisions concerning the military have greater impact than decisions in any other realm of U.S. national governmental policy. Critical as such decisions are, the U.S. Constitution is scant help in an effort to determine *how* military policy is made. Specific situations frequently place two or more provisions of the Constitution into conflict. This is true even when each provision is clear on its face, which is not always the case. The sections of the Constitution which create the framework for establishing U.S. military posture are examples of just such ambiguity: Congress shall "provide for the common Defense and general Welfare," "raise and support Armies," and "provide and maintain a Navy," but the president is commander-in-chief of the Armed Services. Does this mean that the president is in supreme and complete command of forces which are selected and armed by Congress? Of course not, but the relationship often remains ambiguous and obscure.

Military policy is not unique. Those who must make the Constitution work find that the generalities of the framers frequently left open the specific rules for policy-making. What the rules are and how they changed between 1945 and the second anniversary of the Nixon presidency are the topics which anchor this essay. Four specific themes recur.

First, members of Congress possess certain techniques and labor under definite limitations as they encounter policies formed in the executive branch. Second, both congressional and executive policy-makers treat *structural* (domestic) aspects of military policy differently from the way they treat *strategic* (international) components. Third, congressional-executive patterns of interaction underscore the importance of strategic decision-making procedures in the executive branch. Finally, changes in forms, formats, and forums of decision-making impose trade-offs; advantages gained through change usually mean that other advantages, previously enjoyed, are lost.

The RS-70 controversy

The RS-70 controversy overflowed with illustrations of decision-making trade-offs. The B-70 bomber was redesignated RS-70 in 1962 and given a reconnaissance strike mission after two presidents and four secretaries of defense refused to fund fully the prototype development program. The B-70 first became an air force budget request item for fiscal year 1954 (FY54). It was conceived as a manned bomber designed to fly at about 2,200 miles per hour at altitudes of about 70,000 feet. The aircraft originally was scheduled to be operational in 1964. The program was terminated some ten years after it began, although cutbacks began in 1958. Spokesmen for the air force continued to hope, during most of the ten years, that by the early 1970's North American Aviation, Inc., would produce and that the air force would have the RS-70, nee B-70.[1]

Air force representatives were active rather than passive in attempting to realize their hopes for the RS-70. They convinced the chairman and members of the House Armed Services Committee that funding for the RS-70 program for FY63 should be $491 million instead of the $171 million asked by President John F. Kennedy and his secretary of defense, Robert S. McNamara.

[1]U.S. Congress, House, Subcommittee of the Committee on Appropriations, *Hearings on Department of Defense Appropriations for 1961,* 86th Cong. 2d sess., 1960, Pt. 2, pp. 249–59; Pt. 6, pp. 33–38; and the *New York Times,* 8 March 1952, p. 14.

Constitutional threats and tests

Chairman Carl Vinson exploited an unusual, possibly unique, tactic as he sought to boost the president's RS-70 budget request to the total sought by air force spokesmen. He and the other members of the House Armed Services Committee threatened a constitutional test between Congress and the executive. Specifically, they threatened to recommend, to the full House, *authorizing* legislation which *directed* the secretary of the air force to enter into contracts that had been forbidden by the secretary of defense. If passed, the legislation would have directed the secretary of the air force to utilize an authorization of $320 million more than President Kennedy requested in FY63 for an RS-70 weapons system.[2]

A move to "direct" expenditures deviated dramatically from the usual approach in committees which authorize the executive to act and to spend. Members of such committees typically recommend to their parent houses that an executive official be *authorized* to spend specific amounts for stated purposes. Each authorization bill, if and when it passes both Houses of Congress, contains two implied conditions. The first condition is that the Appropriations Committees and the Congress will appropriate enough money to fulfill the authorization, which often does not happen. The second condition is that the president or his subordinates will spend any or all of the appropriated money, which sometimes does not occur either.

Threats by members of Congress to direct specific action by an executive official exposed the sensitive, gray area where congressional and executive authority overlap. Implemented to its fullest, this concept would leave the commander in chief with command of his forces and also with his forces armed with weapons selected and supplied against the presidental will by another authority—Congress.

The threatened directive also set Congress against itself in compli-

---

[2]U.S. Congress, House, Committee on Armed Services, *Hearings on Military Posture and H. R. 9751, Authorizations for Aircraft, Missiles, and Naval Vessels,* 87th Cong. 2d sess., 1962, pp. 3171–77, 3897–3920, and 3988. Cited hereafter as *Hearings on H. R. 9571,* 1962.

cated ways. Members of the House Armed Services Committee raised a potential challenge to several other committees, especially the Senate Armed Services Committee and the Appropriations Committee in each house. Even if the threatened directive were accepted in the House, members of the Senate Armed Services Committee might be unwilling to recommend such a proposal to their parent body. Should they be both willing and able to engineer the directive through the Senate, the House and Senate Appropriations Committees would be severely challenged. In the Appropriations Committees, particularly the House Committee, members traditionally exercise their own independent judgment about how much money should be *appropriated* regardless of how much more has been *authorized*. This is as true for the two Military Appropriations Subcommittees as it is for the parent committees.

Some of the questions raised by the threatened directive suggest why the participants were delighted when the dispute was resolved without the conflict and disruption which answers would have required. (1) If the directive to the air force secretary passed in the House, would members of the House Military Appropriations Subcommittee be denied their independent judgment on how much money should be appropriated? (2) What would the relevant Senate committees do? (3) If the secretary of defense or the president refused to permit their subordinate to execute the RS-70 contracts, would any of the three of them be subjected to impeachment proceedings? (4) Would the legal duty imposed upon the secretary of the air force result in the release of funds by the president? (5) What would occur if the secretary of the air force executed contracts against the orders of his superiors in the executive branch?

Whether or not such questions were ever formally posed, they were never answered. President Kennedy and Chairman Vinson reached a compromise the day before the proposal went to the floor of the House. The offending word, "directed," was struck, and "authorized" was substituted. In exchange for the revised wording, the president and Secretary McNamara agreed to have the RS-70 reevaluated, a commitment McNamara had made more than a month earlier. Vinson made certain, however, that the "proper" interests were represented in the RS-70 reevaluation group.[3]

[3]U.S. Congressional Record, 87th Cong. 2d sess., 1962, CVIII, pp. 4309–10. Cited hereafter as *C. R.,* CVIII, 1962.

Relationships under stress

Neither the president nor Vinson nor anyone else forced answers to questions such as those posed above. Answers will not be forced in this essay either. Instead, this examination is of the relationships among those who shared in governing as they attempted to avoid the tests of strength and will which answers would have required.

The RS-70 disputants did not sink the ship of state; they did rock the boat a bit. When Vinson proposed to *direct* the secretary of the air force, he exposed many links which bind together those who share in governing—bind them in ways which make them appear on the verge of flying apart. The particular links which ultimately withstood Vinson's tests were not only within Congress but also within the executive branch and between the two.

Consider the ways in which congressmen are alert to chinks in executive solidarity. Fragmentation in the executive branch often is generated by its three parts: the career bureaucracy (military and civilian); politically appointed members of the administration; and members of the president's staff, institutionalized in the executive office of the president.

Bureaucracy. In the RS-70 controversy, the *bureaucracy* was a major spokesman. Bureaucrats constitute the permanent government. They are on the job when any particular president is inaugurated, and they will be there when he leaves. Members of the bureaucracy are often understood to be civilians only, but the military is also a career bureaucracy. Bureaucrats obtain their positions, are retained, and are promoted upon the basis of merit rather than patronage. They are charged with implementing policies made by themselves or by others in the executive branch of Congress, but the ways of implementation may subtly affect these policies or even change them radically.

Administration. Of the 8000-odd presidential appointees who constitute a president's administration, the ones considered here are department heads and their deputy, under, and assistant secretaries, plus a few others. Appointed by the president, these officials can find their loyalties whipsawed from above and below. A department head must rely upon the bureaucrats of his department in many essential ways. However, they may, and often do, have policy preferences contrary to the president's and/or the department head's. The buffeting which a member of the administration takes is compounded when his personal preferences differ from those of both his subordinates and his superiors.

Executive Office of the President. Members of the president's staff are often lumped under the term "administration" with department heads and other appointed members of the line organization, but here the "presidency" or the "president's staff" refers to those 1,500 men and women in the Executive Office of the President. With their offices in the White House or next door in the Executive Office building, they are physically closer to the president than are bureaucrats and administrators. The members of the president's staff often are psychologically closer to the president, also. If a president is to realize his preferences over those of his administration and the bureaucracy, he usually must rely heavily upon those in the Executive Office of the President. They include, among others, the White House Staff, the Bureau of the Budget (BOB) (and its beefed-up successor, the Office of Management and Budget), the Council of Economic Advisors, and the National Security Council.

Participants from Congress, the bureaucracy, the administration, and the Executive Office were involved in the RS-70 controversy and had vested interests in its resolution.

Congressional-executive relations

The floors of the two congressional houses are major stages where representatives and senators go to posture and to be on display. Committee rooms are where they work, and this is the reason for the emphasis upon committees throughout this essay.

Members of Congress in their committees do not deal with the president; they deal with personnel from the Executive Office of the President. They deal sometimes with department heads, their deputies, and assistants; but most often, they deal with the bureau chiefs and those who work in the bureaus. During their annual pilgrimage to Capitol Hill, some bureau spokesmen confront members of committees who seek to *control* them, others who seek to *supervise* them, and others who are content merely to *oversee* them.[4] Some congressmen ask questions that direct attention and tend toward *control:* "Which problems shall we examine?" Another type of question goes toward *supervision,* solving problems and setting priorities: "Which course of action is better?" Other questions simply seek to find out the score so that congressmen can watch over what takes place in the bureau: "How well are we doing?"[5]

Control

The most vigorous efforts at *control* occurred in the pre-Constitution period (1775–1781) when members of Congress attempted to administer government through their committees. In the last half of the twentieth century, however, legislators can be said to *control* when they gain their preferences by employing either or both of two techniques: 1) when they specify the exact organizational structure for the bureaus with which they deal; or 2) when they compel bureau personnel to clear administrative decisions with committee members or with committee staff personnel before they can be implemented. *Control* may be exercised by members of Congress individually or collectively, through their committee or through their committee's staff.

Members of the House Armed Services Committee have established their *control* over a limited range of issues, especially real estate transactions. A relatively common device was engineered in 1951; it required personnel in the Defense Department to "come into agreement" with the Armed Services Committees on any military real estate purchase or sale which 1) exceeded $25,000, or 2) equaled $25,000 for a lease of one

[4]Malcolm E. Jewell and Samuel C. Patterson, *The Legislative Process in the United States* (New York: Random House, 1966), pp. 484–509; Cornelius P. Cotter, Legislative Oversight, *Congress: The First Branch of Government,* coordinator, Alfred de Grazia (Washington, D.C.: America Enterprise Institute for Public Policy Research, 1966); William E. Rhode, *Committee Clearance of Administrative Decisions* (East Lansing: Michigan State University Bureau of Social and Political Research, 1959); Joseph P. Harris, *Congressional Control of Administration* (Garden City, N.Y.: Doubleday, Anchor Books, 1964), pp. 9, 195–97, 233–36, and 246–48.

[5]See James G. March and Herbert A. Simon, *Organizations* (New York: John Wiley and Sons, 1963) pp. 161–62.

year or more. After several actual and threatened vetoes, the tactic was changed. Members of the House Armed Services Committee in 1960 substituted the requirement that all military real estate transactions for $50,000 or more be submitted in advance to them and their counterparts in the Senate. A simple resolution passed in either house could negate any transaction.

When administrative decisions, before they are implemented, must first be cleared through committee members or committee staff members, there is the possibility that attention directing, problem-solving, and scorecard questions will be asked both in the Congress and in the executive branch. *Control* does not necessarily mean that every issue will be scrutinized in a congressional committee to determine which problems to solve, how to solve them, or how previous decisions are working. The potential for questioning every issue is there, however. Risks for bureaucrats and their superiors are higher when they ignore that potential with committees which *control* than when they ignore it with committees which *supervise* or *oversee*.

When committee members *control* the bureaucracy, policy initiation and innovation (new ideas, new decisions, new policies) flow or grind from complex interactions among committee and bureau personnel. It is usually impossible to determine who proposed 1) problems for solution, 2) alternative solutions, or 3) methods of evaluating the solutions chosen; in any case, congressmen are more likely to initiate and innovate for those issues they *control* than they are for those they *supervise* or *oversee*.

Supervision

Supervision is a less restrictive form of intervention into administrative activities by members of congressional committees. *Supervision* occurs when congressmen basically take for granted that personnel in the Executive Office are looking at the proper problems. The questions posed by members of such committees are basically limited to *problem-solving*. Instead of considering all possible courses of action, congressmen tend to question the specific emphases or priorities established in the executive branch. This means that the persons who decide *what* is

sions on the amount, procurement, and distribution of supplies; and 4) organizational decisions on methods and forms utilized in organizing and administering the armed forces. Structural decisions are made in the "currency of domestic politics": economic prosperity, individual freedom and welfare, inexpensive government, low taxation, economic stability, social welfare. "Participation" in the real estate aspects of structural decisions tended to be in the form of committee *control* by the Armed Services Committees.[7]

During the same 1945 to 1960 period, Professor Huntington found that Congress *did not* play a decisive part in decisions on *strategy*. Strategy includes 1) program decisions dealing with a) the strength, composition and readiness of military forces, and b) the readiness, number, type, and development rate of their weapons (for example, *the RS-70*); and 2) use decisions dealing with deployment, commitment, and employment of military forces. Strategic decisions are made in the "currency of international politics": conquest, influence, power, territory, trade, wealth, empire, security.

Members of Congress, between 1945 and 1960, appeared unwilling to interject themselves more decisively into strategic policy-making for two reasons. First, members of Congress and executive personnel were generally in agreement concerning foreign policy goals. Such agreement relegated controversy to disputes over alternative solutions rather than disputes over goals. Disputes over programs to reach strategic goals were between and among officials from several executive agencies: the separate branches of the armed services, the Defense Department, the State Department, the Treasury Department, the Budget Bureau, and a few others. Second, no congressional committee possesses either the legal power or the political capability to: 1) bring together and balance all the conflicting interests existing among the executives agencies involved; or 2) effect a compromise among them on strategic programs.

---

[7]Samuel P. Huntington, *The Common Defense: Strategic Programs in National Politics* (New York: Columbia University Press, 1961), pp. 3–4, 131–32, 146–74, 304. Unless otherwise noted, discussions concerning military policy-making between 1945 and 1960 are from this source.

The *site* of strategic decision making between 1945 and 1950 was in the executive branch, but its *character* was legislative. The traditional patterns of legislative conflict and compromise occurred among executive personnel. A detailed study of the defense budget for fiscal 1950 essentially confirms these conclusions about the *site* and *character* of strategic decision-making.[8]

Between 1945 and 1960, members of the two Armed Services Committees and the two Military Appropriations Subcommittees manipulated both control and oversight techniques. Issues which were defined by decision participants as structural (domestic) drew committee *control* or at least *supervision.* On the other hand, when committee members defined an issue as strategic (international), they resorted to *oversight.*[9]

Dispersion of authority in Congress makes it difficult for members of any committee to generate more than *oversight* on strategic issues. Secretaries of state and defense must cultivate close ties with ten committees or subcommittees, and they often must confront some fifteen more committees in justifying important programs or parts of programs.[10] Chairman of the Senate Foreign Relations Committee J. William Fulbright (D., Arkansas) has observed that Congress occasionally initiates marginal policies (Fulbright exchange scholars, for example) and serves as "legitimator" of executive policies.[11] This means that when members of Congress approve programs originated within the executive branch, such programs are viewed as legitimate and worthy of citizen compliance.

Insofar as the Indo-Chinese War and Fulbright's committee are adequate indicators of current trends, two tentative conclusions appear rea-

[8]Warner R. Schilling, Paul Y. Hammond, and Glenn H. Snyder, *Strategy, Politics, and Defense Budgets* (New York: Columbia University Press, 1962), pp. 1–272.

[9]Elias Hunzar in his *The Purse and the Sword: Control of the Army by Congress, 1933–1950* (Ithaca, N.Y.: Cornell University Press, 1950) suggests that this relationship pre-dated 1945.

[10]Holbert N. Carroll, "The Congress and National Security Policy," *The Congress and America's Future,* ed. David B. Truman (Englewood Cliffs, N.J.: Prentice-Hall, 1965), p. 152.

[11]James A. Robinson, *Congress and Foreign Policy* rev. ed. (Homewood, Ill.: Dorsey Press, 1967), pp. 171–213.

sonable. First, when members of *just one* committee withhold or withdraw their stamp of legitimacy, this rare event has important, restrictive implications for future strategic decisions made by executive personnel. Second, members of a committee do not necessarily *control,* even when they can develop restrictions upon executive flexibility such as the 1971 Cooper-Church resolution, which formally prevents U.S. ground troops from entering Cambodia and Laos. They can put certain decisions off-limits, but they do not then come forward with their own coherent plan for ending or withdrawing from the Indo-Chinese War. They say, in essence, "You have not decided well. With this new guidance and with specific alternatives denied (ground troops in Laos or Cambodia), rethink your strategic problems and alternative solutions."[12]

This approach is somewhat stronger but similar to the mode of the Armed Services Committees and Military Appropriations Subcommittees between 1945 and 1960. When members of these four committees contested strategic decisions, during this fifteen year period, they operated, for all practical purposes, as lobbyists. They challenged, petitioned, and harrassed decision-makers within the executive branch to examine again and defend again their original decision.

If not greater, complexities in military strategy and other foreign policy are less familiar to congressmen than complexities in domestic affairs. Relatedly, only a small portion of the citizenry is attentive to, or conversant about issues of foreign policy. Constitutional, institutional, and behavioral obstacles largely bar congressional initiative and innovation in international relations.[13] Nonetheless, members of the Armed Services Committees, in 1959, engineered through Congress a statutory change with the potential to rearrange their docility in strategic decisions.

[12]Eugene P. Dvorin, ed., *The Senate's War Powers: Debate on Cambodia from the Congressional Record* (Chicago: Markham Publishing Co., 1971), particularly pp. 38ff.

[13]Gabriel A. Almond, *The American People and Foreign Policy* (New York: Frederick A. Praeger, 1961); James N. Rosenau, *Public Opinion and Foreign Policy* (New York: Random House, 1961); and Robert A. Dahl, *Congress and Foreign Policy* (New York: W. W. Norton, 1964).

The Military Construction Act of 1959: Section 412(b)

From the Senate Armed Services Committee emerged the impetus for section 412(b) of the Military Construction Act of 1959, Public Law 86–149.[14] This section requires *authorizations* prior to appropriations for procurement of aircraft, missiles, or naval vessels (strategic weapons). The authorization measure for fiscal 1963 expanded §412(b) to include all authorizations prior to appropriations for research, development, test, and evaluation for strategic weapons.[15] Subsequent expansions of §412(b) have been for tactical weapons.

Prior to §412(b) members of the two Armed Services Committees had contented themselves with granting general authorities such as one to the secretary of the army in 1956. He was to procure "guided missiles," with no item particularized.[16] To obtain particular authority over strategic weapons, members of the Armed Services Committees made their move through structural legislation, a construction bill.

Strategic weapons such as the RS-70 are the concrete manifestations of abstract goals, concepts, and plans. With specific weapons certain strategic goals probably can be realized and particular concepts can be operationalized; others cannot. In other words, a strategic goal such as the defense of Western Europe requires strategic concepts about how that goal can be attained. Strategic weapons become the tools through which the concepts are put into operation. When committee members have an opportunity to ask questions about strategic weapons they possess the potential to question the concepts and the goals those weapons are designed to fulfill. Should questions about strategic concepts and goals flow from questioning about weapons, the trend could be toward *control* and attention direction: Which strategic problems shall we look

[14]Edward A. Kolodziej, *The Uncommon Defense and Congress, 1945–1963* (Columbus: Ohio State University Press, 1966), pp. 372ff.; and Bernard K. Gordon, "The Military Budget: Congressional Phase," *Journal of Politics* 23, no. 1 (November, 1961): 689–710.

[15]*U.S. Congressional Record,* 87th Cong. 2d sess., 1962, CVIII, pp. 5833, 5932–33.

[16]Peter Woll, *American Bureaucracy* (New York: W. W. Norton, 1963), p. 119.

at? Alternatively, questions about strategic weapons might move toward *supervision*, problem-solving and priority-setting: "Which course of action is better?" Instead, it appears that members of the Armed Services Committees continued to *oversee;* they continued to ask scorecard questions: "How well are we doing?" Under §412(b), they had greater access to and they could focus upon strategic weapons decisions, but they exercised *oversight* techniques; they neither *controlled* nor *supervised* those decisions.[17] House Armed Services Committee Chairman, Carl Vinson, said as much in 1961:

> Up to this time the Departments merely had to request and obtain appropriations for the procurement of these items under these very broad authorities. I am afraid that the end result of this procedure was that members of the Appropriations Committee were the only ones in Congress who actually had very much knowledge of the tremendous programs and expenditures which the Congress was called upon to pass each year. It is my hope that Section 412 has called to a halt this situation. If it did nothing else, it brought 37 more members of the House into the heretofore exclusive area of knowledge of these very large problems.[18]

Lessons from the RS-70

If new congressional access to and focus upon strategic decisions lie unexploited for control or supervision, what purpose is served by §412(b)? In the RS-70 case, Chairman Vinson and his colleagues employed their broadened warrant to threaten several of those who must deal with them regularly. Without §412(b), the threats would have been unlikely; with §412(b), they were possible. If Vinson settled for no more than a reexamination of the RS-70 that he had already been promised, the threats which §412(b) permitted did not accomplish much—or did they?

---

[17]Raymond H. Dawson, "Congressional Innovation and Intervention in Defense Policy: Legislative Authorization of Weapons Systems," *American Political Science Review* 56, no. 1 (March 1962): 42–57; and John Malcolm Moore, "Military Strategy and Legislative Oversight" (Ph.D. diss. University of Georgia, 1969), pp. 60–2, 213–15, 243–55. See, also, Kolodziej, *op.cit.*, pp. 374–401.

[18]*U.S. Congressional Record*, Daily Edition, 24 May 1961, p. 8218.

Vinson told his fellow members of the House that his accomplishments were fourfold. First, he had dramatized the unwillingness of thoughtful men to rely upon a strategy of massive retaliation only. Second, he had impressed upon the executive the dangers to the nation of junking manned bombers. Third, he emphasized the depth with which members of the Committee felt about these two issues. Fourth, he wrung from the secretary of defense a reversal of his previous unwillingness to spend more than the requested $171 million for the RS-70.

Vinson explained to the House how this had been accomplished:

> The president is interested now. He has injected himself right into the middle of the whole matter. And another thing, the committee will get a full assurance that the group making this study will have not only scientists and representatives of the secretary of defense in it, but will have people from the air force, not only the technical ones but the policy ones; not only civilians, but military people whose background and experience in the development and operation of bombers gives them special understanding of the problem we are talking about.[19]

At least Vinson and the other members of his committee had put the president and his secretary of defense on notice that some members of Congress have definite expectations concerning the proper composition of decision-making groups within the executive branch. The RS-70 restudy was left to the executive branch, but those participants were selected, at least in part, by Chairman Vinson with the backing of his committee.

Authority in Congress is scattered among many committees, however. The effects of this dispersion appear in a subsequent agreement between Secretary McNamara and members of the House Appropriations Committee. Their authority to reach independent judgments about appropriations also was threatened by Vinson's proposed "direction" to the secretary of the air force and, more generally, by §412(b). Their agreement with McNamara assured members of the House Appropriations Committee that he would not spend the entire appropriation which was itself a reduction to $362 million from the $491 million authorized.[20]

[19] *C. R.,* CVIII, 1962, p. 4310.
[20] Richard F. Fenno, Jr., *The Power of the Purse: Appropriations Politics in Congress* (Boston: Little, Brown, 1966), p. 72; and Woll, *op.cit.,* p. 128.

Chairman Vinson overtly grasped for *control* in the RS-70 conflict. Without influential allies in the House Appropriations Committee, it is unclear whether McNamara could have withstood Vinson's use of §412(b) to exercise greater *control* over strategic decisions. The argument here is that the short-run implications of the RS-70 conflict are different from the long-run implications. In the short-run, that is, in the RS-70 incident itself, Vinson had particular types of decision makers added. This would fit the earlier definition of *control,* if the change in decision-makers had produced a different outcome. It did not, which leads to consideration of long-run outcomes.

"Congress does not want to run the department of defense—Congress just wants to sit at the table and get across an idea once in a while."[21] In this quotation, Vinson indicates that his goals might not have been as grand as *control.* In future decisions, what might members of Congress demand? What might they object to? The RS-70 case gave Secretary McNamara a firm clue. When he cut particular types of personnel from specific decision-making forums, some members of Congress would consider that decision questionable. And they would question it, even if this required constitutional confrontations. Thus constrained, executive decision-makers might be encouraged to let Congress "sit at the table and get across an idea once in a while."

Strategic decisions within the executive branch

Whether Secretary McNamara was inhibited by what he anticipated that members of Congress might do is a moot point. When Chairman Vinson and members of the House Armed Services Committee disputed the RS-70 decision, McNamara was already in the throes of major changes which rearranged the participants in and their impact upon strategic decision-making.

McNamara's program of change centered upon four types of processes for making decisions, introduced here but explained and illustrated subsequently. At the time of the RS-70 confrontation, McNamara already had taken dynamic strides toward introducing *extreme rational-*

---

[21]*C. R.,* CVIII, 1962, p. 4312.

ity into the executive decision-making processes which he inherited, barely a year earlier. His special targets were processes characterized as *pluralistic, log-rolling,* or *procedurally inclusive.*[22] It is doubtful that Congress could sit at McNamara's table; there was hardly room for many who had sat there previously.

McNamara's format for strategic decision-making eventually overwhelmed many who had participated in such decisions between 1945 and 1960. McNamara and the personnel of his office gained the ability to *direct* or *command* strategic decisions by imposing the extreme rationality of systems (ends-means) analysis. Ends-means analysis requires that the links between needs, objectives, and capabilities be confronted head-on: all were to be exposed, articulated, scrutinized, and examined critically. A program and performance budget system (PPBS) and cost-effectiveness analysis were utilized by McNamara and his staff to accomplish this change which centralized strategic decision-making in them. They were able to direct or command particular decisions as a look at an organization chart might mislead one to believe secretaries of defense had done all along. Of course, directions from the secretary's office might be resisted from within a branch of service, as the RS-70 illustrates.

McNamara's techniques struck at the decision-making format utilized at each of three levels: 1) where the size of the military slice from the national budgetary pie was set; 2) where the size of the slice was determined for each branch of service; and 3) where its share was divided within each branch of the armed forces. As the national budgetary pie sliced and the military portion was determined, McNamara's extreme rationality replaced the pluralistic conflict and compromise format which had existed among personnel from several executive agencies: the separate branches of service; the Defense, State, and Treasury Departments; the Budget Bureau; and a few others. As the size of the slice to be devoured by each service branch was determined, McNamara's extreme rationality replaced the pluralistic conflict and compromise format which had existed among the Joint Chiefs of Staff (JCS) as they sought to gain

---

[22]Cf. Paul Y. Hammond, "A Functional Analysis of Defense Department Decision Making in the McNamara Administration," *American Political Science Review* 57, no. 1 (March 1968): 58–64. Subsequent discussion relies heavily upon this article.

all that they could for their individual service branches. As strategic plans were budgeted within each branch of the armed forces, McNamara's extreme rationality replaced both log-rolling and procedurally inclusive processes. Personnel from one branch of service did not meddle with the internal plans of another branch (log-rolling). These internal plans were produced through procedures which had been designed so that personnel were included in decisions which affected their areas of responsibility.

Pluralism

Conventional notions of the free marketplace assume that the "best" product or idea prevails over its competitors, because consumers somehow possess the skills and tools to determine the "best." This is the heart of the pluralist argument.

There are real problems with the pluralist approach. In practice, pluralistic decision-making produces a definition of "best" that does not mean "maximum." "Best" more nearly means "satisfactory," that is, that most, if not all, of those affected by a decision can live with it. A way to insure that decisions are tolerable to those directly affected is to have their spokesmen included in the decision-making group. They can put their positions before spokesmen for different economic, ideological, organizational, or other interests. Spokesmen can learn the assumptions and restraints operating among those representing other interests. This does not mean necessarily that anyone will persuade anyone else. It does place participants in a forum where they can bargain, trade, and possibly reach tolerable accommodations.[23]

Bargains, trades, and tolerable solutions were the characteristics of pluralistic decisions which, between 1945 and 1960, allocated dollars for defense and dollars for each branch of service. Pluralism reigned as decisions were made concerning the ratio of military expenditures to domestic expenditures as well as the division of funds among the various branches of the armed forces.

[23]See Almond, *op.cit.*; Robert A. Dahl, *Who Governs?* (New Haven, Conn.: Yale University Press, 1961); and Dahl, *Pluralist Democracy in the United States* (Chicago: Rand McNally, 1967), Cf., March and Simon, *op. cit.,* Ch. 6.

Dollars for defense. Strategic posture for the U.S. was set by the same officials who set specific money amounts which would be asked of Congress for implementation. In the pluralistic format identified by Professor Huntington in the 1945-60 period, participants answered three questions: What are the problems? What are we going to do about them? How much are we going to spend doing it? This latter question throws strategic policy into conflict with domestic programs since money spent for one is not available for the other.

The participants in strategic planning and funding decisions between 1945 and 1960 brought to their task several different perspectives and priorities. These differences were reconciled through pluralistic or command compromise rather than by direction or command from the president or anyone else. The chief of staff and members of his staff for each branch of service spoke for the various army, navy, air force, and marine corps interests which they represented in the Defense Department. The secretary of defense and other civilian appointees of the president in the Defense Department spoke from their perspectives, wedged as they were between the priorities of the president and the priorities of the diverse interests of each service branch which they purportedly directed. The secretary of state and his staff members brought to strategic decisions the demands that their particular foreign policies might impose. For example, the North Atlantic Alliance, constructed by Secretary of State John Foster Dulles, demanded particular numbers and placement of military personnel and equipment as well as certain amounts of money. The Treasury Department houses not only the revenue collectors and the revenue but also economists who project future revenue collections and needs. Personnel from Treasury, therefore, possess data concerning levels of funding available for strategic programs as well as domestic programs. Secretary of the Treasury, George Humphrey, also was reportedly President Eisenhower's closest advisor on matters of the economy as was Dulles for foreign affairs.[24] Presidential budgeting expertise during the 1945 to 1960 period was in the Bureau of the Budget (BOB). BOB personnel traditionally have enforced presidential priorities upon the bureaucracy and funneled disputes about funding upward to

[24]Patrick Anderson, *The President's Men* (Garden City, N.Y.: Doubleday, Anchor Books, 1969), p. 176.

the president. Personnel from the White House staff as well as those from BOB (both in the Executive Office of the President) supported presidential priorities, domestic and foreign, when they differed from those of departmental participants. Conflict followed by compromise among these officials specified strategic problems, general solutions to those problems, and how much of the national treasure the president would ask Congress to devote to solutions.

Dollars for each branch of service. Answers to a pair of questions were left to those charged with putting strategic plans into operation: 1) Who is to spend what monies; and 2) For what are the monies to be spent? The first of these questions was also answered in a pluralistic format by the Joint Chiefs of Staff (JCS) during the 1945 to 1960 period. The second of these questions was answered differently, and it will be discussed in the context of log-rolling and procedural inclusiveness.

Members of the JCS wear two hats. Individually, they are the ranking members of their branch of the armed forces: Chief of Staff of the Army, Chief of Naval Operations, Chief of Staff of the Air Force, and Commandant of the Marine Corps. With their Chairman added, they serve collectively as the top military committee advising the president and the secretary of defense. Much of their behavior in the executive branch and in front of congressional committees suggests that they are more comfortable in their individual than in their collective roles.

Decisions about who was to spend what monies illustrate the pluralistic conflict generated by the bias toward individual rather than collective responsibility. After the Joint Chiefs of Staff (JCS) knew how much money the president would request, they were left to divide it among their respective service branches. A bitter battle ended with an obscure but real compromise among the Chiefs of Staff which gave the Air Force 46 percent, the Navy (and Marine Corps) 28 percent, and the Army 23 percent of all military appropriations.[25]

[25]Theodore H. White, "An Inside Report on Robert McNamara's Revolution in the Pentagon," *Look,* 23 April 1963, p. 34; and Huntington, *op.cit.,* p. 424.

Log-rolling and procedural inclusiveness

Once each chief of staff captured the largest possible share of the budget for his service branch in pluralistic settings, log-rolling triumphed among branches. Personnel within a branch of service adopted a posture of noninterference in respect to each other branch. Within each branch, procedural inclusiveness characterized much of the interaction among decision-makers during the 1945 to 1960 period. The combination of log-rolling noninterference between services and procedural inclusiveness within each service contained tremendous potential for uncoordinated strategic decisions. This potential will be illustrated following the description of log-rolling and procedural rationality.

Log-rolling is typically associated with legislatures, but legislators are not alone in swapping support and restraint, particularly restraint. An exchange such as "you support my measure; I'll support yours" contains an important understanding of noninterference. A close approximation of the mutual restraint exercised among the individual services between 1945 and 1960 is contained in the implied provision of a log-rolling trade: "Don't criticize my proposals, and I won't criticize yours."

Log-rolling noninterference by personnel of one service made for another service meant that formats for decision-making did not need to be coordinated. Although they were not coordinated, formats were similar in that they were procedurally inclusive.

Procedures are inclusive when they insure that everyone who is affected is consulted for a statement of his needs, preferences, and recommendations before a decision is made. Carbon copies marked "For your information" and "For your action" abound. What is often labeled "red tape" slowed final decisions between 1945 and 1960. In the sense of slower decisions, procedural inclusiveness produced inefficiency. In the sense of providing decision-makers with the available information, procedural inclusiveness was probably more efficient than pre–World War II techniques. Before World War II, for example, supply personnel selected the equipment which they would procure without consulting those who had to utilize the supplies. Procedural inclusiveness between 1945 and 1960 permitted operating personnel to put in their bid for what they needed, as they saw it, not as it was seen for them by procurement personnel.[26]

Procedural inclusiveness does not preclude decisions made by direction or command, pluralistic, or log-rolling techniques. Every affected person might be consulted and then one in a superior organizational position might direct or command his subordinates to follow a particular course of action. On the other hand, he might let or encourage his subordinates to fight out their differences and reach pluralistic compromises. Still another alternative would be for a superior to permit his subordinates to practice log-rolling noninterference in the area of expertise of another. We lack data which would indicate the mix of command, pluralism, and log-rolling within the various branches of the armed forces during the period of procedural inclusiveness between 1945 and 1960. Trends would seem to be toward command and away from log-rolling. Whether decisions were directed, pluralistically compromised, or log-rolled, the ultimate decision-maker(s) seldom had to articulate his criteria and analysis in formal and explicit terms.

Uncoordinated decisions. No matter how rational the procedures used within each branch of the armed forces, the procedures seldom incorporated those from other branches who might have been affected by within-branch decisions. Log-rolling restraint among branch personnel was dominant, and this lack of coordination produced duplication and inflated costs.

During the 1945 to 1960 period, requirements for the armed forces were calculated branch-by-branch within the budgetary lines established previously by the JCS. Army strategists would plan not only the role of the army but also the role for each branch of service. If their best plan cost more than was allotted, they would produce another total plan until they were within budgetary limits. Budget requests for the army then would be based upon the army role in the army plan. So it was with each other branch of service. Duplication was rampant. If strategic plans of

---

[26]Hammond, *op.cit.,* pp. 58–64; and Peter Blau, *Bureaucracy in Modern Society* (New York: Random House, 1962), pp. 13–14.

one service fit with others, the fit was by accident rather than by design.[27]

Requirements were established to fulfill missions which were assumed by the Joint Chiefs of Staff or assigned by higher authority. An example of such a mission would be the defense of Western Europe from invasion by the Soviet Union. In setting its requirements, the army might place heavy emphasis upon quickly air-lifting many U.S. and allied troops from these homeland or other stations to Western Europe. There would be no assurance that the air force personnel would build transport aircraft into their requirements. In comparison to the army, the air force would not need to move many people and mountains of equipment quickly. Besides, glory and morale for aviators are not in hauling cargo; headlines are garnered by demolishing the enemy. Moreover, both the air force and the navy might purchase aircraft to provide close air support for troops the army could not get into position because of a lack of transportation.

Between and among the branches of service, strategists neither scrutinized nor criticized the planning of other strategists. If strategists could not fit their concepts into their money amounts, they sought additional funds from Congress. They pleaded the merits of their case, asking for more total rather than asking for part of someone else's share. This was the case for years as air force personnel sought more B-70 funding.

Extreme rationality

Robert S. McNamara's form of *extreme rationality* took under seige each of the *pluralistic, log-rolling,* and *procedurally inclusive* decision-making practices which he inherited in January of 1961 when he became secretary of defense. His brand of rationality was extreme in that it forced decision-makers to spell out what they knew, perceived, understood, or believed, and it forced them to distinguish among knowing, perceiving, understanding, and believing. Criteria for making judgments about what was needed were made explicit, and then, these criteria were utilized to compare proposals against similar proposals.

Secretary McNamara and the personnel of his office imposed the

[27]White, *op. cit.,* p. 34, and William W. Kaufmann, "The McNamara Strategy," *The Politics of the Federal Bureaucracy,* ed. Allan A. Atlshuler (New York: Dodd, Mead, 1968), pp. 179–96, particularly p. 181.

extreme rationality of systems (ends-means) analysis. Ends-means analysis requires that the links between objectives, capabilities, and needs be confronted head-on: All were to be exposed, articulated, scrutinized, and examined critically. A program and performance budget system (PPBS) and cost-effectiveness analysis were utilized by McNamara and his staff to accomplish this change. The cost of each alternative was weighed against its projected effectiveness. If a weapons system could provide eighty percent protection for half the cost of a similar weapons system which could provide ninety-five percent protection, McNamara wanted to know. During the 1945 to 1960 era of *procedural inclusiveness,* decision-makers within each branch of service tended to choose the greater protection so long as they had money enough to buy it.[28] McNamara's changes had additional impact upon decision-making both within and outside of the Department of Defense (DOD).

Extreme rationality in DOD. No longer was it enough for a service chief or JCS collectively to say, "In my (our) professional judgment, . . ." Program budget categories were established in the office of the secretary of defense and cost versus effectiveness calculations were made to compare the capabilities of different weapons systems which accomplish the same function or purpose. For example, sea-based missiles (intermediate range and intercontinental) were compared to similar land-based missiles and to strategic bombers (such as the B-70) under the Strategic Retaliatory Forces category. Thus, sea-based missiles no longer competed for funds with naval air, conventional submarines, fleet escorts, mine sweepers, etc. Sea-based missiles began to compete for funds with the land-based missiles and strategic bombers of the air force. The Marine Corps, a part of the naval service, began to compete with similar forces of the army under the General Purpose Forces budget category.[29]

[28]Cf. Robert J. Art, *The TFX Decision: McNamara and the Military* (Boston: Little, Brown, 1968), pp. 32–33, note 58.

[29]The six additional program budget categories which were established are Continental Air and Missile Defense Forces, Airlift and Sealift Forces, Reserve and Guard Forces, Research and Development, General Support, and Civil Defense. See *Study Report on Programming for the Secretary of Defense,* prepared by the Office of the Assistant Secretary of Defense (Comptroller), Programming Directorate for Systems Planning, 25 June 1962.

Different decision-makers perceive, understand, and know the same facts differently. They attach different weights to criteria of cost, risk, and advantage. Under McNamara, the disputes among the service branches were settled by decisions from his and others in his office. This centralization replaced the pluralistic conflict, bargaining, and compromise among the Joint Chiefs of Staff which preceded his administration. Decisions in the office of the secretary of defense went more deeply into the service branches themselves where the chief of staff, members of his staff, line officers, and decision-making committees previously had prevailed. [30] When the Joint Chiefs of Staff were united, early in McNamara's term, he was forced to compromise on missile procurement rather than pay (and have the president pay) the political price of public disputes before Congress.[31] As his tenure endured, this type of trade-off became less and less characteristic of McNamara's style.

Members of the Joint Chiefs of Staff made their strategic and budgetary recommendations and were essentially through with their portion of budget construction in the spring of each year. McNamara's systems analysts would render their decisions on the basis of cost-effectiveness analysis. Then in September and October, McNamara would preside over efforts to reconcile differences between personnel from components of DOD and Bureau of the Budget (BOB) officials.[32]

Extreme rationality outside DOD. McNamara also had a major impact on BOB officials, whom presidents regularly use to enforce their priorities upon their administrations as well as the bureaucracy.[33] Indeed, McNamara was able to marshal such a mass of data and analysis

[30]Art, *op.cit.*, particularly pp. 157–66; and cf., Adam Yarmolinski, "Ideas into Programs," *The Presidential Advisory System,* eds. Thomas E. Cronin and Sanford D. Greenberg (New York: Harper and Row, 1969), pp. 284–94.

[31]David Halberstam, "The Programming of Robert McNamara," *Harper's Magazine,* February, 1971, p. 54.

[32]*New York Times,* 29 September 1969, pp. 1 and 27.

[33]Richard E. Neustadt, "Presidency and Legislation: The Growth of Central Clearance," *American Political Science Review* 48, no. 3 (September, 1954): 642–50; Kermit Gordon, "The Budget Director" in Cronin and Greenberg, *op. cit.,* pp. 284–94; and James W. Davis and Randall B. Ripley, "The Bureau of the Budget and Executive Branch Agencies: Notes of their Interaction," *Politics, Programs, and Budgets,* ed. James W. Davis, Jr. (Englewood Cliffs, N.J.: Prentice-Hall, 1968), pp. 63–77.

that few chose to contest with him before the president. Neither experienced strategists nor experienced budgeteers harbored many hopes of winning a dispute with the secretary of defense.

One former director of BOB argues that the person in that position is valuable and viable to a president only insofar as the director makes the same decision that the president would make were he there. If the director's decisions are appealed to the president and regularly overruled by him, more and more decisions will be appealed, eliminating the usefulness of BOB.[34] It seems as likely from their experience with McNamara that BOB personnel might quit contesting with members of the administration who regularly won appeals to the president.

What appears to have happened until near the end of the Johnson presidency is that those involved in constructing budgets and strategists at top levels found that Secretary McNamara was making the decisions the president would make if called upon to do so. McNamara took precedence over persons of equal and closer organizational position to the president.

Trade-offs

Secretary McNamara's *extreme rationality* provided highly coherent, coordinated programs, but it traded away the advantages of fragmented and decentralized decision-making which included among its advantages the involvement of a greater number and range of participants. Whether or not it was a worthwhile trade is a judgmental question. In the ongoing business of government, probably the most important judgments to examine are those of a different president and his secretary of defense. Richard M. Nixon and Melvin Laird, during their first two years in office, have made changes which undoubtedly reflect their evaluation of McNamara's techniques.

The changes they have wrought within DOD are the products of the Defense Programs Review Board. This board is chaired by the president's foreign policy advisor, Henry Kissinger, and its other members are the deputy secretary of defense, the under secretary of state, the director of

[34]Gordon in Cronin and Greenberg, *op. cit.,* pp. 284–94.

the Office of Management and Budget (BOB expanded and strengthened), the chairman of the Council of Economics Advisors (CEA), and the chairman of the Joint Chiefs of Staff. They review and evaluate programs devised in the armed services in response to strategic decisions made in the National Security Council. The institutional homes of these officials, with one exception, are the same as the pre-McNamara, top-level military strategy/budget setters. The chairman of the CEA has been substituted for a Treasury representative. Otherwise, the board is structured much the same as the key group which determined the size of the military slice from the national budget between 1945 and 1960.

President Nixon appears willing to trade the highly coherent, centralized strategic and budgetary planning of McNamara for a return to a *pluralistic* format similar to the one McNamara abandoned in a shower of cost-effectiveness data.

Trade-offs within DOD

Similar, recent changes have been made in DOD, and they constitute a postscript on the RS-70 dispute. During Laird's first year as secretary, cost-effectiveness analysts were downgraded in the office of the secretary of defense. At the same time, members of JCS—wearing, also, their other hats as ranking member of their particular branch of service—were upgraded, and cost-effectiveness analysis was made a tool for use by them rather than by the secretary of defense. Secretary McNamara turned the strategic and budgetary recommendations of the Joint Chiefs over to his cost-effectiveness analysts in the spring. On the other hand, Secretary Laird plans to continue the participation of the Chiefs of Staff throughout the annual budget-preparation cycle.[35] This seems to place the service chiefs in a better position to resist decisions which go against their preferences. Before the McNamara changes, the chiefs of staff and those around them (so long as they stayed within preestablished budgetary ceilings) essentially could seek the interests of their separate services without outside interference. There is a considerable difference between a chief of staff being able to resist the preferences of others.

[35] *New York Times,* 29 September 1969, pp. 1 and 27.

It is not yet clear how much influence and authority the Chiefs of Staff have gained from Laird's changes. Whatever their current influence and authority, it exceeds that which they had during the McNamara period; they participate longer, in more decisions, with more data and better analyses. The potential implications of these recent changes are analyzed in the context of the 1961 dispute over the RS-70.

The RS-70

The RS-70 incident was among the first where McNamara rearranged 1945–1960 patterns; he intervened in allocations of research and development funds for the air force. The controversy foreshadowed changes to come and illustrates two important trade-offs. First, McNamara's categories for analysis, no matter how rational they were, traded away certain types of comparison. Second, extremely rational decisions require articulated, explicit, formal reasoning but deny the intuitive hunch, the nagging doubt of the experienced professional.

It is not certain that McNamara's embryo, functional categories, forced air force strategists to redesignate the B-70 as the RS-70. Nonetheless, the redesignation and the subsequent conflict spotlight the capabilities of different analytic schemes. Air force strategists quit attempting to add the B-70 as a first-strike weapon. They argued instead that the RS-70 could follow a missile strike. After missiles had eliminated surface-to-air defenses, the RS-70 could reconnoiter the damage and strike priority targets which survived the missile attack.[36] McNamara continued to compare its capabilities to those of first-strike missiles.

Chairman Vinson of the House Armed Services Committee, on the other hand, utilized a different method of analysis. He ascertained that no other existing or projected weapons system would be available for the reconnaissance-strike task, and he judged that task to be important. Vinson needed no more cost-analyses before attempting to strengthen the RS-70 program.

The first trade-off is that functional categories which permit (not

[36]U.S. Congress, House, Committee on Armed Services, *Authorization for Aircraft, Missiles, and Naval Vessels,* 87th Cong., 2d Sess., 1962, *H. Rept. 1406* to accompany *H. R. 9751,* p. 9.

necessarily insure) results to be judged in terms of costs may shut out weapons systems or even strategic concepts which do not fit the categories of analysis. Vinson perceived that use of McNamara's categories was producing a single strategy—massive retaliation.[37]

Throughout the RS-70 conflict, a more general and troubling trade-off seemed to motivate Vinson. He preferred to satisfy the parochial interests and the stated needs of air force spokesmen. He feared that centralized decision-makers would overlook a national vulnerability that might be covered, at least partially, by fragmented, log-rolling strategists in the separate service branches. Centralized decision-making might promise short-run savings at tremendous long-run costs.

Centralized decision-making does not necessarily insure lower costs any more than fragmented decision-making insures that all reasonable strategic contingencies will be covered. Vinson opted for the latter probability, however. He supported the intuitive, nagging concern of professional strategists and rejected the *extreme rationality* of McNamara's professional budgeteers, whom he considered unreliable as strategists. Vinson had no guarantee that the McNamara-type *extreme rationality* could differentiate valid professional concerns from efforts simply to enhance the position of a service branch.

These trade-offs cannot be evaluated here. It is impossible to judge the strength of arguments in favor of fragmented professionalism until more is known about how many and which decisions were directed, pluralistic, or log-rolled within each branch of service before McNamara's changes. Whatever the earlier combination, McNamara's lasting change may be in the use of systems analysis and program and performance budgeting within the branches of the armed forces. Insofar as these techniques continue, it is safe to predict that more and more decisions will be decentralized in the chief of staff for each branch.

[37] *C. R.,* CVIII, 1962, p. 4310; and Roland Evans, Jr., "The Sixth Sense of Carl Vinson," *Reporter,* 12 April 1962, p. 26.

29

The President
as Leader and Clerk:
Command, Persuasion,
and Public Prestige

Richard E. Neustadt

In form all presidents are leaders, nowadays. In fact this guarantees no more than that they will be clerks. Everybody now expects the man inside the White House to do something about everything. Laws and customs now reflect acceptance of him as the Great Initiator, an acceptance quite as widespread at the Capitol as at his end of Pennsylvania Avenue. But such acceptance does not signify that all the rest of government is at his feet. It merely signifies that other men have found it practically impossible to do *their* jobs without assurance of initiatives from him. Service for themselves, not power for the president, has brought them to accept his leadership in form. They find his actions useful in their business. The transformation of his routine obligations testifies to their dependence on an active White House. A president, these days, is an invaluable clerk. His services are in demand all over Washington. His influence, however, is a very different matter. Laws and customs tell us little about leadership in fact.

Why have our presidents been honored with this clerkship? The answer is that no one else's services suffice. Our Constitution, our traditions, and our politics provide no better source for the initiatives a president can take. Executive officials need decisions, and political protection, and a referee for fights. Where are these to come from but the White House? Congressmen need an agenda from outside, something with high status to respond to or react against. What provides it better than the program of the president? Party politicians need a record to defend in the

Reprinted with permission of author and publisher. From *Presidential Power: The Politics of Leadership* (New York: John Wiley, Science Editions, 1962), pp. 6–8, 9–10, 32, 33–34, 56, 57, 58, 58–59. Footnotes have been renumbered. 401

next national campaign. How can it be made except by "their" administration? Private persons with a public axe to grind may need a helping hand or they may need a grinding stone. In either case who gives more satisfaction than a president? And outside the United States, in every country where our policies and postures influence home politics, there will be people needing just the "right" thing said and done or just the "wrong" thing stopped *in Washington*. What symbolizes Washington more nearly than the White House?

A modern president is bound to face demands for aid and service from five more or less distinguishable sources: from executive officialdom, from Congress, from his partisans, from citizens at large, and from abroad. The presidency's clerkship is expressive of these pressures. In effect they are constituency pressures and each president has five sets of constituents. The five are not distinguished by their membership; membership is obviously an overlapping matter. And taken one by one they do not match the man's electorate; one of them, indeed, is outside his electorate. They are distinguished, rather, by their different claims upon him. Initiatives are what they want, for five distinctive reasons. Since government and politics have offered no alternative, our laws and customs turn those wants into his obligations.

Why, then, is the president not guaranteed an influence commensurate with services performed? Constituent relations are relations of dependence. Everyone with any share in governing this country will belong to one (or two, or three) of his "constituencies." Since everyone depends on him why is he not assured of everyone's support? The answer is that no one else sits where he sits, or sees quite as he sees; no one else feels the full weight of his obligations. Those obligations are a tribute to his unique place in our political system. But just because it is unique they fall on him alone. *The same conditions that promote his leadership in form preclude a guarantee of leadership in fact.* No man or group at either end of Pennsylvania Avenue shares his peculiar status in our government and politics. That is why his services are in demand. By the same token, though, the obligations of all other men are different from his own. His cabinet officers have departmental duties and constituents. His legislative leaders head *congressional* parties, one in either House. His national party organization stands apart from his official family. His political allies in the states need not face Washington, or one another. The private groups that seek him out are not compelled to govern. And friends abroad are not compelled to run in our elections. Lacking his position and prerogatives, these men cannot regard his obligations as their own. They have their jobs to do; none is the same as his. As they perceive their duty they may find it right to follow him, in fact, or they may not. Whether they will feel obliged *on their responsibility* to do what he wants done remains an open question.

The power to command

In the early summer of 1952, before the heat of the campaign, President Truman used to contemplate the problems of the general-become-president should Eisenhower win the forthcoming election. "He'll sit here," Truman would remark (tapping his desk for emphasis), "and he'll say, 'Do this! Do that!' *And nothing will happen.* Poor Ike—it won't be a bit like the Army. He'll find it very frustrating."

Eisenhower evidently found it so. "In the face of the continuing dissidence and disunity, the president sometimes simply exploded with exasperation," wrote Robert Donovan in comment on the early months of Eisenhower's first term. "What was the use, he demanded to know, of his trying to lead the Republican party. . . ." And this reaction was not limited to early months alone, or to his party only. "The president still feels," an Eisenhower aide remarked to me in 1958, "that when he's decided something, that *ought* to be the end of it . . . and when it bounces back undone or done wrong, he tends to react with shocked surprise."

Truman knew whereof he spoke. With "resignation" in the place of "shocked surprise" the aide's description would have fitted Truman. The former senator may have been less shocked than the former general, but he was no less subjected to that painful and repetitive experience: "Do this, do that, and nothing will happen." Long before he came to talk of Eisenhower he had put his own experience in other words: "I sit here all day trying to persuade people to do the things they ought to have sense enough to do without my persuading them. . . . That's all the powers of the president amount to."

In these words of a president, spoken on the job, one finds the essence of the problem now before us: "powers" are no guarantee of power; clerkship is no guarantee of leadership.

* * *

_____

The power to persuade

The limits on command suggest the structure of our government. The constitutional convention of 1787 is supposed to have created a government of "separated powers." It did nothing of the sort. Rather, it created a government of separated institutions *sharing* powers.[1] "I am part of the legislative process," Eisenhower often said in 1959 as a reminder of his veto.[2] Congress, the dispenser of authority and funds, is no less part of the administrative process. Federalism adds another set of separated institutions. The Bill of Rights adds others. Many public purposes can only be achieved by voluntary acts of private institutions; the press, for one, in Douglass Cater's phrase, is a "fourth branch of government."[3] And with the coming of alliances abroad, the separate institutions of a London, or a Bonn, share in the making of American public policy.

What the Constitution separates our political parties do not combine. The parties are themselves composed of separated organizations sharing public authority. The authority consists of nominating powers. Our national parties are confederations of state and local party institutions, with a headquarters that represents the White House, more or less, if the party has a president in office. These confederacies manage presidential nominations. All other public offices depend upon electorates confined within

---

[1] The reader will want to keep in mind the distinction between two senses in which the word *power* is employed. When I have used the word (or its plural) to refer to formal constitutional, statutory, or customary authority, it is either qualified by the adjective "formal" or placed in quotation marks as "power(s)." Where I have used it in the sense of effective influence upon the conduct of others, it appears without quotation marks (and always in the singular). Where clarity and convenience permit, *authority* is substituted for "power" in the first sense and *influence* for power in the second sense.

[2] See, for example, his press conference of July 22, 1959, as reported in the *New York Times* for July 23, 1959.

[3] See Douglass Cater, *The Fourth Branch of Government* (Boston: Houghton-Mifflin, 1959).

the states.[4] All other nominations are controlled within the states. The president and congressmen who bear one party's label are divided by dependence upon different sets of voters. The differences are sharpest at the stage of nomination. The White House has too small a share in nominating congressmen, and Congress has too little weight in nominating presidents for party to erase their constitutional separation. Party links are stronger than is frequently supposed, but nominating processes assure the separation.

The separateness of institutions and the sharing of authority prescribe the terms on which a president persuades. When one man shares authority with another, but does not gain or lose his job upon the other's whim, his willingness to act upon the urging of the other turns on whether he conceives the action right for him. The essence of a president's persuasive task is to convince such men that what the White House wants of them is what they ought to do for their sake and on their authority.

Persuasive power, thus defined, amounts to more than charm or reasoned argument. These have their uses for a president, but these are not the whole of his resources. For the men he would induce to do what he wants done on their own responsibility will need or fear some acts by him on his responsibility. If they share his authority, he has some share in theirs. Presidential "powers" may be inconclusive when a president commands, but always remain relevant as he persuades. The status and authority inherent in his office reinforce his logic and his charm.

Status adds something to persuasiveness; authority adds still more. . . .

[In his efforts to persuade, a president's actions are his trading stock.] Behind each action lay a personal choice, and these together comprised his control over the give-and-take that gained him what he wanted. . . . *his power was protected by his choices.*

By "choice" I mean no more than what is commonly referred to as "decision": a president's own act of doing or not doing. Decision is so often indecisive and indecision is so frequently conclusive, that choice becomes the preferable term. "Choice" has its share of undesired conno-

---

[4]With the exception of the vice-presidency, of course.

tations. In common usage it implies a black-and-white alternative. Presidential choices are rarely of that character. It also may imply that the alternatives are set before the choice-maker by someone else. A president is often left to figure out his options for himself. Neither implication holds in any of the references to "choice" throughout this book.

If presidents could count upon past choices to enhance their current influence, as Truman's choice of men had done for him, persuasion would pose fewer difficulties than it does. But presidents can count on no such thing. Depending on the circumstances, prior choices can be as embarrassing as they were helpful in the instance of the Marshall Plan. . . .

But adequate or not, a president's own choices are the only means *in his own hands* of guarding his own prospects for effective influence. He can draw power from continuing relationships in the degree that he can capitalize upon the needs of others for the presidency's status and authority. He helps himself to do so, though, by nothing save ability to recognize the pre-conditions and the chance advantages and to proceed accordingly in the course of the choice-making that comes his way. To ask how he can guard prospective influence is thus to raise a further question: what helps him guard his power stakes in his own acts of choice?

Professional reputation

A president's persuasiveness with other men in government depends on something more than his advantages for bargaining. The men he would persuade must be convinced in their own minds that he has skill and will enough to *use* his advantages. Their judgment of him is a factor in his influence with them. . . .

The men who share in governing this country are inveterate observers of a president. They have the doing of whatever he wants done. They are the objects of his personal persuasion. They also are the most attentive members of his audience. These doers comprise what in spirit, not geography, might well be termed the "Washington community." This community cuts across the president's constituencies. Members of Congress and of his administration, governors of states, military commanders in the field, leading politicians in both parties, representatives of private organizations, newsmen of assorted types and sizes, foreign diplomats (and principals abroad)—all these are "Washingtonians" no matter what their physical location. In most respects the Washington community is far from homogeneous. In one respect it is tightly knit indeed: by definition, all its members are compelled to watch the president for reasons not of pleasure but vocation. They need him in their business just as he needs them. Their own work thus requires that they keep an eye on him. Because they watch him closely his persuasiveness with them turns quite as much on their informed appraisals as on his presumed advantages.

In influencing Washingtonians, the most important law at a president's disposal is the "law" of "anticipated reactions," propounded years ago by Carl J. Friedrich.[5] The men who share in governing do what they think they must. A president's effect on them is heightened or diminished by their thoughts about his probable reaction to their doing. They base their expectations on what they can see of him. And they are watching all the time. Looking at themselves, at him, at the immediate event, and toward the future, they may think that what he might do in theory, he would not dare to do in fact. So MacArthur evidently thought before he was dismissed. They may think that the president has tied his hands behind his back, as Faubus thought, apparently, before and after Newport. They may conclude with Arnall that the president has more to lose than they do, should he not support them. Or they may conclude, as Sawyer evidently did, that they risk more than he does if they do not support him. A Marshall and a Vandenberg may decide that the president can be relied upon to put his "powers" and his status at their service. A Charles E. Wilson, after Key West, may decide the opposite.

What these men think may or may not be "true" but it is the reality on which they act, at least until their calculations turn out wrong.

[5]Carl J. Friedrich, "Public Policy and the Nature of Administrative Responsibility," *Public Policy*, Vol. 1 (Cambridge: Harvard University Press, 1940), pp. 3–24.

30

Reorganization Plan No. 2 of 1970

Richard M. Nixon

To the Congress of the United States:

We in government often are quick to call for reform in other institutions, but slow to reform ourselves. Yet nowhere today is modern management more needed than in government itself.

In 1939, President Franklin D. Roosevelt proposed and the Congress accepted a reorganization plan that laid the groundwork for providing managerial assistance for a modern Presidency.

The plan placed the Bureau of the Budget within the Executive Office of the President. It made available to the President direct access to important new management instruments. The purpose of the plan was to improve the administration of the Government—to ensure that the Government could perform "promptly, effectively, without waste or lost motion."

Fulfilling that purpose today is far more difficult—and more important—than it was 30 years ago.

Last April, I created a President's Advisory Council on Executive Organization and named to it a distinguished group of outstanding experts headed by Roy L. Ash. I gave the Council a broad charter to examine ways in which the Executive Branch could be better organized. I asked it to recommend specific organizational changes that would make the Executive Branch a more vigorous and more effective instrument for creating and carrying out the programs that are needed today. The Council quickly concluded that the place to begin was in the Executive Office of the President itself. I agree.

The past 30 years have seen enormous changes in the size, structure and functions of the Federal Government. The budget has grown from less than $10 billion to $200 billion. The number of civilian employees has risen from one million to more than two and a half million. Four new Cabinet departments have been created, along with more than a score of independent agencies. Domestic policy issues have become increasingly complex. The interrelationships among Government programs have become more intricate. Yet the organization of the President's policy and management arms has not kept pace.

Over three decades, the Executive Office of the President has mushroomed but not by conscious design. In many areas it does not provide the kind of staff assistance that support the President needs in order to deal with the problems of Government in the 1970s. We confront the 1970s with a staff organization geared in large measure to the tasks of the 1940s and 1950s.

One result, over the years, has been a tendency to enlarge the immediate White House staff—that is, the President's personal staff, as distinct from the institutional structure—to assist with management functions for which the President is responsible. This has blurred the distinction between personal staff and management institutions; it has left key management functions to be performed only intermittently and some not at all. It has perpetuated outdated structures.

Another result has been, paradoxically, to inhibit the delegation of authority to Departments and agencies.

A President whose programs are carefully coordinated, whose information system keeps him adequately informed, and whose organizational assignments are plainly set out, can delegate authority with security and confidence. A President whose office is deficient in these respects will be inclined, instead, to retain close control of operating responsibilities which he cannot and should not handle.

Improving the management processes of the President's own office, therefore, is a key element in improving the management of the entire Executive Branch, and in strengthening the authority of its Departments and agencies. By providing the tools that are needed to reduce duplication, to monitor performance and to promote greater efficiency throughout the Executive Branch, this also will enable us to give the country not only more effective but also more economical government—which it deserves.

To provide the management tools and policy mechanisms needed for the 1970s, I am today transmitting to the Congress Reorganization Plan No. 2 of 1970, prepared in accordance with Chapter 9 of Title 5 of the United States Code.

This plan draws not only on the work of the Ash Council itself, but also on the work of others that preceded—including the pioneering Brownlow Committee of 1936, the two Hoover Commissions, the Rockefeller Committee, and other Presidential task forces.

Essentially, the plan recognizes that two closely connected but basically separate functions both center in the President's office; policy determination and executive management. This involves (1) what Government should do, and (2) how it goes about doing it.

My proposed reorganization creates a new entity to deal with each of these functions:

—It establishes a Domestic Council, to coordinate policy formulation in the domestic area. This cabinet group would be provided with an institutional staff, and to a considerable degree would be a domestic counterpart to the National Security Council.

—It establishes an Office of Management and Budget, which would be the President's principal arm for the exercise of his managerial functions.

The Domestic Council will be primarily concerned with *what* we do; the Office of Management and Budget will be primarily concerned with *how* we do it, and *how well* we do it.

Domestic Council

The past year's experience with the Council for Urban Affairs has shown how immensely valuable a Cabinet-level council can be as a forum for both discussion and action on policy matters that cut across departmental jurisdictions.

The Domestic Council will be chaired by the President. Under the plan, its membership will include the Vice President, and the Secretaries of the Treasury, Interior, Agriculture, Commerce, Labor, Health, Education and Welfare, Housing and Urban Development, and Transportation, and the Attorney-General. I also intend to designate as members the

Director of the Office of Economic Opportunity and, while he remains a member of the Cabinet, the Postmaster General. (Although I continue to hope that the Congress will adopt my proposal to create; in place of the Post Office Department, a self-sufficient postal authority.) The President could add other Executive Branch officials at his discretion.

The Council will be supported by a staff under an Executive Director who will also be one of the President's assistants. Like the National Security Council staff, this staff will work in close coordination with the President's personal staff but will have its own institutional identity. By being established on a permanent, institutional basis, it will be designed to develop and employ the "institutional memory" so essential if continuity is to be maintained, and if experience is to play its proper role in the policy-making process.

There does not now exist an organized, institutionally-staffed group charged with advising the President on the total range of domestic policy. The Domestic Council will fill that need. Under the President's direction, it will also be charged with integrating the various aspects of domestic policy into a consistent whole.

Among the specific policy functions in which I intend the Domestic Council to take the lead are these:

—Assessing national needs, collecting information and developing forecasts, for the purpose of defining national goals and objectives.

—Identifying alternative ways of achieving these objectives, and recommending consistent, integrated sets of policy choices.

—Providing rapid response to Presidential needs for policy advice on pressing domestic issues.

—Coordinating the establishment of national priorities for the allocation of available resources.

—Maintaining a continuous review of the conduct of on-going programs from a policy standpoint, and proposing reforms as needed.

Much of the Council's work will be accomplished by temporary, ad hoc project committees. These might take a variety of forms, such as task forces, planning groups or advisory bodies. They can be established with varying degrees of formality, and can be set up to deal either with broad program areas or with specific problems. The committees will draw for staff support on Department and agency experts, supplemented by the Council's own staff and that of the Office of Management and Budget.

Establishment of the Domestic Council draws on the experience gained during the past year with the Council for Urban Affairs, the Cabinet Committee on the Environment and the Council for Rural Affairs. The principal key to the operation of these Councils has been the effective functioning of their various subcommittees. The Councils themselves will be consolidated into the Domestic Council; Urban, Rural and Environment subcommittees of the Domestic Council will be strengthened, using access to the Domestic Council staff.

Overall, the Domestic Council will provide the President with a streamlined, consolidated domestic policy arm, adequately staffed, and highly flexible in its operation. It also will provide a structure through which departmental initiatives can be more fully considered, and expert advice from the Departments and agencies more fully utilized.

Office of Management and Budget

Under the reorganization plan, the technical and formal means by which the Office of Management and Budget is created is by redesignating the Bureau of the Budget as the Office of Management and Budget. The functions currently vested by law in the Bureau, or in its director, are transferred to the President, with the provision that he can then re-delegate them.

As soon as the reorganization plan takes effect, I intend to delegate those statutory functions to the Director of the new Office of Management and Budget, including those under section 212 of the Budget and Accounting Act, 1921.

However, creation of the Office of Management and Budget represents far more than a mere change of name for the Bureau of the Budget. It represents a basic change in concept and emphasis, reflecting the broader management needs of the Office of the President.

The new Office will still perform the key function of assisting the President in the preparation of the annual Federal budget and overseeing its execution. It will draw upon the skills and experience of the extraordinarily able and dedicated career staff developed by the Bureau of the Budget. But preparation of the budget as such will no longer be its dominant, overriding concern.

While the budget function remains a vital tool of management, it will be strengthened by the greater emphasis the new office will place on fiscal analysis. The budget function is only one of several important management tools that the President must now have. He must also have a substantially enhanced institutional staff capability in other areas of executive management—particularly in program evaluation and coordination, improvement of Executive Branch organization, information and management systems, and development of executive talent. Under this plan, strengthened capability in these areas will be provided partly through internal reorganization, and it will also require additional staff resources.

The new Office of Management and Budget will place much greater emphasis on the evaluation of program performance: on assessing the extent to which programs are actually achieving their intended results, and delivering the intended services to the intended recipients. This is needed on a continuing basis, not as a one-time effort. Program evaluation will remain a function of the individual agencies as it is today. However, a single agency cannot fairly be expected to judge overall effectiveness in programs that cross agency lines—and the difference between agency and Presidential perspectives requires a capacity in the Executive Office to evaluate program performance whenever appropriate.

The new Office will expand efforts to improve interagency cooperation in the field. Washington-based coordinators will help work out interagency problems at the operating level, and assist in developing efficient coordinating mechanisms throughout the country. The success of these efforts depends on the experience, persuasion, and understanding of an Office which will be an expediter and catalyst. The Office will also respond to requests from State and local governments for assistance on intergovernmental programs. It will work closely with the Vice President and the Office of Intergovernmental Relations.

Improvement of Government organization, information and management systems will be a major function of the Office of Management and Budget. It will maintain a continuous review of the organizational structures and management processes of the Executive Branch, and recommend needed changes. It will take the lead in developing new information systems to provide the President with the performance and other data that he needs but does not now get. When new programs are launched, it will seek to ensure that they are not simply forced into or grafted onto existing organizational structures that may not be appropriate. Resistance to organizational change is one of the chief obstacles to effective government; the new Office will seek to ensure that organization keeps abreast of program needs.

The new Office will also take the lead in devising programs for the development of career executive talent throughout the Government. Not the least of the President's needs as Chief Executive is direct capability in the Executive Office for insuring that talented executives are used to the full extent of their abilities. Effective, coordinated efforts for executive manpower development have been hampered by the lack of a system for forecasting the needs for executive talent and appraising leadership potential. Both are crucial to the success of an enterprise—whether private or public.

The Office of Management and Budget will be charged with advising the President on the development of new programs to recruit, train, motivate, deploy, and evaluate the men and women who make up the top ranks of the civil service, in the broadest sense of that term. It will not deal with individuals, but will rely on the talented professionals of the Civil Service Commission and the Departments and agencies themselves to administer these programs. Under the leadership of the Office of Management and Budget there will be joint efforts to see to it that all executive talent is well utilized wherever it may be needed throughout the Executive Branch, and to assure that executive training and motivation meet not only today's needs but those of the years ahead.

Finally, the new Office will continue the Legislative Reference functions now performed by the Bureau of the Budget, drawing together agency reactions on all proposed legislation, and helping develop legislation to carry out the President's program. It also will continue the Bureau's work of improving and coordinating Federal statistical services.

Significance of the changes

The people deserve a more responsive and more effective Government. The times require it. These changes will help provide it.

Each reorganization included in the plan which accompanies this message is necessary to accomplish one or more of the purposes set forth in Section 901(a) of Title 5 of the United States Code. In particular, the plan is responsive to Section 901(a)(1), "to promote the better execution of the laws, the more effective management of the Executive Branch and of its agencies and functions, and the expeditious administration of the public business;" and Section 901(a)(3), "to increase the efficiency of the operations of the Government to the fullest extent practicable."

The reorganizations provided for in this plan make necessary the appointment and compensation of new officers, as specified in Section 102(c) of the plan. The rates of compensation fixed for these officers are comparable to those fixed for other officers in the Executive Branch who have similar responsibilities.

While this plan will result in a modest increase in direct expenditures, its strengthening of the Executive Office of the President will bring significant indirect savings, and at the same time will help ensure that people actually receive the return they deserve for every dollar the Government spends. The savings will result from the improved efficiency these changes will provide throughout the Executive Branch—and also from curtailing the waste that results when programs simply fail to achieve their objectives. It is not practical, however, to itemize or aggregate these indirect expenditure reductions which will result from the reorganization.

I expect to follow with other reorganization plans, quite possibly including ones that will affect other activities of the Executive Office of the President. Our studies are continuing. But this by itself is a reorganization of major significance, and a key to the more effective functioning of the entire Executive Branch.

These changes would provide an improved system of policy-making and coordination, a strengthened capacity to perform those functions that are now the central concerns of the Bureau of the Budget, and a more effective set of management tools for the performance of other functions that have been rapidly increasing in importance.

The reorganization will not only improve the staff resources available to the President, but will also strengthen the advisory roles of those members of the Cabinet principally concerned with domestic affairs. By providing a means of formulating integrated and systematic recommendations on major domestic policy issues, the plan serves not only the needs of the President, but also the interests of the Congress.

This reorganization plan is of major importance to the functioning of modern government. The national interest requires it. I urge that the Congress allow it to become effective.

Richard Nixon

The White House,
March 12, 1970

Reorganization Plan No. 2 of 1970

Prepared by the President and transmitted to the Senate and the House of Representatives in Congress assembled, March 12, 1970, pursuant to the provisions of chapter 9 of title 5 of the United States Code.

Part I. Office of Management and Budget

Section 101. *Transfer of functions to the President.* There are hereby transferred to the President of the United States all functions vested by law (including reorganization plan) in the Bureau of the Budget or the Director of the Bureau of the Budget.

Sec. 102. *Office of Management and Budget.* (a) The Bureau of the Budget in the Executive Office of the President is hereby designated as the Office of Management and Budget.

(b) The offices of Director of the Bureau of the Budget and Deputy Director of the Bureau of the Budget, and the offices of Assistant Directors of the Bureau of the Budget which are established by statute (31 U.S.C. 16a and 16c), are hereby designated Director of the Office of Management and Budget, Deputy Director of the Office of Management and Budget, and Assistant Directors of the Office of Management and Budget, respectively.

(c) There shall be within the Office of Management and Budget not more than six additional officers, as determined from time to time by the Director of the Office of Management and Budget (hereinafter referred to as the Director). Each such officer shall be appointed by the Director, subject to the approval of the President, under the classified civil service, shall have such title as the Director shall from time to time determine, and shall receive compensation at the rate now or hereafter prescribed for offices and positions at Level V of the Executive Schedule (5 U.S.C. 5316).

(d) The Office of Management and Budget and the Director shall perform such functions as the President may from time to time delegate or assign thereto. The Director, under the direction of the President, shall supervise and direct the administration of the Office of Management and Budget.

(e) The Deputy Director of the Office of Management and Budget, the Assistant Directors of the Office of Management and Budget designated by this reorganization plan, and the officers provided for in subsection (c) of this section shall perform such functions as the Director may from time to time direct.

(f) The Deputy Director (or during the absence or disability of the Deputy Director or in the event of a vacancy in the office of Deputy Director, such other officials of the Office of Management and Budget in such order as the President may from time to time designate) shall act as Director during the absence or disability of the Director or in the event of a vacancy in the office of Director.

Sec. 103. *Records, property, personnel, and funds.* The records, property, personnel, and unexpended balances, available or to be made available, of appropriations, allocations, and other funds of the Bureau of the Budget shall, upon the taking effect of the provisions of this reorganization plan, become records, property, personnel, and unexpended balances of the Office of Management and Budget.

Part II. Domestic Council

Sec. 201. *Establishment of the Council.* (a) There is hereby established in the Executive Office of the President a Domestic Council, hereinafter referred to as the Council.

(b) The Council shall be composed of the following:

The President of the United States

The Vice President of the United States

The Attorney General
Secretary of Agriculture
Secretary of Commerce
Secretary of Health, Education, and Welfare
Secretary of Housing and Urban Development
Secretary of the Interior
Secretary of Labor
Secretary of Transportation
Secretary of the Treasury

and such other officers of the Executive Branch as the President may from time to time direct.

(c) The President of the United States shall preside over meetings of the Council: *Provided,* That, in the event of his absence, he may designate a member of the Council to preside.

Sec. 202. *Functions of the Council.* The Council shall perform such functions as the President may from time to time delegate or assign thereto.

Sec. 203. *Executive Director.* The staff of the Council shall be headed by an Executive Director who shall be an assistant to the President designated by the President. The Executive Director shall perform such functions as the President may from time to time direct.

Part III. Taking Effect

Sec. 301. *Effective date.* The provisions of this reorganization plan shall take effect as provided by section 906(a) of title 5 of the United States Code, or on July 1, 1970, whichever is later.

• • •

Summary of Executive Office Reorganization Plan

The President has long been concerned about the need to improve the functioning of the Executive Branch. To develop sound and fresh approaches, he appointed last April the President's Advisory Council on Executive Organization under the Chairmanship of Roy Ash. Shortly thereafter, the President concluded with the Council that a most important opportunity for improvement was in the Executive Office of the President itself—a conclusion reached in several previous administrations as well.

The Executive Office of the President

The Executive Office of the President was created over thirty years ago and has grown without adequate design or planning. Improvements in the Executive Office would provide a strong impetus for improving the operations of the entire Executive Branch.

Under the guidance of the President, the Ash Council's study of the Executive Office lasted for some eight months. Extensive interviews were conducted with many past and present officials of the President's office and other agencies of the Executive Branch, and with distinguished authorities outside of government. Studies over the past thirty years were analyzed along with a wide variety of other written material.

The President is in agreement with the unanimous recommendations of the Ash Council study and is submitting to the Congress Reorganization Plan 2 of 1970. The basic objective of the Plan is to modernize the Executive Office in a way that strengthens the role of the agencies by providing the support the President needs particularly in:

—Development of domestic policies and programs

—Program performance and coordination

—Evaluation of existing programs and improvement in the flow of information about them

—Formulation of programs for recruitment, training, and development of executive talent

---

The Office of Management and Budget

The Reorganization Plan transfers to the President all functions vested by law in the Bureau of the Budget and designates the Bureau as the Office of Management and Budget. The intention is that the President will delegate the functions of the Bureau to the new Office and that additional staff resources will be sought for the non-budgetary aspects of the Office's work. This new Office, in addition to its units which work on the budget and program evaluation, will probably have five units whose work will involve:

1. program coordination
2. legislative reference
3. executive development
4. organization and management systems
5. management information systems

The Plan authorizes Level V officers for the new Office of Management and Budget to be appointed by the Director subject to the President's approval, in the classified civil service.

The Domestic Council

Late last year the President created the post of Assistant to the President for Domestic Affairs and developed the "mission oriented" approach for forming specific project groups to analyze policy options. The Reorganization Plan enhances these steps by establishing a Domestic Council which brings together under one roof many of the sources for developing domestic policy and designing specific programs.

The Cabinet level Council will be chaired by the President and includes the Vice President and the heads of nine departments (all but State, Defense and the Post Office), although additions can be made by the President as he desires: e.g., the Postmaster General and the Director of the Office of Economic Opportunity. He might want to name heads of agencies without cabinet status from time to time. The plan provides for an Executive Director who shall be an assistant to the President and direct the Council staff.

The Domestic Council and its staff will serve as a pool from which to create various committees or groupings that will advise the President in an integrated way on domestic policy. It can be an important adjunct to the direct contact between the President and the agency heads.

Anticipated benefits

When the Reorganization Plan takes effect there will be:
—Reduction of the number of separate councils, groups and committees now advising the President on domestic policies and coordination
—Improvement in the President's capability to deal with the complex management, organization, and administrative issues raised by the problems and programs of the 1970's
—Significant long-run savings from these improvements
—More effective and appropriate use of the President's personal White House staff
—Reversal of the trend toward operational decision-making in the White House. This will permit greater reliance upon the agencies.

The President
Executive Order 11541

By virtue of the authority vested in me by the Constitution and statutes of the United States, including section 301 of title 3 of the United States Code, and pursuant to Reorganization Plan No. 2 of 1970 (hereinafter referred to as "the Plan"), it is ordered as follows:

Section 1. (a) All functions transferred to the President of the United States by Part I of the Plan (including the function vested by section 102 (f) of designating the officials of the Office of Management and Budget who shall act as Director during the absence or disability of the Deputy Director or in the event of a vacancy in the office of Deputy Director) are hereby delegated to the Director of the Office of Management and Budget in the Executive Office of the President. Such functions shall be carried out by the Director under the direction of the President and pursuant to such further instructions as the President from time to time may issue.

(b) All outstanding delegations, rules, regulations, orders, circulars, bulletins, or other forms of Executive or administrative action issued or taken by or relating to the Bureau of the Budget or the Director of the

Bureau of the Budget prior to the effective date of this order shall, until amended or revoked, remain in full force and effect as if issued or taken by or relating to the Office of Management and Budget or the Director of the Office of Management and Budget.

Sec. 2. (a) Under the direction of the President and subject to such further instructions as the President from time to time may issue, the Domestic Council in the Executive Office of the President shall (1) receive and develop information necessary for assessing national domestic needs and defining national domestic goals, and develop for the President alternative proposals for reaching those goals; (2) collaborate with the Office of Management and Budget and others in the determination of national domestic priorities for the allocation of available resources; (3) collaborate with the Office of Management and Budget and others to assure a continuing review of ongoing programs from the standpoint of their relative contributions to national goals as compared with their use of available resources; and (4) provide policy advice to the President on domestic issues.

(b) The organizations listed herein are terminated, and the functions heretofore assigned to them shall be performed by the Domestic Council:

Council for Urban Affairs (Executive Order No. 11452 of January 23, 1969)

Cabinet Committee on the Environment (Executive Order No. 11472 of May 29, 1969, as amended by Executive Order No. 11514 of March 5, 1970)

Council for Rural Affairs (Executive Order No. 11493 of November 13, 1969)

Sec. 3. This order shall be effective July 1, 1970.

The White House,
July 1, 1970.

31

Organization as Overlays

John Pfiffner and
Frank Sherwood

The formal structure of an organization represents as closely as possible the deliberate intention of its framers for the processes of interaction that will take place among its members. In the typical work organization this takes the form of a definition of task specialties, and their arrangement in levels of authority with clearly defined lines of communication from one level to the next. (See Chart 2-1.)

It must be recognized, however, that the actual processes of interaction among the individuals represented in the formal plan cannot adequately be described solely in terms of its planned lines of interaction. Coexisting with the formal structure are myriad other ways of interacting for persons in the organization; these can be analyzed according to various theories of group behavior, but it must not be forgotten that in reality they never function so distinctively, and all are intermixed together in an organization which also follows to a large extent its formal structure.

These modifying processes must be studied one at a time; a good way to do so without forgetting their "togetherness" is to consider each as a transparent "overlay" pattern superimposed on the basic formal organizational pattern. The totality of these overlays might be so complex as to be nearly opaque, but it will still be a closer approach to reality than the bare organization chart so typically used to diagram a large group structure.

Five such overlay patterns will be considered here; many more or

Reprinted with permission of author and Prentice-Hall, Inc., Englewood Cliffs, New Jersey. From *Administrative Organization,* © 1960, pp. 18–27. Footnotes have been renumbered.

less might be chosen from the kinds of studies that have been made, but these five might well be considered basic:
- •The sociometric network
- •The system of functional contacts
- •The grid of decision-making centers
- •The pattern of power
- •Channels of communication[1]

The idea that these processes are overlays upon the conventional job-task pyramid does not require that the latter take a subordinate position, although much of the research in organization might give this impression. The overlay approach aims to be realistic in recognizing that organization also consists of a wide variety of contacts that involve communication, sociometry, goal centered functionalism, decision-making, and personal power. Let us consider this complex of processes one at a time.

The job-task pyramid

The job-task pyramid constitutes the basis from which all departures are measured. It is the official version of the organization as the people in the organization believe that it is and should be. It would be correct to say that in most production organizations today, whether private or public, this official version of the organization-as-it-should-be reflects the view of those in the top echelons of the job-task pyramid. The actual operating organizations may differ in some respects from the formal organization; this difference can be expressed by showing the manner in which the other networks vary from the job-task hierarchy.

---

[1]For much of the conceptual underpinnings of this chapter we are indebted to John T. Dorsey, Jr., "A Communication Model for Administration," *Administrative Science Quarterly* 2 (December 1957):307–324. While Dorsey would seem to view communication as the central component of administration, we would put it on a level with others dealt with here.

CHART 2-1
The Typical Job Pyramid of Authority and Some of Its Interacting Processes

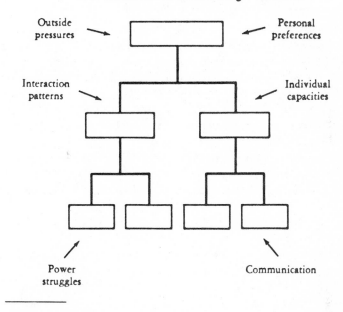

Outside pressures

Personal preferences

Interaction patterns

Individual capacities

Power struggles

Communication

Job-task hierarchy as foundation

Variations of the other networks from the job-task hierarchy should not be taken as an indication that the latter is being undermined or has no acceptance in the organization. It is well recognized in practice that there is an operating organization that varies from the chart with the full knowledge of those in authority. Day-to-day and hour-to-hour adjustments must be made, and there is no need to revise the chart for each of these. Nevertheless, the job task hierarchy as depicted by the organization manual does set forth the grid of official authority as viewed by those in the organization. Without it the other networks would simply not exist.[2]

[2]William Brownrigg deals with the job-task hierarchy most provocatively in *The Human Enterprise Process and Its Administration* (University, Ala.: University of Alabama Press, 1954).

The sociometric overlay
(See Chart 2-2a)

In any organization there is a set of relationships among people which is purely social in nature; it exists because of a net feeling of attraction or rejection. This pattern of person-to-person contacts is called sociometric because it is revealed in the kind of group testing that was given that name by its originator, J. L. Moreno. Some investigators have felt that individual attitudes lending themselves to sociometric measurement include as many as the following:

1. The *prescribed* relations, which are identical with the official or formal organization.
2. The *perceived* relations, which consist of people's interpretation of the meaning of the official network.
3. The *actual* relations are those interactions which in fact take place among persons.
4. The *desired* relations are people's preferences regarding interactions they want with other persons.
5. The *rejected* relations are the relationships with other people which are not wanted.[3]

It is, however, the last two categories that are primarily sociological in nature, and it is these that will be considered sociometric here. Desired and rejected relationships are fairly easy to ascertain with statistical reliability, and are found to be very responsive to the other dynamics of the group. Ohio State studies of naval leadership have effectively utilized sociometric charts (sociograms—graphic representations of social relations) superimposed on the traditional job-task charts.[4]

[3]Fred Massarik, Robert Tannenbaum, Murray Kahane, and Irving Weschler, "Sociometric Choice and Organizational Effectiveness: a Multi-Relational Approach," *Sociometry* 16 (August 1953):211–238.

[4]Ralph M. Stogdill, *Leadership and Structure of Personal Interaction* (Columbus: Ohio State University, Bureau of Business Research, Monograph No. 84, 1957), p. 10.

CHART 2-2a
Social Overlay—The Special Friendships in the Organization

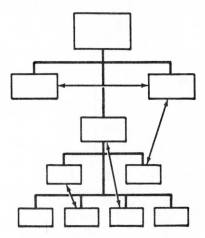

The functional overlay
(See Chart 2-2b)

There is in the organization a network of functional contacts that is important to and yet different from the formal authority structure. Functional contacts occur most typically where specialized information is needed; through them the staff or other specialist, the intellectual "leader," exerts his influence upon operations without direct responsibility for the work itself. This relationship, something like that between a professional man and his client, is a phenomenon of the twentieth century, and more markedly of the mid-century period.

Frederick Taylor was so perceptive as to understand the importance of the network of functional contacts in a management institution. Taylor called these functional contacts "functional supervision"; this term upset many theorists who worshipped the concept of clear cut supervisor-subordinate authority relationship.[5]

[5]A collection of excerpts from the literature of the early scientific management movement relating to staff specialization and functionalism is contained in Albert Lepawsky, *Administration* (New York: Alfred A. Knopf, 1949), pp. 299–306.

CHART 2-2b
Functional Overlay—the Direct Relationships Between the
Specialist Assistant and the Operating Departments

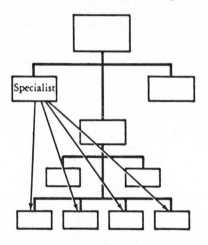

While Taylor's original concept of multiple supervision was rejected as a theoretical instrument at the time, it is still true that most organizations exhibit a system of functional supervision. Many charts of formal authority structures, such as those of the military, also show functional contacts through such devices as broken connecting lines.

The decision overlay
(See Chart 2-2c)

Simon maintains that the best way to analyze an organization is to find out where the decisions are made and by whom.[6] It can perhaps be assumed that normally in an organization the decision pattern follows the structure of the formal hierarchy, that is, the job-task pyramid. However, the power and authority network, together with the functional network,

---

[6] Herbert A. Simon, *Administrative Behavior,* 2d ed. (New York: Macmillan Company, 1947), p. xix. Simon's decision model is discussed in detail in Chapter 21.

may cut across hierarchical channels. It is in this sense that they take on the configuration of a grid or network. Thus the network pattern of approach is helpful, not in undermining the concept of hierarchy but in conveying the picture of actual practice. It modifies the harsh overtones of hierarchy by pointing out that actual organizations permit a great many cross-contacts.

CHART 2-2c
Decision Overlay—Flow of Significant Decisions in the Organization

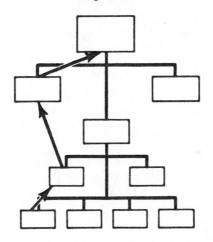

Network of influence

It might be more correct to say that there is a network of influence, not a network of decison. This, of course, depends upon one's definition of decision-making and if one insists upon there being a clear cut choice between alternatives by a person in authority, then decision-making usually follows clear hierarchical paths and channels. However, if we think in terms of a decision *process* rather than a decision *point,* the sense of interaction and influence is more appropriately conveyed. In this connection it is helpful to refer to Mary Parker Follett's concept of order giving in which she says "an order, command, is a step in a process, a moment in the movement of interweaving experience. We should guard against thinking this step a larger part of the whole process than it really is."[7]

The power overlay
(See Chart 2-2d)

Any discussion of power as a factor in organizational dynamics rather quickly encounters difficulties of definition and terminology. Since this is a subject upon which there will be considerable discussion at a later point in this book, let it be noted here that many of these problems arise from a confusion of the terms *power* and *authority*.[8] They are not necessarily synonymous; yet there has been a tendency to look at the organization chart, note the various status levels, and to assume that power increases as one rises in the pyramid. Much of this attitude is based on old concepts of authority as they are found in jurisprudence. Within this framework there is an assumption that a rule laid down by a political superior who is ultimately sovereign can be enforced by the imposition of sanctions. Translated into the terminology of management institutions, this means that authority, and hence power, rests with those at the top echelons of the job-task pyramid.

Power no longer viewed as synonymous with authority

However there has been a considerable rebellion against this narrow view of the power factor in organization environment. Almost everyone who has had any experience in a management institution has encountered a situation where the boss's secretary, or his assistant, or the executive officer, is the "person to see." For a great variety of reasons, these people may be effective decision-makers in the situation. Thus power is

[7]Henry C. Metcalf and L. Urwick, eds., *Dynamic Administration: The Collected Papers of Mary Parker Follett* (New York: Harper and Brothers, 1940), p. 49.

[8]See Chapter 5, "Authority, Policy, and Administration as Organization Factors."

CHART 2-2d
Power Overlay—Centers of Power in the Organization

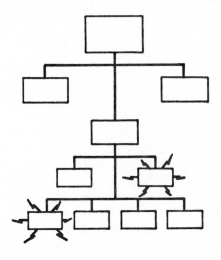

really personal; it is political; and it may or may not be legitimate in that it has been authorized by formal law or has achieved hierarchical legitimization. Involving a person-to-person relationship, power exists when one has the ability to influence someone to behave in a particular way or to make decisions. As a result the mapping of power centers would seldom follow the pattern of a typical hierarchy.

Management institutions are political

It seems desirable to emphasize that management institutions are political in nature and that the basis of politics is power. While the use of the adjective "political" may be jarring to students of business administration who regard politics and government as being synonymous, the fact remains that business organizations are also political to an important degree. The maneuvering for proxies to gain control of an industrial corporation is certainly a political act and the same is true of struggles on the part of individuals to "build empires," or the use of artifice to gain the ear of the president.

The important consideration from the standpoint of organization theory is that there is a network or a grid of personal power centers, though sometimes latent and not expressed.[9] They may or may not coincide with the official structure of authority. Power is not institutionalized in the sense that one can look in the organization manual and find out where it resides. As a matter of fact one might find it in unsuspected places. The person of comparatively low status may be a power center because he has been around so long that only he knows the intricate rules and the regulations well enough to make immediate decisions.

The communication verlay
(See Chart 2-2e)

Perhaps nowhere is the interrelationship of the various overlays more clearly to be seen than in communication. As will be observed at countless points in this book, the information process is central to organizational system. It affects control and decision-making, influence and power, interpersonal relationships, and leadership, to name only a few facets. Dorsey, in making a case for the significance of communications, says that "power consists of the extent to which a given communication influences the generation and flow of later communications. Points in the patterned flow where this occurs ... are positions of power. ..."[10] Furthermore, the communication net "consists physically of a complex of *decision centers* and *channels* which seek, receive, transmit, subdivide, classify, store, select, recall, recombine and retransmit *information.*"[11] This net consists not only of the technical information apparatus, but also of the human nervous systems of the people who make up the organization.

It is important to recognize that communication is itself a clearly identifiable facet of behavior. Redfield tells, for example, of the consult-

---

[9]Robert Dubin, *Human Relations in Administration: The Sociology of Organization* (Englewood Cliffs, N.J.: Prentice-Hall, 1951), p. 173. See also Dubin, *The World of Work* (Englewood Cliffs, N.J.: Prentice-Hall, Inc., 1958), pp. 47–54.

[10]Dorsey, *op. cit.,* p. 310.

[11]*Ibid.,* p. 317.

CHART 2-2e
*Communications Overlay—The Route of Telephone Calls on
a Particular Matter*

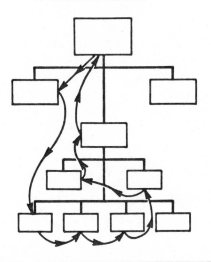

ant who "starts his studies in the mail room, for, by plotting the lines of actual communication, he can sometimes build a more accurate organization chart than the one that hangs on the wall in the president's office."[12] Such a chart is, of course, one of communications. And it may tell a great deal more about how life is really lived in an organization than the formal authority picture. Thus an important and useful means of taking a look at an organization is to ask the question, "Who talks to whom about what?"

Answers to the question will often reveal that patterns of communication are at variance with official prescriptions. That is something the consultant mentioned in the previous paragraph frequently found. Furthermore there have been enough experiments with small groups to give great strength to the proposition that "the mere existence of a hierarchy sets up restraints against communication between levels."[13] Gardner has

[12]Charles Redfield, *Communication in Management* (Chicago: University of Chicago Press, 1953), p. 7.

[13]Burleigh B. Gardner and David G. Moore, *Human Relations in Industry,* 3d ed. (Homewood, Ill.: Richard D. Irwin, 1955), pp. 213ff.

pointed out that factory production reports on productivity are sometimes rigged in order to give higher echelons the type of information which will make them happy.[14] Such blockages and distortions are certainly frequent enough to force us to recognize that the communications overlay represents an important dimension of organization analysis.

[14]Leon Festinger, "Informal Social Communication," in Dorwin Cartwright and Alvin Zander, *Group Dynamics* (Evanston, Ill.: Row Peterson, 1953), p. 201.

32

The Diffusion
of Sovereignty
Don K. Price

"Faceless technocrats in long, white coats are making decisions to-day which rightfully and by law should be made by the Congress," said Senator E. L. Bartlett of Alaska as he urged that Congress set up its own corps of scientific advisers. His complaint reflects a fear that is probably shared by many citizens. In view of the esoteric nature of the scientific processes that now seem to dominate our policies, can the elected repre-sentatives of the people maintain control over the major decisions of the government?

The typical liberal who supported the extension of governmental control over business in the early twentieth century was not very greatly worried about weakening the independent status of private property as a check on centralized power. To protect his freedom, he was inclined to trust the responsible processes of representative government. No matter how much power might be vested in the government, it would still be under popular control; the experts in the civil and military services would function only as the agents of policies that had been initiated by the processes of party leadership and legislative debate.

But now that great issues turn on new scientific discoveries far too complicated for politicians to comprehend, many people doubt that rep-resentative institutions can still do their job. The fear that the new powers created by science may be beyond the control of constitutional processes, and that scientists may become a new governing clique or cabal of secret advisers, has begun to seem plausible. The intellectual world in general, especially in Europe, is tempted to believe that modern man faces a political dilemma and is now obliged to choose between the two kinds of authoritarian governments that have taken over the control of many countries. One is the type that is guided by military or clerical leaders who affirm traditional values; the other is the type of dictatorship based on the materialist dialectic, professing science as its basic faith.

If American scientists, like American politicians, have generally not been persuaded that they had to choose either horn of this dilemma, it was probably because their actual experience was quite different from that of their counterparts in many other countries. In most of Europe, the reactionaries and the radicals shared a basic assumption not only with each other, but also with the parliamentary liberals against whom they rebelled. That assumption was the idea of sovereignty, the notion that the government of a nation was in some sense an expression of a single authoritative national purpose, and the embodiment of a unified will. This sovereign will, or the parliament that expressed it, would define a set of policies, based on a coherent set of principles, to be administered by a coordinated and disciplined bureaucracy.

To any newspaper reader, it should be obvious how little this ideal of sovereignty corresponds to the actual nature of the American political system, although some scholars try to make the facts fit the ideal. Some of the most obvious differences appear in the different role of scientists, and in the organization of the new programs they have initiated. For American scientists have played a significant role in the development of a system of political responsibility that does not work on the principles of parliamentary government and does not work on the principles of the new dictatorships of either the right or the left that have been supplanting the parliamentary system in many countries. It is a system that—along with some considerable disadvantages—has one great advantage: it does not assume that within the government there must be a single sovereign will, and therefore additional functions can be given to government without adding to the concentration of power within society.

We need a theory of the relation of science to political authority that will more accurately reflect the American experience. Before we Americans try to outline such a theory—or at least an approach toward it—we need to take a careful look at the facts. We cannot understand science in relation to politics unless we understand the way scientists behave in relation to politicians, both individually and in the organizations to which they belong. We should therefore ask three elementary questions that seem relevant to any theory of political responsibility, and take special note of the role of scientists as we answer each of them: (1) What kind of men make a career of running the government? (2) Who initiates new policies? (3) Who controls the organization and procedures of the government departments?

Scientists and professionals in administration

The classic parliamentary system is based on the collective responsibility of a cabinet to an elected assembly. Since that responsibility is collective—that is, all members of the cabinet are equally responsible for the policies of the government as a whole—it is necessary for the actual administration of the government to be under the coordinated control of a single disciplined administrative corps. It is hard to imagine such a corps composed of men whose education and early careers had been devoted to the intense specialization of the modern sciences. At any rate, none of the major nations whose governments are set up on the parliamentary model have ever tried to do without an elite corps of career administrators, and in such a corps scientists are rare indeed.

In the United States, on the other hand, men trained in the sciences, and in the professions based on the sciences, find it easy to move up into high administrative positions.

In Great Britain, which is the classic example of a parliamentary government, the Administrative Class, the top corps of the civil service, is still dominated by men trained in the humanistic and historical studies; not one man in twenty among these guardians of public policy has had a scientific or technical education. In spite of recurrent criticism of its role, the Administrative Class still maintains a professional monopoly (though in a studiously amateur and nonscientific way) over the organization of the government departments, and a major share of influence in the formation of national policy. It thus has no great interest in making it easy for scientists to move up into its membership, or the universities to work closely with it on its major policy problems.

Now that we are both constitutional democracies, it makes much less difference that Great Britain has a king and the United States a president, but a great deal of difference how we set up the professional group of men who actually run the government. Our Jacksonian revolution indeed destroyed the hopes of John Quincy Adams for a continuation of the Jeffersonian alliance between science and republicanism. At the same time, by wiping out the beginnings of a career system, it prevented the development of an elite administrative corps and thus cleared the channels of promotion for the scientists who, decades later, were to begin to move up in the civil service. The frontier radicalism of the day distrusted all forms of Establishment; this was the era in which state constitutions forbade clergymen to hold public office and prohibited educational qualifications for admission to the bar. But as the business of government got more complicated, the frontier had to admit that certain skills were necessary. Its essentially pragmatic temper insisted, as it became necessary to hire civil servants for merit rather than patronage, that the requirements be defined in terms of the needs of the specific jobs, rather than by general educational status. It was easiest to prove the need for special skills in technical fields, partly on account of the objective nature of the problem, partly because scientific societies were determined to raise and maintain their professional standards in the civil service as well as in private practice.

As a result, it was in the scientific and professional fields that the career civil service system was first pushed up to the higher ranks. As we developed our top civil service, we made it something quite different from a career Administrative Class; most of its members are not only nonpolitical, but nonadministrative as well, and they are not career officials in the same sense as a U.S. navy officer or a British civil servant.

In recent years, scientists and engineers, though rare among those in high political office, have done reasonably well in the civil service. The program of Rockefeller Public Service Awards, recognizing distinguished achievement in the federal civil service between 1952 and 1960, gave two-fifths of its awards to men engaged in scientific or technological programs, and having scientific or technical educations. Similarly, a recent study of 7,640 federal civil servants in the top ranks showed that as undergraduates a third of them had specialized in engineering, and nearly a quarter in the physical or biological sciences. By contrast, only 16 percent had specialized in applied studies like business, education, and administration, 16 percent in the behavioral sciences, and only 9 percent in the humanities. One-tenth of them had doctors' degrees, and one quarter masters' degrees; among those who did graduate work, the proportion with training in the physical and biological sciences was even higher than at the undergraduate level. On their way up to administrative responsibilities, whether in government service or private life, many of these officials had served at length in the sciences and related professions; as late as fifteen years after starting their careers, 18 percent had been engineers, 8 percent scientists, and 2 percent medical doctors; only 3 percent had been lawyers.

The top positions within the career civil service, for administrative continuity and bureaucratic power, are those of the bureau chiefs. A study in 1958 of the 63 bureau chiefs showed that 9 of them had advanced degrees in the natural sciences, and 17 others had been trained in lesser ways as engineers or technicians. By comparison with these 26 from various branches of technology, there were 9 economists and only 8 lawyers, and 20 from miscellaneous administrative or business careers. Aside from the positions of bureau chief, the top career positions are the so-called "supergrade," which were added above the regular civil service grades to let the government compete for scarce talent. The favorite justification for creating these positions is the need to employ capable scientists and engineers, notably in the technical branches of the Defense Department and the National Aeronautics and Space Administration. Administrators have ridden along to higher salaries on the political coat tails of scientists.

Scientists who become bureau chiefs in the U.S. service are, of course, no longer practicing scientists; they are doing work that in the United Kingdom would be done by a member of the Administrative Class educated in history or the classics. Their training may not be ideally suited for their administrative duties, but neither was that of their English counterparts. Macaulay, after all, used to argue that he wanted to recruit university graduates in the classics not because they had been studying the classics but because the classics attracted the best minds which could adapt themselves to anything. And the scientific training of many

American administrators puts them on a level with their English humanist counterparts in at least one respect: their lack of interest in management as a science, or sometimes at all.

The inductive initiation of policy

Though the scientists in top civil service posts have not been deeply interested in administration, they have been interested in policy. And this is the second major way in which the scientific civil servant in the United States differs from his British or European counterpart: he takes a direct role in initiating policies and publicly advocating them.

In their influence on policy, as in their advancement in the hierarchy, the scientists in American government have had a special opportunity because they have not had to work under a tightly organized corps of administrators, or a tightly knit political leadership. After the Civil War, there was no strong conservative tradition based on a landed interest, and no national party with a coherent ideology to take control of the programs of government. As a result, policy tended to develop separately in every field. There was no one with sufficient authority to tell the scientific experts that they belonged in a subordinate role.

Indeed they were listened to all the more readily because they were usually not thought of as bureaucrats. There was no one from whom Congress wanted advice less than from the regular career service. But each group of scientists had one foot in government, so to speak, and one outside, and the policy views that the insiders developed would come back to the Congress from the National Academy or the scientific societies. In a government of limited constitutional powers, a research program could be justified in a given field when an action program could not. But the research ultimately seemed to lead to action, in spite of the lawyers' scruples and the party bosses' lack of interest in policy issues. Research was influential not merely because the politicians were persuaded by objective data; an even more important reason may have been that scientists (and in some fields, the economists) were the major organized communities of professional opinion with a continuous interest in specific public programs. This has been the pattern of the development of many new federal programs: you can trace it in agriculture, in natural resources, in the regulation of business, in labor and welfare, and we now see its beginnings in the support of education.

The most influential pattern was set in agriculture. Washington and Jefferson had been interested in fostering scientific improvements in agriculture, and in federal support of a national university. They were blocked by the lawyers' scruples about states' rights. But the agricultural scientists found a way to their goal by a different route—one that evaded constitutional barriers by merging federal and state interests through federal grants of either land or money to the states, and by building up a program on scientific and educational bases. The principal basis was, of course, the land-grant college; from it grew the experiment station, the extension program, and the whole interlocking system of institutions which has let the federal government play a more effective role in the agricultural economy than the government of any supposedly socialized state.

In all this development, the land-grant colleges and the associations of various kinds of agricultural scientists maintained an important influence on the Department of Agriculture, supplied most of its career personnel, and generally provided the intellectual leadership for national agricultural policy. Thus in effect they greatly weakened the old constitutional distinction between state and federal functions, but without subjecting the field of agriculture to the control of a centralized bureaucracy.

The pattern of grants-in-aid, with its new set of administrative relationships, met two cardinal needs: (1) to provide money, as well as national policy direction, from Washington, and (2) to enlarge the operating responsibilities of the states, while preserving a large measure of their autonomy. It accordingly became the basis on which new programs were developed—highways, public health, social security, welfare, housing, and others. This was what political scientists came to call the "New Federalism," which has given the scientists and specialists in each field of policy a chance to work out programs without too much constraint by any party doctrine.

The classic theory of parliamentary government calls for something like a deductive method in the formulation of policy. That is to say, it suggests that policy originates in the doctrines or platforms of the political parties, and that it is then expressed in the enactments of the legislature. The role of administrators and their scientific and technical subordinates is merely to carry out the predetermined policy, to deduce specific actions from the statutory general principles.

It was of course not the scientists, but the lawyers, who saved us from this dogmatic belief. Some people still think that the function of judges is simply to interpret and apply the laws that legislatures enact, and the function of administrators merely to administer such laws. This was the conception of the extreme doctrinaires of both the American and French revolutions; sovereignty was in the people, and could be expressed only through their elected representatives in deliberative assembly. So for a time in France, during the Revolution, judges were required to go back to the legislature and ask for guidance whenever they found a case not covered explicitly enough by statute. But the lawyers in the tradition of the common law never held with such nonsense. They knew that justice required a great deal of initiative and inventiveness from a profession with a corporate tradition. They knew that the political authority of a legislature would be destroyed, rather than enhanced, if the legal profession and the judiciary looked to it for all ideas and initiative, and failed to exercise their own.

In Great Britain the career administrators, for all their formal public deference to members of the cabinet, were soon accorded a powerful role in the initiation of policy, but the notion persisted rather strongly that the scientists were instruments for predetermined ends. In the United States, on the other hand, the politicians were rather more ready to accord to scientists than to general administrators the right to press their policy views.

The leaders of political parties or members of an elite administrative corps may like to look on scientists as properly subordinate, and science as a way of thinking that should deal with the means to support a policy, a tradition, or an ideology, rather than an end in itself. We can understand this relationship in other countries if we recall how, until recent years, our military services thought that civilian scientists in military laboratories should conduct their research only pursuant to "requirements" defined by military staff work. This notion was exploded as it became apparent that what scientists discovered by unrestricted research might be of greater military importance than the things the military officers thought they wanted—in short, that the means might determine the ends.

Weapons development provides the extreme (and almost the only conspicuous) example in American politics in which scientists have been faced with difficulties in getting a direct political hearing for their policy ideas. For members of Congress usually want their scientific advice on a specific problem undiluted by either party doctrine or the policy views of general administrators.

This attitude is something like an inductive approach to policy. It distrusts the deduction of specific decisions from general political principles, or from a party's ideology. It distrusts the presentation of facts by either bureaucrats or party managers who may distort them for their special purposes; it is afraid of the doctrine that the end determines the means, for it suspects that the politician does not really know in precise terms what is the chief end of man, and may be tempted to define it to suit purposes of his own. This approach may have been furthered, in American history, by the influence of scientific ideas along with rationalism during the Revolution. Later it may have been furthered by a dim realization that science, if not too much constrained by predetermined political ends (or, if you like, political teleology), could help develop a higher set of goals and purposes than had yet been dreamed of. But mainly, I suspect, it was given a chance because people were sick of the results of exaggerated party doctrine and of the Civil War to which it led.

So the president was not expected to run for office, or run his administration, according to a doctrinaire platform, or to coordinate his departments so closely as to suppress a certain amount of policy initiative from his technical subordinates. Similarly, the congressional committees, which were fiercely partisan with respect to the spoils of office, became nearly nonpartisan, or at least weakly disciplined by their parties, in the consideration of new policies. And both the executive and the legislature developed the habit of turning for policy advice and assistance not only to the scientists in government, but to their colleagues in the universities and foundations. Both land-grant colleges and private universities were drawn into the processes of policy-making, partly because they were, in the absence of a career bureaucracy, the main reservoir of expertise on which politicians could draw for advice, and partly in response to the influence of the philanthropic foundations.

By the 1920's, some of the major foundations had lost interest in the charitable alleviation of social problems, and had begun to hope that science might solve them. This idea led them to a strategy of supporting scientific research—and not only research but demonstration projects to test its application. After being tested, the research could be extended by the greater resources of government. The foundations' aid to scientific education and research is a familiar story in almost every branch of science. Equally important, they went on to help strengthen the professional organizations of scientists, to pay for the efforts of governmental agencies to reform their own systems of organization and administration, and to pay for research projects undertaken at the request of public officials who could not persuade legislatures to appropriate the necessary funds.

By the time of the Second World War, the leading scientists knew that a grant-making agency like a foundation could initiate nationwide programs by making grants to independent universities and governmental agencies. Hookworm control, the foundation of public libraries, and the reform of medical education had amply proved the point. And political leaders were inclined to turn to private funds to help them explore future policy opportunities, or experiment with them, as when President Hoover sought foundation financing for his Committee on Social Trends and for a National Science Fund. The Public Administration Clearing House provided the initial administrative costs for President Roosevelt's Science Advisory Board.

The process of responsible policy-making is thus not something that begins with the definition of a political ideal according to some partisan doctrine, and concludes by using administrative and scientific means to attain that end. It is a process of interaction among the scientists, professional leaders, administrators, and politicians; ultimate authority is with the politicians but the initiative is quite likely to rest with others, including the scientists in or out of government.

Political decentralization of the executive

The presence of scientists and professionals in the civil service and their unusual degree of policy initiative are not the only differences that science has helped to bring about in the American constitutional system. The third difference is perhaps the most profound: the idea that the very organization of government itself is not something to be controlled by the insiders, but may be determined by the processes of open politics. Though the American scientific civil servant has policy initiative, and thus may seem to be tipping the balance of power against the politician, the politician more than makes up for it by assuming control over the internal structure of government organization and over its procedures.

The scientists were of course not the major influence in support of this tendency to open the inner workings of government to popular political control; that tendency came from many social and political sources. But it was encouraged by the early rationalism of the Jeffersonians, who believed that politics itself should be an experimental process. It was encouraged by the desire to give independent status within governments to agencies with scientific functions, like the Smithsonian Institution, or agencies that were supposed to make their decisions more on technical than political grounds, like the regulatory commissions. And it was encouraged by the desire of scientific and professional services to have special status of their own apart from the general civil service, a desire which accounted for separate uniformed corps like those of the Coast and Geodetic Survey and the Public Health Service.

One of the classic principles of administration holds that with responsibility should go a corresponding degree of administrative authority. Within a limited managerial context, this is the proverbial wisdom, and sound enough. And at the political level, it is the key idea in the classic theory of parliamentary responsibility. The cabinet within the parliament, and the prime minister within the cabinet, were able to take control by saying, in effect, that they could not continue to carry the responsibilities of His Majesty's Government if not given full control over the means to their proposed ends. But in the United States the idea of authority commensurate with responsibility is contradicted by the history as well as the theory of our constitutional system.

For the Jacksonian revolution completed the efforts of the Jeffersonian rationalists to abolish all types of establishments. The Constitution had forbidden a national established church, and the Founding Fathers had moved rapidly to rely on the volunteer state militias rather than a national standing army. And the Jacksonians proceeded to root out the beginnings of a career administrative service, in order to prevent the democratic control of policy from being influenced by a vested interest within the government. In Great Britain, as A. V. Dicey was to point out, the civil servant (unlike his French counterpart) was kept subject to the same law and the same courts as the private citizen, in order to make sure that he did not exceed the authority granted him by law. The United States went one step further; the civil servant was kept, in effect, a part of the private labor market, rather than being made a part of a lifetime service with a corporate tradition. He worked for a bureau that was likely to be fairly independent of any general government policy, and rather more under the control of the particular congressional committees to which it looked for legislative authority and for the appropriation of its funds. His Majesty's Civil Service was the embodiment of a national ideal; the U.S. civil service had only a nominal existence—it was only a set of rules and procedures that imposed negative restraints on a collection of nearly autonomous bureaus.

The president, in short, could not effectively demand control over the civil service or the form of organization of the executive departments, in order to control the means toward the ends legislated by Congress. For federal administration, like the process of policy-making, was supposed to work on something like a parody of the inductive method. The existence of a general bureaucracy, committed to an integrated national purpose, was not to be taken for granted on general principles; each position in the civil service was supposed to be set up by law, or later by a formal proof of its necessity under a system of job classification, and the men recruited for their ability to fill these particular jobs were supposed somehow to constitute an organization capable of fulfilling a national purpose. The end did not determine the means; in congressional procedure, the committee in charge of legislation defined the ends, and the appropriations subcommittee sometimes supplied the means.

This was the logical corollary of the peculiarly American assumption that it was just as appropriate for the voters and legislators to control the administrative organization and procedures of government as its policies, that is to say, to control the means as well as the ends. This was a radical departure from British or European assumptions. The parliamentary progression from conservatives to liberals to socialists never changed the fundamental European assumption that, although governments might be responsible to legislatures for the substance of their policies, it was better for politics and legislation not to meddle with internal administrative organization or the management of the bureaucracy. The socialist political leaders took the unity of the state and its bureaucracy for granted. If anything, they tended to make it all the more monolithic, and to push to its logical conclusion the tendency of Benthamite liberalism to abolish the privileges of guilds and public corporations.

But in the United States the current of radicalism ran in the opposite direction; after the age of Jackson, lobbyists and legislators were likely to concern themselves at least as much with the details of administrative organization as with major policies, generally with the purpose of creating centers of independence within government. Thus, in the nineteenth century, the states and cities adopted constitutions and charters that made them loose collections of independent agencies, with no responsible executive.

This decentralizing tendency was pushed so far that it destroyed the unity of administration, and sometimes had disastrous effects on the competence and the political responsibility of government. But it also disproved the idea—often assumed both by those who admired and those who feared socialism—that an extension in the scope of governmental functions in the United States would automatically bring a corresponding centralization of power.

The extension of the New Federalism

Those three peculiarities of the American political system had made it possible, by the time of the New Deal, to bring the major programs of state and municipal government and the major programs affecting the agricultural economy within the scope of federal government policy, without destroying the operating autonomy of the states and cities or the land-grant colleges. The New Federalism, in short, had worked best in those aspects of public affairs in which the power of government and the power of the great industrial corporations were not in rivalry. Leaders of private universities and scientific institutions, partly with this example in mind and partly in view of their experience with the programs of private foundations, were beginning to wonder, a decade before the Second World War, whether they would have to accept some comparable relationship to the federal government.

The system of federal grants and contracts by which universities and industrial corporations now have been brought into a relation of dependence on federal policy and federal funds, but with a high degree of independence with respect to their internal affairs, was not the result of an immediate flash of wartime inspiration. Its essential idea can be traced back to the depths of the Great Depression. By that time the naive nineteenth-century faith in the contribution of science to democratic politics was less prevalent in the more important universities and the more advanced fields of science than in the agricultural colleges. Scientists in the major private universities were supported more by private corporations and foundations than by government, and leaders in the newer fields like nuclear physics and biochemistry had closer intellectual ties with their European counterparts than with the agronomists or engineers of the land-grant colleges. The scientists in institutions that derived their support from industrial wealth and were interested in problems of the industrial urban economy saw the constitutional model in a very different perspective. Among them, accordingly, were to be found both those conservative scientists who were most distrustful of government and those radicals who tended to take a Marxist view of the role of science in society.

It was from such institutions that the Science Advisory Board of 1934–35, set up by President Roosevelt to prepare a program to combat the depression, drew its rather conservative members. They came up with a report that shocked their colleagues, for they actually proposed government research grants to private institutions, citing as a precedent the previous programs of aid to the land-grant colleges. The federal government, however, or at any rate Public Works Administrator Harold L. Ickes, did not think it proper to give federal subsidies to private institutions, and rejected the proposal.

But the reluctance of private institutions to accept government support, and the reluctance of the government to grant funds outside the framework of complete political responsibility, broke down under the pressure of the Second World War.

The scientists who were then put in charge of the most advanced weapons programs (including some of the same leaders who had served on the earlier Science Advisory Board) were ready to work out a thoroughly pragmatic set of arrangements for the conduct of weapons research, based on the same procedures that had worked in the foundation programs with which they were familiar. The approach that they adopted in the two great scientific programs of the war—the Office of Scientific Research and Development (OSRD) and the Manhattan District of the Army Engineers—was simply to enlist institutions rather than individuals.

To those who expect wartime crises and military authority to produce a centralization of authority, this approach must have been as surprising as if the Army had used the war as an excuse to increase, rather than decrease, its reliance on the state militias. But in the hands of Vannevar Bush, James B. Conant, and Karl T. Compton, the government contract brought private corporations within the scope of a still newer and more flexible type of federalism, one that was founded on the government contract rather than the grant-in-aid. Under the OSRD, the Massachusetts Institute of Technology took on the responsibility for developing radar, and the California Institute of Technology rockets. Under the Manhattan District, the University of Chicago set up the first sustained nuclear reaction and the University of California fabricated the first atomic bomb, while Du Pont, General Electric, Union Carbide, and other industrial giants built the facilities to produce the fissionable materials.

The postwar extension of this system, already described, has brought private scientific institutions—universities as well as business corporations—into a connection with the federal government as intimate and active as that of any land-grant college. And in at least some parts of the industrial system it may now be bringing about a relation between government and business entirely different from the one that existed during the quarrels of the depression era, much as the grants-in-aid system transformed federal-state relations some decades after the Civil War. Indeed, it may now be breaking down the political opposition to federal programs even more effectively than did the system of grants to the states.

State and local governments and private corporations used to join in their jealousy of purely federal activities and to consider extension of them as socialistic. The federal grants to states in the field of agriculture, however, were no longer socialistic in the eyes of the governors and the farm bloc; they were a defense of the American way of life, even though they entailed government controls. And now that the atomic energy and space and military programs support such a large share of the nation's business, and so much of its enterprise and innovation spills over quite naturally and properly into related commercial fields, it is no wonder that private business corporations are less jealous of government. More accurately, their jealousy no longer takes the form of fighting socialism, but of haggling over the administrative provisions of contracts. A great deal of private enterprise is now secreted in the interstices of government contracts. In short, what the grants-in-aid programs did to the arguments for states' rights, the new contractual systems are doing to those for pure private enterprise.

The argument for a measure of independence from central authority still remains valid in either case, and so does the need to recognize that the fundamental responsibility of government cannot be delegated. Policy decisions remain the responsibility of government. But "policy" here means simply those aspects that government authorities believe ought to be controlled, either because they think them of major importance or because they realize that voters or congressmen think so.

This means that they will consider as policy certain aspects of management (for example, fair employment practices or prevailing wage rates). But, so long as they retain ultimate control, they may act on the advice of contractors upon the most momentous new issues, or delegate major segments of the business whenever they can specify the purposes to be accomplished. The complex and costly nature of certain types of military studies, and the sophistication of the new techniques of operations research, make the possibility of such delegation very broad indeed. There is nothing in the nature of the contract itself (or the grant, which differs from it only symbolically and in technical detail) to determine whether a central bureaucracy will control every detail of the contractor's management or will leave him free to decide matters in secret that ought to be determined by the president and Congress.

But the general effect of this new system is clear: the fusion of economic and political power has been accompanied by a considerable *diffusion* of central authority. This has destroyed the notion that the future growth in the functions and expenditures of government, which seems to be made inevitable by the increase in the technological complexity of our civilization, would necessarily take the form of a vast bureaucracy, organized on Max Weber's hierarchical principles, and using the processes of science as Julian Huxley predicted to answer policy questions. Where scientists have shaped this development, its political and administrative patterns have reflected the way scientists actually behave rather than the way science fiction or Marxist theory would have them behave; they have introduced into stodgy and responsible channels of bureaucracy the amiable disorder of a university faculty meeting.

Take, for example, our oldest and least scientific federal agency having a large operational mission—the Post Office—and compare it with the air force or the Space Administration. The Post Office is a relatively self-contained hierarchy. The air force develops its policies and runs its programs with the advice and cooperation of several dozen of the most influential universities and industrial corporations of the country, whose executives and faculty members consequently have independent bases from which to criticize any policies, strategic plans, or administrative arrangements they dislike—and they can always find a congressional committee to listen to them.

The role of science in this difference does not seem to be merely accidental. For one thing, the pursuit of science itself is a non-hierarchical affair; the best scientists either personally prefer, or are taught by their guilds that they should prefer, the university's combination of research, teaching, and undisciplined administration—and to get the best scientists the government took them on their own terms. But more important is the long-range and indirect connection; when the revolution of the Enlightenment proposed that the organization and procedures of government as well as its policies should be open to scientific inquiry and independent criticism, it started a process which has had deep effects on the constitutional system. These effects showed first in the relation of scientific administrators to their executive superiors and to congressional committees, and later in the new structure of federalism, and in the new contractual relationships between the federal government and private institutions.

The involvement of scientists in these contractual relationships since 1945 has extended their earlier influence on our system of political responsibility.

In the first place, scientists have acquired an even higher degree of initiative and independence in policy. Scientists who advise government or carry on research for government, but are not primarily on the government payroll, have an even greater freedom of enterprise than scientists in the civil service. A government department that gets its research or its advice from scientists on the staffs of private institutions, and pays for it through a contract or grant, is not going to be able to train such men in the disciplined habits of anonymous discretion. On the contrary, these scientists have plenty of opportunity to take the initiative in policy matters and to further the contribution that research can make to the opening up of new political alternatives. The stories of the most awesome decisions of recent years—such as the decision to make the H-bomb, or to establish a Distant Early Warning system, or to try to work out an agreement with the Russians for ending nuclear tests—reveal a great deal of political enterprise on the part of scientists. Many of them were men whose primary formal status was with private corporations or universities.

In the second place, the developments since 1945 have given a new push to the decentralization of political responsibility. Already the American political concern with the means as well as the ends—the disposition to legislate (or even to establish by Constitutional provision) details of organization and procedure—has made it possible, within the framework of government, to decentralize administration even while centralizing our policies. What we did after the Second World War was to extend this process to a broader system that amalgamated public and private interests. For example, we have nationalized the support of research in the medical schools of the country through the grants of the National Institutes of Health. But administratively—which in this case means effectively—we have *denationalized* the process of controlling federal expenditures for this purpose. For Congress has by law provided that the principal control over medical research grants be exercised by a network of committees of scientists who are not primarily government officials.

If you think sovereignty is something real, this is not the way you will wish to run a government. You are more likely to deduce from the ideal of sovereignty the corollaries that the state is something like a person, and that its personality should be integrated and its ideas consistent with one another.

Since in the modern industrial world there is no way to keep government and business from being dependent on each other, this assumption of the reality of sovereignty, and the effort to find a system of legislative procedures and administrative institutions to translate its ideal purposes into actual practice, may lead to a continuous concentration of political and economic power. On what principles is that concentration to be controlled and held responsible?

Those who have abandoned the traditional value system of Western Europe, or who never held it, are likely to create a new ideology and a new elite to determine the ends of the state, and to control the entire society toward those ends. It may be argued (and this point will be considered later) that this is the way to let science control politics. But it is not a system of political responsibility, and need not be discussed now.

Those who hold to traditional values are likely to seek some new version of Plato's Guardians: the elite who are set apart from the rest of the citizens and trained and dedicated to the purposes of the state. The cruder way to do this, and the way that has been taken by a good many parliamentary democracies, is to rally round some military leader, or to give special responsibility to the career military corps. This is what has been done by those nations that lack the traditions and the skills of the nation that invented the parliamentary system. The United Kingdom can rely instead on its Administrative Class and its parliamentary leadership. The Administrative Class of its civil service is a corps that can continue to embody the purposes of the state as long as it is careful to avoid a role of authority or public responsibility. And the leadership of the House of Commons is a bipartisan group carefully self-schooled in the art of never letting the internal workings of Her Majesty's Government and Her Majesty's Services become objects of political or legislative determination. But under any type of Guardians—military, administrative, or parliamentary—the system of political responsibility is designed to test any new proposal in relation to the general purposes of the state, the ideal policies of the governing parties, or the effectiveness of the administrative establishment. It is not very much inclined to turn scientists loose to experiment with policy issues, or to license irresponsible private institutions to explore the inner workings of government, or to permit any of its parts to work at cross purposes with the rest.

In short, if you start by believing that sovereignty is something real, you are likely to design your constitutional system to focus political attention on the ends of the sovereign state, and to insist that the work of scientists supported by government be treated as a means toward the predetermined ends.

Politics in the United States has always seemed impossibly irresponsible to those who think from those premises. And this is perhaps because the United States started from a quite different premise. It not only abolished its allegiance to a particular sovereign, but abandoned the ideal of sovereignty, and treated it as only a word. Those who used the word most gave it the least reality. Those who talked most about the sovereignty of the several states were careful not to give the idea any administrative substance; if they had, they might have won the Civil War.

In the period of the American Revolution, its theorists appealed against the idea of sovereignty to both the past and the future. They appealed to the past when they asserted, with the lawyers, that the king was under the law, and that even the parliament itself did not have unlimited power to make law; indeed they were just as eager to set up Constitutional safeguards against unlimited legislative power as against executive authority. But the Revolution appealed also to the future, as men like Franklin and Jefferson sought to free both politics and science from the monarchical and ecclesiastical institutions that defined traditional values.

By consequence, democratic politics assumed the right to deal with the means of government as well as the ends, or even to put the means ahead of the ends. This meant that hardly anyone worried if neither the president nor the congressional committees paid much attention to party doctrine in dealing with questions of policy, or to discipline and coordination in dealing with the administrative departments. This gave the scientists a chance to move back and forth between the government and private institutions, and from either base to take a lively initiative in matters of policy. And it made possible the development of more centers of dissent and criticism with respect to public policy even in those fields which government undertook to finance and direct.

This system makes it impossible to maintain an institutional distinction between ends and means, between policy decisions on the one hand and scientific research or administration on the other. Hence it makes party responsibility in the parliamentary sense impossible, and it greatly complicates the task of coordinating either policy or administration.

On the other hand, to blur the distinction between ends and means is a part of the scientific approach: no scientist likes to feel that his basic values and objectives have been set by others so rigidly that he cannot follow where his research leads him. It may be even more necessary to blur the distinction between ends and means, in an institutional sense, in the twentieth century, when it is the requirements of new ideology, rather than old orthodoxy, that threaten freedom. For science itself, by introducing so many complexities into public policy, destroyed the comfortable nineteenth-century notion that public issues could really be determined by the parliamentary competition of two opposing doctrines. At the same time science, by developing new techniques of mass communication, made possible the means for producing disciplined support of authoritarian government. If the structure of political institutions does not specifically encourage some social experimentation based on scientific initiative, with some degree of deliberate freedom from the constraints of policy as determined by either partisan theorists or an administrative elite, it will narrow the range of free scientific and political development. Perhaps our eighteenth-century Constitution, with its implied distrust of party discipline, will yet prove to be more adaptable to our scientific era than the classic nineteenth-century parliamentary model of Walter Bagehot or Woodrow Wilson.

American scientists, who have tended to be a little disillusioned about their relationship with politicians ever since the Jacksonian period, are now entitled to look with a little more satisfaction on the system of political responsibility that they have helped to establish. For it is a system that is congenial to the pragmatic and inductive approach that appeals to most scientists, especially those who profess no interest in philosophy. It puts a premium on their qualifications for promotion within the bureaucracy, and gives their policy views a respectful hearing. And it is based on principles quite different from either the classic parliamentary system or the single-party system that characterizes the new dictatorships.

But all this gives no grounds for self-satisfaction; it only helps us diagnose our troubles more accurately. It suggests that in the United States the main danger to political freedom and responsibility is not likely to come from the secrecy of scientific advice, or an excess of central executive authority, or a drift toward socialism. There is much less reason to worry that the great decisions of a scientific or technological nature will be secret than that they will be *popular;* the temptation of scientists to lobby for particular scientific programs, and to promise technological miracles in order to get funds for basic research may be a demoralizing one. There is much less reason to fear that the executive will dominate the Congress than that the Congress as a whole will surrender its power to its own committees, and that they will be too obsessed with new technological toys to deal with broader issues of policy. And there is much less danger of a drift toward a socialist dictatorship than toward a system in which the government will pay all the costs of a series of expensive programs each of which will be contracted out to private corporations and managed in their private interests.

We do not need to believe in the traditional ideal of sovereignty to think that a modest measure of coherence in our national policies, and of discipline in our administrative system, may be desirable in the interest of political responsibility. Some argue that in order to attain those ends we need to strengthen the political influence of the traditional learning or religious values. Only by a return to traditional values, they argue, can party leaders be guided by moral and political theory, and career civil servants be trained in a philosophy of the public interest. Is this true? Or should we press ahead to a system in which science forms the basis for a new set of political dogmas, enforced by a new kind of establishment? Or do we have another and better choice?

The answers to these questions depend on the basic relation of the sciences to traditional values.

33

Systems Analysis Techniques for Planning–Programming–Budgeting

E. S. Quade

Broadly speaking, any orderly analytic study designed to help a decision-maker identify a preferred course of action from among possible alternatives might be termed a systems analysis. As commonly used in the defense community, the phrase "systems analysis" refers to formal inquiries intended to advise a decision-maker on the policy choices involved in such matters as weapon development, force posture design, or the determination of strategic objectives. A typical analysis might tackle the question of what might be the possible characteristics of a new strategic bomber and whether one should be developed; whether tactical air wings, carrier task forces, or neither could be substituted for United States ground divisions in Europe; or whether we should modify the test-ban treaty now that the Chinese Communists have nuclear weapons and, if so, how. Systems analysis represents an approach to, or way of looking at, complex problems of choice under uncertainty that should have utility in the Planning–Programming–Budgeting (PPB) process. Our purpose is to discuss the question of extending military systems analysis to the civilian activities of the government, to point out some of the limitations of analysis in this role, and to call attention to techniques that seem likely to be particularly useful. I will interpret the term "technique" broadly enough to range from proven mathematical algorithms to certain broad principles that seem to be often associated with successful analysis.

Reprinted with permission of author and publisher. From E. S. Quade, "Systems Analysis Techniques for Planning–Programming–Budgeting," Report P-3322 (Santa Monica, California: The Rand Corporation, 1966), pp. 292–312 E. S. Quade is a consultant at the Rand Corporation.

Some fifteen years ago a similar extension raised quite some doubt. When weapons system analysts (particularly those at The RAND Corporation) began to include the formulation of national security policy and strategy as part of their field of interest, experienced "military analysts" in the Pentagon and elsewhere were not encouraging. They held that the tools, techniques, and concepts of operations analysis, as practiced in World War II, or of weapons system optimization and selection—in which analysts had been reasonably successful—would not carry over, that strategy and policy planning were arts and would remain so.

Fortunately, these skeptics were only partially right. It is true that additional concepts and methodologies significantly different from those of earlier analysis had to be developed. But there has been substantial progress, and the years since 1961 have seen a marked increase in the extent to which analyses of policy and strategy have influenced decisionmakers on the broadest issues of national defense.

Today's contemplated extension to PPB is long overdue and possibly even more radical. Systems analysis has barely entered the domain of the social sciences. Here, in urban planning, in education, in welfare, and in other non-military activities, as Olaf Helmer remarks in his perceptive essay:

> . . . we are faced with an abundance of challenges: how to keep the peace, how to alleviate the hardships of social change, how to provide food and comfort for the inaffluent, how to improve the social institutions and the values of the affluent, how to cope with revolutionary innovations, and so on.[1]

Since systems analysis represents an approach to, or way of looking at, any problem of choice under uncertainty, it should be able to help with these problems.

Actually, systematic analysis of *routine* operations is widespread throughout the civil government as well as in commerce, industry, and the military. Here analysis takes its most mathematical form and, in a certain sense, its most fruitful role. For example, it may help to determine how Post Office pick-up trucks should be routed to collect mail from deposit boxes, or whether computers should be rented or purchased to handle warehouse inventories, or what type of all-weather landing system should be installed in new commercial aircraft. Such problems are typically an attempt to increase the efficiency of a man-machine system in a situation where it is clear what "more efficient" means. The analysis can often be reduced to the application of a well understood mathematical discipline such as linear programming or queuing theory to a generic "model," which, by a specification of its parameters, can be made to fit a wide variety of operations. An "optimum" solution is then obtained by means of a systematic computational routine. The queuing model, for example, is relevant to many aspects of the operations of the Post Office, airports, service facilities, maintenance shops, and so on. In many instances such models may actually tell the client what his decision or plan ought to be. Analysis of this type is usually called operations research or management science rather than systems analysis, however.

There are, however, other decisions or problems, civilian as well as military, where computational techniques can help only with sub-problems. Typical decisions of this latter type might be the determination of how much of the federal budget should be allocated to economic development and what fraction of that should be spent on South America; or whether the needs of interstate transportation are better served by improved high speed rail transport or by higher performance highway turnpikes; or if there is some legislative action that might end the growth of juvenile delinquency. Such problems will normally involve more than the efficient allocation of resources among alternative uses; they are not "solvable" in the same sense as efficiency problems in which one can maximize some "pay-off" function that clearly expresses what one is trying to accomplish. Here, rather, the objectives or goals of the action to be taken must be determined first. Decision problems associated with program budgeting are mainly of this type—where the difficulty lies in deciding what ought to be done as well as in how to do it, where it is not clear what "more efficient" means, and where many of the factors in the problem elude quantification. The final program recommendation will thus remain in part a matter of faith and judgment. Studies to help with these problems are systems analyses rather than operations research.[2]

Every systems analysis involves, at one stage, a comparison of alternative courses of action in terms of their costs and their effectiveness in attaining a specified objective. Usually this comparison takes the form of an attempt to designate the alternative that will minimize the costs, subject to some fixed performance requirement (something like reduce unemployment to less than 2 percent in two years, or add a certain number of miles to the interstate highway system); or conversely, it is an attempt to maximize some physical measure of performance subject to a budget constraint. Such evaluations are called cost-effectiveness analyses.[3] Since they often receive the lion's share of attention, the entire study also is frequently called a cost-effectiveness analysis. But this label puts too much emphasis on just one aspect of the decision process. In analyses designed to furnish broad policy advice, other facts of the problem are of greater significance than the comparison of alternatives: the specification of sensible objectives, the determination of a satisfactory way to measure performance, the influence of considerations that cannot be quantified, or the design of better alternatives.

The essence of the method

What is there about the analytic approach that makes it better or more useful than other ways to furnish advice—than, say, an expert or a committee? In areas such as urban redevelopment or welfare planning, where there is no accepted theoretical foundation, advice obtained from experts working individually or as a committee must depend largely on judgment and intuition. *So must the advice from systems analysis.* But the virtue of such analysis is that it permits the judgment and intuition of the experts in relevant fields to be combined systematically and efficiently. The essence of the method is to construct and operate within a "model," a simplified abstraction of the real situation appropriate to the question. Such a model, which may take such varied forms as a computer simulation, an operational game, or even a purely verbal "scenario," introduces a precise structure and terminology that serve primarily as an effective means of communication, enabling the participants in the study to exercise their judgment and intuition in a concrete context and in proper relation to others. Moreover, through feedback from the model (the results of computation, the countermoves in the game, or the critique of the scenario), the experts have a chance to revise early judgments and thus arrive at a clearer understanding of the problem and its context, and perhaps of their subject matter.[4]

The process of analysis

The fundamental importance of the model is seen in its relation to the other elements of analysis.[5] There are five all told, and each is present in every analysis of choice and should always be explicitly identified.

1. *The objective (or objectives).* Systems analysis is undertaken primarily to help choose a policy or course of action. The first and most important task of the analyst is to discover what the decision-maker's objectives are (or should be) and then how to measure the extent to which these objectives are, in fact, attained by various choices. This done, strategies, policies, or possible actions can be examined, compared, and recommended on the basis of how well and how cheaply they can accomplish these objectives.

2. *The alternatives.* The alternatives are the means by which it is hoped the objectives can be attained. They may be policies or strategies or specific actions or instrumentalities and they need not be obvious substitutes for each other or perform the same specific function. Thus, education, anti-poverty measures, police protection, and slum clearance may all be alternatives in combating juvenile delinquency.

3. *The costs.* The choice of a particular alternative for accomplishing the objectives implies that certain specific resources can no longer be used for other purposes. These are the costs. For a future time period, most costs can be measured in money, but their true measure is in terms of the opportunities they preclude. Thus, if the goal is to lower traffic fatalities, the irritation and delay caused to motorists by schemes that lower automobile speed in a particular location must be considered as costs, for such irritation and delay may cause more speeding elsewhere.

4. *A model (or models).* A model is a simplified stylized representation of the real world that abstracts the cause-and-effect relationships essential to the question studied. The means of representation may range from a set of mathematical equations or a computer program to a purely verbal description of the situation, in which intuition alone is used to predict the consequences of various choices. In systems analysis (or any analysis of choice, the role of the model, (or models, for it may be inappropriate or absurd to attempt to incorporate all the aspects of a problem in a single formulation) is to estimate for each alternative the costs that

would be incurred and the extent to which the objectives would be attained.

5. *A criterion.* A criterion is a rule or standard by which to rank the alternatives in order of desirability. It provides a means for weighing cost against effectiveness.

The process of analysis takes place in three overlapping stages. In the first, the formulation stage, the issues are clarified, the extent of the inquiry limited, and the elements identified. In the second, the search stage, information is gathered and alternatives generated. The third stage is evaluation.

To start the process of evaluation or comparison, the various *alternatives* (which may have to be discovered or invented as part of the analysis) are examined by means of the *models*. The models tell us what consequences or outcomes can be expected to follow from each alternative; that is, what the *costs* are and the extent to which each *objective* is attained. A *criterion* can then be used to weigh the costs against performance, and thus the alternatives can be arranged in the order of preference.

Unfortunately, things are seldom tidy: too often the objectives are multiple, conflicting, and obscure; alternatives are not adequate to attain the objectives; the measures of effectiveness do not really measure the extent to which the objectives are attained; the predictions from the model are full of uncertainties; and other criteria that look almost as plausible as the one chosen may lead to a different order of preference. When this happens, we must take another approach. A single attempt or pass at a problem is seldom enough. The key of successful analysis is a continuous cycle of formulating the problem, selecting objectives, designing alternatives, collecting data, building models, weighing cost against performance, testing for sensitivity, questioning assumptions and data, re-examining the objectives, opening new alternatives, building better models, and so on, until satisfaction is obtained or time or money force a cut-off.

In brief, a systems analysis attempts to look at the entire problem and look at it in its proper context. Characteristically, it will involve a systematic investigation of the decision-maker's objectives and of the relevant criteria; a comparison—quantitative insofar as possible—of the cost, effectiveness, risk, and timing associated with each alternative policy or strategy for achieving the objectives; and an attempt to design better alternatives and select other goals if those examined are found wanting.

Note that there is nothing really new about the procedures I have just sketched. They have been used, more or less successfully, by managers throughout government and industry since ancient times. The need for considering cost relative to performance must have occurred to the earliest planner. Systems analysis is thus not a catchword to suggest we are doing something new; at most, we are doing something better. What may be novel though, is that this sort of analysis is an attempt to look at the entire problem systematically with emphasis on explicitness, on quantification, and on the recognition of uncertainty. Also novel are the schemes or models used to explore the consequences of various choices and to eliminate inferior action in situations where the relationships cannot be represented adequately by a mathematical model.

Note that there is nothing in these procedures that guarantees the advice from the analysis to be good. They do not preclude the possibility that we are addressing the wrong problem or have allowed our personal biases to bar a better solution from consideration. When a study is a poor one it is rarely because the computer was not powerful enough or because the methods of optimization were not sufficiently sophisticated, but because it had the wrong objective or poor criteria. There are some characteristics of a study, however, that seem to be associated with good analysis. Let me identify some of these.

Principles of good analysis

1. It is all important to tackle the "right" problem. A large part of the investigators' efforts must be invested in thinking about the problem, exploring its proper breadth, and trying to discover the appropriate objectives and to search out good criteria for choice. If we have not chosen the best set of alternatives to compare we will not discover the best solution. But if we have chosen the wrong objective then we might find a solution to the wrong problem. Getting an accurate answer to the wrong question is likely to be far less helpful than an incomplete answer to the right question.

2. The analysis must be systems oriented. Rather than isolating a

part of the problem by neglecting its interactions with other parts, an effort should be made to extend the boundaries of the inquiry as far as required for the problem at hand, to find what interdependencies are important, and to study the entire complex system. This should be done even if it requires the use of purely intuitive judgment.

An interdisciplinary team of persons having a variety of knowledge and skills is helpful here. This not so merely because a complex problem is likely to involve many diverse factors that cannot be handled by a single discipline. More importantly, a problem looks different to an economist, an engineer, a political scientist, or a professional bureaucrat, and their different approaches may contribute to finding a solution.

3. The presence of uncertainty should be recognized, and an attempt made to take it into account. Most important decisions are fraught with uncertainty. In planning urban redevelopment we are uncertain about city growth patterns, about the extent to which freeways or rapid transit systems will be used, about costs, about tax revenues, about the demand for services. For many of these things, there is no way to say with confidence that a given estimate is correct. The analyst attempts to identify these uncertainties and evaluate their impact. Often he can say the value of a parameter will be more than A but less than B. Sometimes it is possible to indicate how the uncertainty can be reduced by further testing and how long that will take. Most important, the analysis should determine the effect of uncertainty on the answers. This is done by a sensitivity analysis that shows the answers change in response to changes in assumptions and estimates.[6]

The study report should include the presentation of a contingency table showing the effectiveness and cost associated with each significant alternative for various future environments and for each set of assumptions about the uncertainties.

4. The analysis attempts to discover new alternatives as well as to improve the obvious ones. The invention of new alternatives can be much more valuable than an exhaustive comparison of given alternatives, none of which may be very satisfactory.

5. While in problems of public policy or national security, the scientific method of controlled repeated experiment cannot be used, the analysis should strive to attain the standards traditional to science. These are (1) intersubjectivity: results obtained by processes that can be duplicated

by others to attain the same results; (2) explicitness: use of calculations, assumptions, data, and judgments that are subject to checking, criticism, and disagreement; and (3) objectivity: conclusions do not depend on personalities, reputations, or vested interests; where possible these conclusions should be in quantitative and experimental terms.

The models

As mentioned earlier, systems analysis is flexible in the models it uses. Indeed, it has to be. Mathematics and computing machines, while extremely useful, are limited in the aid they can give in broad policy questions. If the important aspects of the problem can be completely formulated mathematically or represented numerically, techniques such as dynamic programming, game theory, queuing theory, or computer simulation may be the means of providing the best solution. But in most policy analyses, computations and computers are often more valuable for the aid they provide to intuition and understanding, rather than for the results they supply.

While a computer can solve only the problems that the analyst knows conceptually how to solve himself, it can help with many others. The objection that one cannot use results which depend on many uncertain parameters represents a lack of understanding of how systems analysis can help a decision-maker. For a study to be useful it must indicate the *relative* merit of the various alternatives and identify the critical parameters. The great advantage of a computerized model is that it gives the analyst the capability to do numerous excursions, parametric investigations, and sensitivity analyses and thus to investigate the ranking of alternatives under a host of assumptions. This may be of more practical value to the decision-maker than the ability to say with high confidence that a given alternative will have such and such a rank in a very narrowly defined situation.

The type of model appropriate to a problem depends on the problem and what we know or think we know about it.

For example, suppose we are concerned with long-range economic forecasting or decisions about the development of a national economy. The type of model to use will depend on the particular economy and on the kind of questions that must be answered. If the questions were about the United States, the model might be mathematical and possibly programmed for a computer because of its size and complexity. (By a mathematical model I mean one in which the relationships between the variables and parameters are represented by mathematical equations.) In the case of the United States, because of the vast amount of data available in the form of economic and demographic time series regarding just about every conceivable aspect of economic life, numerous mathematical and computer models have been formulated and used with more or less success.

If we are not able to abstract the situation to a series of equations or a mathematical model, some other way to represent the consequences that follow from particular choices must be found. Simulation may work. Here, instead of describing the situation directly, each element making up the real situation may be simulated by a physical object or, most often, by a digital computer using sets of random numbers, and its behavior analyzed by operating with the representation. For example, we might use computer simulation to study the economy of some Latin American country. The distinction between a computer simulation and the use of a computer to analyze a mathematical model is often a fuzzy one, but the fundamental difference is that in simulation the over-all behavior of the model is studied through a case-by-case approach.

For studying the economy of a newly emerging nation such as is found in Africa, where the situation is even more poorly structured and where we have little firm knowledge of existing facts and relationships, a possible approach would be through the direct involvement of experts who have knowledge of the problem.

Ordinarily, we would like to have the judgment of more than one expert, even though their advice usually differs. There are several ways to try for a consensus; the traditional way has been to assemble the experts in one place, to let them discuss the problem freely, and to require that they arrive at a joint answer. They could also be put to work individually, letting others seek methods for the best combined use of their findings. Or they could be asked to work in a group exercise—ranging from a simple structured discussion to a sophisticated simulation or an "operational game"—to obtain judgments from the group as a whole.

This latter approach is a laboratory simulation involving role-playing by human subjects who simulate real-world decision-makers. To study the economy of an underdeveloped country the various sectors of the economy might be simulated by specialized experts.[7] They would be expected, in acting out their roles, not so much to play a competitive game against one another, but to use their intuitition as experts to simulate as best they could the attitudes and consequent decisions of their real-life counterparts. For instance, a player simulating a goods-producing sector of the economy might, within constraints, shut down or expand manufacturing facilities, modernize, change raw material and labor inputs, vary prices and so on. There would also need to be government players who could introduce new fiscal or monetary policies and regulations (taxes, subsidies, tariffs, price ceilings, etc.) as well as social and political innovations with only indirect economic implications (social security, education, appeals to patriotism, universal military service, etc). In laying down the rules governing the players' options and constraints and the actions taken within these rules, expert judgment is essential. It is also clear that for this problem political and sociological experts will be needed, as well as economists.

There is, of course, no guarantee that the projections obtained from such a model would be reliable. But the participating experts might gain a great deal of insight. Here the game structure—again a model—furnishes the participants with an artificial, simulated environment within which they can jointly and simultaneously experiment, acquiring through feedback the insights necessary to make successful predictions within the gaming context and thus indirectly about the real world.

Another useful technique is one that military systems analysts call "scenario writing." This is an effort to show how, starting with the present, a future state might evolve out of the present one. The idea is to show how this might happen plausibly by exhibiting a reasonable chain of events. A scenario is thus a primitive model. A collection of scenarios provides an insight on how future trends can depend on factors under our control and suggests policy options to us.

Another type of group action, somewhat less structured than the operational game, attempts to improve the panel or committee approach by subjecting the views of individual experts to each other's criticism without actual confrontation and its possible psychological shortcomings. In this approach, called the Delphi method, direct debate is replaced by the interchange of information and opinion through a carefully designed sequence of questionnaires. At each successive interrogation, the participants are given new refined information, and opinion feedback is derived by computing consensus from the earlier part of the program. The process continues until either a consensus is reached, or the conflicting views are documented fully.[8]

It should be emphasized that in many important problems it is not possible to build really quantitative models. The primary function of a model is "explanatory," to organize our thinking. As I have already stated, the essence of systems analysis is not mathematical techniques or procedures, and its recommendations need not follow from computation. What counts is the effort to compare alternatives systematically, in quantitative terms when possible, using a logical sequence of steps that can be retraced and verified by others.

The virtues

In spite of many limitations, the decision-makers who have made use of systems analysis find it extremely useful. In fact, for some questions of national defense, analysis is essential. Without calculation there is no way to discover how many missiles may be needed to destroy a target system, or how arms control may affect security. It may be essential in other areas also; one cannot experiment radically with the national economy or even change the traffic patterns in a large city without running the risk of chaos. Analysis offers an alternative to "muddling through" or to settling national problems by yielding to the strongest pressure group. It forces the devotees of a program to make explicit their lines of argument, to calculate the resources their programs will require as well as the advantages they might produce.

It is easy, unfortunately, to exaggerate the degree of assistance that systems analysis can offer the policy-maker. At most, it can help him understand the relevant alternatives and the key interactions by providing an estimate of the costs, risks, pay-offs and the time-span associated with each course of action. It may lead him to consider new and better alternatives. It may sharpen the decision-maker's intuition and will certainly broaden his basis for judgment, thus helping him make a better decision. But value judgments, imprecise knowledge, intuitive estimates, and uncertainties about nature and the actions of others mean that a study can do little more than assess some of the implications of choosing one alternative over another. In practically no case, therefore, should the decision-maker expect the analysis to demonstrate that, beyond all reasonable doubt, a particular course of action is best.

The limitations

Every systems analysis has defects. Some of these are limitations inherent in all analysis of choice. Others are a consequence of the difficulties and complexities of the question. Still others are blunders or errors in thinking, which hopefully will disappear as we learn to do better and more complete analyses.

The alternatives to analysis also have their defects. One alternative is pure intuition. This is in no sense analytic, since no effort is made to structure the problem or to establish cause-and-effect relationships and operate on them to arrive at a solution. The intuitive process is to learn everything possible about the problem, to "live with it," and to let the subconscious provide the solution.

Between pure intuition, on one hand, and systems analysis, on the other, other sources of advice can, in a sense, be considered to employ analysis, although ordinarily of a less systematic, explicit, and quantitative kind. One can turn to an expert. His opinion may, in fact, be very helpful if it results from a reasonable and impartial examination of the facts, with due allowance for uncertainty, and if his assumptions and chain of logic are made *explicit.* Only then can others use his information to form their own considered opinions. But an expert, particularly an unbiased expert, may be hard to find.

Another way to handle a problem is to turn it over to a committee. Committees, however, are much less likely than experts to make their reasoning explicit, since their findings are usually obtained by bargaining. This is not to imply that a look by a "blue ribbon" committee into such problems as poverty or the allocation of funds for foreign aid might not be useful, but a committee's greatest usefulness is likely to be in the critique of analysis done by others.

However, no matter whether the advice is supplied by an expert, a committee, or a formal study group, the analysis of a problem of choice involves the same five elements and basic structure we discussed earlier.

It is important to remember that all policy analysis falls short of being scientific research. No matter how we strive to maintain standards of scientific inquiry or how closely we attempt to follow scientific methods, we cannot turn systems analysis into science. Such analysis is designed primarily to recommend—or at least to suggest—a course of action, rather than merely to understand and predict. Like engineering, the aim is to use the results of science to do things well and cheaply. Yet, when applied to national problems, the difference from ordinary engineering is apparent in the enormous responsibility involved in the unusual difficulty of appraising—or even discovering—a value system applicable to the problems, and in the absence of ways to test the validity of the analysis.

Except for this inability to verify, systems analysis may still look like a purely rational approach to decision-making, a coldly objective, scientific method free from preconceived ideas, partisan bias, judgment and intuition.

It really is not. Judgment and intuition are used in designing the models; in deciding what alternatives to consider, what factors are relevant, what the interrelations between these factors are, and what criteria to choose; and in interpreting the results of the analysis. This fact—that judgment and intuition permeate all analysis—should be remembered when we examine the apparently precise results that seem to come with such high-precision analysis.

Many flaws are the results of pitfalls faced by the analyst. It is all too easy for him to begin to believe his own assumptions and to attach undue significance to his calculations, especially if they involve bitter arguments and extended computations. The most dangerous pitfall or source of defects is an unconscious adherence to a "party line." This is frequently caused by a cherished belief or an *attention bias*. All organizations foster one to some extent; RAND, the military services, and the civilian agencies of the government are no exception. The party line is "the most important single reason for the tremendous miscalculations that are made in foreseeing and preparing for technical advances or changes in the strategic situation."[9] Examples are plentiful: the political adviser whose aim is so fixed on maintaining peace that he completely disregards what might happen should deterrence fail; the weaponeer who is so fascinated by the startling new weapons that he has invented that he assumes the politician will allow them to be used; the union leader whose attention is so fixed on current employment that he rejects an automatic device that can spread his craft into scores of new areas. In fact, this failure to realize the vital interdependence of political purpose, diplomacy, military posture, economics, and technical feasibility is the typical flaw in most practitioners' approach to national security analysis.

There are also pitfalls for the bureaucrat who commissions a study or gives inputs to it. For instance, he may specify assumptions and limit the problem arbitrarily. When a problem is first observed in one part of an organization, there is a tendency to seek a solution completely contained in that part. An administrator is thus likely to pose his problems in such a way as to bar from consideration alternatives or criteria that do not fit into his idea of the way things should be done; for example, he may not think of using ships for some tasks now being done by aircraft. Also, to act wisely on the basis of someone else's analysis one should, at the very least, understand the important and fundamental principles involved. One danger associated with analysis is that it may be employed by an administrator who is unaware of or unwilling to accept its limitations.

Pitfalls are one thing, but the inherent limitations of analysis itself are another. These limitations confine analysis to an advisory role. Three are commented on here: analysis is necessarily incomplete; measures of effectiveness are inevitably approximate; and ways to predict the future are lacking.

Analysis is necessarily incomplete

Time and money costs obviously place sharp limits on how far any inquiry can be carried. The very fact that time moves on means that a correct choice at a given time may soon be outdated by events and that goals set down at the start may not be final. The need for reporting almost always forces a cut-off. Time considerations are particularly important in military analysis, for the decision-maker can wait only so long for an answer. Other costs are important here, too. For instance, we would like to find out what the Chinese Communists would do if we put an end to all military aid to Southeast Asia. One way to get this information would be to stop such aid. But while this would clearly be cheap in immediate dollar costs, the likelihood of other later costs precludes this type of investigation.

Still more important, however, is the general fact that, even with no limitations of time and money, analysis can never treat all the considerations that may be relevant. Some are too intangible—for example, how some unilateral United States action will affect NATO solidarity, or whether Congress will accept economies that disrupt cherished institutions such as the National Guard or radically change the pattern of domestic military spending. Considerations of this type should play as important a role in the recommendation of alternative policies as any idealized cost-effectiveness calculations. But ways to measure these considerations even approximately do not exist today, and they must be handled intuitively. Other immeasurable considerations involve moral judgments—for example, whether national security is better served by an increase in the budget for defense or for welfare, or under what circumstances the preservation of an immediate advantage is worth the compromise of fundamental principles. The analyst can apply his and others' judgment and intuition to these considerations, thus making them part of the study; but *bringing them to the attention of the decision-maker,* the man with the responsibility, is extremely important.

Measures of effectiveness are approximate

In military comparisons, measures of effectiveness are at best reasonably satisfactory approximations for indicating the attainment of such vaguely defined objectives as deterrence or victory. Sometimes the best that can be done is to find measures that point in the right direction. Consider deterrence, for instance. It exists only in the mind—and in the enemy's mind at that. We cannot, therefore, measure the effectiveness of alternatives we hope will lead to deterrence by some scale of deterrence, but must use instead such approximations as to the potential mortalities that we might inflict or the roof cover we might destroy. Consequently, even if a comparison of two systems indicated that one could inflict 50 percent more casualties on the enemy than the other, we could not conclude that this means the system supplies 50 percent more deterrence. In fact, since in some circumstances it may be important *not* to look too dangerous, we encounter arguments that the system threatening the greatest number of casualties may provide the *least* deterrence!

Similarly, consider the objective of United States government expenditures for health. A usual measure of effectiveness is the dollar value of increased labor force participation. But, this is clearly inadequate; medical services are more often in demand because of a desire to reduce the every day aches and pains of life. Moreover, we cannot be very confident about the accuracy of our estimates. For example, one recent and authoritative source estimates the yearly cost of cancer to the United States at $11 billion, while another, equally authoritative, estimates $2.6 billion.[10]

No satisfactory way to predict the future exists

While it is possible to forecast events in the sense of mapping out possible futures, there is no satisfactory way to predict a single future for which we can work out the best system or determine an optimum policy. Consequently, we must consider a range of possible futures or contingencies. In any one of these we may be able to designate a preferred course of action, but we have no way to determine such action for the entire range of possibilities. We can design a force structure for a particular war in a particular place, but we have no way to work out a structure that is good for the entire spectrum of future wars in all the places they may occur.

Consequently, defense planning is rich in the kind of analysis that tells what damage could be done to the United States given a particular enemy force structure; but it is poor in the kinds of analyses that evaluate how we will actually stand in relation to the Soviets in years to come.

In spite of these limitations, it is not sensible to formulate policy or action without careful consideration of whatever relevant numbers can be discovered. In current Department of Defense practice, quantitative estimates of various kinds are used extensively. Many people, however, are vaguely uneasy about the particular way these estimates are made and their increasingly important role not only in military planning but elsewhere throughout the government.

Some skepticism may be justified, for the analytical work may not always be done competently or used with its limitations in mind. There may indeed be some dangers in relying on systems analysis, or on any similar approach to broad decisions. For one thing, since many factors fundamental to problems of federal policy are not readily amenable to quantitative treatment, they may possibly be neglected, or deliberately set aside for later consideration and then forgotten, or improperly weighed in the analysis itself, or in the decision based on such analysis. For another, a study may, on the surface, appear so scientific and quantitative that it may be assigned a validity not justified by the many subjective judgments involved. In other words, we may be so mesmerized by the beauty and precision of the numbers that we overlook the simplifications made to achieve this precision, neglect analysis of the qualitative factors, and overemphasize the importantce of idealized calculations in the decision process. But without analysis we face even greater dangers in neglect of considerations and in the assignment of improper weights!

The future

And finally, what of the future? Resistance by the military to the use of systems analysis in broad problems of strategy has gradually broken down. Both government and military planning and strategy have always involved more art than science; what is happening is that the art form is changing from an ad hoc, seat-of-the-pants approach based on intuition to one based on analysis *supported by* intuition and experience. This change may come more slowly in the non-military aspects of government. For one thing, the civilian employees of the government are not so closely controlled "from the top" as those in the military; also the goals in these areas are just as vague and even more likely to be conflicting.[11] The requirements of the integrated Planning–Programming–Budgeting System will do much to speed the acceptance of analysis for other tasks, however.

With the acceptance of analysis, the computer is becoming increasingly significant—as an automaton, a process-controller, an information processor, and a decision aid. Its usefulness in serving these ends can be expected to grow. But at the same time, it is important to note that even the best computer is no more than a tool to expedite analysis. Even in the narrowest decisions, considerations not subject to any sort of quantitative analysis can always be present. Big decisions, therefore, cannot be the *automatic* consequence of a computer program or of any application of mathematical models.

For broad studies, intuitive, subjective, even *ad hoc* study schemes must continue to be used—but supplemented to an increasing extent by systems analysis. The ingredients of this analysis must include not only an increasing use of computer-based models for those problems where they are appropriate, but for treatment of the non-quantifiable aspects, a greater use of techniques for better employment of judgment, intuition, and experience. These techniques—operational gaming, "scenario" writing, and the systematic interrogation of experts—are on the way to becoming an integral part of systems analysis.

Concluding remarks

And now to review. A systems analysis is an analytic study designed to help a decision-maker identify a preferred choice among possible alternatives. It is characterized by a systematic and rational approach, with assumptions made explicit, objectives and criteria clearly defined, and alternative courses of action compared in the light of their possible consequences. An effort is made to use quantitative methods, but computers are not essential. What is essential is a model that enables expert intuition and judgment to be applied efficiently. The method provides its answer by processes that are accessible to critical examination, capable of duplication by others, and, more or less, readily modified as new information becomes available. And, in contrast to other aids to decision-making, which share the same limitations, it extracts everything possible from scientific methods, and therefore its virtues are the virtues of those methods. At its narrowest, systems analysis has offered a way to choose the numerical quantities related to a weapon system so that they are logically consistent with each other, with an assumed objective, and with the calculator's expectation of the future. At its broadest, through providing the analytic backup for the plans, programs, and budgets of the various executive departments and establishments of the federal government, it can help guide national policy. But, even within the Department of Defense, its capabilities have yet to be fully exploited.

Notes

Any views expressed in this paper are those of the author. They should not be interpreted as reflecting the views of the RAND Corporation or the official opinion or policy of any of its governmental or private research sponsors. Papers are reproduced by The RAND Corporation as a courtesy to members of its staff.

A condensed version of this paper was presented in the course Executive Orientation in Planning, Programming, and Budgeting, sponsored by U.S. Bureau of the Budget and the U.S. Civil Service Commission, Washington, D.C., February 24–25, 1966.

1. Helmer, O., *Social Technology,* The RAND Corporation, P-3063, February 1965; presented at the Futuribles Conference in Paris, April 1965.

2. For a further discussion of this distinction, see Schlesinger, J. R., "Quantitative Analysis and National Security," *World Politics,* Vol. XV, No. 2 (January 1963), 295–315.

3. Or, alternatively, cost-utility and cost-benefit analysis.

4. C. J. Hitch in Quade, E. S., (ed.), *Analysis for Military Decisions,* (Chicago: Rand McNally, 1964), p. 23, states: "Systems analyses should be looked upon not as the antithesis of judgment but as a framework which permits the judgment of experts in numerous subfields to be utilized—to yield results which transcend any individual judgment. This is its aim and opportunity."

5. Olaf Helmer, *op. cit.,* p. 7, puts it this way: "The advantage of employing a model lies in forcing the analyst to make explicit what elements of a situation he is taking into consideration and in imposing upon him the discipline of clarifying the concepts he is using. The model thus serves the important purpose of establishing unambiguous intersubjective communication about the subject matter at hand. Whatever intrinsic uncertainties may becloud the area of investigation, they are thus less likely to be further compounded by uncertainties due to disparate subjective interpretations."

6. See, for example, Fort, Donald M., *Systems Analysis as an Aid in Air Transportation Planning,* The RAND Corporation, P-3293, January 1966, pp. 12–14.

7. Helmer, O., and E. S. Quade, "An Approach to the Study of a Developing Economy by Operational Gaming," in *Recherche Operationnelle et Problèmes du Tiers-Monde,* Colloquium organized by the French Society of Operational Research, with the participation of the Institute of Management Sciences, Operations Research Society of America (Paris: Dunod, 1964), pp. 43–54.

8. Helmer, O., and Norman C. Dalkey, "An Experimental Application of the Delphi Method to the Use of Experts," *Management Sciences* 9, no. 3 (April 1963):458–467; and Helmer, O., and Nicholas Rescher, "On the Epistemology of the Inexact Sciences," *Management Sciences* 6, no. 1 (October 1959):25–52.

9. *Ibid.*

10. Kahn, H., and I. Mann, *Ten Common Pitfalls,* (Santa Monica, Calif.: The RAND Corporation, RM-1937, 17 July 1957.)

11. James R. Schlesinger, *op. cit.,* has a slightly different view: "Thus the mere uncovering of ways to increase efficiency is not sufficient. Even where a decision is clear to the disinterested observer, it is difficult to persuade committed men that their programs or activities should be reduced or abandoned. The price of enthusiasm is that those who have a commitment will be 'sold' on their specialty and are incapable of viewing it in cold analytical terms. This may be especially true of the military establishment, where the concepts of duty, honor, and country *when particularized* lead to a certain inflexibility in adjusting to technological change and the new claims of efficiency. But it is also true in the civilian world: for conservationists, foresters, water resource specialists, businessmen, union leaders, or agrarians, some aspects of their value-systems run directly counter to the claims of efficiency. The economic view strikes them all as immoral as well as misleading. (After all, is it not a value judgment on the part of economists that efficiency calculations are important?).

"Even in the case of fairly low-level decisions, if they are political, systematic quantitative analysis does not necessarily solve problems. It will not convince ardent supporters that their program is submarginal. Nevertheless, quantitative analysis remains most useful. Certain operational decisions, it either provides the decisionmaker with the justification he may desire for cutting off a project or forces him to come up with a non-numerical rationalization. It eliminates the purely subjective approach on the part of devotees of a program and forces them to change their lines of argument. They must talk about reality rather than morality. Operational research creates a bridge to budgetary problems over which planners, who previously could assume resources were free, are forced, willingly or unwillingly, to walk."

34

Dysfunctional Consequences
of Performance Measurements

V. F. Ridgway

There is today a strong tendency to state numerically as many as possible of the variables with which management must deal. The mounting interest in and application of tools such as operations research, linear programming, and statistical decision-making, all of which require quantifiable variables, foster the idea that if progress toward goals can be measured, efforts and resources can be more rationally managed. This has led to the development of quantitative performance measurements for all levels within organizations, up to and including measurements of the performance of a division manager with profit responsibility in decentralized company. Measurements at lower levels in the organization may be in terms of amount of work, quality of work, time required, and so on.

Quantitative measures of performance are tools, and are undoubtedly useful. But research indicates that indiscriminate use and undue confidence and reliance in them result from insufficient knowledge of the full effects and consequences. Judicious use of a tool requires awareness of possible side effects and reactions. Otherwise, indiscriminate use may result in side effects and reactions outweighing the benefits, as was the case when penicillin was first hailed as a wonder drug. The cure is sometimes worse than the disease.

It seems worthwhile to review the current scattered knowledge of the dysfunctional consequences resulting from the imposition of a system of performance measurements. For the purpose of analyzing the impact of performance measurements upon job performance, we can consider separately single, multiple, and composite criteria. Single crite-

Reprinted with permission of author and publisher. From *Administrative Science Quarterly* I, no. 2 (September 1956): 240–47.

ria occur when only one quantity is measured and observed, such as total output or profit. Multiple criteria occur when several quantities are measured simultaneously, such as output, quality, cost, safety, waste, and so forth. Composite criteria occur when the separate quantities are weighted in some fashion and then added or averaged.

Single criteria

A single criterion of performance was in use in a public employment agency studied by Peter M. Blau.[1] The agency's responsibility was "to serve workers seeking employment and employers seeking workers." Employment interviewers were appraised by the numbers of interviews they conducted. Thus the interviewer was motivated to complete as many interviews as he could, but not to spend adequate time in locating jobs for the clients. The organization's goal of placing clients in jobs was not given primary consideration because the measurement device applied to only one aspect of the activity.

Blau reports another case in a federal law enforcement agency which investigated business establishments. Here he found that work schedules were distorted by the imposition of a quota of eight cases per month for each investigator. Toward the end of the month an investigator who found himself short of the eight cases would pick easy, fast cases to finish that month and save the lengthier cases till the following month. Priority of the cases for investigation was based on length of the case rather than urgency, as standards of impartiality would require. This is one of many instances in which the existence of an "accounting period" adversely affects the over-all goal accomplishment of the organization.

Chris Argyris also reports this tendency to use easy jobs as fillers toward the end of a period in order to meet a quota.[2] In this case, a factory supervisor reported that they "feed the machines all the easy orders" toward the end of the month, rather than finish them in the sequence in which they were received. Such a practice may lead to undue delay of

---

[1]Peter M. Blau, *The Dynamics of Bureaucracy* (Chicago, Ill., 1955).
[2]Chris Argyris, *The Impact of Budgets on People* (New York, 1952).

the delivery of some customers' orders, perhaps the most profitable orders.

David Granick's study of Soviet management reveals how the attention and glory that accrues to a plant manager when he can set a new monthly production record in one month leads to the neglect of repairs and maintenance, so that in ensuing months there will be a distinct drop in production.[3] Similarly, the output of an entire plant may be allowed to fall off in order to create conditions under which one worker can make a production record, when the importance of such a record is considered greater than overall plant production.

Joseph S. Berliner's report on Soviet business administration points out sharply how the accounting period has an adverse effect upon management decisions.[4] The use of monthly production quotas causes "storming" at the end of the month to reach the quota. Repairs and maintenance are postponed until the following month, so that production lags in the early part of the month, and storming must again be resorted to in the following month. This has impact upon the rate of production for suppliers and customers who are forced into a fluctuating rate of operations with its attendant losses and wastes.

Standard costs as a criterion of performance is a frequent source of dissatisfaction in manufacturing plants.[5] The "lumpiness" of indirect charges that are allocated to the plants or divisions (indirect charges being unequal from month to month), variations in quality and cost of raw materials, or other factors beyond the control of the operating manager, coupled with inaccuracies and errors in the apportionment of indirect charges, causes distrust of the standards. A typical reaction of operating executives in such cases seems to be to seek explanations and justifications. Consequently, considerable time and energy is expended in discussion and debate about the correctness of charges. Only "wooden money" savings accrue when charges are shifted to other accounts and there is

[3]David Granick, *Management of the Industrial Firm in the U.S.S.R.* (New York, 1954).

[4]Joseph S. Berliner, "A Problem in Soviet Business Management," *Administrative Science Quarterly* 1 (1956): 86–101.

[5]H. A. Simon, H. Guetzkow, G. Kozmetsky, G. Tyndall, *Centralization vs. Decentralization in Organizing the Controller's Department* (New York, 1954).

no increase in company profits. It should be pointed out, however, that having charges applied to the proper departments may have the advantage of more correctly directing attention to problem areas.

Granick discusses two measures of the success of the Soviet firm which have been considered and rejected as overall measures by Soviet industrial leaders and economists.[6] The first, cost-reduction per unit of product, is considered inadequate because it does not provide a basis for evaluating new products. Further, variations in amount of production affect the cost-reduction index because of the finer division of overhead costs, quality changes, and assortment. The second overall measure of a firm's performance, profitability, has been rejected as the basic criterion on the grounds that it is affected in the short run by factors outside the control of management, such as shortages of supplies. Profitability as a measure of success led to a reduction in experimental work and deemphasized the importance of production quantity, quality, and assortment. Neither cost-reduction nor profitability was acceptable alone; each was only a partial index. The Soviets had concluded by 1940 that no single measure of success of a firm is adequate in itself and that there is no substitute for genuine analysis of all the elements entering into a firm's work.

Difficulties with single criteria have been observed in operations research, where one of the principal sources of difficulty is considered to be the choice of proper criteria for performance measurement.[7] The difficulty of translating the several alternatives into their full effect upon the organization's goal forces the operations researcher to settle for a criterion more manageable than profit maximization, but less appropriate. The efficiency of a subgroup of the organization may be improved in terms of some plausible test, yet the organization's efficiency in terms of its major goal may be decreased.

In all studies mentioned above, the inadequacy of a single measure of performance is evident. Whether this is a measure of an employee at the working level, or a measure of management, attention is directed

[6]Granick, *op. cit.,*

[7]Charles Hitch and Roland McKean, "Suboptimization in Operations Problems" in J. F. McCloskey and Flora F. Trefethen, eds., *Operations Research for Management* (Baltimore, Md., 1954).

away from the overall goal. The existence of a measure of performance motivates individuals to effort, but the effort may be wasted, as in seeking "wooden money" savings, or may be detrimental to the organization's goal, as in rushing through interviews, delaying repairs, and rejecting profitable opportunities.

Multiple measurements

Recognition of the inadequacies of a single measure of success or performance leads organizations to develop several criteria. It is felt then that all aspects of the job will receive adequate attention and emphasis so that efforts of individuals will not be distorted.

A realization in the employment office studied by Blau that job referrals and placements were also important led eventually to their inclusion in measuring the performance of the interviewers.[8] Merely counting the number of referrals and placements had led to wholesale indiscriminate referrals, which did not accomplish the employment agency's screening function. Therefore, to stress the qualitative aspects of the interviewer's job, several ratios (of referrals to interviews, placements to interviews, and placements to referrals) were devised. Altogether there were eight quantities that were counted or calculated for each interviewer. This increase in quantity and complexity of performance measurements was felt necessary to give emphasis to all aspects of the interviewer's job.

Granick relates that no single criterion was universally adopted in appraising Soviet management.[9] Some managers were acclaimed for satisfying production quotas while violating labor laws. Others were removed from office for violating quality and assortment plans while fulfilling production quotas. Apparently there is a ranking of importance of these multiple criteria. In a typical interfirm competition the judges were provided with a long list of indexes. These included production of finished goods in the planned assortment, an even flow of production as between different ten-day periods and as between months, planned mastery of new types of products, improvement in product quality and reduction in waste, economy of materials through improved design and

[8]Blau, *op. cit.*
[9]Granick, *op. cit.*

changing of technological processes, fulfillment of labor productivity tasks and lowering of unit cost, keeping within the established wage fund, and increase in the number of worker suggestions for improvements in work methods and conditions and their adoption into operation. But no indication of how these indexes should be weighted was given. The preeminence of such indexes as quantity, quality, assortment of production, and remaining within the firm's allotment of materials and fuels brought some order into the otherwise chaotic picture. The presence of "campaigns" and "priorities" stressing one or more factors also has aided Soviet management in deciding which elements of its work are at the moment most important.

Without a single over-all composite measure of success, however, there is no way of determining whether the temporarily increased effort on the "campaign" criteria of the month represents new effort or merely effort shifted from other criteria. And the intangibility of some of these indexes makes it impossible to judge whether there has been decreased effort on other aspects. Hence even in a campaign period the relative emphases may become so unbalanced as to mitigate or defeat the purpose of the campaign.

The Soviet manager is working then under several measurements, and the relative influence or emphasis attached to any one measurement varies from firm to firm and from month to month. Profits and production are used, among other measurements, and these two may lead to contradictory managerial decisions. Granick hypothesizes that some managers have refused complicated orders that were difficult to produce because it would mean failure to produce the planned quantities. Acceptance of these orders would have been very profitable, but of the two criteria, production quantity took precedence.

Numerous American writers in the field of management have stressed the importance of multiple criteria in evaluating performance of management. Peter Drucker, for example, lists market standing, innovation, productivity, physical and financial resources, profitability, manager performance and development, worker performance and attitude, and public responsibility.[10] This list includes many of the same items as the list used by Soviet management.

[10] Peter M. Drucker, *The Practice of Management* (New York, 1954).

The consensus at a round-table discussion of business and professional men[11] was that although return on investment is important, additional criteria are essential for an adequate appraisal of operating departments. These other criteria are fairly well summed up in Drucker's list above.

Thus we see that the need for multiple criteria is recognized and that they are employed at different levels of the organization—lower levels as in the employment agency, higher levels as considered by Granick and Drucker. At all levels these multiple measurements or criteria are intended to focus attention on the many facets of a particular job.

The use of multiple criteria assumes that the individual will commit his or the organization's efforts, attention, and resources in greater measure to those activities which promise to contribute the greatest improvement to over-all performance. There must then exist a theoretical condition under which an additional unit of effort or resources would yield equally desirable results in overall performance, whether applied to production, quality, research, safety, public relations, or any of the other suggested areas. This would be the condition of "balanced stress on objectives" to which Drucker refers.

Without a single over-all composite measure of performance, the individual is forced to rely upon his judgment as to whether increased effort on one criterion improves over-all performance, or whether there may be a reduction in performance on some other criterion which will outweigh the increase in the first. This is quite possible, for in any immediate situation many of these objectives may be contradictory to each other.

Composites

To adequately balance the stress on the contradictory objectives or criteria by which performance of particular individual or organization is appraised, there must be an implied or explicit weighting of these criteria. When such a weighting system is available, it is an easy task to

---

[11]William H. Newman and James P. Logan, *Management of Expanding Enterprises* (New York, 1955).

combine the measures of the various subgoals into a composite score for overall performance.

Such a composite is used by the American Institute of Management in evaluating and ranking the managements of corporations, hospitals, and other organizations.[12] These ratings are accomplished by attaching a numerical grade to each of several criteria, such as economic function, corporate structure, production efficiency, and the like. Each criterion has an optimum rating, and the score on each for any particular organization is added to obtain a total score. Although there may be disagreement on the validity of the weighting system employed, the rating given on any particular category, the categories themselves, or the methods of estimating scores in the A.I.M. management audit, this system is an example of the type of overall performance measurement which might be developed. Were such a system of ratings employed by an organization and found acceptable by management, it presumably would serve as a guide to obtaining a balanced stress on objectives.

A composite measure of performance was employed in air force wings as reported by K. C. Wagner.[13] A complex rating scheme covering a wide range of activities was used. When the organizations were put under pressure to raise their composite score without proportionate increases in the organization's means of achieving them, there were observable unanticipated consequences in the squadrons. Under a system of multiple criteria, pressure to increase performance on one criterion might be relieved by a slackening effort toward other criteria. But with a composite criterion this does not seem as likely to occur. In Wagner's report individuals were subjected to tension, role and value conflicts, and reduced morale; air crews suffered from inter-crew antagonism, apathy, and reduced morale; organization and power structures underwent changes; communications distortions and blockages occurred; integration decreased; culture patterns changed; and norms were violated. Some of these consequences may be desirable, some undesirable. The net result, however, might easily be less effective over-all performance.

[12] *Manual of Excellent Managements* (New York, 1955).

[13] Kenneth C. Wagner, "Latent Functions of an Executive Control: A Sociological Analysis of a Social System under Stress," *Research Previews,* vol. 2 (Chapel Hill: Institute for Research in Social Science, March 1954), mimeo.

These consequences were observable in a situation where goals were increased without a corresponding increase in means, which seems to be a common situation. Berliner refers to the "ratchet principle" wherein an increase in performance becomes the new standard, and the standard is thus continually raised. Recognition of the operation of the "ratchet principle" by workers was documented by F. J. Roethlisberger and William J. Dickson.[14] There was a tacit agreement among the workers not to exceed the quota, for fear that the job would then be rerated. Deliberate restriction of output is not an uncommon occurrence.

Although the experiences reported with the use of composite measures of performance are rather skimpy, there is still a clear indication that their use may have adverse consequences for the overall performance of the organization.

Conclusion

Quantitative performance measurements—whether single, multiple, or composite—are seen to have undesirable consequences for overall organizational performance. The complexity of large organizations requires better knowledge of organizational behavior for managers to make best use of the personnel available to them. Even where performance measures are instituted purely for purposes of information, they are probably interpreted as definitions of the important aspects of that job or activity and hence have important implications for the motivation of behavior. The movitational and behavioral consequences of performance measurements are inadequately understood. Further research in this area is necessary for a better understanding of how behavior may be oriented toward optimum accomplishment of the organization's goals.

[14]F. J. Roethlisberger and William J. Dickson, *Management and the Worker* (Cambridge, Mass., 1939).

35

Is There a Public Interest Theory?

Glendon Schubert, Jr.

My investigation has been concerned primarily with the usages of the public interest concept to be found in the writings of political scientists during the last three decades. Although I recognize that members of our profession have no copyright on the term, and that, indeed, the uses of the concept by nonpolitical scientists are doubtless of vastly greater significance—at least if one is to measure importance in terms of what goes on in the world—than its appropriation and exemplification in our professional literature, nevertheless, I believe that there is a justification (other than that of convenience) to support the sample that I have chosen to examine. Without any intention of denigrating our professional reputation as a group of, shall we say, independent thinkers, I think it is fair to assume that a broad sampling of political science writings of the past generation is likely to reflect with reasonable faithfulness the larger universe of meanings attributed to the public interest concept in the behavior of American society—and I mean by this to include specifically, of course, American *political* society, which is the relevant body of data with which one must be concerned if he is interested in the contemporary theory of the public interest in the United States.

In a brief paper, it is manifestly impossible for me to discuss the data upon which my findings and conclusions are based.[1] I shall therefore direct my remaining remarks to a brief summary of my own classification

Reprinted from Carl J. Friedrich (ed.), *The Public Interest,* (New York: Atherton Press, 1966); copyright © 1962 by Atherton Press, pp. 162–76. Reprinted with permission of author and publisher.

[1]The data are presented and discussed at length in my book, *The Public Interest: A Critique of the Theory of a Political Concept* (1961).

of public interest theorists, and to an even briefer summary of the research of other critics of public interest theory.

I

In the larger study from which these conclusions are drawn, I have employed two principal bases for classifying the data, which consist of theoretical statements about the public interest in various kinds of decision-making situations.

First, I have identified five types of roles relating to decision-making by the national government; I have limited the analysis to the national level of government for the purpose of simplicity. The first of these, which I call the "constituency" factor, involves political decison-making by persons who are not public officials: the public, political parties, and interests groups. Congress, the presidency, administrators (including regulatory commissioners), and the judiciary comprise the other four factors; obviously, these are all *official* decison-makers.

The other major basis for classifying the data borrows from a conceptual scheme suggested by Wayne A. R. Leys, in an article in which he took issue with the orthodox theory of administrative discretion that had dominated thinking in the field of administrative law for the preceding half-century—and that, indeed, continues to hold sway in the writings of lawyers and political scientists alike. The godfather of orthodoxy was Ernst Freund, formerly Professor of Law at the University of Chicago, who taught that the solution to the problem of the official endowed with discretionary powers was to increase the *definiteness* of legal standards ("legal," in this context, meaning primarily statutes and administrative rules). The essence of Leys' critique is that Freund had oversimplified the problem by dealing with only one aspect of it. Leys himself would distinguish three classes of discretionary powers: (1) technical discretion, which is freedom in prescribing the rule but not the criterion or end of action, (2) discretion in prescribing the rule of action *and also* in clarifying a *vague* criterion—this is the authorization of social planning, and (3) discretion in prescribing the rule of action where the criterion of action is *ambiguous* because it is in dispute—this amounts to an instruction to the official to use his ingenuity in political mediation.[2]

I have adapted Leys' basic system of classification in the following way. I shall divide contemporary theorists of the public interest in governmental decision-making into three groups: rationalists, idealists, and realists. The rationalists, who correspond to Leys' first category, envisage a political system in which the norms are all given, in so far as public officials are concerned, and the function of political and bureaucratic officials alike is to translate the given norms into specific rules of governmental action. The idealists, who correspond to Leys' second category, conceive of the decision-making situation as requiring the exercise of authority in order to engage in social planning by clarifying a vague criterion. The realists are the counterpart of Leys' third category; these theorists state that the function of public officials (both political and bureaucratic) is to engage in the political mediation of disputes; the goals of public policy are specific but in conflict. Both the rationalists and the realists are opposed to the idealists, in the sense that both groups are positivists; but there are important differences in their respective theories of the public interest, and retaining Ley's classification system is of considerable help in discriminating among the differences.

II

The rationalists are a propublic, proparty, and anti-interest group. They postulate a common good, which reflects the presumed existence of various common—frequently majoritarian—interests. The common good (or commonweal, to use the older term) finds expression in a popular will (public will, will of the people); the common obligation of all public officials is faithfully to execute the popular will. To this extent, there is consensus among rationalists. Differences of opinion are many, however, as to the appropriate channels for authentic interpretation of the public will. Basically, there are two factions: party rationalists and popular rationalists. Party rationalists defend a stronger two-party system as the cho-

---

[2]Wayne A. R. Leys, "Ethics and Administrative Discretion," *Public Administration Review* 3 (1943): 18.

sen instrument for expressing the public will; popular rationalists would do away with political brokers and consult public opinion directly in order to discover the will of the people. Party rationalists tend to be Anglophiles with regard to the political party system, the relationship between legislators and political parties, the relationship between the executive and the legislative departments. (Incidentally, the model of British political processes envisaged by the Anglophiles bears no necessarily close correspondence to contemporary reality.) The party rationalists urge, therefore, that congressmen ought to be the disciplined members of a majority or a minority party, with the two parties dividing over issues of public policy. Popular rationalists think that congressmen ought to carry out the wishes of their constituents.

The Anglophiles believe that the presidency should be weakened and subjected to the control and policy direction of Congress, which they have already defined as the legitimate expositor of the public will. Other party rationalists, however, would link presidential leadership to a stronger two-party system, thus strengthening the presidency. Popular rationalists would accomplish the same result by casting the president in the role of instrumental leader of direct popular majorities. At this point, the distinction between party and popular rationalists disappears, because all rationalists agree that the proper function of the bureaucracy is to carry out the policy norms supplied by hierarchical superiors (Congress and the president). Administrative rationalists would use scientific management to rationalize the behavior of administrators; legal rationalists would accomplish the same result among judges according to the prescriptions of analytical jurisprudence. In both instances, administrators and judges are supposed to exercise technical discretion to carry out norms which they do not make, but which are supplied to them in the form of constitutional provisions, statutes, and executive orders—made, of course, by the representatives of the people, who implement the public will. There is a schism among rationalists regarding how best to rationalize the independent regulatory commissions; administrative rationalists want to place the commissions within the ambit of presidential control, and legal rationalists want the commissions to be subject to the administrative direction of the judiciary. Either way, it is variously argued, the commissions would become subservient to the will of the people, and the common good would be assured.

The idealists are propublic, antiparty, and anti-interest group. By "propublic," I mean, of course, that idealists support the true interests of the public, which do not necessarily coincide with the interests of the public as perceived by the public itself. Idealists believe that the public interest reposes not in the positive law made by men, but in the higher law, in natural law. They describe the public interest as a thing of substance, independent of the decisional process and absolute in its terms. They advise the public official to excogitate the true essence of the public interest by means of a mental act of extrasensory perception. This does not necessarily imply communion with the public will, because no will may yet have been formulated regarding the relevant issues; in any event, there is no assurance that the public will will be right. The public interest becomes whatever the still, small voice of conscience reveals to each official.

Such an approach renders superfluous, if not downright dangerous, such orthodox appurtenances of democratic politics as political parties and interest groups. These latter are perceived as disturbing interferences with official excogitation of truth, virtue, and justice. According to idealist thought, congressmen are responsible neither to political parties nor to their constituencies; they have a higher obligation to God and to their own consciences. Those who advocate converting the presidency into a plebiscitary dictatorship emphasize the evils of party influence; proponents of the stewardship theory of the presidency wish to surmount the pernicious demands of selfish special interest groups. In either case, the president is urged to rise above the mundane level of democratic political processes and to become the Father of his Country, the patron of all of the people, a leader of crusades both at home and abroad who should receive love and adulation—not criticism—from his subjects.

The same images recur in idealist discussion of administrative decision-making. Administrative engineers advise administrators to be creative manipulators and to resist the seductions of interest groups. Guild idealists warn—almost in the words of Madison—of the danger of party politics, and demand that administrators be given elbowroom for the exercise of craft and conscience. Substituting judges for administrators, equivalent prescriptions are offered by the spokesmen for sociological jurisprudence and scientific idealism, respectively. Thus, the themes which permeate idealist public interest theory are the invocation of natural-law ideals; hostility to the instrumentalities of democratic politics—i.e., political parties and interest groups; elitist notions of superior intelligence and wisdom; and the abetment of public officials, from the president on down, to become aggressive evangelists who will strive mightily—and ruthlessly, if necessary—in behalf of the public interest. The public interest, of course, is what the elite thinks is good for the masses. Idealist dogma, as dogma, is basically antithetical to democratic theories of governance.

The realists are a prointerest group. It is not accurate to say that they are antiparty or antipublic. However, they define "party" and "public" in such a way that these terms lose the identity that we have ascribed to them in discussing rationalist and idealist thought, to say nothing of their usual, everyday meaning in American speech. Political parties become merely a special kind of interest group, and "public" becomes segmented as "publics," in which form it, too, merges in the concept of "interest group." The realists, in other words, do not oppose the public and political parties; they devour them.

There are three major strands of realist theory, and as befits a pattern of thought so colored with pluralism, the three major strands are each primarily oriented to one or more of the other social sciences. Bentleyan realism draws predominantly upon the outmoded sociology of the turn of the century; the source of inspiration for psychological realism is self-evident; and law and economics are the wellsprings for due process-equilibrium realism.

The Bentleyans direct attention to the competition among multifarious interest groups and assert that this is the reality of political behavior at all levels of governmental (as well as nongovernmental) decision-making. The official responds to these pressures; his decisions register the thrust of the balance of power for the time being. It makes no difference whether the decision-maker is a congressman, the president, an administrator, or a judge; his role is essentially the same, although the patterns of access and the particular constellations of groups that enter the lists will vary according to the institutional context in which the official decision maker functions. To the Bentleyans, the public interest has significance only as the slogan which symbolizes the compromise resulting from a particular accommodation or adjustment of group interaction.

Psychological realists go beyond the essentially mechanical formulations of the Bentleyans, and focus attention upon the conflict of interests within the mind of the decision-maker. The rather fuzzy Bentleyan notion of unorganized groups is redefined by the psychological realists in terms of Dewey's concept of a self-conscious search for the consequences of choice. Thus, the role of official mediation described by the psychological realists adds a significant factor to the formulations of the Bentleyans: the personal value system of the decision-maker. He is limited, of course, to the values that he understands and recognizes, but he is not necessarily limited to the values with which he personally agrees. His acceptance of such broad components of the democratic ethic as the concepts of "freedom, equality, and opportunity" may lead him to take into consideration interests other than those actively pressing in behalf of specific alternatives of choice in a particular decision.

At this point, the line between psychological realism and social engineering may seem to be pretty shadowy, but the distinction is nonetheless viable. The social engineers write on a blank slate: creative manipulation leads to the fabrication of any interest group pattern needed to support the predetermined goals established by the decision-maker. Official mediation looks to the interstices of a framework provided by the interaction of activated groups and asks what the effect would be, upon this pattern, if certain other interests were weighed in the final decision. In this sense, the official mediator functions as a catalyst; but since the critical conflict is internal to the decision-maker rather than in the external environment, psychological realism's search for consequences is a more operational concept than Bentley's mystical notion of the leadership of unorganized groups. Nevertheless, both are different ways of thinking about the same processes.

As we have seen, psychological realists apply the concept of official mediation to congressmen, the president, administrators, and judges alike. There is a close functional relationship, however, among politicization, constituency size, and the limits of official horizon. In Harlan Cleveland's image, the president stands a little higher on the mountain than anyone else, and consequently can see further; district court justices and subordinate administrators, presumably, have much more limited horizons. But what of the Supreme Court? Are the justices on a separate alp? I do not think a meaningful answer to this question is possible at the present stage of underdevelopment in the measurement of power by the political science profession; but the question raises doubts, in any event, about the application of Cleveland's hierarchical image, rather than about psychological realism's concept of official mediation.

The next logical step beyond psychological realism is to prestructure the environment of decision-making and to condition the mental processes of the decision-maker. It is to these matters that the due process realists call attention. Although all realists premise their theories of the public interest upon a philosophy of ethical relativism, rather than the absolutism characteristic of rationalists and idealists, the due process-equilibrium realists lean most heavily upon what is, at least crudely, a mathematical probability theory. According to the theory, people accept democratic decision-making processes because these provide the maximum opportunity for diverse interests to seek to influence governmental decisions at all levels. A plurality of decision-making points afford access to a plurality of interests, which can seek to change or to provoke particular decisions. The job of official decision-makers—irrespective of whether we speak of congressmen, the president, administrators, or judges—is to maximize continuity and stability in public policy, or, in other words, to minimize disruption in existing patterns of accommodation among affected interests. The extent to which agitation continues, before the same or other decision-makers, provides a rough measure of the extent to which adjustment has, in terms of the equilibrium standard, been successful or "satisfactory."

Now this kind of thinking is quite conservative in its general overtones. It underscores the adjectives in advocating gradual, peaceful, evolutionary, orderly change. It does not tilt, it slants, the scales of judgment in favor of the status quo. The votaries of liberalism preach a brand of ethics in which most Americans feel they ought to believe; but it is not a way of life, nor is it the basis for our system of government. It is the Constitution, not the Declaration of Independence, that provides the model for the American political system. The general model leaves largely unspecified, however, the structure and functioning of decision-making processes in Congress, the presidency, administrative agencies, and the courts. It is particularly upon administrative decision-making processes that the due process-equilibrium realists have focused their attention.

Instead of leaving the "representativeness" of the administrator's personal value system, or the particular configuration of interests in a specific type of decision, up to chance, due process theory would so structure both of these factors in the decision-making process as to maximize the probability that the resulting decision has been made, in fact, after consideration of all relevant interests and perspectives. Due process theorists do not claim that any particular substantive result will automatically be the "right" decision; they do not guarantee that every decision arrived at after such full consideration will be "in the public interest." This is the point that seems so difficult for absolutists, who live in a world of dichotomies, to comprehend. What the due process theorists do claim is that decisions reached as a result of such full consideration are more likely to meet the test of equilibrium theory—i.e., "satisfaction," acceptance, and the like—and to do so most of the time, than are decisions arrived at as the necessary consequence, at least in a statistical sense, of processes that assure less than full consideration. *Decisions that are the product of a process of full consideration are most likely to be decisions in the public interest.*

There has been some, but very limited, application of the concept of "administrative due process" to congressional, presidential, and judicial decision-making. Although some critics have decried placing "the organization man in the presidency," the fact remains that the applicability of the model of "administrative due process" to these other decision-makers is a function of bureaucratization of congressional, presidential, and judicial decision-making processes. Certainly, there is considerable evidence to support the proposition that the trend in each of these areas is towards greater bureaucratization. To this extent, the potential extension of the public interest theory of the due process-equilibrium realists is correspondingly enhanced.

III

Two decades elapsed after Beard's historical studies of the national interest as a concept, before any systematic analyses of the public interest concept appeared in the literature of political science. Beginning in 1955, however, several political scientists and philosophers have ventured independent (from each other, and from my own work) exploratory critical essays on the subject of public interest theory. A survey of the findings of these critics suggests, however, that they have little to add to the results of my own investigation of public interest theory. Some of them (e.g., Banfield, Sorauf, Leys and Perry) suggest differing perspectives from which the literature may be viewed and appraised. Such alternative formulations do not appear to lead to insights or to comprehension of public interest theory significantly different from that produced by the conceptual schema that I have employed, however. Any systematic typology may have utility for analytical purposes, but no matter how the literature is classified and the data are compared, no systematic body of "public interest theory" appears extant. American writers in the field of political science have evolved neither a unified nor a consistent theory to describe how the public interest is defined in governmental decision-making; they have not constructed theoretical models with the degree of precision and specificity necessary if such models are to be used as description of, or as a guide to, the actual behavior of real people. A theory of the public interest in governmental decision making ought to describe a relationship between concepts of the public interest and official behavior in such terms that it might be possible to attempt to validate empirically hypotheses concerning the relationship. If extant theory does not lend itself to such uses, it is difficult to comprehend the justification for teaching students of political science that subservience to the public interest is a relevant norm of official responsibility.

Moreover, critical investigation has failed to reveal a statement of public interest theory that offers much promise as a guide either to public officials who are supposed to make decisions in the public interest or to research scholars who might wish to investigate the extent to which governmental decisions are empirically made in the public interest. For either of the latter purposes, it would be necessary to have operational definitions of the public interest concept; and neither my analysis nor that of other contemporary critics suggests that the public interest theory prevalent in America today either is or is readily capable of being made operational.

IV

Rationalist theory has limited relevance to the empirical world, since it speaks primarily of faithful execution of decisions that somebody other than the actor has made; it offers little guidance to the decision-maker who is expected to make policy in the face of the conflicting demands of an articulate and organized clientele. In fact, the more important the decision—and as a usual consequence, the more complex the decision-making milieu—the less guidance has rationalist theory to offer. It might, for instance, indicate what would be responsible presidential behavior in signing commissions for the promotional lists of the armed forces; it most certainly will not be very helpful to the president in deciding whether and how to get a man to the moon. To get back down to earth, it will not even tell him when, and in terms of what criteria, he should exercise his veto power, since the Constitution clearly did not presume that the president would take his orders from Congress (or vice versa) in exercising his power to grant or to withhold his approval of enrolled bills —even if we assume, with the rationalists, that constitutional intent is the fundamental consideration in such circumstances. The theoretical apparatus of the rationalists, however elegant it otherwise may be, is limited precisely by their insistence that a science of political behavior cannot be concerned with political choice. The model constructed by the rationalists is a sausage machine: the public will is poured into one end and out of the other end drop neat little segments of the public interest, each wrapped in its own natural casing.

Idealist theory, to the contrary, speaks precisely to the macroscopic type of decision with which the rationalists cannot be concerned. But what does idealism have to offer, other than moralistic exhortations to do good? It leaves the decision-maker to rely upon his own best lights whether these are conceived of as a Platonic soul, a Calvinistic conscience, or as Catholic natural law. It may be that any of these provides the best standards available for guiding some decision-makers in some situations; but labeling as "the public interest" either such a process or the result that it produces adds nothing to what we would have—except from the point of view of the engineering of consent—if there were no such phrase as the public interest. With or without the label, we must rely upon the prior political socialization and the ethical preconditioning of the individual decision-maker for whatever kind or degree of responsibility that ensues in such circumstances.

Moreover, the concept of the public interest logically is irrelevant to decision-making in accordance with idealist theory, in which ultimate obligations and responsibility are nonpolitical. It is neither to the public nor to hierarchical superiors nor to the affected clientele that the decision maker looks for guidance; his responsibility lies in faithfulness to his personal perception of other abstractions, such as "justice," that are at least equally as devoid of a predictable content as "the public interest." Unless the idealists are prepared to advocate the "brainwashing" of candidates for public employment to assure the establishment of a single party line among government officials, the practical utility of their theory would seem to be quite limited unless, in the alternative, they can explain how men with differing value orientations are to commune with the infinite and come up with common answers. Idealist theory really implies an officialdom of supermen, which in turn evokes all the difficulties to be encountered in breeding a race of official heroes—or, if it makes a difference, of heroic officials. None of the idealist writers in recent years seem to have improved very much upon Plato's discussion of this subject, nor do they appear to have resolved the age-old dilemma: how to keep the tyrants benevolent.

Realists advise the decision-maker that his job is to resolve the conflicting claims of competing interest groups, and to keep the boat from rocking so far as possible. Except on the merely mechanical and purportedly descriptive level of naive Bentleyanism, he should do this with as much consideration as he is capable of giving, or as he can be made capable of giving—by the structuring of the decision-making situation—to the probable consequences of his choice. The principal difficulty with the theory, even in its most sophisticated form, lies in its generality, for the due process-equilibrium realists describe wondrous engines (including the human mind) into which are poured all sorts of miscellaneous ingredients which, after a decent period of agitation, are spewed forth from time to time, each bearing a union label reading: "Made in the Public Interest in the U.S.A." But their hero is neither the Charlie Chaplin of modern times nor Prometheus unbound; he is the counterpart of the politician described by Herring in *The Politics of Democracy.*

The problem facing realist theorists is to demonstrate how it is possible to bridge the hiatus between the ideal they posit and the empirical world. It is true that the statements of at least the administrative-due process realists do suggest the possibility of constructing more detailed models of specific decisional processes in particular agencies with iden-tifiable functions to perform. Such models, whether as descriptions of existing agencies or as blueprints for reorganized or new agencies, might lend themselves, at least in principle, to empirical verification. Assuming, for the sake of argument, that the paperwork can be done, it would still be necessary to construct and implement, upon an experimental basis, at least one model prefabricated political decision-making process; bud-get estimating might be a good place to begin. Assuming that this also could be done, ahead lie questions of continuous reorganization to cope with predictable problems of obsolescence, the development of more genuinely interchangeable human cogs, and—not least—the impatience of the American public after it becomes known to the world that the Russians have perfected a successfully functioning (and much bigger) organization of the same type several months before the American proto-model is announced. And that announcement, we might as well antici-pate, will come at the same time that the American team of responsible budget analysts is about to produce its first underbalanced budget—which will be made, needless to say, in the public interest.

V

It may be somewhat difficult for some persons to accept the conclu-sion that there is no public-interest theory worthy of the name and that the concept itself is significant primarily as a datum of politics. As such, it may at times fulfill a "hair shirt" function, to borrow Sorauf's felicitous phrase; it may also be nothing more than a label attached indiscrimi-nately to a miscellany of particular compromise of the moment. In either case, "the public interest" neither adds to nor detracts from the theory and methods otherwise presently available for analyzing political behav-ior.

I recognize also that there may be some who will consider this paper incomplete, since I have criticized the public interest theories of other persons without making any attempt to "do something positive" by sug-gesting a public interest concept of my own. The expectation that the iconoclast ought to pick up the pieces and build a new and better temple on the ruins of the old runs like a steel thread through the moral fiber of most Americans, including academicians. I would dispute the premise. I would also argue, in any event, that if the public interest concept makes no operational sense, notwithstanding the efforts of a generation of capable scholars, then political scientists might better spend their time nurturing concepts that offer greater promise of becoming useful tools in the scientific study of political responsibility.

36

An Electronic
Data Processing System
Bill G. Schumacher

The purpose of this appendix is not to explain the electronic operations of an EDP system, but rather to present an orderly description of the basic units and their functions in such a manner as to dispel any mystery about such systems. An EDP system could be explained first by considering its application; yet, such an approach would be too broad. If a problem can be defined and the required resource employed, then the problem can be solved.

To begin such a task, there is a need to define basic terminology. The basic elements in both the machine and man portions of the relationship should be identified. The present method of application development should also be examined. EDP systems are usually divided into "hardware," which pertains to the machine elements or units, and "software," which includes the human elements or the instructional devices, manipulative programs, and the like.

Basic terminology

There are two basic types of computers: digital and analog. Data processing is associated with the digital. The digital computer, as its name implies, is a counting machine; it receives and manipulates numerical data, and can produce output made up of alphabetic and numerical characters. The analog computer, as its name implies, represents vari-

Reprinted with permission of author and publisher. From Bill G. Schumacher, *Computer Dynamics in Public Administration,* ® 1967, Spartan Books, New York, pp. 163–71.

ables through physical analogies. Of the two, the digital is more common. The slide rule is a simple analog computer; the abacus is a simple digital computer.

The word "system" is often used in the rational approach to administration. In this discussion of electronic data processing systems, a system is an organized collection of parts united by a regulated interaction.

Hardware

Input

The parts of the machine system of a computer may be divided into input, processing, and output. The input portion of the computer usually consists of a machine which converts punched holes in cards to electronic impulses that can be machine interpreted. This input unit is called a card reader.

The use of 80-column cards is almost standard, as is the rectangular punch through which the machine receives the electronic signal. Most data are deliberately created by key punching, an action performed on a Printing Card Punch. Using a keyboard, the operator electrically produces a punched hole and prints the character of the punch in any of the 80 columns. The validity of the operation can be checked by a similar machine called a Verifier. The results of these two operations are data that are almost error free. There are a multitude of other mechanical and electronic ways to punch cards, including the use of the computer itself. The input device described as a card reader is usually associated in one unit with a punching device. In addition to punched cards, other media can be used, such as magnetic tape, paper tape, magnetic ink characters, optical character sensing, etc. The basic machine input unit is usually the card reader/punch.

Processing

After the data are converted into electronic signals, processing or handling of data begins. It consists of storing and retrieving data, controlling the validity of the data, manipulating data logically or arithmetically, as well as performing the desired operation upon the data. All of this is carried out in a unit known as a processing unit.

Data storage and retrieval. Storage of data refers to placing given electronic signals for letters or numbers in identified locations in the system. These locations or electronic "pigeonholes" in the processing unit are called core storage. The number of individual letters or numbers that can be stored is commonly measured by the thousand or "kilo." The core-storage capacity of the computer is designated by the abbreviation "K." A processing unit having a capacity of 8000 storage locations would be called an 8K computer. Other storage devices can be connected either directly or indirectly with the central processing unit. The most common direct or inline types are the sequential and random access. The sequential are magnetic tape units, which operate like a tape recorder. To use a musical analogy, data, like notes, can be scanned in the same sequence in which they were recorded. On the other hand, the random access unit is like a juke box. The data are stored on disks that are arranged vertically. The random access unit can recover a particular item or group of characters from any part of any disk.

Each possible location for a single character is numbered. This number is called the address. By referring to this address it is possible to place a character at a given spot or to recover a character stored there; however, it is much easier to tag or label the address of each individual or group of characters and refer to them only by this name. The computer, if properly instructed, can locate the label, the label address, and then the data. Data retrieval is thus possible on an anthropocentric basis. The elapsed time or access time to recover data in this manner can be measured in billionths of a second. The administrator-user should be concerned with the validity, security, and accessibility of the data rather than with the electronic mechanics of storage and retrieval.

Control of data. While the processing unit provides basic storage, it also controls data as they are processed. This checking process is automatic in some instances. For example, the hardware is constantly checking the validity of the signals which it is handling to ensure that no change occurs. One such check is called bit parity. This is one of the reasons why high-fidelity data are a characteristic of the system. Most computers also have a marginal check. This is an automatic control feature, a preventive maintenance check, that locates defective units in the system. The computer can also be instructed to double-check any item, but the most important control feature of this nature is its capability of controlling its own operations. Once correctly instructed, the computer follows the plan of the user with speed and accuracy and without fatigue or prejudice.

Manipulation of data. With high-fidelity control the computer handles the data as required. Basically, three functions are executed by the processing unit. The first is the arithmetic and logical function. The machine is capable through proper instructions of adding, subtracting, multiplying, and dividing. It can also perform a function based on a condition. For example, if two groups of characters are equal, certain operations or sequences can be performed. If other conditions are tested, then other operations or sequences can be involved, etc.

Secondly, the data in the same form in which they were introduced, or with alterations resulting from arithmetic or logical manipulation, can be transferred or moved from one designated area to another designated area. Finally, the operation of all parts of the hardware system function is designated by the user. These operational functions include starting, stopping, input/output operations, etc.

The processing unit is, therefore, the prime apparatus of the system. It is here that the plan of the user is executed upon the data. The interrelation of these functions gives the user a highly potent information system.

The future of manipulation of data is in the heuristic area. Simon envisions EDP systems capable of judging their own performance, recognizing errors, and making necessary adjustments.

Output

The principal output unit of a computer system is the printer. This device is basically mechanical and usually prints at a rate ranging from 400 to 1200 lines a minute. Another standard output is the punched card. This can be produced by the reader/punch unit, as mentioned above. The punched cards produced by the computer have holes only, which are not interpreted into print. If it is necessary for humans to read the cards, they can be interpreted by a separate device, which prints on the card, or on a separate listing, the characters which the punched holes represent. Some keypunching devices can perform this same function. The speed and accuracy with which the computer punches cards make it an unrivaled source of this type of output. Since the printer and the card reader/punch are in separate units, it is possible for most basic computer systems to print and punch essentially at the same time. In addition to these basic output media, additional equipment can produce magnetic tape, paper tape, cathode ray images, drawings, or maps.

Some devices have both input and output capabilities. Console type-writers and other terminal units can communicate directly with a computer system. Both input/output devices as well as individual output units can be used at a distance from the basic computer system. The use of normal and special telephonic systems allows for teleprocessing of data.

The speed of the processing unit often exceeds that of the input/output devices. Optical scanning of data could increase the input speed of future systems, and photochemical printing techniques will possibly operate at 6000 lines per minute. The future of this method as a printer of computer output should be outstanding.

Software

Software is a collective name for the devices that instruct the computer. The various units of the computer are controlled by electronic signals, which are initiated by certain symbols coded into some input media. The collection of these symbols is called machine language. This vocabulary is designed for the convenience of the mechanism rather than that of man, the user. In fact, to use these symbols in the sequence required is very tedious.

In order for man to use the apparatus more readily, intermediate languages which are easier for man have been developed. These devices generate anthropocentric codes into apparatocentric codes. Some have a one-code-for-one-function relationship; these are called assembly programs. Others are capable of translating one anthropocentric code into several machine functions; these are compilers. In both assembly programs and compilers the entire problem must be stated in exact detail before the computer will respond properly. There are other language methods, but the compiler is the most common. Regardless of the method used, the primary unit of the software package is the language program.

A language is, therefore, a general problem form. The products of its utilization are the specific "machine language" instructions presented to the computer for substantive outputs. These plans of instruction are programs. The elements of the program relate to the machine unit functions and are arranged in groups or routines. Such arrangement allows for repetition of routines without a redundancy of instructions. The total collection of programs, together with the language device, makes up the software package.

Systems development

Since the cost of machine and man hours is considerable, adequate preparation is needed to avoid waste. This preparation is called systems development, or "systems." It is a rational development of computer programs to produce certain defined output. Present systems techniques are somewhat inefficient. At the point of translation from a human problem to a machine problem there are many chances for error. The administrator cannot usually translate his problem directly to the computer because of the difficulty of using present languages. Since he must allow systems personnel to translate his plan to the machine, there is danger of professional or transcription error. All through the process the input, processing, and output instructions are jumbled at the caprice of the systems personnel. The development of a software system should be deductive in methodology. It usually includes a feasibility study, systems analysis, programming, and testing.

Feasibility study

Feasibility studies are becoming less important; most people realize that application depends as much on ingenuity as on resources. Anticipated savings were the criteria for judgment of the results of many early systems. Quite often savings did not materialize. Instead the competence of the organization increased. Some feasibility studies have had the detrimental effect of developing micro rather than macro systems.

Systems analysis

Systems analysis is sometimes completed concurrently with the feasibility study. Regardless of when it is done, it is a highly underestimated part of systems development. Without proper definition the problem will never be solved. This direction toward specific results is often lacking because of the failure of administrators to be involved. Lacking this support, the systems analyst often has to include inefficient, parasite routines in order to gain staff support necessary for survival of the system.

With the support of the administrator the systems analyst can determine the criteria necessary to judge the desired results. These criteria should not be primarily cost but, rather, maximum results. Quite often the latter can be cheaper than just automation of manual systems. Automation of the entire process should be the goal. When a particular process requires that man be used on a routine basis, such a process should be re-examined for the possibility of using the computer. Practically any job can be automated, if the job has been clearly defined.

The deductive analysis proceeds by defining the end results, then the intermediate results, and finally the source data necessary to produce both. Source data can best be obtained by automation. If the data are not in the form of some input media, the computer can assist by producing every variation of data that is expected. (It was necessary to know these variations before the problem could be defined.) Those cards not reflecting the variation that actually does occur should be destroyed. To automate source data ensures high-fidelity results. The same source data should be used by all levels of the organization.

This de novo type of definition is the preferred method. Sometimes it is necessary to define an existing system. This can be done by searching the regulations, manuals, procedure guides, and job descriptions. But this is not always productive. Interviews with key personnel are helpful, provided the discussions follow a predetermined line of questioning.

Systems people in an organization are usually limited in number. This delays the development of a total system and encourages the more routine applications. This situation can be avoided by training personnel in each subsection of the organization in basic systems analysis. Not only does this give the resulting system the characteristic of being a local product, but also the system analyst extends his production through consultation rather than through operation. Such training sessions can include the historic background of scientific management and automation, present systems techniques, and finally the analysis of some system of the organization.

This should be done in narrative as well as graphic form. Quite often it is necessary to teach the techniques of flow-charting. A flow chart is a collection of graphic symbols which show the interrelationship of each function or unit of a proposed solution. These symbols are connected by arrows which indicate the flow from source documents to results. When completed, it is the skeletal framework of the processes and resources to be employed. The complete systems presentation should include a flow chart and a narrative analysis. The latter should include exhibits of the source documents and output samples. Such documentation can save the professional system analysts weeks of work.

Programming

Once the problem has been defined, preferably de novo, the interaction with the machine technology begins. By using the analyst's report, the programmer writes the instructions for the input, processing, and output functions required. This ordered listing of the individual and groups of instructions is called "coding." Once it is complete the list is keypunched and verified. If the program was coded in a language other than machine language, the next step is to take the deck of cards (source deck) containing the instructions and have them processed by the computer using the language compiler, which changes them into machine code. Some errors of omission or commission on the part of the program can be determined by a diagnostic listing produced at this time. The resolving of these errors is called "debugging." When the program is essentially error free, the deck of machine codes (object deck) is ready for machine operation with typical input data.

The testing period continues until every variable condition has been tested. The program may be operated parallel with any other similar system. During this time documentation and training aids are finalized. The importance of this process cannot be underestimated.

Summary

These hardware and software elements should be constantly developed into more efficient systems. The greatest dysfunction of the technology is the absence of enough persons who are knowledgeable in its use. This can be enhanced by improving the languages, achieving better functional division of the technology, and offering more extensive training. With these improvements the full ingenuity of the administrative-user can be utilized.

37

Leadership in Administration

Philip Selznick

The argument of this essay is quite simply stated: *The executive becomes a statesman as he makes the transition from administrative management to institutional leadership.* This shift entails a reassessment of his own tasks and of the needs of the enterprise. It is marked by a concern for the evolution of the organization as a whole, including its changing aims and capabilities. In a word, it means viewing the organization as an institution. To understand the nature of institutional leadership, we must have some notion of the meaning and significance of the term "institution" itself.

Organizations and institutions

The most striking and obvious thing about an administrative organization is its formal system of rules and objectives. Here tasks, powers,

Reprinted with permission of author and publisher. From *Leadership in Administration* by Philip Selznick. Copyright © 1957 by Harper & Row, Publishers, Inc., pp. 4–6, 7–9, 10–11, 12 13–19, 20–22, 24–25, 26, 27–28. Footnotes have been renumbered.

and procedures are set out according to some officially approved pattern. This pattern purports to say how the work of the organization is to be carried on, whether it be producing steel, winning votes, teaching children, or saving souls. The organization thus designed is a technical instrument for mobilizing human energies and directing them toward set aims. We allocate tasks, delegate authority, channel communication, and find some way of co-ordinating all that has been divided up and parceled out. All this is conceived as an exercise in engineering; it is governed by the related ideals of rationality and discipline.

The term "organization" thus suggests a certain bareness, a lean, no-nonsense system of consciously co-ordinated activities.[1] It refers to an *expendable tool,* a rational instrument engineered to do a job. An "institution," on the other hand, is more nearly a natural product of social needs and pressures—a responsive, adaptive organism. This distinction is a matter of analysis, not of direct description. It does not mean that any given enterprise must be either one or the other. While an extreme case may closely approach either an "ideal" organization or an "ideal" institution, most living associations resist so easy a classification. They are complex mixtures of both designed and responsive behavior.

When we say that the Standard Oil Company or the Department of Agriculture is to be studied as an institution, we usually mean that we are going to pay some attention to its history and to the way it has been influenced by the social environment. Thus we may be interested in how its organization adapts itself to existing centers of power in the community, often in unconscious ways; from what strata of society its leadership is drawn and how this affects policy; how it justifies its existence ideologically. We may ask what underlying need in the larger community—not necessarily expressed or recognized by the people involved—is filled by the organization or by some of its practices. Thus, the phrase "as a social institution" suggests an emphasis on problems and experiences that are not adequately accounted for within the narrower framework of administrative analysis.

[1]C. I. Barnard, *The Functions of the Executive* (Cambridge: Harvard University Press, 1938), p. 73.

* * *

The relation of an organization to the external environment is, how ever, only one source of institutional experience. There is also an internal social world to be considered. An organization is a group of living human beings. The formal or official design for living never completely accounts for what the participants do. It is always supplemented by what is called the "informal structure," which arises as the individual brings into play his own personality, his special problems and interests. Formal relations co-ordinate roles or specialized activities, not persons. Rules apply to foremen and machinists, to clerks, sergeants, and vice-presidents, yet no durable organization is able to hold human experience to these formally defined roles. In actual practice, men tend to interact as many-faceted persons, adjusting to the daily round in ways that spill over the neat boundaries set by their assigned roles.

The formal, technical system is therefore never more than a part of the living enterprise we deal with in action. The persons and groups who make it up are not content to be treated as manipulable or expendable. As human beings and not mere tools they have their own need for self-protection and self-fulfillment—needs that may either sustain the formal system or undermine it. These human relations are a great reservoir of energy. They may be directed in constructive ways toward desired ends or they may become recalcitrant sources of frustration. One objective of sound management practice is to direct and control these internal social pressures.

The relations outlined on an organization chart provide a framework within which fuller and more spontaneous human behavior takes place. The formal system may draw upon that behavior for added strength; it will in its turn be subordinated to personal and group egotism. Every official and employee will try to use his position to satisfy his psychological needs. This may result in a gain for the organization if he accepts its goals and extends himself in its interests. But usually, even in the best circumstances, some price is paid in organizational rigidity.

Similarly, when a technically devised organizational unit becomes a social group—a unity of persons rather than of technicians—newly deployable energy is created; but this, too, has inherently divisive and frustrating potentialities. For the unity of persons breaks through the neat confines of rational organization and procedure; it creates new strivings, primarily for the protection of group integrity, that exert an unceasing influence on the formal pattern of delegation and control. This search for security and fulfillment is reflected in the struggle of individuals for place and preferment, in rivalry among units within the organization, and in commitment to ingrained ways of behaving. These are universal features of organizational life, and the problems they raise are perennial ones.

Of these problems, organizational rivalry may be the most important. Such rivalry mobilizes individual egotism while binding it to group goals. This may create a powerful force, threatening the unity of the larger enterprise. Hence it is that within every association there is the same basic constitutional problem, the same need for an accommodative balance between fragmentary group interests and the aims of the whole, as exists in any polity. The problem is aggravated in a special-purpose enterprise because the aims of the whole are more sharply defined, and therefore more vulnerable to divisive activity, than in the natural community.

* * *

Once we turn our attention to the emergence of natural social processes within a formal association, and the pressure of these on policy, we are quickly led to a wide range of interesting questions. Thus, the tendency for a group to develop fixed ways of perceiving itself and the world, often unconsciously, is of considerable importance. With this sort of problem in mind, a study of a military intelligence agency, for example can go beyond the more routine aspects of administrative efficiency. The study should also consider whether any institutional factors affect the ability of the agency *to ask the right questions.* Are its questions related to a general outlook, a tacit image of itself and its task? Is this image tradition-bound? Is it conditioned by long-established organized practices? Is there a self-restricted outlook due to insecurities that motivate a safe (but narrow and compartmentalized) concept of military intelligence? A study of these problems would explore the conditions under which organizational self-protection induces *withdrawal* from rivalry rather than participation in it. More needs to be known about such pathological withdrawal for it, too—no less than excessive rivalry itself—may frustrate the rational development of organizations and programs.

The dynamics of organizational rivalry—not the mere documentation of its existence—has received very little systematic attention. This is a good example of an area of experience not adequately accounted for within the conceptual framework of administrative analysis. Organizational struggles are usually thought of as adventitious and subversive. This outlook inhibits the development of a body of knowledge *about* organization rivalry, e.g., stating the conditions and consequences of factional victory, defeat, and withdrawal, or indicating the way external pressures on an organization are reflected in internal controversy.

* * *

Taking account of both internal and external social forces, institutional studies emphasize the *adaptive* change and evolution of organizational forms and practices. In these studies the story is told of new patterns emerging and old ones declining, not as a result of conscious design but as natural and largely unplanned adaptations to new situations. The most interesting and perceptive analyses of this type show the organization responding to a problem posed by its history, an adaptation significantly changing the role and character of the organization. Typically, institutional analysis sees legal or formal changes as recording and regularizing an evolution that has already been substantially completed informally.

* * *

This emphasis on adaptive change suggests that in attempting to understand large and relatively enduring organizations we must draw upon what we know about natural communities. In doing so we are led to consider such matters as the following:

1. The development of administrative ideologies as conscious and unconscious devices of communication and self-defense. Just as doctrinal orthodoxies help natural communities to maintain social order, so, too, in administrative agencies, technical programs and procedures are often elaborated into official "philosophies." These help to build a homogeneous staff and ensure institutional continuity. Sometimes they are created and manipulated self-consciously, but most administrative ideologies emerge in spontaneous and unplanned ways, as natural aids to organizational security. A well-formulated doctrine is remarkably handy for boosting internal morale, communicating the bases for decisions, and rebuffing outside claims and criticisms.

2. The creation and protection of elites. In the natural community elites play a vital role in the creation and protection of values. Similarly, in organizations, and especially those that have or strive for some special identity, the formation of elites is a practical problem of the first importance. Specialized academies, selective recruiting, and many other devices help to build up the self-consciousness and the confidence of present and potential leaders. However, again as in the natural community, counter-pressures work to break down the insulation of these elites and to warp their self-confidence. A problem of institutional leadership, as of statesmanship generally, is to see that elites do exist and function while inhibiting their tendency to become sealed off and to be more concerned with their own fate than with that of the enterprise as a whole. One answer, as in the Catholic Church, is to avoid selectivity in the *choice* of leaders while emphasizing intensive indoctrination in their *training*. The whole problem of leadership training, and more generally of forming and maintaining elites, should receive a high priority in scientific studies of organization and policy.

3. The emergence of contending interest-groups, many of which bid for dominant influence in society. The simple protection of their identity, and the attempt to control the conditions of existence, stimulate the normal push and pull of these groups; and the bid for social dominance

is reflected in the crises that signify underlying shifts in the distribution of power. The same natural processes go on within organizations, often stimulating the rivalry of formal administrative units, sometimes creating factions that cut across the official lines of communication and command. Here, too, there is normal day-to-day contention, and there is the attempt to become the dominant or "senior" unit, as when a personnel department replaces an accounting division as the source from which general managers are recruited; or when a sales organization comes to dominate the manufacturing organization in product design. These changes cannot, however, be accounted for as simply the products of bureaucratic maneuver. The outcome of the contest is conditioned by a shift in the character and role of the enterprise. Many internal controversies, although stimulated by rather narrow impulses, provide the channels through which broader pressures on the organization are absorbed.

The natural tendencies cited here—the development of defensive ideologies, the dependence of institutional values on the formation and sustaining of elites, the existence of internal conflicts expressing group interests—only illustrate the many elements that combine to form the social structure of an organization. Despite their diversity, these forces have a unified effect. In their operation we see the way group values are formed, for together they define the commitments of the organization and give it a distinctive identity. In other words, to the extent that they are natural communities, organizations have a history; and this history is compounded of discernible and repetitive modes of responding to internal and external pressures. As these responses crystallize into definite patterns, a social structure emerges. The more fully developed its social structure, the more will the organization become valued for itself, not as a tool but as an institutional fulfillment of group integrity and aspiration.

Institutionalization is a *process*. It is something that happens to an organization over time, reflecting the organization's own distinctive history, the people who have been in it, the groups it embodies and the vested interests they have created, and the way it has adapted to its environment. For purposes of this essay, the following point is of special importance: The degree of institutionalization depends on how much leeway there is for personal and group interaction. The more precise an organization's goals, and the more specialized and technical its operations, the less opportunity will there be for social forces to affect its development. A university has more such leeway than most businesses, because its goals are less clearly defined and it can give more free play to internal forces and historical adaptation. But no organization of any duration is completely free of institutionalization. Later we shall argue that leadership is most needed among those organizations, and in those periods of organizational life, where there is most freedom from the determination of decisions by technical goals and methods.

In what is perhaps its most significant meaning, "to institutionalize" is to *infuse with value* beyond the technical requirements of the task at hand. The prizing of social machinery beyond its technical role is largely a reflection of the unique way in which it fulfills personal or group needs. Whenever individuals become attached to an organization or a way of doing things as persons rather than as technicians, the result is a prizing of the device for its own sake. From the standpoint of the committed person, the organization is changed from an expendable tool into a valued source of personal satisfaction. Some manifestations of this process are quite obvious; others are less easily recognized. It is a commonplace that administrative changes are difficult when individuals have become habituated to and identified with long-established procedures. For example, the shifting of personnel is inhibited when business relations become personal ones and there is resistance to any change that threatens rewarding ties. A great deal of energy in organizations is expended in a continuous effort to preserve the rational, technical, impersonal system against such counter-pressures.

Less generally recognized is the effect of this personal involvement on the rational choice of methods and goals. We have already hinted at the importance of "self-images" in, say, restricting the outlook of military-intelligence and similar agencies. These self-images are natural products of organizational experience. They provide the individual with an ordered approach to his day-to-day problems, a way of responding to the world consistently yet involuntarily, in accordance with approved perspectives yet without continuous reference to explicit and formalized rules. This consistent outlook or orientation is indicated when organizational names are applied to individuals as labels for characteristic ways of thinking and working, as when we speak of a "regular army" or a "Foreign Service" man. By long habituation, sometimes also as a result of aggressive indoc-trination, the individual absorbs a way of perceiving and evaluating his experience. This reduces his anxiety by lending the world of fact a famil-iar cast; and it helps assure an easy conformity with established practice.

As in the case of all institutionalization, the development and trans-mission of self-images is useful but potentially frustrating. To mold the minds of individuals according to a definite pattern creates a homoge-neous organization, and this is an enormous aid to communication. A broad context of "understood" meanings ensures that in the perfor-mance of assigned tasks the spirit as well as the letter will be observed. Similarly, emotional identification with the organization creates re-sources of energy that may increase day-to-day effort and, especially, be summoned in times of crisis or threat. But these commitments are costly. They bind the organization to specific aims and procedures, often greatly limiting the freedom of the leadership to deploy its resources, and reduc-ing the capacity of the organization to survive under new conditions.

The test of infusion with value is *expendability.* If an organization is merely an instrument, it will be readily altered or cast aside when a more efficient tool becomes available. Most organizations are thus expend-able. When value infusion takes place, however, there is a resistance to change. People feel a sense of personal loss; the "identity" of the group or community seems somehow to be violated; they bow to economic or technological considerations only reluctantly, with regret. A case in point is the perennial effort to save San Francisco's cable cars from replace-ment by more economical forms of transportation. The Marine Corps has this institutional halo, and it resists administrative measures that would submerge its identity. In 1950, President Truman became irritated with political pressure favoring Marine Corps membership on the Joint Chiefs of Staff. He wrote a letter calling the marines the navy's "police force" and likening their "propaganda machine" to Stalin's. This raised a storm of protest which ended with a presidential apology.

From the standpoint of social systems rather than persons, organiza-tions become infused with value as they come to symbolize the communi-ty's aspirations, its sense of identity. . . .

Both personal and social commitments combine to weaken the

purely technical significance of organizations. Beginning as a tool, the organization derives added meaning from the psychological and social functions it performs. In doing so it becomes valued for itself. To be sure, the personal and group bonds that make for institutionalization are not wholly separable. As the individual works out his special problems, seeking his own satisfactions, he helps to tie the organization into the community's institutional network. Personal incentives may spark this absorption, and provide the needed energy; but its character and direction will be shaped by values already existent in the community at large. Similarly, although organizational controversy may be directly motivated by narrow personal and group aims, the contending programs usually reflect ideological differences in the larger arena. In this way, the internal struggle for power becomes a channel through which external environmental forces make themselves felt. This is, indeed, a classic function of the American political party system; but less formal and recognized groupings within administrative organizations follow the same pattern. Organizations do not so much create values as embody them. As this occurs, the organization becomes increasingly institutionalized.

The transformation of expendable technical organizations into institutions is marked by a *concern for self-maintenance*. A living association blends technical aims and procedures with personal desires and group interests. As a result, various elements in the association have a stake in its continued existence. Moreover, the aims of the organization may require a certain permanence and stability. There is a need to accommodate internal interest and adapt to outside forces, in order to maintain the organization as a "going concern," minimize risks, and achieve long-run as well as short-run objectives. An important sign of this development is that the leaders become security-conscious and are often willing to sacrifice quick returns for the sake of stability. The history of the labor movement is replete with efforts to win union security through provisions for compulsory membership and automatic deduction of dues payments from wages. These objectives look to the long-run maintenance of the union rather than to immediate gains for the members.

There is a close relation between "infusion with value" and "self-maintenance." As an organization acquires a self, a distinctive identity, it becomes an institution. This involves the taking on of values, ways of acting and believing that are deemed important for their own sake. From then on self-maintenance becomes more than bare organizational survival; it becomes a struggle to preserve the uniqueness of the group in the face of new problems and altered circumstances.

To summarize: organizations are technical instruments, designed as means to definite goals. They are judged on engineering premises; they are expendable. Institutions, whether conceived as groups or practices, may be partly engineered, but they have also a "natural" dimension. They are products of interaction and adaptation; they become the receptacles of group idealism; they are less readily expendable.

Some premises about leadership

Leadership is not a familiar, everyday idea, as readily available to common sense as to social science. It is a slippery phenomenon that eludes them both. What leaders do is hardly self-evident. And it is likely that much failure of leadership results from an inadequate understanding of its true nature and tasks. Most of this essay will be devoted to identifying and analyzing the chief functions of institutional leadership. By way of introduction, however, it may be helpful to state a few simple guiding ideas here.

1. *Leadership is a kind of work done to meet the needs of a social situation.* Possibly there are some individuals more likely to be leaders than others, possessed of distinguishing personal traits or capacities.[2] Whether or not this is so, we shall here be concerned with leadership as

---

[2]This problem has received considerable attention, with largely negative but still inconclusive results. See Ralph M. Stogdill, "Personal Factors Associated with Leadership: A Survey of the Literature," *J. Psychology* 25 (1948): 35–71; also William O. Jenkins, "A Review of Leadership Studies with Particular Reference to Military Problems," *Psychological Bulletin* 44 (1947): 54–77.

a specialized form of activity, a kind of work or function. Identifying what leaders do certainly bears on (and is perhaps indispensable to) the discovery of requisite personal attributes; but the questions are of a different kind and may be treated separately.

* * *

2. *Leadership is not equivalent to office-holding or high prestige or authority or decision-making.* It is not helpful to identify leadership with whatever is done by people in high places. The activity we have in mind may or may not be engaged in by those who are formally in positions of authority. This is inescapable if we are to develop a theory that will be useful in diagnosing cases of inadequate leadership on the part of persons in authority. If this view is correct, it means that only some (and sometimes none) of the activities of decision-makers are leadership activities. Here again, understanding leadership requires understanding of a broader social process. If some types of decisions are more closely related to leadership activities than others, we should learn what they are. To this end in this analysis let us make a distinction between "routine" and "critical" decision-making.

3. *Leadership is dispensable.* The word "leadership" has its own halo, easily inviting the tacit assumption that, being a good thing, it is always in order. It may indeed be that all human groups require at all times *some* leadership activities. But if leadership is anything determinate, we should know how to distinguish its presence from its absence; similarly, if there are some social situations that especially require leadership, we should know how to tell them apart from other social situations. The idea is developed in this essay that leadership is not equally necessary in all large-scale organizations, or in any one at all times, and that it becomes dispensable as the natural processes of institutionalization become eliminated or controlled. This will provide some clues to the general conditions that call for leadership decisions.

These premises emphasize the futility of attempting to understand leadership apart from the broader organizational experience of which it is a phase. A theory of leadership will necessarily reflect the level of sophistication we have reached in the study of organization. We are dealing with an activity, with a function, with work done; we can make no more sense of it than is allowed by our understanding of the field within which that activity takes place.

The default of leadership

When institutional leadership fails, it is perhaps more often by default than by positive error or sin. Leadership is lacking when it is needed; and the institution drifts, exposed to vagrant pressures, readily influenced by short-run opportunistic trends. This default is partly a failure of nerve, partly a failure of understanding. It takes nerve to hold a course; it takes understanding to recognize and deal with the basic sources of institutional vulnerability.

One type of default is the failure to set goals. Once an organization becomes a "going concern," with many forces working to keep it alive, the people who run it can readily escape the task of defining its purposes. . . .

Another type of default occurs when goals, however neatly formulated, enjoy only a superficial acceptance and do not genuinely influence the total structure of the enterprise. Truly accepted values must infuse the organization at many levels, affecting the perspectives and attitudes of personnel, the relative importance of staff activities, the distribution of authority, relations with outside groups, and many other matters. . . .

The default of leadership shows itself in an acute form when *organizational* achievement or survival is confounded with *institutional* success. To be sure, no institutional leader can avoid concern for the minimum conditions of continued organizational existence. But he fails if he permits sheer organizational achievement, in resources, stability, or reputation, to become the criterion of his success. A university led by administrators without a clear sense of values to be achieved may fail dismally while steadily growing larger and more secure.

Finally, the role of the institutional leader should be clearly distinguished from that of the "interpersonal" leader. The latter's task is to smooth the path of human interaction, ease communication, evoke personal devotion, and allay anxiety. His expertness has relatively little to do with content; he is more concerned with persons than with policies. His main contribution is to the efficiency of the enterprise. The institutional leader, on the other hand, *is primarily an expert in the promotion and protection of values.* The interpretation that follows takes this idea as a starting point, exploring its meanings and implications.

38

What's Really Ahead for Middle Management

Donald R. Shaul

During the past few years, thousands of hard-working middle managers have looked on with rising uneasiness while theoreticians of all hues have been cheerfully debating what effects the inexorable spread of electronic data processing will have on their future. Has the death knell sounded for middle management? A good many authorities have intimated as much, forecasting that, with the widespread reorganization necessitated by EDP, a vast number of middle-management jobs will either vanish altogether or become so structured that for all practical purposes their incumbents will become mere supervisors, denuded of their decision-making powers and stripped of their status.

Moreover, say these prophets of doom, much of the innovating and planning now being done by middle managers will be taken away from them by top management. The planning of work activities will become programmed. The middle managers who remain will be highly specialized, adept at systems analysis, operations research, model building, and advanced EDP techniques. For the most part, their control function will be taken over by the computer itself.

The proponents of this school of thought have not had it all their own way, however. At the opposite extreme there are some authorities who maintain that, as a result of EDP, either more middle managers will be needed than ever or, at worst, that there will be a minimal change in the demand for them. These writers say that middle managers will have to be more able, that their decisions will become more important and far-reaching, and that their status will be enhanced. Between these two

Reprinted with permission of author and The American Management Association. From *Personnel* 41 (November-December 1964): 9–16.

opposing viewpoints are the inevitable fence-straddlers, who have hypothesized that either side may be right in the long run.

There has been argument also over what effect the new technology will have on the locus of authority and decision making in the enterprise. One group believes that EDP must lead to the centralization of authority as well as of activities, and that the EDP elite will eventually make most of the decisions. Another holds that EDP should be used to assist individual managers at all levels to make better decisions and hence should remain decentralized.

Nearly all those who have written on the subject agree, though, on one thing: EDP will relieve middle managers of a vast amount of detailed administrative work, since all decisions that do not require the exercise of individual judgment will be made by the system.[1]

How do these varying speculations square with actual experience? With the aim of throwing some light on this question, I recently interviewed 53 middle managers and 14 top managers in eight companies, all of which had had at least two years' operating experience with an EDP system. The companies studied included representatives of both manufacturing and service industries—aircraft, petroleum, electronics (solely government work), radio and TV, banking, life insurance, finance, and telephone. All the managers interviewed had had several years' service with their companies.[2]

The interviews, which were conducted with the aid of a written questionnaire, focused on the effects of EDP on these aspects of the middle manager's job: (1) the nature and scope of his functions; (2) his decision-making authority; and (3) his status. Before I go on to discuss my findings in detail, I may perhaps summarize their general tenor by saying that the prophesied demise of the middle manager, like the reported death of Mark Twain, seems to have been greatly exaggerated.

---

[1][Footnote omitted].

[2]For the purposes of this study, the term "middle manager" included any manager above the level of first-line supervisor and below the level of division manager or the equivalent. The term "EDP" was defined as a system that (1) makes an original entry or records data in an electronically or mechanically usable form, (2) communicates and processes these data automatically, and (3) integrates or coordinates all related data processing activities and procedures to provide swift and orderly information for managerial planning and control.

Changes in management functions

To assess what effect EDP had had on the nature of the middle manager's job, I took as my yardstick the traditional executive functions —planning, organizing, staffing, directing, and controlling. Let's see now what changes, if any, my interviewees reported under each of these heads:

Planning

Sixty percent of the managers interviewed said they work longer on planning activities now than they did before the EDP system was installed. This, they said, was due in the main to three reasons: (1) the increased volume and reliability of the data received; (2) the speed-up in the flow of information; and (3) the demands of their superiors for more detailed analyses, as well as for greater output from the system. All these pressures are compelling managers to plan more intensively and make more decisions than they used to before EDP came on the scene.

Some typical comments on this score:

—Things are moving much faster today. Our decisions must be made more quickly and yet our plans have to take into account the increased complexity of interrelationships involved in the information system.

—The computer is performing calculations that formerly were impossible, and I now use this information in formulating my plans.

—Just being an integral part of an information circuit forces us to plan more carefully as well as to make decisions more quickly.

Organizing

EDP seems to have had little effect on this function. Nearly all the managers reported that there had been practically no change in their organizing activities.

Staffing

Somewhat more change was noted here. EDP requires higher-caliber managers to fill the same positions now, my respondents said. Hence, additional time is needed to train people for them. Nearly everyone agreed that all managers should be familiar with the capabilities and limitations of their own company's EDP system.

Directing

A high percentage of the managers I talked with agreed that they now have to spend more time on directing the work of their departments. Several reasons were advanced for this change: (1) when a department is an integral part of an information circuit, the manager must have a thorough knowledge of its operation; (2) more complex relationships with interdependent departments have arisen because of the overriding influence of the EDP system; (3) there is more information to digest and use; (4) the addition of new activities has enlarged the manager's span of control; and (5) the increased reliance on EDP now makes it necessary for the manager to spend more time with his subordinates to insure that they are aware of the relationships involved in the new system, as well as what it can—and cannot—do.

As a result, the installation of an EDP system tends to expand the middle manager's personal contacts with his subordinate managers. As a rule, though, his contacts with his superiors at the top echelons are no more frequent than they used to be. Apparently, having discovered the wealth of information the computer can provide, the top managers are now demanding more analytical studies, most of them in greater depth, than of old. They often ask, my respondents said, for information that has not hitherto been available, and demand to be supplied immediately with facts that actually take considerable time to extract from the tape files. Such requests usually entail more frequent consultations between the top-level middle manager and his subordinates, but do not require him to see his own boss more often than before.

Controlling

Approximately two-thirds of my interviewees agreed with the prediction that the computer will reduce the time managers need to spend on controlling. However, they rejected the notion that the middle-management ranks will be thinned as a result. In fact, they said, the computer has made it possible for managers to devote more time to their other (and previously neglected) functions. In general, the respondents felt that as more sophisticated techniques of computer usage were developed they would spend even less time controlling, because fewer exceptions requiring action would be brought to them for decisions. Thus, they would have more time for considering opportunities, because they would no longer be so preoccupied with solving problems. In any event, they said, human judgment would always have to make the final appraisal of the exceptions reported by computers. Moreover, they pointed out, the fact that computers were now helping in their control function did not relieve them of responsibility for the performance of their departments.

There was no evidence in these conversations substantiating the gloomy predictions that (1) the position of middle managers will become highly structured; (2) they will become mere specialists in computer techniques and operations; and (3) their job will take on the characteristics of straight leadership and supervision. It is true that the repetitive types of decisions, involving such matters as control of inventories, optimum shipping routes, product mix, credit checks, and maintaining quality-control standards, have been programmed into the computer; but this accomplishment now permits managers to spend more time on important decisions—the decisions involving risk and uncertainty.

In fact, it appears that middle managers are being forced to go on making full use of their experience and judgment by the nature of the EDP system itself. In the first place, the increased volume of information forthcoming from the computer necessitates evaluation by experienced personnel if it is to be effectively used. Second, decisions are becoming increasingly complex because of the interdependency of relationships within the information system.

The effects of decisions on interdependent departments now have to be carefully weighed before action is taken. Managers are finding it increasingly necessary to confer with their peers on mutual problems—problems that involve the new information system as well as the departments themselves. As a result, *coordination*—the very essence of management—has become more vital than ever before to successful managerial performance.

In short, the experience of the managers I interviewed has not borne out the prediction that EDP would bring about basic changes in the nature of the middle-management job. No executive functions have been eliminated nor has the advent of the computer led to the creation of "functional" managers—one group for planning, another for organizing, and a third for control, for example. There has been a shift, though, in the amount of time middle managers spend on their individual functions. They now do less controlling and more planning, staffing, and directing. More time is available for motivating, leading, and training—functions the computer cannot handle—as well as for weighing new opportunities, and devising better work methods and better ways to provide service to customers or other departments.

Changes in scope

Far from contracting the scope of the middle manager's job, EDP is expanding it, my respondents reported. A number of the managers I interviewed said that, on balance, more activities had been assigned to them since the system was installed. Many entirely new activities had been added, because the computer had made it possible to develop new services. Moreover, managers are now expected to make more thorough evaluations and to make more planning decisions because of the increased volume of information available to them.

Because middle managers are receiving more information—and more accurate information—faster than before, the expectation is that the quality of their decisions will improve. In some of the companies studied, an improvement in decision-making has been noted, but this is not likely to become wide-spread for a long time to come. It will be many years before the EDP system will be available to middle managers seeking optimum solutions to simulation problems involving the use of different variables. The high investment in programmed information, the heavy volume of work handled by the computers, and the higher priority of top management and staff work all preclude the use of the system at lower levels at the present time.

My respondents agreed with the prediction that EDP would increase the visibility and speed of business decisions and make it possible to "see" more in a shorter planning period. They also confirmed that a continuous and rapid feedback permits faster adjustment to a new conditions. Plans can now be made for longer periods ahead; alternatively, more accurate forecasts are possible for the short run. Either way, the result is that middle managers are developing an increasing awareness of their responsibility to engage in planning decisions at their level, and they are making more planning decisions, not fewer, as some experts have prophesied.

Busy top managers, in fact, are finding the EDP system is an important aid in delegating decision making to their subordinates. From my interviewees' comments it seems evident that they will continue to do so.

Broader and faster

Actually, then, EDP has made the middle manager's job more complex. Now, the manager must not only have some knowledge of the capabilities and limitations of the system itself; he must also be constantly coordinating his activities with those of other departments. Moreover, he is expected to react faster, make decisions more quickly (and take more facts into account in making them), and make more elaborate plans.

Almost half the middle managers I interviewed thought that EDP had definitely helped them to make better decisions. The rest said that they had not noticed any change. So far as planning was concerned, it was generally agreed that the system now enables detailed forecasts to be made for considerably longer periods ahead. On the other hand, because more accurate information is now available much faster than before, many operational activities do not have to be planned so far in advance.

Among the top managers interviewed, there was unanimous agreement that EDP itself does not create positions whose incumbents perform both line and staff functions; it has no effect on the number of middle managers rotated between line and staff positions; and it is not used to concentrate authority in top managers. However, this group was divided about the effect EDP had on rotating line and staff positions. Some felt that staff personnel would make the transition more easily because they had had the opportunity to familiarize themselves with all the ramifications of the information system, whereas line managers had a restricted viewpoint—the nature of their jobs and the vastly increased demands on their time did not permit them to become so familiar with the system's over-all operations. Other top managers took the view, however, that line managers are being kept sufficiently well informed of the operations and interrelations of the EDP system to make the transfer to a staff position without difficulty.

Changes in authority

There has been a slight drift away from rigid enforcement of the rules governing middle managers' decision-making authority, my study shows. The computer has aided in this change by being instrumental in providing better controls. As superior managers gain confidence in their subordinates they sometimes grant approval, *ex post facto,* for actions taken during their absence. For example, one division manager now gives tacit consent to certain of his subordinates to exceed expenditure limits while he is away. On his return, he approves the transactions. But, in general, there has not been any change in the number of rules imposed upon middle managers.

Changes in the authority delegated to middle managers coincide with the increase or decrease in the number of activities assigned to departments, according to my respondents. The considerable reduction in the decision-making authority granted to middle managers predicted by some experts has not taken place. Apparently, the EDP system itself has had no significant influence upon the decision-making authority of middle managers.

In fact, half the managers studied are now using more of their experience and judgment in rendering decisions, while the rest are using at least as much as before. A number of reasons were offered in explanation of the greater demands on experience and judgment. There is more information now and many new classifications to analyze; the manager must understand the EDP system and all interrelated activities to perform his job properly; new ways to use the information provided by the system are constantly being sought; decisions must be made faster and more often; and problems now have to be probed more deeply.

There was general agreement that middle managers are not sharing their decisions with top managers or staff specialists, nor are they being denied the opportunity to continue making decisions on subjects under their control. While corporate policies are being improved and better information is available to all levels of management much more quickly, the operating decisions continue to be made at the lowest level at which sound judgment, based on the available facts, can be brought to bear on the problem.

Changes in status

My respondents were also unanimously of the opinion that, contrary to many predictions, the status of middle managers had not been lowered since EDP came on the scene. In fact, they pointed to a number of reasons substantiating the belief that, rather, the middle manager's status has been raised: (1) his job is more complex; (2) he has a greatly increased volume of information to analyze in greater depth; (3) he is using more experience and judgment; and (4) EDP has either added to his activities or replaced some with more responsible functions.

Several of the top managers interviewed made these points:

—The middle manager's job is more complex today because he has more controls to adhere to daily—quality, budget, cost. In effect, a manager today must have at least a working knowledge of the EDP system and is handling a job that a superintendent was handling before.

—Middle-manager jobs are more complex because there are more things going on in our department and they are more elaborate than they used to be. We do more of the total procedure now, instead of a simple part of it. Timing is much more important and reactions must be faster. What used to be one department is now three departments.

—The administration of the system will require managers to have a thorough knowledge of its operations, so that they can be placed in spots where they can coordinate activities that are not related to each other in their daily operations, yet, being an integral part of the information system, must be supervised so that no action is taken that would be detrimental to broad company goals. A production line can have only one person making decisions that affect the administrative processes.

From the above findings it should be evident that while EDP has undoubtedly eliminated a vast amount of monotonous, detailed administrative work, there has been no accompanying reduction in the need for middle managers. Indeed, some of the companies studied are now finding it necessary to establish new criteria for determining the salaries of middle managers instead of compensating them on the basis of the number of subordinates assigned to them. Where there have been reductions in the number of workers, these have usually been compensated for by new activities being assigned to existing departments, or by the creation of new departments. Thus, the centralization of *activities* has not been accompanied by the elimination of managerial positions. On the contrary, the reorganization necessitated by the installation of EDP, and the new types of activities, coupled with the expansion of existing operations, all of which the system has made possible, have resulted in the addition of over 50 middle-management positions in the companies studied.

Moreover, in many of these companies the top managers are finding that they require more specialists. Several told me that the volume of data now being received may well require additional managerial personnel with the requisite experience to interpret it properly. One manager said he thought that in his company several supervisors and a few lower-echelon middle managers would eventually be eliminated; but he also visualized that the upper-echelon middle managers would require experienced staff personnel of their own.

All in all, then, instead of middle managers' facing a drastic reduction in their decision-making power and a lowering of their status, my survey indicates that this vital component of the management hierarchy is recognized as being more important than ever. Certainly, overall, no serious threat to middle managers seems to be posed by EDP. Their real menace is still the traditional causes of business failure, whether stemming from poor performance within the enterprise, from technological changes such as automation, or from external forces over which the company has little or no control.

39

Representative Bureaucracy: A Reassessment

V. Subramaniam

The term "representative bureaucracy" was first given currency in 1949 through Donald Kingsley's book with the same title[1] and since then it has gained popularity through the discussions of a few American political scientists and British sociologists.[2] The underlying concept, however, is still subject to some confusion owing in part to its normative overtones. This paper attempts, in the first place, to analyze some important sources of confusion and, secondly, to show the practical difficulties in the realization of a representative bureaucracy by comparing the social backgrounds of civil servants in different countries.

I. Conceptual confusion

Kingsley himself was partly responsible for injecting some ambiguity into the meaning of the term. He pointed out—though without giving precise figures—the actual dominance of the middle class in Britain's higher civil service and traced its history. He was generally satisfied that this class "mirrored the dominant forces in society" and so "can be entrusted with power" and at the same time he was anxious that the civil

Reprinted with permission of author and publisher. From *The American Political Science Review* 59 (December 1967): 1010–19. Some footnotes have been renumbered.

[1] J. Donald Kingsley, *Representative Bureaucracy* (Yellow Springs, Ohio: The Antioch Press, 1944).

[2] E.g. Van Riper, Long and Warner (American), Kelsall and Bottomore (British). Their published research is referred to in detail in other footnotes that follow.

service should draw proportionately more from the working class.[3] In other words, he was happy in one part of his book to see the same class which called the political tune well represented in the higher civil service —thereby ensuring harmony between the body politic and body administrative and sorry in another part that the working class was left out. This ambivalence confuses the straight meaning of the term "representative bureaucracy." Literally, it would mean a civil service in which *every* economic class, caste, or region or religion in a country is represented in exact proportion to its numbers in the population. In practice, its American proponents interpret it less literally to mean a bureaucracy drawn "from all social, racial and religious groups on the basis of ability"—but not necessarily in exact numerical proportion to produce "a copy of the total society."[4] European research workers on the social backgrounds of higher civil servants would agree by implication with the American definition.

There is thus broad agreement on the basic meaning of the concept —though people can and do disagree about the desirable degree of representation and the categories to be represented.[5] But two other basic confusions still remain. The first of these, found usually among European left wing critics of middle-class dominated civil services, shows itself in their disappointment with the simultaneous and apparently incongruous evolution of representative democratic political institutions and unrepresentative civil services in the course of the last 150 years. The second confusion inheres in the naive and dogmatic argument advanced in favor of representative bureaucracy—that it is necessarily responsive to the needs of all the classes it is drawn from and to the general public. I shall analyse each confusion in turn.

To understand the disappointment of left-wing critics with the pro-

---

[3] See Kingsley, *op. cit.,* pp. 282–283, for the social harmony argument; and the second half of the chapter "The New Aristocracy" for the working class representation argument.

[4] Warner et al., *The American Federal Executive* (New Haven: Yale University Press, 1963), p. 5.

[5] For example, the Western critics would be interested in the proportionate representation of economic classes while an Indian politician would lay stress on representation by caste, region and language.

cesses of recent history it is revealing to examine them with the help of the sociological categories, "ascriptive" and "performance-oriented," rather than use normative political terms such as representative and unrepresentative. These twin sociological categories are used as modes of reference—in judging men and things in different societies.[6] In the ascriptive mode some abilities are "ascribed" to those who belong to certain families or clans, or groups—and whenever and wherever such abilities are required, the "ascribed" are automatically called up. In the latter mode, the presence of such abilities is tested for by actual performance. The first mode is historically older and *prima facie* less rational than the second, but neither mode has a necessary logical relation with a representative or unrepresentative bureaucracy. But the first mode has been associated with an unrepresentative upper-class-dominated bureaucracy just as the latter has come to be associated with representative bureaucracy. We shall see why. Until about a century and a half ago, the higher positions in government and administration in all countries were filled by men from a numerically small upper class, regardless of whether the social organization was feudal, mercantile, or semi-industrial and the form of government parliamentary, monarchic, or aristocratic. This was justified by the ascription of certain abilities to members of that upper class. It was replaced by a performance-oriented mode of reference in the course of the eighteenth and nineteenth centuries, for two reasons. The first was the general growth of rationalism in Europe from the Renaissance onwards and its increasing influence in the late eighteenth century. In such a climate it appeared rather indefensible to ascribe abilities where they could be tested for by performance. The second reason was the patent failure of "ascribed" groups in some European countries to deliver the goods. It was most dramatic in France where the decadent *ancien regime* with its tradition of patronage appointments and sale of offices collapsed suddenly. It was more gradual in countries such as Prussia and Britain but nevertheless evident.[7]

[6]Concerning the two modes of reference, see Talcott Parsons, *The Social System* (London: Tavistock, 1952), pp. 63–65.

[7]For the gradual introduction of the middle class element in British administration, see Kingsley, *op. cit.,* chapter 7. For Prussia, see H. Rosenberg, *Bureaucracy, Autocracy and Aristocracy* (Cambridge, Mass.: Harvard University Press, 1958).

The most important historical feature from our point of view—of this replacement of ascription by performance-testing—was that it coincided in time with the spread of democratic institutions. Again, France provides the dramatic example. The fall of the *ancien regime* was followed simultaneously by the rise of two most powerful slogans—that of liberty, equality and fraternity and that of a career open to talents. In Britain too, the introduction of competitive examinations went on *pari passu* with the enlargement of the franchise. This historical association, not unnaturally, led some to look upon selection by performance tests and representative democracy as complementary and even corollary and raised expectations, not altogether logical, that these two in combination should lead to a representative bureaucracy. The disappointment implied even in academic discussions about the nondevelopment of representative civil services is largely the result of such association. The expectation was not altogether logical as it was based on the somewhat temporary and sporadic phenomenon of some unrepresentative "ascribed" groups being replaced in power by more representative groups who had perforce to prove their ability by performance. As we shall see a little later, ascription and performance-orientation are both to be found fairly well mixed up in stable societies both old and new—and the representativeness of a bureaucracy and its selection by performance-testing (or merit) are logically separate. Whether they are practically compatible or otherwise is a matter of observation and political manipulation.

Historical developments in the United States followed a different path wherein these implications were sorted out more clearly.[8] Representative democracy started more or less with a clean slate, ascription played too insignificant a part in American modes of thought to produce any reaction against it and the Jacksonian democrats were not without some logic in their rejection of a whole corpus of contemporary European ideas and practices. They set their face against the European concept of property in office and instituted rotation in office. As against ascription of abilities to a few noble-born, or a test for their presence by examination performance, they attributed a minimum of ability to all citizens—which they declared was ample for the performance of the simple duties of a public office. Conceived as a rejection of decadent European ideas about

[8]This paragraph is based upon Paul Van Riper, *History of the United States Civil Service* (Evanston: Row, Peterson & Co., 1958), chapter 3.

property in office and the mystique of bureaucratic work, this Jacksonian theory as a whole was self-consistent. Its results were rather mixed. Its immediate consequence was the spoils system, which withered away in due course. A more lasting effect was a moral commitment to keep public services in America open to, and representative of, all sections and classes of the general public and this has, since then, influenced all procedures of selection to official posts. To sum up the different developments in Europe and the U.S.A. somewhat sweepingly: in the former, the parallel growth of representative political institutions and performance tests for civil service recruitment raised some misplaced expectations about the automatic evolution of a representative bureaucracy; whereas in the U.S.A. representative political institutions and representative civil services were developed in fact simultaneously, separately and deliberately as partly soft-pedalling the need for, and the rigor of, performance tests.

II. Ascription v. performance-testing

We shall now examine the related question—whether ascription and performance-testing are so sharply different and whether they were and are practiced in all their theoretical rigor anywhere. Ascription of a certain ability or quality, say, (a) to those who possess another quality, (b) such as membership of a class, family or clan, is by itself neither irrational nor opposed to the practice of testing for this quality by actual performance. It is not irrational, if observation over a period suggests that (a) and (b) have a significant correlation and concrete tests for ability (a) might themselves have suggested earlier or conformed later such correlation. It failed in those societies where the correlations were false or overrated or never tested. Conversely, performance-testing to be perfectly rational, would test one's performance of a single act—before entrusting him with further performances of that specific act—a procedure somewhat expensive and elementary.[9] In actual practice, perfor-

---

[9]Such elementary rationality—i.e., taking into account specific ability for the duties of a specific post—is shown in traditional Australian public service definitions of fitness or efficiency in the respective State and Commonwealth Public Services Acts. But good sense has mitigated its literal application.

mance tests or examinations in the recruitment of civil services are usually based on a more complex chain of correlations. Some of these examinations are relatively specific—when technicians are tested broadly in their subjects and techniques, and professionals such as doctors and engineers are recuited on the basis of proven ability through professional examinations. Even here the test is for general technical or professional performance and not for ability to perform a specific act. Other examinations are based on somewhat conjectural correlations; thus the competitive examination for the British Administrative class is not based on actual performance in any given administrative situation but rather on a tenuous chain of Macaulayan reasoning:[10] that those who show ability in their teens and early twenties keep it to the end of their career; that such ability is best revealed by a competitive examination— which tests intelligence, academic ability and self-discipline; that ability is general, i.e., ability of one type is easily transformed into another type and therefore the ability revealed by competitive examination is transformed into administrative ability. There seems to be plenty of room for ascription to slip into this long chain of reasoning, relating examination performance in the humanities to administrative ability, as there is even more in reliance upon a short interview. In other words, ascription is not as irrational or unfunctional as appears at first sight even as performance-testing is not so rigorously rational. It is therefore possible for the social composition of civil services elected by the latter to be not so strikingly different from those selected by the former.

Moreover, in actual practice, ascription was modified in older societies in many ways so as to include some recruits from all ranks of society. Thus entry into, and advancement in, institutions based on celibacy such as the Catholic Church and various eunuch groups of the Turkish and Chinese Empires was always open to all classes and it was possible to climb to high administrative positions through them. Even where a small class controlled administrative recruitment tightly, it could accept members of somewhat less well-placed classes through marriage

---

[10]For the two famous speeches of Macaulay, see *Speeches—Parliamentary and Miscellaneous by Rt. Hon. Thomas Babington Macaulay* (London: Clarke Beeton & Co.), p. 183, vol. I for the speech of 1853, pp. 267–273, vol. II, for the speech of 1855.

and adoption. The commercial classes of England and Japan penetrated the ranks of the landed aristocracy by the former methods as many talented Roman and Turkish slaves rose up socially through the latter. Again, a new king or a new dynasty, keen to break the control of an older class over administrative recruitment might encourage men of lower social origins to enter and advance in the governmental bureaucracy.[11] In some bureaucratic empires, the king tried continuously to gain control of civil service recruitment and even instituted elementary performance criteria for this purpose.[12] Absolute practice of ascription and continuous monopoly of one social class was much less usual in nondemocratic regimes than popularly supposed.

Nor were ascriptive assumptions taken too seriously by the ruling class even as they were preached. There were other important reasons for recruitment by an upper class from its own ranks to the state bureaucracy. In the first place it provided some guarantee of loyalty to the existing regime on the part of the recruit—out of sheer self-interest.[13] Secondly, the recruit could be expected to understand the unstated major premises of the regime without tedious explanation and might even have picked up some of the finer details of administration through the vicarious experience of watching his family elders at work. As a last resort, a blatantly inefficient or disloyal person could be silently removed or relieved in the interests of the class image by some established methods.

III. The argument for representative bureaucracy

I have dealt with the confusion flowing from some naive expectations of the establishment of representative bureaucracy in the wake of repre-

---

[11] Re the efforts of kings to gain greater control of bureaucracies in bureaucratic empires, see S. N. Eisenstadt, *The Political Systems of Bureaucratic Empires* (The Free Press of Glencoe, 1963), chapter 10, particularly pp. 278–279.

[12] For an early advocacy of selection by performance, see Shamasastry, *Kautilya's Arthasastra,* p. 13, and chapter X for details of tests.

[13] In this regard, aristocrats, imperialists, and communists are all the same in trying to recruit members of a given class for key administrative positions on grounds of politicial reliability.

sentative democracy. I shall now examine briefly the confusion attaching to the argument in support of the former. The essential case is that a civil service which includes members of all classes *therefore* ensures that all their different values and interests are articulated and hence brought to bear upon the decisions taken and policies formulated by it.[14] This argument is implied by some and explained by others. We may set aside Kingsley's argument, which is really a case for political harmony, and summarize—as an example—Kelsall's use of the foregoing pattern of argument to plead for a wider representation of all classes.[15] In his view, the attitudes and sympathies of the British civil servant such as "smugness and complacency" and "lack of touch with working class problems" are those of the middle class he is drawn from. He has unconsciously imbibed a sense of superiority to the working class and with no "memory of misery, hunger, squalor, bureaucratic oppression, and economic insecurity," his perception of such problems lacks depth. The greater representation of the working class through various means would make for a truly representative and *therefore* responsive civil service. The American proponents are more direct and precise in presenting this case. Thus Van Riper makes it clear that a representative bureaucracy must "(1) consist of a reasonable cross section of the body politic in terms of occupation, class, geography, and the like, and (2) must be in general tune with the ethos and attitudes of the society of which it is part," and he would attribute the success of American democracy in part at least to the representative character of the federal civil service.[16] Norton E. Long goes even further to say that it is "a better sample of the mass of the people than the Congress," that "important interests which are unrepresented or malrepresented" in the Congress receive "more effective and more responsible representation through administrative channels," that it has saved the democratic process from bogging down and should be duly recognized as "our great fourth branch of government."[17]

[14]The argument becomes stronger, the greater the power of the civil service.

[15]R. K. Kelsall, *Higher Civil Servants in Britain* (London: Routledge & Kegan Paul, 1955), pp. 189–193.

[16]Van Riper, *op. cit.*, pp. 549–559.

[17]Norton E. Long, "Bureaucracy and Constitutionalism," this *Review* 46 (1952): 808–818.

The arguments for representative bureaucracy (or rather guaranteed representation for some unrepresented groups) put forward in India around the turn of the century followed the foregoing basic pattern with local variations.[18] Indian society, it was argued, was really divided into caste and religious groups rather than economic classes, but these divisions were more rigid, being based on birth, and had more influence on their members than class. The case for equitable and proportionate representation of each caste and religious group was founded frankly on the probability of the sectional sympathies or even sectional loyalties of recruits causing harm to unrepresented sections. The danger was held to be very real in the late nineteenth- and early twentieth-century India more than elsewhere because (1) India had a purely bureaucratic form of government with little democratic control, and membership in the civil service meant more power than elsewhere, which power could be used and was often alleged to be used by the administrator in favor of one's community; and also because (2) membership in the civil service conferred significant financial security, a prize most sought after in Indian society. It was argued that there was a strong case for the more equitable, i.e., proportionate, distribution of the two scarce commodities of power and security, particularly because competition for them was weighted heavily in favor of the more fortunate early starters (the higher Hindu castes) who could deliberately use it to keep out the latecomers.

Thus the basic argument—stated in different ways in different contexts—is that bureaucrats carry their class attitudes and prejudices into their official life and only when all classes (or castes) are properly represented in the civil service will their different needs and interests find due consideration. Norton E. Long would stretch this further to say that such a representative bureaucracy would even make up for the sins of unrepresentative political institutions such as the Congress in U.S.A.[19]

How good is this basic case founded on the inevitability of one's sympathies for one's class of origin? Is it as self-evident as its proponents make it out? Of course, Freudians and behaviorists are agreed that child-

---

[18]For further details and references regarding the Indian arguments, see V. Subramaniam, "Graduates in the Public Service—A Comparative Study of Attitudes," *Public Administration* (London), 35, 377–378.

[19]Long, *op. cit.;* see in particular the latter half of the article.

hood influences are long-lasting. There is also plenty of empirical research evidence (in regard to the U.S.A.) to show that the middle and working classes differ substantially in several regards, from toilet training for children to the style of promiscuity, from the nature of their mental disorders to their marital lives. But all this neglects the existence of deviants from class norms, in both the upper and lower classes. We are familiar with aristocrats and rich heirs who have passionate sympathy for the working class. On the other hand, the proportion of deviants among the members of the lower classes who work their way up is held by many observers to be high. Leaving aside the familiar upstart and the climber, they point out that those founders of Britain's industry in the nineteenth century who came from poor families were not conspicuous for their sympathy to their class of origin and that leadership studies of working class parties and unions reveal the same story. It has been suggested that the men who climb out of the lower classes, the upward-mobiles, under present conditions anyway, shed their class sympathies either at the beginning of the climb itself or halfway through. The proven existence of deviants from class norms and the probability of their high proportion among recruits from the lower classes, shakes to the foundations the basic argument for representative bureaucracy.[20]

Besides this, one has still to explain—in more detail than its advocates have done—the process by which a representative bureaucracy becomes responsive to sectional *as well* as general interests. If the various classes represented have all different and conflicting interests and if their members in the bureaucracy advocate mainly class interests—in accord with the basic argument—the result is likely to be a divided and even ineffectual bureaucracy. It might work after a fashion—on the basis of a hostage theory according to which bureaucrats of each class do not

[20]Re the several differences in attitudes and customs of the middle and working classes, see Harold M. Hodges, Jr., *Social Stratification: Class in America,* (Cambridge Mass.: Schenkman, 1964), the two chapters of Values and Behaviour, and the chapter on Social Class and Social Intimacy. Regarding lack of class sympathies among successful men from the lower classes, see Maurice Duverger, *Political Parties,* chapter III, section III, and Kenneth Robinson, "Selection and the Social Background of the Administrative Class," *Public Administration* (London), 35, 388. All this evidence is impressionistic and Hodges produces no evidence about deviants to rebut this impression.

harm the interests of others for fear of retaliation.[21] Or to think of a less gruesome picture, bureaucrats with different social backgrounds may influence each other by formal and informal contacts and bargaining. This is known to happen but such mutual influence and bargaining is not half as free as in the open legislative forum between politicians of different persuasions—for it is severely cramped by the hierarchical position of the incumbent.[22] The actual picture is often brighter than the foregoing ones at least in the United States, mainly because the majority of bureaucrats cherish some common values which are part of the nation's sociopolitical consensus and they also expose themselves to all influences regardless of their class origins. In other words, this responsiveness is more a reflection of the consensual and equalitarian ethos of the community as a whole than a direct result of its representativeness only.

The old Wilson-Goodnow argument against "elective" bureaucracy may not hold good in its old form against "representative" bureaucracy but it is not without relevance. The original argument may be paraphrased thus.[23] Political institutions such as parliaments and presidents should reflect, shape and so represent the popular will—and it is right they should be constituted on the elective-representative principle. Administrators carry out this will—and should be selected solely on the basis of competence in execution—as revealed by professional qualifications or (competitive) performance tests. It is disastrous to apply the ethos of one to the other—to apply the principle of appointment by performance-testing to political institutions and that of election (or representativeness?) to administrative establishments. The main flaw in this argument has been recounted *ad nauseam* by proponents of representative bureaucracy, namely, that the dichotomy does not work as strictly as stated and that administrators influence political decisions and make them too. But this does not make an automatic case for representative

[21]For a version of the hostage theory, see *Speeches and Writings of Mohammed Iqbal,* Speech in the Punjab Legislative Council, July 19, 1927.

[22]For hierarchy and the inhibition of free communication, see Blau and Scott, *Formal Organizations* (San Francisco: Chandler, 1962), pp. 121–124.

[23]For the original argument and detailed references, see R. S. Parker and V. Subramaniam, "Public and Private Administration," (section II) *International Review of Administrative Sciences,* Brussels, vol. 30, no. 4.

bureaucracy, though it weakens the original argument against elective offices. From a purely logical and dichotomist standpoint, if an administrative position involves a large proportion of political decisions, it should be made a purely political position—perhaps even elective or politically responsible in some way. For many practical reasons this proved extremely difficult in the American governmental framework. At the same time, administrators have progressively grown politically responsive without going embarrassingly partisan—a fortunate development that seems to have saved American democracy from the need for drastic reorganization. This development owes something to the "representative" character of the federal service and a lot more to other factors too. It is clearly stretching the evidence somewhat to claim that "representative" bureaucracy is the only or even the most effective answer to the problem of increasing bureaucratic power. It is stretching it too far to assert, as Norton E. Long does, that it is a part-cure for unrepresentative political institutions.

IV. Social backgrounds of civil servants

I have so far pointed out some conceptual and logical shortcomings of the idea of representative bureaucracy—even while conceding its limited advantages. I shall further justify this cautious approach by a comparative analysis of the social backgrounds of higher civil servants in different countries. In the present stage of my research I would not like to hazard any firm conclusions on the subject because reliable data are not available for many countries and even the readily available data need some reprocessing and reinterpretation.[24] Even so, it is difficult to resist the tentative conclusion about the widely prevalent middle class domination of higher civil services in the six countries listed in Table 1, in spite

[24]I am processing material for a book entitled *Social Composition of Public Bureaucracies* to be published M/S Longman Green in a series under the general editorship of J. W. Grove. The present paper is a preview of the general argument of the book.

of their different economic, social and political backgrounds.[25] The extent of the domination is nearly the same (from 80 to 95 percent) and the differences relate mainly (a) to the degree or coefficient of over-representation of the middle class as a whole, and (b) to the different degrees of representation of different sections of the middle class. To illustrate; the percentage of the sons from middle-class occupational categories does not differ very much between U.S.A. (81%) and India (87.6% for the Accounts Services and 96% for the Administrative Service) but in the former, these categories constitute something near 60 percent of its working population and so, the degree of over-representation is of the order of 1.35. In India, however, they constitute just about 9 percent of the working population and the degree of their over-representation is near 10. Thus, while the middle class share is about the same in different countries, the degree of its over-representation depends on its size, and the larger it is, the more representative the bureaucracy. Secondly, the representation of different sections of the middle class differs sharply from one country to another even when its total representation is about the same. Thus in India, Turkey and France, the sons of civil servants form more or less half (46 to 50%) of the total number of recruits—whereas in Denmark and Britain, their percentage comes down to about 25 and to even less in the case of the U.S.A., in all of which countries the skilled workers, business executives, farmers and businessmen are better represented. These variations may be explained in part by the different origins and history of the middle class in different countries. In India and Turkey it was artificially created in response to Western occupation or influence

[25]Please see Table 1 for details. The sources for the figures for different countries are as follows:

For Denmark—Henry Stjernquist, "Centraladministrationens Embedsmaend 1848–1946," *Centraladministrationen 1848–1948,* Ministerialforeningen, Copenhagen, 1948.

For Turkey—C. H. Dodd, "The Social and Educational Background of Turkish Officials." *Middle Eastern Studies,* London, vol. I, p. 271.

For U.S.A.—Warner *et al, op. cit.,* p. 321.

For Great Britain—R. K. Kelsall, *op. cit.,* pp. 150–51.

For France—T. B. Bottomore, "Le Mobilité Sociale dans la Haute Administration Française," *Cahiers Internationaux Sociologie,* vol. XII, Sommaire, p. 169.

The Indian figures are based on my own research.

TABLE 1
Comparative Table of the Occupations of the Fathers of Higher Civil Servants in Six Countries

Name of Country	Middle Classes						Others	
	Shopkeepers Businessmen etc.	Governmental (incl. Army) Employees	Business Employees	Professionals	Skilled Workers	Total for Middle Classes	Unskilled Workers	Agricultural Workers and Farmers
	%	%	%	%	%	%	%	%
1. Denmark (1945)	19.5	25.1	4.3	38.3	—	87.2	4.3	8.5
2. Great Britain (1949-52)	17.8	27.0	13.3	30.4	8.7	97.2	1.5	1.3
3. France (1945-51)	11.4	50.2 (41.8)	8.3	23.1	3.3	96.4	—	3.6
4. U.S.A. (1959)	20.0	?	24.0	20.0	17.0	81.0	4.0	15.0
5. Turkey (1960)	16.0	45.5	—	29.0	—	90.5	1.0	8.5
6. India (1947-56) (a) I.A.S.	12.0	50.6	4.5	29.2	—	96.3	—	4.7
(b) A/cs Services	7.5	46.7	5.2	28.2	—	87.6	4.2	8.6

N.B.: Research workers differ about the inclusion of skilled workers in the middle class. In this table, it affects the size of middle class representation only in the case of the U.S.A. and to a much lesser extent to the case of Great Britain. The inclusion can be justified in the former case on the basis of (a) their nearness to the professional and clerical middle classes in their earnings and ethos and (b) the significant proportion of them that transfer to the professional and clerical middle classes in one generation.

—and is still largely made up of salaried employees of government and business.[26] As the sons of the former have a traditional predilection for following in their father's footsteps the degree of overrepresentation is very high indeed. The middle class of France is more varied but seems to be nearly as tradition-bound as its counterparts in Eastern countries with the result that civil servants' sons are just as well represented in her civil service as in India's and Turkey's. Greater occupational mobility and lack of traditionalism seem to have weakened the urge to follow the father's profession in U.S.A. which has a more varied pattern of middle class representation, with Denmark and Britain standing midway.

* * *

To reiterate the main point, the higher civil service is drawn to an equally large degree from the middle class in all these countries, in spite of their different social, economic and political backgrounds—and is more "representative" just where the middle class itself is large. This is rather sobering but it can be explained by the combination of skills and qualities cultivated by the middle class—which increases immensely its chances of success vis-à-vis the working class. If civil servants were chosen through a random number table from the whole population, it is highly probable that each class (i.e., the upper middle, lower middle, and working class) might be represented in the civil service more or less in proportion to its numbers. In practice the selection is restricted by several requirements operating more or less in favour of the two branches of the middle class. Let us take note of four important requirements relating to age, intelligence, a certain level of education, and eagerness to compete. We can see that the middle class has *prima facie* a higher probability of meeting the last three requirements than the working class and the final combined probability which is a product of the separate probabilities is therefore so much higher than that for the working class. Let us see how.

We may assume that under normal conditions the age distribution in all the three classes is the same—with perhaps a slightly higher proportion of the working class in their twenties and thirties—perhaps enjoying a very slight advantage in regard to their numbers in the recruitable age groups. During some periods of history this advantage may constitute a

[26]Regarding the evolution of the Indian middle class, see B. B. Misra, *The Indian Middle Classes* (London: Oxford University Press, 1961).

significant factor against an aging and infertile middle class—whose depleted ranks may be filled up rapidly from below. We are not concerned with this rare occurrence at the moment and may proceed on the assumption of the same age distribution in all classes.

We do not have any reliable knowledge about the distribution of native intelligence in the different classes.[27] Some researchers suggest that it is about the same in all classes, others that it is slightly higher in the city working class than in the middle class and still others that it is lower. At the same time, psychologists have identified different areas of intelligence and suggested that different groups may excell or fail in different areas, women in shape and color perceptions, working class children in manipulative tests and middle class children in verbal ability. Perhaps there is no conclusive evidence of advantage to any one class in regard to *general* intelligence, but we may accept the evidence in regard to the greater verbal ability of middle class children. Thus they have an edge on others in something which matters a great deal in competitive examinations.

We know a little more about the opportunities for school and university education for different classes. In most industrial and developed societies, the differences in the proportion of school-leavers in different economic classes are not very large; they are rather small at the junior school level and somewhat larger at the secondary school level. But the difference is more striking in regard to university education even in industrial societies—the proportion of the university trained in the middle classes often being a hundred times their proportion in the working classes.[28] Thus any system which recruits university graduates in their early twenties is bound to give a striking advantage to the middle class at the expense of the working class and the peasantry.

[27]For summaries of I.Q. surveys, see N. Eysenck, *Uses and Abuses of Psychology* (Pelican); P. E. Vernon, *Intelligence and Attainment Tests* (University of London Press, 1960); and John B. Miner, *Intelligence in the United States* (Springer, N. Y., 1957). It would appear from Miner, *op. cit.*, pp. 78–84 and C. O. Carter, *Human Heredity* (Pelican), pp. 132–135, that I.Q. increases proportionately with social class, but this I.Q. is based somewhat heavily on verbal ability.

[28]The distribution of university education among the middle class and the working class and its bearing on civil service recruitment has been discussed by Kelsall, *op. cit.*, Kingsley, *op. cit.*, pp. 146–147, and Bottomore, *op. cit.* It seems that the opportunity for university education for the middle class boy was about 35 times that for the working class boy in Britain according to Kingsley and about three to four times in the U.S.A. according to Hodges, *op. cit.*, pp. 260–261. In other Western countries the ratio might be in between the two, whereas in India, it may be well over 100.

There is little doubt that the middle class boy—by the very nature of his class—is more aware of the existence of professions and salaried jobs in the civil service and realizes that he has to look after himself by competing for life's prizes. As against this middle class competitive individualism, the working class boy suffers by his proneness to, and training in, cooperative effort.[29]

* * *

V. Conclusion

Let us now sum up the thesis and end on a practical note. There are serious weaknesses in the case for representative bureaucracy and in practice the sons of the middle class occupy over eighty percent of the posts of the higher civil service in several (non-communist) countries regardless of their stage of economic development—because of possessing a combination of advantages. We have also suggested that the U.S. federal civil service is representative because U.S. society is largely middle class. In fact, there are further reasons to justify caution about the possibility or benefits of a representative bureaucracy outside the American context.[30] If the representativeness of the U.S. Federal bureaucracy is based on its middle class society, its responsiveness flows much from factors other than mere representativeness. Reference has been made to the general American consensus transcending class barriers and covering a wide field of political and social values—and the reflection of this in bureaucratic attitudes. An important element in this consensus is one's general accessibility regardless of class or position and this exposes the bureaucrat to many prevailing winds of opinion and interest. Indeed his sensitivity is heightened to public and professional needs because he moves in and out of the Federal bureaucracy frequently into the private practice of his profession or to private enterprise. In short, a numerically representative bureaucracy may not be possible to establish when torn from its American context except with immense difficulty, and its consequences would be certainly unpredictable and perhaps even undesirable.

[29]For some evidence of the competition-proneness of the middle class vis-à-vis the working class, see Hodges, *op. cit.,* p. 265.

[30]As against the enthusiasm of Norton E. Long, Van Riper has doubts about the exportability of representative bureaucracy and would anyway treat it as only one of several possible devices to ensure democratic administration: *op. cit.,* p. 559.

40

Evaluation and Program Administration

Edward Allen Suchman

Evaluation is a form of programmatic activity in two major respects. First, the purpose of an evaluation is usually applied—its main objective is to increase the effectiveness of program administration. Second, the conduct of an evaluation study itself constitutes a form of program activity—the planning and execution of evaluation studies requires administrative resources. We might call the former evaluation *in* administration, while the latter could be classified as the administration *of* evaluation.

Evaluation as an aspect of program administration becomes an essential part of the entire administrative process related to program planning, development, and operation. In fact, as we shall see, it plays a central role in the growth of the new field of administrative science. At the same time, the conduct of evaluation studies, especially on a systematic, continuing basis, requires an administrative apparatus of its own and presents unique problems of organizational structure and function. In this chapter we will examine the first aspect of evaluation *in* program administration. . . .

Evaluation and administrative science

Before looking specifically at the role of evaluation in program administration, let us examine briefly the concept of evaluation as a basic process in administrative science. Lewis offers the following useful prop-

Reprinted with permission of author and publisher. From chapter 8 of *Evaluative Research* by Edward A. Suchman, Ph.D., © 1967 by Russell Sage Foundation, Basic Books, Inc., Publishers, New York.

osition concerning the relationship of evaluation to knowledge and action: "Knowledge, action, and evaluation are essentially connected. The primary and pervasive significance of knowledge lies in its guidance of action: knowing is for the sake of doing. And action, obviously, is rooted in evaluation. For a being which did not assign comparative values, deliberate action would be pointless; and for one which did not know, it would be impossible."[1]

Thus, evaluative research as the study of planned social change supplies much of the knowledge base for the developing field of administrative science. The social experiment, involving the formulation and carrying out of programs designed to produce some desired change, is the main form of scientific research for the testing of administrative principles. Evaluative hypotheses are largely administrative hypotheses dealing with the relationship between some programmatic activity and the attainment of some desired action objective.

The evaluation study in social action is as essential to an empirically based administrative science as clinical or drug evaluation is to the practice of scientific medicine. In general, however, many administrators who may have done excellent work in measuring existing public needs, resources, and community attitudes, in following the general steps for defining objectives, and in carrying out of the requisite public service activity, seem unwilling to proceed with an evaluation of their efforts. If a need for a particular service appears to exist, then supplying that service in accord with the best available knowledge seems to them to be sufficient justification in itself. Thus, evaluation has not received the amount of attention it deserves from the field of public service as the basis for the formulation and development of policies of program administration.

Knutson is particularly critical of evaluation studies in the area of health education for neglecting these broader aspects of policy. He states: "The field of evaluation in health education is particularly weak in the program and policy design levels of research planning. If studies of evaluation are planned in terms of these broader frameworks, the evidence that accumulates will gradually satisfy the long-term as well as the short-term needs of health education and provide a sound basis for program planning."[2]

Evaluative research on a policy level has the important function of challenging traditional practices. James maintains, "Evaluation research is one of the few ways open to us for methodically changing the direction of our activities."[3] In particular, he distinguishes between programs of the past, present, and future.[4] Programs of the past are based upon needs which are well understood and accepted by both the professional and the community at large. In public health, for example, these constitute the traditional communicable disease programs, such as diptheria and smallpox. Public health activities in these areas need little further validation and the major problem is one of maintaining the existing barriers to these diseases. Evaluative research, however, can perform the worthwhile function of streamlining these activities and making them more efficient. Challenging the need for some of these programs through evaluation studies may also show that many of them have been oversold to the community and that changing conditions may have made them ineffective or even unnecessary. Thus, evaluation studies of past programs serve the valuable function of weeding out unproductive effort.

In regard to programs of the present, the need for such programs is also generally recognized, and while adequate resources may be available, they may not, as yet, be fully committed. Current programs do not have the established validity of programs of the past, but they do constitute acceptable targets for attack—even if only on a limited scale and with tentative backing. A significant problem still exists regarding the development of effective services for many current problems. Such programs in public health include tuberculosis control, infant and child supervision, dental programs, and health education in general. The greatest need for evaluation of these types of programs involves built-in evaluative research to assess current progress and to indicate promising new lines of attack. Such evaluation studies may also help to secure support for personnel and financial resources needed to meet existing problems.

Programs of the future are ill-defined except in general terms. Community services are scarce, developmental in nature, and inadequate in terms of the social problem. Similarly, community attitudes are unknown or generally apathetic. Examples of such problem areas in public health include accidents, heart disease, mental illness, cancer, and diabetes. Important as these problems are today as major causes of illness and death, effective public health activities remain to be developed in the future.

Evaluative research has a major contribution to make toward defining objectives and developing new control programs for the future. Demonstration programs of an experimental nature and incorporating evaluative research designs can serve five important functions: (1) to measure the impact of new activities upon the specific social problem; (2) to show their impact upon the other programs and activities of the service agency; (3) to test their acceptance by the public; (4) to serve as a framework for further research; and (5) to help the gradual development of future programs. Such evaluations of demonstration programs constitute perhaps one of the most important research activities of operating agencies.

Evaluation as part of the administrative process is closely tied to such important administrative functions as program planning, development, and operation. We usually think of evaluation as coming at the end of a sequence which proceeds as follows:

1. Research
2. Planning
3. Demonstration
4. Operation
5. Evaluation

However, in a general sense, evaluation as a study of effectiveness may occur at each stage of this process. We may evaluate the findings of a research study, the proposals of a planning project, the feasibility of a developmental program, the accomplishments of an operational program, and even the significance of an evaluation study. It is important to keep in mind our definition of evaluation as the study of the desirable and undesirable consequences of planned social change and to recognize that each of the steps in the diagram above represents a form of human activity designed to achieve certain valued objectives, and, hence, subject to evaluative research.

Research

More specifically, each stage of the administrative process does present somewhat different problems for evaluation. Research programs raise both basic and applied problems of evaluation. As a form of basic research, they are subject to evaluation according to scientific criteria of study design, the reliability and validity of the measurements made, and the significance of the inferences or generalizations. The canons of the scientific method represent evaluative criteria for judging the success or failure of a research project.

Even as scientific projects, moreover, research programs may still be evaluated in terms of administrative criteria of input versus output. From the point of view of administrative science, however, the main criteria for evaluating research will usually relate to its *utility* to the administrator or program director. A great deal has been written about the problems of evaluating how well or poorly the findings of a research project have been utilized.[5] An oft-quoted remark is, "The road to inaction is paved with research reports."

Merton's discussion of "gaps" between research and policy is relevant here. He finds that (1) the research may not have been adequately focused on the practical problem, and (2) concrete forecasts may have been contingent upon uncontrolled conditions.[6] To these inherent "research" gaps must be added a wide range of "organizational" or "interpersonal" gaps between research and policy, that is, "the framework of values (organizational) precludes examination of some practicable courses of action"; "the policy-maker may be more willing to take the risks involved in decisions based on past experience than risks found in research-based recommendations"; "limitations of time and funds may at times condemn an applied research to practical futility"; "lack of continuing communication between policy-maker and research staff"; "status of researcher vis-à-vis the operating agency." This enumeration of barriers to successful research utilization is directly applicable to evaluative research as a form of applied research. We will view this problem in more detail in the next chapter when we discuss the administration *of* evaluative research projects.

Planning

In regard to program planning, evaluation is absolutely essential at all stages of the planning process. Planning proceeds step by step and each step must be evaluated before the next step can be taken. This principle is the basis of a rather ambitious attempt to make the planning process a systematic one involving the development of a network of events or activities related to each other along a time dimension and evaluated according to different estimates of resources and objectives. Known as PERT, this program for systematic planning has been applied to a wide range of administrative activities ranging from airplane production to classroom instruction.[7]

The First National Conference on Evaluation in Public Health assigned an important role to evaluation during program planning. Such evaluation should be built into any planning activity in order to provide for a check on the adequacy of the plan and to permit redirection before the plan becomes too fixed. During this planning stage, evaluative research can feed back information which would permit a redefinition of objectives and a rechanneling of resources. Conducting such evaluation studies at strategic points in the program plan can provide a check on intermediate results and measure progress toward the long-range objective.[8]

James points out that the planning of public service programs involves three main factors: needs, resources, and attitudes.[9] For productive planning, all three of these factors have to be evaluated separately. "A public health need is a problem affecting the health of our population and which, according to prevalent cultural values, requires solution." Such needs, to be evaluated, have to be translated into administrative terms dealing with immediate and ultimate objectives. "To carry out a public health program, secondly, *resources* of trained personnel, vaccines, drugs, x-rays, special diets, clinics, etc., are required." The evaluation of available resources, both their quantity and quality, is a prerequisite to adequate planning. Finally, "effective public health programs can only rarely be conducted in the present era, unless the community attitude toward them is satisfactory." The evaluation of community attitudes involves public opinion studies designed to determine what the public knows, believes, and is willing to do or accept in regard to any specific social problem. The correct evaluation of needs, resources, and attitudes is a prerequisite for administrative program planning.

Demonstration

Given a program plan, the next step is to try it out on a demonstration basis, if possible. Quite often the demand for services and action to meet an obvious threat is so great that one cannot wait to carry out a pilot project. However, whenever possible, high priority needs to be given to the constant development of demonstration programs in order to keep up with new problems and utilize new knowledge. To be worthwhile, such demonstration programs require evaluative research. The entire rationale of a demonstration program is to test the desirability of some proposed course of action. In the absence of such a test, one learns very little from a demonstration program. As stated by Herzog, "A demonstration necessarily involves research . . . a built-in evaluation."[10] She goes on to caution, however, that while such evaluative research is essential, it should be simple "but not 'unscientific.' " The objective of a demonstration project is to demonstrate the *application* of knowledge and not to produce such knowledge.

A somewhat different attitude toward the research functions of a demonstration program is taken by James, who believes that the demonstration program offers an unusual opportunity for conducting research. He finds that the limited generalizability of demonstration projects permits a more flexible approach and the ability to experiment with new ideas involving small populations without having to adhere to the rigid requirements of a research project. He would rank systematic program development by means of demonstration projects high as a source of new ideas and practices. He cautions that "great stress should be laid upon selection of objectives, exploration of the strategic factors involved, building evaluation into the project, and retaining enough flexibility to keep the demonstration useful during its entire development. Instead of stressing only the services to be achieved, careful attention must be given in program development to the elements of failure and what can be done about them. Rather than be annoyed at the problems which arise, their appearance should be welcomed as learning opportunities."[11]

The Office of Vocational Rehabilitation sees demonstration projects as occupying a position midway between research and service. As such they have some of the characteristics of both—one learns and acquires new knowledge at the same time that one tries out new services. The Office of Vocational Rehabilitation defines the demonstration project as "the application in a practical setting of results, derived from either fundamental research or from experience in life situations, for the purpose of determining whether these knowledges or experiences are actually applicable in the practical setting chosen."[12]

Criteria for evaluating demonstration projects, as proposed by the Office of Vocational Rehabilitation, include: (1) Novelty—demonstration programs should offer something new and as yet untried. Hypotheses should be offered as to why this new approach is desirable. (2) Evaluation —systematic evaluation of the effectiveness of the demonstration must be carried out with as high standards of excellence as a basic research study. The requirements of such evaluative research involve conceptualization of the desired objectives and the development of before and after measures of the attainment of these objectives. In addition, these measures of outcomes should permit differentiation of relevant aspects rather than one overall measure and should permit the formulation of hypotheses showing the relationship between the procedures used and the behavioral outcomes.[13] (3) Generalizability—results should be practical and meaningful to normal situations and not limited to particular personnel, equipment or services. (4) Desirability—the significance and value of the project should be clear from the demonstration and its evaluation.

There is some disagreement as to whether the evaluation of a demonstration project should stress its practical or its ideal nature. On the one hand, the argument goes, "When we set out to demonstrate something we are demonstrating to ourselves and to others the relative values of meeting certain community needs in certain ways. But it goes beyond that. If our original hypotheses are proved sound, the techniques we have demonstrated should be carried on in an intensified and expanded program. 'Demonstration' connotes a limited effort with the goal of providing its validity for application on a much broader basis."[14] According to this approach, the evaluation of a demonstration program should indicate the extent to which the demonstration program is practical and can serve as a model for similar programs on a broader scale.

The opposing point of view would plan the demonstration program to stress what is ideally possible in a high quality program. Borgatta finds that "under the concept of demonstration programs, whether they be in the health services or welfare, emphasis is placed on the exemplary application of a service that is assumed already to be effective."[15] In this sense the demonstration program becomes a model program rather than a prototype for similar operating programs. This approach will often be used when there is skepticism or antagonism toward a new program and the emphasis of the evaluation is upon knowing that something worthwhile can be done, provided the required resources are made available.

Both the "typical" and the "model" demonstration programs have their own justifications. A serious error is committed, however, when an evaluation is made without taking into account the type of program and its purpose. Many operating programs prove unsuccessful despite the favorable evaluation of a demonstration project because the demonstration project was a "model" one and was conducted under more favorable circumstances than are possible for an operational program. On the other hand, while the demonstration program should attempt to reproduce conditions realistically, it is important that such conditions offer at least a reasonable possibility of success. The evaluation of a demonstration program which is weak to begin with will only prove its ineffectiveness and interfere with future opportunities for action.

Despite the obvious fact that there is little point in undertaking a demonstration program that is doomed from the start, many program directors do so anyway, probably with the mistaken notion that any demonstration program is better than none. Perhaps this is the reason that so many evaluation studies of public service and community action show negative results—the programs were never really given a fair trial. To some extent this may also explain why, as we shall see in the next section, so many program directors resist building-in evaluation to their demonstration programs. They never really had faith in the program to begin with and an evaluation could only prove embarrassing.

In evaluating a demonstration program, particular attention should be paid to the analysis of process—how and why various aspects of the program failed or succeeded, among whom the effects were most noticeable, when these effects occurred, how long they lasted, and so forth.[16] Of special importance are the possible "boomerang" or negative side effects. Detection of these in the demonstration program offers the possibility of avoiding or lessening them in the operating program. A parallel might be drawn between this aspect of program evaluation and the field trials or demonstration stage of drug research. After a new drug has been proven effective in the laboratory or clinic, it must still undergo evaluation by a field demonstration involving its use in a wide variety of actual treatment programs.

At the present time, the major emphasis of many action research projects is upon demonstration programs on the federal, state, and local levels. These demonstration programs appear to offer an acceptable compromise between research projects which are too slow and operational programs which are too experimental or expensive. The demonstration program seems to be the administrator's answer to public demand that "something be done" to meet a problem. It is quite likely, as Blum and Leonard predict:

> We predict that with motivation of public administration, many, if not most, public-service programs can and will be started as demonstrations. Quality evaluation will be built in such a way as to permit maximum flexibility. Even at what superficially seems to involve major costs, demonstrations that determine whether extensive or long-term efforts should be adopted will be the means of getting better and more extensive service at less cost than today's unevaluated, skimpy, and often ineffective programs. With improved quality of administration and scientific programming, demonstrations in one area should provide some pilot experience for others.[17]

Operation

A successful operational program is, of course, the ultimate goal of program planning, demonstration, and evaluation. The general purpose of program planning is to define the problem and to formulate program objectives and devise the means or activities for accomplishing these objectives. The demonstration program helps to indicate the probable success of the planned program, to try out procedures, and to suggest modifications. The evaluation provides a measure of the extent to which the demonstration or operational program attains the desired results. But it is this operational program with its actual "delivery of services" which provides the ultimate rationale for all of the other administrative processes.

Evaluative research is a basic ingredient of "scientific" program management. To the extent that operational programs are closely linked to the attainment of some desired objective rather than to the perpetuation of their own existence, they will make constant use of evaluation studies. Such evaluation studies may serve the following valuable functions for program operation.

1. Determine the extent to which program activities are achieving the desired objectives. Measure the degree of progress toward ultimate goals and indicate level of attainment.

2. Point out specific strong and weak points of program operation and suggest changes and modifications of procedures and objectives. Increase effectiveness by maximizing strengths and minimizing weaknesses.

3. Examine efficiency and adequacy of programs compared to other methods and total needs. Improve program procedures and increase scope.

4. Provide quality-controls. Set standards of performance and check on their continuous attainment.

5. Help to clarify program objectives by requiring operational definition in terms of measurable criteria. Challenge the "taken-for-granted" assumptions underlying programs. Point out inconsistencies in objectives or activities.

6. Develop new procedures and suggest new approaches and programs for future programs.

7. Provide checks on possible "boomerang" or negative side effects. Alert staff to possible changes of the program.

8. Establish priorities among programs in terms of best use of limited resources—funds, personnel, and time.

9. Indicate degree of transferability of program to other areas and populations. Suggest necessary modifications to fit changing times and places.

10. Advance scientific knowledge base of professional practice by testing effectiveness of proposed preventive and treatment programs. Suggest hypotheses for future research.

11. Advance administrative science by testing effectiveness of different organizational structures and modes of operation.

12. Provide public accountability. Justify program to public. In-

crease public support for successful programs and decrease demand for unnecessary or unsuccessful ones.

13. Build morale of staff by involving them in evaluation of their efforts. Provide goals and standards against which to measure progress and achievement.

14. Develop a critical attitude among staff and field personnel. Increase communication and information among program staff resulting in better coordination of services.

It must be remembered that the foregoing list is probably more applicable to the potential than the actual advantages of evaluative research. This is what evaluative research tries to accomplish; in very few instances does it actually succeed. Fleck distinguishes three types of evaluation research in relation to program operations: (1) *Ritualistic*—the development of activity indices, most often found when the goal of the program is short-term stability. "Organizational changes need not take place if the factors that produce the index are to a large extent irrelevant to the organization." (2) *Operational*—the measure of efficiency or the maximum yield per unit of cost. "The unequivocal precision obtainable by the operational method is more than offset by its failure to describe accurately the conditions under which an organization will act." (3) *Behavioral* —aimed at change to meet new conditions. Objective is long-range survival versus short-term stability. "The evaluation study revealed a great trend and provided guidelines for deliberate action."[18] It is probably true that at the present moment most evaluation studies are likely to be of the ritualistic type.

This is not too difficult to understand. Operational programs are often highly entrenched activities based upon a large collection of inadequately tested assumptions and defended by staff and field personnel with strong vested interests in the continuation of the program as it is. It is obvious from this description that an evaluation study which proposes to challenge the effectiveness of an established operational program poses a real threat to program personnel. Therefore, it is not surprising to note how rare and how difficult it is to conduct an evaluation study of an existing program. To a large extent such evaluations are limited to new programs which are still open to change. And yet the need for evaluation is undoubtedly greatest for established operating programs.

James recognizes this problem when he talks about the need "to build dissatisfaction" into traditional programs. Since it is unlikely that this dissatisfaction will come from within the program itself, he strongly suggests the use of an advisory committee of outsiders that meets regularly to review the current status of the program. This type of critical review can also be furthered through the use of interdisciplinary program teams. Given a mixture of disciplines or backgrounds, it is more likely that some member will challenge the existing program. Unless there is some dissatisfaction, James sees very little likelihood of an evaluation of an operating program. This point is underscored by Borgatta, who finds that "when conditions are bad enough and social conscience is brought into play, both the need and the potential for improvement may lead to the development of a program designed to be corrective. Most programs that receive systematic attention for evaluation occur in the context of correcting an existing situation."[19]

Change is often a stimulus to evaluating existing programs. If the state of a problem changes, or if a new method of meeting this problem is discovered, it is more likely that an attempt will be made to evaluate the desirability of continuing a traditional program. Sometimes even a change in personnel, especially at the administrative level, will provide the opportunity to reevaluate a program. A change in available resources, either in personnel or funds, may require a decision concerning the relative priority of an old or a new approach which would encourage evaluative research. Competition can be an effective stimulus toward evaluation.

It is obvious from these brief remarks that the evaluation of an ongoing, established, operational program is fraught with administrative considerations. Quite often these may lead to what we might call an "abuse" of evaluative research; that is, the evaluation is done with some other purpose than program improvement in mind. For example, we may list the following forms of evaluative "abuse" or pseudo-evaluation:

1. *Eye-wash*—an attempt to justify a weak or bad program by deliberately selecting only those aspects that "look good." The objective of the evaluation is limited to those parts of the program that appear successful.

2. *White-wash*—an attempt to cover up program failure or errors by

avoiding any objective appraisal. A favorite device here is to solicit "testimonials" which divert attention from the failure.

3. *Submarine*—an attempt to "torpedo" or destroy a program regardless of its worth in order to get rid of it. This often occurs in administrative clashes over power or prestige when opponents are "sunk" along with their programs.

4. *Posture*—an attempt to use evaluation as a "gesture" of objectivity and to assume the pose of "scientific" research. This "looks good" to the public and is a sign of "professional" status.

5. *Postponement*—an attempt to delay needed action by pretending to seek the "facts." Evaluative research takes time and, hopefully, the storm will blow over by the time the study is completed.

6. *Substitution*—an attempt to "cloud over" or disguise failure in an essential part of the program by shifting attention to some less relevant, but defensible, aspect of the program.

These are only some of the many ways an ingenious administrator can utilize evaluative research to further his own rather than the program's objectives. All of these occur constantly in the "games people play" in administrative circles, but when they become systematized as "evaluation research," we feel justified in labeling them "abuses." As we shall see later in our discussion of administrator-evaluator role relationships, these misuses of evaluation pose a major ethical problem for the evaluator as researcher and may become a serious source of conflict between himself and the program staff.

Borgatta lists some of the many ways in which the results of even a well-conducted evaluation study may be rationalized so as to avoid the need to act upon negative findings.[20] These rationalizations may be used before the fact to prevent the initiation of any evaluative research, or after the fact to dismiss the findings as not significant. For example, rationalizations for avoiding evaluation include the following:

1. The effects of the program are long-range; thus, the consequences cannot be measured in the immediate future.
2. The effects are general rather than specific; thus, no single criterion can be utilized to evaluate the program, and, indeed, even using many measures would not really get at complex general consequences intended.

3. The results are small, but significant; thus, they cannot be measured effectively because instruments are not sufficiently sensitive.
4. The effects are subtle, and circumstances may not be ordered appropriately to get at the qualities that are being changed. The measurement would disturb the processes involved.
5. Experimental manipulation cannot be carried out because to withhold treatment from some persons would not be fair.

Rationalizations of negative findings, even when the evaluation study is well conducted, include:

1. The effectiveness of the program cannot really be judged because those who could use the services most did not participate.
2. Some of the persons who received the services improved greatly. Clearly, some of the persons who recovered could not have done so if they had not received attention.
3. Some of the persons who most needed the program were actually in the control group.
4. The fact that no difference was found between the persons receiving services and those not receiving services clearly indicates that the program was not sufficiently intensive. More of the services are obviously required.
5. Persons in the control group received other kinds of attention.

Occasionally one will even find the research worker being attacked because his evaluation study "failed" to find the desired effects. Thus, a "good" evaluation of a "bad" program may often be dismissed as a research failure—and not infrequently, the evaluator will apologize for his lack of positive findings.

A major effort to place the evaluation of operational programs on a "scientific" basis and to decrease the possibilities of bias or abuse is represented by the rapidly growing field of operations research. Using a systematic and comprehensive approach which involves all four processes of program planning, demonstration, operation, and evaluation, operations research attempts to develop models of interaction, often utilizing mathematical concepts, which provide guidelines for the most productive and efficient use of available resources to meet specified objectives. This method is highly technical and requires detailed treatment in its own right. Several excellent books deal with the theory and practice of this approach.[21]

In general, operations research consists of the following steps:

1. Statement of Objective;
2. Process of Attaining Objective;
3. Development of Model;
4. Evaluation of Model;
5. Application of Model.

This approach has been used quite successfully in relation to hospital operation and other health services.[22] As described by James, "Operations research has helped greatly to clear the air for public health evaluation by stressing and not glossing over the compromises between research findings and the art of public health practice. If it should reveal, for example, that restaurant sanitation emphasizes goals that are aesthetic rather than disease-preventing, then attention can be switched to technics which can achieve a maximum aesthetic return for the least effort."[23]

An important aspect of evaluation in relation to operations research is the continuous check it provides upon determining the optimal combination of program practices related to the desired goal. By stating the conditions under which certain procedures will attain predetermined goals, operations research provides for the "establishment of evaluation machinery with an apparatus for new decision-making when the key variables change beyond predetermined limits."[24] Evaluation is thus an essential feature of all aspects of operations research.

One component of evaluative research that is often neglected and that constitutes an important aspect of operations research is the cost of a program. Few programs can be justified at any cost. Priorities among public services must often be determined on the basis of the most desirable allocation of resources—money, personnel, facilities. Competition among service programs sets the stage for a public demand for evaluation of results in terms of required resources. Weisbrod points out that while improved health is desirable, so are improved housing, highways, flood control, recreation facilities, and so on. Since we cannot have everything, we must economize. He concludes, "To make choices in a rational manner requires estimation of the relative importance of the various alternatives. . . . With this general possibility in mind, increasing attention has come to be paid to estimating in money terms the real importance of good health—or, what is the same thing, estimating losses from poor health. . . .[25]

Arbona stresses the importance of evaluating the positive effects of action programs in a nation's economy. "It is very important to design a methodology that will demonstrate to the satisfaction of all, but especially of the economists, how investments in health result in the improvement of a nation's economy. This need is especially vital in developing countries where resources are limited and other services generally absorb so large a proportion of national budgets that health services' support is meager compared to needs."[26] The development of program and performance budgeting for public service programs represents an attempt to introduce the "cost" criterion into evaluative research.[27,28] In using these cost criteria, however, one must keep in mind the social aspects of such a financial evaluation. As Flagle cautions, "The construction of a table or scale of utilities, although cast in terms of economics, is essentially a psychological experiment involving social values."[29]

Resistance and barriers to evaluation

Few individuals with strongly vested interests in the programs they are conducting can be expected to welcome an objective evaluation. Many of them have been "socialized" into taking the worthwhileness of their activities for granted and are naturally resistant to having these activities and their underlying assumptions challenged.[30] Furthermore, many of them are sincerely convinced that evaluative research is not really "scientific" and cannot be relied upon to produce reliable and valid results. Others are too caught up in the daily demands of providing "obviously necessary" services to take the time for research, especially if this requires an interruption or modification of services or the reallocation of limited resources.

A good example of such administrative resistance is offered by Wright and Hyman in describing their experiences in evaluating the Encampment for Citizenship.

> . . . There is reason for the researcher to be apprehensive about such matters. The staff of such institutions as the Encampment often have invested considerable time, effort, and sentiment in their programs. They may be

ego-involved in their activities. They may be sensitive to the cold-blooded, objective probings of the scientific researcher. Even under favorable circumstances, it is common to find that action-oriented and dedicated persons are unreceptive to social science. . . . How much more likely a hostile reaction may be if such measurements threaten to reveal unfavorable information![31]

The literature on evaluative research contains some examples of evaluation studies which have produced "negative" results. Yankauer and his colleagues discuss the doubtful benefits of annual school physical examinations;[32] Wilner and his associates after a careful evaluation of housing projects point out the minor health advantages of such projects despite optimistic claims to the contrary;[33] Meyer and Borgatta could find very little positive impact in a well-planned rehabilitation program for mental patients.[34] And, as James points out, for each of these tested programs there are dozens of untested programs which continue in existence despite any convincing evidence of their accomplishments.[35]

Administrative resistance is also likely to be magnified if there is the possibility of a conflict between the goals or objectives of the program and the goals or objectives of the organization itself. Organizations and administrative structures will tend to perpetuate themselves. The organizational goals thus become those of survival, stability, power, and growth. These may conflict with the program goals of the organization, which may be to do away with a problem—and hence the need for the organization. If the results of the evaluation study tend to weaken the power of the organization, such a study will tend to be resisted. Even if the study is conducted and the results indicate that the organization has done such a good job that it is in danger of putting itself out of business, organizational pressures will tend to seek a new problem area to justify the continuation of the organization. The proposition as stated by Berelson and Steiner reads, "There is a tendency for organizations to equate power with purpose, or even to place power above purpose, so that survival as an organization becomes an end in itself. . . . An oversimplified way to put this is to say that most organizations will adjust rather than die: after all, they are made up of human beings who will do the same."[36]

Notes

1.   C. I. Lewis, "An Analysis of Knowledge and Valuation, *The Paul Carus Foun dation Lectures VII* (La Salle, Ill.: Open Court Publishing Co., 1946), p. 3.
2.   Andie L. Knutson, "Evaluating Health Education," *Public Health Reports* 67 (January 1952): 73–77.
3.   George James, "Research by Local Health Departments—Problems, Methods, Results," *American Journal of Public Health* 48 (March 1958): 354.
4.   George James, "Planning and Evaluation of Health Programs," in *Administration of Community Health Services* (Chicago: International City Managers' Association, 1961), chapter 6.
5.   Alvin W. Gouldner, "Theoretical Requirements of the Applied Social Sciences," *American Sociological Review* 22 (February 1957): 92–102.
6.   Robert K. Merton, "The Role of Applied Social Science in the Formation of Policy," *Philosophy of Science* 16 (July 1949): 161–81.
7.   J. W. Blood (ed.), *PERT: A New Management Planning and Control Technique* (New York: American Management Association, 1962).
8.   "Evaluation in Public Health," *Public Health Reports* 71 (June 1956): 526–27.
9.   George James, "The Present Status and Future Development of Community Health Research—A Critique from the Viewpoint of Community Health Agencies," *Annals of the New York Academy of Sciences,* 22 May 1963, p. 761.
10.   Elizabeth Herzog, "Research Demonstrations and Common Sense," *Child Welfare,* June 1962, p. 245.
11.   James, "Planning and Evaluation of Health Programs," *op. cit.,* p. 133.
12.   John W. Criswell, *The Place of Demonstration Projects in the Program of the Office of Vocational Rehabilitation,* Washington, D.C., August 1962, p. 1. Mimeographed.
13.   *Ibid.,* p. 2.
14.   *Planning Evaluations of Mental Health Programs* (New York: Milbank Memorial Fund, 1958), p. 49.
15.   Edgar F. Borgatta, "Research Problems in Evaluation of Health Service Demonstrations," *Milbank Memorial Fund Quarterly* 44, pt. 2 (October 1966): 196.
16.   As stressed by Blum and Leonard, "If the demonstration ultimately proves successful and accomplishes its objectives, the key to its adoption or usefulness elsewhere may be not so much in the proof of effectiveness as in knowledge of the steps that resulted in its development and secured participation and acceptance." Hendrik L. Blum and Alvin R. Leonard, *Public Administration: A Public Health Viewpoint* (New York: Macmillan, 1963), p. 318.
17.   *Ibid.,* p. 320.

18. Andrew C. Fleck, "Evaluation Research Programs in Public Health Practice," *Annals of the New York Academy of Sciences,* 22 May 1963, pp. 721-23.

19. Borgatta, *op. cit.,* pp. 183-84. To some extent, the conditions specified by Merton and Devereux for creating public concern about a social problem also promote evaluative research: "(1) A *perceived discrepancy* between some existing (or future) external situation, on the one hand, and the values or goals of an individual or organization, on the other; (2) A feeling of a *need for adjustive activity* or for creative action of some sort; (3) A 'puzzle element'—an *awareness of ignorance or doubt* about at least some of the facts and relationships believed to be relevant to a decision about what, if anything, should be done." Robert K. Merton and Edward C. Devereux, Jr., "Practical Problems and the Uses of Social Science," *Trans-action,* July 1964, pp. 18-21.

20. Borgatta, *ibid.,* pp. 186-87.

21. Joseph F. McCloskey and Florence N. Trefethen (eds.), *Operations Research for Management* (Baltimore: Johns Hopkins Press, 1954); C. West Churchman, Russell L. Ackoff, and E. Leonard Arnoff, *Introduction to Operations Research* (New York: John Wiley, 1957).

22. Charles D. Flagle, "Operational Research in the Health Services," *Annals of the New York Academy of Sciences,* 22 May 1963, pp. 748-59; Martin S. Feldstein, "Operational Research and Efficiency in Health Service," *The Lancet,* March 1963, pp. 491-93.

23. James, "Research by Local Health Departments—Problems, Methods, Results," *op. cit.,* p. 355.

24. Otis L. Anderson, "Operations Research in Public Health," *Public Health Reports* 79 (April 1964): 297-305.

25. Burton A. Weisbrod, "Does Better Health Pay?," *Public Health Reports* 75 (June 1960): 557.

26. Guillermo Arbona, "Public Health Progress in Puerto Rico," *Public Health Reports* 79 (January 1964): 42.

27. L. J. Taubenhaus, R. H. Hamlin, and R. C. Wood, "Performance Reporting and Program Budgeting: Tools for Program Evaluation," *American Journal of Public Health* 47 (April 1957): 432-38.

28. George James, Daniel Klepak, and Herman E. Hilleboe, "Fiscal Research in Public Health," *American Journal of Public Health* 45 (July 1955): 906-14.

29. Flagle, *op. cit.,* p. 758.

30. Such resistance to changes in established values and practices extends beyond the administrator to the community itself. This has been substantiated by many studies of attempts to change community programs. For example, as described by Lewis: "Those who enter a community to engage in an action program must recognize the implications of the fact that they are not entering a power vacuum. In every human community there exists a network of relations between individuals. It is to the interest of many of these individuals to maintain this system of relationships. Any group of

outsiders moving into a community will be seen by some as potentially disruptive, even if they plan no action. If they do plan action, whatever positive measures they undertake, no matter how benign, will be perceived by some community members as a threat to their own status and interests." Oscar Lewis, "Medicine and Politics in a Mexican Village," in Benjamin D. Paul (ed.), *Health, Culture, and Community* (New York: Russell Sage Foundation, 1955), p. 431.

31.   Charles R. Wright, and Herbert H. Hyman, "The Evaluators," in Philip E. Hammond (ed.), *Sociologists at Work* (New York: Basic Books, 1964), p. 123.

32.   A. Yankauer et al., "A Study of Periodic School Medical Examinations," *American Journal of Public Health* 45 (January 1955): 71–78; 46 (December 1956): 1553–62; 47 (November 1957): 1421–29; 52 (April 1962): 656-57.

33.   Daniel M. Wilner, R. P. Walkley, T. C. Pinkerton, and M. Tayback, *Housing Environment and Family Life* (Baltimore: Johns Hopkins Press, 1962).

34.   Henry J. Meyer and Edgar F. Borgatta, *An Experiment in Mental Patient Rehabilitation* (New York: Russell Sage Foundation, 1959).

35.   George James, "Research by Local Health Departments—Problems, Methods, Results," *op. cit.* Specifically, he points out, "One of the simplest methods of doing this is to carry out a survey to collect relevant data concerning needs, resources, and attitudes, carry out the program, and then to repeat the survey to evaluate the changes. Curiously enough, although steps one and two are fairly common, health officers have done relatively little with step three. By the time step three is reached, the program is deemed a success and evaluation relegated to a low priority. This has been the case with both child guidance and crippled children's programs, two amazing instances of the lack of priority given to the follow-up of the hundreds of thousands who have received such care in every section of the country during the past two decades" (p. 356).

36.   Bernard Berelson and Gary Steiner, *Human Behavior: An Inventory of Scientific Findings* (New York: Harcourt, Brace and World, Inc., 1964). A good example of this process may be seen in the National Foundation which shifted its goals from poliomyelitis to children's disabilities in general after the former problem had been brought under control. MacIntosh goes so far as to claim that the major objective of many voluntary agencies which are focused upon some specific social problem should be aimed at "self-extinction." From a talk before the Eastern States Health Conference on "Voluntary Action in the British Health Services," New York, 27 April 1961.

41

Leadership:
A Frame of Reference*

Robert Tannenbaum and
Fred Massarik

Introduction

The word *leadership* has been widely used. Political orators, business executives, social workers, and scholars employ it in speech and
writing. Yet, there is widespread disagreement as to its meaning. Among
social scientists, the theoretical formulations of the leadership concept
have continued to shift, focusing first upon one aspect and then upon
another. Much still needs to be done to develop a basic, systematic
theory. The time seems ripe for attempting a careful statement of a frame
of reference which may serve to make available research more meaningful, and which may guide future research and practice.[1] Specifically, such
a frame of reference can perform the useful function of pointing to the

Reprinted from *Leadership and Organization: A Behavioral Science Approach,* by Robert Tannenbaum, Irving R. Weschler, and Fred Massarik, pp. 22–
42. Copyright © 1961 by McGraw-Hill, Inc. Used by permission of McGraw-Hill
Book Company and the authors.

*This chapter is a slightly modified version of an article under the same title
by Robert Tannenbaum and Fred Massarik, *Management Science,* vol. 4, no. 1, pp.
1–19, October, 1957.

[1]The evolution of the frame of reference proposed in this chapter cannot be
attributed to any one individual; rather, most persons who have been members of
the Human Relations Research Group, Institute of Industrial Relations and School
of Business Administration, UCLA, during the past few years have played a significant role in its development. These persons, in addition to the present authors, are
Paula Brown, Raymond Ezekiel, Arnold Gebel, Murray Kahane, Verne Kallejian,
Gertrude Peterson, Clovis and Pat Shepherd, Eugene Talbot, and Irving R.
Weschler.

variables which need to be measured. It can help us to state hypotheses concerning the key variables underlying leadership effectiveness. It can also provide meaningful objectives for the development of more adequate leaders.

A brief historical view

The history of the "leadership" concept highlights the shifting focus in theoretical orientation. Early leadership research focused on the *leader* himself, to the virtual exclusion of other variables. It was assumed that leadership effectiveness could be explained by isolating psychological and physical characteristics, or traits, which were presumed to differentiate the leader from other members of his group. Studies guided by this assumption generally proved none too fruitful. Almost without exception universal traits proved elusive, and there was little agreement as to the most useful traits. Gouldner reviews some of the empirical and conservatively interpreted evidence relating to "universal traits," such as intelligence and psychosexual appeal. However, he concludes: "At this time there is no reliable evidence concerning the existence of universal leadership traits."[2] It does not now seem surprising that this approach proved rather sterile. Leaders do not function in isolation. They must deal with followers within a cultural, social, and physical context.

With the fall from grace of the trait approach, the emphasis swung away from the leader as an entity complete unto himself. Instead, the *situationist* approach came to the fore. The situationists do not necessarily abandon the search for significant leader characteristics, but they attempt to look for them in situations containing common elements. Stogdill, after examining a large number of leadership studies aimed at isolating the traits of effective leaders, comes to the following conclusion: "The qualities, characteristics and skills required in a leader are determined to a large extent by the demands of the situation in which he is to function as a leader."[3]

[2]Alvin W. Gouldner, ed., *Studies in Leadership* (New York: Harper & Brothers, 1950), pp. 31–35, especially p. 34.

[3]See Ralph M. Stogdill, "Personal Factors Associated with Leadership: A Survey of the Literature," *Journal of Psychology* 25 (January 1948): 63.

More recently the *follower* has been systematically considered as a major variable in leadership research. This approach focuses on personal needs, assuming that the most effective leader is the one who most nearly satisfies the needs of his followers.[4]

There have been many attempts to assess recent developments in leadership theory. The trait approach, the situationist approach, and the follower-oriented approach have variously been discussed and evaluated by a number of authors including Stogdill, Jenkins, Gouldner, and Sanford.[5] On the basis of their work, it has become increasingly clear that, in the words of Sanford,[6]

> It now looks as if any comprehensive theory of leadership will have to find a way of delaing, in terms of one consistent set of rubrics, with the three delineable facets of the leadership phenomenon:
>
> 1. the leader and his psychological attributes
> 2. the follower with his problems, attitudes and needs, and
> 3. The group situation in which followers and leaders relate with one another.
>
> To concentrate on any one of these facets of the problem represents oversimplification of an intricate phenomenon.

Consequently, the frame of reference which we present is an attempt to take into account these three facets.

A basic definition of leadership

We define leadership as *interpersonal influence, exercised in situation and directed, through the communication process, toward the attain-*

[4]For example, see Fillmore H. Sanford, *Authoritarianism and Leadership* (Philadelphia: Institute for Research in Human Relations, 1950), chap. 1.

[5]See Stogdill, *op. cit.;* Gouldner, *op. cit.* (Introduction); William D. Jenkins, "A Review of Leadership Studies with Particular Reference to Military Problems," *Psychological Bulletin* (January 1947): 54–79; Fillmore H. Sanford, "Research in Military Leadership," in his *Current Trends: Psychology in the World Emergency* (Pittsburgh: University of Pittsburgh Press, 1952), pp. 45–59.

[6]Sanford, "Research in Military Leadership," p. 60.

ment of a specified goal or goals.[7] Leadership always involves attempts on the part of a *leader* (influencer) to affect (influence) the behavior of a *follower* (influencee) or followers in *situation.*

This definition has the virtue of generality. It does not limit the leadership concept to formally appointed functionaries or to individuals whose influence potential rests upon the voluntary consent of others. Rather, it is applicable to *all* interpersonal relationships in which influence attempts are involved. Relationships as apparently diverse as the superior-subordinate, the staff-line, the consultant-client, the salesman-customer, the teacher-student, the counselor-counselee, the husband-wife, or the parent-child are all seen as involving leadership. Thus, our proposed frame of reference, based on the definition and given continuing substance through a flow of relevant research findings from many disciplines, can be useful in understanding a wide range of social phenomena.

One way of characterizing our definition of leadership is to say that it treats leadership as a *process* or *function* rather than as an exclusive attribute of a *prescribed role.* The subordinate often influences the superior; the customer, the salesman; and the group member, the chairman. In any given relationship, the roles of the influencer and the influencee often shift from one person to the other. Conceptually, the influence process or function is present even though the specific individuals taking the roles of influencer and influencee may vary. Thus, the leader role is one which is rarely taken continuously by one individual, even under specific conditions with the same persons. Instead, it is one that is taken at one time or another by each individual.

[7]Essentially, our definition subsumes definitions 1B, 1C, and 1E in the Ohio State "Paradigm for the Study of Leadership," all of which have to do with influence. The Ohio State definitions follow.

"1B. (The leader is the) individual who exercises positive influence acts upon others.

"1C. (The leader is the) individual who exercises more, or more important, positive influence acts than any other member in the group.

"1E. (The leader is the) individual who exercises most influence in goal-setting and goal-achievement."

See Richard T. Morris and Melvin Seeman, "The Problem of Leadership: An Interdisciplinary Approach," *American Journal of Sociology* 56, no. 2 (September 1950): 151. Reasons for our use of *situation* rather than *a situation* are presented on page 26.

One criticism of our definition is that it unrealistically focuses on what appears to be a two-person relationship to the exclusion of group phenomena. For a number of reasons, we find this criticism unconvincing. First, the influencee at any given time may be more than one individual; an entire group may be considered to be the "follower." Second, since the leader role is not restricted to a formally prescribed person, the notion of shared leadership is consistent with our view. Finally, the presence of other persons—with their values, beliefs, and customary modes of behavior—in the context of any given (and often momentary) interpersonal relationship represents a complex of variables which we take into account as a part of the situation. Our focus is on a relationship which is often transitory and always affected by situational contexts.

The components of leadership

Having made these general observations about the definition, we will now discuss in greater detail some considerations that arise in connection with its major components.

Interpersonal influence

The essence of leadership is interpersonal influence, involving the influencer in an attempt to affect the behavior of the influencee through communication. We use the word *attempt* advisedly, in order to draw a distinction between influence efforts and influence effects.

To many, an act of leadership has occurred only if specified goals have been achieved. Under this interpretation, whether or not an individual may be called a leader in a given influence instance depends upon whether or not he is successful. If he is not, no leadership has occurred. Were we to accept this notion of leadership, we would be faced with the necessity of finding a satisfactory term for labeling unsuccessful influence efforts. It is our preference to let leadership refer to influence attempts and to treat the assessment of leadership effectiveness as a separate matter. Thus a person who attempts to influence others but is unsuccessful is still a leader in our view, although a highly ineffective one.

It is useful to draw a distinction between power and leadership. Power is potential for influence. However, even though an individual may possess considerable power in relationship to another, he may for a number of reasons (his personal values, apparent lack of necessity to do so, misjudgment) not use all of the power available to him. A leadership act reflects that portion of the power available to an individual which he chooses to employ at the time.[8]

It should be noted, in contrast to the above view, that the concept *power* frequently connotes a potential for coercion, based, for example, upon physical force, informal social pressure, law, and authority. In actuality, a given leader typically has available not only these external sources providing him with power, but also power derived from such inner resources as understanding and flexibility.

Exercised in situation

The concept *situation* is to be found in much of the recent writing on leadership. An analysis of this literature indicates that the term has been variously used to denote an activity or a particular set of activities engaged in by a group; group characteristics, including interpersonal relationships; group goals or needs; and the cultural context.[9]

It seems appropriate to us to define *situation* as including only those aspects of the objective context which, at any given moment, have an attitudinal or behavioral impact (whether consciously or unconsciously) on the individuals in the influence relationship, and to recognize that the

---

[8]For a relevant discussion of power, see D. Cartwright, *Toward a Social Psychology of Groups: The Concept of Power,* presidential address delivered before the Society for the Psychological Study of Social Issues, Cleveland, Ohio, 5 Sept. 1953, p. 19. Mimeographed.

[9]For varying views of "situation," see Daniel Bell, " 'Screening' Leaders in a Democracy," *Commentary* 5, no. 4 (April 1948): 368–375; Gouldner, *op. cit.;* J. K. Hemphill, *Situational Factors in Leadership,* The Ohio State University Studies, Bureau of Educational Research Monograph no. 32 (Columbus: The Ohio State University, 1949); Jenkins, *op. cit.;* Paul Pigors, *Leadership or Domination* (Boston: Houghton Mifflin Company, 1935); Sanford, *Authoritarianism and Leadership;* Melvin Seeman, "Role Conflict and Ambivalence in Leadership," *American Sociological Review* 18 (August 1953): 373–380; Stogdill, *op. cit.*

situation of the leader and that of the follower may differ from each other in many respects. Both the phenomenological field and unconscious modes of response to external stimuli are relevant here. Stimuli having independent empirical reality, but having no impact on one or the other of the individuals, cannot be viewed as components of their respective situations. It is thus important to know, though not always easy operationally to ascertain, which stimuli external to the leader and to the follower affect each as they interact in the influence relationship.

The objective context of any influence relationship might include any or all of the following:

1. Physical phenomena (noise, light, table and chair arrangement, etc.)

2. Other individuals, including the members of the specific group of which the leader and follower are a part

3. The organization

4. The broader culture, including social norms, role prescriptions, stereotypes, etc.

5. Goals, including personal goals, group goals, and organizational goals

In reality, goals are an essential part of the concepts of group, organization, and culture. However, because of their special importance to the study of leadership, we here treat them separately.

An individual may influence the behavior of others by manipulating elements of their environment (situation). Thus, placing physical facilities in close proximity so that people can work near each other rather than in isolation may promote higher levels of productivity and/or job satisfaction. Since our definition limits leadership to interpersonal influence exercised through the communication process, we would not associate manipulation of situational components with leadership except in a special case—that in which such manipulation is intended by the leader as a communication symbol per se, carrying with it such implications as "this is a good place to work," "they always have our interests at heart," and the like.

_____

The communication process

Our definition of leadership concerns only that interpersonal influence which is exercised through the communication process. We thus exclude, for example, the direct physical manipulation of another person, since such coercion, in its pure form, does not utilize symbolic means. On the other hand, we include threats and other coercive devices which can be imparted only by means of communication.

There are many problems involved in differentiating conceptually between the communication[10] and the leadership processes. We view communication as the sole process through which a leader, as leader, can function. The objective of a communicator, as communicator, is to transmit a message from himself to a communicatee which the latter will interpret as the former desires. The communicator's goal is to convey meanings, or ideas, without distortion.

The leader is interested in more than simply conveying ideas for their own sake. With rare exceptions, the leader's final objective is not solely to bring about attitude change. Rather, the leader makes use of communication as the medium through which he tries to affect the follower's attitudes so that the follower will be ready to move or will actually move in the direction of the specified goal. Of course, there is often a time lag between a change in the follower's attitude and the actual or potential goal movement.

An individual may communicate effectively without being an effective leader. He may desire, for example, that another individual leave the room, and he tells him so. The other individual may say, "I understand you want me to leave the room," and yet remain seated. The leader has been understood, the meaning he has transmitted presumably has been received without distortion, and effective communication has taken place. However, the leader has not succeeded in changing the follower's attitudes in such a way that this follower has been motivated to behave in accordance with the specified goal (overt behavior involving leaving the room). Thus, the leadership attempt has been ineffective.

As our later discussion will suggest, a leader, in order to be effective,

---

[10]For two excellent discussions of the communication process, see Franklin Fearing, "Toward a Psychological Theory of Human Communication," *Journal of Personality,* 22 (September 1953): 71–88; Wendell Johnson, "The Fateful Process of Mr. A. Talking to Mr. B.," *Harvard Business Review* 31 (January-February 1953): 49–56.

needs to select those communication behaviors from his repertory which are likely to "strike the right chord" in the follower's personality make-up, resulting in changed attitudes and behavior in line with the desired goal.

Directed toward the attainment of a specified goal or goals

All leadership acts are goal-oriented. The leader uses his influence to achieve some desired (although often unconscious) goal or goals. These goals toward which individuals exert their influence fall into four categories, whose differences have considerable relevance for leadership theory. The following classification should not suggest that any given influence effort is necessarily aimed exclusively at one single goal. Often a complex of goals is involved, as when a leader brings about the attainment of organizational goals and at the same time satisfies some of his own needs.

1. *Organizational goals.* In formal organizations, managers (as leaders) are those who are held responsible by their superiors for influencing others (subordinates) toward the attainment of organizational goals.[11] These goals are the rationally contrived purposes of the organizational entity. Since these goals often have little or no direct motivational import to the followers, the manager's task of leadership often requires him to use other inducements which do have relevance to the need systems of the followers.

2. *Group goals.* In small, informal, face-to-face groups the relevant goals are those which evolve through the interaction of the members of the group. They reflect (although not necessarily unanimously) "what the group wants to do." In such a situation, the leader is anyone who uses his influence to facilitate the group's attainment of its own goals. The achievement of a position of effective influence in such groups depends upon an individual's sensitivity to the group's objectives and upon his skill in bringing about their realization.

3. *Personal goals of the follower.* In such activities as teaching, training, counseling, therapy, and consulting, the leader often uses his influence to assist the follower in attaining his own (the follower's) personal

[11][Footnote omitted.]

goals.[12]For example, through the establishment of an atmosphere of warmth, security, and acceptance and through the use of facilitative methods, the leader aids another person to reach ends he has not been able to reach by himself.

4. *Personal goals of the leader.* Leaders also use their influence primarily to meet their own needs. At times such personal motives are at the level of consciousness and can be made explicit, but often they lie at the unconscious level where they are hidden from the leader. A teacher may think that he lectures to a class because "this is the best way to teach," without realizing that in so doing he feels more secure because the students never have a chance to "show him up." Likewise, a supervisor may harshly discipline a subordinate because "it is important to keep people in line," although a deep-felt need to express hostility receives some satisfaction through his behavior.

The issue of conscious and unconscious intent poses some knotty problems for both leadership theory and research. Should we be concerned only with objectives that can be made explicit by the leader, or should we admit unconscious motives? If we attempt the latter, by what operational methods do we define the hidden purposes? Unconscious purposes frequently do motivate the leader even though, with the exception of projective techniques, we have few methods available for operationalizing such hidden motives.

Leadership effectiveness

Our definition of leadership focuses on influence efforts rather than upon influence effects. However, once leadership has been exercised, it becomes appropriate to raise questions about the effectiveness of such leadership.

The effectiveness of any influence attempt must always be assessed

[12]See, for example, Carl R. Rogers, *Client-centered Therapy* (Boston: Houghton Mifflin Company, 1951); and Thomas Gordon, *Group-centered Leadership* (Boston: Houghton Mifflin Company, 1955). No selflessness on the part of the leader is implied. His need satisfaction comes through remuneration for his services and/or gratification from serving others.

with reference to the leader's intended goal or goals. This again points up the crucial nature of the conscious-unconscious intent issue discussed above. No leadership act is inherently effective or ineffective; it might be either, depending upon the goals with reference to which it is assessed. Further, regardless of the leader's intended purpose, a given act of a leader might be seen as effective when viewed by his superior in terms of organizational goals, and at the same time be seen as ineffective when viewed by his subordinates in terms of informal-group goals.

Many operational problems are involved in assessing leadership effectiveness. The very multiplicity of coexisting goals encountered in most real-life situations makes clear-cut measurement difficult. Further, the usual goal clusters contain elements that have differential weight in the attainment of still "higher" goals in a hierarchy. An industrial organization, for example, may have many goals: high employee morale, labor peace, high productivity, contribution to community welfare, etc. These several goals may all contribute to a more inclusive goal, as culturally or organizationally espoused: increased profits. High productivity and labor peace may be viewed as "more important" subgoals for the attainment of profits than employee morale or community welfare. Or, indeed, the opposite may be the case.

Specific leadership acts may also assist the attainment of certain goals while retarding the attainment of others. Finally, all leadership acts are in fact intertwined with numerous nonleadership acts (involving perhaps such factors as accounting procedures, production control, and technological progress), all of which may contribute to organizational success. Therefore, one often encounters real difficulty in the assessment of leadership effectiveness per se.

Our concept of leadership effectiveness is nonmoral in that it implies nothing about the goodness or badness of the goals of influence, nor, for that matter, about the influence methods used to achieve these goals. The ethical evaluation involves factors different from those involved in effectiveness evaluation. For example, a gangster's effort—involving lies and coercion—to lead a teen-ager into a life of crime may prove to be a highly effective, although repugnant, leadership act.

Perhaps the most challenging question relating to leadership effectiveness is the one which focuses upon the variables most closely associated with such effectiveness. What can be said about the leadership process which may help us better to understand that which makes for leadership effectiveness?

Consistent with our definition of leadership, we feel that effectiveness in leadership is a function of the dynamic interrelationship of the personality characteristics of the leader, the personality characteristics of the follower, and the characteristics of the situation within the field of each individual.

We have already pointed out that the *situation* has a differential impact on both the leader and the follower as they interact. The *personality of the follower* (as it manifests itself in a given situation) becomes a key variable with which the leader must deal. The needs, attitudes, values, and feelings of the follower determine the kinds of stimuli produced by the leader to which the follower will respond. The *personality of the leader* (also manifesting itself in a situation) influences his range of perception of follower and situation, his judgment of what is relevant among these perceptions, and thence his sensitivity to the personality of the follower and to the situation. The leader's personality also has impact on his behavioral repertory (action flexibility) and on his skill in selecting appropriate communication behaviors.

In the sections which follow, we will examine in greater detail the interrelationship of these elements of the leadership process for the purpose of better answering the question: "What makes for leadership effectiveness?"

The dynamics of leadership

The principal dramatis personae of the leadership process, it has been noted, are the leader, who wishes to initiate interpersonal influence through communication, and the follower, whose attitudes and behavior are to be influenced toward the attainment of a specified goal. The complete leadership process ... is subsequently discussed, and a brief summary is presented in the next few paragraphs.

In order to understand the leadership process, it becomes necessary to consider the *personality of the leader* in relation to the *personality of*

the follower and to the *characteristics of situation* as appropriate starting points. We shall speak primarily of the leader, recognizing the shifting nature of the leadership role.

The leader's *needs* and his related *perceptual capacities* (potential
for responding to a variety of external stimuli) affect his response to the
many stimuli which confront him. These stimuli are received from the
follower and from the situation (physical phenomena, other individuals,
groups, organizations, the broader cultural context, and goals). His needs
and perceptual capacities in relation to the quality and quantity of available stimuli determine his *perceptual flexibility* (the range of perceptions), which provides him with a basis for influence attempts.

A mere range of perceptions is not all that is necessary. The leader
must distinguish those perceptions which he believes to be *relevant* to
the attainment of the specified goal from those which he considers *irrelevant.* He may, of course, err in making this distinction, as defined by some
external, "actual" criterion of relevance.

Further, not all perceptions may be accurate or "correct" in the sense
that they agree with a stipulated criterion of "reality." When such agreement does exist in the leader's perception, one may speak of *sensitivity*
(here used as a synonym for accuracy of perception)—*social sensitivity*
in re follower, other individuals, groups, organizations, and cultures; *nonsocial sensitivity* in re physical phenomena. When no such agreement
exists, one may speak of *insensitivity.*

The perceptual preliminaries that we have described thus far do not
necessarily proceed in a logical, conscious, or rational sequence. Nor are
perceptions equivalent in the sense that one accurate perception is as
good as another, if "goodness" is measured by the extent to which a
perception may lay the groundwork for subsequent effective influence
attempts.

Once the leader has taken a look at the "buzzing, blooming confusion" which initially may confront him, and once he has sized up the
factors which he deems to be goal-relevant, he has available his *psychological map,* which may provide a basis for action. It is at this point that
his personality once more comes into play. His *needs* and his related
action capacities (capacities for behavior) determine his *action flexibility*
(range of available communication behaviors).

Communication serves as the process through which influence is exerted.[13] It aims to bring about coincidence between the meaning of information transmitted by the communicator (the information input) and the meaning of information received by the communicatee (the information output). The leader uses communication stimuli as tools by which he may affect the perceptual-cognitive structure of the follower. He attempts to select from his alternative communication behaviors those which he believes will appropriately affect the follower so that the desired attitude changes may in turn result in the desired behavioral changes. Certain *communication behaviors* are therefore *judged appropriate* by the leader and *selected,* and others are *judged inappropriate* and *rejected.* The selected behaviors may, may not, or may partially attain the specified goal. The degree to which the leader-selected behaviors are actually appropriate, i.e., succeed in moving the follower toward attainment of the specified goal, is a measure of *leadership effectiveness.*

The series of events just described may be viewed as a particular sequence in an ongoing cycle. Events at any one step of the series may be "fed back" to the leader, resulting in modifications in his behavior and altering other parts of the sequence. The leadership process, although analyzable in terms of discrete events, is not a mechanical addition of such events, but a process involving the principle of feedback.

We now discuss in more detail each of these aspects of the leadership process.

Leader personality: needs, perceptual capacities, action capacities

Past attempts to define leadership in terms of leader characteristics were generally fruitless; however, the topic of leader personality can not

---

[13]Consistent with our definition of leadership, influence in the present context is limited to influence exercised through communication. Like a manager, the more comprehensive concept, the individual here viewed as leader may also engage in actions, limited by his action capacities, which may constitute influence efforts of a noncommunication type: physical manipulations, redesign of plant layout, development of new office systems, etc. Ultimately, managerial effectiveness is a resultant of the effectiveness of leadership actions and of other goal-oriented actions which are of a nonleadership character and which do not involve communication.

be ignored. Two attributes of the leader's needs are of particular importance. First, his needs significantly determine what he can see or do in the course of his influence attempts. His fear of rejection may cause him to suspect rejection when in fact he has acceptance. This fear may also prevent him, for example, from disciplining a subordinate when this is in order. Second, his needs, by affecting other aspects of his personality structure, have impact on how he is perceived by the follower. In many subtle respects these reciprocal perceptions condition the follower's responses to influence attempts.

Perceptual capacities and action capacities, as aspects of leader personality, are conceptually analogous to personality variables such as intelligence and emotional stability. They are viewed as "internal" bases for subsequent behavior, characterized by some stability and generality.

Conceivably, tests developed for the measurement of perceptual and action capacities should provide some probability indication of actual behavior that may be expected under real-life conditions. Under the stresses of reality, effective intelligence may not correspond to intelligence as abstractly predicted by a test. There may be a gap between the leader's perceptual and action capacities and his actual perceptions and behaviors under a given set of real circumstances. The development of adequate operational tests for perceptual and action capacities is a task which needs to be undertaken.

Perceptual capacity is viewed as a potential for responding to a variety of external stimuli. Action capacity is viewed analogously as a potential for responding behaviorally under a variety of conditions. However, not all action capacities can be utilized in the exertion of interpersonal influence. In our view, communication capacities are the exclusive focus. They are seen as potential skills for the production of symbolic stimuli, including verbal behavior, facial expression, gestures, etc.

Perceptual flexibility

Perceptual flexibility is defined as the range of stimuli of which the leader is cognitively aware in an actual leadership situation. It constitutes the *realized potential* for perception (as defined by perceptual capacities); it is what a person in fact is aware of under a given set of circumstances. The perceptual flexibility concept implies nothing about the correctness or incorrectness of the leader's perceptions. It deals solely with the range of perceptions which he may have available as he seeks understanding of follower and situation.

The range of perceptions which the leader may have is typically a function of the quantity of stimuli available. However, the relationship certainly need not involve a one-to-one correspondence between stimuli and the perceptual response to them. In some cases, a particular leader may have available only a few stimuli about the follower, but by means of his personality resources (e.g., experience in presumably similar situations), he may give evidence of considerable perceptual flexibility. One might distinguish pathological conditions of perceptual flexibility involving cases in which a person gives evidence of a wide range of perceptions, none of which have a consensually significant relation to reality. Certain types of schizophrenics might exemplify this extreme, which undoubtedly has many milder counterparts found in ordinary leadership situations.

In line with the distinction between follower and situation, as entities toward which the leader must respond, we may distinguish *perceptual flexibility regarding attributes of the follower* and *perceptual flexibility regarding attributes of the situation.*

How does perceptual flexibility fit within the frame of the leadership process? The leadership process begins with a wide variety of stimuli impinging upon the leader. Some of these stimuli may have no discernible perceptual impact upon him. Others are received by him at various points of the conscious-unconscious continuum. The distinction between stimuli having no impact and those having impact at an unconscious level is, of course, difficult to make in operational terms, although it seems to be conceptually necessary.

The perceptual processes concerning follower and situation are complex. For instance, with respect to perceptual flexibility regarding follower attributes, the leader may seek to share cognitively the follower's total phenomenological field—to see things from the latter's point of view. He may seek to assess the impact upon the follower of stimuli derived from the various elements of the situation. And the leader may wish to predict how he himself is perceived by the follower. Thus, as the leader responds to the follower, the former deals not simply with the latter's relatively stable personality characteristics, but rather with the interaction of these characteristics with stimuli emitted by the leader and by elements in the follower's situation.

Relevance judged by leader and "actual" relevance

The processes of "structuring the situation" and of "understanding the follower" imply that the leader has some purpose in mind. Ordinarily, he does not make a total or comprehensive attempt to make explicit *all* possible perceptions, i.e., to make fully explicit all available perceptual flexibility. Perhaps intuitively and automatically he does not even bother with certain perceptions because they do not seem to hold much promise as guidelines to the actions which he contemplates.

Whether it occurs as a result of careful thinking, or whether it happens spontaneously, the leader makes some kind of judgment, sorting perceptions which he judges to be relevant from those he believes irrelevant. The notion of relevancy clearly stipulates a link in the mind of the leader between the stimulus perceived and the goal desired. No perception is intrinsically relevant, nor is a given perception equally relevant for the attainment of all goals. Further, it is possible to distinguish those perceptions which the leader holds relevant or irrelevant from those which are "actually" relevant or irrelevant as judged by an external third party.

The ability of the leader to ignore or quickly discard actually irrelevant stimuli may be a correlate of leadership effectiveness. In routine leadership acts the leader habitually judges certain stimuli as relevant and disregards others. The skill to see relevancy in stimuli which on prior occasions were irrelevant may facilitate the leader's task under changing conditions of follower and situation. A leader's skill in judging relevancy probably varies for different judgmental tasks, e.g., judging relevance re follower attributes and re attributes of situation.

Social (and nonsocial) sensitivity

General considerations. As soon as the explicit or implicit judgment or relevancy has been made by the leader, the question arises as to whether the perceptions that are believed to be relevant are also correct. All perceptions which agree with a specified criterion of "reality" are classified as correct, or sensitive; those which do not, as insensitive.

The leader obviously seeks to maximize those perceptions which are both relevant and correct. Sensitivity to irrelevant items, insensitivity to relevant items, and, of course, insensitive perceptions of irrelevant items contribute nothing toward providing the leader with an accurate psychological map with which to guide his choice of influence efforts.

It is probably most important for the leader to be socially sensitive to relevant dynamics of the follower whom he seeks to influence, including the follower's needs, feelings, and motivations, although sensitivity alone is not necessarily a guarantee of leadership effectiveness. His sensitivity to other entities is also important. One may consider, for example, social sensitivity to particular groups, organizations, and cultures, as well as sensitivity to the various goals, as discussed in the section "Directed toward the Attainment of a Specified Goal or Goals." In addition, nonsocial sensitivity to physical aspects frequently is necessary for the leader.

The types of social sensitivity. Much current research has been concerned with a detailed explication of the social sensitivity concept. While detailed treatment can not be given here, a few observations may suggest the scope and complexity of this concept. ...[14]

Social sensitivity (here used synonymously with social perceptual accuracy) covers a wide variety or processes. We have already indicated that the content of the perceptions may vary, and that in this sense one may distinguish numerous social sensitivities, ranging from interpersonal sensitivity toward individuals to sensitivity for broad cultures. A

[14]As noted earlier, current usage sometimes views social sensitivity as a particular skill and social perceptual accuracy as a resultant, including all accurate social perceptions regardless of their origin. For relevant theory, see, for instance, F. Massarik, "Socio-perceptual Accuracy in Two Contrasting Group Settings," unpublished doctoral dissertation, University of California, Los Angeles, 1957; N. L. Gage and L. J. Cronbach, "Conceptual and Methodological Problems in Interpersonal Perception," *Psychological Review* 62 (November 1955): 411–422; American Psychological Association, "The Status of Empathy as a Hypothetical Construct in Psychology Today," a symposium at the Convention of the American Psychological Association, Cleveland, Ohio, 1953.

sensitivity toward self ("insight" into self) also has been investigated as a possible correlate of sensitivity toward others and as a correlate of interpersonal effectiveness.

Social sensitivity as a generic concept has been studied under a number of headings, some of which have referred to fully synonymous phenomena while others have involved somewhat diverse nuances of meaning. These headings include "empathy," "diagnostic skill," "understanding others," etc. The leader's attempt to "understand" the follower involves a type of social sensitivity, containing a number of components which cause it to be a complex concept.

There are many aspects of the follower's personality and of the follower's situation which the leader may need to understand. Empirical research has reflected this by requiring various subjects in the many experiments to make predictions regarding such diverse attributes of other persons as their self descriptions, their perceptions of others, their attitudes toward social issues, and their views of group characteristics. A leader may have a particular reason for maximizing his social sensitivity to the follower's self concept and motivations, to the follower's perception of other individuals (including the follower's perception of the leader), to the follower's perception of social relationships, and to the follower's perception of his own situation.

Frequently, a leader is concerned with predicting the social characteristics of groups or organizations.[15] His concern may be with eventual influence efforts directed toward these groups and organizations, or else he may wish to be socially sensitive to them as an aid to assessing their impact on individual followers. The functions of political leaders and the activities of anthropologists may require comprehension of broad cultural entities as well as the understanding of groups and organizations. It is probable that the psychological attributes facilitating social sensitivity to groups, organizations, and cultural entities differ from those necessary for interpersonal sensitivity.

[15]For example, see K. Chowdry and T. M. Newcomb, "The Relative Abilities of Leaders and Non-leaders to Estimate Opinions of Their Own Groups," *Journal of Abnormal and Social Psychology* 47 (January 1952): 51–57.

Levels of difficulty in social sensitivity. For each of the various types of social sensitivity, one may distinguish various "levels of depth" which affect the accuracy with which particular predictions can be made. On the whole, certain judgments are easier to make than others. The average leader, for example, may have a better "batting average" in making a rough estimate of a follower's age, or an approximate judgment on the size of a group of subordinates, than he has with respect to a follower's unconscious dynamics, or a group's state of interpersonal tension. The determination of level of difficulty undoubtedly is statistical and empirical in nature. In individual instances, it certainly is a function of (1) the psychological attributes of the leader which determine his skills in social perception (his perceptual capacities) and (2) the quantity and quality of stimuli, or cues, available to the leader.

With respect to prediction, it may be that superficial behavioral characteristics, public attitudes, feelings and attitudes privately held, and unconscious processes represent increasing degrees of depth and therefore of difficulty. Further, the task of prediction becomes increasingly difficult as the leader is required to make many and complex extrapolations from available stimuli to the desired judgment.

The effect of assumed similarity. If a leader closely resembles a follower in relevant attributes, the dynamic of "assuming similarity" (sometimes called "naive projection") may prove to be a boon in achieving social sensitivity.[16] If the leader does not resemble the follower, this same dynamic may prove to be a burden. If the leader assumes that the follower whom he is trying to understand is essentially a "carbon copy" of himself, the leader may be tempted to attribute all his own feelings and attitudes to this follower. Of course, if this "carbon-copy hypothesis" is borne out, such naive projection may make for a condition resembling successful understanding of the follower. Unfortunately from the standpoint of ease of social perception, the hypothesis is seldom fully correct, and often it is quite false. As a result, more than a naive faith in the similarity between himself and others is necessary if the leader wishes

[16]See A. H. Hastorf and I. E. Bender, "A Caution Respecting the Measurement of Empathic Ability," *Journal of Abnormal and Social Psychology* 47 (April 1952): 574–76.

to increase his social sensitivity toward the follower, particularly in view of the usual changing and heterogeneous nature of interpersonal relationships.

While it is self-evident that followers are not exact replicas of the leader, nor replicas of each other, there are, of course, important similarities among people. Certain groups may preselect their members by numerous explicit and implicit criteria. The formation of subcultures creates conformity to various norms, and thence varying degrees of homogeneity. This suggests that the leader needs to be skillful in assessing similarities between himself and a follower, and among followers, in addition to being skillful in the assessment of individual differences.

Other variables affecting social sensitivity. Many unanswered questions remain regarding the processes themselves that help or hinder social sensitivity, and regarding the attributes and dynamics of the socially sensitive individual. Factors associated with the total organization of personality, the leader's ego involvement with the follower, and his affective relationships with the follower are among other variables that may affect these processes.

The psychological map

The point now has been reached in our analysis of the leadership process at which we may assume that the leader has completed the cognitive perceptual structuring of follower and situation. The end result of this structuring process may be called the *psychological map*.[17] The leader assesses follower and situation as a preliminary to action. In doing so, he forms a mental image of the barriers and facilitating circumstances that bear on the desired goals of his leadership behavior. He further visualizes (sometimes explicitly and sometimes implicitly) those action pathways open to him which he believes will lead to leadership effectiveness. However, the psychological map that is available to him undoubtedly is a combination of accurate and inaccurate notions regarding relevant and irrelevant items. Whatever the nature of its components, this

[17]For an explication of an earlier, related concept, see E. C. Tolman, "Cognitive Maps in Rats and Men," *Psychological Review* 55 (July 1948): 189–208.

map provides the basis for the course which the leader follows in his attempt to exert influence through communication.

_____

Action flexibility

At any given time, a person has available a repertory of behaviors which, singly or in combination, he may bring into play in his attempt to deal with his environment. The scope of this repertory, the range of behaviors of which the person sees himself as capable, is defined as his *action flexibility*. It constitutes the realized potential for action (as defined by action capacities) under a given set of circumstances. By the present definition of leadership, we are concerned solely with the communication aspect of action flexibility. Therefore, our emphasis is upon the leader's repertory in communication, his skills in transmitting meanings through the use of symbols. The context in which communication occurs involves more than "sending" *verbal messages;* it includes also the leader's behaviors which affect the follower's receptivity or blocking of the meanings which the leader transmits. For example, *listening* by the leader to the follower may facilitate the extent to which the latter subsequently lends himself to "hearing" or "understanding" the former's messages. Nonverbal communication is clearly relevant.[18]

Action flexibility is related to the leader's personality resources, particularly to his action capacities. Rigidities in the personality structure, lack of experience and training, and similar impediments may restrict the leader's capacities for behavior, and thence his flexibility in communicating.

Construction of operational tests for action flexibility (as, indeed, also for perceptual flexibility) involves a host of difficulties. Mere verbal, conscious answers by the leader to the inquiry "What can you do or say to influence the follower?" are likely to give an incomplete picture, to say the least. More searching approaches may be required involving exploration of the leader's underlying dynamics and inferred capacities for richness of behavior.

_____

[18]See J. Ruesch and W. Kees, *Nonverbal Communication* (Berkeley and Los Angeles: University of California Press, 1956).

Selection of communication behaviors judged appropriate by leader and "actual" appropriateness

The very fact that the leader seeks to exert influence on a follower presupposes that some communication behaviors, though available, are quickly and automatically judged by the leader to be inappropriate to the task at hand. Some may be so clearly inappropriate that they are not even perceived. Other communication behaviors, however, may not lend themselves to such quick and automatic choice or to such facile disregard. In this latter case, the leader may need to make explicit his attempt to study his psychological map of follower and situation which is the end result of the perceptual preliminaries (perceptual flexibility, judging relevance, sensitivity). Having evaluated the information provided by this map, the leader may seek to select communication behaviors which he judges to be most appropriate in the light of available information. He seeks to exert influence toward the attainment of a specified goal by the follower, and one may assume that an adequate psychological map, which contains actually relevant and accurate information, will facilitate his endeavors.

Misinformation in varying quantities and of varying significance is also likely to be contained in the map. The leader may discard (judge as inappropriate) some communication behaviors which actually are appropriate, as externally defined, while in turn he may select some actually inappropriate ones which should have been discarded. The ultimate test, of course, is the degree to which the behaviors chosen prove actually appropriate, i.e., effective, as measured by the criterion of goal attainment. For instance, if a sharp command motivates an employee quickly to perform a defined task, this command-giving behavior is judged as appropriate. On the other hand, if the same behavior causes an altercation and subsequent hostility, the behavior, at least in the short run, is inappropriate.

Some final thoughts about leadership effectiveness

Finally, we wish to highlight some key variables, suggested by the preceding analysis, that may underlie leadership effectiveness.

Though still vaguely defined, some attributes of leader personality appear to be associated with leadership effectiveness. These attributes are the leader's needs, perceptual capacities, and action capacities. They are of importance only (1) to the extent to which they affect what the leader sees in his attempt to understand follower and situation and (2) to the extent to which they have impact on his communication skills. Needs that reduce the leader's perceptual capacities, that impair his perceptual flexibility, that mar his judgments of relevance, and that reduce his sensitivities are likely to be negatively associated with leadership effectiveness. Similarly, needs that adversely affect his action capacities, action flexibility, and selection of appropriate communication behaviors are also likely to hinder leadership effectiveness.

The follower is an important variable in the psychological map that forms the basis for the leader's communication behaviors. It is of crucial importance that the leader be sensitive to relevant attributes of the follower. The relevant attributes seldom will be of a superficial kind, such as the follower's appearance or his publicly held attitudes. Rather, the leader needs to assess correctly attributes such as the follower's feelings, his motives, and his perceptions of others. As there are many types of social sensitivity, leaders whose followers are entire groups may need to develop different perceptual skills than leaders dealing principally with individuals.

While social sensitivity (and perhaps accuracy in the psychological map generally) is assumed to facilitate leadership effectiveness, such facilitation does not necessarily proceed in a linear fashion. "Too much" social sensitivity, for example, may pose a threat to the follower, thus potentially impeding leadership effectiveness, unless the leader finds appropriate behavioral skills by means of which to offset the possible threat. Constant preoccupation with "understanding the follower" conceivably may prove paralyzing and may interfere with the development of an adequate psychological map.

An adequate psychological map is economical in the sense that it is confined to the minimum pattern of relevant and correct perceptions. This implies that the effective leader is skillful in ignoring or discarding irrelevant and incorrect perceptions.

The leader needs to utilize his psychological map as a guideline for the exertion of interpersonal influence. In this connection, the effective leader clearly recognizes, or has fully internalized at an unconscious level, the goals toward which he wishes to direct influence.

Further, the effective leader has available an adequate repertory of communication behaviors (as part of his action flexibility). In the utilization of this repertory, the effective leader will be skillful in selecting those behaviors which are most appropriate for the accomplishment of the goals which he seeks. There may be some cases in which unconscious internalization of goals by the leader is so complete that he selects appropriate behaviors even though the psychological map is not accurate or clear.

Some researchable questions generated by this frame of reference can focus on the leader as a component within an interacting system whose ends are the attainment of specified goals. It then becomes possible to examine the variance of goal attainment (leadership effectiveness) accounted for by the various parts of the system as spelled out in this frame of reference. Also, our experience has indicated that the frame of reference can provide a basis for and facilitate a systematic analysis of the sensitivity training process. This is a process through which members of unstructured training groups can gain increased social sensitivity and action flexibility.

42

PPBS in Perspective
Augustus B. Turnbull III

This article seeks to put into perspective the concept of a planning-programming-budgeting system. PPBS has been immersed in argument since it was first given wide notoriety by President Johnson in 1965 when he announced that the federal government was going to identify national goals, establish their priority, promote efficiency and economy and spotlight program changes. The debate at first centered on theory and philosophy since there was little practice to evaluate. But the pure theories have been sullied by applications in governments large and small, and the debate has moved to more pragmatic levels.

The stated needs for PPBS are simple and clear cut. Government is doing a poor job of allocating its scarce resources because it has separated planning from budgeting. Important decisions are made on an incremental basis during the hectic pressure of budget preparation time with no one making any real effort to examine anything except the immediate, direct effects of the decision. Indirect results, as well as future year implications, are almost completely ignored. Formal cost-benefit analysis of alternative means of reaching explicit goals are absent in the pre-PPB administrative environment.

Proponents of PPBS assert that through a systematic and comprehensive effort to specify objectives, analyze alternatives, and evaluate costs and benefits on a multi-year time horizon, the efficiency and effectiveness of government decision-making can be greatly improved. Opponents of PPBS assert that the nature of the American political system not only makes PPBS impracticable but also makes it unnecessary. Such coordination as is really needed is provided by spokesmen for partisan factions through the multiple interactions of the democratic political process.

Why is PPBS impracticable? Opponents cite a multitude of reasons. It is challenged first on conceptual grounds. The putative initial step in a PPB process is to isolate explicit measurable goals and then to evaluate alternative means of reaching those goals. Political scientist Aaron Wildavsky and economist Charles Lindblom are prominent among the critics of this concept. They point out that in fact the American political system rarely makes a distinction between goals and the programs designed to effect them. Political battles are fought over specific programs, not isolated statements of goals, and the favored goal preference often can only be inferred from the details of the successful program.

A related conceptual problem is raised by the effort of PPBS administrators to place all activities of a given government jurisdiction into a program structure. Activities which contribute to like results (outputs) should be grouped together for purposes of comparative analysis. The difficulties in accomplishing this task are manifold. Specific outputs of governmental programs are often difficult to specify. For example, what are the outputs of a university? How should they be measured? With what other governmental outputs should they be grouped for analysis? If a single government activity produces more than one output how can one realistically charge resources (inputs) to the several outputs? If a governmental organization unit produces more than one output, or if it produces no output which reaches the public (as is the case with many "staff" agencies), a program structure based on outputs will have little correspondence with the organizational structure of the government. When one looks at the relationships among programs and organization units the conceptual difficulties with PPBS merge into serious practical difficulties.

Government activities and programs are carried out by organizational units established for a multitude of reasons, some of which are long since forgotten. Through the years these units take on a distinctive ethos underpinned by statutes, administrative regulations, and the often-ritualized behavior of the resident bureaucrats, their clients, and their legislative supporters and detractors. Any analysis of these activities and programs, which does not take into full account the organizational units in which they are housed, has a fundamental, if not a tragic, flaw. This point, however, should not be overstated. Examination of similar programs sponsored by different organizations can be revealing indeed in any analytic sense and may well suggest the need for important policy changes. Yet implementing these policy changes requires a careful analysis of the organizations affected and an understanding of why they have been involved in the programs. In addition, managerial effectiveness, as distinct from allocative effectiveness, requires careful and continued concern with the operational details of the organizational unit which is consuming resources (inputs) in order to produce outputs.

At this point PPBS, which is basically a concept of how better decisions can be made, becomes entangled with broader organizational theory and the issue of how the will of a democratic people can best be carried into practice by government.

The somewhat spurious question has been raised as to whether the people's elected representatives, either legislative or executive, should be making the government's decisions rather than leaving them to mysterious "analysts" buried in the bowels of the bureaucracy. A quick and legitimate answer to this query is that in any event most decisions never get to the attention of the elected representatives and that both they and the career government employees who make the routine decisions could benefit from the "sharpening of judgment" that good analysis can provide.

Another organizational question is whether PPBS has a centralizing bias. The argument that it does is based on the assumption that since the starting points for analysis and thus decisions, are a clearly defined statement of goals and an across-the-board program structure, then those who determine the goals and the program structure will have effective control over the system. A standard example is Secretary of Defense McNamara's success in effectively moving the locus of decisions to his office by forcing the military services to compete with each other on the basis of their similar programs (i.e., programs contributing to the same national defense goals) as defined by Secretary McNamara's analytic staff.

Serious questions as to the effectiveness of such centralization may be raised in very large governmental jurisdictions and in the American federal structure of government where federal, state, and several local governments are often involved in implementing parts of the same program. If the federal government provides funds for expenditures in a broad area of concern, e.g., protection of the environment, and these funds are expended by local governments or even by private corporations on specific projects authorized by the state government, it is difficult to see how a systematic means-end analysis can be carried out. In addition, recent behavioral research suggests that in some circumstances highly decentralized forms of organization are more effective than the traditional, hierarchial forms based on functional specialization. These findings suggest that care be taken to see that PPB systems are sensitive to the needs of all levels of the organization.

Governments which have begun to implement PPB systems have had to contend with a number of practical difficulties. One problem, a lack of understanding of the concept, can be fairly easily remedied insofar as the government officials who do not need a technical understanding of PPBS are concerned. The rudiments of PPBS can be covered in one and two-day sessions. A fairly thorough understanding (though not necessarily acceptance) of the key concepts can be provided in one- or two-week sessions. Such training meets the needs of the government generalists, but two problems remain. Implementing a new system of decision-making requires that the decision-makers change their method of making decisions. This statement is tautological, but failure to recognize its implications has led to the downfall of more than one attempt to implement PPBS.

Even if decision-makers are prepared to incorporate the results of PPB analysis in their decisions, it is difficult to find and employ analysts who can provide such analyses to the decision-makers. It takes far more than a few days of training to create a PPB analyst. The U.S. Civil Service Commission has attempted to meet the problem by reclassifying a number of employees with a wide variety of analytic backgrounds, by instituting short courses in analytic techniques, and by encouraging universities to develop new programs of study, but the shortage of analysts continues to be a major limiting factor in the implementation of PPBS at the federal level. The situation is far worse at state and local levels.

Data overload can become a major practical problem in PPBS. If an agency is required to justify its programs on the basis of *analysis* rather than rhetoric, yet it is not sure how to do the requested analysis, experience at the federal and state level indicates the agency is very likely to provide a flood of rhetoric instead of the requested analyses.

This result intensifies a traditional conflict between planners and budgeters. Planners tend to produce comprehensive but somewhat vague planning documents; budgeters must contend with very specific, often very narrow decisions and must do it very quickly. They do not have time to relate the broad planning documents to specific budget decisions. Jack Carlson, an assistant director of the Bureau of the Budget, has revealed that this is precisely what happened when the federal government first attempted to integrate PPB analysis with the traditional budget process. The Bureau of the Budget did not have time to read the analyses because it had to get the budget to Congress before the deadline.

Supporters of PPBS put great emphasis on cost-benefit analysis only to find their opponents turning the argument against them. It is alleged that the costs in money and time required for the PPBS effort do not result in sufficient savings to justify the expenditures. Development of the data necessary for PPB analysis requires an extraordinary amount of costly effort. Agencies and their reviewers must look at the base (existing programs) as well as the increment (requested new programs) and they must do it in the unfamiliar context of a program structure that largely ignores traditional organizational lines.

If the data are to have any correspondence with reality, accounting and management information systems must develop considerable new flexibility and an ability at hairsplitting. For example, how much of a professor's salary should be charged against preparing examinations and syllabi (i.e., the instruction output) and how much against researching and writing manuscripts (i.e., the research output)? If such apportionment can be made, through what systems and at what cost is it going to be reported and aggregated at higher levels in the organization?

Another question often raised covertly if not openly is whether the organizational unit really wants such information to be available at higher levels. The old adage that knowledge is power is well understood by most administrators. The program that is clearly defined and explicitly costed-out may well be the one that feels the bite of the economizer's axe. In any case, it will be susceptible to more precise administrative direction from higher levels in the organization.

Administrators may also instinctively fear that the trend in budgetary practice may swing back toward the control orientation through the device of PPBS *in combination* with traditional object-of-expenditure budgeting. Allen Schick has developed a very useful taxonomy of budgetary reform as moving from a control, to a management, to a planning orientation. PPBS is seen by many as the culmination of the planning orientation in which top administrators and legislators will devote their primary attention to resource allocation among major program categories and alternative programs within categories while administrators wrestle with the most effective use of inputs (objects-of-expenditure) in the production of program outputs. Yet where legislative or budget bureau specification of program requirements is an addition to rather than a replacement for the traditional object-of-expenditure budget, the administrator's flexibility is lessened rather than enhanced.

* * *

This article has concentrated on the obstacles to implementing a PPB system. It has noted the difficulty of defining goals, identifying outputs and developing an across-the-board program structure. The need for a clear examination of both programs and organizations has been stressed. PPBS is grounded in analysis yet analytic talent is hard to find, and the fruits of analysis are inordinately difficult to inject into the decision-making process. Agencies may legitimately complain about the high cost of developing data for PPB analysis and fear both that it will or will not be used by reviewing authorities.

Yet despite these obstacles PPBS has not died the early death predicted by some. It has survived the first, and most critical, presidential transition at the federal level and is becoming a standard part of the lexicon of state budget agencies. In some form it has been tried in local governments across the nation. The reason for the persistence of this radical new approach to the allocation of resources seems to lie in the increasing relative scarcity of taxpayer-provided resources. At every level of government the close of the 1960's brought a new awareness of the magnitude of the problems facing American governments, but the period was also marked by a growing unwillingness of American taxpayers to assign more of their income to the public coffers.

This concern with scarce resources comes at a time when governments are faced with urgent social and environmental problems. It is apparent that the complex tasks now facing government, e.g., reducing poverty, attacking pollution, providing consumer protection, and calming ethnic and racial hostilities, are of a different order of magnitude from those of even a decade ago. It is no longer relatively simple to determine the cause of problems and the effect of government programs. As a result, the choice among alternative programs must be made on the basis of more than statements of political values; technical questions of effectiveness become critical issues. These technical issues cannot be resolved through political votes. Analysis is necessary to narrow the areas of disagreement to a point where political value judgments can play a valid role. Providing such analyses is a major responsibility of a PPB system.

In addition, the managed economy and what Murray Weidenbaum has termed "the modern public sector" of the 1970's reflect tremendous extensions of governmental action into areas where traditional decision-making criteria provide little guidance.

These changes coincide with and in part result from a realization that the incremental political decision-making process is inadequate when major social changes are taking place and when significant elements in the political system have inadequate opportunities to participate in the decisions made through that system.

The combination of scarcity of resources and new kinds of responsibilities is forcing public officials to develop new tools for evaluating the effectiveness and the relative desirability of competing programs. Some hope these new tools in combination can become a new system of decision-making. Despite all of the obstacles and difficulties outlined above, the concepts associated with a planning, programing, budgeting system are winning acceptance. It has been recognized that governmental ability to integrate plans—often vision without power—and budgets—often power without vision—must be strengthened. The task is not an easy one, nor is it completed, but any current perspective must assign to PPBS a key role in the integrative process.

Selected References

Hovey, Harold A. *The Planning-Programming-Budgeting Approach to Government Decision-Making.* New York: Frederick A. Praeger, 1968.
Lindblom, Charles. *Intelligence of Democracy.* New York: Macmillan, 1965.

Schultze, Charles L. *The Politics and Economics of Public Spending.* Washington: The Brookings Institution, 1968.

Turnbull, Augustus B., III. *The PPBS Systems Analyst: Skills and Training Requirements.* Washington: U.S. Civil Service Commission, 1969.

U.S. Congress, Joint Economic Committee, Subcommittee on Economy in Government. *The Analysis and Evaluation of Public Expenditures: The PPB System, A Compendium of Papers.* Ninety-first Congress, 1st Session, 1969 (3 volumes).

Weidenbaum, Murray. *The Modern Public Sector.* New York: Basic Books, 1969.

Author Index

Subject Index